Land Legislation in
Mandate Palestine

Land Legislation in Mandate Palestine

VOLUME 8

OFFICIAL REPORTS AND MEMORANDA,
PART IV

Editor: Martin Bunton

CAMBRIDGE UNIVERSITY PRESS

Cambridge, New York, Melbourne, Madrid, Cape Town, Singapore, São Paulo

Cambridge University Press
The Edinburgh Building, Cambridge CB2 2RU, UK

Published in the United States of America by Cambridge University Press,
New York

www.cambridge.org
Information on this title: www.archiveeditions.co.uk

© Copyright in this edition including research, selection of documents, arrangement,
contents lists and descriptions: Cambridge Archive Editions Ltd 2009

Cambridge Archive Editions is an imprint of Cambridge University Press.

Facsimiles of original documents including Crown copyright material are published
under licence from The National Archives, London, England. Images may be used only
for purposes of research, private study or education. Applications for any other use
should be made to The National Archives Image Library, Kew, Richmond, Surrey
TW9 4DU. Infringement of the above condition may result in legal action.

Subject to statutory exception and to the provisions of relevant collective licensing
agreements, no reproduction of other parts of the work may take place without written
permission of Cambridge University Press.

The publisher also acknowledges with thanks permission and facilities to photograph
the maps from the Report of the Ango-American Committee of Enquiry regarding the
Problems of European Jewry and Palestine (Supplement to CMD 6808) provided by
St Antony's College, Oxford.

Every reasonable effort has been made to contact all copyright holders; in the event of
any omission please contact the publisher.

First published 2009

Printed and bound by CPI Group (UK) Ltd, Croydon, CR0 4YY

British Library Cataloguing in Publication Data
Land Legislation in Mandate Palestine.
  1. Land tenure–Law and legislation–Palestine–History–
  20th century. 2. Land tenure–Law and legislation–
  Palestine–History–20th century–Sources. 3. Palestine–
  Politics and government–1917-1948.
  I. Bunton, Martin P.
  346.5'6940432-dc22

ISBN-13: 978-1-84097-260-3 (set) (hardback)
          978-1-84097-307-5 (volume 8)

Land Legislation in Mandate Palestine

CONTENTS

VOLUME 8:

OFFICIAL REPORTS AND MEMORANDA, PART IV

Section 8: Agricultural Credit, 1930–1936   1

8.01 Government of Palestine, 'Report by Mr. C.F. Strickland of the Indian Civil Service on the Possibility of Introducing a System of Agricultural Cooperation in Palestine', 1930

8.02 'Agricultural bank, Palestine', memorandum by H.F. Downie, 12 December 1932 [CO 733/223/14]   59

8.03 A. Wauchope, High Commissioner for Palestine, Jerusalem, to P. Cunliffe-Lister, Secretary of State for the Colonies, London, 29 July 1933, regarding the funding of cooperative societies, and enclosing brief explanatory memoranda by the Attorney General, (22 February 1933) and by C.F. Strickland, (8 April 1933) [CO 733/233/6]   71

8.04 Government of Palestine, 'Co-operative Pamphlet 1: The Co-operative Organisation of the Arab Population of Palestine.' Issued by the Registrar of Co-operative Societies, Jerusalem, April 1933, English and Arabic [CO 733/233/6]   79

8.05 C.F. Strickland, 'Memorandum on the Cooperative Societies Ordinance' [CO 733/233/7]   97

8.06 A. Wauchope, High Commissioner for Palestine, Jerusalem, to P. Cunliffe-Lister, Secretary of State for the Colonies, London, 16 April 1935, regarding agricultural credit for hill villages, and enclosing brief report by an appointed committee [CO 733/274/5]   105

Section 9: Memoranda on restricting land sales, 1930–1936

9.01 'Palestine. Statement with regard to British Policy' (Passfield White Paper, 1930) [CO 733/183/1]   123

9.02 'Letter from the Prime Minister [J. Ramsay MacDonald] to Dr. Ch. Weizmann', 18 February 1931, reiterating British policy on land legislation [CO 733/199/7A]   135

9.03 Chancellor, High Commissioner for Palestine, Jerusalem, to Lord Passfield, Secretary of State for the Colonies, London, 29 March 1930, on proposals to control the disposition of agricultural land in order to prevent the dispossession of the indigenous population, with seven enclosures: (I) draft ordinance to establish control over certain dispositions of agricultural land; (II) draft ordinance to amend the protection of cultivators ordinance 1929; memoranda by (III) the Solicitor-General, (IV) the Attorney General and, (V), the Chief Secretary on same; (VI) draft bill prepared by Attorney General and (VII) explanatory note by Attorney General on same [CO 733/185/2] — 145

9.04 'Note for the Secretary of State on the draft protection of Cultivators Ordinance' by H.F. Downie, 9 June 1933; Memorandum on Draft Protection of Cultivators ordinance, 1933, by H.F. Downie, 24 May 1933; 'Policy in Palestine: Memorandum by the Secretary of State for the Colonies', (Confidential Print 16(33)), February 1933 [CO 733/234/3]; H.H. Trusted, Officer Administering the Government, Jerusalem, to Sir P. Cunliffe-Lister, Secretary of State for the Colonies, 11 May 1933, regarding recommendations on the issue of landless Arabs with three enclosures, draft of legislation and memoranda, thereon [CO 733/234/3] — 195

9.05 A. Wauchope, High Commissioner for Palestine, Jerusalem, to Sir P. Cunliffe-Lister, Secretary of State for the Colonies, 23 August 1934, regarding protection of cultivators ordinance, and enclosing: an erratum notice and a letter dated 27 April 1934 from himself to Sir P. Cunliffe-Lister covering to a memorandum by L. Andrews, Development Officer, entitled 'Memorandum by the Development Officer on the subject of the measures taken by the Palestine Government for the protection of cultivators' [CO 733/252/14] — 257

9.06 A. Wauchope, High Commissioner for Palestine, Jerusalem, to A.C.C. Parkinson, 21 December 1935, enclosing a draft memorandum on restricting land sales [CO 733 272/12]; with Cabinet memorandum, 'The Palestine land question" [CO733/272/12] — 283

9.07 Memorandum by the Secretary of State for the Colonies entitled 'Palestine. Arab grievances', including appendices (Confidential Print 3(36)), January 1936 [CO 733/290/7] — 319

9.08 A. Wauchope, High Commissioner for Palestine, Jerusalem, to A.C.C. Parkinson, 2 May 1936, enclosing 'Brief on government's proposals for the protection of small owners by the reservation of subsistence areas' [CO 733/290/7] — 339

9.09 A. Wauchope, High Commissioner for Palestine, Jerusalem, to J.H. Thomas, Secretary of State for the Colonies, 4 May 1936, transmitting 'Report of Committee of Proposed Restriction of Land Sales' and 'Report of Sub-committee Appointed to Enquire into Proposals to Restrict Sales of Land' [CO 733/290/7] — 357

Contents   vii

9.10   A. Wauchope, High Commissioner for Palestine, Jerusalem, to W.G.A. Ormsby-Gore, Secretary of State for the Colonies, 12 August 1936, regarding proposals for the restriction of land sales in Palestine [CO 733/290/7]   395

9.11   'Memorandum regarding Mr. Ramsay MacDonald's letter to Dr. Weizmann of 13th February 1931, with special reference to its bearing upon the proposals recently approved in principle for restricting the sale of land in certain areas of Palestine' with appendices [CO 733/290/8]   403

9.12   'Extract from Cabinet Paper C.P. 36, January 1936. Secret. The prohibition by law of the transfer of Arab lands to Jews' [CO 733/290/8]   427

9.13   'Land Transfers Regulations: Notes on Legal Aspects' [CO 733/418/13]   433

Section 10: Peel Commission

10.01   'Palestine Royal Commission. Memoranda Prepared by the Government of Palestine.' (Colonial No. 133. London H.M. Stationery Office, 1937). Extracts as follows:
"Memorandum No. 7. Statistics of agricultural population, cultivable and uncultivable land in Palestine and area of land alienated to Jews."
"Memorandum No. 8. Description of different kinds of land, and of agricultural production of each."
"Memorandum No. 9. Description of measures being taken by government (i) by education (ii) by research (iii) by irrigation (iv) by other means to improve productivity of different types of land and indication of extent to which (i) Arabs (ii) Jews benefit."
"Memorandum No. 10. Description of various forms of ownership and tenure of land."
"Memorandum No. 11. Description of the activities of the department of development in connection with the re-settlement of displaced Arab cultivators."
"Memorandum No. 12. Description of land registration system."
"Memorandum No. 13. Rural indebtedness."
"Memorandum No. 14. Measures taken to provide agricultural credit."
"Memorandum No. 15. Measures taken to encourage co-operation."
"Memorandum No. 16. Account of system of land taxation and of effect of recent changes."
"Memorandum No. 17. Description of measures adopted in Palestine to protect cultivators."
"Memorandum No. 38. State domain."   445

10.02   'Memoranda Prepared by the Government of Palestine for the Use of the Palestine Royal Commission, Volume 2.' (Printed at the Government Printing Press, Jerusalem, 1937). Extract:"Memorandum No.3C. Development of Forestry"   511

10.03 Palestine Royal Commission. Minutes of Evidence Heard at Public Sessions (with Index). (Colonial No. 134. London, H.M. Stationery Office, 1937); Notes of evidence taken on Tuesday 24th November 1936, witnesses present: D.G. Harris, Irrigation Adviser; Col. F.J. Salmon, Commissioner for Lands and Surveys; L.Y. Andrews, Development Officer; M.C. Bennett, Department of Lands and Surveys 521

10.04 Chapter IX. "The Land", Palestine Royal Commission Report (Peel Report) (London, H.M. Stationery Office, 1937) 539

10.05 High Commissioner for Palestine, Jerusalem, to W.G.A. Ormsby-Gore, Secretary of State for the Colonies, 18 November 1937, enclosing a copy of the 'Report of the Committee appointed to Enquire into the Implementation of the Royal Commission's Recommendations', 10 September 1937 [CO 733/329/4] 603

10.06 Sir E. Dowson, Kent, to Under-Secretary of State, Colonial Office, 21 June 1938, regarding the settlement and registration of title to land and associated fiscal reforms in Palestine' (pp. 59–64), and enclosing four memoranda: 'Revision and Amendment of the Land Law'; 'Acceleration of settlement of title'; 'Associated fiscal measures'; 'Compilation of land statistics' [CO 733/361/12] 617

10.07 Letter from Sir E. Dowson, 16 August 1938, regarding the settlement of title in Palestine, and enclosing 'Memorandum II: Reviewing the history of cadastral survey settlement of title and associated measures in Palestine between 1913 and 1936' [CO 733/361/12] 641

Section 11: Anglo-American Committee of Enquiry, 1945–1946

11.01 'A Survey of Palestine: Prepared in December 1945 and January 1946 for the Information of the Anglo-American Committee of Inquiry (Regarding the Problems of European Jewry and Palestine)', Vol I, Chapter 8 only. [PRO 30/78/28] 683

Supplement to Volume IV. Maps. From "A Survey of Palestine: Prepared in December 1945 and January 1946 for the Information of the Anglo-American Committee of Inquiry (Regarding the Problems of European Jewry and Palestine)" [Cmd. 6808]. See Map Box, maps 12–16.

Section 12: Memorandum on land registration at the termination of the Mandate

12.01 Sir J.F. Spry, 'Memorandum on the history, law and practice of land registration in Palestine and the organisation of the Department of Land Registration, with a note on the custody of the records of title to land at the termination of the British Mandate' [CO 733/494/3] 771

Section 8: Agricultural Credit, 1930-1936

8.01

GOVERNMENT OFFICES
JERUSALEM

21st August, 1930

I was directed by the Secretary of State in his letter No. 77288/30 dated 3rd July, 1930, "to proceed to Palestine to study the economic position of the fellahin and to instruct the officers of the District Administration and the fellahin as to the objects and methods of the working of cooperative credit societies". I interpret this mission as covering all forms of cooperative societies, not merely credit.

I arrived in Palestine on July 10th, and have travelled to all parts of the country, visiting Arab villages and Jewish colonies with the assistance of Area and District Officers and of Jewish cooperators. The recommendations contained in this report depend for their fulfilment to a large extent on the measures which may be introduced in accordance with the report of Sir John Hope Simpson and, to the best of my belief, do not conflict at any important point with the recommendations which he is likely to make.

2. The Arab cultivator of Palestine is a man similar in temperament, standard of life and agricultural practices to many of the Muslim cultivators with whose conditions I have been familiar in the north-west of India. He appears, however, to enjoy a slightly higher percentage of literacy and a very acute intelligence. He may be compared favourably in the latter respect with certain of the peasant classes in Southern Europe. *Prima facie* there is no reason why he should not attain the same level of

The fellah and his debt

prosperity and adopt equally progressive methods of agriculture. His trouble, however, is his debt; so long as a small cultivator sees the burden of his debt to be so great and the rate of accruing interest so high, that not only the present produce of his fields but even the increased amount of produce which he may hope to secure by minor agricultural improvement are insufficient to pay off his creditors, he will make no sincere attempt to alter his plan of cultivation. If his present crops allow him only to pay one-half of the interest upon his debt, there is little inducement to make such improvements as will enable him to pay three-quarters of the amount. The benefit will fall entirely into the hands of his creditors, while he will only labour the harder without hope of reaching freedom. His debt is declared on all sides to have increased seriously in recent years; it is due partly to a succession of bad seasons which have rendered him unable to pay his tithe and other taxes, but more than all to the disastrous fall in agricultural prices which has marked the last two years. I make no comment on the scale of taxation, which does not fall within my terms of reference. To these troubles must be added the natural unpunctuality of an illiterate cultivator, which leads to an accumulation of compound interest; a tendency to extravagance on the occasion of marriages (instances ranging up to £P.2000 have been brought before me, though I do not suggest that they are frequent or general), and the lack of control over the credit which he has received, at cruel rates of interest, from the merchants or professional money-lenders. These rates appear to vary from a nominal 30% to a nominal 200% per annum, the actual rate being, on account of deductions and frequent compounding, somewhat higher than the figures here shown. Since the Turkish law prohibits a rate of interest in excess of 9% the pro-note is drawn up in a form concealing the exact nature of the transaction; either it shows that the borrower has received a larger sum than that which was actually paid, *e.g.* £P.15 instead of £P.10, or a fictitious sale of goods is included in the terms, and if the goods change hands at all they are immediately returned to the lender. The case of a cat, which carried two tablets of soap across a table from the creditor to the debtor, who thereupon agreed to buy for £50 "the load of soap borne by this animal" may be mythical, but indicates a common method of evading the law. The total amount of debt has been estimated at £P.2,000,000 and the number of cultivating families may be 80,000 to 100,000. The average per family would thus be £P.20, and a normal cultivator's holding may be 100 dunums or 23 acres. These figures, however, are uncertain, and it is not always clear, when they are quoted, whether they include the debts of the Beduin and of the Jewish colonists, and whether they include recent productive as well as old and unproductive debt. I have made no attempt to arrive at a more accurate figure, but my enquiries in the villages have shown me a number of cultivators whose debt ranges from £P.10 to £P.1000. There are also a few who are entirely free. It appears in any case, that the amount of debt is not only burdensome and such as to hamper any attempt at progressive agriculture, but that no small percentage of the cultivators are entirely insolvent, and neither cooperative credit nor any form of State loans can place them on a solvent footing, if the whole nominal claim of their creditors is to be repaid.

3. The cultivating methods of the small Arab farmer are as primitive as in the majority of undeveloped countries. In the hills at least he uses the nail plough which merely scrapes the surface, and it is not easy, in consequence of the stony soil, to introduce a more powerful implement. The terracing of hillsides, though excellent in some places, is unsatisfactory in others, and a progressive denudation of the slopes is clearly proceeding where the terraces are not well maintained. It is not surprising therefore that his estimated out-turn of wheat is about 60 or 70 kilograms per dunum or between 500 and 600 lbs. per acre, while the milk output of his cows is optimistically guessed at 200 gallons per annum. A casual observer might prefer a much lower figure. His backwardness is due to lack of opportunity as well as lack of security in the past, to instability of character and to the load of debt which hampers all his operations. It is useless to suppose, for

4

the reasons given above, that a serious attempt at agricultural improvement will be made, before he has been relieved from this debt or has been led to realise that a sustained effort can in the end relieve him from it. The insistence of his creditors leaves him at present barely enough for his subsistence, and it is only natural that if easy and uncontrolled credit be given to him from any source, he will misuse a bounty the value of which he has had no chance to learn. It may be possible, in addition to affording him a controlled source of credit, to proceed direct to the organisation of marketing, but here again the difficulty will be the character of the Arab peasant. So long as his outlook on life is hopeless and his attitude towards his fellow villagers is one of suspicion, he will seldom be loyal to a marketing association, and without the *intention* of loyalty on his part it will be difficult to enforce any marketing contract which he may enter and break. The problem is very similar to that of Ireland and Germany fifty years ago and of many peasant countries in Eastern Europe and in Asia. Stability of character is a plant of slow growth, but without it there is no hope of freeing the peasant permanently from the debt which he has learned to regard as inevitable; still less is it practicable to undertake those more advanced forms of cooperation or agricultural organisation which require a broad view beyond the confines of the village. It may be argued that certain countries have undertaken marketing as their chief form of cooperation, but wherever the peasant was originally indebted, as in Ireland, it must be remembered that the credit societies, though they have now receded in the background, were the first stage in the building, on which the creameries and other bodies have now been superposed.

Cooperative credit

4. The first essential therefore for the organization of the Arab fellah is to provide him with current resources through a cooperative credit society (leaving the clearance of his major debt to a later time), to form his character slowly in such a society during a term of years, and to train him to watch his expenditure and submit it to the criticism of his fellow members, to be punctual in payment, and to be

loyal to his society rather than to those creditors who are the cause of his afflictions. It *must* be realised that it will not be possible to achieve this result through an Agricultural Bank. In almost every village when I asked the fellahin to offer their own solution for their difficulties they replied with a demand for an Agricultural Bank. In many cases I am convinced, and a short cross-examination strengthened me in my opinion, that they had no idea what such a bank is. They were merely repeating the catch-word which they had heard from other people. Whatever be the merits of an Agricultural Bank for long-term loans, it is much less efficient than cooperative credit for the supply of current needs, and it makes no attempt at the building of character. A cultivator may take his crop loans from an Agricultural Bank for the whole of his life, but unless he is an exceptional man he will be no less under the necessity of continuing the process as an old man than he was in his youth. Through an Agricultural Bank he builds up no owned capital of his own, it is a palliative, not a remedy, so far at least as short-term credit is concerned. There are also many inconveniences in combining the issue of short- and long-term loans in the same institution; and the supervision, which a prudent institution must exert over the use of long-term money by a simple-minded cultivator, renders it impossible for him to learn the value of economic independence and self-government. In an Agricultural Bank he is always a borrower; in a cooperative credit society he rapidly becomes borrower and lender at the same time.

5. There will of course be difficulties in organising any self-governing group among fellahin who are limited in their views and for the most part illiterate. On the other hand their illiteracy is less than in many parts of India, where cooperation has attained a measure of success. The schoolmasters of Palestine are said to be of a type which will readily assist the village movement, and, in natural intelligence and in readiness to consider and accept the cooperative idea when placed before him, the Arab appears to me to stand above the Indian, and in many cases, also the European peasant. Faction is rife in every village

The credit society

and will no doubt prove a serious obstacle. It may often be necessary to create more than one society in a village, but since the villages are for the most part large, and contain often a population of several thousand persons, it would in any case be dangerous to organise in a single society all the members of a village community who may wish to cooperate. Where therefore, there is a demand for separate societies in each faction, their creation, though unpleasant, may be less harmful than it would be in small villages. I recommend that a second society in a village be not registered unless the society already existing is likely to exceed a manageable number of members (e. g. from 50 to 100 persons). This, however, will be a matter for the Registrar to decide on the basis of local experience. The system therefore, which should be created among the Palestine Arabs, is that known in Germany and Europe as the "Raiffeisen" society, characterised by a small area of operations, modest contributions towards the share capital, equality of voting power among the members, unlimited liability towards the creditors of the society and a close internal control over the borrowings and repayments of every member. This system, which has now won almost universal acceptance in peasant countries, will afford the Arab villager a means of drawing together the threads of his social and economic life in the village. In many Asiatic countries which have been exposed to the impact of European influences, the village community has been violently broken up or gradually dissolved. The experience of Palestine has been the same. In one respect the Arab has been fortunate, in that the plan of joint borrowing under the title of the *"kafala mutasalsila"* is still generally understood and practised; there can be no better introduction to the Raiffeisen system and the cooperative idea.* But a cooperative society of credit will be based not on the property of the joint borrowers but on their honesty of character and punctuality of dealing. It will therefore readily admit landless men, whether tenants

---

(*) In one hill village my explanation of a society's working was greeted by a peasant, an old soldier, with the remark, "That is like the societies I have seen in Rumania. They are very good".

7

or labourers, if their character is satisfactory, and will exclude persons of the highest status, whether effendis or mukhtars, in whom the members of the society have no confidence. The procedure of forming a society has been explained to the British and Palestinian officers who accompanied me to the villages, and a draft of model rules with a number of standard forms will be supplied for the benefit of the future Registrar. By means of small subscriptions paid by each man according to his capacity over a period of ten years, the society will gradually build up a capital of its own; but in the earlier years will need assistance in the form of a loan either from Government or from the commercial banks. A sum of about £P.22,000 is already in the Treasury on account of the old Ottoman Agricultural Bank, and it is probable that further recoveries will be made from the debtors of that institution. This money, which was derived from the pre-war inhabitants of the country, should be made available for small initial loans to the first cooperative societies, on the basis of unlimited liability, not of a mortgage of their property, and repayable by instalments over a term of years. The rate of interest should not be less than 8%, since a lower rate will impede the formation of a Central Cooperative Bank when the time is ripe. Such a Bank will not be able to lend at less than 8%. In addition to this sum, or, if any society prefers, as an alternative to it, it will be possible to continue the excellent system of joint loans which are made by Barclay's Bank in Nazareth, and which that Bank would no doubt be willing to extend to its other branches, if societies recommended by the Registrar were to approach it. The present rate of interest is the legal maximum of 9%, plus a commission, and if the formation of societies were to relieve the Bank of the necessity for maintaining a field staff for recoveries and enquiries, it would presumably be possible to dispense with the commission entirely.

6. The ultimate solution of the question of cooperative finance will no doubt be, as in other countries, the registration of a Cooperative Central Bank. The object of such a bank is to receive deposits from the public, and loans from Government or from the commercial banks as

A Cooperative Bank

8

well as share money from its own shareholders, and to make loans to the primary societies affiliated to it. These shareholders should be (1) leading individuals who are interested in the welfare of the cultivators and who are willing, on this account, to subscribe one or two shares each of £P.10, and (2) the primary societies to which loans are to be made. The directorate is drawn from both these classes of shareholder and, in such a country as Palestine, it is usual to appoint a high officer of Government (not the Registrar) as President of the Bank. Deposits for a cooperative bank will not be forthcoming until the movement itself is fairly well established, and I do not advise that such an institution be formed for several years. When it does come into existence, the commercial banks will no doubt prefer to finance it, whether by advances against Government securities or by cash credit in a simple form, rather than to deal directly with the primary societies. The Bank is not however guaranteed by Government.

Registration of banks

7. A cooperative society or bank, which lends only to its own members, receives the bulk of its deposits (whether from members or non-members) for a fixed term and opens current accounts for its members only, is not exposed to the risks of a commercial bank. I recommend therefore that a cooperative institution, which does not receive deposits at call or for a short term from non-members and does not open current accounts for non-members, be exempted from registration under the Banking Ordinance.

Payment of debt

8. Borrowing from an outside institution while its own funds are growing, and lending to members at higher rates of interest than that at which it borrows, a village society should be able at the end of ten years to exhibit a substantial capital of its own, sufficient for the current agricultural needs of the members. It will not in the earlier years be able to undertake on a large scale the repayment of outside creditors; and I have explained in the villages that so long as interest on that debt is being charged at excessive rates, it is virtually impossible for the debtor

to reduce the principal. The right procedure, though I admit that it may be too heroic for some of the villages, is for the society to call upon the creditors of its members to agree to a reasonable settlement, reducing the rate of interest to a moderate figure on condition that the payment of such instalments as may be fixed is rendered possible by loans from the society. If, as must be anticipated, many of the merchants and money-lenders refuse to accept these terms, the right remedy—again heroic but in my opinion indispensable—is to discontinue all payments to the creditors, leaving them to seek their remedy through the Civil Court. The Civil Court, in giving a decree, will often consent to fix instalments, and in any case brings down the interest to a lower rate. In either of these cases the society, if it does not consider that the judgment debtor is totally insolvent, *i.e.*, if the amount decreed is not more than he can ever hope to repay—in which case he should apply for insolvency—will either help him in meeting the instalments, or will apply to its financing institution for a special loan in order to pay the decree money in a lump sum. Such action will only be taken by the society if the member has been constantly loyal to his obligations towards it. The higher judicial authorities should be approached if it is found that instalments are not fixed by the Courts in such amounts or at such intervals as it may be possible for a cultivator to pay. I do not for a moment suggest that this long struggle against the weakness of their own characters and against the pressure of angry creditors will be comfortable or easy to the members of the cooperative credit societies; but I have never pretended that the process of cooperative self-education is comfortable and easy. I only claim that for the illiterate cultivator who is indebted it is the only possible way of securing freedom. I, at least, know no other.

9. It will be evident from what has been said above on the subject of the rates of interest charged, that the legal rate of 9% prescribed by the Turkish law is a dead letter. It is evaded by the merchants in the form of fictitious sales and of deductions from the nominal loan, *The rate of interest*

while the commercial banks find it necessary to charge a commission which substantially increases the total debit against the borrower. I have been assured both by banks and by merchants that loans at 8% or 9% without commission are habitually made to sound men on good security. But it is obvious that 9% is not a possible rate for a merchant to allow to a cultivator in a distant village, whose inclination and intention is frequently to avoid repayment if he can. The bad debts of merchants are no doubt considerable, and since the legal rate of interest is in practice a dead letter (as a legal rate of interest has always been, to the best of my belief, in every country and in every century in which it has been laid down), it will be better to abolish it entirely. At present it merely serves to mislead the observer, and to force the lender into unsatisfactory methods of evading the law or enhancing by commission the actual charge. If for any reason the maximum rate be nominally retained, I recommend that cooperative societies be formally exempted from it. If a society is borrowing from its financing institution at 8% or 9%—and it will seldom be able to obtain money for less—it must itself charge 12%, in order to collect as rapidly as possible a capital of its own. In no village in which I have mentioned this figure has a word of protest been uttered, and it is clear that men who are paying 50% or more will gladly accept a rate of 12%. Any attempt to force the lending rate of societies down to 9% or 10% will result in impeding the creation of their own capital and postponing the day of their financial independence.

The Registrar

10. Though it is desirable that the cooperative societies shall receive the general assistance of the District Officers and their administrative superiors, it will nevertheless be clear that the technical organisation and the supervision of the Raiffeisen credit societies, such as I have described, will need not only a separate Registrar but also a man of high and specialised qualifications. He should be entirely free from other duties and should be encouraged to spend the maximum number of days outside his office. In order to retain a trained man on this duty he must be well paid and in the event of an officer junior to him acting

44

in a superior post, he should be seconded and draw also the same acting pay. The remarks of the Royal Commission on Agriculture in India have already been brought to the attention of the Palestine Administration, but I include them again in order that they may be studied in this immediate connexion.

Paragraph 376 of the Report of the Royal Commission on Agriculture in India. Cmd. 3132.

"376. If, as we hold, an efficient department must be retained to perform the essential duties of education, supervision and inspection; if the time has not yet come when the department can be weakened either in numbers or quality, the personality of the Registrar is a matter of the greatest importance. In the circumstances we have described in the opening paragraph of this chapter, it was inevitable that, at the outset, the Registrar should be the foundation of the movement. It was for him to study the experience of other countries and to bring his knowledge to the examination of the economic problems of the "agriculturists, artisans and persons of limited means" for whose relief legislation was undertaken. It was never intended that he should be merely a registering officer. He was expected to provide supervision, assistance, counsel and control and, though he was warned that he must not allow cooperation to become an official concern managed by State establishments, he was held to be primarily responsible for seeing that societies were formed on a sound basis and was given wide powers to ensure this. The Committee on Cooperation, after a careful enquiry into the movement throughout India, expressed their considered view of the qualifications required and the duties to be performed, in no ambiguous terms. "He must be continually studying cooperative literature, which is now most extensive; he must make himself acquainted with economic conditions and practices both throughout India and in his own province; he must know the principles and methods of joint stock banking; and must examine the systems of developing thrift and inculcating coopera-

"The Registrar"

tion which have been tried in other countries. He is also head of a teaching establishment and must devise effective means for impressing a real knowledge of cooperation on the bulk of the population. He has further to control a large staff and to draft model by-laws and rules, to collect statistics and write reports, to advise Government on various subjects, and to keep in close touch with the higher finance of the movement as managed by provincial banks and central banks."

From such a survey as we have been able to make of the movement, we are inclined to doubt whether these words were before some local governments when appointments to the post of Registrar were made. When the Committee on Cooperation toured India in 1914-15, the cooperative movement was still almost entirely confined to credit, and development even in that direction was still far from the stage which it has now reached. To the list of qualifications laid down by the Committee we would now add others, for the modern Registrar must be fully abreast of the activities of all departments working for the improvement of rural conditions; he must see that there is a sound foundation of Better Business to support the superstructure of Better Farming and Better Living; the more efficient the movement, the more will other departments make use of it to promote their own special activities. If our view is accepted, that the experts of other departments will find, in a wide-spread and efficient cooperative movement, the one agency enabling them to reach the mass of the rural population, the Registrar of the future will need to be very carefully selected.

We, therefore, recommend that local governments should select the best man available as Registrar; on no account should the post be regarded as a convenient refuge for an official promoted by seniority to Collector's rank. Administrative experience, knowledge of the people and their economic conditions and ability to enlist the cooperation of honorary workers are essential qualifications. A Registrar, once appointed and proved efficient, should not be transferred from the post until the full benefit of continuity of policy has been assured. The minimum period during which he should hold the appointment should not be less than five years, on the assumption that he has already had two years service as Assistant or Joint Registrar, and the maximum not more than ten. Within these limits, it should be possible, on the one hand, to gain the advantage of long experience and, on the other to avoid committing the movement, for longer than would be prudent, to the charge of a single individual. If, during his period of office, the time should come when the Registrar would, in the normal course, be promoted to some higher post such as that of Commissioner of a division, we consider that he should retain his appointment with the emoluments and position of the higher rank. The movement is gathering force so rapidly in some provinces that the post of Registrar is becoming one of the most important under the local government and should be recognised as such.

In order to ensure that future Registrars should possess the technical qualifications we have enumerated above, we recommend that there should be an officer under training in all provinces. He could fill a leave vacancy, act for the Registrar, if he were sent on deputation to study conditions in Europe, or himself be placed on deputation for such study. Evidence of the value of deputation for this purpose was given by several officers who appeared before us and we consider it desirable that it should be encouraged. We think that it should usually be preceded by considerable study and experience of the movement in India, in order to ensure a full acquaintance with the nature of the problems on which further light is to be sought. Full advantage should, we think, be taken by officers on deputation of the opportunities of obtaining a special training in technique and field work which are provided by the Horace Plunkett Foundation in London and the Irish Agricultural Organisation in Dublin respectively. Both these institutions have very generously offered to train a limited number of honorary workers free of charge. If honorary workers willing to take advantage of this offer are forthcoming, we consider that they should be encouraged to do so, by a grant from Government towards the expenses involved in a visit to Great Britain and Ireland.

In this connection, we would suggest that the Government of the Central Provinces should consider the desirability of appointing a whole time Registrar in that province. The number of societies in the Central Provinces falls little short of the number in Bombay, whilst the population of the province is greater than that of Burma. We are aware that the total membership of societies is much smaller than it is in either of the two provinces mentioned, but we cannot regard as satisfactory the present arrangement under which the Registrar of Cooperative Societies in the Central Provinces is also Director of Industries and Registrar of Joint Stock Companies. We consider that the appointment of a whole-time incumbent would assist in removing the defects on which we have had occasion to comment in the earlier paragraphs of this chapter."

His training 11. The Palestine Government should therefore select the most competent man available from its existing officers who are familiar with village work, offering him the pay of Grade 1 together with a Settlement Officer's allowance, requiring him to remain on cooperative duty for at least five years (subject to ordinary periods of leave) and seconding him for acting appointment. In order that he may speak with authority on the technical subject with which he is dealing, he should be sent for a period of six months' deputation to examine rural conditions in general and the cooperative movement in particular in several selected countries. His tour might include a visit to the Punjab in India, where he should become thoroughly acquainted with the management of the rural societies and the training of the cooperative staff. Certain special types of society deserve his notice in Bengal, Bombay and Madras, and a fortnight spent in Ceylon will show him the defects which may appear in the cooperative movement under an imperfect plan of supervision and the manner in which a fully trained officer proceeds to correct them. His movements in Europe will to a large extent be influenced by the European languages which he knows. The cooperative organization in France is so dependent on State finance that it is not suitable for imitation, but if he knows French he can make a useful tour in Italy, Belgium and South Holland: while German would take him with advantage through Germany and Czechoslovakia. He should in either case visit the Jewish societies in Poland, since his understanding of the Jewish movement in Palestine will be helped by an observation of Jewish methods in the earlier homes of the members. If he has time, it will also be profitable to visit the International Institute of Agriculture in Rome, the Cooperative Section of the International Labour Office in Geneva, the Horace Plunkett Foundation in London and the Cooperative Union in Manchester. Time will scarcely permit him to study the Irish Movement, though there is much to be learned of value from its recent developments.

12. On his return he should select two Arab officers to work under him as Inspectors of Cooperation, but the appointment of a Jewish assistant or inspector might be discussed with the Cooperative Council when formed. Such an officer would in my opinion be able to render valuable service, but the right man may be expensive and only the right man will be worth appointing. It is improbable that the right man will be found in the legal profession, since the principal requirement is not legal knowledge but a cooperative spirit and a capacity to win the confidence of cooperators. I attach great importance to the Registrar learning Hebrew, whereby he can establish direct relations with the Jewish societies, and care must be taken that the premature appointment of a Jewish assistant does not cut off the Registrar from the Jewish community. *His staff*

The training of inspectors in the Punjab extends over a period of 18 months, the candidates being for the most part graduates of an Indian University, and being required to pass, towards the end of their training, an examination in economics of a post-graduate standard. So

16

high a standard may not be attained by the Palestinian staff in the beginning, but the Registrar should devote himself largely to their training, insisting upon a full course of reading as well as practical work with their own hands in the village societies. If it should be desired to send them also overseas, they would find in the Punjab a certain number of persons who know Arabic, and would also be able to work in English with the Indian staff of the Punjab Registrar. The intensive course of study for cooperative inspectors in the Punjab is held in the winter during four months, from November to February, and their admission to this class, which is held in English, could, perhaps, be obtained.

Need for caution

13. The Registrar will proceed with caution. There can be no greater mistake than the hasty registration of half-baked societies. It is better to disappoint an eager group of fifty persons, teaching them and wearying them until only fifteen remain, than to extend credit to a number of indebted cultivators whose sole idea with regard to the proposed society is that it will give them money at 12%. Government should not be disappointed if the first society is only registered when the Registrar himself has been six months at work in Palestine.

His position

14. The present position of the Registrar of Cooperative Societies under the Attorney-General is not appropriate to the duties now proposed for him. His primary function is not legal, as is that of the Registrar of Companies. If the cooperative movement among the Arabs is successful, an increase of his subordinate staff, both in the field and in the office, will be unavoidable, and will justify the creation of an independent Cooperative Department. In addition to Arab Inspectors and to a Jewish Inspector, possibly also a marketing organiser, he will require such an office staff, familiar with Arabic and Hebrew, as to obviate the necessity for frequent translation into English, a process which results in delay and inconvenience. The language difficulty will however be minimised if all model rules and forms, whether in Arabic or Hebrew, are printed or lithographed, in order that a divergence from

17

the normal may be easily perceptible. Contract and mortgage forms also should be standardised and printed. The Registrar will prepare the Arabic forms and rules, and will invite the Cooperative Council to collaborate with him in respect of Hebrew documents. If manuscript or non-standard forms are used, a measure of delay in examination cannot be avoided.

In the event—which I should regret—of additional duties being given to the Registrar, they should be of a nature to take him into the villages and bring him into touch with the land administration and the social and economic life of the people.

15. The utilisation of Jewish societies to extend a knowledge of cooperation to the Arabs does not seem to me practicable in the case of cooperative credit. I visited a Jewish society to which Arabs from several surrounding villages have been admitted, and found the Arab members unwilling to consider the idea of separate societies. But I did not feel that, whatever the goodwill of the Jewish organisers, the Arab members were regarded as being on a level with the other members of the society, nor was there any hope of the Jewish community admitting into their own society the large number of Arabs whom separate societies in each village could embrace. The reluctance of the Jews on this point is very natural; a society including numerous persons from several villages would be cumbrous and uncooperative. It will be better in every case to organise separate rural societies of credit for the Arabs. The question of marketing is discussed later. *[margin: Arabs in Jewish societies]*

16. If the Trans-Jordan Government should desire to send a candidate for cooperative training under the Registrar, the training given to him should be similar to that of the Registrar's inspectors. A note on the Trans-Jordan Agricultural Bank has been given to the High Commissioner and the British Resident. *[margin: Cooperation in Trans-Jordan]*

17. A touring officer will be in a better position to exercise the duties of registration, inspection, audit and *[margin: Powers of the Registrar]*

18

dissolution of societies than a Registrar who is confined, as has hitherto been the case, to his office chair. He should exercise the fullest powers of control, and a revised Ordinance and revised regulations under the Ordinance have been laid before the Palestine Government for consideration.

Jewish societies

18. The manner of exercising his powers will be different in the case of the Jewish and the Arab communities; the Jews are familiar with cooperation, the community is closely knit and the societies are, on the whole, well organised. What is required in the case of this community is a more efficient audit and a stricter regulation of those societies which are not truly cooperative. I find it, for instance, impossible to believe that the cooperative system can cover the principle of lottery, or that a group of persons residing principally in Rumania is entitled to operate in land transactions in Palestine under the shelter of the cooperative law. There is no reasonable doubt that the better Jewish cooperatives will welcome action by the Registrar, in consultation with them, to restrain the eccentricities of the more erratic societies. The bulk of the Jewish societies are good, and there is a healthy cooperative spirit among them. I therefore support the proposal which is already under discussion for the formation of audit unions, which will be recognised by the Registrar as competent to appoint an auditor to carry out the audit of the societies affiliated to them. The Registrar will retain his full power of inspecting the audit unions under the Ordinance, and if he is a genuine cooperator and a trained man, I have no doubt that cordial relations can be established.

Cancellation and liquidation

19. As regards the treatment of unsatisfactory societies, whether Jewish or Arab, the Registrar will take action not only to cancel registration but also to liquidate the funds of the societies. It is not sufficient to strike a society off the register, leaving the funds in the possession of any person who may be fortunate enough to hold them. If a society is shown by its audit—a copy of which should in every case be sent to the Registrar—to be persistently

uncooperative or unbusinesslike, it should be liquidated after due warning. There are at present a number of societies which have never submitted an audit report or a balance sheet; and though I recognise that the other duties of the Registrar have rendered it impossible to insist on a full compliance with the law, there should be no laxity on this point when the Registrar is in a position to deal with it.

20. The existing system of audit is definitely unsatisfactory. Each society is free to select an auditor at its own discretion from a large number of competitors, whose procedure is in no way checked and upon whom therefore an undesirable pressure may be exerted to be lax in their examination, if a renewal of the engagement is to be secured. Moreover laxity is not the only defect. A cooperative audit differs in kind and intention from a mere business audit, and a cooperative auditor should deal with a number of questions, with which a commercial auditor does not usually concern himself. These relate to the cooperative quality of the society and its proceedings, and should always be discussed in a special report to the members, which should without fail be mentioned in the auditor's certificate. (Provision for this report has been made in the draft of regulations). A cooperative audit of this type will, it is hoped, be provided for the Jewish societies by the organisation of audit unions, and all societies which do not join a union should be audited by a person appointed by the Registrar (as empowered in my draft of an Ordinance). The Registrar should prescribe the fee to be paid by each such society, and since in these cases a charge for supervision of audit may reasonably be made, the fee need not be limited to the amount paid to the auditor, and the balance may be credited to an audit fund.

The Arab village societies can be adequately audited by the Registrar and his inspectors. Their accounts will be very simple, and I am taking steps to obtain model account books for the use of such societies, which the Registrar can adopt in Arabic to the purposes of this

Audit

20

country. Though audited by the official staff, the Arab societies should from the first pay an audit fee into a non-official fund, temporarily controlled by the Registrar but intended to form the nucleus of a future Arab audit union. Whether a number of such unions will hereafter spring up cannot be foreseen, but it appears preferable that all the rural societies should directly join a single union as the centre of their movement. Certain of the Arab marketing societies may find it convenient to join a Jewish audit union, but in view of the difference of language and script their admission should be subject to the approval of the Registrar, and provision should be made accordingly in the rules of the Jewish unions, if the possibility of admitting Arab societies is contemplated by them at all.

An Arab union cannot be organised in the near future, but must await the growth of a sufficient number of societies.

Cooperative Council

21. For dealing with the Jewish societies and as a means of ascertaining their views, a Cooperative Council will be of assistance both to the Registrar and to the movement. This body, whether registered as a cooperative society or not, might consist of eight or nine persons, five being representative of Jewish audit unions (no union having more than one representative), and three being non-officials appointed by the High Commissioner from other individuals interested in cooperation but not on the committee of an audit union. The Registrar should be entitled to attend all meetings and to bring with him any other servant of Government who can contribute usefully to the discussion of a specific subject, but there is probably no advantage in allowing the Registrar a vote. The functions of the Council should be advisory, and the Registrar should bring before it all questions of importance, while retaining unimpaired his official powers. So long as the Arab societies are few and immature, I do not recommend the appointment of an Arab to the Council. Their representatives will hereafter be found among the Presidents of flourishing societies, and it cannot at this

stage be foreseen whether they will join the Cooperative Council now proposed, or will create a similar body of their own, which will unite with Jewish representatives for the discussion, with the Registrar, of matters of common interest.

22. It is a recognised principle that cooperative societies shall receive privileges and shall be exempted from the formalities of the law so far as may be practicable. It is for this reason that a special cooperative law is required. Those who enter a cooperative society agree thereby to submit themselves to the control of their fellow members and also to the control of the Registrar, subject always to an appeal from the society to the Registrar and from the orders of the Registrar to the executive authority which placed him in his post. I regard it therefore as highly undesirable that there should be an appeal from a trained Registrar to a Court of Law where this can be avoided. An appeal against an order refusing to register a society should lie to the executive superior and not to a judicial Court. An order of cancellation of registration, when financial interests have already been built up, stands on a different footing and an appeal to a Court must naturally be allowed. In general, however the fewer the formalities and the fewer the appeals, the better. No man need enter a society unless he wishes, and if he desires to maintain a right to a technical and exactly prescribed procedure, he and his friends should register under the Companies Ordinance. The liquidation of societies should therefore be conducted by the Registrar through a liquidator appointed by him, on principles of general equity and on lines laid down in the Ordinance and regulations. I recommend that the recent amendment of the Cooperative Societies Ordinance whereby Part 6 of the Companies Ordinance was made applicable to the winding-up of societies, be cancelled, and that cooperative societies be similarly released from section 117 of the Companies Ordinance.

Informality of cooperative procedure

23. A summary procedure is also needed for recovery of debts from stubborn defaulters. There are two alternative courses : a society may be permitted, as in many

Settlement of disputes

European countries, to protest a bill which has not been paid, and in the event of no objection being raised by the defaulter within a few days, to take out execution against him through the Execution Office. This plan seems suitable to the Jewish societies which are relatively skilled in methods of business. For the Arab rural societies I prefer the other course whereby every dispute between the society and any member, including the failure to pay a debt which is due, shall be compulsorily referred to the Registrar, or to an arbitrator appointed by him, for decision by an award in arbitration. The jurisdiction of the Courts is in such cases totally excluded. The award of the arbitrator is presented to the Civil Court which, without hearing objections or summoning the other party, proceeds to execute it. The Execution Office is not entitled to interfere with the award in any way, such as the granting of instalments not contemplated by the arbitrator. All appeals *ad misericordiam* have been heard in advance by the arbitrator, and there is no occasion for the Execution Office to entertain them. Moreover, if a defaulter against whom execution has been taken out repents and asks the society to treat him with lenience, my experience is that the societies are only too inclined to be mild and to grant unjustified extensions. If the societies are involved in the complexities of execution procedure and objections in Court, it will be difficult to find villagers who will accept office in them and will sacrifice the necessary time for prosecuting the claims of the society. Service as an office-holder in a rural credit society is honorary, and entry into the society is, as stated above, entirely voluntary.

Execution difficulties

24. Various complaints have been brought before me with regard to the cost of execution and the delays therein involved. I am not able to make many useful suggestions on this point. Cooperative societies should be exempted from as many stamps and fees as possible; and the cost of execution on a protested bill or an arbitrator's award should be reduced to 4 per cent, as levied in execution under the Arbitration Ordinance. It is not unlikely that the execution of cooperative warrants would be more efficient and more prompt if carried out by bailiffs than by policemen.

25. A further reasonable privilege for rural societies in outlying areas will be the transmission of funds by Government order from the nearest sub-Treasury to a bank or a Government Treasury elsewhere. Villagers cannot be expected to understand in full the methods of commercial payment, and it is not safe for them to retain large sums in their possession or to carry them by hand throughout the country. There may also be cases in which a society will desire for the sake of security to keep its surplus cash in the safe of the District Officer. This privilege would also be helpful, though the surplus cash ought to be reduced at all times to the minimum possible. Those funds which for the time being are not required, should be repaid to the financing institution.

Custody of cash

26. A Registrar who is to receive special training and to be entrusted with great responsibilities must be prepared to take a wide view of his function. He is not merely relieving the peasants from debt but is undertaking a reconstruction of their lives and of the future of the country. He must aim at adult education and at the teaching of citizenship in a community in which these ideas are at present almost unknown. He cannot succeed in isolation but will need the help of every Department, and in his turn will make himself and his societies a means for carrying out the objects at which the other Departments aim. A cooperator has first to relieve the rural population from debt, but having done so, he proceeds to his real task, which is to serve the purposes of other people. The cooperative society is the most valuable agency which can be found in a village for the promotion of agriculture, education and public health; and though it is difficult for the officers of those Departments to grasp the fact at first, while the Registrar is fighting the evil of debt and is therefore postponing his approach to his ultimate duty, they will realise the real object of the society when the members, having learnt by cooperation in credit the value of cooperation in the abstract, will go on at the instigation of the Registrar and his staff to demand new schools, to adopt measures of health and to accept the improvements offered to them by the agricultural

Wide scope of cooperation

and veterinary officers. One of the first allies of the Registrar is the schoolmaster, and the special class for schoolmasters now projected at the Tulkarem Agricultural School should provide him with men qualified and ready to work with him for the general welfare of the village.

Economic study

27. In order to understand the scope of his duties the Registrar must be a continual reader. It is not enough to fight the evils of the countryside with empirical weapons. He must always be strengthening himself by the study of what has been done elsewhere and must soak his mind in rural economics and in cooperation. He must live his work as well as perform it. For this purpose he will need a large and growing library of economic books. I have drawn up a small preliminary list, but Government will be well advised to give him a special grant from which he may add to his official library year by year. He should similarly insist on his subordinate staff maintaining their studies, and if books suitable to the purposes of Palestine do not exist, it will be the pleasant duty of the Registrar to write them.

Function of District Officers

28. I have referred above to the need for collaboration with the District Officers. It will be impossible for a District Officer to acquaint himself with all the technicalities and conventions of cooperation, nor is it convenient that he should attempt to do so. The District Officer, when visiting a village should not fail to enquire as to the progress of the society, to *see the cash* in the hands of the treasurer in order to avoid embezzlement, and to admonish any leading member who may be causing trouble whether by taking an undue amount of the funds as a loan to himself or by other means. The Registrar will find that he cannot dispense with the help of the District Officer and the latter will soon discover that the activity of the Registrar, at all events, after the first year or two, means much for the progress and the peace of the village.

Agricultural improvements

29. The society is the natural channel by which agricultural improvements will be brought to the knowledge

of the small cultivators. It is comparatively simple for an agricultural officer to discuss an improvement with a large landowner or a man of education, and there is a hydra-headed theory that agricultural knowledge filters down. I believe this theory to be totally mistaken and the enquiries which I have made in Palestine tend to show that those improvements which have been adopted by well-to-do men have not been imitated by their simpler brethren. The poor man believes that the rich landowner either enjoys facilities which he himself does not possess, or that he is willing to submit to an economic loss in order to gratify an officer of Government. If the Agricultural Department wish to establish satisfactory relations with the small cultivators, especially in the hills and the backward areas, they should approach the credit societies, in which they will find a group of men accustomed to work together and to trust one another. A village demonstration plot, on which a cultivator selected by the society agrees to try the seed or the implement recommended by an agricultural expert, side by side with the seed and the implement which he ordinarily uses, will, if properly conducted, carry conviction to fifty persons, each of them cultivating a small holding, whom it would have been impossible for the agricultural expert to convince individually. The societies when convinced will be able to take over in bulk selected seed, stock and implements, swarms of bees and the lighter cross-bred poultry. The Registrar's staff and the agricultural officers will be able by joint meetings to reinforce the lessons of such demonstrations, and within a few years the supply of selected animals and seed and implements to the societies should exceed anything which the Agricultural Department are at present able to supply.

30. I am anxious in passing to deprecate the use of the name "cooperative" by any Department except with reference to registered cooperative societies. A village demonstration plot is not a cooperative plot, unless it is actually in the hands of a registered society, and a scheme for joint purchases or manufacture of milk or other products at an Agricultural School is not cooperation unless

The "co-operative" name

the capital is supplied by the producing fellahin and unless the management is solely and entirely in their hands. All such schemes are to be welcomed on the ground of the valuable instruction which they give, but it is advisable to avoid a lax use of the cooperative term which can only cause misunderstanding in the minds of the people.

Cooperative marketing of oranges

31. Such minor operations of agricultural purchase as are appropriate to the need of the majority of Arab villages can be carried out through credit societies. Marketing, however, is a more difficult matter, and one which can only be successfully conducted if the final contact with the market is made through an organisation commanding skilled employees and a large bulk of produce. There is therefore little hope that Arab societies will be able to set up their own marketing organisation in the near future; nor will it often be necessary for them to do so, since in this sphere the efforts of the Jews and Arabs can be combined with advantage to all parties. Separate marketing societies should be formed in each Arab village where there is a prospect of commanding a sufficient quantity of produce, *e.g.* oranges, to deserve the attention of a large marketing organisation. The association of the two communities in the same society will not ordinarily be convenient, but the affiliation of local Jewish and Arab societies to a single federation where a small committee of educated and broad-minded men can be brought together, does not suffer from the same social disadvantages and will prevent needless competition in the market. A meeting of orange growers which I attended at Jaffa put forward a strong demand for the creation of marketing societies, but few concrete suggestions with regard to the manner of forming them. The first step is to be taken by the growers themselves, who should approach Government asking for the imposition of a cess, *e.g.* 10 mils on every case of oranges exported. On the export of three million cases this cess would yield a sum of £P. 30,000. The policy in question has been adopted with regard to oranges in South Africa and tea, cotton and jute in India. There are similar instances in other countries. The

proceeds of the cess would be devoted to technical research and to advertising in the foreign market. A part could also be employed to pay a special organiser familiar with the conditions of the orange industry in Palestine, who should, with the assistance of Jewish cooperators and the Registrar, encourage the Arab orange growers to form marketing societies and to bind themselves by a contract of sale. The cess could be managed by a semi-official committee of growers and Government nominees, which would be in a position to voice the demands of the producers for reduced railway freights, abolition of import duties on box-wood, and the establishment of a Government mark to be applied only to oranges of approved grade and packing (as in Denmark, Ireland and England). The committee would also plan out a scheme of packing-house areas throughout the whole orange country in order to avoid overlapping. Similar measures can subsequently be taken with regard to tobacco, almonds and other crops. The Orange Growers' Federation or Exchange, which will be formed by the Jewish and Arab societies, should insist on the use of a standard contract approved by the legal experts of Government, and any defect which may subsequently be found in the contract in consequence of judicial decisions should be promptly remedied by legislation with retrospective effect.

32. I am myself a convinced believer in the compulsion of minorities in the field of agricultural marketing. Such countries as South Africa, Queensland, and Jamaica have taken powers, when 75 or 90 per cent of the growers are combined in a single selling organisation, to compel the remainder to use the same channel, in order that the process of placing the crop on the market may be orderly and controlled. It is instructive to note that the Agricultural Marketing Bill recently outlined by the British Minister for Agriculture, appears to contemplate similar action in England. The failure of Hop Growers Limited, which handled 90% of the British output of hops but was unable to bring in the owners of the remaining 10%, is a well-known instance of the trouble which a negligible minority may cause to the agriculture of any country. When the

Compulsion of minorities

28

large majority of orange growers or other farmers in Palestine are united in a single organisation, compulsion of a recalcitrant minority will be entirely justified.

Sale of Barley

33. A demand for assistance in respect of barley was strongly expressed by the settled and the nomadic Beduin in the Beersheba and Gaza districts, but the problem in their case is rather to produce and sell at a remunerative rate a crop of which the value has fallen throughout the world than to obviate internal competition. Palestinian barley has apparently been displaced in the British market by Californian barley, and the only visible remedies are: (1) greater production per acre, and (2) better grading and cleaning. For the former, I suggest that an agricultural station or a series of demonstration plots be created at Beersheba, and selected Beduin be persuaded to grow the improved barleys of the Agricultural Department side by side with their own varieties. If the leaders of the tribes can be convinced that the selected barleys are better than their own, it may then be possible to collect a large stock of the better types and exchange it in the sowing season, weight for weight, with that which the Beduin would otherwise sow. Thereafter arrangements should be made for the maintenance of a small stock in the Beersheba district for replacement of grain which has become mixed in the hands of the growers. The Agricultural Department has already applied for a special grading and cleaning plant at Haifa, and if funds permit, I recommend that in the interests of the growers this plant be set up. There is no immediate prospect of the Beduin or other barley growers keeping their grain clean on the threshing floors.

Sale of milk

34. The cooperative sale of milk under hygienic conditions would confer great benefit on Palestine, the present supply of this quality being unequal to the demand. It is useless to provide Arab peasants with valuable cows which at their present stage of understanding they will not feed or maintain in the proper way. If any progress on these lines be made it will be in the neighbourhood of the Jewish dairying colonies; but no Jewish dairy can be

expected to accept a dirty or an excessively fluctuating supply of milk. On the other hand the Arab clients of such a society must be assured that their milk will be accepted, during periods of surplus, on an equal footing with that of the original members. The proposed milk installation at Tulkarem school will no doubt also teach Arab cattle owners the advantages of milk manufacture, and the Registrar may be able to form milk supply societies in the surrounding villages. These should at first bind themselves only to supply their milk to the school, but may at some future date become competent to take over the plant and contribute to the capital.

35. The need for Arab cooperation is not confined to the villages. No less than the Jews, Arabs in the towns require money for the opening of small businesses, the purchase of their raw materials and the meeting of unforeseen domestic needs. The first principle of urban credit is thrift. The ultimate ideal of an urban credit society should be to lend to each member only what he himself has saved. From the beginning therefore urban credit societies should require every member (1) gradually to subscribe a share of considerable size and (2) to open a regular savings deposit account, against which he would be entitled to borrow when necessary at a reduced rate of interest, paying a higher rate on any sum which he borrows in excess of such savings. I am here speaking of the individual urban member. A producer's society on the other hand cannot be expected to supply a large part of its initial capital, though its rules should prevent the hasty distribution of profits before an adequate reserve fund has been built up. Where real security in the form of a mortgage on property or a lien on materials can be offered by a producer's society, the financing institution should accept this in addition to the usual personal guarantees. The financing of urban producers' societies involves some risk, and the Jewish societies appear to incur occasional bad debts, as do similar bodies in other countries. It is therefore prudent to build up a reserve fund or a bad debt fund in the financing body, to meet this possibility. It is however, not inconceivable that in the interests of

Urban cooperation

30

      communal harmony and of the unity of labour, some of the Jewish urban societies will be willing to finance Arab societies of producers. There is no cooperative objection to such a policy.

Handicrafts   36. Attention should also be paid by the Registrar to the small handicrafts, which are in danger of disappearance under the pressure of factory competition. Such crafts are particularly deserving of assistance from Government, in the form of loans, of technical instruction and of guidance in marketing. I have had no time to examine the mother-of-pearl industry at Bethlehem, the weavers of Mejdel and Ramallah or the soap-makers of Nablus. These and such other industries as exist in Palestine should not only be conserved, if it is possible to find a market for their produce, but also taught to produce goods of a respectable quality and to avoid Europeanised and uniform designs. It is however much easier to provide societies of handicraftsmen with their raw material than to market their output.

Short-term loans from Government   37. In consequence of the indebtedness of the rural population and of the slow rate at which healthy cooperative societies of credit will be organised, it is advisable to continue the issue of short-term loans from Government on occasions of local or general scarcity. In a year of average crops the peasant should be able to finance himself until the following harvest from the sale of his produce, if only he will have the strength of mind to refuse to deliver it over to his creditors. So long as he surrenders everything to them, I see no hope for his ultimate redemption; and the plan for clearance of heavy debts (apart from the credit societies) which I outline in a later part of this report, will render it possible for a man, who wishes to free himself from the yoke, to face his creditor with a certain amount of courage. But it is not the business of any Government to finance a cultivator who is not willing to make an effort to save himself when an opportunity is offered to him. Crop loans issued by Government should therefore be issued not as a normal annual event but in times when the harvest is insufficient to carry the cultivator on until the next harvest.* I recommend that crop loans be issued to individuals through the District Officer under the general supervision of the Area Officer, so far as concerns non-members of credit societies, and that a sum proportionate to its membership be similarly lent through the District Officer to any credit society of which the members are in difficulties. It would not be fair to deny special assistance to the members of a society on the ground that they possess funds sufficient for their needs in an ordinary year. Crop loans if limited as I suggest, will be issued in extraordinary years, and the societies will be as well entitled to them as are non-members. The rate of interest charged by Government might be 9% to individuals and 8% to societies, but in any case the rate at which the society re-issues the loan should not be restricted by Government. A member will often prefer to pay 12% in order to strengthen his society, rather than 9% to a body in which he feels no personal stake. When at some future time a central bank is created, the crop loans in special years which are needed by members of the society will naturally be advanced by Government in a lump sum to the central bank, leaving that body to distribute to the societies at its discretion.

Jewish credit or agricultural societies can also be used as a channel for the issue of crop loans to their members, provided the societies are not engaged also in long-term business. A combination of short- and long-term credits makes it difficult to ascertain the correct position of a society.

Long-term credit

38. I now turn to the question of long-term credit. I propose to deal only with the rural question. Short-term credit, the usual requirement of the towns, is not seriously deficient; the Anglo-Palestine Company and the General

---

(*) There have in the past been defaults in payment, and a sum of £P.45,000 is still outstanding. Much of this is said to date from the years immediately after the war, when animals in poor condition were bought from the Army and failed to survive. Later defaults have been less frequent, and there is no reason to anticipate serious trouble in future.

Mortgage Bank advance also long-term loans for urban building. Rural long-term credit on the other hand is available only to a limited degree from the Palestine Corporation, which has sanctioned about £P. 50,000 for the development of orange groves for a maximum period of 12 years; from the Palestine Mortgage and Credit Bank for the housing and equipment of workers' settlements, the sum advanced being between £P.15,000 and £P. 20,000 for a maximum period of 15 years; and the Central Bank of Cooperative Institutions in Palestine, which has lent £P.20,000 for orange groves for periods up to 10 years.

Credit societies not suitable

39. Cooperative credit societies are not suitable agencies for the distribution of long-term loans. The bases of short- and long-term lending are different, and confusion will arise in the minds of the managing committee if both functions are undertaken by a single body. A cooperator borrows from his society on the basis of his character and his capacity to use the money wisely, while a person demanding a long-term loan offers his property as security in the first place, though character is not ignored. It is important to prevent the intrusion of this idea of property as the basis of credit into the transactions of a cooperative society. As the owned funds of a society increase, it will be able to make loans of moderate amounts, repayable over periods of four or five years, without taking mortgage security at all; and if loans of an excessive amount are issued through the society from a mortgage institution to an individual member, an undue burden is thrown on the unlimited liability of the other members. While therefore a mortgage institution will do well in the interests of all parties to refer to a credit society before making an advance to one of its members, an advance should not be made to or through a credit society of the ordinary type.

Credit in the hills

40. So far as I can judge from a short stay in the country and from enquiries in the district, long-term credit is seldom justified in the hilly areas. If there is much terracing to be done it can be carried out piecemeal by the family labour of a small cultivator and by the

private resources of a larger landowner. If the landowner is so heavily indebted that he cannot undertake an even gradual terracing of the land, it is doubtful whether the return from such an undertaking will be sufficient in the hills to repay the cost of the work. Where irrigation is not concerned, the planting of fruit trees is not extremely expensive, and I have little faith in a landowner, whether indebted or not, who will not agree to a scheme of piecemeal development when no reduction of costs is secured by operating on a larger scale. The only exception to the general rule would appear to be the formation of a dairy herd; and if good security can be offered by a landowner whose requirements exceed the means of a credit society, this would be a legitimate object for a mortgage loan.

41. Long-term credits are then justified if required for (1) development of *irrigated* land in the plains; (2) repayment of old debt. Preference should undoubtedly be given to development. It is not impossible to combine the clearance of debt with the development of land where the security is sufficiently good, but normally the indebted man has contributed in a greater or less degree to his own troubles. Whatever weakness there may be in his character could be corrected if he were dealing in short-term credit in a cooperative society under the supervision of his fellows, but long-term loans from a mortgage institution bring him under no such supervision, and it is not unlikely that he will be an unsatisfactory client. If he really means business, I consider that he should sell part of his land or lease the whole of it for a term of years. I realise that this suggestion will be intensely unpopular, but I will be no party to involving Government or a mortgage institution in a series of embarrassing disputes with prominent persons throughout the country, which may end in the unpopular process of foreclosure and sale. Long-term credits for the repayment of debt should therefore be given, if at all, with great caution and against security which is not only theoretically sound but can be realised in case of need without difficulty and without communal protest. There remains the principal

<small>Credit for old debt</small>

34

object of long-term credits in Palestine, the development of irrigated lands in the plains.

No general campaign of debt clearance

42. Reference has been made to the need for caution. Intensive agriculture is expanding at a rapid rate and there have been instances in the past of a fall in values in consequence of over-rapid growth. It will therefore be dangerous for Government or any body financed or guaranteed by Government to become the creditor of a large percentage of the rural population. The debtors have in such a case everything to gain by a change of Government, and the gratitude which they might at first feel for financial assistance is apt to be short-lived. It is also difficult, if not impossible, for Government or any institution in which Government is involved, to recover its debts from a large majority of the population in any area in which the debtors declare themselves (for good or bad reasons) unable to repay. An Agricultural Bank guaranteed by Government stands in this respect on the same footing as Government itself, and I consider it therefore unwise for a general campaign of debt redemption or mortgage loans for development to be undertaken throughout the country. Whatever is done should be done by measured stages, while the future of the agricultural market in Palestine and abroad is closely watched. I do not wish to assume a pessimistic attitude with regard to the orange or any other market, but there can be no question that the issue of loans for orange groves amounting perhaps to several millions of pounds in a short period would be a rash venture.

Long-term credit agencies

43. The agency for the issue of long-term credit may theoretically be one of three types. Each of these involves Government help in some form. I have found no support for the idea that without such help a mortgage institution of any kind can be created at present in Palestine.

A consortium

(1) A consortium of commercial banks might be formed on the analogy of the Agricultural Mortgage Banks of Great Britain and the Irish Free State, the capital being provided or guaranteed partly by Government and partly

by the banks in the consortium. Any odium which might result from foreclosures and other strenuous action would to some extent be reduced, since the debtor and his sympathisers could not deny that private money was at stake. On the other hand there is no likelihood of commercial banks entering at present into a consortium of this type, which should undertake to guarantee long-term loans to Arab borrowers on more than a negligible scale. The distrust of the agricultural classes as independent borrowers is deeply rooted, and in my opinion, so long as the borrowers remain independent and imperfectly controlled, is well grounded. Such a mortgage bank therefore would be compelled to pay a high rate of interest on any debentures which it might issue, and it is notable that the Agricultural Mortgage Bank in England was not able to place the whole of its issue of debentures at 5%. A mortgage bank lending to Jewish cultivators would have more chance of success, and I will return to this question below.

44. (2) The second agency for long-term credits is a nominally independent Agricultural Bank as commonly demanded by the articulate Arabs of this country. It will, however, have no hope of raising funds or making progress without a Government guarantee, and will then be exposed to all the odium of a frankly official body in case of taking stringent measures. If, as may be assumed, it has a non-official or largely non-official Board of Directors and a separate office, it will need to operate on a comparatively large scale in order to meet its expenses. Both for this reason and on account of the natural inclination of business men to expand any institution which they are directing and to show a large and progressive balance sheet, there will be a strong temptation to issue a large number of loans on security which may be excellent, but to individuals who may fail to meet their obligations for lack of close supervision and control. It seems to me impossible that a Board of commercial men should exercise that continuous supervision or possess that detailed knowledge, which the temperament of the Arab borrower renders desirable. The experience of many countries also

An Agricultural Bank

shows that an Agricultural Bank lending to individual borrowers on a mortgage of land or other immovable property is entirely unsuited to the temperament and the methods of small cultivators. The Agricultural Bank of Kenya, recently created, will deal with estate-holders and men of relatively advanced business understanding; it is in no way comparable with an agricultural bank in Palestine. The small Agricultural Bank in Trans-Jordan, inherited from the Turkish Government, is also compelled to foreclose on and sell the property of about 4% of its borrowers in each year, and defaults are far more frequent among the individuals who borrow on a single mortgage than among the groups of joint borrowers who offer as primary security their collective personal guarantee. The sale of 4% per annum of the properties mortgaged to an agricultural bank in Palestine would provoke political and possibly racial feeling of the most dangerous kind. The classical instance however, which shows the unsuitability of such a bank to the purposes of the small cultivator, is the Agricultural Bank of Egypt. I have described in some detail on a previous occasion* the experience of this Bank, and the reasons which have caused it almost entirely to discontinue dealings with the Egyptian fellahin. It would be invidious at the present time to say more than that a simple and often illiterate cultivator does not recognise the obligation of prompt repayment to an imposing institution in a distant town which he regards as either an oppressive or an enormously wealthy creditor who need only be paid if and when it is able to enforce payment. I am in any case deeply and immovably convinced that an agricultural bank in Palestine dealing on a commercial basis with small farmers would be as great an evil as any Government could introduce; supervision would be impossible, repayments would be reluctant and sales of land would be unpleasantly frequent

The Agricultural Bank of Cyprus

The Agricultural Bank of Cyprus works in a different manner. It is financed by means of fifty-year bonds issued

---

(*) Studies in European Cooperation, Volume II: Government

by the Ottoman Bank, the interest being guaranteed at 4% by the Cyprus Government. It has advanced £250,000 at 8% to cooperative societies throughout the island. The societies lend to their members for periods extending up to 20 years, and the mortgages taken from the members are passed on by the societies to the Bank, which now holds a considerable percentage of the rural mortgages in Cyprus. It should be noted that (1) the Ottoman Bank is not increasing its bond issues, in spite of keen demand, beyond the limit of £ 250,000, and (2) that advances to small cultivators on mortgage security for a long term through rural credit societies are by no means the most sound form of cooperation, and I should be very sorry to see them imitated in Palestine. Since I have not visited Cyprus, I do not think it appropriate to comment more frankly, but the brevity of my remarks on agricultural banks in general as a means of financing small cultivators should not be taken as weakening in any way the vigour with which I reject this entirely unsatisfactory solution of the problem so far as the Arabs are concerned.

45. (3) There remains the only possible method of finance (in the absence of a cooperative mortgage system through separate mortgage institutions, which cannot be created until the cooperative system has been working for at least ten or fifteen years) namely, a Government Loan Fund, from which advances should be made with the full knowledge and supervision which the circumstances require. A Government fund administered by a small committee consisting, for instance, of the Treasurer, the Commissioner of Lands, the Director of Agriculture and if necessary one commercial banker, will involve less expense, and will be less liable to expand its lending operations in order to show an imposing balance sheet. The staff of the District Administration and of the Agricultural Department will be at its disposal, and since there is no prospect of a separate agricultural bank or a consortium being set up without a large contribution of State capital or State guarantee, nothing is lost by placing the administration directly in the hands of the State. I

<small>A Government loan fund</small>

38

realise that official procedure will be slow and is always considered a fair subject of attack, but in the peculiar circumstances of this country it is preferable to any other arrangement which will not secure both caution in lending, and control over the use of the money by the borrowers.

A Jewish Mortgage Bank

46. I have now to consider the methods by which such a fund can be administered and the purposes to which it can be applied. It is in the first place unnecessary to subject Jewish borrowers, who offer sufficient security, to the same close control as Arabs, who as a community tend to be less prudent. I would therefore offer to the Jewish community that if they will arrange for the issue of long-term debentures, either through a mortgage bank specially created by them or through a consortium of those Jewish institutions (the Central Bank of Cooperative Institutions, the Palestine Corporation, and the Palestine Mortgage and Credit Bank, possibly also the Anglo-Palestine Company) which are already engaged in long-term rural business, the Government will take up an amount of the debentures equal to those which they sell to other persons or bodies, subject to a maximum limit which might be, at all events in the first place, £P. 250,000. The term of the debentures might be 25 years, and there should be no implied promise that Government will take up new debentures on their expiry. The bank ought by that time to be well established. Government could claim a seat on the Board of Directors, a right to approve the auditors and in the last resort, if the operations of the Bank are held by Government to involve undue financial risks, Government should be entitled to recall its capital in five annual instalments of £P. 50,000. It could be provided that this power should in any case not be exercised during the first five years of the bank's life, and that notice of two years should be given before the first instalments become payable. An arrangement of this kind would leave the Jewish community, which is familiar with mortgage credit and has carried out with success a number of similar transactions in the Jewish settlements, free to develop on its own lines and to attract additional capital as required from its symphathisers throughout the world. If on con-

sideration the community does not welcome this proposal, it may be necessary to deal with Jewish applicants also directly from the Government loan fund, but the loanable capital available for the Jewish community would then be smaller, since there would be no private subscriptions, and the procedure of Government Departments would lead to friction from time to time.

47. The remainder of the fund, whether intended for Arabs alone or also for Jews (in case of the failure to create a Jewish Mortgage Bank), should be devoted to the development of irrigated or irrigable land in the plains. It would be possible, if on general grounds it were held advisable, to develop a village or group of villages as a whole. It has been suggested that in about 200 villages, owning about three and a half million dunums in the maritime plain, a total of perhaps 300,000 dunums is both capable of irrigation and also suitable for plantation with orange groves. The figures are not exact, since in the absence of an exact land record and a detailed water survey it is not certain how much land is really suitable for oranges, how much for other fruits and how much is irrigable. The cost of developing a dunum of orange grove for a Jewish settler is put at about £P.100, while for an Arab who uses more labour of his own, requires no new house, and has ordinarily other land to live on while the grove is being developed, it is in the neighbourhood of £P.40 or £P.50. ' I do not propose to enter into the details of such a scheme, which would involve major questions of policy. Legislation would clearly be required. There is in general much to be said for encouraging the fellah to sell a part of his irrigable land through the agency of the Loan Fund Committee, and to repay the reasonable claims of his creditors from the sale proceeds and develop the remainder of his irrigable land with any surplus remaining and with such additional money as the Fund will advance. If such a general scheme is not approved, loans to single applicants for development can be advanced in the usual way, but (1) an arrangement for irrigation cannot often be made for single individuals (2) a redistribution of holdings will be necessary if water

Development of land

is not to be wasted; and (3) the amount of debt, required to clear the old creditors and also pay for development, will be such as to overburden some of the borrowers. The total interest on this larger amount, at the lower rate charged by the Fund, may not exceed that which a fellah formerly owed to his creditors on a smaller amount, but he will now be made to pay it punctually and in full, whereas formerly he did not do so. He may in consequence be sold up or compelled to sell before the land yields him its enhanced return, and will thus be worse off than before. If he is a member of a cooperative society, the latter also will suffer in case of such a forced sale. Or the fellah, seeing prosperity before him, may begin to spend money more freely and be less interested in the society on which he has hitherto depended. He will be a less satisfactory member, and if foolish enough to become unduly embarrassed, may sell the whole of his property and disappear, leaving the society unable to recover its dues. From every point of view therefore it is essential that, whether borrowing singly or as a sharer in a wide project of development, his use of the money be watched by the Agricultural Department, and it seems preferable that he should first clear his debts, if considerable, by surrendering part of his land.

Rate of interest

48. The old Ottoman Agricultural Bank charged 6% interest plus 1% commission and also placed ½% or 1% on the tithe. The result was probably a net income equivalent to about 9%. The funds which, in accordance with my proposal, will be administered by the Government, can, I assume, be raised in the open market at a rate not exceeding 6%, and if they are lent out at 9% to individuals and 8% to groups or to cooperative societies, the surplus thus accruing will not only ensure the fund against possible losses but will also cover that portion of it which from time to time will lie unused. Even if not more than half of the money is actually in use at the rate of 8%, and the balance is earning 4% on short-term deposit, the cost of the loan at 6% will be met. It is obviously reasonable to reduce the rate of interest when a group of persons or a society such as a society of cooperative irrigation offers collective security.

41

49. The banks at present engaged in long-term credit are issuing their loans for periods up to 15 years; it may be wise for the rules of the Loan Fund to prescribe a maximum of 20 years, but it will not often be necessary to exceed ten or twelve years. — Term of loans

50. No loan should be made to a member of a cooperative society without informing the committee of the society and listening to any objections which they may have to offer. — Relation with cooperative societies

51. Loans should ordinarily be given only against a first mortgage and to not more than 60% of the value. The valuation will be carried out by persons appointed by Government, though the absence of a crop record in Palestine, to which reference is made below, will render the process of valuation more difficult. In order to avoid overlapping with credit societies, a minimum of £P.50 should be fixed for every loan, and a sum of less than £P.100 should not be advanced to a member of a credit society unless the Government is assured that the society is unable to finance the borrower. It will not be prudent of Government to lend to any member of a society whom the committee, though having funds at their disposal, consider to be untrustworthy and refuse to finance. — Amount of loans

52. The terms on which land is at present held by settlers under the Jewish National Fund preclude the possibility of an absolute mortgage. If a separate Jewish Mortgage Bank is founded, the position can be discussed by this body with the National Fund, which will possibly be prepared to guarantee such loans or to modify the the terms of land tenure. If the mortgage is laid only upon the lease of the settler, i.e. upon his right to hold the land for the balance of 49 years, the amount advanced by a mortgage institution will clearly be less than if a full mortgage were available. — Jewish National Fund lands

53. To meet this case, and also for the convenience of those Jewish societies which are taking chattel mortgages, it will be convenient if an entry of such chattel mortgages — Chattel mortgages

42

is made in the Land Register and if a "caution" is also there entered whenever future crops have been mortgaged without the land. It should be the duty of the Land Registry to draw the attention of all persons, who may examine the entry concerning such a plot of land, to the existence of this "caution".

A Palestine Loan

54. In order to finance the Loan Fund, the share of Government in a Jewish Mortgage Bank if created, and the short-term advances to cooperative societies and to individual non-members, it will be necessary for the Palestine Government to raise a loan. The amount of such a loan will depend upon the decision of Government with regard to the development of the orange-growing areas, whether by accepting individual applications or by taking up a group of villages as a whole, and on the rate at which such development is to be carried out. I recommend that in the first place the loan be of £P.1,000,000, and that an offer to invest £P.250,000 in a Jewish Mortgage Bank (or in a consortium of existing banks which do long-term rural business) be made to the Jewish community. The balance will be at the disposal of Government for development and for long- and short-term loans; but it does not appear prudent to embark on a larger loan than this in the first stage of the undertaking. If a development policy is approved and if any part of the orange lands is offered to Jewish purchasers in order to clear the debt of the Arab owners, I have no doubt that the debentures issued by the Jewish Mortgage Bank will be rapidly taken up. There will then remain from £P.500,000 to £P.750,000 in the hands of Government for the use of both communities, but needed primarily for the Arabs who are not in a position to raise a large sum.

General recommendation

55. Having dealt with the questions of Cooperation and of long-term credits, I have now to consider other matters which concern "the economic condition of the fellahin". I recommend in the first place that the use of metrical weights and measures be made compulsory throughout the entire country at the earliest possible date. The co-existence of a different *rotl* and *oka* etc., etc., in a number

of districts exposes the countryman to the risk of unfair treatment when he is dealing with the merchant. I have raised this question in many villages, asking the fellahin in particular whether the change would involve any inconvenience to their women-folk; they have, in all villages except one, approved of my proposal and have added that their women would soon adapt themselves to the new measures. A curious clause in the Weights and Measures Ordinance lays down that the metrical system may only be made compulsory within five years from the issue of the Ordinance. This period is rapidly passing and I recommend that no further time be lost. Government should arrange for the manufacture and distribution at cost price of metrical weights and measures bearing an official stamp. The possession, apart from the use, of the older weights and measures should be prohibited, and the shops should be inspected from time to time in order to ensure compliance. Article 262 of the Turkish Penal Code prohibits the use of other weights and measures than those prescribed, but apparently does not forbid their possession. The Weights and Measures Ordinance penalises the use or the possession of false weights and measures, but not of others than those prescribed. A legislative amendment will apparently be needed.

I have reason to believe that the Trans-Jordan Government will be prepared to follow the policy of the Palestine Government if the metrical system is compulsorily introduced.

56. The holdings of the cultivators consist at present, in the majority of cases, of a number of scattered strips and patches of land in all directions around a village. The system of inheritance also tends to a progressive subdivision of each holding. It is clear that this fragmentation and sub-division materially reduces the value of the fellah's holding as a working farm, and in almost every village in which I have discussed the matter, the fellahin have agreed that if two or three classes of land were established and each man were given in one place the amount of land which he formerly held in each class, or

Consolidation of holdings

44

if compensation in the form of a larger area were given when land of a lower quality is taken in exchange for land of a better quality, they would all gain considerably from the transaction. They admit that they would grumble at first, but add that if the re-allotment were honestly carried out and under the orders of Government they would soon be thoroughly content. It is evidently impossible for the fellahin to carry out such a re-allotment by consent. The schemes of partition which they themselves will propose are for the most part conservative, and such as to perpetuate, if they do not aggravate, the sub-division of holdings and the fragmentation of plots. The allotment of strips at Samakh is a striking instance of the evil which results from following the wishes of the people. The partitioning officer, being associated with a committee with which he had to reach agreement, was unable to carry out a radical plan of re-allotment, and though he reduced the number to four strips for each person, the strips are of enormous length, and I found one measuring 2,150 metres from end to end and $4^{1}/_{2}$ metres in width. The lie of the land does not appear to necessitate this curious elongation; it is merely the result of old habit and prejudice. The Land Settlement Ordinance gives the Settlement Officer considerable powers to reject a scheme put forward by the people, if unsatisfactory, and to insist on a better scheme of his own. Where the land is undivided in practice as well as in theory, few obstacles arise, and he can assign to each sharer a single block, or a block in each class of land, which can be economically farmed. If a partition has been privately made but not registered, he can achieve the same result with a little more argument and difficulty, taking account, in his assignment of blocks, of the improvements actually made in any parcel by one of the co-sharers. I propose therefore that the undivided villages be settled before those which have been legally divided, because a consolidation of holdings can easily be secured by partition in the former. The desire for an acceleration of settlement should not compel or induce a Settlement Officer to accept any method of partition, preferred by the people, which is less sound from the economic and agricultural standpoint. Every partition of undivided land should be in the form of block holdings. I recommend that orders of Government be issued to this effect. If the present opportunity is missed, it will never recur.

The need for block assignments is most pressing in the orange-growing belt of the maritime plain, where effective irrigation is dependent on it. The settlement of such villages should on no account be so hurried as to lead to imperfect partition, whether the land be really undivided or privately partitioned.

The case of the fully partitioned villages in the orange belt is somewhat different. A complete re-allotment of parcels without the consent of the people can here only be carried out with the aid of legislation. Since the treatment of the undivided villages will occupy the Settlement Officers and the Survey Department for some time, I suggest that all fees be remitted when any legally divided land is, during and after the settlement, the subject of sale or exchange with a view to consolidation of any holding, and that the Land Registrar be authorised to decide whether a doubtful transfer falls within this description or not. Some transfers for the purpose of consolidation have already been made, and a remission of fees will increase their number. Eventually, when the settlement of undivided villages has been finished, legislation will be needed. Compulsory repartition is familiar to every European country, and I have seen it proceeding without difficulty in Scandinavia* and Switzerland and have conducted it by cooperative consent in India. The law which I suggest for imitation is that of Holland, but all the laws on the subject can be obtained from the International Institute of Agriculture in Rome. No appeal from a proceeding in consolidation should be allowed to a judicial Court, except on a strict question of law. In Norway, the only country which I know where appeals to the Courts are allowed on other points, the result is

---

(*) See the section on Consolidation of Holdings in my Studies in European Cooperation. Volume II.

frequently to delay the completion of repartition for a number of years.

Crop records

57. While the advantages of a clear record of rights in land will be secured on the completion of the Land Settlement now proceeding, there is no provision for the future record of crops and cultivators. Under the Indian Revenue System there is in each village a Village Accountant on a pay of about £ 2 a month (plus certain fees), who maintains, in addition to the village field map and a copy of the record of land right, a register showing the name of the cultivator of each field in each harvest, the kind of crop sown, the area of the crop and the area matured and failed. This record is of great utility both to Government in the Statistical Department, to the officers of the District Administration, to the Agricultural Department and to the cooperative societies. He also surveys and demarcates the parcels or holdings assigned to each co-sharer in a partition of joint land, thus relieving the Survey Department. If the extra expense of such a staff can be afforded, it will be of value in Palestine; and it will be difficult in its absence for the District Officer or other person to estimate the annual income of an individual who applies, on the plan which I shall describe below, for a settlement of his debts. The Indian Headman of the village is rewarded for his services by a payment of 5% of the land revenue which he collects. The Mukhtar in this country receives 2% only, and many enquiries show that the sum thus paid to him is in many cases very small. If his remuneration were raised to 5% he might well be able to carry out a collection of all village taxes, thus dispensing with need for a rural tax-collector, and also to maintain a crop record either personally or, if he is illiterate, through the help of the clerk whom he at present employs.

Sale of land in execution

58. Several cases have been brought to my notice in which a Civil Court executing a decree against a judgment debtor has attached and sold the whole land of the debtor or the whole of his crop. The Turkish law appears to exempt from sale such amount of land, etc., as is needed

for the support of the debtor and his family. It may be argued that the judgment debtor should be familiar with this law and should raise an objection before the executing officer, but it is not reasonable to expect a fellah to raise a legal objection of this kind. A Civil Court, before selling any agricultural land, should be required to call for a report from the District Officer, showing how much land the debtor possesses, and how much can be sold without reducing his holding below the minimum necessary for his subsistence. In the course of this enquiry, the District Officer might with advantage refer to the Land Register to discover whether there are any charges on the land. The assertion of such a charge is at present, at all events in some cases, left to the charge-holder, who may happen to be unaware of the proceedings.

59. Certain villages have put forward a request for the total prohibition of the sale of agricultural land, whether voluntary or by order of the Court. I do not wish to enter upon this question, with which Sir John Hope Simpson is primarily concerned. *Prohibition of transfers*

60. It is admitted that the number of warrants of imprisonment issued against judgment debtors is deplorably large, and that the prisons contain an excessive proportion of persons thus arrested. The draft Imprisonment for Debt Ordinance reduces from 91 to 21 days the period of imprisonment, and lays upon the creditor the burden of payment for his debtor while in jail. It also requires a Court to be satisfied that the judgment debtor is in a position to pay and is wilfully withholding payment, before a warrant is issued against him. If the Ordinance is passed in this form, the debtor, whether honest or dishonest, will be in a stronger position than hitherto, and it may be well for Government to consider whether they will not make a more marked distinction between the two cases. An honest debtor who is unable to pay is sufficiently protected by the requirement that his ability to pay be proved—the burden of proof being presumably on the creditor—and there is no need to reduce the period of imprisonment in his case, since he will not be *Imprisonment for debt*

imprisoned at all. A stubborn debtor, on the other hand, who is able to pay and refuses to do so, is not a deserving object for leniency, and the reduction of the maximum period of imprisonment in his case is not easily justified. A cooperative society for instance, which has lent to an apparently respectable and loyal member, but finds that on account of some internal quarrel within the village he is unwilling to meet his obligations, should be entitled, after obtaining an award against him in compulsory arbitration—in the course of which the arbitrator hears everything that the defaulter has to say—to commit him to prison at the society's own expense for a sufficient period to deter other members from likewise breaking their promises. In the case of a stubborn debtor the maximum period of imprisonment should be not 21 or 91 days but six months or a year. There will be no fear of the prisons being crowded with debtors, since no creditor will hold a debtor in jail at his own expense merely for the pleasure of doing so. Reference is sometimes made to the fact that the debtors who are now committed to prison seldom complete the entire sentence of 21 days. This only means that the creditor has bullied them into signing some still more unreasonable pro-note or bond than before. He will have no opportunity of doing this, if he has to prove to the Court or Executing Officer that his debtor is in a position to pay. He will also bear in mind the procedure, which I have now to recommend, for a settlement of debts in the case of an honest debtor who is completely or partially insolvent. I recommend therefore that the maximum period of imprisonment be not reduced, but that, as provided in the draft Ordinance, the Executing Officer be satisfied that the debtor is able to pay, and the creditor be charged with his maintenance while under confinement.

Bankruptcy for farmers

64. Not only will the growth of the cooperative societies be slow but there will always be a number of persons who, on account of unstable character or of heavy indebtedness, or of faction in the villages, will not be admitted to the societies by the other members. The economic problem of the rural Arabs is not solved unless those persons are also offered a way of escape from their diffi-

culties. The most obvious remedy is to extend to the cultivator the law of bankruptcy, which under the Turkish Code is applicable only to merchants. It is, however, demoralising to a peasant to pass through a formal Insolvency Court, which lends him an opportunity by means of fictitious debts and concealment of assets—neither of which can always be detected by a stationary Court—to avoid the payment of a fair dividend to his creditors. Bankruptcy is an infectious disease among farmers, since it does not often carry in an agricultural community the stigma which is attached to it by the commercial classes. Bankruptcy is not therefore a sufficient answer to the question of rural debt.

62. Various proposals have been made to me for penal action against the usurer. It is demanded that he be imprisoned for charging more than 9%, that his property be confiscated, or that the whole of his claim be cancelled. Stringent action of this kind is not likely to bring about the desired result. The lenders will either cease to lend entirely, in which case the fellahin will be distressed, or will find new ways of evading the new law as they evade at present the existing law. It is quite certain that a lender cannot be compelled by legislation to make advances at a rate which he does not consider high enough to cover his risks in view of the class of person to whom he is lending. Another suggestion is that all debts be registered in a Court or before an officer of Government or in an agricultural bank, and that no debt which is not so registered be recoverable at law. Such a procedure, which may be practicable in a very simple community, seems to me unduly restrictive in a country where commercial life is active. Commercial debts cannot be subjected to such a rule without serious derangement of trade, and it will be impossible so to define the kind of debt between a merchant and a fellah which it is desired to register, as to avoid encroaching on the commercial field. It will be inconvenient, too, to differentiate between the various communities in Palestine, some of which would be unwilling to limit in this way their agricultural credit. Moreover, the fellahin have also their commercial dealings, and it

Penalties for usury

would be comparatively easy to evade the suggested rule by making advances not only nominally but actually in the form of goods. A case came before me in Beersheba where one of the Beduin who required a loan in cash was given 20 kantars of barley in kind at £P.2 per kantar, and was obliged to sell the whole amount forthwith to the son of the lender at the prevailing market price of £P.1.100 mils per kantar.

The only remedies for usury, which I believe to have any effect, are (1) the provision of alternative credit to honest men on reasonable terms, *i.e.*, Cooperation: (2) publicity of the terms of the loan. The fellahin whom I have questioned have nearly always known exactly what they owed, and at what rate of interest. This is ensured by the annual renewal of bonds. (3) The imposition of a duty on the Courts, instead of allowing a discretion, to enquire into the terms of a transaction between a non-cultivator (merchant, moneylender or landlord) and a cultivator (small landowner or tenant), when it comes before them. This result can best be attained by prescribing compulsory issues, on which a definite finding must be reached, such as (a) Is the transaction one involving the relation of creditor and debtor, in form or in reality, between a non-cultivator and a cultivator? (b) Were the terms of the transaction reasonable and fair, and without undue influence? (c) What equitable relief should be granted to the debtor? The present Ordinance admitting oral evidence with regard to usurious dealings is said to be defeated by a transfer of the pro-note to a third party, whose rights are reserved by the Ordinance, and I recommend that when the debtor is a cultivator, the reservation of third party's rights on transfer of the pro-note be cancelled.

A settlement of debts 63. The demoralising effect of bankruptcy cannot entirely be escaped. It may nevertheless be reduced by employing a special procedure which the fellahin will regard as exceptional and which need not be permanent. I have pointed out on a previous page that no Government can allow itself to become the creditor of a very large percentage of the population. If this is correct, the idea of assessing each debtor's capacity to pay and giving him a loan from an Agricultural Bank or from Government to pay off all his creditors is ruled out of consideration. Any procedure in fact which leaves the initiative directly in the hands of the debtors, will lead to a swamping of the Courts, or other officers concerned, with a deluge of eager applicants. If the District Officer were authorised to make a summary settlement of the debts of the fellahin, at least 50% of the population would be at the door of his office within a week. If on the other hand, a judgment debtor (if honest) is protected from imprisonment by the new Imprisonment Ordinance, and if, as required by the Turkish Law, the Courts exempt from sale that amount of land and agricultural necessaries which is sufficient for the support of the fellah and his family, the initiative towards the settlement of debt can safely be left with the creditor. I recommend that legislation be passed providing that any owner or tenant of agricultural land, against whom a warrant of arrest or attachment of land is issued by a Civil Court in execution of a decree obtained against him by his creditors, be entitled to apply to the District Officer — or, if hereafter the increase of such cases justifies the establishment of a Special Court or Officer then to that Court or Officer—for a settlement of his debts and an assessment of his capacity to pay. The existing Courts have not time to undertake this new work, nor would they be well adapted to a special and summary procedure. A strictly judicial treatment will not touch the evil, and the ordinary rules of judicial evidence should be set aside. The District Officer, acting under the general guidance of the Area Officer, will notify the case in the Gazette or otherwise as Government may think fit, and will invite all persons having a claim against the debtor to put forward such claim, together with the documents in support of it or a brief written statement of evidence, within a limited period of time. On the receipt of the application the District Officer will inform the Civil Court or Execution Officer, who will stay the proceedings in execution. Other suits pending, or thereafter instituted, against a person thus notified, should be stayed or refused, and the claimant referred to the District Officer or Special Court.

The debtor, when filing his petition before the District Officer, will add a statement of his land and other assets, together with an estimate, countersigned by the Mukhtar or such other authority as the District Commissioner may direct, of the annual produce of his land and his other earnings. (It is obvious that a system of crop records would be invaluable for such a purpose). The District Officer, after hearing the creditors and the debtor in a summary manner, and after a visit to the village and an examination of the debtor's lands, will assess the maximum sum which the debtor, while maintaining himself and his family, is able to repay in an average year; and will consult the creditors as to the method of payment. Under the Alienation of Land Act in several provinces in Northern India, the land of an agriculturist may be leased to a creditor or to another person for 20 years, at the end of which time the debt is totally extinguished. It would be possible in Palestine to follow the same course or, if the creditors prefer, to leave the debtor in possession and to fix the instalments which he should pay into the District Officer's Court on each harvest. The lease or the instalments will not necessarily extend over twenty years, but should in no case be longer. It may be possible to pay off all reasonable debts in a shorter period. The District Officer will investigate so far as possible—and I quite realise the difficulties of doing so—the origin of such debt, the real rate of interest and the amount which would still remain due to the creditor if interest had been calculated from the first at a moderate rate, say 12%. If the transactions of a creditor and debtor extend over a long period of years, the limit might be set at the date of the British occupation of the country. The claims of Government should be separately calculated, and should not be scaled down, though it will be for Government to consider whether in case of such a special settlement, which will set a broken man on his feet again, some concession with regard to the older official claims might not be made. Loans advanced to the debtor at a reasonable rate of interest and for useful purposes on honest terms, such as those of Barclay's Bank at Nazareth and similar institutions, should be included in the total without reduction. The process of scaling down is intended only for those who have gambled in loans to a semi-insolvent fellah at an exorbitant rate. The District Officer, after estimating the annual surplus of the debtor and hearing the proposals of the creditors, will decide whether the land shall be leased for a term of years, leaving the fellah to earn his living by cultivation as a tenant or by labour, or whether the debtor shall be left in possession subject to the obligation of punctually paying his instalments. In the event of unjustified default in any instalment, the District Officer will of his own motion either proceed to execute his original order by distraint as though the over-due instalment were a sum due to Government, or will, if he thinks fit, revise his order and give the land on lease. The share of each creditor in the annual instalments should be fixed by the District Officer's original order, and all payments by the debtor should be made into the District Officer's Court and not direct to any creditor. Care must be taken that a debtor does not, by collusion with a friend, set up against himself an imaginary debt, which he will proceed to admit in order to reduce the balance available for his genuine creditors. I do not expect that the number of cases with which a District Officer will have to deal at any given moment will be such as to make a full enquiry impossible. If, however, the number becomes large, the appointment of a special officer or Court will be inevitable, and in the interests of the country, the outlay will be justified. The Officer or Court must be itinerant, and visit the village of the debtor wherever possible.

An appeal against the order of a District Officer should be to the District Commissioner, whose decision should be final. The order of a Special Court should be final.

64. The proposal for settlement of debts which I have here outlined is open to attack from several directions. It is an attempt to exclude the jurisdiction of the Courts. This cannot be denied, and the justification lies in the need for a special and summary course of action. It may be criticised as unjust to the creditors, but since the

Objections

54

debtor in question is *ex hypothesi* insolvent, the creditors are not entitled to hope for a full payment. The procedure will differ from that of an Insolvency Court in discriminating between debts at a reasonable and debts at an exorbitant rate of interest. From the point of view of the fellahin it may be objected that no general shaking off of burdens is contemplated. This is true. A general shaking off could only be carried out with funds of Government, and I do not consider that Government can safely finance it. In reality it is open to any fellah who really wishes to free himself, - to discontinue all payments towards his creditors. It is not necessary or advisable for Government to declare a moratorium, as has often been suggested to me. Each debtor will declare it for himself and put it in practice. The creditors will then be forced into the Court if they wish to recover anything at all, and this will, whether they like it or not, enable their debtor to claim the benefit of the special law. They will no doubt cease to lend to any debtor who ceases to repay, but the only reason why a cultivator of reasonably thrifty habits is at present obliged to seek credit from a money-lender is that he has delivered the whole of his produce to his creditor at the last harvest, and has nothing to live on and no seed to sow. This will no longer be the case, if he abstains from delivering his produce to his creditors, and the loss of new credits will therefore not hurt him in any way. In case of a failure of the harvest, Government will advance crop loans, either directly to him, or if he is a member of a cooperative society, then to his society. There will be no fear of his starvation, his creditor will be forced to take the initiative if he himself has the courage to stand firm, and the essential point which I wish to make is this: that a man who has not the courage to stand firm against his creditors, when a road of escape is open to him if he does so, is a man whom no procedure and no bounty can finally release from debt. He lacks the necessary character, and if he is cleared once, he will in a short time be indebted again to the maximum limit of his credit.

Full payment

65. There may be special cases in which for sufficient reason a cooperative society or Government itself may be

willing to advance to a cultivator the full sum assessed against him by the District Officer and to recover from him by instalments. The action of a cooperative society in this respect will depend upon the past behaviour of the debtor as a member of the society. I do not recommend that Government should often take such a step on its own account.

66. My final recommendation is that if possible a public utility company be formed under the partial control of Government, and if necessary with a subsidy from Government, for the broadcasting of news in Arabic throughout the villages in Palestine. The Arab is an intelligent man but frequently illiterate. His ideas are subject to perversion by biased or inflammatory news. I should like to see a receiving set and loud speaker owned or leased by the village as a whole, installed in the village meeting house and kept in order by the touring staff of the broadcasting company. I find it incredible, though I have been frequently assured, that an Arab village will not subscribe for the maintenance of such an installation at a moderate figure. The news supplied should of course not merely be Government statements or instructive material. General news which at present reaches the village in a distorted form could thus be supplied in a true form; there should also be amusing matter, music and other entertainment. The idea may be novel, but I am convinced that the great lack of rural life throughout the world is the lack of novelty and variety in interests. The effect would not be immediate, but I do not doubt that in the end Government would be well repaid both financially and from many more important points of view.

Rural broadcasting

8.02

AGRICULTURAL BANK, PALESTINE.

1. In Turkish times there was an institution called the Ottoman Agricultural Bank (founded in 1898). The capital of this Bank was obtained partly from the assets and accrued interest of a previous Government credit institution (The Caisses d'Utilité Publique) and partly from an additional 10% (reduced in 1905 to 1/20) on the tithe, which was to be payable until the capital of the Bank reached £T.10,000,000.

2. The Ottoman Agricultural Bank was put into liquidation at the end of the War. The process of liquidation is not yet complete, but so far assets amounting to £20,500 have been taken over by the Government of Palestine and outstanding local assets (probably bad debts) are estimated to amount to £86,000.

3. The Occupied Territory Administration continued to collect the addition on the tithe, crediting the proceeds to general revenue.

4. Until 1923 arrangements were made with the Anglo-Egyptian Bank to make advances to the Administration for loans to cultivators not exceeding in the aggregate £500,000.

5. It was at one time contemplated that a portion of the 1924 Guaranteed Loan should be allocated for the purpose of an Agricultural Bank, but it was found impossible to include this item in the Loan Schedule. From time to time the Government of Palestine has made small loans to individual cultivators for purchase of
seed

seed, live stock, etc., and it has recently been found necessary to write off part of the unpaid instalments of such loans.

6. The Shaw Commission (page 122 of their Report) drew attention to the point that one of the grievances of the Arabs was that the Palestine Government had not revived the Ottoman Agricultural Bank, and they suggested that it was a matter for consideration whether credits for Arab agriculturists should not be provided either by loans or by reviving the Agricultural Bank, or by some other means. They did not, however, devote detailed consideration to this question.

(See No.(1) in 77067/30))

7. Late in 1929, Sir John Chancellor appointed a Committee to consider the desirability of establishing an Agricultural Bank. The Committee submitted proposals for the establishment of such a Bank on the basis of a minimum capital of £500,000, which they suggested might be raised by means of a loan. This scheme was carefully considered in the Colonial Office and Sir J. Campbell's views were obtained. In March 1930,

(No.4 in 77067/30).

the High Commissioner was informed that the Secretary of State was unable to accept the Committee's recommendations for the following reasons:-

(a) that there was no possibility of the Government of Palestine raising a loan to provide the necessary capital of £500,000, and the Government was not in a position to furnish the capital without recourse to a loan.

(b) Objection was taken to the Committee's recommendation that the proposed Agricultural Bank should

should be financed, controlled and administered by the Government, as experience elsewhere had shown how difficult it was for a Government to recover advances of this kind owing to political pressure. It was also pointed out that in the case of Palestine the Government would always be exposed to charges of showing favour to the Arabs or to the Jews in its conduct of the Bank's operations.

(c) It seemed unlikely that the majority of the Arab agriculturists, both small-holders and tenants, were in fact in a position at the time to avail themselves of the credit facilities which would be offered by an Agricultural Bank;

> (1) owing to the uncertainty of land titles in Palestine, and
>
> (2) to the absence of Arab Co-operative Credit Societies.

It was pointed out that the Arab smallholder had at best only a doubtful security to offer for an Agricultural loan, and that the Arab tenant cultivator, standing alone and unsupported by a Co-operative Credit Society, had no real security to give.

8. It was suggested that the first step to be taken was to provide machinery under which legal titles could be secured by smallholders (this was being done under the Land Settlement Scheme) and legal security of tenure could be obtained by tenants; and that for this purpose the settlement of title should be accelerated in regions which were specially suited for intensive cultivation.

simultaneously

Simultaneously every effort should be made to organise Village Co-operative Credit Societies, and for this purpose an expert should be appointed to visit Palestine and outline a scheme. It was suggested that the funds required for the Co-operative Credit Scheme might be found from the sum of £20,500, which was in the hands of the Treasurer as part of the assets of the Ottoman Agricultural Bank.

At the same time, steps should be taken to encourage the Banks in Palestine to finance those small-holders who possess legal titles to their land and to finance Co-operative Societies Organisations on sound lines.

77299/30.

9. Sir John Chancellor concurred with these suggestions and Mr. C. F. Strickland, late of the Indian Civil Service, was sent out in July 1930 to advise the Government of Palestine on the subject of Co-operative Institutions and Co-operative Credit Societies.

10. Sir John Hope Simpson was at this time continuing his investigations in Palestine, and on pages 89 to 91 of his report he emphasises the importance of instituting Arab Co-operative Societies and expressed satisfaction at the appointment of an expert to deal with this question.

11. In May, 1930, the Jewish Agency sent us a copy of a memorandum on the development of the Jewish National Home which contained the following proposals relating to the provision of long term credit:-

Paragraph 33. - "It (i.e., the Government of Palestine) could contribute materially to a radical solution of the problem of the landless fellaheen by

supplementing

supplementing the amounts of compensation paid by the
Jewish Institution with long term credits - a facility
which would enable the tenants to become owners of
land elsewhere in predominantly Arab regions.
This would obviate the need for a drastic measure of
expropriating the Arab land-holder for the benefit of
the fellaheen and at the same time would help to
consolidate Jewish land settlement."

Paragraph 38.

"As an illustration of the methods for putting
such a policy into effect we would suggest the
formation, under the auspices of the Jewish Agency, of
a suitably equipped Irrigation and Settlement Company
for the development on a comprehensive scale of
intensive methods of cultivation on the holdings of
fellaheen who are willing to exchange part of their
land for the irrigation and other important schemes
carried out by the Company; the Palestine Administration to supervise that the value of loans so effected
are in proper and economic relation to that of the
land disposed of by the peasant, and generally to
demand such safeguards as may be deemed necessary in
the interests of the rural community as a whole:
The surplus thus concentrated in the hands of the said
Company to be used for Jewish close settlement."

/2. Mr. Strickland's Report was received in
August, 1930. Its general features are:-

(a) That for purposes of private short term
credits for agriculturists an Agricultural Bank was
much less efficient than a system of Co-operative
Credit Societies.

(Paragraph 4)

Paragraph 4. That the formation of Co-operative Credit Societies amongst the Arab Agriculturists should be encouraged forthwith through the medium of a Registrar of Co-operative Societies working with the District Administration's Staff, and that the balance held by the Treasury on account of the old Ottoman Agricultural Bank should be made available for small initial loans to the first Co-operative Societies on the basis of unlimited liability, not of the mortgage of their property and repayable by instalments over a term of years. The rate of interest should not be less than 8%.

(b) That the ultimate solution of the question of Co-operative finance would no doubt be, as elsewhere, the registration of a Co-operative Central Bank which would not be guaranteed by the Government.

(c) Government should continue to issue short term loans on occasions of local or general scarcity. Such loans should be issued to individuals through the District Officers, and sums proportionate to membership should be similarly lent through the District Officer of any Credit Society of which the members mightbe in difficulties.

(d) As for long term loans, Co-operative Credit Societies were not suitable agencies for this purpose. Long term credits were seldom justified in the hilly areas, but were justified if required for :-
    (1) Development of irrigated land in the plains;
    (2) Repayment of old debt. But long term credits
        for the latter purpose should only be given,

if

if at all, with great caution and against security which is not only theoretically sound, but can be realised without difficulty.

(e) As regards long term credits for development of irrigated lands, Mr. Strickland emphasised the need for caution in view of the dangers of over-rapid growth. There were three possible methods:-
- (1) A consortium of Commercial Banks.
- (2) A nominally independent Agricultural Bank, as demanded by the Arabs.
- (3) A Government Loan Fund.

(1) The capital would be provided, or guaranteed partly by Government and partly by the Banks in the consortium, and any odium which might result from foreclosures, etc., would to some extent be reduced, since private money would be at stake. There was, however, no likelihood of Commercial Banks at present entering into a consortium of this type in view of their distrust of the agricultural classes as independent borrowers.

(2) An Agricultural Bank would have no hope of raising funds or making progress without a Government guarantee, and would then be exposed to all the odium of a frankly official body in case of taking stringent measures. It was impossible that a board of commercial men could exercise that continuous supervision, or possess that detailed knowledge which the temperament of the Arab borrower rendered desirable.

(3)

(3) A Government Loan Fund would be administered by a small Committee consisting of three officials and a banker who would be able to make advances with the full knowledge and supervision which the circumstances required. The staff of the District Administration and of the Agricultural Department would be at its disposal. Mr. Strickland suggested that the Government should raise a loan of one million pounds in order to provide capital for such a Loan Fund, and the details of the scheme are contained in paragraphs 46 to 54 of his Report. He proposed that £250,000 out of the loan of £1,000,000 should be used for the purchase by the Government of debentures in a Jewish Mortgage Bank or a consortium of Jewish Credit Institutions.

13. In October 1930, was published Sir John Hope-Simpson's Report, and the White Paper (Cmd.3692) which adopted Sir John Hope-Simpson's proposals for the initiation by the Government of a development scheme on a large scale. Under this scheme the Government would re-distribute the agricultural population on a more economic basis, thus increasing the amount of land available for new settlement. Excess land occupied by Arabs would be expropriated by Government with compensation and would be 'developed' for intensive cultivation. By this means land might be found in the first place for the "displaced" Arabs, and later for further Jewish settlement. It may be noted that a scheme of this kind

kind, under which the improvement of the land
(irrigation, etc.) is carried out by the Government,
renders unnecessary the institution of a Land Bank
for the provision of long term credit for the
cultivators.

14. Mr. French was appointed Director of
Development in 1931, for the purpose of preparing a
Registry of the "displaced" Arabs and of working out
the details of the proposed Development Scheme.
In paragraph 110 of his first report Mr. French
refers to the impending appointment of a Registrar
of Co-operative Societies, and states that he is
himself not qualified to advise on this highly
technical subject, though he is optimistic enough
to agree with Mr. Strickland's estimate of the
possibilities of Co-operative Credit Societies in
the Arab villages.

15. In paragraphs 54 to 60 of his Supplementary
Report, Mr. French subjects to devastating criticism
a suggestion of the Jewish Agency for the participation
of the Government in a Jewish Agricultural and
Settlement Bank (concerned purely with the promotion
of further Jewish settlement and not with the
provision of credits for Arab cultivators.)

8.03

PALESTINE.

HIGH COMMISSIONER FOR PALESTINE,
JERUSALEM.

CONFIDENTIAL.

July, 1933.

Reference No. V/32/33

RECEIVED
7 AUG 1933
C. O. REG'Y

Sir,

I have the honour to refer to paragraph 9 of your Confidential despatch of the 26th May, with regard, inter alia, to my proposal to utilize the sum of LP. 20,000 representing the funds of the Ottoman Agricultural Bank, which are held on deposit by the Public Custodian, for the purpose of making advances to co-operative societies which will, in turn, make loans to their members. As you surmise, the words "a year" were inserted by inadvertence in paragraph 30 of my despatch No. 342 of the 15th April.

2. This proposal arose out of a suggestion by Mr. C.F. Strickland, C.I.E., during his recent visit to Palestine: I attach a copy of his explanatory memorandum on the subject to the Treasurer. I also forward a memorandum by the Attorney-General, advising that there is, in principle, no legal objection to utilizing the funds of the Ottoman Agricultural Bank in the manner proposed.

Enclosure I.
Enclosure II.

3. The proposal has been modified in the course of subsequent discussion, particularly in respect of the form of security for loans, and the maximum amount and term of loans. Finally, after consideration in Executive Council, I recommend that the proposal be adopted in the following form:

(1)/

The Right Honourable
Sir Philip Cunliffe-Lister, G.B.E., M.P., etc., etc.,
    His Majesty's Principal Secretary of State
                for the Colonies.

-2-

(1) An annual credit should be supplied by the Treasurer to the Registrar of Co-operative Societies out of the funds of the Ottoman Agricultural Bank in Liquidation for the purpose of granting loans to Co-operative Societies for specific purposes on the understanding that such credit can only be used where the Registrar is able to convince the Treasurer that Co-operative Societies cannot otherwise be financed by Commercial Banks.

(2) Loans granted from this source to Co-operative Societies should bear interest at the rate of 1% above bank rate with a maximum of 7%.

(3) The maximum term of any such loan should be three years and the maximum amount not ordinarily in excess of LP. 500;

Provided that any such loan issued by a Society to any of its members from the funds in question shall be repayable within a period of three years and shall be covered by adequate security, and

Provided further that loans to Co-operative Societies shall be granted on the unlimited joint and several liability of members and that the Treasurer shall have the right, as a condition of any such loan, to require the Society to take a charge on members' crops or such other security available as he may consider necessary, and to assign such charge or charges to Government.

4./

-3-

4. I am satisfied that this source of credit, judiciously distributed, will be the means of establishing on a sound basis many of the Arab Co-operative Societies which it is hoped to register under the new Co-operative Societies Ordinance, and which may not for various reasons be in a position to obtain credit from commercial banks.

                I have the honour to be,

                    Sir,

                  Your most obedient,

                    humble servant,

                    Arthur Wauchope

                    HIGH COMMISSIONER
                    FOR PALESTINE.

ENCLOSURE No. 1 TO PALESTINE DESPATCH
No. .... Date ...10.7.33
Enclosure II

Copy.

Government of Palestine.

22nd February, 1933.

Treasurer.

    I have good reason to hope that the Arab co-operative societies will be financed by commercial banks, but there may be cases in which such a bank, either because it does not know a particular neighbourhood or because it cannot come to terms with the Registrar, is not willing to finance a society which the Registrar recommends. Negotiations may then have been prolonged until sowing time is very near, and if the Registrar asks for a loan from Government, it will be needed quickly if it is to be of use. Such demands are not likely to exceed the surplus of the old Agricultural Bank, and should be very few. Is it possible for the Treasury to give the Registrar an annual credit out of the surplus in question, on which he could draw to finance a society? Government will have to rely very largely on the judgment of the Registrar whom they have trained for a specific purpose and any other checks which Government might apply to test the application, would be of a material nature and not necessarily valid in the co-operative field.

    If not, how long would elapse between an application from the Registrar and the actual receipt of the money?

    The annual credit seems the best method.

    The rate of interest should not be too low, since a low rate would make societies reluctant thereafter to borrow from banks. I suggest 9%, and if Government think this high, they can specifically allocate part of it to a co-operative purpose suggested by the Registrar.

                    (Sgd) C.F. Strickland.

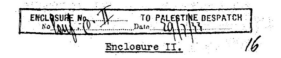

Enclosure II.

Memorandum.

The Proclamation of March, 1921, (published in the Gazette of the 15th May, 1921) directing the liquidation of the Ottoman Agricultural Bank provides in paragraph 9 as follows :-

> "The assets resulting from the liquidation shall be disposed of as the High Commissioner shall direct regard being had to the purpose for which the Ottoman Agricultural Bank was founded."

2. Those purposes are set out in Young's Corps de Droit, Volume V page 342, as follows:- (I do not take any responsibility for the translation)

> "(1) To lend, in accordance with the present regulation, money to cultivators against mortgage of matters which are capable of being sold, or against good guarantee.
> "(2) To receive money on deposit on interest.
> "(3) To serve as an intermediary in respect of financial transactions which it should favour. It is however stipulated that the total amounts bearing interest, received by the Bank within the period of one year, may not exceed the one half of the cash in hand at the commencement of that year."

3. There would seem no objection to the suggestion in principle, but I am not clear what security, if any, Government proposes to take for the loans.

(Sgd) H.H. Trusted.
ATTORNEY-GENERAL.

8-4-33.

8.04

GOVERNMENT OF PALESTINE

CO-OPERATIVE PAMPHLET 1

THE CO-OPERATIVE ORGANISATION OF THE ARAB POPULATION OF PALESTINE

Issued by the Registrar of Co-operative Societies

P. O. B. 649 Jerusalem.

April 1933

The condition of agricultural depression existing in the country has been long a matter of serious concern to everyone interested in the economic welfare of the rural population. With a view to improving the position of the cultivators, the Government has recently appointed an officer to the post of Registrar of Co-operative Societies, whose duties will include the approval of the rules of societies, the registration of societies, and the exercise of such control over the operations of societies as may be provided in the new co-operative law now under consideration. In addition to these statutory duties, the Registrar will assist in every possible manner the rural population in organizing themselves into co-operative societies, providing model rules and helping them with advice, educating them in the methods and principles of co-operation, and extending aid and supervision in particular to newly founded societies. It is hoped that the progressive spreading of a network of co-operative societies all over the country will tend, by providing facilities for the obtaining of loans under reasonable conditions, to the reduction of debt, and will result in the obtaining of better prices for agricultural produce by organized and collective sale in the most favourable markets, and in economies in the purchase of the requirements of the cultivators by joint purchase in bulk. And generally through the co-operative organization of the people, it is hoped to secure a higher standard of life among cultivators by obtaining for them a higher return for their labours, by the limitation of their expenditure on unnecessary objects, and the discouraging of extravagance, and by providing a means for the amicable settlement of disputes, thus reducing the large amounts which are at present expended in many villages on unnecessary and frivolous litigation. The Registrar will also assist the urban population in co-operative organization of industrial production societies, thrift and loan societies and other societies aimed at the securing of advantages to their members by joint and collective action.

2. The following are types of co-operative societies, which, it is contemplated, may be adapted to conditions in Palestine.

— 2

(a) Rural Credit Societies:—The usual type of rural credit society which it is considered is most suited to conditions in Palestine, is that associated with the name of Herr Raiffeisen, a German reformer, who first organized credit societies about eighty years ago. The Raiffeisen credit societies have been adopted in most European countries, also in India, China and in South Africa. The principles governing these societies involve a small share qualification of members, their unlimited joint and several liability for the debts of the society, the non-payment of a dividend on share capital or the restriction of the dividend to a low rate, and that each member should have one vote irrespectively of the number of shares held by him. This type of society usually grants short term loans only, for productive purposes either repayable at the harvesting of the member's crops, or in the case of loans for the purchase of cattle or more expensive implements repayable in two annual instalments.

(b) Societies for the Sale of Agricultural Products:-

Such societies might be formed for the sale of general agricultural produce or for the sale of separate commodities such as citrus fruit, bananas, tobacco and olive oil. A condition of membership should be that the members bind themselves to the delivery of their products for sale to their society to the exclusion of any other agency of sale. The Registrar during his recent tour in Egypt visited a well-organized society in Alexandria, conducting a whole-sale market for the sale of the vegetables of about 1000 small-holders, which appeared to be securing important advantages for its members. Another society was selling the general produce of farmers collectively, obtaining for them better prices, than in the case of sales by individual farmers to the local merchants.

(c) Societies for the Purchase of the Agricultural Requirements of the Farmers:- Such as implements, machinery, seeds, fruit trees, fertilizers, packing materials for citrus fruits etc. By means of collective purchase the members of such societies would be able to obtain their requirements at lower prices than individual purchasers. It is possible that as is the custom in many countries, it will be found possible to combine in one society the objects described under (b) & (c).

(d) **Agricultural Societies for Special Purposes**:-

Such as the carrying out of irrigation projects, including the joint sinking of wells and the purchase of pumping plant; joint ownership and working of agricultural machinery such as mechanical ploughs; societies for the conservation and use of manure; dairy societies; bee-keeping and poultry societies; societies for the fumigation of fruit trees; societies for the reclamation of marshy lands or for the terracing and planting of hills; olive pressing societies etc. etc. In Egypt a co-operative society was visited, which conducted a dairy for the making of butter and cheese from its members' milk; another society owned a tractor which was used for ploughing the land of members and for pumping water for irrigation, while a third society undertook with the help of Government the fumigation of citrus trees.

(e) **Societies for Social and Moral Purposes**:- e.g. for the restraint of extravagance in marriage and other ceremonies, to prevent unnecessary expenditure in entertaining, to reduce the high rates of dowry required from bridegrooms, to limit unnecessary expenditure on litigation by providing for the settlement of disputes by arbitration, to put an end to such undesirable and harmful practices as the wilful destruction of trees and other property as a result of village feuds, and to promote village education and social intercourse in the villages. It may be observed that among the Moslem population of the Punjab a considerable number of societies exist for the purpose of the restraint of extravagance and for the settlement of disputes by arbitration which have contributed to an important degree to the improvement of the economic and social welfare of their members.

(f) **Urban Societies**:- Societies may be formed in the towns for the purposes of thrift and credit, for industrial purposes such as the joint exercise of a trade or the manufacture of handicrafts, for the marketing of vegetables, and fish, for the supply of domestic necessities, for building and other contracting and for the purpose of the transport of passengers and merchandise. Building societies and garden suburb societies may also be organised.

(g) Further developments in co-operative organization may be the formation of central societies for specific purposes, the

— 4 —

shares in which are held by the village societies. Examples of this type of society are:- Central banks receiving the surplus funds of credit societies, and making loans to societies either from the funds of the central bank or by borrowing from the commercial banks; central marketing of produce societies, receiving the products of the local societies and selling them in bulk such as a central citrus growers' society; central agricultural purchase societies purchasing in bulk the requirements of the local societies

3. As a first step, it is hoped, as soon as the new Co-operative Law is enacted, to proceed this year with the formation of a few credit societies, and these societies will only be founded in such villages, where after instruction of the villagers by the Registrar and his staff and the making of careful enquiries regarding the position of the founders, there appears to be a fair prospect of the successful development of a society. No attempt will be made at the outset to found societies with a large number of members but the procedure will be to organize groups of a comparatively small number of persons, say from ten to twenty five, who are of good reputation and have confidence in each other. The condition of mutual confidence is essential as it cannot be expected that persons will enter into a bond of unlimited joint and several liability for the debts of the society unless this condition is present. The idea of such mutual responsibility is not a new one in this country; cultivators are accustomed to the "Kefala Mutasalsila" in connection with the payment of tithes to the Turkish Government, which, it may be remarked, was a form of co-operation, and Barclays Bank at Nazareth has for a number of years been making short term loans to groups of villagers, secured on their crops and by a "Kefala Mutsalsila". In forming such societies the rich man, if he is not of good reputation and does not enjoy the confidence of his fellow villagers, will be rigorously excluded, while the poor man provided he is of good character and hard-working, will be admitted. After the expiration of a period of training and experience, the members of co-operative credit societies should gradually add to their number by admitting new members, who would naturally be persons in whom they have confidence. The difficulty, which a person of indifferent reputation would encounter in obtaining admission to

— 5 —

a society performing useful service in the village might be an incentive to him to mend his ways. A well defined area of operations will be insisted upon, which in the case of small villages will be the area of the village, and in larger villages, societies will comprise a quarter of the village, or the members of a "Hamuleh", "ruba᠈" or "thulth". Where the circumstances of a village are such that it is impossible to found a single society to represent all the people in the village, a second society may be established.

4. Members of a credit society will be required to acquire at least one share in the share capital of the society, and it is suggested that these shares shall be of a value of £P. 5 which may be paid by instalments spread over a period of ten years. Richer members will be encouraged to acquire more than one share. The society will be granted loans either by the Government or by one of the commercial banks and will lend to their members at a rate of interest exceeding the rate at which the society borrows by at least 3%. This difference in the rates of interest will be utilized to pay the expenses of administering the society, which in the case of a village credit society will be small, and the balance will be credited to reserve fund, which will be gradually built up in this manner until the society possesses sufficient capital to supply loans to its members from its own accumulated funds, without the necessity of borrowing money from the Government or a bank. Efforts will also be made to induce members to deposit their savings with their local credit society.

5. On the registration of a credit society, and the election of a Managing Committee, the Committee with the help of the Registrar or one of his staff, will draw up a list of loans to be granted to their members. Loans will be approved in the first place for specific productive agricultural purposes such as the purchase of seed, implements, fertilizers, ploughing cattle, etc., and it will be the duty of the Committee to ascertain whether the objects of the loans are necessary and reasonable and to watch that the loan is used for the purposes for which it was granted. A condition under which the loan is granted should be, that if it is not used for the authorised purpose, the loan shall immediately be recoverable. An essential condition will be the

— 6 —

capacity of the borrower to repay the loan at due date. When the list of applications has been revised and if necessary scaled-down, the Registrar will assist the Committee to obtain a credit either from the Government or a bank, and the usual course will be to place the credit at the disposal of the society with a local bank. It must be emphasized to borrowers that they must repay their loans to their society immediately they fall due in preference to their other debts in order to build up the credit of their society and thus facilitate the obtaining of loans in succeeding years.

6. The affairs of co-operative credit societies will be directed by the Managing Committee, of say five to seven members, who will be elected at the annual general meeting for a period of service of one year. In addition supervising committees may also where desirable be similarly elected to supervise and check the accounts of the society. A secretary will be appointed, who should not be a member of either of these committees, nor in receipt of a regular salary but a small honorarium may be granted to him in respect of his services by the General Meeting. During the early stages, officers of the Co-operative Department will visit the societies frequently, instructing the Managing Commites in their duties, the keeping of the books and the preparation of the annual balance sheet. Trial checks will from time to time be made of the books and the cash balances verified. It is intended that the accounts of small rural societies will be audited for the present by officers of the Department.

7. The Registrar of Co-operative Societies and his staff will from an early date tour the villages with the object of instructing the cultivators in co-operative methods and principles. It must however be emphasized that it would be unsound and unwise to attempt to create immediately a large number of societies composed of members with little or no understanding of co-operative principles and ideals. In the first year a few societies only will be created; in successive years it is hoped that the rate of expansion will progressively increase until a network of societies will spread all over the country. It is hoped by this means to raise the general economic level of the people and to reduce the state of indebtedness particularly among the rural population. It must also be realized that co-operation aims at

— 7 —

much more than the securing of economic benefits to the people. Among its fuller objects are the education of the people to be self-reliant and to depend on themselves, and the general improvement in the social and moral conditions of life and with this object in view attempts will be made to establish welfare societies for such purposes as those described in para2(e) above.

8. The Registrar of Co-operative Societies will be glad to give any further information on the proposed development of the co-operative movement to any person interested and enquiries should be addressed to him at P.O.B. 649, Jerusalem; he will also be ready to grant interviews which should be arranged in advance for the purpose of obtaining additional information, either at his office or at the District or Sub-District Offices at the times of his periodical visits. In this connection it cannot be too strongly stressed that the success of his efforts will depend largely on the sympathetic and well-informed interest in the movement of all officers working in the villages, of the press and of influential members of the public.

حكومة فلسطين

النشرة الاولى

نظام التعاون بين اهالي فلسطين العرب

وضعها

مسجل جمعيات التعاون

صندوق البريد ٦٤٩ . القدس

نيسان ١٩٣٣

١ — إن سوء الحالة الزراعية في هذه البلاد ما فتئ يشغل كبير عناية الذين يهمهم صالح القرويين الاقتصادي . ولاجل تحسين هذه الحالة عينت الحكومة مؤخراً مسجلا لجمعيات التعاون عهدت اليه الموافقة على انظمة الجمعيات وتسجيلها والاشراف على اعمالها لدى الذي يجيزه قانون التعاون الجديد الذي لا يزال قيد البحث . وعدا عن الواجبات التي يفرضها عليه القانون سيساعد القرويين بجميع الطرق الممكنة في تنظيم جمعيات التعاون بينهم ، وتزويدهم بانظمة نموذجية ينسجون على منوالها ، واسداء النصح لهم ، وتدريبهم على طرق ومبادىء التعاون ، والاشراف بصورة خاصة على الجمعيات الحديثة وشد ازرها . ومن المأمول ان يؤدي انتشار جمعيات التعاون التدريجي في هذه البلاد الى تسهيل الاقتراض بشروط معقولة ، وانقاص الديون ، والحصول على اجود الاسعار للحاصلات الزراعية في الاسواق الملائمة وذلك بالبيع المشترك المنظم ، والتوفير في شراء حاجات الزراع بالاشتراك في ابتياعها بالجملة . وعلى العموم ينتظر بواسطة تنظيم جمعيات التعاون بين الاهالي ان نرفع مستوى المعيشة بين المزارعين وذلك بان نحصل لهم على ايراد حسن لقاء اتعابهم ، وان نحدد ما يصرفونه في السبل الغير الضرورية ، وان نكبح جماح الاسراف ، وان نهىء الاسباب لفض الخلافات بطرق ودية وبذلك نوفر على القرويين المبالغ الطائلة التي يصرفونها اليوم في التقاضي التافه الذي لا حاجة لهم به . وسيساعد المسجل اهالي المدن ايضاً في تنظيم جمعيات تعاونية للانتاج الصناعي ، وجمعيات للتوفير والتسليف ، وغيرها من الجمعيات التي تعود على اعضائها بالخير عن طريق العمل المشترك .

٢ — وانواع جمعيات التعاون الآتية هي التي نفكر في تطبيقها بفلسطين بعد جعلها ملائمة لحالة البلاد .

(١) جمعيات التسليف القروية : جمعيات التسليف القروية التي تلائم حالة

— ٢ —

فلسطين هي التي تقترن باسم الهر رايفايزن ، المصلح الالماني ، الذي كان له فضل السبق في تنظيم جمعيات تسليفيه من هذا النوع لثمانين سنة خلت . وقد انتشرت هذه الجمعيات في اكثر البلدان الاوروبية وفي الهند والصين وجنوبي افريقيـــا ايضاً . ووفقاً لهذه المبادىء يكون اعضاء الجمعيات من ذوي الاسهم الصغيره ، ويكفلون بالتضامن والتكافل ديون الجمعية كفالة متسلسلة ، ولا يستوفون حصصاً في الارباح على مقياس اسهمهم وان استوفوا اي ارباح فتكون قليلة جداً . ويكون لكل عضو صوت واحد فقط بغض النظر عن عدد اسهمه . وتمنح هذه الجمعيات قروضاً قصيرة الاجل لاغراض منتجة يستحق دفعها في موسم الحصاد او تدفع على قسطين سنويين اذا كان الاقتراض لشراء المواشي والآلات الغالية .

(ب) جمعيات بيع الحاصلات الزراعية : بالاستطاعة ان تشكل مثل هذه الجمعيات اما لبيع الحـــاصلات الزراعية على الاطلاق او لبيع صنف معين منها كالاثمار الحمضية والموز والتبغ والزيت . ومن شروط العضوية ان يتعهد الاعضاء بتسليم حاصلاتهم الى الجمعية لبيعها وان لا يبيعوها باية طريقة اخرى . ولقد زار المسجل اثناء سياحته في مصر جمعية محكمة التنظيم في الاسكندرية تأخذ على عاتقها بيع خضروات ما يقارب الالف من صغار المنتجين ، وتبين له انها تعود على اعضائها بالخير العميم . وزار جمعية اخرى تبيع حاصلات الزراع عموماً بالتضامن وتحصل لهم على اسعار افضل من الاسعار التي يحصل عليها الزراع الذين يبيعون بانفسهم حاصلاتهم من التجار المحليين .

(ج) جمعيات شراء الحـــاجات الزراعية للزارعين : كالادوات الزراعية والآلات والبذار والاثمار المثمرة والاسمدة ومواد تعبئة الاثمار الحمضية وما شاكل ذلك . ويستطيع اعضاء هذه الجمعيات بواسطة الشراء المشترك ان يحصلوا على حاجاتهم بأثمان مخفضة تقل عن الاثمان التي يدفعونها فيما لو اشتروها بانفسهم . وبالامكان ، كما هي العادة المتبعة في بلدان مختلفة ، ان يجمع في جمعية واحدة بين الاغراض المبينة في الفقرتين (ب) و (ج) .

— ٣ —

(د) الجمعيات الزراعية لاغراض خاصة : وهي كالقيام بمشاريع الري بما فيها حفر الآبار وشراء المضخات بالتضامن ، وامتلاك الآلات الزراعية واستعمالها كالمحاريث الميكانيكية بالتضامن ايضاً ، وتاسيس جمعيات لحفظ السماد واستعماله ، وجمعيات لصنع الالبان ، وتربية النحل والطيور الداجنة ، وتخمير الاتجار المثمرة ، وتجفيف المستنقعات ، وتحدير التلال وزراعتها ، وعصر الزيتون وما شاكل ذلك . وقد زرنا في مصر جمعية تعاونية تصنع الزبدة والجبن من الحليب الذي يقدمه لها اعضاؤها ، واخرى تمتلك آلة بخارية تستعمل لحرث الارض ونزح المـــاء. للري ، وثالثة تاخذ على عاتقها تخمير الاتجار الحمضية بمساعدة الحكومة .

(ه) الجمعيات الاخلاقية والاجتماعية : إن اغراض هذه الجمعيات هي كبح جماح الاسراف في الاعراس والولائم ، وانقاص المهور الباهظة ، ووضع حد للمصارف غير الضرورية التي تنفق في المداعاة وذلك بفض الخلافات بالتحكيم ، والقضاء على العادات الضارة المكروهة التي تتسبب عن المنازعات والضغائن كقطع الاتجار واتلاف غيرها مما يملكه الفلاحون . ومن هذه الغايات ايضاً رفع مستوى التعليم والحالة الاجتماعية بين القرويين . ولا بد من الملاحظة هنا بانه يوجد بين اهالي البنجاب المسلمين في الهند عدد لا يستهان به من الجمعيات التي ترمي الى صد تيار الاسراف وفض الخلافات بالتحكيم ، والتي كان لها فضل كبير في تحسين حالة اعضائها الاقتصادية والاجتماعية .

(و) جمعيات المدن : يمكن ان تؤسس في المدن جمعيات للتوفير والتسليف لاغراض صناعية كالاتجار المشترك وعمل المصنوعات اليدوية ، وبيع الخضروات والسمك ، ولتقديم الحاجات البيتية ، وللبناء . وغيره من المقاولات ، ولنقل الركاب والبضاعة . ويمكن ايضاً تنظيم جمعيات لبناء بيوت وضواح (احياء خاصة تكتنفها الاتجار) لاعضائها .

(ز) والخطوة الثانية في النظام التعاوني هي تأسيس جمعيات مركزية لاغراض معينة تكون اسهمها ملكاً للجمعيات القروية . ومن الامثلة على هذا النوع البنوك

— ٤ —

المركزية التي تستلم من جمعيات التسليف المبالغ الزائدة عن حاجاتها . والبنك المركزي يقرض الجمعية من اموالها او من الاموال التي يستدينها من البنوك التجارية . ومنها الجمعيات المركزية لتصدير الحاصلات التي تستلم حاصلات الجمعيات المحلية وتبيعها بالجملة كالجمعية المركزية لمزارعي الاثمار الحمضية . ومنها ايضاً الجمعيات المركزية الزراعية للشراء التي تبتاع حاجيات الجمعيات المحلية بالجملة .

٣ — وكخطوة اولى في سبيل الوصول الى الغاية التي نرمي اليها نؤمل بعد صدور القانون الجديد في هذا العام ان ننظم بضع جمعيات تعاونية تسليفية . وسيقتصر على تأسيس هذه الجمعيات في القرى التي يرجى فيها النجاح ، وذلك بعد ان يدلي المسجل ومفتشه بالتعليمات الى القرويين ويتأكدا من حالة المؤسسين . ولن نحاول في البدء تأسيس جمعيات تضم عدداً كبيراً من الاعضاء. بل سنبذل جل عنايتنا في تنظيم جماعات قليلة العدد تتراوح مثلا بين العشرة والخمسة والعشرين شخصاً على ان يكونوا من ذوي السمعة الطيبة الذين يثق بعضهم ببعض . فتبادل الثقة امر ضروري اذ انه ليس من المنتظر ان ترتبط عدة اشخاص بكفالة واحدة متسلسلة بالتكافل والتضامن لدفع ديون الجمعية ما لم يتوفر فيهم هذا الشرط . إن فكرة المسؤولية المشتركة ليست بالامر المستحدث في هذه البلاد فقد اعتاد الفلاحون على الكفالة المتسلسلة فيما يتعلق بدفع الاعشار في عهد الحكومة التركية ، الامر الذي لا يخرج عن كونه نوعاً من التعاون . وهذا فرع بنك باركليس في الناصرة قد اخذ منذ سنين يقرض الفلاحين قروضاً قصيرة الاجل بضمانة حاصلاتهم وبالكفالة المتسلسلة. وعند تأسيس هذه الجمعيات لن يقبل فيها على الاطلاق الغني السيء السمعة الذي لا يتمتع بثقة اخوانه القرويين ، بينما يقبل الفقير الذي يتحلى باخلاق حميدة ويكون عاملا مجداً. وعند انقضاء دور التدريب والتجربة يسعى اعضاء الجمعية بالتدريج الى ضم اعضاء آخرين اليهم ممن يثقون بهم . وقد تكون الصعوبة التي تحول دون دخول من لا يتحلى بسمعته في جمعية تقوم بخدمات نافعة للقرية مشوقاً له على اصلاح سيرته . وسنجعل نطاق العمل محدداً ، ففي القرية الصغيرة يتناول اختصاص الجمعية القرية بكاملها وفي القرى الكبيرة اعضاء الحامولة او ,,الربع،، او ,,الثلث،، .

— ٥ —

وان تعسر انشاء جمعية واحدة في القرية تمثل جميع اهلها لا مانع من ان تؤسس فيها جمعيتان .

٤ — سيطلب من كل عضو في الجمعية التسليفية ان يشتري سهماً واحداً على الاقل من الرأسمال الاسهمي للجمعية . ويقترح ان تكون قيمة السهم خمسة جنيهات تدفع باقساط على مدار عشر سنوات . وسيشجع الاعضاء الاغنياء على شراء اكثر من سهم واحد . وستمنح الجمعية قروضاً من الحكومة او من احد البنوك التجاريه . وتتقاضى من الاعضاء فائدة بمعدل ٣٪. على الاقل فوق معدل الفائدة التي تدفعها على القرض الذي استلفته . ويستعمل الفرق بين قيمة الفائدتين لدفع نفقــات ادارة الجمعية ، وهي قليلة في الجمعية التسليفية القروية ، وما تبقى يضاف الى المال الاحتياطي الذي يزداد بهذا الشكل شيئاً فشيئاً حتى يصبح للجمعية رأسمال كافٍ فستطيع حينئذ ان تقرض اعضاءها من اموالها المتراكمة بدون ان تلجأ الى الحكومة او احد البنوك لاقراضها . وستبذل الجهود لحمل الاعضاء على ايداع ما يوفرونه في صندوق جمعيتهم التسليفية المحلية .

٥ — وعند تسجيل الجمعية وانتخاب هيئة الادارة تضع هذه اللجنة بمساعدة المسجل او احد موظفيه قائمة بالقروض التي ستمنحها الى اعضائها . وستمنح في الدرجة الاولى قروض لاغراض زراعية معينة كشراء البذار والادوات الزراعية والاسمدة ومواشي الحراثة وما شاكل ذلك . ويكون من واجب لجنة الادارة ان تتحقق ان الغاية التي طلب القرض من اجلها ضرورية معقولة ، وان تاخذ الحيطة لاستثمار القرض في سبيل الغاية المتوخاة. ويجب ان يكون من شروط الاقراض استرداد القرض في الحال اذا لم يصرف في هذه الغاية . وستكون قدرة المقترض على سداد القرض في موسم الحصاد شرطاً اساسياً . وبعد ان تعدل قائمة القروض وتخفض اذا دعت الحاجة الى ذلك ، يساعد المسجل لجنة الادارة في الحصول على قرض من الحكومة او احد البنوك . والطريقة العاديه هي ان يفتح للجمعيه اعتماد في احد البنوك المحلية . ويجب ان يوقع المقترضون بان من واجبهم ان يسددوا ما عليهم من

— ٦ —

الديون الى جمعيتهم عند حلول الاجل وان يميزوها على غيرها من القروض حتى يتمكنوا من تشييد اعتماد جمعيتهم المالي وبذلك يسهلون عليها الاستقراض في السنين المقبلة .

٦ — وتشرف على شؤون جمعية التعاون التسليفية لجنة الادارة التي تتألف مثلا من خمسة الى سبعة اعضاء . ينتخبون لمدة سنة في الاجتماع السنوي العام . وفضلا عن ذلك يمكن عند الحاجة انتخاب لجان مراقبة لتشرف على حسابات الجمعية وتدققها . ويعين سكرتير للجمعية يشترط فيه ان لا يكون من اعضاء لجنة الادارة ولا من لجنة المراقبة وان لا يتقاضى راتباً معيناً ، على انه يجوز ان تمنحه الهيئة العمومية مكافأة ضئيلة لقاء خدماته . وفي الادوار الاولى يكثر موظفو دائرة التعاون من زيارة الجمعية ليبينوا للجان الادارة وظائفها ويشرحوا لها كيفية مسك الدفاتر واعداد الميزانية السنوية . وسيقومون من حين لآخر بفحص الدفاتر واحصاء رصيد الصندوق . وفي النية الآن ان تراقب حسابات الجمعيات القروية الصغيرة من قبل موظفي دائرة التعاون .

٧ — سيتجول مسجل جمعيات التعاون وموظفوه في القرى واضعين نصب اعينهم تدريب الفلاحين على مبادىء التعاون وطرقه . ونؤكد بانه من الخطأ والخطل ان نؤسس في الحال عدداً كبيراً من الجمعيات تضم اعضاءً ممن لا يعرفون شيئاً عن مبادىء التعاون ومثله العليا او ممن يعرفون عنها النذر القليل . في السنة الاولى سنؤسس بضع جمعيات آملين في السنين التالية ان تتسع هذه الحركة شيئاً فشيئا فتعم جميع انحاء البلاد . وبهذه الواسطة نأمل ان نرفع المستوى الاقتصادي بين الاهلين وان نخفف من وطأة الدين الذي ينوء بحمله القرويون خاصة . ويجب ان لا يغرب عن البال بان التعاون يرمي الى هدف اسمى من نفع الاهالي المادي ، فمن جملة اغراضه تعليم الناس الاعتماد على النفس وتحسين الاحوال الاخلاقية والاجتماعية . وسنحاول ، واضعين هذا الهدف نصب اعيننا ، تأسيس جمعيات اخلاقية لتحقيق الغايات التي وصفناها في الفقرة ٢ (ج) المذكورة .

— ٧ —

٨ — إنه ليسر مسجل جمعيات التعاون ان يقدم اية معلومات اضافية عن الحركة التعاونية المنوى انشاؤها الى اي شخص يهمه هذا الموضوع ، على ان يوجه الطلب الى عنوانه : صندوق البريد ٦٤٩ — القدس . وهو على استعداد لمقابلة هؤلاء . في مكتبه او في دوائر حكام الالوية والقائمقامين اثناء زيارته لها بعد ان تحدد المقابلة بميعاد سابق . وبهذه المناسبة لا بد من القول بان توفيق المسجل فيما يبذل من جهود لانشاء المؤسسات التعاونية يتوقف لدرجـــة كبرى على ما يبديه جميع موظفي الحكومة الذين يشتغلون في القرى ، والصحافة وذوي النفوذ والكلمة المسموعة من افراد الامة الذين يهمهم صالح القرويين ، من العطف والدراية نحو هذه الحركة .

8.05

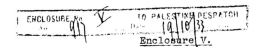

Enclosure V.

Memorandum on the Co-operative Societies Ordinance.

The Palestine Co-operative Societies Ordinance, 1920, is based in many respects on the Indian Co-operative Societies Act, 1912. It differs in not contemplating an active and peripatetic Registrar, who would (as in India, Ceylon, Malaya) take a considerable part in the organization of societies, and subsequently in their guidance and inspection, and if necessary in their liquidation. Under such an Ordinance the Jews have proved competent to organize societies, but the Arabs have not. They require a trained Registrar as their leader, and in a certain measure their controller, since they are unfamiliar with the movement and need education in it. This trained Registrar has now been appointed.

Such a Registrar must have powers, in excess of those given to him by the present Ordinance, in order to avert serious mistakes. It is not desirable to enact two Ordinances for the two communities, and the powers must therefore be applicable to Jewish as well as Arab societies. The Registrar will use them sparingly in the case of Jewish co-operators, but the Jewish movement, which has grown up without the active help of Government, presents certain defects which he cannot ignore.

In order to leave a Registrar, trained for his duties, in a position free from obstruction by individual members who are not genuine co-operators, appeals against his orders are to lie to the High Commissioner and not to the Courts. This is the ordinary rule in India and elsewhere, and it is essential if the Registrar's work is not to be continually hampered by litigious persons. The

High/

-2-

High Commissioner will be able to prevent an unreasonable use of authority.

Arab societies will gradually build up their own share capital and surplus funds, but will need additional finance, which it is hoped to secure from the commercial banks. Advances from Government are less stimulating, and will only be necessary in villages which a commercial bank regards as inaccessible.

2. The new Ordinance, in addition to providing for the exercise of a temperate authority by the Registrar, will authorize the registration of central co-operative societies for credit, marketing and other purposes, will secure to marketing societies the validity of contracts made with their members for the delivery and sale of their produce, and will permit the High Commissioner, in case a society includes 75% of the producers of a given commodity and 75% of the crops, to enforce the marketing of the remaining 25% through the same channel, in order that the market may not be wrecked by a few recalcitrant persons. The same principle is applied in co-operative legislation in Australia, North America, South Africa and the West Indies; it is found in the Agricultural Marketing Act of Great Britain, and has recently been approved by the Colonial Office in the Co-operative Ordinance of Tanganyika. The High Commissioner is at liberty to refuse the demand of such a majority for a compulsory order, if he foresees communal friction or finds it inadvisable for other reasons.

All these provisions are beneficial to Jews and Arabs alike.

Co-operative societies which distribute no dividend on their shares are also released by this

Ordinance/

Ordinance from the statutory limitation of interest at 9%. This old Turkish law is frequently evaded by the charging of a commission in addition to interest or by the entry of an unreal sum of principal money in a bond; the limitation thus affects only the honest creditor and not the dishonest. It is therefore of little value. In any case, co-operative societies, which pay no dividend on shares but carry their surplus to a reserve fund, are saving money for the benefit of their own members, and may be left free to fix their own rates. Creditor and debtor are the same person.

The Ordinance follows the Indian model, as does that of Tanganyika. In authorizing the High Commissioner to exempt societies from such taxes, duties and fees as he thinks fit. Arab societies in particular are unlikely to have such a capital as to meet these charges, and since the co-operative movement is of great value to the country, it is well to encourage it by concessions which cost Government very little.

3. The Jewish societies, though vigorous and very creditable to the courage of their members, are not without blemishes. The Ordinance as drafted endeavours to remove these, and protests may be evoked from men who have wandered from the true co-operative path. They have for instance a system of preference shares conferring no right of vote, a class of associate members who are excluded from the vote, a habit of issuing lottery or premium debentures, of using proxies in an unco-operative manner, and of giving loans to non-members. There are other defects, such as the admission of a paid Manager to a seat in the managing committee, which he then tends to dominate. But the worst evils in a

movement/

movement which on the whole is highly creditable, are
(1) unsatisfactory audit and (2) duplication of membership and cross-lending.

For the improvement of audit a system of audit unions is proposed, and is acceptable to the Jewish co-operators. (The Arabs will reach this stage somewhat later, and will for the present be audited by persons appointed by the Registrar). Duplication of membership, i.e. an individual joining and borrowing from several societies, is altogether unsafe and unco-operative, but has spread widely among the Jews. The regulations which it is intended to issue under the new Ordinance will prohibit this practice, but the Registrar has agreed with leading Jewish co-operators that he will consult them as to measures leading to its gradual abandonment. No violent enforcement is contemplated, but a fundamental co-operative principle cannot be surrendered.

Many of the sections in the draft Ordinance, against which the Jewish co-operators, who have been consulted, have raised protests, are already in the present Ordinance, but have never been enforced. The protests are thus made against a Law which would have been peacefully obeyed if it had from the first been applied. In reality, no serious objection will arise to the suggested changes. A prudent traveller cries out before he is hurt, in order to secure more than his share of the road.

The High Commissioner has power, in the new Ordinance, to exempt a society from any of its provisions. This is a common rule in Asia, since it is impossible to foresee every future emergency. The section can be

used/

-5-

used in Palestine to allow a temporary exemption of certain old societies from the new provisions which they dislike and which are not fundamental.

(Sgd) C.F. Strickland.
15th March, 1933.

8.06

HIGH COMMISSIONER FOR PALESTINE,
JERUSALEM.

PALESTINE

CONFIDENTIAL

REFERENCE NO. CF/290/34

16 April, 1935.

Sir,

I have the honour to refer to your Confidential despatch of the 26th May, 1933, and connected correspondence with regard to the provision of agricultural credits in the Schedule to the new Palestine Government Guaranteed Loan of LP. 2,000,000, and in particular to the provision of credits for long term development loans in the hills.

2. I enclose herein a copy of the report submitted on the 7th March by a Committee which I appointed under the Chairmanship of the Director of Agriculture and Forests to formulate the general principles which should govern the application and security for the grant of loans of this kind out of the allocation of LP. 50,000 in the Schedule. It will be observed that the recommendations in the report are founded upon an actual survey of characteristic hill villages in each district so as to determine the nature and extent of assistance required, bearing in mind economic and soil conditions. For convenience of reference I attach a summary of the recommendations in the report.

3. I considered the report in Executive Council and decided to accept the recommendations in it, subject to the following modifications:-

THE RIGHT HONOURABLE
 IR PHILIP CUNLIFFE-LISTER, G.B.E., M.P., etc., etc.,
  HIS MAJESTY'S PRINCIPAL SECRETARY OF STATE
                              FOR THE COLONIES.

2.

(a) That while the loans might be issued to co-operative societies at 6%, the Government Board should stipulate the rate at which the societies should charge their members;

(b). Loans granted on security of title deeds should not be granted at a lower rate than that (7%) to be charged by the Agricultural Mortgage Company for similar loans;

(c) Loans granted on the security of crops should be at 9% in view of the agreement with Barclays Bank for short-term crop loans;

(d) Thus, the rates of interest would be as follows:-

Where the security is title deeds	7%	To be revised according to rate of interest charged by Agricultural Mortgage Company of Palestine on loans against similar security.
Where the security is joint and several guarantees of a co-operative society	7%	
In other cases where the security is the crop	9%	

(e) Sheep and cattle dips should be included in the purposes for which loans will be granted.

4. I am anxious that the cultivators in the Hill districts who are urgently in need of this form of assistance should begin to enjoy the benefits of the allocation in the Loan Schedule with the least possible delay, and I shall be grateful, therefore, if I may be allowed to make the sum of LP. 50,000 available for the purpose immediately from Surplus Balances in anticipation of the issue of the new Loan. In the event of

3.

your approval, the allocation will be administered by a Board of Control consisting of the Director of Agriculture and Forests, Development Officer and a senior Assistant Treasurer.

                I have the honour to be,
                      Sir,
                Your most obedient,
                    humble servant,

Arthur Wauchope
HIGH COMMISSIONER FOR PALESTINE.

#C/13/18

ENCLOSURE No. 1
Conf.
IN PALESTINE DESPATCH
No. 16.4.35

DEPARTMENT OF AGRICULTURE
AND FORESTS.
JERUSALEM.

7th March, 1935.

CHIEF SECRETARY.

Subject: £P. 50,000 Loan Scheme for Hill Villages.

Reference: Your CF/290/34 of the 3rd October, 1934.

I have the honour to refer to your above-quoted letter and to Despatch No. 17448/33 of the 10th of June, 1933, addressed to His Majesty's Treasury, intimating, inter alia, that the Lords Commissioners of the Treasury have been asked to approve of the High Commissioner's proposals with regard to the provision of facilities for long term development loans in the hill districts and of the inclusion of the necessary provision of £P. 50,000 in the Loan Schedule.

2. In your letter No. CF/290/34 of the 3rd October, 1934, His Excellency directed that machinery should be set in motion at once to ensure that the sum of £P.50,000 set aside in the Schedule of the new loan of £P. 2,000,000 for the grant of long term loans to villagers in the hill districts shall, when the time comes, be applied without delay to the best advantage. In that letter, I was instructed to consult with the District Commissioners and the Development Officer to formulate the general principles which should govern the application and security for the grant of loans of this kind. The late Registrar of Cooperative Societies, Mr. F.G. Lowick, and Mr. M.F. Abcarius, O.B.E., Senior Assistant Treasurer, were subsequently also associated with this enquiry.

- 2 -

3. Two meetings of the Committee referred to above were held, on the 12th of October, 1934, and the 12th of February, 1935. Between these dates, preliminary surveys of typical villages in the hill districts were carried out. Two surveys were made in the Jenin District by the Assistant District Commissioner, Mr. H.M. Foot. The first village selected was Yaabed, a typical hill village with a population of 2,383. The second village selected was Kufeir, which has only a population of 107, but which is closely associated with the neighbouring villages of Sir (population 233) and Talfit (population 120). This group of three villages is owned by one family. The third survey was made in Dura village in the District of Hebron - this village has a population of about 9,000, inhabiting 119 Khirbets. The survey of this village was made jointly by Mr. A.F. Nathan, O.B.E., Assistant Director of Agriculture and Forests, and Mr. A. Kardus, M.B.E., District Officer, Hebron.

4. The Committee are now able to make their recommendations under the following heads :-

    I. Objects of the loan.
   II. Security for the loan.
  III. Period of the loan.
  IV. The amounts to be loaned to applicants.
   V. Rate of interest.
  VI. To whom loans should be made.
 VII. Procedure for the application and grant of loans.

- 3 -

I. <u>Objects of the Loan.</u>

It is recommended that the main objects for which loans should be devoted should be the following :-

(a) Fruit and vine growing (including terracing and fencing).
(b) Animal husbandry (including sheep, cows, goats and poultry).
(c) Water conservation for irrigation (including dams, reservoirs, canalisation and wells).
(d) Purchase of agricultural machinery and implements (such as ploughs, grain cleaners, threshing machines and spraying machines).

It is agreed that there is no need to distinguish loan schemes in order of priority.

II. <u>Security for Loan.</u>

The security for the loans should, <u>in general</u>, be based on <u>title deeds</u> or <u>collective guarantees</u>. If the scheme is to be operated on a sound business basis, loans should be restricted to persons whose lands are registered, and the security should be a mortgage on registered lands. In the absence of title deeds, however, the reputed owners, it is suggested, should produce deeds of inheritance. But difficulties must be envisaged regarding shares and co-owners. It must be borne in mind that the proposed total loans of £P. 50,000 will, in all probability, not suffice for all the applications to be received, and if therefore, loans are in fact restricted to persons whose lands are registered and have clear titles, this might prevent some <u>75% of</u> the people in the hills from applying for loans. Consequently, in view of these considerations.

- 4 -

the Committee recommend that three kinds of security should be accepted :-

    (a) For individuals - registered title to the lands.

    (b) For communities - collective or joint and several guarantees.

The security offered by such groups would in most cases be Kafaleh Mutasilsileh.

    (c) For Cooperative Societies - joint and several guarantees.

It is suggested that these guarantees should be made by the members of the Society, and that the Society as a juristic body should create a charge on its own assets in favour of Government, under Section 28 of the Cooperative Societies Ordinance, and that as an additional guarantee, they should assign to Government, charges on the crops of members under Section 27 of the Ordinance. For the purpose of such loans, new societies with limited liability may have to be formed, in accordance with a scheme proposed by the late Registrar of Cooperative Societies, thus :-

> "In the case of a Government loan to a group registered as a co-operative society, the rules should provide for a small capital investment say £P.1.- or 500 mils per member and a very small entrance fee. The maximum liability of the members would be in the form of a multiple of the share capital sufficient to cover amply (say twice) the amount of the loan. The members would be jointly and severally responsible for the debts of the society to the extent of their maximum liability. The loan should be made to the society, and should be re-lent to the members in amounts to be prescribed by Government at a slightly higher rate of interest than that charged by Government to provide for working expenses and to build up a reserve fund. The society would assign to Government the members' bonds for repayment of their loans. Where the members were unable to give a mortgage as security, which will be the rule rather than the exception in the hills, the society would cause them to give a charge on all their crops for the period covered by the loan. This charge would be registered with the District Officer under Section 26 of the Co-operative Societies Ordinance, 1933 and assigned to the Government. I suggest that in view of the legislation for the protection of cultivators, a crop charge is better security than a mortgage on real estate."

- 5 -

In this connection the late Registrar of Cooperative Societies stated that if Government sanctions the necessary staff, his Department would be prepared to undertake the following duties in conjunction with the District Officers :-

(1) Drafting of Rules.
(2) Registration of Societies (free of fees).
(3) Organisation of their routine business (as distinct from the technical work involved in the use of the loan).
(4) Periodical inspections.
(5) Audit of their accounts.
(6) Provision of model account books at reasonable rates.

The late Registrar of Cooperative Societies emphasised the advantages of collective effort as compared with sporadic individual effort and the suitability of the adoption of cooperative organisation whenever it is found desirable and feasible to grant loans for similar purposes to a number of cultivators in the village.

III. Period of the Loan.

It was agreed that the period of the loan would be determined by the nature of each individual scheme, the principal consideration being that recovery should not begin before the production of a saleable crop. The Treasurer has stated that "ordinarily he would not recommend a 40 year loan for any of the objects proposed. He understands that the maximum period of any loan by the proposed Agricultural Mortgage Company is 10 years, but the period must be within the average life of the asset

- 6 -

or improvement created by any loans, and repayment instalments must be determined by the additional benefit or revenue resulting from the asset or improvement".

In the view of the District Commissioner, South, the maximum period of 10 years would not cover all cases. For example, olive trees which do not come into full bearing before 15 years. In the case of newly planted olives, the Rural Property Tax is not collectable until 10 years. The Committee recommend that the period of the loans should vary from about three to seventeen years, it being anticipated that the bulk of the loans would be from 5 to 10 years. With regard to cooperative societies, however, it is pointed out that they may not have a life of 17 years so that there may be difficulties in recovery of the loans from such societies. The Development Officer suggests that this difficulty might be solved by providing in the Rules of the Society that the Society may not terminate its activities before a given date. Similar provisions are usually made in building societies which raise long term loans, (vide Regulation 14 (e) of the Cooperative Societies Regulations, 1934, page 33 of Pamphlet No.4.).

IV. **Amounts to be loaned to Applicants.**

The actual amounts issued would depend on the details of each scheme. In general, they should be limited to 50% of the valuation of the land at the time the loans are issued, less existing mortgages.

The Committee recommend that loans to individuals should normally be from £P.25 to £P. 250 and to communities from £P. 50 to £P. 1,000, the Board to have discretionary power to vary the amount of the loan within these limits. The Development Officer, however, suggests that in the case

– 7 –

of Cooperative Societies no limit should be laid down, that is, the sum to be loaned should be calculated on the requirements of the individual members within the maximum which will be laid down for individuals. For example, if there are 100 members in a society and the limit for an individual is £P. 25, the Society's application to borrow £P. 2,500 should be favourably considered.

V. Rate of Interest.

At present, Cooperative Societies borrow at 6% and lend to their members at 9%, the surplus of 3% being put into the Society. The terms of the "principal loan" are not known, but the Committee note that the following items have to be considered :-

    (a) Interest.
    (b) Sinking Fund.
    (c) Provision for bad debts.
    (d) Costs of administration.

Too high a rate would lead to uneconomic undertakings, and result in inability to repay the loan. The Committee consequently recommend that the rate of interest should not be less than 6 or more than 7%. The Development Officer, however, points out that unless Cooperative Societies are given better terms than other bodies, as regards interest charges, there is the possibility that such Societies may refrain from participating in the loan, although, of course, individual members of such Societies could obtain any sums required in the same manner as other villagers. In that event Government would lose the control of expenditure which is maintained by Cooperative Societies.

VI. To whom Loans should be made.

The majority of the Committee hold the view that the middle-class person is likely under this scheme to be the main beneficiary, as he will be in a better position to offer adequate security. It is clear that if the conditions as to security are too stringent, the poorer individual may not, as a rule, benefit. Communities and Cooperative Societies should also be eligible for loans. At a meeting held in the offices of the District Commissioner, Jerusalem, on the 12th of December, 1934, the District Officers of the Jerusalem Division were assembled and the late Registrar of Cooperative Societies pointed out that Cooperative Societies cannot get loans from banks for long terms. The multiplication of Cooperative Societies in the same village, he said, would not in itself present serious difficulties, but wherever possible, such Societies should be encouraged to combine.

VII. Procedure for Application and Grant of Loans.

The following steps are recommended for adoption when it is decided to call for applications for loans and grant loans :-

(a) A Press Communiqué should be issued as to the policy of Government on this subject.

(b) Applications for loans should be made on a prescribed form. The form of application should show the intended uses of the loan, the conditions and the security offered. The forms should be addressed in the first instance to the District Officer.

(c) District Officers would examine and certify applications in collaboration with Land Registrars particularly with regard to the question of security.

- 9 -

(d) Applications would be submitted through the District Commissioner or Assistant District Commissioner to the Director of Agriculture and Forests, with their observations.

(e) The Director of Agriculture and Forests would cause a detailed inspection to be made of the property and the scheme, and embody the results in a technical report.

(f) The papers would then be referred to the Board who will examine each case on its merits and authorise the issue of loans and prescribe the terms and the conditions for repayment of the loans. (It is understood that the Board is to consist of the Director of Agriculture and Forests, the Development Officer, and the Assistant Treasurer. Despatch Secre A dated 8.4.33. from the Secretary of State refers.)

(g) The Board would then request the District Commissioner or Assistant District Commissioner to issue the loans. They would be responsible for the custody of the documents and recovery of the loans.

NOTE: A draft of the proposed form is attached.

5.   Survey of Typical Hill Villages.

The following is a summary of the recommendations contained in the report on the preliminary survey of Dura Village:-

(a) Drainage and water collection scheme, namely : construction of canals and collection of the drainage water location and improvement of the subterranean springs and collection of their output.

- 10 -

(b) Planting of fruit trees.
(c) General improvement of holdings.
(d) Release from cumbersome mortgages.
(e) Terracing for the planting of fruit trees.

The Committee are of the opinion that the release from mortgages (Item d) should not be regarded as an object for which loans may be granted.

Arising out of Item (a) the Committee observed that, as the Village Water Supply Fund exists for the express purpose of improving drinking supplies (subject to 10% contributions from the village), this would not ordinarily of itself be an appropriate object for the loans.

The following is a summary of the recommendations contained in the report on the survey of Yaabed and Kufeir villages :-

(a) Most pressing needs are for tractors and ploughs, also agricultural machinery.
(b) Improvement of stock.
(c) Boring plants and improvements to simple irrigation systems.
(d) Tree planting.

The Committee recommend with reference to (a) that loans for tractors should not ordinarily be included since loans are primarily for hill development in areas where there is little plain land. Agricultural machinery, however, such as ploughs, grain cleaners, threshing machines and spraying machines, etc. would be suitable objects.

With regard to item (c), the Committee consider that loans to bore for water would be inappropriate since this matter is dealt with by the Underground Water Survey Committee and the Public Works Department. The improvement of simple irrigation systems, however, is a suitable object

AB.

DIRECTOR OF AGRICULTURE
AND FORESTS.

GOVERNMENT OF PALESTINE
APPLICATION FOR LONG TERM LOAN.

1. Sub-District . . . .
2. Village. . . . .
3. Name of Applicant . . . .
4. Amount of Loan applied for . . . .
5. Term of Loan . . . . years.
6. Security offered . . . .
7. Purpose for which loan is required (to be given in detail showing the various items of improvements and the estimated cost of each.

Particulars	Amount £P. Mil

8. I/We hereby undertake if the loan is granted to utilise the money on the proposed improvements or on such other improvements as may be authorised; and I/We understand if this money is diverted to any other purpose I/We shall be liable to refund the amount of loan on demand. Interest at the rate of . . . . per annum shall accrue on the loan and I/We undertake to pay the interest and instalments as they fall due.

. . . .
Signature of Applicant

Date:. . .

9/

9. Observations by District Officer as to:-
(a) Security.

(b) Financial standing and business morality of applicant.

(c) Desirability of the proposed improvements.

Date...................   Signature......................

---

10. Remarks by the competent officer of the Department of Agricu[lture] and Forests:-

Date...............   Signature....................

---

11. Decisions by the Board :-
(a) Amount approved...
(b) Period of loan............................years,
(c) Amount of annual instalment..................................
(d) Date of 1st instalment......................................

Date......

Conf.² 16.4.35

SUMMARY OF RECOMMENDATIONS AS IN THE REPORT DATED THE 7TH MARCH, 1935, FOR THE GRANT OF LOANS IN HILL DISTRICTS OUT OF THE PROVISION OF ₤ 50,000 IN THE NEW LOAN.

(1) The main objects should be the following:

    (a) Fruit and vine growing (including terracing and fencing).

    (b) Animal husbandry (including sheep, cows, goats and poultry).

    (c) Water conservation for irrigation (including dams, reservoirs, canalization and wells).

    (d) Purchase of agricultural machinery and implements (such as ploughs, grain cleaners, threshing machines and praying machines).

(2) No order of priority of objects.

(3) Security to be title deeds (or in their absence deeds of inheritance) in the case of individuals; collective or joint and several guarantees in the case of communities; and joint and several guarantees in the case of Cooperative Societies.

(4) Period 3 to 17 years and any cooperative society to be bound not to cease its activities before the term of any loan.

(5) Amount of loan to be limited to 50% of the valuation of the land less existing mortgages; to individuals normally from LP. 25 to LP. 250 to communities from LP. 50 to LP. 1000. Development Officer suggests no limit in the case of Cooperative Societies.

(6) Interest not less than 6% or 7%.

(7) Middle class persons to be main beneficiaries but communities and cooperative societies also to be eligible.

(8) The procedure for application in grant of loans is given under Head VII in the Report.

Section 9: Memoranda on restricting land sales, 1930-1936

9.01

PALESTINE

Statement with regard to British Policy

*Presented by the Secretary of State for the Colonies
to Parliament by Command of His Majesty
May, 1930.*

LONDON:
PRINTED AND PUBLISHED BY HIS MAJESTY'S STATIONERY OFFICE.
To be purchased directly from H.M. STATIONERY OFFICE at the following addresses:
Adastral House, Kingsway, London, W.C.2; 120, George Street, Edinburgh;
York Street, Manchester; 1, St. Andrew's Crescent, Cardiff;
15, Donegall Square West, Belfast;
or through any Bookseller.

1930.

Price net.

Cmd.

3

Despatch from the Secretary of State for the Colonies to the High Commissioner for Palestine.

DOWNING STREET,
21st May, 1930.

SIR,

I have the honour to transmit to you, for your information, the accompanying copy of a statement with regard to British Policy in Palestine, by the British Accredited Representative at the forthcoming Special Session of the Permanent Mandates Commission. A copy is also enclosed of a letter addressed to the Foreign Office forwarding copies of the above statement for communication to the Members of the Permanent Mandates Commission.

2. Steps are being taken to publish this despatch and enclosure as a Command Paper.

I have, etc.,
PASSFIELD.

Letter from the Colonial Office to the Foreign Office.

DOWNING STREET,
19th May, 1930.

SIR,

I am directed by Lord Passfield to transmit to you, to be laid before Mr. Secretary Henderson, the accompanying copies of a statement with regard to British Policy in Palestine, by the British Accredited Representative at the forthcoming Special Session of the Permanent Mandates Commission.

2. As Mr. Henderson is aware, the Members of the Permanent Mandates Commission have expressed a wish to be furnished with the text of the above statement in advance, if possible a fortnight before the meeting of the Council. Lord Passfield would accordingly be glad if arrangements could be made for copies of the statement as now finally approved to be circulated with the least possible delay to the Members of the Permanent Mandates Commission and to the Secretary-General of the League of Nations.

I am, etc.,
O. G. R. WILLIAMS.

PALESTINE.

Statement by the British Accredited Representative to Permanent Mandates Commission.

1. The Permanent Mandates Commission are aware of the circumstances in which a Special Commission, under the Chairmanship of Sir William Shaw, was appointed by the British Government in September last " to enquire into the immediate causes which led to the recent outbreak in Palestine and to make recommendations as to the steps necessary to avoid a recurrence." After an exhaustive investigation conducted on the spot, the Commission presented its report on the 12th March, 1930. The Report was published in Great Britain as a Parliamentary Paper at the beginning of April, and copies were at the same time forwarded to the Secretary-General of the League of Nations, for distribution to members of the Permanent Mandates Commission.

2. Following upon the publication of the Report, the Prime Minister of Great Britain made a statement in the following terms in the British House of Commons on the 3rd April, 1930 :—

" His Majesty's Government will continue to administer Palestine in accordance with the terms of the Mandate as approved by the Council of the League of Nations. That is an international obligation from which there can be no question of receding.

" Under the terms of the Mandate His Majesty's Government are responsible for promoting ' the establishment in Palestine of a National Home for the Jewish people, it being clearly understood that nothing shall be done which might prejudice the civil and religious rights of existing non-Jewish communities in Palestine or the rights and political status enjoyed by Jews in any other country.'

" A double undertaking is involved, to the Jewish people on the one hand, and to the non-Jewish population of Palestine on the other; and it is the firm resolve of His Majesty's Government to give effect, in equal measure, to both parts of the Declaration, and to do equal justice to all sections of the population of Palestine. That is a duty from which they will not shrink, and to the discharge of which they will apply all the resources at their command.

" The Report of the Shaw Commission, which is in the hands of Honourable Members, covers a wide field. The Commission was appointed to consider the immediate causes of the deplorable disturbances of August last, and to suggest means of preventing a recurrence. In endeavouring faithfully to carry out the terms of

---

Cmd. 3530.

reference, the Commission must have found it difficult to draw lines very rigidly. The Government is now studying the various recommendations of the Commission, with a view to dealing with the immediate causes of the outbreak and to preventing a recurrence, and is in consultation with the interests concerned. I wish it to be understood that this statement includes the immediate provision of the police forces required to secure Civil peace under existing circumstances."

3. His Majesty's Government have now given further consideration to the various conclusions and recommendations of the Commission of Enquiry. But before proceeding to the discussion of details, they would wish to offer some preliminary observations of a more general nature. The difficulties arising out of the peculiar character of the Palestine Mandate are well known. There is no need to labour this aspect of the question, since it is one with which the Permanent Mandates Commission are already familiar. It was discussed in detail in the course of the Observations recorded by the Commission (in November 1924) on the first report on the administration of Palestine that came under their examination. The Commission then remarked that, whereas all the other mandates the application of which they had hitherto examined were only intended to give effect to the general principles of Article 22 of the Covenant of the League of Nations, the mandate for Palestine was " of a more complex nature," in that it imposed upon the Mandatory Power a " twofold duty," viz., that of promoting the establishment of a National Home for the Jewish people, in addition to that of administering the country in conformity with the interests of the population as a whole. The result, as the Commission pointed out, was to create a " conflict of interests " between which the balance had to be held. The observations recorded by the Permanent Mandates Commission in November 1924 have lost none of their relevance at the present time. The conflict of interest remains, and the task of holding the balance has certainly not decreased in difficulty. The situation is one of great delicacy, calling for the exercise of all possible patience and circumspection. That it has certain unsatisfactory features, as is pointed out in the Report of the Commission of Enquiry, His Majesty's Government are not concerned to dispute. Rather, they are more concerned to provide a remedy; and to this task they mean to address themselves with all the resources at their disposal. They do not underrate the difficulties. The conditions under which remedial measures can be applied are strictly limited; they are governed by the terms of the Mandate and by the dual obligation which it imposes. Such measures cannot be devised or introduced at a moment's notice. Caution is essential, and the ground must be carefully examined before an advance can safely be made. For these reasons His Majesty's Government are not in a position to formulate precise

and concrete proposals in regard to all the points that the Commission have raised. On some at least of these points they can do no more than indicate provisionally the lines on which they hope to proceed.

4. Turning to the questions of detail, His Majesty's Government accept generally the findings of the Commission of Enquiry under the following five heads, viz. :—

(i) Nature of the outbreak (page 158);

(ii) Zionist complaints against the Grand Mufti of Jerusalem (pages 158 and 159);

(iii) Zionist complaints against the Palestine Arab Executive (page 159);

(iv) Zionist complaints against the Government (pages 159 to 161); and

(v) Minor Arab grievances (page 163).

His Majesty's Government do not consider that these conclusions in themselves call for special action on their part. It will be noted, in connection with (ii), that Mr. Snell, one of the three Commissioners, in his Note of Reservations, has attributed to the Grand Mufti a greater share in the responsibility for the disturbances than is attributed to him in the Report, and has expressed the view that the Mufti must bear the blame for his failure to make any effort to control the character of agitation conducted in the name of a religion, of which, in Palestine, he was the head (page 172). As to this, reference is invited to the statement made on page 77 of the Commission's Report to the effect that, whatever activities he may have indulged in outside the knowledge of the Government, in public the Mufti, both at noon on the 23rd August and thereafter throughout the period of the disturbances, exerted his influence in the direction of promoting peace and restoring order. On this point, the Report states, there was an absolute unanimity of opinion among the many official witnesses with whom the question of the Mufti's conduct was raised during the course of the Commission's enquiry. Mr. Snell also dissents from the conclusions in the Report " acquitting the Moslem religious authorities of all but the slightest blame for the innovations introduced in the neighbourhood of the Wailing Wall." On this point it is to be observed that the Report (paragraph 7 on page 159) does not purport to assign any specific degree of blame to the Mohammedan authorities. The conclusion which it records is that " in the matter of innovations of practice little blame can be attached to the Mufti in which some Jewish religious authorities also would not have to share." His Majesty's Government do not feel that they can usefully offer any further comments on this branch of the question.

7

5. It may be convenient to deal in one paragraph with two important economic questions which are closely inter-related, viz., those concerning Immigration and the Land problem. The Conclusions and Recommendations of the Commission of Enquiry on these questions appear on pages 161, 162, 165, and 166 of their Report. Mr. Snell has also expressed certain views and has made supplementary recommendations with regard to these questions in his Note of Reservation. It is in relation to these questions, and to that of immigration in particular, that the dual character of the Mandate assumes its most significant aspect. This was recognised, in effect, by the Permanent Mandates Commission when, in the course of the Observations of November, 1924, from which quotation has already been made, they selected the problem of immigration ("perhaps the dominant issue of the present situation in Palestine") as best illustrating their general exposition upon the operation of the Mandate. The following passage from the Observations states the problem so clearly that it may be quoted in full :—" It is obvious that if the Mandatory Power had only to take into consideration the interests of the population, its immigration policy ought to be dictated primarily by considerations of the economic needs of the country. It is, moreover, equally clear that if the Mandatory Power had not to take into account the interests of the Arab population, and if its sole duty was to encourage Jewish immigration in Palestine, it might be in a position to pursue an agrarian policy which would facilitate and expedite to a greater extent than its present policy the creation of a Jewish National Home." That, stated succinctly, is the dilemma which has confronted, and still confronts, the Mandatory Government. The policy which they have adopted, and which they had endeavoured to follow, is based upon the principle that immigration shall " not exceed the economic capacity of the country at the time to absorb new arrivals." The soundness of this principle will hardly be challenged; but its practical application is not without difficulty. The absorptive capacity of the country must be correctly gauged; everything turns upon that. But to gauge it correctly, many intricate considerations of land settlement, development, etc., must be taken into account; and the margin for miscalculation is necessarily wide. If there had been mistakes in the past, they must be avoided in future. But the question is too important, and too vital to the prosperity of Palestine, to be tackled hastily or without due consideration. His Majesty's Government have felt unable to formulate specific proposals without further expert examination of the whole problem in all its aspects. A highly qualified investigator has accordingly been appointed to proceed to Palestine on a temporary mission, in order to confer with the High Commissioner and report to His Majesty's Government on land settlement, immigration, and development. For this Mission Sir John Hope-Simpson, who is employed under the League of Nations as Vice-Chairman of the Refugee Settlement Commission in Greece, has been selected. He is now on his

8

way to Palestine. The whole question of future policy in regard to immigration, land settlement and development will be considered and determined on receipt of Sir J. Hope-Simpson's report. In the meantime, temporary measures are being taken with a view to safeguarding the position of certain elements in the population of Palestine. The question of a temporary suspension of immigration is under examination; and legislation is to be introduced with the object of controlling the disposition of agricultural lands in such a manner as to prevent the dispossession of the indigenous agricultural population. These temporary measures will be superseded in any case by such permanent enactments as may be decided upon when future policy is determined in the light of Sir J. Hope-Simpson's report.

6. His Majesty's Government are also making enquiries with regard to this statement on page 161 of the Report (paragraph 30), that the selection of immigrants under the Labour Schedule ought not to be entrusted to the General Federation of Jewish Labour in Palestine. They are further in consultation with the High Commissioner for Palestine regarding the question, referred to at (c) on page 166 of the Commission's Report, of providing credit facilities for Palestinian agriculturists.

7. On the important subject of constitutional development, the Commission of Enquiry have made no formal recommendation, beyond urging that when the question again comes under review, regard should be had to their conclusion that the absence of any measure of self-government greatly aggravated the difficulties of the local administration. This is a question in which the Permanent Mandates Commission have from the first displayed an active interest. In their original Observations of November, 1924, they expressed their appreciation of " the persistent efforts of the High Commissioner to secure the co-operation of the Arab majority in the central administration of the country." A year later, in October, 1925, they expressed the hope that " an extension of co-operation, particularly in the conduct of municipal and district affairs " might become possible in the near future. Further references to the subject appeared in the Commission's " Observations " both of June, 1926, and of July, 1927. The position, stated quite briefly, is as follows : The questions of " self-governing institutions " and of " local autonomy " are dealt with in Articles 2 and 3 respectively of the Palestine Mandate. Article 2 makes the Mandatory responsible for placing the country under such political administrative and economical conditions as will secure (*inter alia*) " the development of self-governing institutions." Article 3 requires the Mandatory, so far as circumstances permit, to encourage local autonomy. The steps taken for the establishment of municipal and local Councils in Palestine are well known to the Commission. Nor is it necessary to refer in detail to the attempts that have been

made in the past to introduce a measure of self-government for the country as a whole. These attempts are fully described in the Report of the Commission of Enquiry. It will be apparent that the absence of any such measure of self-government in Palestine is not due to any lack of good will on the part of the Mandatory Power. It must be a primary condition of any constitutional change in Palestine that the Mandatory Government should reserve to itself the power of carrying out the obligations imposed upon it by the Mandate. The question formed the subject of conversation with the Delegation of Palestinian Arabs which lately came to England for the purpose of representing their views on future policy in Palestine. It has been made clear to the Delegation that no measure of self-government could be considered which was not compatible with the requirements of the Mandate. The matter is, of course, one which also deeply concerns the Jewish Agency.

8. On page 163 of the Report, the Commission expressed certain views on the difficulties inherent in the Mandate. Their recommendations on this point as recorded on pages 164 and 165, include the issue of a clear statement of policy—

(1) containing a definition in clear and positive terms of the meaning which His Majesty's Government attach to the passages in the Mandate for the safeguarding of the rights of the non-Jewish community in Palestine ; and

(2) laying down, for the guidance of the Government of Palestine, directions more explicit than any that have yet been given as to the conduct of policy on such vital issues as land and immigration.

The statement of British policy in Palestine, of which a copy is reproduced on pages 196-199 of the Report of the Commission, was issued in 1922. The administration of the country has since been conducted on the general lines laid down in that statement, except that, for reasons already explained, the proposed Legislative Council has never been brought into being. His Majesty's Government do not challenge the view that a further and more explicit statement of policy is required ; and it is their intention in due course to issue such a statement. Since, however, no such statement could be adequate or complete which ignored the vital questions of land settlement, immigration and development, it will be necessary to await the Report of Sir J. Hope-Simpson before giving effect to the Commission's recommendation. Their further recommendations relating to the functions of the Zionist Organization and to the Palestine Zionist Executive (page 167 of the Report) will also be adopted when the proposed statement is drawn up.

9. As regards defence and security, the Commission on page 163 of their Report have expressed the view that the policy of reducing the garrison in Palestine and Trans-Jordan was carried out too far. In this connection the remarks made on page 157 of the Report

should be borne in mind. As is there admitted, the presence of troops or of British police in larger numbers on the 23rd August, 1929, would not necessarily have prevented an outbreak. The experience of April 1920 and May 1921, when racial disturbances occurred despite the strength of the garrison, points the other way. His Majesty's Government have at present under their earnest consideration the question of the composition and strength of the garrision to be retained in Palestine in the future. In the meantime, they do not propose to disturb the existing garrison of two battalions of infantry plus units of the Royal Air Force. Arrangements have also been made with a view to ensuring the despatch of reinforcements to Palestine with the least possible delay if need should arise. As regards the police, effect has already been given to recommendation (c) on page 168 of the Commission's Report, that an independent enquiry should be made by an experienced police officer from some other dependency into the organisation of the Department of Police in Palestine. The officer selected for this enquiry, Mr. H. L. Dowbiggin, Inspector of Police, Ceylon, arrived in Palestine in January, and his final report is expected shortly. In the meantime, an additional 400 British police have been recruited for Palestine, and steps have been taken to increase the mobility of the British police. Mr. Dowbiggin has presented an *ad interim* report on the specific subject of the protection of outlying Jewish colonies; and action is being taken on the lines recommended by him. A further increase in the number of British and Palestinian police is involved, and a scheme of defence, including the establishment and control of sealed armouries, is being brought into force. His Majesty's Government are fully satisfied as to the need for sealed armouries; without them, the adequate defence of the colonies can be ensured only at a prohibitive cost. The question of improving the Intelligence Service and of forming a reserve of special constables, which formed the subject of the recommendations in paragraph 53 on page 167 and paragraph 55 (*d*) on page 168, are being taken up with the High Commissioner for Palestine.

10. With regard to the recommendation in paragraph 50 on page 166, the Permanent Mandates Commission are no doubt aware that the Council of the League have approved of the appointment of a Commission to define and determine Jewish and Moslem rites at the Western or Wailing Wall.

11. There remain the recommendations in paragraph 52 on page 167 under the heading " Press Incitement." The High Commissioner has at present under consideration the enactment of legislation to provide for the better control of the press. The suggestion made in paragraph 52 (*b*) will be duly considered in this connexion. The High Commissioner's attention will also be drawn to the remarks on Press incitement included in the Note of Reservations by Mr. Snell (page 181).

May, 1930.

9.02

Printed for the use of the Colonial Office.

Middle East.
No. 39.

<u>*Confidential.*</u>

Palestine

Letter from the Prime Minister to Dr. Ch. Weizmann.

13th February, 1931.

Palestine

Letter from the Prime Minister to Dr. Ch. Weizmann.

10, DOWNING STREET,
WHITEHALL,
13th February, 1931.

Dear DR. WEIZMANN,

IN order to remove certain misconceptions and misunderstandings which have arisen as to the policy of His Majesty's Government with regard to Palestine, as set forth in the White Paper of October, 1930,* and which were the subject of a Debate in the House of Commons on the 17th November, and also to meet certain criticisms put forward by the Jewish Agency, I have pleasure in forwarding you the following statement of our position, which will fall to be read as the authoritative interpretation of the White Paper on the matters with which this letter deals.

2. It has been said that the policy of His Majesty's Government involves a serious departure from the obligations of the Mandate as hitherto understood, that it misconceives the Mandatory obligations, and that it foreshadows a policy which is inconsistent with the obligations of the Mandatory to the Jewish people.

3. His Majesty's Government did not regard it as necessary to quote *in extenso* the declarations of policy which have been previously made, but attention is drawn to the fact that, not only does the White Paper of 1930 refer to and endorse the White Paper of 1922,† which has been accepted by the Jewish Agency, but it recognises that the undertaking of the Mandate is an undertaking to the Jewish people and not only to the Jewish population of Palestine. The White Paper placed in the foreground of its statement my speech in the House of Commons on the 3rd April, 1930, in which I announced in words which could not have been made more plain, that it was the intention of His Majesty's Government to continue to administer Palestine in accordance with the terms of the Mandate as approved by the Council of the League of Nations. That position has been reaffirmed and again made plain by my speech in the House of Commons on the 17th November. In my speech on the 3rd April I used the following language :—

"His Majesty's Government will continue to administer Palestine in accordance with the terms of the Mandate as approved by the Council of the League of Nations. This is an international obligation from which there can be no question of receding.

---

* Cmd. 3692. † Cmd. 1700.

3

"Under the terms of the Mandate His Majesty's Government are responsible for promoting 'the establishment in Palestine of a National Home for the Jewish people, it being clearly understood that nothing shall be done which might prejudice the civil and religious rights of existing non-Jewish communities in Palestine or the rights and political status enjoyed by Jews in any other country.'

"A double undertaking is involved, to the Jewish people on the one hand, and to the non-Jewish population of Palestine on the other; and it is the firm resolve of His Majesty's Government to give effect, in equal measure, to both parts of the Declaration, and to do equal justice to all sections of the population of Palestine. That is a duty from which they will not shrink, and to the discharge of which they will apply all the resources at their command."

That declaration is in conformity not only with the articles, but also with the preamble of the Mandate, which is hereby explicitly reaffirmed.

4. In carrying out the policy of the Mandate the Mandatory cannot ignore the existence of differing interests and viewpoints. These, indeed, are not in themselves irreconcilable, but they can only be reconciled if there is a proper realisation that the full solution of the problem depends on an understanding between the Jews and the Arabs. Until that is reached, considerations of balance must inevitably enter into the definition of policy.

5. A good deal of criticism has been directed to the White Paper upon the assertion that it contains injurious allegations against the Jewish people and Jewish Labour organization. Any such intention on the part of His Majesty's Government is expressly disavowed. It is recognised that the Jewish Agency have all along given willing co-operation in carrying out the policy of the Mandate, and that the constructive work done by the Jewish people in Palestine has had beneficial effects on the development and well-being of the country as a whole. His Majesty's Government also recognise the value of the services of labour and trades union organization in Palestine, to which they desire to give every encouragement.

6. A question has arisen as to the meaning to be attached to the words "safeguarding the civil and religious rights of all inhabitants of Palestine, irrespective of race and religion," occurring in article 2, and the words "ensuring that the rights and position of other sections of the population are not prejudiced." occurring in article 6 of the Mandate. The words "safeguarding the civil and religious rights," occurring in article 2, cannot be read as meaning that the civil and religious rights of individual citizens are to be unalterable. In the case of *Suleiman Murra*, to which reference has been made, the Privy Council, in construing these words of article 2, said:

4

"It does not mean . . . that all the civil rights of every inhabitant of Palestine which existed at the date of the Mandate are to remain unaltered throughout its duration; for if this were to be a condition of the Mandatory jurisdiction, no effective legislation would be possible." The words, accordingly, must be read in another sense, and the key to the true purpose and meaning of the sentence is to be found in the concluding words of the article: "irrespective of race and religion." These words indicate that, in respect of civil and religious rights, the Mandatory is not to discriminate between persons on the ground of religion or race, and this protective provision applies equally to Jews, Arabs, and all sections of the population.

7. The words "rights and position of other sections of the population," occurring in article 6, plainly refer to the non-Jewish community. These rights and position are not to be prejudiced, that is, are not to be impaired or made worse. The effect of the policy of immigration and settlement on the economic position of the non-Jewish community cannot be excluded from consideration. But the words are not to be read as implying that existing economic conditions in Palestine should be crystallised. On the contrary, the obligation to facilitate Jewish immigration and to encourage close settlement by Jews on the land, remains a positive obligation of the Mandate, and it can be fulfilled without prejudice to the rights and position of other sections of the population of Palestine.

8. We may proceed to the contention that the Mandate has been reinterpreted in a manner highly prejudicial to Jewish interests in the vital matters of land settlement and immigration. It has been said that the policy of the White Paper would place an embargo upon immigration, and would suspend, if not, indeed, terminate, the close settlement of the Jews on the land, which is a primary purpose of the Mandate. In support of this contention particular stress has been laid upon the passage referring to State lands in the White Paper, which says that "it would not be possible to make these areas available for Jewish settlement in view of their actual occupation by Arab cultivators, and of the importance of making available additional land on which to place the Arab cultivators who are now landless."

9. The language of this passage needs to be read in the light of the policy as a whole. It is desirable to make it clear that the landless Arabs, to whom it was intended to refer in the passage quoted, were such Arabs as can be shown to have been displaced from the lands which they occupied in consequence of the lands passing into Jewish hands, and who have not obtained other holdings on which they can establish themselves or other equally satisfactory occupation. The number of such displaced Arabs must be a matter for careful enquiry. It is to landless Arabs within this category that His Majesty's Government feel themselves under

an obligation to facilitate their settlement upon the land. The recognition of this obligation in no way detracts from the larger purposes of development, which His Majesty's Government regards as the most effectual means of furthering the establishment of a National Home for the Jews.

10. In framing a policy of land settlement, it is essential that His Majesty's Government should take into consideration every circumstance that is relevant to the main purposes of the Mandate. The area of cultivable land, the possibilities of irrigation, the absorptive capacity of the country in relation to immigration are all elements pertinent to the issues to be elucidated, and the neglect of any one of them would be prejudicial to the formulation of a just and stable policy.

It is the intention of His Majesty's Government to institute an enquiry as soon as possible to ascertain, *inter alia*, what State and other lands are, or properly can be made, available for close settlement by Jews under reference to the obligation imposed upon the Mandatory by article 6 of the Mandate. This enquiry will be comprehensive in its scope, and will include the whole land resources of Palestine. In the conduct of the enquiry provision will be made for all interests, whether Jewish or Arab, making such representations as it may be desired to put forward.

11. The question of the congestion amongst the fellahin in the hill districts of Palestine is receiving the careful consideration of His Majesty's Government. It is contemplated that measures will be devised for the improvement and intensive development of the land, and for bringing into cultivation areas which hitherto may have remained uncultivated, and thereby securing to the fellahin a better standard of living, without save in exceptional cases, having recourse to transfer.

12. In giving effect to the policy of land settlement, as contemplated in article 11 of the Mandate, it is necessary, if disorganization is to be avoided, and if the policy is to have a chance to succeed, that there should exist some centralised control of transactions relating to the acquisition and transfer of land during such interim period as may reasonably be necessary to place the development scheme upon a sure foundation. The power contemplated is regulative and not prohibitory, although it does involve a power to prevent transactions which are inconsistent with the tenor of the scheme. But the exercise of the power will be limited and in no respect arbitrary. In every case it will be conditioned by considerations as to how best to give effect to the purposes of the Mandate. Any control contemplated will be fenced with due safeguards to secure as little interference as possible with the free transfer of land. The centralised control will take effect as from such date only as the authority charged with the duty of carrying

6

out the policy of land development shall begin to operate. The High Commissioner will, pending the establishment of such centralised control, have full powers to take all steps necessary to protect the tenancy and occupancy rights, including the rights of squatters, throughout Palestine.

13. Further, the statement of policy of His Majesty's Government did not imply a prohibition of acquisition of additional land by Jews. It contains no such prohibition, nor is any such intended. What it does contemplate is such temporary control of land disposition and transfers as may be necessary, not to impair the harmony and effectiveness of the scheme of land settlement to be undertaken. His Majesty's Government feel bound to point out that they alone of the Governments which have been responsible for the administration of Palestine since the acceptance of the Mandate have declared their definite intention to initiate an active policy of development which it is believed will result in substantial and lasting benefit to both Jews and Arabs.

14. Cognate to this question is the control of Immigration. It must, first of all, be pointed out that such control is not in any sense a departure from previous policy. From 1920 onwards, when the original Immigration Ordinance came into force, regulations for the control of Immigration have been issued from time to time, directed to prevent illicit entry and to define and facilitate authorised entry. This right of regulation has at no time been challenged.

15. But the intention of His Majesty's Government appears to have been represented as being that " no further immigration of Jews is to be permitted so long as it might prevent any Arab from obtaining employment." His Majesty's Government never proposed to pursue such a policy. They were concerned to state that, in the regulation of Jewish immigration, the following principles should apply, viz., that " it is essential to ensure that the immigrants should not be a burden upon the people of Palestine as a whole, and that they should not deprive any section of the present population of their employment " (White Paper, 1922). In the one aspect His Majesty's Government have to be mindful of their obligations to facilitate Jewish Immigration under suitable conditions, and to encourage close settlement of Jews on the land; in the other aspect they have to be equally mindful of their duty to ensure that no prejudice results to the rights and position of the non-Jewish community. It is because of this apparent conflict of obligations that His Majesty's Government have felt bound to emphasise the necessity of the proper application of the absorptive capacity principle. That principle is vital to any scheme of development, the primary purpose of which must be the settlement both of Jews and of displaced Arabs upon the land. It is for that

reason that His Majesty's Government have insisted, and are compelled to insist, that Government control of immigration must be maintained and that immigration regulations must be properly applied. The considerations relevant to the limits of absorptive capacity are purely economic considerations.

16. His Majesty's Government did not prescribe and do not contemplate any stoppage or prohibition of Jewish immigration in any of its categories. The practice of sanctioning a " Labour Schedule " of wage-earning immigrants will continue. In each case consideration will be given to anticipated labour requirements for works which, being dependent on Jewish or mainly Jewish capital, would not be or would not have been undertaken unless Jewish labour was made available. \ With regard to public and municipal works falling to be financed out of public funds, the claim of Jewish labour to a due share of the employment available, taking into account Jewish contributions to public revenue, shall be taken into consideration.] As regards other kinds of employment, it will be necessary in each case to take into account the factors bearing upon the demand for labour, including the factor of unemployment amongst both the Jews and the Arabs. Immigrants with prospects of employment other than employment of a purely ephemeral character will not be excluded on the sole ground that the employment cannot be guaranteed to be of unlimited duration.

17. In determining the extent to which Immigration at any time may be permitted, it is necessary also to have regard to the declared policy of the Jewish Agency to the effect that in " all the works or undertakings carried out or furthered by the Agency it shall be deemed to be a matter of principle that Jewish labour shall be employed." His Majesty's Government do not in any way challenge the right of the Agency to formulate or approve and endorse such a policy. The principle of preferential and, indeed, exclusive employment of Jewish labour by Jewish organizations is a principle which the Jewish Agency are entitled to affirm. But it must be pointed out that if in consequence of this policy Arab labour is displaced or existing unemployment becomes aggravated, that is a factor in the situation to which the Mandatory is bound to have regard.

18. His Majesty's Government desire to say finally, as they have repeatedly and unequivocally affirmed, that the obligations imposed upon the Mandatory, by its acceptance of the Mandate, are solemn international obligations, from which there is not now, nor has there been at any time, an intention to depart. To the tasks imposed by the Mandate His Majesty's Government have set their hand, and they will not withdraw it. But if their efforts are to be successful there is need for co-operation, confidence, readiness on all sides to appreciate the difficulties and complexities

8

of the problem, and, above all, there must be a full and unqualified recognition that no solution can be satisfactory or permanent which is not based upon justice, both to the Jewish people and to the non-Jewish communities of Palestine.

I am, my dear Dr. Weizmann,

Yours very sincerely,

J. RAMSAY MACDONALD.

The President of the
    Jewish Agency.

9.03

PALESTINE.  **GOVERNMENT OFFICES,
JERUSALEM.**

<u>CONFIDENTIAL.</u>
<u>REFERENCE NO.</u> 3 6 7/3 0.

29th March, 1930.

RECEIVED
7 APR 1930
COL. OFFICE

My Lord,

77050/30
See +

    I have the honour to refer to paragraph 84 of my Confidential despatch of the 17th January, 1930, in which I informed Your Lordship that I proposed to submit a Bill to control the disposition of agricultural land in order to prevent dispossession of the indigenous agricultural population.

  2. The present position in regard to cultivable land and the main features of the policy of the Palestine Government in regard to the disposition of such land are set forth in paragraph 65 to 85 of the Confidential despatch to which I have referred.

  3. In view of the fact that the Solicitor-General had been charged with responsibility for preparing information for the Commission of Inquiry in regard to the land question, I requested him to draft legislation on the lines suggested in paragraph 84 of my Confidential despatch of the 17th January.

  4. I enclose copies of two Bills prepared by the Solicitor-General with that object, entitled:

Enclosure I.
  (1) An Ordinance to establish control of certain dispositions of agricultural land;
  and

(2)/

The Right Hon'ble. Lord Passfield, P.C.,
 His Majesty's Principal Secretary of State
    for the Colonies.

-2-

Enclosure II.

Enclosure III.

(2) An Ordinance to amend the Protection of Cultivators Ordinance, 1929, together with a memorandum by him explaining the intention of the Bills.

5. The former Bill is based upon Section 11 of the Tanganyika Ordinance – the Law of Property and Conveyancing Ordinance, No.2 of 1923.

It provides that a disposition of agricultural land belonging to a person who is an Arab in favour of a person who is not an Arab shall not be operative unless it is in writing and unless and until it is approved by the High Commissioner.

With regard to Clause 7 of the Bill I am informed that:

(i) the number of existing registered mortgages of miri land in Arab ownership created since the 1st October 1920 is 1354;

(ii) the areas so mortgaged are approximately 190,125 dunums; and

(iii) the amount for which the areas are mortgaged is approximately £.512,000.

The possible financial consequences to Government resulting from the provisions in Clause 7 as to attachments should not be substantial.

It would appear that any ultimate loss to Government would be limited to the result of errors of assessment in the value of the land, since the land will be available for the recovery of the debt due to Government by a sale which will not involve dispossession of occupying cultivators, and the

amount/

-3-

amount payable by Government to the mortgagee is not to be greater than the value of the land if that value is less than the amount of the mortgage.

6. When the two Bills were considered in Executive Council the Attorney-General and the Acting Chief Secretary expressed doubt as to whether the Transfer of Agricultural Land Bill was the best remedy having regard to the circumstances in which Palestine was administered under the Mandate.

<u>Enclosures IV and V.</u>   I enclose copies of Memoranda which they submitted on the subject.

Briefly, it is argued in these Memoranda that the objections to the Transfer of Agricultural Land Bill are:

(a) that it introduces discrimination between Arabs and non-Arabs; and

(b) that by imposing restrictions on a larger number of transactions than is necessary the Bill will affect credit adversely and will be administratively inconvenient.

7. After discussion of the matter in Executive Council it was decided that the objects to be attained by means of legislation were:-

(i) that no disposition of agricultural land which has the effect of dispossessing cultivators should be permitted until arrangements have been made for them to be provided with suitable land elsewhere;

(ii)/

—4—

(ii) that evictions from agricultural land should not be permitted unless provision is made for the occupants to be provided with land elsewhere.

8. I requested the Attorney-General to draft a Bill framed in such a way as to attain these objects and, at the same time, to avoid the objections which he and the Acting Chief Secretary had made to the Bill prepared by the Solicitor-General.

9. The Bill prepared by the Attorney-General was considered and amended in Executive Council and I enclose the amended draft together with a copy of his explanatory memorandum.

<u>Enclosure VI.</u>
<u>Enclosure VII.</u>

With regard to existing mortgages the Attorney-General states that, in his opinion, no provision is necessary unless mortgages of large areas are outstanding.

10. Clause 14 of the Attorney-General's Bill contains an important provision which runs as follows:-

" Where notice has been given to determine a tenancy under this Ordinance and the High Commissioner is satisfied that hardship would be caused if the tenants were evicted, he may, by Order, direct that no proceedings shall be taken for eviction of the tenants until he is satisfied that the tenants will retain, or will be able to acquire elsewhere, sufficient land for the maintenance of themselves and their families, and

no/

-5-

"no Court or Judge shall make or execute an Order of eviction against such tenants so long as the Order of the High Commissioner is in force."

11. I have the following observations to make on this clause:-

(i) the power given to the High Commissioner is an arbitrary power but it will not be exercised where notices to quit have been given for failure to pay rent or to cultivate according to the rules of good husbandry;

(ii) the existence of an arbitrary power may have the effect of compelling purchasers to be careful to make adequate provision for occupying cultivators, since it would be embarrassing to them if the power were used against them when their arrangements for developing the land were well advanced;

(iii) it is, therefore, possible that the power given to the High Commissioner will only rarely have to be invoked.

12. The Solicitor-General argues against this clause as follows:-

(a) legislation controlling dispositions will be evaded, if possible;

(b) the classification, by area, of dispositions to be controlled by the Bill is arbitrary and, therefore, evasion is possible;

(c)/

-6-

(c) Clause 12(3) recognises a possible method of evasion which, if successful, is validated by clause 12(5);

(d) it is unfair to purchasers, who have evaded the Ordinance, but whose title is validated by the Ordinance in spite of their evasion, that they should be prevented from putting into operation the project which was the ultimate object of the purchase at a time when the consideration will have passed and all the arrangements for the establishment of a settlement will have been made;

(e) it is also unfair to purchasers who have complied with the Ordinance that the ultimate object of the purchase should be defeated by the exercise of the power contained in clause 14;

(f) the power will probably have to be exercised when vacant possession of land which has been acquired for land reserves is required and it will be much more difficult for the High Commissioner to resist pressure to refrain from exercising his power then than it would be for him to refuse consent to the original disposition;

(g) the larger the transaction, the greater may be the need for the exercise of the power contained in clause 14 and the greater will be the hardship to the purchaser if the power is exercised; consequently the greater

will be/

-7-

will be the pressure put upon the High Commissioner not to exercise the power;

(h) so long as surplus land is not available, and purchases from Arabs by non-Arabs continue, clause 14 will frequently be put in operation.

13. Two courses appear to be open to this Government:-

(i) to enact the two Bills drafted by the Solicitor-General;

(ii) to enact the Bill drafted by the Attorney-General.

14. As regards the first course, the Bills would achieve the object in view with the minimum interference with credit. They would require the minimum administrative action.

15. As regards the second course, while evasion of the Bill seems possible and its efficacy may therefore depend ultimately on the power to control evictions, it is not open to the objections made by the Attorney-General and the Acting Chief Secretary to the Bill prepared by the Solicitor-General.

16. I have felt it necessary to submit alternative draft Bills for Your Lordship's consideration because I recognise that the objections to the differentiation in the Solicitor-General's Bill between Arabs and non-Arabs may be sufficiently strong to render it

expedient /

—3—

expedient to adopt an alternative method. The Bill prepared by the Attorney-General is the only detailed alternative proposal before me, although the Treasurer has suggested that the acquisitions of Jewish purchasing agencies could be controlled by providing that all acquisitions of agricultural land by corporate bodies, without distinction, should be subject to the consent of the High Commissioner.

17. If His Majesty's Government should decide to take steps to secure the amendment of certain articles of the Palestine Mandate and any consequential amendments of the Palestine Order in Council, then I see no difficulty in proceeding with the Bills drafted by the Solicitor-General.

It may be that Your Lordship will see no difficulty in following this course, even if it is not possible to consider changes in the Palestine Mandate at present, but, if it should not be considered wise to proceed now with the Bills prepared by the Solicitor-General, then it is my opinion that, subject to any advice which Your Lordship may have to offer and to further consideration of the question of existing mortgages and attachments, the Bill prepared by the Attorney-General should be enacted without delay in view of the paramount necessity of ensuring that Arab cultivators shall not be evicted from lands which they and their

ancestors /

—9—

ancestors have long occupied unless provision is made for them to obtain an adequate area of agricultural land elsewhere.

                    I have the honour to be,
                          My Lord,
                    Your Lordship's most obedient,
                        humble servant,

J. R. Chancellor.

                        HIGH COMMISSIONER
                         FOR PALESTINE.

ENCLOSURE I TO CONFIDENTIAL DESPATCH OF "B" 29/3/30.

An Ordinance to establish control over certain
dispositions of Agricultural land.

BE IT ENACTED BY THE HIGH COMMISSIONER FOR PALESTINE, WITH THE ADVICE OF THE ADVIROSY COUNCIL THEREOF.

Short Title. 1. This Ordinance may be cited as the Transfer of Agricultural Land Ordinance, 1930.

Definitions. 2. In this Ordinance, unless the context otherwise requires:-

"Land" means "miri" land and includes an undivided interest in "miri" land but does not include miri land or an undivided interest in miri land which lies within an urban area as defined in any order made under the Urban Property Tax Ordinance, 1928, or within a municipal area which is not, or does not form part of, an urban area so defined.

"Disposition" means a sale, transfer, mortgage, lease, sub-lease, transfer of possession, partition and every other disposition of land, whether similar to those before enumerated or not and includes an agreement for a disposition and a disposition of land in execution of any order of a Court but does not include any order of Court except an order for foreclosure of a mortgage of land.

Dispositions of land by Arabs in favour of persons who are not Arabs. 3.(1) A disposition of land belonging to a person who is an Arab in favour of a person who is not an Arab or conferring on a person who is not an Arab any rights over the land of a person who is an Arab

shall/

-2-

shall not be operative unless it is in writing and unless and until it is approved by the High Commissioner.

(ii) In the event of any dispute arising as to whether a person is or is not an Arab for the purposes of the preceding sub-section, such dispute shall be referred to the High Commissioner whose decision shall be final.

Mode of indicating approval.	4. It shall be sufficient if the approval required by this Ordinance is endorsed on the instrument effecting the disposition whether before or after execution or on a draft or copy thereof.
Registrar of Lands not to register until approval given.	5. A Registrar of Lands shall not register or give effect to any disposition for which approval is required by this Ordinance until he is satisfied that such approval has been given.
High Commissioner may dispense with necessity for approval of foreclosure, etc.	6. The High Commissioner, in giving his approval under this Ordinance to a mortgage, may, if he thinks fit, declare that his approval shall not be required to the foreclosure of the mortgage or to the sale under the mortgage to a person who is not an Arab.
Provisions as to existing mortgages where approval of foreclosure or sale refused.	7.(i) If the High Commissioner shall refuse to approve of the foreclosure of a mortgage executed and registered prior to the day of 1930, or of a sale under such a mortgage to a person who is not an Arab, the mortgagee may apply to the High Commissioner for payment of the amount due/

-3-

due under the mortgage and the High Commissioner shall cause to be paid out of the general revenues of Palestine the amount due under the mortgage or if the value of the land mortgaged shall be less than the amount due under the mortgage, the High Commissioner shall cause to be paid to the mortgagee the value of the land.

(ii) In the event of any dispute arising as to the value of such land the High Commissioner and the mortgagee shall each appoint a person to determine the value of the land and the persons so appointed shall before entering upon such valuation appoint an umpire and shall thereafter proceed to their valuation, and if they agree as to the value of the land their valuation shall be final and binding, but if they fail to agree the matter shall be referred to the umpire and the valuation of the umpire shall then be final and binding as to the value of the land.

(iii) If the High Commissioner shall under the provisions of this section cause to be paid to a mortgagee the amount due upon the mortgage or the value of the land mortgaged, as the case may be, then the mortgage shall be deemed to be satisfied, but the amount of such payment shall be a debt due by the mortgagor and his heirs to the Government of Palestine and the same may be sued for and recovered in a Court of Law at any time within fifteen years from the date when such payment was made.

(iv) /

—4—

(iv) For the purposes of this section the value of the land shall mean the amount which it might be expected/if sold in the open market by a willing seller immediately prior to the date of the commencement of this Ordinance. [to realise]

(v) For the purposes of this Section the word "mortgage" shall include an attachment of land made by a Court prior to the   day of   1930, the word "mortgagee" shall include the person in whose favour the attachment was made, the word "mortgagor" shall include the person whose land is attached, the phrase "land mortgaged" shall include the land attached and the phrase "amount due under the mortgage" shall include the amount in respect of which the land is attached.

(vi) Any person appointed under sub-section (ii), not being a public officer, may receive such fee for his services as the High Commissioner shall direct and any expenses necessarily incurred for the purposes of the said sub-section shall be borne by the Government.

ENCLOSURE II TO CONFIDENTIAL DESPATCH "B" OF 29.3.30.

An Ordinance to amend the Protection of Cultivators Ordinance, 1929.

BE IT ENACTED BY THE HIGH COMMISSIONER FOR PALESTINE, WITH THE ADVICE OF THE ADVISORY COUNCIL THEREOF.

Short Title. 1. This Ordinance may be cited as the Protection of Cultivators (Amendment) Ordinance, 1930, and the Protection of Cultivators Ordinance, 1929 (hereinafter referred to as the Principal Ordinance) and this Ordinance may together be cited as the Protection of Cultivators Ordinances 1929 and 1930.

Amendment of Section 3 of the Principal Ordinance.
2. Section 3(3) of the Principal Ordinance is hereby amended as follows:-

(a) The words "The landlord shall send a copy of the notice to the District Commissioner" shall be deleted from sub-section (3) of the said section; and

(b) The following sub-section shall be added to the said section:-

"(4) Every notice given under this section shall be void and of no effect unless a copy thereof be served by the landlord on the District Commissioner of the District in which the land is situate within 30 days after the notice has been served on the tenant and, if the object of the notice is to determine a tenancy in order that the land may be transferred with vacant possession, unless the notice contain a declaration by the landlord to that effect.

3./

-2-

Amendment of Section 4 of the Principal Ordinance.

3. Section 4 of the Principal Ordinance is hereby amended as follows:-

(a) Sub-section (2) is hereby repealed and in place thereof the following sub-section shall have effect:-

"(2) If the tenant is not willing to pay the increased rent he shall within one month of the date of the notice refer the question to the Board who shall decide what, having regard to all the circumstances, is a reasonable amount of rent to be paid. If the tenant is not willing to pay the amount of rent awarded by the Board he shall, within one month of the date of the award, notify the landlord who may thereupon give him notice to quit expiring on the date when the rent awarded by the Board would come into force".

(b) The following sub-section shall be added to Section 4:-

"(3) Every notice given under this section shall be void and of no effect unless a copy thereof be served by the landlord on the District Commissioner of the District in which the land is situate within 30 days after the notice has been served on the tenant".

Addition of new Section.

4. The following section shall be inserted in the Principal Ordinance as Section 8 (A):-

"Orders/

—3—

"Orders for Eviction.

8.(A) No Court or Judge shall make an order for eviction of a tenant pursuant to a notice given under this Ordinance unless the landlord satisfies the Court or Judge that the tenancy has been validly terminated under this Ordinance and unless the landlord declares whether the object of the termination of the tenancy is a transfer of the land with vacant possession and, if that be the object of the termination of the tenancy, unless the landlord satisfies the Court or Judge that, if the transfer is a disposition to which the Transfer of Agricultural Land Ordinance 1930 applies, the approval of the High Commissioner to such disposition has been obtained."

ENCLOSURE **III** TO CONFIDENTIAL DESPATCH "B" OF 29.1.30.

by H.C. to S.S.

MEMORANDUM

by the Solicitor-General on the Transfer of Agricultural Land Bill and the Protection of Cultivators (Amendment) Bill.

The Transfer of Agricultural Land Bill is designed to enable the Government to meet the problem created by the present position in regard to cultivable land which is summarised in paragraph 77 of Despatch Confidential to the Secretary of State of the 17th January, 1930, as follows:-

   (a) all cultivable State domain is occupied.

   (b) Government owns waste land such as the coastal sand dunes, the desert area south-east of Beersheba and the mountainous region between the Jerusalem-Hebron road and the Dead Sea. These areas are not cultivable.

   (c) Government owns large areas of land in the hilly parts of the country which are fit only for afforestation.

   (d) The cultivable land in the occupation of the indigenous population is fully occupied and cannot support a larger population under existing methods of cultivation.

   (e) Any change from extensive to intensive methods of cultivation must take time and money, and is unlikely to proceed at a more rapid rate than that required to permit of the absorption on the land of the annual natural increase of the Arab population.

   (f) If more land now in the occupation of the indigenous population is sold for the purpose of Jewish settlement, either the existing cultivators

will /

—2—

will be dispossessed of their land and will cease to be cultivators or their holdings must be reduced below what is now regarded as the average area sufficient to support an Arab agricultural family.

2. In the situation thus created the interests of the indigenous population and the interests of the Jews are in direct conflict; for, so long as surplus land does not exist, further purchases of agricultural land by Jews can, generally speaking, be made only by dispossessing Arab cultivators of the land they are occupying and so creating a class of landless peasantry.

3. The case of the Wadi Hawareth lands illustrates the problem created for the Government, as a result of the purchase of Arab agricultural land, and the existing state of the law which does not enable the Government to prevent the creation of a class of landless peasantry.

4. It is part of the policy of the Zionist Organisation, as expressed in resolutions passed at Zürich in July-August, 1929, to create, in the immediate future, land reserves in all parts of the country; and it is known that further purchases of Arab agricultural land are being negotiated. It is likely, therefore, that the case of the Wadi Hawareth lands will be repeated.

5.   Prior to the promulgation of the Protection of Cultivators Ordinance on the 1st August, 1929, it was provided by Section 6 of the Land Transfer Ordinance, 1920 (as amended) that the consent of the Government to a disposition of land which was required by the Ordinance should be withheld in the case of agricultural land unless the tenants in occupation retained sufficient land in the district or elsewhere for the maintenance of themselves and their families. This provision was repealed by the Protection of Cultivators Ordinance, 1929, for the reason (among others) that it could be evaded and, in fact, in four cases, it had been evaded, by the purchaser refusing to purchase the land except with vacant possession and so compelling the vendor to remove all tenants from the land before the sale took place.

For this reason legislation reviving the principle embodied in the Land Transfer Ordinance, 1920, would be ineffective.

6.   The only effective measure which can be taken is to provide that the transfer of Arab agricultural land, except between Arabs, and the creation of rights over such land, except in favour of Arabs, should be allowed only with the consent of the High Commissioner.

The principle of such a measure is the same, *mutatis mutandis*, as is contained in Article 6 of the Mandate for Tanganyika.

Dispositions/

Dispositions are not prohibited but only made subject to consent; and consent will only be withheld in those cases which are described in paragraph 2. There will undoubtedly be individual cases in which consent will be granted, because it will be possible to make adequate provision of land for occupying cultivators.

7. The Transfer of Agricultural Land Bill (Clauses 1-6) has, therefore, been based on Section 11 of the Tanganyika Ordinance, No.2 of 1923, entitled "the Law of Property and Conveyancing Ordinance". This Section gives legislative effect to Article 6 of the Tanganyika Mandate.

8. The definition of "disposition" in the Bill (Clause 2) need not include a will since "miri" land cannot be disposed of by will but it must be wide enough to include all forms of disposition which by collusion, can be the means of a sale. The definition also provides that a disposition includes an agreement for a disposition and, consequently, under Clause 3, no agreement for a disposition of the character described in that clause is operative unless it has been approved by the High Commissioner. This provision should be more effective than the provision in the Land Transfer Ordinance which required consent to the transfer but not to the contract. Furthermore, when land is being bought for a land reserve, it may be purchased subject to existing tenancies since immediate possession will not be required: in such a case, the purchaser can be asked, on the occasion of application for consent

to the/

to the contract, what his intentions are in regard to existing tenants and, if consent is then withheld, it will be less embarrassing to him than if it were withheld at the time of the transfer.

9. Clause 3 defines precisely the transactions which will be controlled under the Ordinance and, although there may be arguments against introducing into an Ordinance the phrases "person who is an Arab" and "person who is not an Arab", there is no other way of obtaining control over the transactions which it is desired to control, except by widening the definition and so including within the scope of the Ordinance, transactions which it is not desired to control and creating a greater interference with credit and a greater administrative problem. For example, the Ordinance might be extended to cover all transactions in agricultural land; but there is no necessity to control transactions as between Arabs or transactions as between Jews.

10. Although, by virtue of Section 3 (14) of the Interpretation Ordinance, 1929, the word "person" includes any company or association or body of persons corporate or unincorporate, the phrase "person who is an Arab" would not include companies or religious orders or religious institutions; but a company and a religious order and a religious institution would be included in the phrase "person who is not an Arab".

11./

—6—

11. The High Commissioner can, under Section 22 of the Interpretation Ordinance, 1929, delegate his powers under Clause 3 of the Bill, but it is suggested that no delegation be made until the system has been in operation and general principles have been evolved.

12. Clause 7 of the Bill is based on Section 11 of the Federated Malay States Enactment No.15 of 1913; this clause must be considered in connexion with the statistics as to mortgages of land owned by Arabs which the Director of Lands has supplied. Attachments are usually temporary and the aggregate amount involved must vary considerably: estimates are, therefore, difficult but the aggregate amount at any time must be small in relation to the amount secured by mortgages.

With regard to mortgages there will not be a default in every case; Government will pay an amount equal to the value of the land if that value is less than the amount outstanding on the mortgage: the land will be available for the recovery of the debt by a sale which will not involve dispossession of occupying tenants; any ultimate loss to Government would probably be limited to the result of errors of assessment.

The Ordinance will, admittedly, interfere with existing mortgages and the Federated Malay States legislation provides the only equitable remedy. The statistics, referred to, enable an estimate to be formed of the possible financial consequences of the clause. It is certain, however, that mortgages and

attachments/

–7–

attachments must be brought within the scope of the Ordinance, if the law is to serve its purpose and enable Government to control transfers, such as that of the Wadi Hawareth land, since a sale can always be effected by means of a collusive mortgage or a collusive default under an existing mortgage or attachment.

It is suggested that the date in clause 7(i) and (v) be the date of publication of the Bill in the Gazette so that mortgages unregistered at that date may not be put on the Register between the date of publication and the date of promulgation.

13. Attempts will doubtless be made to evade the provisions of the Ordinance: for example, there may be an oral arrangement under which the vendor agrees to evict his tenants in accordance with the Protection of Cultivators Ordinance, 1929, and to enter into a written agreement when such eviction is complete: the consent of the High Commissioner will then be sought to the disposition which has, in fact, been preceded by a wholesale eviction of which the High Commissioner may not be aware.

There does not appear to be any absolute remedy against such a method of evading the object of the Ordinance except the drastic remedy of controlling evictions. The Protection of Cultivators (Amendment) Bill is, however, designed to ensure that the Government shall be made aware, at any early date, of the fact of eviction notices having been served and of the reasons therefor and to prevent the demand of a
prohibitive/

—8—

prohibitive increase in rent being used to secure eviction.

The object of clause 4 is to throw upon the landlord the onus of proof of compliance with the Ordinance and not to leave it to the tenant to attack the validity of the notice when the landlord has proved service thereof.

14.   It is possible that the Transfer of Agricultural Land Ordinance may be challenged on the ground that it discriminates on the ground of race, and is therefore repugnant to Article 15 of the Mandate for Palestine. I do not think, however, that that Article of the Mandate extends to discrimination in any other matters than those referred to in the Article, namely, freedom of conscience and free exercise of worship.

Article 17 of the Palestine Order in Council may go further than Article 15 in the matter of discrimination although the reason for any such difference is not apparent.   Unless an adequate reason exists, it would seem that Article 17 of the Palestine Order in Council should be amended so as to conform with Article 15 of the Mandate: if this amendment were made the Transfer of Agricultural Land Bill could not, I think, be challenged successfully on the ground that it is ultra vires either the Mandate or the Order in Council.

ENCLOSURE IV TO CONFIDENTIAL DESPATCH "B" OF 29.3.30.

NOTE
on the Transfer of Agricultural Land Bill,
by the Attorney-General.

I think that the legislation proposed is not in conformity with the terms of the Mandate for Palestine, and further that it imposes excessive restrictions on dealings in land and therefore might be economically harmful to the country as a whole. I think too, that the postulates for such drastic measures are in part exaggerated. While paragraphs A, B, and C on page 1 of the memorandum are broadly justified, it is submitted that paragraphs D, E, and F in the statement of the problem do not represent correctly the present or the prospective position. Considerable areas of cultivable land now in the occupation of the indigenous population are not fully occupied or fully cultivated, and can support a larger population even under existing methods of cultivation. This is shown by what has happened in the Jordan Valley lands where the Arab transferees, being unable to cultivate the whole of the area allotted to them under the agreement, have sold portions of it. Moreover, the change from extensive to intensive methods of cultivation which is necessary for the economic prosperity of the country is most likely to be brought about amongst the Arabs by the sale of part of their present extensive holdings. It has been the experience in the past that the establishment of Jewish settlements has fostered intensive cultivation in the neighbouring Arab villages; and it is the money obtained by sale of their land to Jews which furnishes

the/

-2-

the Arabs with the capital required for the new methods of agriculture. It is noted by Professor Mead, the head of the Experts of the Survey Commission which reported in 1928, that "the rural contact of Arabs and Jews is raising fellaheen in the efficiency and manner of their living rather than lowering the Jew".

It is submitted therefore that the corollary drawn in paragraph 2 of the memorandum, that the situation is one in which the interests of the indigenous population and the Jews are in direct conflict, and that further purchases of agricultural land by Jews can be made only by creating a class of Arab landless peasantry, is not justified. The case which is held up as illustrating this conflict, namely, the sale of the Wadi Hawareth lands, illustrates also the possibility of closer settlement of the land without doing injury to the present Arab cultivators. Here there is an area of 30,000 dunums which can be converted into plantation land. Only some 6000 dunums of it are said to be cultivated now in a rough way by 130 Arab families, while the land, if properly cultivated, would support some 300 families; so

that/

-3-

that there would be room for new Jewish settlers and the Arabs together. The principal difficulty which arises from the close settlement of the land, whether by Jews or other persons, is not with Arab agricultural tenants but rather with the Arab tribes who have grazed their flocks and herds over large areas of half cultivated land for many years, and who when removed from the land cannot find other grazing grounds. The agricultural tenants if they were to receive compensation on being dispossessed will usually acquire other land: but the Arabs of tribal areas whose principal living is from their animals require special treatment and consideration.

The draft legislation is open, I think, to objection as contrary to three principles of the Palestine Mandate –

(1) it runs counter to the direction that the country shall be placed under such ... economic conditions as will secure the establishment of the Jewish National Home. Land settlement is an essential part of that Home and a way must be found to enable Jews to acquire land while seeing that the other sections of the population are not victimized.

(2) it runs counter to the direction in two articles for the encouragement of close settlement by Jews on the land, and for introducing a land system appropriate to the needs of the country which shall have regard to the desirability of promoting the close settlement and intensive cultivation of the land.

It is /

—4—

It is true that the former article makes it a condition of this development that the rights and position of other sections of the population shall not be prejudiced; but a system which would tend to the maintenance of the present position of extensive land-holding does not carry out the intention of the Mandate.

3. It is framed in the form of discrimination on the ground of race. And although the prohibition of any such discrimination is contained in an article of the Mandate which deals in the first place with complete freedom of conscience and religious worship, it is to be noted that the widest interpretation has already been given to the article of the Mandate in Article 17(1)(a) of the Palestine Order in Council, which lays down that no Ordinance shall be promulgated which ... . shall tend to discriminate in any way between the inhabitants of Palestine on the ground of race, religion or language.

In this connexion it is observed that the statement in paragraph 14 of the memorandum that the Tanganyika Mandate contains a similar article as to discrimination is not correct. The Mandate for East Africa does contain a clause about economic equality of subjects of all countries which are members of the League of Nations; but it has nothing to correspond with the clause in the Palestine Mandate against discrimination. There is a fundamental difference in the system of the 'B' Mandate to which Tanganyika belongs and the Palestine Mandate, particularly with

regard/

-5-

regard to land holding. The B Mandates require that in framing laws relating to the holding or transfer of land the Mandatory shall safeguard the interests of the native population and not allow any transfer except between natives without the consent of the public authorities. The basic idea is that the native must be protected against the foreign settler. On the other hand the Palestine Mandate expressly contemplates that the Jews shall settle on the land and that a system of intensive cultivation shall be framed with a view to the placing of an increased agricultural population. It is a guiding idea of the Mandate that Jews and Arabs have equally historical rights to the land; and therefore there should not be differentiation against one or the other.

At the same time it is certainly necessary that the Government shall control large transactions in land so as to prevent the disposition of whole villages without arrangements for the future living of the old tenants. There is no need, I think, to restrict to this end all transactions and to require the approval of the High Commissioner to every disposition of land by an Arab to a non-Arab. The effect of such complete restriction would inevitably be the depreciation of the value of the land which would arouse the resentment of the Arabs, as happened in 1920 and 1921. There must be many small and innocent dealings in rural land between individuals in different places which should not be checked. Now that steps have been taken to protect tenants from sudden eviction and to secure them

compensation/

-6-

compensation from eviction the need of further legislation is, I think, restricted to keeping control of the larger transactions where a village or tribe or a considerable number of persons is in danger of being dispossessed by a disposition.

The history of the Government control over land transactions since the Occupation is as follows. From 1918 to July 1920 land transactions were forbidden, although in practice many were carried out surreptitiously. In 1920 the original Land Transfer Ordinance prescribed that every transaction must be approved by the Administration, and where a disposition affected property exceeding in value £3000, or an area of 300 dunums in the case of agricultural land, it had to obtain the consent of the High Commissioner who might refer the application to a commission appointed by him to report on the closer settlement of the land. It was laid down that the High Commissioner might consent to the transfer of large areas where he was satisfied that it would be in the public interest. A campaign was conducted in the country against these restrictions; and the Ordinance of 1921 relaxed them save in the case of a transfer of agricultural land on which there were tenants in possession. Then in 1929, when experience had shown that landlords evaded the check for the protection of their tenants, the Protection of Cultivators Ordinance was enacted to secure full notice to tenants of eviction and money compensation for improvements and disturbance.

I am of the opinion that some further legislative
measure/

measure is required to prevent any wholesale dispossession of old tenants without provision for their replacement elsewhere; and I am in agreement with the proposed amendments of the Protection of Cultivators Ordinance so as to secure that the District Commissioner shall have knowledge of any eviction notice served by a landlord on his tenants. The Commissioner would then be forewarned of any attempt to eject the whole or a part of the villagers with a view to the transfer of the land. Further it would be necessary to provide that the transfer of large areas, which might be defined as areas exceeding 1000 dunums or possibly 500 dunums, should be referred to His Excellency before being approved. To prevent evasion through the breaking up of one large transaction into a number of smaller transactions, it would be stipulated that the disposition of a number of small contiguous areas amounting together to more than the prescribed area should be deemed a disposition within the clause. Under the legislation the High Commissioner would be able to refer dispositions of the kind to a body in the nature of the old Land Commission, which would have to be satisfied that the tenants were either provided with land on part of the area to be transferred or elsewhere in Palestine, or would be employed on the transferred land, or prefer to acquire land elsewhere in Palestine or Trans-Jordan. The control would apply generally to all large transactions and no discrimination would be expressed as between dispositions of Arabs or non-Arabs.

                        (Initialled) N.B.

ENCLOSURE V TO CONFIDENTIAL DESPATCH "B" OF 29-3.30.

Transfer of Agricultural Land Bill and Protection of Cultivators (Amendment) Bill.

Observations by the Acting Chief Secretary.

1.   The Transfer of Agricultural Land Bill differentiates between "persons who are Arabs" and "persons who are not Arabs".

It therefore discriminates between the inhabitants of Palestine on the ground of race and, possibly, on the grounds of religion and language. It appears therefore to be contrary to Article 17(1)(a) and Article 18 of the Palestine Order in Council 1922 as amended by the Palestine (Amendment) Order in Council 1923. It is therefore, I think, unconstitutional.

In so far as the Protection of Cultivators (Amendment) Bill requires action founded on what may or may not be done under the Transfer of Agricultural Land Bill, it may be unconstitutional. Since Article 17 (1) (a) and Article 18 of the combined Palestine Order in Council reproduce the paragraph concerning discrimination in Article 15 of the Mandate, the two Ordinances being inconsistent with those two Articles of the combined Order in Council are repugnant to or inconsistent with the provisions of the Mandate. Under Article 17(1)(c) and Article 18 of the Combined Order in Council no Ordinance may be passed which has that character.   If the Bills pass into law they may be held to be ultra vires.

-2-

2. The Transfer of Agricultural Land Bill by restricting a free market for real estate is uneconomic for the following reasons:-

   (i) It will depress the value of land and so diminish the wealth of the country;
   (ii) It will add greatly to the difficulties of the difficult problem of provision of credit in this country;
   (iii) It will tend to discourage close settlement of the land and so will be against the interests and well being of the people for which the mandatory is responsible, it being admitted that close settlement of the land is to be encouraged in all countries, provided that sub-division does not become so fine as to be uneconomic to the individual cultivator.
   In so far as the Bill tends to discourage intensive cultivation and close settlement of the land it is repugnant to the provisions of Article 11 of the Mandate, and would be *ultra* *vires* if passed into law;
   (iv) The Government Agricultural Bank will be obliged to make smaller loans by reason of the fact that the land will have diminished in value and so in that respect will not be as great a security, and by reason of the fact that to recover debts the market will be restricted, and by reason of
   the/

—3—

the consequential fact that the Bank may have to administer mortgaged estates and so not recover debts of considerable magnitude, and consequentially the capital of the Bank will be prejudiced.

3. The Transfer of Agricultural Land Bill tends to political segregation of Jews and non-Jews. This may be inevitable but it is questionable whether it should be adopted as a policy by Government and encouraged by legislation.

4. The Tanganyika Mandate recognises essentially the need for the development of Africa by white people and the need to protect the inferior black people from exploitation by individual interests of the white people. It therefore recognises an inferiority of status attached to the black people. It does not seem to be a model for a mandate in regard to people whose independence is provisionally recognised.

5. On the analogy of the Tanganyika Mandate the Transfer of Agricultural Land Bill inevitably draws a sharp distinction between modern development and unprofitable cultivation. The doctrine behind the Transfer of Agricultural Land Bill seems to be that the protection of the non-Jews is to be found in maintaining them in "economic reservations" in the knowledge that the system of unprofitable cultivation may be thereby perpetuated.

It follows that the protection of non-Jews may not be in their interests or for their ultimate well-being.

—4—

Moreover, since there is a parity of exchange among all marketable commodities, agricultural credits based on
(i) depressed values of land due to restrictions on a free market; and
(ii) inability to dispose of mortgages on a free market, will not be economic in the sense that they will not have that parity of exchange with commodities required for agricultural development which have their values determined by ordinary economic laws.

It follows that even where agricultural credits can be given those credits will be smaller in magnitude than they should be for proper development; and, consequently, that this form of protection may not be in the interests of non-Jews.

6. On the assumption that the Bills pass into law, it may be anticipated that much ingenuity will be exercised by interested parties in regard to "persons who are Arabs" and "persons who are not Arabs". It will be burdensome on the High Commissioner to determine the cases particularly since under Royal Instruction XXVII the High Commissioner must observe the principles of Cmd.1700 and so treat all Palestinians, no matter what may be their racial origin, as one in the eye of the law. Ethnologically, it is doubtful if many *feilahin* are racially Arab. Many are descended directly from the ancient inhabitants. The so-called Arabs of Nablus may be
lineally/

-5-

lineally descended from the Samaritans; and so on.

A Moroccan Arab is certainly an Arab. Such a person could indubitably obtain rights over land in Palestine if he became a Palestinian and possibly if he did not acquire citizenship. If he did the Palestinian "Arabs" would have no protection under the Bill.

P.I.C.A. might very well employ such an agent, who might be a trained agriculturist, who could evict unprofitable tenants merely because he wished to establish more profitable cultivation. It is true that he could not then employ as cultivators "persons who are not Arabs" without consent; but the point is that evictions would have occurred for other quite good reasons, and an increment would have been added to the "landless peasantry". Rather than let the land lie idle it is possible that the High Commissioner in the end would consent to his employing as cultivators "persons who are not Arabs".

Unless the Ordinance itself make provision it is difficult to see how under § 3(14) of the Interpretation Ordinance "a person who is an Arab" would not include companies or religious orders or institutions.

7. The provisions of § 7 of the Bill will surely encourage mortgagors not to pay their debt. If the mortgagors have left Palestine before proceedings are begun, it will be difficult matter to secure the redemption of the debt to the Government.

Moreover,/

-6-

Moreover, unless the country were facing economic disaster it is difficult to see how to justify to the taxpayer the use of revenue for the purposes contemplated.

Furthermore the administration of mortgaged estates may be embarrassing to the Government.

8. I do not think the problem is insoluble by other methods.

The present problem is caused by three factors:-

(i) Since there is no conscription there are more young men in the villages and tribal areas than was the custom;

(ii) The improvement in sanitation has turned a stationary or declining population into an ascending population;

(iii) The need for land for immigrant Jews.

In course of time Malthusian principles will apply and the population and the resources will be adjusted one to the other.

Until that happens a temporary solution must be found. The problem is not acute in long established villages, and, so far, it is apparent only in those areas where there are semi-nomads who have no titles to ownership of land but have beneficial practices and possibly prescriptive rights of different kinds. Generally speaking they are wasteful and unprofitable cultivators.

Development/

-7-

Development of the country will by ordinary evolutionary processes displace these people from the land; the impulse given to this displacement by the needs of the immigrant Jews is accelerating the displacement beyond its proper rate with a resulting discomfort for both non-Jews and the Government.

9. Two "braking" factors are required:-

(i) No dispositions of land which displace persons for whom no arrangements for maintenance of their livelihood have been made should be permitted until such livelihood is assured;

(ii) No evictions for any cause should be permitted except where provision has been made for the livelihood of those who are evicted.

10. As to 9(i) and (ii) District Commissioners should by law be in a position to receive early information of intended evictions or dispositions of land affecting the livelihood of tenants and should have statutory duties in regard to these matters. Normally, where any large disposition of land is in contemplation it should be provided that those persons already cultivating it, in whole or in part, however rudely, shall be given a proper area of land within the estate under a long lease so that they either disappear as a result of natural and economic laws or become efficient cultivators under the influence of their more efficient neighbourhood. Eviction for the sake of vacant possession should not be permitted.

11. Evasions will be possible under any legislation and it is better I submit to have legislation which will encourage honest dealing rather than dishonest dealing in land.

12. I am therefore of opinion that the present proposals should be abandoned, at any rate until it is shewn that other principles, open to fewer and less grave objections, have not the desired effect.

24.2.30. (Initialled) E.M.

ENCLOSURE VI TO CONFIDENTIAL DESPATCH "A" OF 29.3.30.

Draft Ordinance to amend the Protection of Cultivators Ordinance 1929 with a view to prevent injury to cultivators by the transfer and close settlement of land.

BE IT ENACTED BY THE HIGH COMMISSIONER FOR PALESTINE, WITH THE ADVICE OF THE ADVISORY COUNCIL THEREOF.

Short Title. 1.   This Ordinance may be cited as the Protection of Cultivators (Amendment) Ordinance 1930, and the Protection of Cultivators Ordinance, 1929 (hereinafter referred to as the Principal Ordinance) and this Ordinance may together be cited as the Protection of Cultivators Ordinance 1929 and 1930.

PART I.

AMENDMENT OF PRINCIPAL ORDINANCE.

Amendment of Section 3 of the Principal Ordinance.   2.   Section 3 of the Principal Ordinance is hereby amended as follows:-

Copy of notice of termination of tenancy to be given to District Commissioner.

(a)   The words "The landlord shall send a copy of the notice to the District Commissioner" shall be deleted at the end of Subsection (3); and

(b)   The following Subsection shall be added to the said section:-

"(4)   Every notice given under this section shall be void and of no effect unless a copy thereof be served by the landlord on the District Commissioner of the District in which the land is situate within 30 days after the notice has been served on the tenant, and unless the notice contain a declaration by the landlord that its

object/

-2-

object is to terminate the tenancy in order that the land may be transferred with vacant possession if such be the object of the notice."

Amendment of Section 4 of the Principal Ordinance.

3. Section 4 of the Principal Ordinance is hereby amended as follows:-

(a) Subsection (2) shall be repealed and the following Subsection shall be substituted therefor:-

"(2) If the tenant is not willing to pay the increased rent he shall within one month of the date of the notice refer the question to the Board who shall decide what, having regard to all the circumstances, is a reasonable amount of rent to be paid. If the tenant is not willing to pay the amount of rent awarded by the Board he shall, within one month of the date of the award, notify the landlord who may thereupon give him notice to quit expiring on the date when the rent awarded by the Board would come into force."

(b) The following subsection shall be added to the Section:-

"(3) Every notice given under this section shall be void and of no effect unless a copy thereof be served by the landlord on the District Commissioner of the District in which the land is situate within 30 days after the notice has been served on the tenant."

−3−

PART II.

ADDITION TO THE PRINCIPAL ORDINANCE.

4. The following sections shall be added to the Principal Ordinance as Sections 11,12,13,14 thereof.

Definitions. 11. In this part of the Ordinance −

"Land" means miri land outside an urban area, as defined in any order issued under the Urban Property Tax Ordinance 1928, or in the case of a Municipality where no such order has been made, outside the municipal area.

"Disposition" means a sale, transfer, mortgage, lease or sub-lease transfer of possession and every other disposition of land, whether similar to those before enumerated or not and includes an agreement for a disposition and a disposition of land in execution of any order of a Court but does not include any order of Court except an order for foreclosure of a mortgage of land.

"Village" includes a tribal area, and any of the villages mentioned in a proclamation issued under Article 11 of the Palestine Order in Council."

Disposition of large areas to be referred to High Commissioner. 12.(1) Any disposition of land of an area of 1000 dunums or more, or any disposition which the Director of Lands has reason to believe forms part of a disposition exceeding such area in one village or neighbouring villages shall not be valid unless it is in writing and is approved by the High Commissioner.

(2)/

—4—

(2) Any disposition of a share or shares of undivided land, where the area of the shares on partition may amount to 1000 dunums or more shall be subject to the same conditions.

(3) Any disposition of an area less than 1000 dunums which forms part of another disposition or a series of dispositions in respect of which the area or the aggregate area involved is 1000 dunums or more forming part of a village or neighbouring villages shall be subject to the same conditions.

(4) Any clause in a disposition, or in any document connected with a disposition which falls under the provisions of this section stipulating for a penalty or payment of damages in case of failure to carry out the disposition shall be void and of no effect unless the disposition is approved by the High Commissioner.

(5) Where a disposition of an area less than 1000 dunums has been registered and subsequently is found to form part of a disposition exceeding such area, it shall not be thereby invalidated.

13. No Court or Judge shall make an order for eviction of a tenant pursuant to a notice given under this Ordinance unless the landlord satisfies the Court or Judge that the tenancy has been validly terminated under this Ordinance and unless the landlord declares wether the object of the termination of the tenancy is a transfer of the land with vacant possession and, if that be the object of the termination of the tenancy, unless the

landlord/

-5-

landlord satisfies the Court or Judge that the disposition has been referred to the High Commissioner in accordance with the provisions of Section 12 hereof and approved by him.

Power of High Commissioner to suspend proceedings for eviction of tenants.

14. Where notice has been given to determine a tenancy under this Ordinance and the High Commissioner is satisfied that hardship would be caused if the tenants were evicted, he may, by Order, direct that no proceedings shall be taken for eviction of the tenants until he is satisfied that the tenants will retain, or will be able to acquire elsewhere, sufficient land for the maintenance of themselves and their families, and no Court or Judge shall make or execute an Order of eviction against such tenants so long as the Order of the High Commissioner is in force.

ENCLOSURE VII TO CONFIDENTIAL DESPATCH "A" OF 29.3.30.

NOTE
on the Protection of Cultivators Amendment Ordinance, by the Attorney-General.

The amendments of the Principal Ordinance of 1929 are designed, on the one hand, to strengthen the provisions with regard to notice of termination of agricultural tenancies and the eviction of agricultural tenants, and to secure that the Government shall have information of a proposed termination of a tenancy at the earliest moment; and on the other hand to give the Government powers of checking dispositions of any large area of land which are likely to involve the disturbance of the present cultivators.

Section 2 of the amending Ordinance amplifies the provision in the principal enactment concerning the communication of notice to the District Commissioner, and prescribes that where the landlord is terminating a tenancy in order that he may transfer the land to a purchaser he must notify the Government of his intention.

Section 3 provides similarly for notice to the Government of an intention to increase the rent of an agricultural tenant, and further for the reference to the Board of any proposed increase of rent which is disputed by the tenant, so that the Board may fix a fair rent.

The second part of the amending Ordinance involves a partial return to the system prescribed by the original Transfer of Land Ordinance which was issued in 1920. Under that system all transactions in land were controlled by the Government, with a view both to preventing speculation and to protecting small

-2-

holders; and all dispositions of more than 300 dunums, (that is, roughly 60 Acres) of agricultural land had to be referred to the High Commissioner for approval. A campaign was conducted in the country against the provisions designed to check speculation; and the Land Transfer Amendment Ordinance 1921 relaxed the restrictions save in the case of a transfer of agricultural land on which there were tenants in possession. After experience had shown that landlords could evade the check for the protection of the tenants, the Protection of Cultivators Ordinance was enacted to secure full notice to tenants of a termination of the tenancy and money compensation for disturbance and improvements carried out by them. Further legislation is required to prevent wholesale dispossession of old tenants without provision for their settlement on the land elsewhere; and it is proposed therefore that the transfer of any large areas of land, which will normally be worked by agricultural tenants, shall be referred to the High Commissioner so that he may be assured that the tenants will be provided for either on the land to be transferred or elsewhere. It is proposed that the control shall be limited to areas of 1000 dunums or more, so as to avoid interference with credit and ordinary day to day transactions. On the other hand the control is to be exercised over every kind of disposition of the larger areas in order to prevent attempts of evasion. Land in an urban area is excluded from the control, because all such land

must/

-3-

must be regarded as building sites and should be dealt with freely.

The new Section 12 aims at preventing the evasion of control by breaking up a large transaction into a number of small transactions. The Director of Lands would have notice from the District Commissioner where agricultural tenants of any considerable area have been served with notice to quit; and he would be in a position to require the reference of any disposition of such land, if there were reason to think that the sale of a parcel of less than 1000 dunums formed part of a larger transaction to be executed either at the time or later. The control is to be applied also to the disposition of shares of any considerable fraction of undivided land.

Subsection (5) has been included to make it clear that a transaction of less than 1000 dunums, which has already been registered, will not itself be invalidated by the staying of subsequent transactions in adjoining land. The disposition of other parcels will be checked till proper arrangements are made for the old cultivators; but it would introduce confusion to annul a transaction already completed and registered, perhaps, some years before.

Section 13 gives power to hold up an eviction when there is evidence that a disposition is to follow the eviction, until it is established that the tenants' position is assured.

Section 14/

—4—

Section 14 is designed to meet the circumstances where a disposition of agricultural land which escapes restriction is made subject to the existing tenancies, and subsequently the purchaser takes steps to obtain vacant possession by evicting the old tenants. The example of the Wadi Hawareth lands has indicated the desirability of giving the High Commissioner a residuary power to hold up eviction in such cases, which affect the lives of a sub-tribe or of a part of a village, until adequate provision is made for placing the existing settlers on the land elsewhere. The power given is on the face of it indefinite; but it seems preferable to give this broad power to the High Commissioner in order to cope with any cases of hardship which come to light than to throw the net of control over agricultural land transactions generally, or over any transactions between Arabs and other persons.

(Signed) N. Bentwich.

9.04

PALESTINE.

Note for the Secretary of State on the
draft Protection of Cultivators
Ordinance.

C.P.16/33.

1. This draft Ordinance embodies adequately the new provisions contained in paragraph 21 of the Cabinet Memorandum and contains a few additional provisions which were not contemplated in the Cabinet Memorandum. None of these call for comment except the definition of "statutory tenant".

2. A "statutory tenant" who has occupied and cultivated for <u>a year</u> gets the protection of the Ordinance. At present <u>an agreement</u> for <u>two years</u> is required.

The Jews will not like the change, but it can be justified on the grounds explained in the despatch, viz., that under the present system landlords avoid the law by letting a tenant in for less than two years. Any period is open to the possibility of evasion of this kind, but it is thought that a year should be a satisfactory period, considering the methods of cultivation employed in Palestine.

3. The Legal Advisers have made a number of suggestions for minor amendments, which can be sent out to Palestine for consideration, but before the despatch goes a few points call for the Secretary of State's decision:-

(a) <u>Trespassers.</u>

Mr. Roberts-Wray has suggested that the definition of "statutory tenant" would include a

mere

mere trespasser who manages to remain on a piece of land for twelve months, and that unless we intended to protect such people it would be as well to exclude them from the definition e.g. by inserting "lawfully" before "occupying" in the definition.

Many of the people whom we wish to protect wandered on to the land of Arab owners many years ago, and have been allowed to remain without any tenancy agreements. Presumably if they have been in possession without the knowledge of the landlord they might be regarded as in unlawful occupation, but if the landlord has tacitly agreed to their continuing in possession, they would not. This depends largely upon local law. For example Mr. Drayton states that under the Ottoman Law of Leasing (1882) all leases must be in <u>writing.</u>

? We should make no attempt to exclude trespassers from the definition.

(b) <u>Sale or mortgage of tenancy rights in subsistence areas.</u>

The draft Ordinance says nothing about this. At a recent discussion with Sir Arthur Wauchope it was agreed that a section should be inserted prohibiting sale or mortgage <u>except with the approval of the High Commissioner.</u> In subsequent talk with the High Commissioner it was pointed out that, while it might be possible to justify sale to the landlord, the proviso underlined above would, on the face of it, allow the sale or mortgage to another Arab, and that this would be unjust to the landlord. The United Kingdom

Kingdom Rent Restriction Acts make it a penal offence to ask or receive payment, as a condition of giving up possession, from any person other than the landlord. There was not, however, time to discuss this point fully with the High Commissioner before he left.

The Legal Adviser has suggested that the tenant should not be allowed to make money out of the protection given by the Ordinance, even by surrendering to the landlord and that if the tenant wishes to leave the subsistence area the landlord should obtain free possession. The Department concur with this view and would suggest that the High Commissioner should be asked to consider whether it would not be best to prohibit sale or mortgage <u>absolutely</u>, but, if he still wishes to retain the proviso, at any rate to make it clear that sale to the landlord only is contemplated on the lines of the attached sub-clause, which has been drafted by the Legal Adviser.

(c) <u>Publication of draft Ordinance.</u>

Sir Arthur Wauchope recently told us that he wished the Ordinance to be enacted without the usual one month's prior publication in the Gazette. His arguments were:-

(i) that if notice were given the Jews would take the opportunity of coming to arrangements with tenants under the existing Ordinance; and

(ii) that there was nothing to be gained by inviting public controversy on legislation which it had been definitely decided to enact.

The

The Palestine Order-in-Council (Section 17(1)(d)) provides as follows:-

> "No Ordinance shall be promulgated unless a draft of the same shall first have been made public for one calendar month at the least before the enactment thereof, unless immediate promulgation shall in the judgment of the High Commissioner be indispensably necessary in the public interest."

The draft Protection of Cultivators Ordinance repeals all the previous relevant legislation, and Section 3(1), (which relates to notice to quit) takes effect "notwithstanding any provision of any contract to the contrary". Assuming that the draft Ordinance were published in the Gazette for one month before enactment, Section 3(1) would adequately secure the position of any tenants who might be induced during that month to enter into agreements with Jewish landlords. There would, however, be nothing to prevent Jewish landlords from issuing notices to quit under the existing legislation and Mr. Roberts-Wray is of opinion that such notices might be held by the Courts not to be affected by the new Ordinance in view of the terms of the Palestine Interpretation Ordinance as to the effect of repeals.

There is, therefore, some weight in the argument that the Ordinance should be published without notice in order to prevent forestalling. But if the draft Ordinance is to be published for a month, this difficulty

difficulty could be met by inserting saving provisions e.g. that any notice to quit issued after the date of the publication of the Ordinance, which would not have been valid if the new Ordinance had been in force, shall be null and void, and that any notice to quit issued after the aforesaid date which would have been valid had the new Ordinance been in operation, shall be deemed to have been issued under the provisions of the new Ordinance.

The High Commissioner's second argument has also some weight. There is everything to be said for avoiding a month's controversy on the draft Ordinance. The Jews will strain every nerve in Palestine and in London to get the Ordinance withdrawn or weakened, and in Palestine there is quite likely to be captious Arab criticism as well. The result may be a serious embitterment of political feeling in Palestine, which should be avoided, if possible, in the public interest.

It is suggested that immediate enactment should be approved, and that this procedure should be defended, if necessary, on the grounds (a) that it was necessary to prevent attempts to forestall the operation of the Ordinance, and (b) that the Secretary of State was fully aware of the views of the Jewish and Arab leaders on the question of restrictive land legislation from their memoranda on the French reports and previous expressions of opinion, and felt justified in the circumstances in approving the High Commissioner's recommendation that the Ordinance should be enacted without prior publication on the grounds of the public interest.

(sd) H. F. Downie
9.6.33

PALESTINE.

DRAFT PROTECTION OF CULTIVATORS ORDINANCE, 1933.

Should a "statutory tenant" be allowed to sell or mortgage his tenancy interest in a "subsistence area"?

Para.9 (v) of No.8 in 97072/32.

1. The High Commissioner originally suggested the inclusion in the proposed new Protection of Cultivators Ordinance of a provision to the effect that a tenant should not be allowed to sell his "lot viable", but that he should be allowed to raise a mortgage on his interest in it subject to certain conditions.

No.13 in 97072/33.

2. In reply we pointed out

(a) that a tenant could not in any case sell his "lot viable" - i.e. the land itself, which would not belong to him - but only his tenancy right:

(b) that it was impossible to prevent a tenant from leaving his "lot viable", and that in the circumstances it was a question whether he should not be allowed to realise his interest in the "lot viable."

We asked whether it was the High Commissioner's object to prevent a Jewish land purchaser from buying out the tenants, or to prevent an Arab tenant who intended to leave his "lot viable" from selling his interest to another Arab, thus perpetuating the tenancy to the disadvantage of the Jewish landlord.

No.1 in 17272/33.

3. Sir Arthur Wauchope replied that his object was to prevent a Jewish purchaser from buying out the tenant, but that on further consideration he agreed that it was not practicable to prevent a tenant from giving up his interest in the "lot viable", whether for a consideration or not.

4. In the light of this reply, the summary of projected land legislation contained in paragraph 21 of the

the Cabinet memorandum on Policy in Palestine included the suggestion (paragraph 21 (6)) that a tenant should be allowed to sell or mortgage his tenancy interest in the "subsistence area", and was approved by the Cabinet in this form.

No.1 in 17272/1/33.

5. We now have the draft of the new Protection of Cultivators Ordinance. The draft contains no reference, positive or negative, to the right of the tenant to sell or mortgage his tenancy interest in the "subsistence area".

Paragraph 10 of the covering despatch (drafted by Mr Mills) says, "as the primary object of the Bill is to ensure, as far as possible, that cultivators remain upon the land, it would seem undesirable to provide in terms a means by which they could at once be displaced".

In his explanatory memorandum appended to the draft Ordinance, the Acting Attorney General comments as follows :-

"It should be noted that the Cabinet memorandum provided in Section 21 (6) :-

'A tenant be allowed to sell or mortgage his tenancy interest in the subsistence area'

A provision to this effect has, however, not been

inserted

inserted[x] as it was felt that there might be some misunderstanding with regard to a subsistence area under this Ordinance and an area which might be retained by reason of any Homestead Ordinance, and it appeared undesirable that a tenant should be allowed to sell his interest in a subsistence area and so immediately become landless.

It is probably impossible to prevent such a tenant from being bribed to leave his area in some cases, but there would seem no reason why there should be a specific provision[x] in the law that he can sell his rights".

6. Sir Arthur Wauchope has now informed us in recent discussions that, after further consultation with his advisers, he is convinced that the new Ordinance should include a definite prohibition of the sale or mortgage of a tenant's interest in a subsistence area, except with the approval of the High Commissioner. (Sir Arthur Wauchope told me that Musa el Alami has advised him that a provision of this kind will greatly help to commend the proposed legislation to the Arabs, and the High Commissioner has reason to understand that it will not unduly perturb the Jews.)

7. It is generally agreed that we cannot stop tenants from abandoning their subsistence areas, and there is little doubt that many will be bribed to do so. At the same time, the prohibition of sale may discourage this tendency and is at any rate consistent with the policy

[x] The intention was, I think, merely that the new Ordinance should not contain any prohibition of sale or mortgage of a subsistence area.

policy of attaching the tenant to the land which has inspired the new Ordinance.

8. If the draft Ordinance is left as it is, i.e. with no reference one way or the other to the right of the tenant to sell his interest, there will be nothing to prevent an Arab statutory tenant from selling his tenancy right in his subsistence area to another Arab, who may be a complete stranger to the neighbourhood and who will, in any case, have no moral claim on the landlord. In this way the tenancy of the subsistence area could be protracted ad infinitum, and this hardly seems fair to the landlord.

This consideration should afford an effective reply to any Jewish criticisms of the prohibition of sale. (Intd.) H.F.D.

? But he new Arab tenant & how to occupy & cultivate for a year before he can obtain protection under the Ord[inance]

9. As to the right of the tenant to mortgage his interest, as the draft Ordinance now stands, the security would not be attractive as the mortgagee could not rely on securing possession on foreclosure. ("No person lawfully occupying a subsistence area shall be ejected therefrom save upon the recommendation of a Board with the approval of the High Commissioner" - see Section 7 (4) of draft Ordinance.)

10. The mortgagee might, however, have some remedy against the crop in the case of default by the mortgagor and seeing that the subsistence area is intended merely to "enable the statutory tenant to maintain his customary means of livelihood" - Section 7 (1) - it would seem to be perfectly justifiable to prohibit the tenant from mortgaging his tenancy interest.

11. It might be argued that if we insert the suggested prohibition of sale or mortgage, we shall have crossed the Rubicon and accepted the principle of interfering with voluntary land transactions, a step which (as has been made clear in the Cabinet memorandum with reference to the small owner) we do not at present intend to take.

12. It is, however, at least doubtful whether the tenant of a subsistence area can fairly be regarded as owning his tenancy right in the full sense of the word. This right has been secured for him by special legislation, and on this ground it would seem that the Government has a claim to control its disposal. The object of the legislation is to secure the tenant's subsistence upon the land and not to enable him to turn his privilege to financial account.

13. On the whole, there would appear no strong objection to adopting the High Commissioner's new suggestion, although it cannot be hoped by this, or by any other means to prevent tenants of subsistence areas from leaving the land. It is, however, difficult to see how the High Commissioner will be able to discriminate between one case and another, and he might be asked to re-consider his suggestion on this point. The arguments used above as to the limited nature of the tenant's right in the subsistence area led to the conclusion that sale or mortgage should be prohibited absolutely, i.e. if a tenant wishes to abandon his subsistence area and go elsewhere, or leave the land altogether for employment in a town, he has no strong claim to any compensatory payment from the landlord.

14. If the draft ordinance is amended as proposed

by the insertion of a provision to the effect that the tenant of a subsistence area may not sell or mortgage his tenancy interest, the Secretary of State will no doubt consider whether it is necessary first to consult the Cabinet, or whether it will be sufficient to inform them after the event of the modification of the original proposals.

M Downs
24.5.33

THIS DOCUMENT IS THE PROPERTY OF HIS BRITANNIC MAJESTY'S GOVERNMENT

Printed for the Cabinet. February 1933.

SECRET.   Copy No. 51

C.P. 16 (33).

CABINET.

POLICY IN PALESTINE.

Memorandum by the Secretary of State for the Colonies.

1. IT has become necessary to take decisions on certain important questions relating to land policy in Palestine. The problem with which we have to deal may be stated quite simply. The Jews have for years been buying land in Palestine for agricultural colonisation. This is part of the fundamental policy of Zionism, and is likely to continue so long as funds are available, and land can be obtained. The Jews pay market prices to Arab landowners, and in many cases generous compensation to tenants and other occupants, who are displaced from the land purchased.

2. In former years when one Arab sold land to another, the landowner changed, but the tenants remained, and those who laboured on the land for regular or seasonal wage still continued to earn that wage. To some extent this practice was, and is, maintained by such organisations as the Palestine Jewish Colonisation Association. But the Zionist Policy is different. When the Jewish National Fund purchase land, not only the landlord is changed, but the tenants and all the wage-earning labourer class are compelled to move; for the Zionist policy is not only to acquire ownership, but also to ensure that all the work required on the land shall be carried out by Jews only. The right of the Zionists to take such action cannot be questioned, but it obviously creates a new situation for the Arab cultivator.

3. The result is the growth of a body of "landless" Arabs, who may be divided into three classes:—
   (a) Tenants.
   (b) Small owner-occupiers.
   (c) Labourers.

In a more highly-developed country, one might expect such persons to be partly absorbed into other occupations, and the remainder dealt with by the Poor Law Authorities, but conditions in Palestine are peculiar. The fellah is usually heavily in debt, improvident and unfitted for urban life. Political exploitation, which is active in Palestine, tends to create in the "landless" class a feeling of disaffection and unrest. Sir Arthur Wauchope is definitely of opinion that this constitutes a potential danger, which should be arrested without delay, if serious consequences are to be averted.

4. The attention of the late Government was drawn to this problem by the Report of the Shaw Commission on the disturbances of 1929 (Cmd. 3530, March 1930), and by the report of Sir John Hope Simpson (Cmd. 3686, October 1930). In the Statement of Policy of October 1930 (Cmd. 3692) and in the Prime Minister's letter of the 13th February, 1931, to Dr. Weizmann, His Majesty's Government accepted responsibility for the resettlement of such Arabs as could be shown to have been displaced from the lands which they occupied, in consequence of those lands passing into Jewish hands, if they had not obtained other holdings or other satisfactory occupation (paragraph 9 of the Prime Minister's letter). They also accepted generally Sir John Hope Simpson's proposal for

[8152]   B

making further land available for Arabs (including Arabs already "landless") and Jews, by means of a comprehensive development scheme; and they contemplated that, in connection with this development scheme, which would involve a guaranteed loan of £2½ million, the Government of Palestine should take legislative powers to control dispositions of land which would be sufficiently wide to protect Arab cultivators for the future. In the meantime, full power was reserved (paragraph 12 of the Prime Minister's letter) to take all steps necessary to protect the tenancy and occupancy rights, including the rights of squatters, throughout Palestine.

5. In August, 1931, Mr. Lewis French was appointed Director of Development for the purpose of—
  (a) Preparing a register of "landless" Arabs;
  (b) Drawing up a scheme for the resettlement of those Arabs; and
  (c) Investigating the methods to be adopted to give effect to the policy of land settlement adumbrated in the White Paper of 1930, and in the Prime Minister's letter.

6. Mr. French presented a report to the High Commissioner in December 1931, and a supplementary report in April last. These reports have been communicated in confidence to the Jewish Agency and the Arab Executive, whose observations upon them are at present awaited by the High Commissioner. It has been publicly announced in Palestine, with my concurrence, that no decisions will be taken upon the French reports until His Majesty's Government have received and considered the High Commissioner's recommendations, together with the observations of the Jewish Agency, and the Arab Executive.

7. A summary of Mr. French's proposals is appended (Appendix II). The reports contain—
  (a) Estimates of the cost of resettling an Arab family on "dry" (unirrigated) land for extensive cultivation, and on irrigated land for citrus cultivation, respectively; based on the assumption that the Government of Palestine will undertake the necessary works of land improvement, and will equip the settlers and maintain them during the early years. Mr. French estimates that the cost would be £500 per family for "dry" farming, and £650 to £800 for citrus growing.
  (b) A general survey of the land resources of the Territory, and of the possibility of making further land available for intensive cultivation, by means of irrigation, drainage, &c.
  (c) Proposals for the enactment of somewhat drastic legislation, designed to provide security of tenure for the Arab cultivator; viz., an "Occupancy Tenants' Ordinance," which would confer an "occupancy right" on existing and future tenants, thus preventing their eviction, and a Homestead Protection Ordinance, which would prevent the owner-occupier or the "occupancy tenant" who wished to dispose of his land or "occupancy tenancy" from parting with a minimum "homestead area."

8. Mr. French has now resigned, and his place has been taken by his deputy, who was formerly a member of the Palestine Administrative Service. There is reason to believe that Mr. French's reports will be received with hostility by both Arabs and Jews, and that any proposals based upon them will be the subject of acute controversy.

9. Apart from this, it is necessary to take into account the change of conditions since the policy of the late Government was formulated in 1930. This policy contemplated a development scheme, to be financed out of a guaranteed loan of £2½ million, and Parliament was informed (see Appendix I, paragraph 11) that, during the first years of the development scheme, it would be necessary to provide from British Votes such annual amounts as might be required to meet the interest and sinking fund charges upon the loan. Though the financial and economic condition of Palestine shows signs of improvement, world economic conditions remain uncertain, and financial stringency at home is still acute. For these reasons, I consider that there is ample justification for postponing the initiation of any large scheme of development in Palestine, and that we should now reconsider our commitments in the light of the changed

3

conditions, and determine how far we must go towards meeting them, and how it is to be done.

10. If the proposal for a development scheme is shelved, we are left with two urgent problems, which call for immediate action:—
  (a) What should be done as regards Arabs who have already become "landless"?
  (b) How can the process of displacement be stopped?

As regards (a), the pledges given by His Majesty's Government were very definite. The claims of "landless" Arabs are actually being accepted for registration at the present time, and any indication that His Majesty's Government do not intend to carry out their undertaking to resettle them would have a deplorable political effect, which would be exploited to the full by the increasingly active Arab Nationalist Party, and by the Communists. The register of "landless" Arabs is nearly complete, and it is estimated that the total may amount to some 800 or 900 families. This figure takes no account of owner-occupiers, or of Arab villagers who have hitherto worked as labourers for Arab landowners, but who will find their means of livelihood vanish when both the ownership of the land and the work on it becomes Jewish in place of Arab. Sir Arthur Wauchope holds, and I agree with him, that we are only pledged to deal with "landless" Arabs, in the sense of those who have lost their land through Jewish action, i.e., tenants. For financial reasons, if on no other grounds, the Palestine Government cannot undertake, in addition, to settle on the land, at a cost of perhaps £500 each, those Arab owner-occupiers, who have voluntarily sold their land, or Arab villagers, who have lost, not land-holdings but their employment upon the land as a result of Jewish land purchases. It is, however, necessary that the existence of the labourer class (estimated at some 3,000 families) should be recognised.

11. I wish to inform the High Commissioner that His Majesty's Government concur with his views as to the limitation of the register to displaced tenants; and I propose to ask him to submit his own recommendations for providing land for the 800 or 900 families who are likely to be registered, with due regard to economy. It may be found unnecessary to provide for this re-settlement on such a costly scale as is suggested in Mr. French's reports. For example, it is hoped that the Wadi Hawareth Arabs, whose settlement constitutes the most urgent problem, will be settled at a cost of about £250 per family; in this case the land is obtainable at an exceptionally low price, and the Arabs already possess tents, agricultural implements and ploughing animals, items for which Mr. French allowed £110 to £120.

12. I am afraid we must recognise that even this limited plan of re-settlement will probably involve a guaranteed loan. This being the case it would, in my opinion, be desirable to provide facilities by means of the same loan for the financing of certain urgent public works in Palestine. The provisional list of these works, of which the greater part are revenue-producing, or will effect savings in annual expenditure, include the provision of married quarters for the infantry garrison, an oil berth for the Iraq Petroleum Company at Haifa Harbour, town water supplies and improvements of the telegraph and telephone systems.

I should like to have approval in principle for such a loan, which, in consultation with the Treasury, I should endeavour to keep within such limits as would be likely to obviate any call on the Exchequer under the guarantee.

13. I have not overlooked the fact that the Prime Minister's letter and Dr. Shiels' speech contemplated that, if funds were available, some assistance would be given to Jewish settlement, and that this was confirmed by Sir Arthur Wauchope in statements which he made, with my approval, to the Arab Executive and the Jewish Agency on the 27th January, 1932 (see Appendix I, paragraphs 6, 8–10). These undertakings were, however, expressly dependent upon the initiation of a development scheme; and if, for the reasons given in paragraph 9, the development scheme is postponed, we are, I consider, free to confine action to the re-settlement of "landless" Arabs.

[8152]

14. At the same time it will probably be found necessary on economic and political grounds to provide on the Palestine Estimates for a Government contribution to the Jewish Agricultural Research Station. It will be noted (Appendix II, paragraph 6) that Mr. French's reports contain a recommendation of this nature.

For the same reasons the High Comissioner urges strongly that the guaranteed loan should include provision for a capital grant of £10,000 or £20,000 to a definitely Jewish institution (agricultural or educational). Further, the High Commissioner desires to include provision for the capital cost, roughly estimated at £60,000, of a Technical School, which he regards as one of Palestine's most urgent needs. This school would be open to both Arabs and Jews, and it is understood that probably it would be used mainly by Arabs, but it would also be of benefit to the Jews. I should be glad to receive approval in principle for these proposals.

15. With regard to (b), in view of the high cost of resettlement, it is obvious that, for financial reasons, quite apart from the question of policy and the preservation of order in Palestine, the process of displacement should be brought to an end as soon as possible. I have discussed the question fully with Sir Arthur Wauchope and I am satisfied that there is no half-way house between leaving things as they are and so aggravating the evil, and some form of legislation to control land transactions. I am also convinced that, in view of the opposition of the Jews to legislation of this nature, any new enactment should not transgress any of our commitments to the Jews and should involve as little interference as possible with the economic life of the country.

16. Reference has been made in paragraph 7 above to the restrictive legislation proposed by Mr. French. Sir Arthur Wauchope considers, and I agree with him, that these ordinances go too far. We agree that the right of a tenant to a holding sufficient for the subsistence of his family must be assured, but, in conformity with the proposal not to register owner-occupiers as " landless " Arabs, we consider that the right of the owner-occupier to sell his land should remain unrestricted, at any rate for the present.

17. It has already been noted that in paragraph 12 of the Prime Minister's letter full power was reserved (pending the establishment of temporary centralised control of land transfers in connection with the development scheme) to take all steps necessary to protect tenancy and occupancy rights, including the rights of squatters, throughout Palestine. In accordance with this policy, a temporary Ordinance with a life of 12 months was enacted on the 28th May, 1931, which amended the Protection of Cultivators Ordinance, 1929, in several important particulars. The life of the amending Ordinance was extended for a further 12 months on the 28th May, 1932.

18. The present Protection of Cultivators legislation provides as follows:—

(1) No tenant of two years' standing, who has paid his rent and cultivated his holding properly and not been declared bankrupt, may be evicted without at least one year's notice, compensation for disturbance and for improvements and (if he is of more than five years' standing and goes without an eviction order) the equivalent of one year's average rent. Any dispute regarding the amount of compensation has to be decided by a Board consisting of a District Officer, one representative of the landlord and one representative of the tenant. The Board's decisions require confirmation by the District Commissioner.

(2) Unless there has been failure to pay rent or to cultivate properly, or unless the tenant has been declared bankrupt, the court will not grant an eviction order unless the High Commissioner is satisfied that "equivalent provision has been secured towards the livelihood of the tenant." (The Ordinance does not specify what this "equivalent provision" must be.)

(3) The tenant's rent cannot be raised except with the consent of a Board constituted as above.

(4) Tenants who have not paid their rent and have not cultivated their land properly may be evicted at 15 days' notice unless they apply for the matter to be referred to a Board constituted as above.

19. Sir Arthur Wauchope tells me that, since the amending Ordinance came into force, few, if any, tenants have been turned off their lands. No case has been referred to the High Commissioner under (2) above, and, therefore, no eviction orders can have been made except after default in regard to payment of rent, or proper cultivation, or after bankruptcy. At the same time the Ordinance does not provide complete security, since it merely impedes, but does not prevent, eviction, and allows of compensation in other forms than land in the case of eviction.

20. The most important parts of the existing legislation expire in May, 1933, and some legislation will, therefore, be necessary in any case within the next few months. Sir Arthur Wauchope's proposal is that the Protection of Cultivators legislation should be made permanent, and that the opportunity should be taken to simplify it and redraft it. The legislation would be "permanent" in the sense that the time-limit would be removed, but the Ordinance would be subject to review in the event of the establishment of the centralized land control contemplated in the Prime Minister's letter.

21. The revised Ordinance would contain the following provisions:—

(1) A tenant who has paid his rent and not neglected his holding grossly may not be evicted unless the High Commissioner is satisfied that an equivalent provision has been made for him *in land* up to the minimum required for subsistence of himself and his family, and unless he is given at least one year's notice, compensation for disturbance and for improvements and, if of more than 5 years' standing, the equivalent of one year's average rent.

(2) A tenant's rent not to be raised except with the consent of a Board constituted as at present.

(3) A tenant who has not paid his rent not to be evicted without at least one year's notice and compensation for improvements, and even then not to be evicted from the minimum area required for subsistence provided he cultivates it fairly.

*(4) Any question as to what is a sufficient subsistence area for any particular tenant to be settled by a Board constituted as at present, and liable to review, say, every 5 years.

(5) A Board to decide, as at present, all questions regarding the amount of compensation due.

(6) A tenant to be allowed to sell or mortgage his tenancy interest in the "subsistence area."

(7) The following clause, taken from Mr. French's Occupancy Tenant's Ordinance:—

"Notwithstanding anything contained in this Ordinance, the District Commissioner may, on the application of the landlord, authorise the resumption by him of a holding or part thereof, upon being satisfied (1) that such resumption is required for some reasonable and sufficient purpose having relation to the good of the holding or of the adjoining lands, including development by drainage or irrigation or by closer settlement or colonization or disposal for building purposes; and (2) that the 'occupancy tenant' will retain sufficient land in the district or elsewhere for the maintenance of himself and his family, or that the purpose for which the resumption of the holding is sought comprises the provision for the 'occupancy tenant' of developed land sufficient for the maintenance of himself and his family, together with adequate subsistence for them pending the development of such lands."

22. Sir Arthur Wauchope is definitely of opinion that no legislation should at present be passed preventing the owner-occupier from disposing of his land. He considers that it would be difficult to justify such an interference with the right of landowners to dispose of their property, and that the inclusion of the

---

* NOTE.—Sir Arthur Wauchope proposed to lay it down that the minimum area to be reserved should be such as to provide the tenant with subsistence by his existing methods of cultivation. I would prefer that the Ordinance should leave the determination of the "subsistence area" in each case to the Board, in order to allow of a reduction of this area in cases where the landlord may be prepared to irrigate the land and to provide for the tenant's subsistence in the meantime.

owner-occupier in the proposed legislation would be likely to strengthen the opposition to anything which it may be decided to do for the tenant. He does not anticipate, at any rate during the next few years, a serious problem arising from the conversion of owner-occupiers into " landless " Arabs.

23. I am in agreement with the High Commissioner's views on the subject of preventive legislation, and I should like to authorise him to prepare and, subject to my approval, to pass a draft Ordinance embodying the provisions which he suggests.

24. It remains to consider whether the line of action proposed in this memorandum affords any substantial ground for complaint on the part of the Jews. It is true (see Appendix I, paragraph 3) that His Majesty's Government have stated that they regard a development scheme as the most effectual means of furthering the establishment of a National Home for the Jews. But it can fairly be contended that the change which has taken place in financial and economic conditions since that statement was made would afford ample justification for postponing the development scheme, and with it any expenditure on Jewish settlement. As regards the resettlement of displaced Arabs, this is an obligation of His Majesty's Government which has already been recognised by the Jews. The Jewish Agency have had an opportunity of examining the case of each applicant for inclusion in the register of " landless " Arabs before final decision, and the Prime Minister's letter and the published instructions to the Director of Development contemplate the resettlement of these Arabs on completion of the register, irrespective of the initiation of any wider scheme of land settlement.

If preventive legislation is confined as proposed above to a strengthening of the Protection of Cultivators Ordinance, it can be justified as falling within the reservation already quoted from paragraph 12 of the Prime Minister's letter, and the Jews will have no grounds for claiming that any such legislation should be dependent on the initiation of a development scheme.

25. I ask the Cabinet to approve—
   (a) that there shall be no new development scheme at present (paragraph 9);
   (b) that the register of " landless " Arabs shall be limited to ex-tenants (paragraphs 10–11);
   (c) that the High Commissioner shall be instructed to prepare and submit plans for re-settling " landless " Arabs registered in accordance with this definition (paragraph 11);
   (d) that the cost of re-settlement of " landless " Arabs and of certain urgent public works shall be met out of a guaranteed loan (paragraph 12);
   (e) that the High Commissioner shall be authorised to meet Jewish demands for some equivalent treatment by granting a contribution from Palestine Government funds to Jewish research, and by including in the guaranteed loan provision for a contribution of £10,000 or £20,000 to a Jewish agricultural or educational institution and for the cost, estimated at £60,000, of a Technical School (paragraph 14);
   (f) that the Protection of Cultivators Ordinance shall be amended on the lines set out above (paragraph 21);
   (g) that no restriction shall be placed on owner-occupiers in disposing of their land (paragraphs 16 and 22).

26. If this line of action meets with approval, I will discuss with Sir Arthur Wauchope the steps to be taken to give publicity, here and in Palestine, to the decisions of His Majesty's Government.

27. Appended to this memorandum are:—
   Appendix I.—A statement of the commitments of His Majesty's Government.
   Appendix II.—A summary of the proposals contained in Mr. French's reports.

P. C.-L.

Colonial Office, Downing Street,
February 1, 1933.

7

APPENDIX I.

Commitments of His Majesty's Government.

1. "LEGISLATION is to be introduced with the object of controlling the disposition of agricultural lands in such a manner as to prevent the dispossession of the indigenous agricultural population. These temporary measures will be superseded in any case by such permanent enactments as may be decided upon when future policy is determined in the light of Sir John Hope Simpson's Report." (Paragraph 5 of Statement with regard to British Policy in Palestine, May 1930, Cmd. 3582.)

2. ".... It is, however, an error to imagine that the Palestine Government is in possession of large areas of vacant land which could be made available for Jewish settlement. The extent of unoccupied areas of Government land is negligible. The Government claims considerable areas which are, in fact, occupied and cultivated by Arabs. Even were the title of the Government to these areas admitted, and it is in many cases disputed, it would not be possible to make these areas available for Jewish settlement, in view of their actual occupation by Arab cultivators and of the importance of making available additional land on which to place the Arab cultivators who are now landless." (Paragraph 15 of Statement of Policy by His Majesty's Government, October 1930, Cmd. 3692).

3. "We may proceed to the contention that the Mandate has been reinterpreted in a manner highly prejudicial to Jewish interests in the vital matters of land settlement and immigration. It has been said that the policy of the White Paper would place an embargo upon immigration, and would suspend, if not, indeed, terminate, the close settlement of the Jews on the land, which is a primary purpose of the Mandate. In support of this contention particular stress has been laid upon the passage referring to State lands in the White Paper, which says that 'it would not be possible to make these areas available for Jewish settlement in view of their actual occupation by Arab cultivators, and of the importance of making available additional land on which to place the Arab cultivators who are now landless.'

"The language of this passage needs to be read in the light of the policy as a whole. It is desirable to make it clear that the landless Arabs, to whom it was intended to refer in the passage quoted, were such Arabs as can be shown to have been displaced from the lands which they occupied in consequence of the lands passing into Jewish hands, and who have not obtained other holdings on which they can establish themselves or other equally satisfactory occupation. The number of such displaced Arabs must be a matter for careful enquiry. It is to landless Arabs within this category that His Majesty's Government feel themselves under an obligation to facilitate their settlement upon the land. The recognition of this obligation in no way detracts from the larger purposes of development, which His Majesty's Government regards as the most effectual means of furthering the establishment of a National Home for the Jews." (Paragraphs 8 and 9 of letter from the Prime Minister to Dr. Weizmann, February 13, 1931.)

4 "It is the intention of His Majesty's Government to institute an enquiry as soon as possible to ascertain, *inter alia*, what State and other lands are, or properly can be made, available for close settlement by Jews under reference to the obligation imposed upon the Mandatory by Article 6 of the Mandate. This enquiry will be comprehensive in its scope, and will include the whole land resources of Palestine. In the conduct of the enquiry, provision will be made for all interests, whether Jewish or Arab, making such representations as it may be desired to put forward." (Paragraph 10 of Prime Minister's letter.)

5. "In giving effect to the policy of land settlement as contemplated in article 11 of the Mandate, it is necessary if disorganisation is to be avoided, and if the policy is to have a chance to succeed, that there should exist some centralised control of transactions relating to the acquisition and transfer of land during

such interim period as may reasonably be necessary to place the development scheme upon a sure foundation. The power contemplated is regulative and not prohibitory, although it does involve a power to prevent transactions which are inconsistent with the tenor of the scheme. But the exercise of the power will be limited and in no respect arbitrary. In every case it will be conditioned by considerations as to how best to give effect to the purposes of the Mandate. Any control contemplated will be fenced with due safeguards to secure as little interference as possible with the free transfer of land. The centralised control will take effect as from such a date only as the authority charged with the duty of carrying out the policy of land development shall begin to operate. The High Commissioner will, pending the establishment of such centralised control, have full powers to take all steps necessary to protect the tenancy and occupancy rights, including the rights of squatters, throughout Palestine."

"Further, the statement of policy of His Majesty's Government did not imply a prohibition of acquisition of additional land by Jews. It contains no such prohibition, nor is any such intended. What it does contemplate is such temporary control of land disposition and transfers as may be necessary not to impair the harmony and effectiveness of the scheme of land settlement to be undertaken. His Majesty's Government feel bound to point out that they alone of the Governments which have been responsible for the administration of Palestine since the acceptance of the Mandate have declared their definite intention to initiate an active policy of development which it is believed will result in substantial and lasting benefit to both Jews and Arabs." (Paragraphs 12 and 13 of Prime Minister's letter.)

6. " . . . . the proper application of the absorptive capacity principle. That principle is vital to any scheme of development, the primary purpose of which must be the settlement both of Jews and of displaced Arabs upon the land." (Paragraph 15 of Prime Minister's letter.)

7. Lord Passfield's despatch to the High Commissioner for Palestine, dated the 26th June, 1931, regarding the development scheme, lays upon the Director of Development the duty, *inter alia*, to prepare a register of displaced Arabs as defined in the Prime Minister's letter and to draw up a scheme of re-settlement for registered displaced Arabs. The despatch goes on to say that when the scheme has been approved by the High Commissioner, re-settlement will be carried out as quickly as possible. (See paragraph 5, iii (*b*), of the despatch.)

This despatch was published at the time and has been reproduced in the Annual Report on Palestine for 1931.

8. "The scheme is intended in the first place to provide for those 'landless' Arabs who can be shown to have been dispossessed as a result of land passing into Jewish hands, and any balance will be available for both Jewish and Arab settlement." (Dr. Shiels' speech in House of Commons on the 17th November, 1930.)

9. "While it is not possible for him at this stage to say anything definite about the provision of funds for development purposes, he could tell them that the object which His Majesty's Government had in view was to take early action, if financial circumstances permit, to put into operation a scheme of development, limited in its scope, providing first for the re-settlement of Arabs . . . . and second for some assistance to Jewish settlement in Palestine." (Report of Sir Arthur Wauchope's speech to Arab Executive and Jewish Agency on the 27th January, 1932.)

10. "His Excellency said that the direct deduction from the instructions he had received was that if a loan was sanctioned then a portion, though what portion he did not know, of the funds would be devoted for the benefit of Jewish settlement."

"His Excellency said he imagined that the first duty of the Development Commission would be to re-settle a number of displaced Arabs; but that did not mean that a portion of the funds should not be spent simultaneously on objects that would be for the benefit of Jewish interests." (Report of Sir Arthur Wauchope's statement to Chairman of Jewish Agency Executive on the 27th January, 1932.)

11. "His Majesty's Government have come to the conclusion that to achieve the object in view it is necessary to provide for an expenditure not exceeding £2,500,000, a large part of which would be devoted to works of a productive character .... namely, irrigation, drainage and other schemes. .... In view of the present financial situation in Palestine, the only way in which a sum of this magnitude can be provided is by means of a loan under the guarantee of His Majesty's Government. During the first years of the development scheme it will be necessary to provide from British Votes such annual amounts as may be required to meet the interest and sinking fund charges upon the loan." (Dr. Shiels in the House of Commons on the 17th November, 1930.)

APPENDIX II.

PALESTINE DEVELOPMENT.

Summary of Mr. French's Proposals.

1. *Landless Arabs.*

Claims received	3,700
Claims examined by 1st April	1,367
*Claims finally accepted...	72
*Claims provisionally accepted	80
Claims rejected	648

As regards the total number of claims which will be eventually accepted, Mr. French cannot give a closer estimate than between 1,000 and 2,000. (*N.B.*—The latest estimate is 800 to 900 families.)

2. *Proposals for settlement of Arabs.*

(a) Not more than 100 or 200 families can be settled within the next eighteen months on such limited areas of " dry " lands (for cereal farming) as are likely to be available. Estimated cost £500 per family.

(b) Any further settlement must be on irrigated lands for intensive farming (*i.e.*, citrus), and might cost as much as £800 per family. This must be a very gradual process, depending not only on the results of enquiries into the question of available land, but on examination of the important question of market prospects for Palestine citrus fruits.

3. *Facilities of Jewish Colonisation.*

The only possible areas are—
  (a) The coastal plain;
  (b) Beisan;
  (c) Huleh; and
  (d) A portion of the Jordan Valley.

The Beersheba district would also have possibilities, if boring investigations now in progress result in the discovery of adequate artesian supplies of water.

(a) The coastal plain is being actively developed for citrus fruit growing, and present progress is as rapid as circumstances warrant, having regard to market possibilities. "The dangers to Palestine of a collapse in the citrus industry must be foreseen. .... If the bottom falls out of the citrus growing industry, there is no evidence that it can be replaced by any other reasonably profitable product."

(b), (c), (d) If these areas should be found technically capable of irrigation, and if then capable of producing economic crops, they would allow of resettlement of landless Arabs and colonization by immigrant Jews by gradual development over a series of years; but the crucial question of *markets* would have to be considered. "There would be no justification for incurring considerable expense in opening up new areas so long as it remains in doubt

* These claims all emanate from Wadi Hawareth Arabs.

10

whether foreign markets will be able to absorb all the fruit that is being and is capable of being produced in the coastal plain, where water is readily obtainable."

4. *Hydrographic Survey.*

A hydrographic survey of the whole country was recommended in the First Report, and, as part of this survey, it is proposed that preliminary surveys of the Baisan, Huleh and Jordan Valley areas should be undertaken as a first step. Cost of hydrographic survey, £8,000.

5. *Immediate aid to Jewish organisations in work of colonization.*

The Jewish Agency considers that assistance for consolidation of colonies already founded would not be an appropriate method of applying development funds. Mr. French agrees that the intrusion of Government into the internal economy of colonies existing or in progress of establishment would be undesirable from every aspect.

As an alternative the Jewish Agency have submitted proposals for a Jewish Agricultural and Settlement Bank. Mr. French analyses this proposal and shows that such a bank would have to charge a higher rate of interest than the settlers could pay, and that the result would be an annual loss to the Government. An annual charge of £60,000 for 40 years would be imposed upon the Palestine taxpayers. "Palestine is predominantly agricultural, and to impose extra taxation on agriculturists generally, in order to provide uneconomic credit facilities for a limited number, would be manifestly unfair."

(Mr. French considers that the only purpose for which the Government would be justified in providing long-term credits for Jewish agriculture, would be the improvement of holdings for the purpose of securing a larger net return from land. He does not think that there is any need at present for the provision of such facilities.)

6. *Government contribution towards cost of Jewish Agricultural Research Station.*

Mr. French proposes that the Government should contribute a sum of £32,365 towards the upkeep of this station, spreading over a period of five years. This would enable the Jewish Agency to expand the Station, especially on the demonstration side. The services of this institution would, of course, be available for both Jews and Arabs.

7. *Land Legislation.*

With a view to preventing additions to the claims of "landless" Arabs in future, Mr. French most strongly recommends the enactment of legislation to control dispositions of land, and he appends to his Report rough drafts of two ordinances, viz., the "Homesteads Protection Ordinance" and the "Occupancy Tenants Ordinance." He remarks "Resettlement will be a very costly operation and the burden which it will impose upon the taxpayers of Palestine can, I submit, be justified only by a simultaneous attempt to prevent a recreation of the problem."

8. *Water supplies.*

Mr. French renews the recommendation made in the First Report that the Government should re-assert its right to the ownership of all water, and the use of all water running to waste.

Minor Recommendations.

1. *Survey Staff.*

Should the work of settlement catch up the work of survey, it may be necessary to provide additional survey staff at a cost of £12,000 spread over eight years.

2. *Partition of mesha'a lands.*

Mr. French suggests the appointment of a small special staff to supervise and accelerate this work. Cost, £7,500, spread over 3 years.

3. *Village Registrars.*

The First Report contains a recommendation for the appointment of a staff of village registrars who will keep records of land ownership and tenancy rights, and transference of such rights. Cost, £20,000 per annum when staff is complete.

4. *Livestock Industry.*

It is recommended that the Government should carry out certain experiments in animal feeding and breeding in the interests of the livestock industry. Cost uncertain.

5. *Arab Co-operative Societies.*

Immediate steps should be taken to promote the formation of co-operative societies among Arab orange-growers.

(N.B.)—A Registrar of Co-operative Societies has now been appointed.)

6. *Expenses of land registration, partition, &c.*

A small Committee should be appointed to examine the scales of fees in connection with land transactions, which are at present so heavy as to discourage partition and registration.

PALESTINE.

HIGH COMMISSIONER FOR PALESTINE,
JERUSALEM.

CONFIDENTIAL. 11th May, 1933.
Reference No. CF/92/33.

Sir,

I have the honour to refer to Sir Arthur Wauchope's despatch No.342 of the 15th April, 1933, in which the High Commissioner made his recommendations on the Reports submitted by Mr. Lewis French, C.I.E., C.B.E., concerned with the problems of agricultural development and land settlement in Palestine.

2. It was explained in that despatch how the special policy of His Majesty's Government in Palestine has led to a situation in which there exists a class of persons conveniently described as "landless Arabs" who have lost their traditional agricultural occupations from which they derived a livelihood as a consequence of displacement from the soil following purchases of land by Jewish persons and institutions in furtherance of the establishment of a Jewish National Home in Palestine.

It was further explained that "landless Arabs" fell into three classes, namely,

(i) owners of comparatively small holdings;

(ii) tenants, as such a term can broadly be used as descriptive of a variety of forms of land tenure;

(iii) agricultural labourers.

Sir Arthur Wauchope propounded solutions of the problems created which are best classified by reference to the past and to the future. So far as remedies for the

past/

The Right Honourable
Sir Philip Cunliffe-Lister, G.B.E., M.P., etc., etc.,
His Majesty's Principal Secretary of State
for the Colonies.

-8-

past are required, administrative measures are in process for resettlement of "landless Arabs" on the land; while, so far as measures preventive of the social and economic evils apprehended from a continuation of the system of displacement of agricultural Arabs are indicated, the High Commissioner made proposals for legislation the substance of which is given in paragraph 19 of his despatch under reference.

3. It should be iterated that displaced Arab cultivators have been owners of small holdings, tenants (as that term may be broadly used) and agricultural labourers. The proposed remedies for the situation arising from the past and the preventive measures at present designed for the future are limited to the class of displaced Arabs described as tenants, and do not extend to persons who may be described as small landowners, about whom, I understand, Sir Arthur Wauchope proposes to address you in due course after further inquiry into the problem.

The proposals to be made in this despatch are limited to the protection of tenants whose livelihood may be threatened by the acts of landlords.

It is not proposed to extend the contemplated protective legislation to agricultural labourers, in so far as these are differentiated from tenants. As will be seen from the following quotation from the Report of the Census taken in 1931, the population of agricultural labourers is comparatively small in relation to the whole body of cultivators (owners and tenants together):

"The/

-3-

> "The farmers, that is, the persons who cultivate their own lands or the lands of a landlord, number 63,190 earners of whom 3,669 are Jews, and 2,376 are Christians. The agricultural labourers number 29,077 earners, of whom 2,582 are Jews and 512 are Christians. There are thus two farmers for every one agricultural labourer among the Moslems, four farmers for every ten agricultural labourers among the Jews, and 45 farmers for every ten agricultural labourers among the Christians. In England and Wales, 1921, there were 17 agricultural labourers for every one farmer. In Bengal, 1921, there were five farmers for every one hired agricultural labourer. In India as a whole there were, in 1911, four farmers for every one agricultural labourer."

4. During Sir John Chancellor's term of office as High Commissioner the Protection of Cultivators Ordinance 1929 was enacted. This was followed in May 1931 by the Protection of Cultivators (Amendment) Ordinance 1931 some of the provisions of which were limited to a period of application of twelve months. In May 1932 the operation of the temporary provisions of this Ordinance was extended by a further period of twelve months. The time has now come when it is necessary to replace the existing Ordinances by more permanent legislation following the inquiries held into the various problems raised.

5. These introductory remarks serve to explain the conditions under which Sir Arthur Wauchope recommended that the contemplated legislation should be framed in order to express the following principles of policy.

> (i) A tenant who has paid his rent and not neglected his holding grossly may not be evicted unless the High Commissioner is satisfied that an equivalent provision has been made for him in land up to the minimum required for subsistence of himself and his family, and unless he is given at least one year's notice, compensation for disturbance and for improvements and, if of more than five years' standing, the equivalent of one year's average rent.
>
> (ii) A tenant's rent will not be raised except with the consent of a Board constituted as at present.

(iii)/

-4-

(iii) A tenant who has not paid his rent may not be evicted without at least one year's notice and compensation for improvements. Where a tenant has applied to the Board in accordance with Section 3(3) of the existing Protection of Cultivators Ordinance, he shall not be evicted unless the Board gives a decision against him and he fails to pay his rent within the time fixed by the Board, and even then only on an Order of the Court.

(iv) Any question as to what is sufficient subsistence area for any particular tenant will be settled by a Board constituted as at present, and liable to review, say, every five years.

(v) A Board will decide, as at present, all questions regarding the amount of compensation due.

(vi) A tenant will be allowed to sell or mortgage his tenancy interest in the "subsistence area".

(vii) The following provision

Notwithstanding anything contained in this Ordinance, the District Commissioner may on the application of the landlord, authorize the resumption by him of a holding or part thereof upon being satisfied:

(a) that such resumption is required for some reasonable and sufficient purpose having relation to the good of the holding or of the adjoining land, including development by drainage or irrigation or by closer settlement or colonization or disposal for building purposes; and

(b) that the "occupancy tenant" will retain sufficient land of such nature as to enable him to maintain his customary means of livelihood in occupations with which he is completely familiar; the land being, as far as possible, in the vicinity of the home from which the transfer may cause his displacement; or

(c) that the purpose for which the resumption of the holding is sought comprises the provision for the "occupancy tenant" of developed land sufficient for the maintenance of himself and his family, together with adequate subsistence for them pending the development of such land.

Enclosure I.   I transmit the draft of an Ordinance to give effect to these recommendations, together with the Law Officers' Enclosure II. Memorandum and Comparative Table setting out the variations Enclosure III. between the draft Bill and existing legislation.

6./

-5-

6. Regarded from the standpoint of general policy the two principal devices employed in the Bill are, first, the definition of statutory tenant (clause 2) and, secondly, the obligation to provide a subsistence area in the vicinity of the holding from which a statutory tenant is to be ejected.

7. It will be seen that the definition of "tenant" differs from that in the existing legislation in an important respect, namely, that it will not depend on the existence of an agreement express or implied but it will depend on the occupation and cultivation of a holding as matters of fact. A further modification is introduced in clause 3(1) of the Bill, in that the statutory tenant must have occupied and cultivated the holding for a period of not less than one year, before what may be called the security provisions of the Ordinance apply. The existing legislation provides for a tenancy of two years before a tenant obtains protection. It may be noticed that there have been instances in which landlords have evaded the intention of the present Ordinances by making agreements for periods of less than two years. Under the proposed provision a landlord might, in contemplation of the sale of his land, make an agreement for tenancy for a period of less than one year; and, ideally, the tenant could only be secured if there were no minimum limitation of time to the occupancy and cultivation of a holding as a condition precedent to the protection afforded by the Ordinance. On the other hand, a tenant could not derive a minimum livelihood on an occupancy for a period of less than one year and a landlord might be hard put to find cultivating tenants on a basis contrary to agricultural custom, while the tenants who would be prepared to conclude

such/

-6-

such agreements would in general not be of the cultivating class and would not, therefore, be entitled to claim the consideration due to tenants of the cultivating class. I should, perhaps, add that objection will probably be taken to the shortening of the minimum period from two years to one year but, in view of the evasions by landlords of the existing legislation by the conclusion of one-year agreements, I consider that it is right to recommend the more stringent protection of tenants afforded by the reduction of the minimum period of occupancy from two years to one year.

8. The device of creating a subsistence area upon which a displaced tenant can be settled is a necessary consequence of the principles upon which the proposed measure is framed. Events of the past years have shown that monetary compensation for eviction has, so far from solving the problem, actually contributed to its complexity. The attraction of ready money among an improvident people has facilitated the very process by which the problem of the "landless Arab" has been created. The money so acquired is rarely, if ever, invested again in land from which the tenant has hitherto derived his livelihood and general thriftlessness makes the gap between the landless cultivator and the vagrant or criminal small, so that to allow the existing process to continue may lead to a social disorder of the graver sort. It follows that every effort must be made to provide the tenant cultivator with a sufficiency of land from which to continue to derive a livelihood in occupations with which he is familiar. The condition that the subsistence area should be, as far as possible, in the vicinity of the land from which the tenant has been displaced follows from the fact that in Palestine

conditions/

conditions under which agricultural occupations are followed vary considerably in the desert regions in the south, the central hill ranges, the coastal plains, and the valleys running easterly from Haifa. A cultivator familiar with husbandry in one such area may not normally derive a satisfactory livelihood from a subsistence area in another. Moreover there is a social discomfort to be apprehended from a physical displacement from old associations to novel surroundings which cannot facilitate the peaceful transfer of lands, particularly when such transfer is one of the foci of political agitation in the country.

It must be admitted that the obligation to provide subsistence areas for displaced tenants in the vicinity of the holdings from which such tenants are evicted will, of itself, provide a check to some extent on the transfer of land from Arab to Jewish ownership; nevertheless I am satisfied that it is essential.

9. A third point of importance arises from clause 17 of the draft Bill. It will be appreciated that the value of the Bill is derived from the definition of tenant as a person determined by the fact of occupancy and cultivation.

Under existing legislation some trouble has been experienced as in certain instances before the provisions could be applied it was necessary to determine whether the persons concerned were or were not tenants within the meaning of the Ordinance. These questions necessitated reference to the Courts; and, for a variety of reasons which it is not necessary to detail in this despatch, decisions have been unduly delayed, attended in one case by disturbance of the peace.

It is manifestly desirable to expedite decisions in matters which may affect public order, and in clause 17

-8-

it is provided that questions which may arise shall be decided by a special tribunal to be appointed by the High Commissioner, from which an appeal to the High Commissioner in Council may lie.

I should be loth in normal circumstances to propose to oust the jurisdiction of the Courts but I am satisfied that the necessity of a speedy and simplified method of trial of the matters likely to be in dispute justify my doing so.

I hope, therefore, that you will find it possible to approve the retention of clause 17 even though in ordinary circumstances the need for the provision might well be questioned.

10. In the preparation of the Bill it became necessary to consider the following points in connection with subsistence areas, which require comment:-

(i) Should a statutory tenant placed on a subsistence area pay rent?

(ii) If he should pay rent, should he be evicted from the area if he fails to do so?

(iii) Should the occupier of a subsistence area be allowed to sell or mortgage his interest therein?

With regard to the first question it would seem reasonable that the occupier of a subsistence area should pay rent therefor.

As to the second it is not possible to extend the full provisions of the Bill to the occupant of a subsistence area as during his first year he would obtain no protection thereunder. It is proposed therefore that he should not be evicted without the consent of the High Commissioner.

With/

With regard to the third question, as the primary object of the Bill is to ensure, as far as possible, that cultivators remain upon the land it would seem undesirable to provide in terms a means by which they could at once be displaced.

11. An additional sub-section (16 (3)) has been added to the existing law dealing with grazing rights etc., but this is a problem of great difficulty and it should be realized that if the Beduin are actually prevented from entering settled areas they may be faced with starvation.

12. The temporary provisions of the present legislation expire on the 28th of May, 1933, and I realize that it will not be possible for you to consider the draft now submitted and give instructions thereon in time for its enactment by that date. At the same time it is important, as I am sure you will recognize, that the new legislation should come into force as soon as possible.

I propose therefore to extend the existing temporary legislation until the end of June next to be repealed together with the other existing legislation by the Bill now submitted as soon as that is ready for enactment. I should add that the High Commissioner is of opinion that this Bill, when it has received your sanction, should be passed for immediate enactment.

13. In submitting this Bill for consideration I should inform you that the High Commissioner was aware of its general terms before he departed to England and gave his approval in principle to the recommendations herein.

I have the honour to be, Sir,
Your most obedient, humble servant,

H. H. Trusted
OFFICER ADMINISTERING
THE GOVERNMENT.

> ENCLOSURE No. I   TO PALESTINE DESPATCH
> No. Confidential   Date 11th May, 1933.

PROTECTION OF CULTIVATORS ORDINANCE 1933.

An Ordinance to provide for the protection of certain cultivators.

BE IT ENACTED by the High Commissioner for Palestine, with the advice of the Advisory Council thereof:-

Short title.
1. This Ordinance may be cited as the Protection of Cultivators Ordinance, 1933.

Interpretation.
2. In this Ordinance, unless the context otherwise requires, the following expressions have the meanings hereby assigned to them, that is to say:-

"Board" means a Board constituted under this Ordinance.

"District Commissioner" means the Commissioner of the District in which a holding or subsistence area is situated. The definition of District Commissioner in the Interpretation Ordinance, 1929, as enacted in the Interpretation (Amendment) Ordinance, 1933, shall not apply to the interpretation of this Ordinance.

"Holding" means a plot of miri land cultivated by a tenant, and where the land of a village is held in undivided ownership or tenure, includes any portion of land so cultivated within the area of the village:

Provided that where a tenant has been moved by the landlord from one or more plots of land to other plots, such plots shall be deemed to be a holding.

"Landlord" means the person to whom the tenant pays or is liable to pay rent and includes the predecessors in title of such person.

"Miri land" includes miri Waqf land.

"Rent" means any payment in money or kind, and includes any share of the produce of a holding.

"Statutory tenant" means any person, family or tribe occupying and cultivating a holding otherwise than as the owner thereof. It includes the son, father brother, wife or other relative of any person occupying and cultivating a holding who may have with the knowledge of the landlord occupied such holding, and where the person occupying a holding has acquired it by succession from his father or other ascendant or descendant it includes such ascendant or descendant. It includes a person who is hired by the landlord to do agricultural work and receives as remuneration a portion of the produce of the holding which he cultivates. It does not include a person who is hired to do agricultural work and who receives as remuneration a money wage or portion of the produce, but does not cultivate a holding.

Termination of tenancy by notice, etc.

3. (1) Notwithstanding any provision of any contract to the contrary where any statutory tenant has occupied and cultivated a holding for a period of not less than one year, the landlord thereof shall not be entitled to terminate the tenancy unless he shall have given to the tenant in writing notice to quit not less than one year from the first day of October following the date of the notice:

Provided that nothing herein shall extend to the case where any agreement between the landlord and the statutory tenant provides for any longer notice than the notice provided for herein.

(2) In case of dispute a Board shall determine after consultation with the local Inspector of Agriculture,

    (a) what having regard to all the circumstances is a reasonable period for the payment of rent due, and

    (b) whether the statutory tenant has neglected his holding grossly.

(3) If the landlord gives notice in writing to a statutory tenant who has occupied and cultivated a holding for a period of not less than one year to terminate the tenancy because such tenant has neglected his holding grossly, the tenant shall be liable to eviction, unless within fifteen days of the receipt of such notice he applies in writing for reference of the question whether he has so neglected his holding to a Board. If such application is made the Board shall give its decision within fifteen days of the receipt of the application.

(4) Every notice to quit given under this section shall be void and of no effect unless a copy thereof is served by the landlord on the District Commissioner of the district in which the land is situated within thirty days after the notice has been served on the statutory tenant, and unless the notice contains a declaration by the landlord that its object is to terminate the tenancy in order that the land may be transferred with vacant possession, if such be the object of the notice.

Order for eviction only to be granted in certain cases.

4. (1) No court or judge or execution officer shall give any judgment or make any order for the eviction of a statutory tenant who has occupied and cultivated

- 4 -

a holding for a period of not less than one year save in accordance with the following provisions:-

(a) Where the tenant

(i) has paid within a reasonable time in accordance with the decision of a Board all rent due in respect of the holding, and

(ii) has not in the opinion of a Board neglected his holding grossly,

no such judgment shall be given or order made,

1. Unless a notice to quit has been given by the landlord in accordance with the provisions of section 3 of this Ordinance, and

2. Unless it is made to appear to the Court that the tenant has been provided with a subsistence area approved by the High Commissioner, and

3. Unless the question whether the statutory tenant is entitled to compensation for disturbance and for improvements made by such tenant to the holding has been referred to a Board, and if such questions have been so referred and any amount of compensation in respect thereof assessed by the Board, ~~unless such amount~~ shall have been deposited with a Notary Public, and

4. If the statutory tenant has cultivated the holding under the landlord for a period of not less than five years consecutively preceding the date when the notice to quit expired, unless the equivalent of one year's average rent of the

holding has been assessed by a Board and deposited with a Notary Public

(b) Where the tenant has not paid all rent due in respect of the holding within a reasonable time in accordance with the decision of a Board no such judgment shall be given or order made,

    1. Unless the question whether the statutory tenant is entitled to compensation for improvements made by such tenant to the holding has been referred to a Board and if such question has been so referred and any amount of compensation in respect thereof assessed by the Board, ~~unless such amount~~ shall have been deposited with a Notary Public, and

    2. Unless a notice to quit has been given by the landlord in accordance with the provision of section 3 of this Ordinance:

Provided that nothing herein shall be deemed to affect the provision for ejectment when no application is made to a Board in section 3 subsection (3) of this Ordinance contained.

(2) Any sum deposited in respect of disturbance or improvements with a Notary Public in accordance with the provisions of subsection (1) hereof shall, if a judgment is given or order made for eviction, be paid to the statutory tenant against whom such judgment or order is given or made, or if no such judgment or order is given or made any such sum shall be returned to the person who made the deposit.

(3) If a judgment is given or order made for

eviction rent shall be payable in respect of the period between the date when the notice to quit expired and the date of eviction at the rate payable prior to the termination of the tenancy as though the tenancy had continued until the date of eviction.

Provisions of the Ottoman Provisional Law for mortgages not to apply in certain cases.

5. The rights under this Ordinance of

   (a) any statutory tenant who has occupied and cultivated a holding for not less than one year, or

   (b) any person lawfully occupying any subsistence area,

shall not be affected by any sale of such holding or area or of any immovable property of which such area or holding forms part effected under the Ottoman Provisional Law for the Mortgage of Immovable Property dated the 25th February 1328.

Constitution of Board, etc.

6.(1) A Board shall consist of a District Officer as President nominated by the District Commissioner and two members nominated with the approval of the District Commissioner, one by the landlord and the other by the tenant.

(2) The decisions of the Board in any matter referred to them under this Ordinance shall be subject to the confirmation of the District Commissioner, and when confirmed by him shall be final.

(3) If within one month of the nomination of the President of a Board either the landlord or the tenant shall fail to submit the name of the member of the Board who will represent him to the District Commissioner for his approval, the District Commissioner shall nominate some person to represent

the party so failing, and such person so nominated shall be deemed to have been nominated by such party.

Subsistence area. 7. (1) A subsistence area shall be determined by a Board. Such area shall as nearly as circumstances permit be in the vicinity of the holding from which the statutory tenant is being ejected, and shall be such land as will enable the statutory tenant to maintain his customary means of livelihood in an occupation with which he is familiar.

(2) The Board shall determine the rent payable by the statutory tenant in respect of a subsistence area.

(3) The landlord or tenant may apply to a Board not less than five years from the last decision of a Board in respect thereof to vary a subsistence area or the rent thereof.

(4) No person lawfully occupying a subsistence area shall be ejected therefrom save upon the recommendation of a Board with the approval of the High Commissioner.

Compensation for disturbance. 8. (1) Where <u>any statutory</u> tenant who has been in occupation of a holding for not less than one year,

    (a) vacates his holding in consequence of a valid notice to quit, or

    (b) is ejected from his holding by reason of any judgment given or order made under the provision of section 4(1)(a) of this Ordinance,

the landlord shall pay to such statutory tenant compensation for disturbance to be assessed by a Board in accordance with the provisions of this section.

- 8 -

(2) The compensation shall be a sum representing such loss or expense directly attributable to the quitting of the land as the tenant may unavoidably incur in connection with the sale or removal of his movable property:

Provided that compensation shall not be payable in respect of the sale of any such movable property unless the statutory tenant has before the sale given the landlord a reasonable opportunity of making the valuation thereof, and

Provided also that no compensation shall be payable under this section

    (a) where the landlord has made the tenant an offer in writing to withdraw the notice to quit and the tenant has unreasonably refused or failed to accept the offer, or

    (b) if the claim for compensation is not made within three months from the date at which the statutory tenant quits the land.

Compensation for improvements.
9. (1) Where a statutory tenant of a holding has made thereon any improvements comprised in the first schedule to this Ordinance, he shall, subject to the provisions of this Ordinance, be entitled on the termination of the tenancy whether by notice to quit or otherwise to obtain from the landlord as compensation for the improvements such sum as represents the value of the improvements to an incoming tenant:

Provided that in ascertaining the amount of compensation payable there shall be taken into account any benefit which the landlord has given or allowed to the tenant executing the improvements whether expressly stated in any contract of tenancy or not.

(2) Compensation under this section shall not be payable in respect of any improvement comprised in part I of the first schedule to this Ordinance unless the landlord has previously to the execution of the improvement consented in writing to the making thereof, and any such consent may be given by the landlord unconditionally, or upon such terms, as to compensation or otherwise, as may be agreed upon between the landlord and the statutory tenant, and, if any such agreement is made, any compensation payable under the agreement shall be substituted for compensation under this section.

(3) Compensation shall not be payable in respect of any improvement comprised in part II of the first schedule to this Ordinance unless the statutory tenant has given to the landlord not less than two months' notice in writing of his intention to execute the improvement, and of the manner in which he proposes to do the work:

Provided that –

(a) if the improvement consists of application to the land of farmyard manure, it shall be sufficient for the statutory tenant to give notice to the landlord once in each year; and

(b) if the improvement consists of repairs to buildings which are necessary for the habitation of the statutory tenant or the proper cultivation or working of the holding, the statutory tenant shall not execute the repairs unless the landlord fails to execute them within a reasonable time after such notic

- 10 -

Where notice is given under this subsection the landlord and statutory tenant may agree on the terms of compensation or otherwise on which the improvement is to be executed; and if such agreement is made, compensation payable under the agreement shall be substituted for compensation under this section.

(4) The amount of compensation payable for improvement made by the statutory tenant under the provisions hereof shall be assessed by a Board:

Provided that no claim for compensation shall be heard by a Board unless particulars of the claim have been given by the landlord to the statutory tenant or by the statutory tenant to the landlord within three months of the termination of the tenancy by a notice to quit, or within three months from the date at which the statutory tenant quits the holding where there has been no notice to quit.

Arrears of rent may be set off against compensation.	10. Where a tenancy of a holding is terminated and any rent is due from the statutory tenant to the landlord in respect thereof such rent may be deducted from any compensation payable by the landlord to the statutory tenant in respect of the disturbance or improvements.
Rent not to be increased without sanction of a Board.	11. The landlord shall not increase the rent of a holding unless he shall have first obtained the sanction of a Board which shall have power after hearing the landlord and the statutory tenant and after taking such evidence and making such enquiries as they think fit to decide by what amount, if any, the rent shall be increased. The increased rent shall not come

- 11 -

into force before one year from the first day of October following the decision of the Board.

Provision where statutory tenant is a sub-tenant.

12. (1) Where a superior landlord recovers against the landlord of a statutory tenant (in this section hereinafter referred to as the immediate landlord), a judgment for possession or order of ejectment for non-payment of rent or otherwise in respect of any land comprised in a holding the estate of the immediate landlord shall be deemed to be determined as if the judgment for possession or order of ejectment had been executed.

(2) No such judgment or order shall be executed against a statutory tenant, and his tenancy of the holding shall not be affected except that the superior landlord shall become the landlord of the statutory tenant and may proceed for the recovery of all rent due from the statutory tenant to the immediate landlord as if it had always been due to the superior landlord, and shall from the date of such judgment or order be entitled to recover the rent of the holding from the statutory tenant.

(3) If the superior landlord recovers from the statutory tenant any rent in respect of any period prior to his becoming the landlord of the statutory tenant he shall be liable to account to the immediate landlord therefor.

Special powers to District Commissioners.

13. Notwithstanding anything contained in this Ordinance the District Commissioner may on the application of the landlord authorise the resumption by him of a holding or part thereof on being satisfied

(a) that such resumption is required for

- 12 -

  some reasonable and sufficient purpose having relation to the good of the holding or of the adjoining land, including development by drainage or irrigation or by closer settlement or colonization or disposal for building purposes, and

(b) that the statutory tenant will retain sufficient land of such nature as to enable him to maintain his customary means of livelihood in occupations with which he is familiar, such land being as far as possible in the vicinity of the home from which the transfer may cause his displacement, or

(c) that the purpose for which the resumption of the holding is sought comprises the provision for the statutory tenant of developing land sufficient for the maintenance of himself and his family, together with adequate subsistence for them, pending the development of such land.

Land not to be transferred until the provisions of this Ordinance satisfied.

14. (1) Where application is made to register a transfer of any miri land on which there is a statutory tenant who has received notice of termination of tenancy in accordance with this Ordinance, the Director of the Department of Lands shall not record the transfer in the Land Registers unless he is satisfied that security has been given by the landlord for carrying out any obligations to the statutory tenant under this Ordinance, or unless the purchaser agrees that he will take over the obligations of the former landlord, and that any compensation that has been or shall be found due to the statutory tenant shall be charged on the land.

(2) Any compensation agreed to be due or found by a Board to be due to a statutory tenant under this Ordinance shall be charged on the land until the whole of such compensation has been paid.

(3) The provisions of this section shall not apply to any holding when the Director of the Department of Lands is satisfied that compensation for disturbance or improvements in respect of such holding has been assessed by a Board and deposited with a Notary Public.

Outgoing tenant to prepare or allow landlord to prepare land.

15. If the landlord desires that a tenant who has received notice to quit in accordance with section 3 hereof shall prepare the land for cultivation in the following year, he shall give notice to the tenant in writing to that effect, and if the tenant complies with the notice shall pay compensation to the tenant for the preparation of the land. If the tenant is unwilling to prepare the land he shall inform the landlord within one month of the receipt of the notice, and the landlord shall be entitled during the year of notice to prepare for cultivation in the following year any land of the tenant which is not under crop.

Provision as to certain rights.

16. (1) No court or judge shall make an order for the eviction of a person who is exercising and has exercised continuously for a period of five years a practice of grazing or watering animals or the cutting of wood or reeds or other beneficial occupation of similar character on the land whether by right, custom, usage or sufferance, unless the landlord satisfies the court or judge that the High Commissioner is satisfied that equivalent provision has been secured towards the livelihood of such person.

- 14 -

(2) Nothing in this subsection contained shall be deemed to authorise any person to enter upon any land save for the purpose of exercising the practice which he has exercised in the past.

(3) No member of any nomadic tribe who has not spent a period of at least five years in one place shall be deemed to have enjoyed any rights to which reference is made in this section continually for a period of five years.

Certain matters to be decided by a Commission.

17. (1) Any dispute

    (a) as to whether any person is a statutory tenant of a holding, or

    (b) as to the length of time that any statutory tenant has occupied and cultivated a holding, or

    (c) as to whether any person is the landlord of a holding, or

    (d) as to whether any person has exercised continuously any practice of grazing or watering animals or cutting wood or reeds or other beneficial occupation of a similar character by custom, usage or sufferance,

shall be referred to a special Commission to be appointed by the High Commissioner.

(2) Any person aggrieved by the decision of any such Commission may appeal to the High Commissioner-in-Council whose decision shall be final and no appeal shall lie therefrom to any court.

(3) Where in any proceedings before any Court it appears that any question material in such proceedings has been decided by a Commission under the provisions of this section such question shall be

deemed to be res judicata, and such Court shall be bound by the decision of the Commission, or if there has been an appeal therefrom by the decision of the High Commissioner-in-Council.

(4) For the purposes of this section the High Commissioner may appoint a Commission consisting of not less than three persons, one of whom shall be a British judicial officer who shall act as chairman of such Commission.

Regulations. 18. The High Commissioner may make, and when made, may vary or revoke regulations as to:-
    (a) the procedure of a Board,
    (b) the fees payable to the members of a Board,
    (c) the practice and procedure to be followed in any enquiry before any commission appointed under the provisions of section 17 of this Ordinance, including the taking of evidence and the right of audience of any persons before any such commission,
    (d) any other matter herein requiring regulation.

Saving. 19. Nothing in this Ordinance shall apply to any person who at the commencement thereof is occupying and cultivating any holding of which the Government of Palestine is the landlord.

Repeal. 20. The Ordinances in the second schedule to this Ordinance are hereby repealed.

FIRST SCHEDULE.

Tenant's Improvements for which Compensation is payable.

PART I.

Improvements to which consent of landlord is required.

1. Erection, alteration or enlargement of buildings.
2. Making or improvement of roads or bridges.
3. Removal of tree-roots, boulders, stones, or other like obstructions to cultivation.
4. Making or improvement of works of irrigation, water courses, ponds, wells or reservoirs, or works for the application of water-power or for supply of water for agricultural or domestic purposes.
5. Making and renewal of permanent fences and walls.
6. Planting of orchards, vineyards, wind-breaks and hedges.
7. Erection and installation of prime-movers, steam, oil and gas engines, turbines, rams, and wind-mills and water-wheels.
8. Erection and installation of power-driven mills or machinery for the grinding, crushing or treatment of agricultural products.

PART II.

Improvements in respect of which notice to landlord is required.

9. Drainage.
10. Embankments and sluices against floods.
11. Application to land of farmyard manure.

12. Application to land of purchased artificial or other purchased manure.

13. Repairs to buildings, being buildings necessary for the habitation of the tenant or the proper cultivation or working of the holding, other than repairs which the tenant is himself under obligation to execute:

    Provided that the tenant before beginning to execute any such repairs shall give to the landlord notice in writing of his intention, together with particulars of such repairs, and shall not execute the repairs unless the landlord fails to execute them within a reasonable time after receiving such notice.

SECOND SCHEDULE.

No.27 of 1929.   Protection of Cultivators Ordinance, 1929.

No.3 of 1931.   Protection of Cultivators (Amendment) Ordinance, 1931.

No.16 of 1932.   Protection of Cultivators (Amendment) Ordinance (No.1) 1929.

No.30 of 1932.   Protection of Cultivators (Amendment) Ordinance (No.2) 1932.

ENCLOSURE No. II TO PALESTINE DESPATCH
Confidential Date 11th May, 1933.

MEMORANDUM.

1. This Ordinance arises out of the proposals for the protection of cultivators which were set out in paragraph 22 of the High Commissioner's despatch No. 342 of the 15th April, 1933, which dealt with the reports submitted by Mr. French on the problems of Agricultural Development and Land Settlement in Palestine.

2. The Ordinance consolidates the Protection of Cultivators Ordinance, 1929, and the amendments thereof, i.e. the Protection of Cultivators Ordinance (No.1) 1932, and (No.2) 1932, and makes permanent, with the amendments, the provisions of that Ordinance which were temporary and extended from year to year.

3. The provisions of the Ordinance have been rearranged in the manner shown in the comparative table which accompanies this memorandum.

4. <u>Clause 2.</u>

The definitions have been arranged in alphabetical order.

A definition of District Commissioner has been inserted, but calls for no comment.

Slight verbal alterations have been made in the definitions of "holding" and "landlord", and a definition of "rent" has been added.

The definition of "Rules of good husbandry" has been omitted as the phrase now used is "has grossly neglected his holding" vide clause 3(2)(b).

The definition of "tenant" has been altered, and such person is now called a "statutory tenant",

and this expression will extend to any person
actually occupying and cultivating a holding. In
this connection it should be noted that the original
definition of tenant applied to any person who had
an agreement, but was modified by the 1931 amendment
to include only any person who had cultivated a holding for not less than two years under an agreement.

This phrase has been taken to mean that a tenant,
either himself or through his predecessor in title,
must have an agreement for two years' tenancy in order
to obtain the protection of the Ordinance, and this
gave the landlord two loopholes:-

(a) He could make an agreement for a period of
less than two years, or

(b) He could maintain that there was no agreement express or implied, and that the Ordinance therefore did not apply, and the tenant
was therefore driven to the Courts to establish
an agreement.

It is clear that any provision for an agreement
of tenancy for any period of time will always be subject to these loopholes, as if, for example, the
period of the agreement is reduced to one year, the
landlord will enter into an agreement with his tenant
for, say, six months. It seems, therefore, that if
this Ordinance is to be really effective and protect
the tenant it should primarily apply to every person
actually occupying and cultivating a holding, and the
subsequent provisions of the Ordinance should be
drafted so as to deal with individuals of different
categories who may come under the general definition
of tenant.

From the foregoing it will be realised that the

definition of "tenant" is the whole crux of the Ordinance, and has presented considerable difficulty.

The expression "statutory tenant" has been adopted as it has been considered desirable to make a distinction between a tenant under this Ordinance and an ordinary tenant, and "statutory" appeared a suitable word to employ.

5. **Clause 3.**

The corresponding section of the principal Ordinance has been amended by section 3 of the 1931 Ordinance. At present it provides for a notice to terminate the tenancy of a tenant who has been cultivating a holding for a period of two years or more. The first few lines have been slightly altered and made to extend to a tenant who has been cultivating a holding for one year.

The present section also provides that it shall not apply to the case of a tenant who has failed to pay rent. This has been omitted in view of the provisions of clause 4 of the draft Ordinance.

The reference to "any law of Bankruptcy" has also been omitted, as at present the Law of Bankruptcy does not extend to cultivators. When, however, the new Bankruptcy Ordinance comes into force it will extend to cultivators, and if this provision is allowed to remain there is a danger of landlords instituting bankruptcy proceedings when the rent is in arrear, and getting the tenant declared bankrupt, so evading this section of the Ordinance.

6. **Clause 4.**

This is one of the most important parts of the draft Ordinance.

It will be seen that its provisions stand to protect a tenant who has occupied and cultivated a holding for not less than one year, and they are divided into two classes -
- (a) the tenant who has paid his rent and not neglected his holding, and
- (b) the tenant who has not paid all the rent due in respect of the holding within a reasonable time in accordance with the decision of a Board.

As regards (a) this clause provides that no order of eviction shall be made unless such tenant has been given notice to quit and provision has been made for a subsistence area, and provision has been made for compensation for disturbance and improvements, and in the case of a tenant of five years' standing provision has been made for the payment to him of one year's annual rent.

The important change is that a tenant must be provided with a subsistence area inter alia before an ejectment order can be made.

As regards (b) where a notice has been given to a tenant by reason of his failure to pay rent an order of eviction will not be made unless notice to quit has been given and provision made for the payment of compensation for improvement.

It should be noted that the existing Ordinance provides that any compensation assessed shall be charged on the land, and that in the case of the transfer of the land the purchaser shall take over the obligations of the former landlord.

In the present draft Ordinance, however, it has been provided that compensation shall be deposited with a Notary Public and paid to the tenant if he is evicted which appeared to be simpler and gives the tenant greater security and saves him the expense of seeking to recover compensation either from his landlord or his landlord's successor in title.

Sub-clause (3) follows the present section 3(B) vide section 5 of the 1931 Ordinance, but it is not clear how this provision can operate if the rent is payable in kind.

7. Clause 5.

This clause is new and seeks to give protection against the forfeiture of a tenant's rights by the sale of property by mortgagee.

8. Clause 6.

The sections of the existing Ordinance having been re-arranged, this clause corresponds to old section 7 as amended by the 1932 (No.2) Ordinance.

The words "two members shall be skilled in agriculture" have been omitted, as the District Commissioner will in practice not approve of unsuitable persons, and it is possible that somebody might challenge the decision of a Board on the grounds that one of the members might not in the opinion of such person be skilled in agriculture.

9. Clause 7.

This clause seeks to define a subsistence area and deals with certain matters in connection therewith.

It should be noted that the Cabinet memorandum provided in section 21(6):- "A tenant be allowed to sell or mortgage his tenancy interest in the subsistence area". A provision to this effect has however not been inserted as it was felt that there might be some misunderstanding with regard to a subsistence area, under this Ordinance. and an area which might be retained by reason of any Homestead Ordinance, and it appeared undesirable that a tenant should be allowed to sell his interest in a subsistence area and so immediately become landless.

It is probably impossible to prevent such a tenant from being bribed to leave his area in some cases, but there would seem no reason why there should be a specific provision in the law that he can sell his rights.

The clause as drafted provides inter alia for payment of rent in respect of the subsistence area, and that no person occupying a subsistence area shall be ejected therefrom save upon the recommendation of a Board with the approval of the High Commissioner.

10. Clause 8.

Compensation for disturbance is the same as the existing law.

11. Clause 9.

Compensation for improvements is the same as in the existing law. Prima facie this provision for compensation for improvements applies for the benefit of the tenant who has neglected his holding grossly, but the question does not appear to be of much practical importance as it is unlikely that where a tenant has taken the trouble to improve his holding he would be found to have neglected it grossly.

- 7 -

12. <u>Clauses 9, 10 and 11</u> follow the provisions of the present law.

13. <u>Clause 12</u> is new and is based upon the Irish Land Law of 1896, and seeks to provide simply for a case of sub-tenancy.

14. <u>Clause 13</u> is new and follows the Cabinet memorandum.

15. <u>Clause 14</u>.
Sub-clauses (1) and (2) are the present law, (3) has been added dealing specifically with the case when compensation has been assessed and deposited with a Notary Public vide clause 4.

16. <u>Clause 15</u>.
This follows the old section 5(6) and makes provision for an outgoing tenant to prepare the land.

17. <u>Clause 16</u>.
Sub-clauses (1) and (2) are the present law. Section 3(A)(2) as enacted in section 4 of Ordinance No.3 of 1931 and amended by section 4 of Ordinance No. 16 of 1932. Sub-clause (3) has been added in an endeavour to exclude from the provision of this clause the rights of nomad&cte graze lands during certain seasons of the year.

18. <u>Clause 17</u>.
This clause is new. It speaks for itself and its object is to overcome the difficulties experienced in getting matters before the Land Courts.

19. <u>Clause 18</u> is the present law with consequential addition.

- 8 -

20. <u>Clause 19</u> is new and has been inserted to meet the case of certain people who have been specially given short term agreements by Government in order to avoid the provisions of the existing Ordinance and whom it is not desired should be protected.

21. <u>Clause 20</u> is the repeal clause, and the schedule of tenants' improvements for which compensation is payable follows the schedule to the 1929 Ordinance.

11th May, 1933.   <u>ACTING ATTORNEY GENERAL</u>.

III
Confidential.   11th May, 1933.

An Ordinance to provide for the
protection of certain cultivators.

COMPARATIVE TABLE.

Clause.

1. Short title as in Ordinance No.27 of 1929.

2. Cf. section 2 of the principal Ordinance as amended by section 2 of Ordinance No.3 of 1931, and sections 2 and 3 of Ordinance No.16 of 1932.

3. Cf. section 3 of the principal Ordinance as amended by section 3 of No.3 of 1931.

4. Cf. section 3(A)(1) of the principal Ordinance as enacted in section 4 of No.3 of 1931, and as amended by section 4 of No.16 of 1932; and section 3(B) of the principal Ordinance as enacted in section 5 of No.3 of 1931; and section 6 of the principal Ordinance.

5. New clause.

6. Cf. section 7 of the principal Ordinance as amended by section 2 of No.30 of 1932.

7. New clause.

8. Cf. section 5 of the principal Ordinance.

9. Cf. section 5 of the principal Ordinance.

10. Cf. section 5(8) of the principal Ordinance.

11. Cf. section 4 of the principal Ordinance as enacted in section 6 of No.3 of 1931.

- 2 -

12. New clause based on Irish Land Law 1896, 12(1) and (2).

13. New clause.

14. Cf. section 8 of principal Ordinance.

15. Cf. section 5(6) of principal Ordinance.

16. Cf. section 3(A)(2) of principal Ordinance as enacted in section 4 of No.3 of 1931, and as amended by section 4 of No.16 of 1932.

17. New clause.

18. Cf. section 9 of principal Ordinance.

19. New clause.

20. Repeal.

First Schedule.

As in Ordinance No.27 of 1929.

Second Schedule.

Ordinances repealed.

9.05

Reference No.CP/214/34.

August, 1934.

My Dear Philip,

You may recall that when the revised Protection of Cultivators Ordinance was being drawn up, I raised the question whether the protection which it was contemplated to afford to tenants should be extended to small owners too. You thought at the time that more definite information was needed before this question could be considered.

I said a year ago that so far as my information went and in the opinion of the Development Officer, the number of small holders which would be affected is not very large.

During the last year the Development Officer has carried out investigations with a view to testing the accuracy of this opinion and has obtained information in respect of certain villages in the Jaffa and Jenin sub-districts where the

landlords/

The Right Honourable
Sir Philip Cunliffe-Lister, G.B.E., M.P., etc.,
His Majesty's Principal Secretary of State
for the Colonies.

- 2 -

landlords are Arab. I attach a memorandum embodying the results of his enquiries and certain complementary information obtained from the Lands Department about the prevalence of sale of land by Arabs to Jews.

It will be seen from the memorandum that although the great majority of owners in the two sub-districts are cultivating areas less than a reasonable lot viable, there are nevertheless considerable areas of land owned by landlords whose holdings are largely in excess of a lot viable.

It is only natural to suppose that Jewish purchasers prefer to buy up large areas in single ownership rather than go to the expense and inconvenience of negotiating sales by a multitude of small holders. The Lands Department's figures tend to confirm this supposition

for/

- 3 -

for the total area of land sold by Arabs to Jews in parcels not exceeding 100 dunums in 1933 formed a very small part of the total areas transferred from Arab to Jewish ownership (namely 9362 dunums out of 61,567 dunums, or less than one-sixth). In these figures no distinction is drawn between sales of urban and sales of rural land respectively and there is no doubt that the majority of the sales of areas of less than 100 dunums represents sales of urban building land.

The knowledge which has been obtained during the past year thus bears out my surmise that there is at present no extensive sale of small parcels of agricultural land and I am accordingly now definitely of the opinion that no legislation should be undertaken at present

to/

- 4 -

to protect small holders though I do not overlook the possibility that some form of protection may be required in the future.

I am informed that owing to the recent purchases of land by Jews in the Gaza Beersheba districts amounting to some 80,000 dunums, a number of small owners will be affected, and probably 100 families will become landless. This is regrettable, but I do not think transactions of this size justify further legislation.

I have approached the Agency as represented by Mr. Ben Gurion on this matter, and am hopeful that a lot viable will be reserved by the Jewish groups concerned for the benefit of about 50 of these 100 families.

Yours very sincerely,

(SD) A. G. WAUCHOPE

The High Commissioner asked in June 1933 for a rough estimate of the number of small owners and the amount of land that would be affected by any legislation which might be introduced to protect small holders.

2. The Development Officer obtained this information in respect of certain villages in the Jaffa sub-district and the Jenin sub-district. For the purpose of compiling this data a *lot viable* was taken to be :-

Citrus plantations	10 dunums.
All other plantations	50 dunums.
Cereal land (Jaffa-Ramleh)	75 dunums.
Cereal land (Jenin)	120 dunums.

3. The data reveal that roughly 90% of the owners hold less than a *lot viable* that is to say that if legislation to protect small owners were introduced, roughly 90% would not be able to sell any land.

	Total No. of Holders.	Total Area of cultivation. Dunums.	Below Subsistence Area.		Above Subsistence Area.	
			No. of owners.	Area Dunums.	No. of owners.	Area Dunums.
Jaffa sub-district	6,322	144,072	5,471	55,892	852	88,180
Jenin sub-district	4,793	260,161	4,294	104,337	499	161,593

It is, however, interesting to note that it is probable that a considerable part of the area of holdings in excess of a subsistence area could be sold without reducing parcels below the subsistence area. In the Jenin sub-district, the Development Officer estimates that 101,725 dunums of the total of 161,593 dunums could be sold.

4. From statistics furnished by the Department of Lands it appears that there is still a considerable

sale/

sale of land by Arabs to Jews.

Sale of land by Arabs to Jews
1st May, 1933 to 31st October, 1933.

	No. of sales.	Area sold.
Sales in which the area is up to 100 dunums	306	3,842
Sales in which the area is over 100 dunums but not more than 500 dunums ..	22	4,378
Sales in which the area is over 500 dunums	22	15,477
	350	23,697

1st November, 1933 to 31st March, 1934.

	No. of sales.	Area sold.
Sales in which the area is up to 100 dunums	373	5,520
Sales in which the area is over 100 dunums but not more than 500 dunums ..	35	5,550
Sales in which the area is over 500 dunums	11	26,800
	409	37,870
Total for year 1933-34	759	61,567

5. In considering these figures it must be borne in mind that a number of the sales, particularly those of large areas represent the completion and registration of sales agreed upon in earlier years and on the other hand the figures do not give any indication of transactions

agreed/

agreed upon but not completed in the period to which the figures relate.

Moreover no distinction is made between urban and rural land and it may be accepted that a large number of the sales of areas up to 100 dunums are of urban building plots.

9th August, 1934.

Government of Palestine

In case of reply please quote the date of this letter and the following number:

V/125/33.

Chief Secretary's Office, Jerusalem, Palestine.

18 May, 1934.

CONFIDENTIAL.

The Chief Secretary to the Government of Palestine presents his compliments to the Under-Secretary of State for the Colonies and with reference to the High Commissioner's Con-
13 fidential despatch of the 27th April, 1934, forwarding a memorandum by the Development Officer on the subject of the steps which have been taken by the Palestine Government to afford protection to cultivators and on the operation of the legislation which is now in force, is directed to request that the following amendment may be made to the statement of claims under the Protection of Cultivators Ordinance heard in the Northern District which appears on page 7 of the memorandum:

13 amended accordingly.

"Appeals applied for .... 3."

[No page follows.]

PALESTINE.

HIGH COMMISSIONER FOR PALESTINE,
JERUSALEM.

CONFIDENTIAL.
Reference No. V/125/33.

21 April, 1934.

Enclosure

Sir,

    I have the honour to refer to correspondence ending with my despatch Confidential C of the 5th April, 1934, regarding the settlement of cases referred to Commissions under Section 19 of the Protection of Cultivators Ordinance, and to transmit herewith for your information a copy of a memorandum prepared on my instructions by the Development Officer on the subject of the steps which have been taken by the Palestine Government to afford protection to cultivators and on the operation of the legislation which is now in force.

    2. I propose to consider the suggestions made in paragraph 20 of the memorandum for the further amendment of the Protection of Cultivators Ordinance, 1933, and shall address you again on this subject in due course.

              I have the honour to be,

                    Sir,

                        Your most obedient,

                              humble servant,

                          J. Hathorn Hall.
                        for HIGH COMMISSIONER
                            FOR PALESTINE.
                           Absent on tour

The Right Honourable
Sir Philip Cunliffe-Lister, G.B.E., M.P., etc., etc.,
       His Majesty's Principal Secretary of State
                          for the Colonies.

CONFIDENTIAL

Enclosure.

Memorandum by the Development Officer
on the subject of the measures taken
by the Palestine Government for the
protection of cultivators.

In September, 1920, the then High Commissioner, Sir Herbert Samuel, enacted the Transfer of Land Ordinance, which contained a section to the effect that the Governor of the District was empowered to withhold his consent to any transfer of land until he was satisfied that in the case of agricultural land, the tenant in occupation, if the property was leased, would retain sufficient land in the district or elsewhere for the maintenance of himself and his family.

2. However, this section was cancelled in 1921 by the Transfer of Land (Amendment) Ordinance, No.2 of 1921, and replaced by the following sections:-

> "Section 5(1). Any person wishing to make a disposition of immovable property must first obtain the consent of the Government.
>
> "Section 8(1). The consent of the Government to a disposition shall be given by the Director of Lands to the Registrar of the District or Sub-District, who shall be satified only that the transferor has a title; provided that in the case of agricultural land which is leased, he shall also be satisfied that any tenant in occupation will retain sufficient land in the district or elsewhere for the maintenance of himself and his family."

3. At the same time as the 1920 Ordinance was promulgated, instructions were issued to the Land Commission as follows:-

> "The Government of Palestine, while desirous to promote in every possibly way the closer settlement of the country, is at the same time anxious that the interests of the present tenants and occupants of land, whether Government property or private property, should be properly protected. It will be necessary on the one hand to take steps to prevent the eviction of tenants by the landlord

on/

-2-

on a sale of land, and on the other to secure for those who have exercised rights of cultivation and grazing, without full legal title, a sufficient area for the maintenance of their families ... "

4. Unfortunately, the Ordinance proved unworkable, as the purchasers gave certain sums of money to the tenants, who in nearly every case were off the land before the transaction was brought to the Land Registry.

5. The Ordinances of 1920 and 1921 remained in force until the 31st of July, 1929, when they were replaced by the Protection of Cultivators Ordinance, No.27 of 1929. This Ordinance provided for the payment to certain classes of tenants of compensation for disturbance or for improvements, on their receiving a valid notice to quit the holding of which they had been in occupation. It further provided for the constitution of Boards to decide disputes as to whether or not compensation for disturbance or compensation for improvement was payable, and as to the amount of any such compensation. <u>It did nothing, however, to secure to those dispossessed "a sufficient area for the maintenance of their families"</u>. It also did nothing to provide for a sub-tenant, and as a result of this loophole, the owner of the village of Shatta, Beisan Sub-District, in order to free himself of his tenants in 1929 and 1930 let the lands of the village to a brother land-owner and, after the termination of this letting, he took proceedings in the Magistrate's Court for the ejectment of 38 cultivators. His application was successful because the Magistrate had no alternative but to find that there was no contract of tenancy between the defendants and the owner: and to order their ejectment.

In/

In 1932 the Protection of Cultivators (Amendment) Ordinance, No.1 was enacted in order to include a sub-tenant.

6. During the period the Land Transfer Ordinances, 1920/21, and the Protection of Cultivators Ordinances, 1929-1933, were in force, many cultivators were displaced from the land; and in 1932-33 the Tribunal appointed for the purpose found that some 584 of them had not obtained other holdings on which they could establish themselves or other equally satisfactory occupation.

This displacement, in so far as the land passed into Jewish possession, was caused as the result of a policy not only to acquire ownership but to ensure that all the work required on the land should be performed by Jews as far as possible; and in the case of the official land-purchasing agency of the Zionist Organization, namely, the Jewish National Fund, by Jews only; and it follows, as the result of this policy, that when land is purchased by Jews, not only is the landlord changed, but the tenants, and practically all the wage-earning class are compelled to move also.

However, in the case of lands purchased by Private Jewish bodies, such as the Palestine Jewish Colonization Association and Hanotaiah Ltd., although tenants have been displaced, they have been employed by these bodies, and in many cases are earning a better livelihood in their new mode of life than previously. As an instance, I would quote the village of Umm Khalid - Tulkarm Sub-District - the major portion of the lands of which were purchased by Hanotaiah Ltd. in 1930, i.e.

before/

before it was the law that a tenant should be provided with a 'subsistence area'. In the case in question, the cultivators not only received generous compensation, but were also employed in the settlement of Nathaniya which has been built on the lands purchased from the owners of Umm Khalid.

7. As a result of the policy mentioned in the preceding paragraph, a number of Arab villages have entirely disappeared, and have been deleted from the official schedule of villages.

8. On his arrival in Palestine, Sir Arthur Wauchope made a particular study of the peculiar problems relating to agricultural development in this country.

As a result of this personal survey, His Excellency found it essential for financial as well as for political and economic reasons to do all in his power to stop, or if that were not possible, to minimize the process of the displacement of Arab cultivators; and on the 31st of August, 1933, His Excellency enacted the Protection of Cultivators Ordinance No.37 of 1933.

This legislation is drafted so as not to transgress any of the existing commitments of His Majesty's Government and to cause as little interference as possible with the economic life of the country.

It repealed the Protection of Cultivators Ordinance, 1929, the three amending Ordinances of 1931-32 and the 'Extension' Ordinance of 1933, which provided for a tenancy of two years before the tenant obtained protection, and a monetary compensation for eviction.

9. The present Ordinance creates a "statutory

tenant/

tenant' and provides that any such tenant who has occupied and cultivated a holding for a period of not less than one year, shall not be ejected therefrom, provided he has paid his rent and has not neglected his holding grossly, unless he has been provided with a <u>subsistence area</u> approved by the High Commissioner; such subsistence area to be, as far as possible, in the vicinity of the land from which he has been displaced.

10. Prior to the enactment of this Ordinance, all disputes as to whether a cultivator was a tenant or not had, in the first instance, to be referred to the Courts, a rather lengthy and expensive procedure.

In order to overcome this difficulty, it was laid down in section 19 of the Ordinance of 1933, that any dispute:-

    (a) as to whether any person is a statutory tenant of a holding, or

    (b) as to the length of time that any statutory tenant has occupied and cultivated a holding, or

    (c) as to whether any person is the landlord of a holding, or

    (d) as to whether any person has exercised continuously any practice of grazing or watering animals or cutting wood or reeds or other beneficial occupation of a similar character by right, custom, usage or sufferance,

shall be referred to a special Commission to be appointed by the High Commissioner, the Chairman of which shall be a British Judicial Officer.

It was also stated that :-

    (2) any person aggrieved by the decision of any such Commission may appeal to the High Commissioner-in-Council whose decision shall be final and no appeal lie therefrom to any Court.

-6-

11. The immediate result of the enactment of this Ordinance was that a considerable crop of disputes arose. These disputes were by no means limited to disputes between Jewish landlords and Arab tenants. (In fact there have been surprisingly few claims to tenancy rights from Arabs in respect of Jewish-owned land).

The fact that few claims to tenancy rights have been submitted in respect of Jewish-owned land is indirect evidence that Jewish land-owners were finding little difficulty, by means of payment of liberal compensation, in persuading Arabs who claimed rights to abandon their claims.

12. The Commission mentioned in paragraph 10(2) of this memorandum was not set up as the Chief Justice held the opinion that a British Judicial Officer should not be Chairman of a Commission with two laymen who might outvote him. He was also of the opinion that the High Commissioner had no power to set up any authority to decide as to rights in land except the Courts established for this purpose under the Order-in-Council.

As a result of this delay, the public began to lose faith in the Ordinance, and it was found impossible to protect the genuine tenant or the honest landlord.

However, on the 3rd of February, 1934, the Protection of Cultivators (Amendment) Ordinance, No.7 of 1934, was enacted, and Section 19 of the Principal Ordinance was amended so as to give the High Commissioner power to appoint one or more Commissions consisting respectively of not less than two persons, and that on a point of law an appeal should lie to the Land Court by leave of that Court by case stated.

Two/

-7-

Two Commissions were set up at once, one for the Southern District and one for the Northern District, constituted as follows:-

<u>Southern District</u>: L. Andrews, Esq., O.B.E.
Development Officer, Chairman.

J.H.H. Pollock, Esq.
Asst. District Commissioner,
Southern District.

<u>Northern District</u>: A.F. Nathan, Esq., O.B.E.
Assistant Director of
Agriculture and Forests, Chairman.

S.H. Perowne, Esq.,
Asst. District Commissioner,
Northern District.

to investigate disputes submitted under Section 19 of the Principal Ordinance.

These Commissions began to sit on the 7th February, 1934, on which date 87 disputes were awaiting investigation in the Southern District, and 48 cases in the Northern District. The Commissions sat on three days a week for the first three weeks and are now sitting when found necessary. In the course of these sittings, additional cases were presented for investigation so that on the 29th of March the state of affairs was as follows:-

<u>Southern District</u>

Number of disputes submitted	319
Number decided	254
Number adjourned	12
Number still to be investigated	53
Appeals applied for	Nil

<u>Northern District</u>

Number of disputes submitted	120
Number decided	102 +
Number adjourned	Nil
Number still to be investigated	18
Appeals applied for	3

+ Includes 36 withdrawn.

The number of disputes listed does not show the actual number of individual claimants nor the number of landlords against whom action was taken.

Claimants/

Claimants varied from one to seventy-two in individual disputes.

From the number of new applications received, it would appear that the public are beginning to realize the advantage of recourse to this new Ordinance.

As an example, I would mention that recently a Jewish land-owner of Jaffa told me that he is only sorry he did not realize some time ago the protection given to landlords by this Ordinance. He added that he had spent thousands of pounds in trying to free his land of spurious tenants. In another case several tenants who insisted on being allowed to cultivate 'subsistence areas' told their landlord on his objecting 'that Government had opened their eyes and they had now become fully aware of their rights under the Ordinance'.

In some cases the less sophisticated cultivators are under the impression that the 'new law' was made in order to give them a right to any land they may be able to plough, whether lawfully or otherwise. In fact, most of the claims in the Gaza Sub-District concern reduction of area to within the limits of a 'subsistence area', and not a refusal on the part of the landlord to lease land to the tenant.

13. In an endeavour further to ensure that villagers were made aware of their rights under the Ordinance, the High Commissioner directed that District Officers be instructed that when an intending sale is brought to their notice, they must at once proceed to the village and inform all concerned of the protection afforded to them by the Ordinance.

14./

-9-

14. To my mind, there is no doubt but that the Protection of Cultivators Ordinance, 1933, gives protection to the tenant who does not wish to be ejected from his holding. It also protects the landlord from false claimants to tenancy rights. It does not, however, prevent the foolish tenant from receiving compensation and renouncing his claims as a 'statutory Tenant'.

In support of this contention, I would quote the following specific cases which have come to my personal notice :-

Tenant Protected:

(a) Abu Shusheh - Ramleh Sub-District.

The Maccabee Land Co. (Jewish) owners of some 3,750 dunums of land, refused to allow the Arab tenants to continue cultivating their lands. Twenty-four of them applied to the Commission and some nineteen of them have been created 'statutory tenants', and are continuing in occupation of the lands in question.

(b) Kheirieh - Ramleh Sub-District.

The Syrian Orphanage (German Christians) owners of 4,000 dunums of land at Kheirieh village, had a dispute with the Arab cultivators, and on enquiry the Commission found that some eighteen of them were statutory tenants.

Landlord Protected:

(a) Salama - Jaffa Sub-District.

Seventy-two Arabs dwelling in tin huts and tents claimed the right to remain on an area of 323 metric dunums. The Commission enquired into their claim and found that they were not entitled to the protection of the Ordinance.

(b)/

(b) <u>Kafr 'Ana - Jaffa Sub-District</u>.

Thirty-four gypsies claimed the right to remain on Jewish land although they had never cultivated same nor had their animals grazed on the area, and the Commission accordingly found that their claim was baseless.

(c) <u>Yahudieh</u>.

Twenty-five Arab labourers living in huts made of empty petrol tins claimed tenancy rights in an endeavour to force the Jewish owners to bribe them to move on, and after due enquiry their claim was dismissed by the Commission.

<u>Foolish Tenants.</u>

On the other hand some 11 cultivators from Na'aneh, Ramleh Sub-District, applied to the Commission asking to be made statutory tenants in the lands of the Jewish Company called Hanotaiah. Their claim was upheld, but three days afterwards they compromised with the landlords for a sum of LP. 600.

15. Since the publication of the new Ordinance, the only big transfer of land from Arab to Jewish hands brought to my notice is the sale of the village of Qira wa Qamun, Haifa Sub-District. The area of this village is some 17,000 dunums, and the number of Arab cultivators was found in 1932 to be 64. The Palestine Land Development Co., who are negotiating the transaction on behalf of the Jewish National Fund, have given me a verbal promise that they will not endeavour to tempt the tenants to evacuate the land on payment of monetary compensation, and have also expressed their willingness to give them holdings in lands which the Jewish National Fund owns in an adjoining village.

16./

16. The Ordinance has passed practically unnoticed in the Hills, as is evidenced by the fact that the return of disputes submitted in the Jerusalem District is Nil. In the Northern District, with few exceptions, all the claims submitted are in respect of lands in the plains.

17. Two claims only were received under Section 18 of the Ordinance, i.e. founded on exercise of a practice of grazing or watering animals or the cutting of wood or reeds, etc. In neither case could claimants substantiate their claims, nor could any entry of their having paid animal tax be found in Government registers.

18. It is yet too early to say if the Ordinance of 1933 will definitely prevent tenants, who would otherwise have been evicted on payment of compensation, from being ejected from the land, for undoubtedly landlords, in the zones where Jews are purchasing land, are making every endeavour by all means at their disposal to circumvent the Ordinance. Also many tenants find it difficult to refuse the offer of ready cash as compensation for giving up their rights and vacating their holdings.

Another factor which induces cultivators to forego their rights is the fact that although the Ordinance gives the statutory tenant the right to occupy and cultivate a holding, there is nothing in the Ordinance which compels a landlord to allow the tenant to cultivate. A cultivator cannot camp on his holding, and if after the close of the agricultural year the landlord refuses to allow him to re-enter the land in order to prepare same for the following season, if I may be permitted to say so, the tenant is 'up in the air', as there is no machinery

which/

which compels the landlord to allow him to cultivate. The tenant then spends many weary hours in appealing to District Commissioners, Magistrates and Police Officers who, although they sympathise with his position, are not able to help him.

In the Southern District, landlords have been quick to realize this apparent omission in the Ordinance, and every time the Commission sits at Jaffa, it is beseiged by statutory tenants asking to be put back on the land.

19. It is said that landlords are becoming particularly cautious in leasing or re-leasing their lands; this is especially so in the Coastal Plain. It is also said that in many cases landlords prefer to leave their lands fallow than run the risk of a claim to tenancy rights. I think that this is the exception rather than the rule, but the tendency to let lands on contract for periods of less than one year and definitely excluding the rights of 'Krab' - the right to cultivate the winter crop immediately succeeding the summer crop (as the summer crop demands more intensive and costly cultivation, the benefit of which has its effect on the next crop) - has come to notice. This practice the Assistant Director of Agriculture and Forests informs me is, agriculturally, undesirable, as the tenant will merely endeavour to get as much out of the land as possible, without any thought as to the future.

In view of this attitude on the part of landlords, it may reasonably be expected that District Commissioners will be flooded with applications from tenants at the beginning of the next cultivation season, say October

next./

next. In fact the District Officer in charge of the Gaza Sub-District anticipates a flood of applications. Should this be so, it will be necessary to re-consider the composition and number of Commissions appointed under Section 19 of the Ordinance.

20. If further amendments are to be made to the Ordinance, it is suggested that the following points should be considered:-

(a) Machinery to enable Courts to place 'statutory tenants' in possession of a 'subsistence area'.

(b) The term year to be defined as to mean an agricultural year, and not the ordinary calendar year, as per the Interpretation Ordinance, 1929.

By an agricultural year, I mean the period required to raise a summer and winter crop. It is not usual for a cultivator to occupy his holding for the whole of a calendar year, as he generally leaves the land for a short period after the harvesting of the summer crop.

(c) That persons who already own or are cultivating a 'subsistence area' should not be capable of being made 'statutory tenants' in the lands of others. At present they can be, and it is then incumbent upon the landlord to approach the High Commissioner for a certificate in accordance with the terms of Section 6(1)(a)2(b) of the Ordinance.

21. I feel confident, now that Commissions have been appointed, that the Ordinance will to a great extent achieve its purpose and will prevent, or at least minimize the process of the displacement of Arab cultivators,

without/

without adequate provision in land for their subsistence, while at the same time placing no obstacle in the way of the buying and selling of land where the transfer of ownership will not adversely affect the tenant. But landlords will undoubtedly be reluctant to permit tenants to cultivate more than the minimum area to which they are entitled under the Ordinance. It may also help if it is found possible to adopt some of the suggestions contained in the preceding paragraph, especially the first one.

As previously stated, it is impossible to legislate for fools, and cases of foolish tenants accepting cash in lieu of a 'subsistence area' are bound to occur.

(Sgd) L. Andrews.
DEVELOPMENT OFFICER.

9.06

HIGH COMMISSIONER FOR PALESTINE,
JERUSALEM.

21 December, 1935.

My dear Parkinson,

    Will you please refer to your telegram No. 394 of the 18th December about a memorandum on land sales to which I referred in paragraph 15 of my despatch Secret 'A' of the 7th December.

    That memorandum took the form of a draft despatch which I had had prepared before I proceeded on leave, and I now enclose a copy.

    One point requires further explanation in view of the time which has elapsed since the despatch was drafted, namely the question discussed in paragraph 4 (ii) of obtaining information to enable me to state how much land would remain in Arab ownership, and how much would pass to Jews, if all available land, excluding the _lots viables_, were sold to Jews. The information which has since been obtained shows that the assumptions made hitherto regarding the minimum size of a _lot viable_ are incorrect, and that all available statistics are insufficient to give an

HIGH COMMISSIONER FOR PALESTINE,
JERUSALEM.

- 2 -

accurate picture of the position.

I am now considering what further steps should be taken in this direction, but in the meantime I shall be glad if I may have the Secretary of State's approval of the general lines of the action proposed in the draft despatch.

I take this opportunity of acknowledging the receipt of your Confidential letter No. 90081/35 of the 11th December, on the legislation which the Government of Cyprus wish to introduce giving the Governor-in-Council power to restrict purchases of immovable property by aliens in any area in which the Governor considers that it is undesirable that further alienation should take place save with his consent.

If the Cyprus law were enacted, it would inevitably attract the attention of the Palestine Arabs. The argument which you put into the mouths of the Arabs is precisely the one they would use, and I think with justification. There would be strong reactions unless some restrictions on the sale of land, as I have recommended, are imposed in Palestine.

Yours always,

Arthur Wauchope

DRAFT

~~Letter~~
~~Telegram~~ to SECRETARY OF STATE.
Despatch

PALESTINE

SECRET

Sir,

        I have the honour to refer to your predecessor's Secret despatch of the 9th April, 1935, on the subject of certain suggestions I put forward for dealing with the situation arising out of the continued sale of land by Arabs to Jews.

2.   The connection between land speculation and the rapid industrialization of the Arab smallholder is an important factor in the situation. The speculative prices which Jewish purchasers pay constitute the principal inducement to the Arab smallholder to sell his land. The present period of industrial expansion enables increasing numbers of Arab villagers to find employment and encourages the sale of land while concealing the extent to which Arab smallholders are disposing of their property.

        With regard to the suggestion made in paragraph 2 of the despatch under reference there was not, at the time when I addressed my Confidential despatch of the 22nd February to Sir

DRAFT

Letter
Telegram   to
Despatch

2.

P. Cunliffe-Lister, any evidence that the high price of land was obstructing Jewish land purchasing activities. I am now advised that Jewish purchases in rural areas have lately decreased, and that the falling-off is due to two main causes, namely the high price of land and the fall in the prices received for oranges.

3.   But my principal preoccupation, as Sir P. Cunliffe-Lister observes, is the protection of the Arab smallholder, and it is mainly with this end in view that I have suggested the enactment of legislation on the lines of the Transfer of Land Ordinance, 1920, to provide that throughout Palestine, with the exception of urban areas, citrus land and the Beersheba sub-district, purchases of land should only be sanctioned if the seller retains a <u>lot viable</u>.

With reference to paragraph 9 of Sir P.Cunliffe Lister's despatch, I am advised that the results of the Mufti's religious campaign against the sale of lands by Arabs to Jews are negligible.

4.   With regard to the specific points raised in paragraph 7 of the

DRAFT

Letter
Telegram to
Despatch

	3. despatch under reference, I submit the following comments:
	(i) The extent of the <u>lot viable</u> will vary according to the locality and the type of land. It is proposed to adopt, so far as it is applicable, the criterion for a "subsistence area" laid down in Section
Annual Volume 1933 page 77.	9(1) of the Protection of Cultivators Ordinance, 1933. The following table sets out the different standards which were provisionally laid down in 1933 for the "subsistence area" in certain localities:

Zone	Type of Land		
	Unirrigated	Irrigated	
		Intensive Citrus & Vegetables	Extensive Cereals & Fodder
1. Hills of Galilee and Judaea	75 dunums	10 dunums	30 dunums
2. <u>Plains</u>			
(a) <u>Maritime Plain</u>			
(i) From Ras el Nakura to a line through Majdal and Hebron	75 dunums	10 dunums	30 dunums
(ii) South of this line	120 dunums	10 dunums	30 dunums
(b) <u>Plain of Esdraelon</u>	75 dunums	10 dunums	30 dunums

(Continued)

DRAFT

Letter
Telegram   to
Despatch

4.

Zone	Unirrigated	Type of Land	
		Irrigated	
		Intensive Citrus & Vegetables	Extensive Cereals & Fodder
(c) Valley of Jezreel			
(i) Western portion	120 dunums	10 dunums	30 dunums
(ii) Eastern portion	150 dunums	10 dunums	30 dunums
(d) Jordan Valley	200 dunums	10 dunums	30 dunums
(e) Hula	100 dunums	10 dunums	30 dunums
3. Plains of Beersheba	200 dunums	10 dunums	30 dunums

Experience of the practical application of these standards has shown that a number of them need to be revised. A Board constituted under section 9(1) of the Protection of Cultivators Ordinance, 1933, is about to be set up in the Gaza sub-district to define minimum subsistence areas for different localities and categories of land.

(ii) The direct practical effect which is expected from securing to the Arab owner a <u>lot viable</u> is, of course, that if he should sell the remainder of his land (if any) and expend the proceeds

DRAFT

Letter
Telegram to
Despatch

5.

unwisely, or fail to obtain, or to retain, other employment, he will at least be assured of his livelihood. I am advised that the proposed restriction would also have the indirect effect of making it more difficult for an Arab smallholder to dispose of any part of his holding to Jewish purchasers, as these would not relish the prospect of an island of Arab land in the midst of their property.

In view of the different sizes of the <u>lot viable</u> in different areas, and of the fact that there must be many smallholders whose entire land is less than the theoretical <u>lot viable</u>, the information at present available is insufficient to enable me to state how much land would remain in Arab ownership, and how much would pass to Jews, if all available Arab land excluding the <u>lots viables</u> were sold to Jews. I have taken steps to obtain further and more reliable information. Returns are being compiled in respect of each village, from which it will be possible to work out the necessary deductions. But these are lengthy and laborious processes, which cannot be completed for some months.

DRAFT

Letter
Telegram to
Despatch

6.

(iii) I consider that it is essential, for the purpose of securing the retention of the <u>lot viable</u>, that all transactions in rural land should be subject to Government approval. To make registration dependent on this condition would, in my opinion, be to saddle Land Registrars with a responsibility which it is not equitable to lay upon officers in the Second Division of the Service.

(iv) I do not recommend that there should be any restriction on the number of transactions to be allowed to each purchaser, or on the number to be allowed to each vendor provided that he retains the prescribed <u>lot viable</u> under the proposed Ordinance and makes any provision for his tenants which may be required under the Protection of Cultivators Ordinance. I consider that sales of areas larger than 1000 dunums should only be permitted as special cases at the discretion of the High Commissioner. I propose that the High Commissioner in exercising his discretion should be guided by the merits of each case as reported by the District Commissioner or

DRAFT

Letter
Telegram to
Despatch

7.

the technical advisers of Government. It is also my intention that the High Commissioner should have power to approve the sale of a <u>lot viable</u>: it is possible that cases might arise where a smallholder's <u>lot viable</u> constitutes a menace to health or effectively blocks an important irrigation or drainage scheme.

(v)   The proposed legislation would prohibit the sale of a <u>lot viable</u> (except with the consent of the High Commissioner) and would be in general terms, prohibiting sale either to an Arab or to a Jew.

I anticipate in the case of smallholders much the same difficulty as has been experienced in the working of the Protection of Cultivators Ordinance, namely that many tenants find it difficult to refuse the offer of ready cash as compensation for giving up their rights and vacating their holdings. There will, however, be this difference that under the proposed Ordinance the smallholder, even though he may be induced to vacate his holding, will not be able to dispose of his rights in his <u>lot viable</u>.

DRAFT

<u>Letter</u>
<u>Telegram</u> to
<u>Despatch</u>

8.

Under article 68 of the Ottoman Land Code, if the owner should desert his <u>lot viable</u> or otherwise fail to cultivate it, Government would have the right to resume possession of the land after it had remained uncultivated for three years.

(vi)   It appears to me most desirable not to prevent genuine mortgages on the <u>lot viable</u>, which are a valuable source of credit and consequently of proper development, and an alternative preferable to the ordinary money-lender. On the other hand mortgages may be fictitious and cases may occur in which money is lent for a short period of one, two or three months, with an outside arrangement for the mortgagor to default so that the mortgagee can buy in the property. To overcome this difficulty I suggest that the proposed Ordinance should provide that there shall be no sale of a <u>lot viable</u> in execution of any mortgage where the principal sum was lent for less than three years.

5.   I appreciate your predecessor's apprehension that the Jews might attack

DRAFT

Letter
Telegram   to
Despatch

9.

the proposed legislation on the ground that it involves control of dispositions of land and infringes the undertaking given in paragraphs 12 and 13 of the Prime Minister's letter to Dr. Weizmann, but I trust that, in the light of the detailed proposals and explanations furnished in this despatch and its enclosure, His Majesty's Government will be satisfied that the proposal is not inconsistent with the Prime Minister's undertakings, although the Government is not proceeding with a comprehensive development scheme.

I remain of the opinion that it is Government's duty, under the mandate of protecting the Arab, to take some positive action, and the measure which I have proposed is the most satisfactory course that I can devise. I agree that there is not at present any indication that the Jewish Agency or Jewish opinion generally would favour any restrictions on Jewish purchase of land from Arabs but I believe, as I indicated in my Confidential despatch of the 22nd February, that it may be possible to secure the cooperation of the Jewish

DRAFT

Letter
Telegram to
Despatch

10.

Agency in the measure which I am proposing, if only as an alternative to something more drastic.

6. I also concur in Sir P. Cunliffe-Lister's view that criticism of the proposals is to be expected from the Arab side, on the ground that the restrictions do not go far enough. But while these critics may argue that the proposal makes no allowance for increase of population, and may cast doubts on its efficacy, I believe that responsible Arab leaders will welcome the measure as a positive step by Government towards the protection of the Arab population of the country. So far as concerns the point that the proposal fails to take into account the increase of the Arab population, it is my hope, as suggested in paragraph 4 of my Confidential despatch of the 22nd February, that improved methods of cultivation will continually increase production so as to compensate to a large extent for the absence of additional land: moreover, consideration of the eventual increase of the population raises such wide issues that I believe that the Arab leaders will recognise that

DRAFT

Letter
Telegram to
Despatch

11.

it is preferable to accept the limited measure which I am proposing, rather than to delay any action by pressing for impossibilities. As regards the argument that the Jews will bribe the Arab owners to abandon their <u>lots viables</u> I have already pointed out that the suggested Ordinance will make it impossible for the smallholder actually to dispose of his right of ownership in the holding: and if any such holdings should escheat to Government I should propose to consider very carefully the possibility of retaining those areas for disposal to landless cultivators who might wish to return to farming for their livelihood.

In short, I am satisfied that the adoption of the measures which I propose would result in real improvement in the condition of the Arab small owners of this and the next generation, and would show both Arab and Jew that while Government certainly encourages the well-being of the National Home, it also has regard to the moral rights of the small owners and of cultivators of the soil.

DRAFT

Letter
Telegram to
Despatch

12.

not enclosed

7. I enclose herein for your consideration a draft Ordinance, based on the Transfer of Land Ordinance, 1920, which sets out the details of my proposal. The further information referred to in paragraph 4(ii) of this despatch will be sent to you at the earliest possible moment.

        I have &c.,

         HCFP.

19.12.35.

The Palestine Land Question.

The Problem.

1. In his confidential despatch of 22nd February, the High Commissioner deals with two interconnected problems relating to land in Palestine, viz.,

(a) the problem of preventing the more or less rapid industrialisation of the small Arab landowners, who are succumbing to the temptation to sell the whole of their land to the Jews and to become employees in the towns (especially in the building industry);

(b) the problem of preventing speculation in land, which has already resulted in a boom and, by raising prices, has made it less easy for the small Arab owner to resist the temptation to sell his land.

2. Neither of these problems is a new one. The Land Transfer Ordinance of 1920 attempted both to forestall the evil consequences of land speculation and to ensure that, when land was sold or leased, the owner or the tenant in occupation retained an area sufficient for the subsistence of himself and his family. This Ordinance was repealed in less than twelve months, except in so far as it protected the rights of tenants in the event of a change of landlord*. Since then no attempt appears to have been made to deal with problem (b) (land speculation) by means of legislation; but problem (a) may be said to have been under continuous consideration, and constituted the main burden of Sir John Hope-Simpson's Report of 1930, and of crucial passages in the White Paper of 1930 and the Prime Minister's letter of 1931. Subsequently, Mr. French dealt with this problem fully in his reports

* These provisions, which were embodied in the Land Transfer Ordinance of 1921, were very soon repealed and replaced by a series of Ordinances for the protection of tenants, ending with the Protection of Cultivators Ordinance of 1933.

of

of December 1931 and April 1932, in general conformity with the principles adumbrated by Sir J. Hope-Simpson.

Attitude of Jews and Arabs to the Problem.

3. As regards the protection of the Arab landowners, the solution suggested (or rather vociferously demanded) by the Arab leaders is simple and drastic, viz., the complete prohibition of further sales of land to the Jews. This has always been one of the chief planks in the Arab political platform, and it will be seen from paragraph 8 of the Mufti's memorandum of 27th December, 1934,* that this is still the first demand of the Arabs and that they demand, in addition, a law prohibiting the transfer of any plot of land to any person whatever unless the owner retains for himself 130 dunums for the maintenance of his family.

* enclosed in (2) in 75072/35.

4. As regards the problem of land speculation, the Arabs have never betrayed any enthusiasm for restrictive measures. In fact, the opposition to the restrictive provisions of the Land Transfer Ordinance of 1920, which led to its repeal within twelve months, emanated primarily from the Arabs*, who suspected the Land Transfer Ordinance as a device for cheapening the market price of land and so making it easier for Jews to buy and less profitable for Arabs to sell. In his memorandum of 27th December, the Mufti makes no suggestion for restricting land speculation, though he comments on the fact that the present high market price of land "allures" Arab smallholders to sell their

* See page 51 of the Report on the disturbances of May, 1921 (Cmd.1540) and Sir H. Samuel's telegram of 22nd November, 1921, in 58411/21.

their properties.

5. The Jews, on the other hand, have always vigorously opposed any Government control over the disposition of land with a view to restricting Jewish purchase of land from Arabs. It is true that they swallowed the Land Transfer Ordinance of 1920, but this Ordinance was hardly in operation sufficiently long to hamper Jewish activities, and we know from Sir H. Samuel's telegram of 22nd November, 1921, that they were as glad as the Arabs to see that Ordinance repealed. It may be taken for granted, broadly speaking, that the Jewish policy is to obtain ownership of as much land in Palestine as possible in the shortest possible time and to fill that land with Jews; and that they do not regard it as a matter of concern to themselves that the small Arab landowner should be converted into a town-worker with no security for his livelihood in times of depression.

6. As regards land speculation, there are signs that responsible Jewish bodies, such as the Jewish Agency, are genuinely worried, especially as regards the situation in urban areas, e.g., Tel Aviv, Haifa and Jerusalem. The high market price of land prejudices the activities of the Jewish Agency and other Jewish colonising bodies and a crash is regarded as inevitable unless official action is taken to stem the tide. In this connection the three articles in the "Palestine Post"*, of which copies are enclosed in

* we had already seen these.

in the High Commissioner's despatch of 22nd February, are significant; but it will be noted that these articles, though they refer to the possibility of the re-introduction of certain of the provisions of the Land Transfer Ordinance of 1920, make little or no reference to the desirability of protecting the small Arab landowner and are concerned (so far as action is suggested) merely with the prevention of speculation in agricultural and urban land. The High Commissioner's suggestion in paragraph 2 of his despatch that these articles indicate that "the situation (by which he means the situation arising out of the continued sale of land by Arabs to Jews) is also engaging the attention of Jewish individuals or bodies" cannot therefore be sustained. There is really no indication that the Jewish Agency or Jewish opinion generally is at present prepared to consider favourably any restrictions on Jewish purchase of land from Arabs, except - as contemplated by Sir John Hope-Simpson and stoutly maintained by the Jews in the discussions arising out of the White Paper of 1930 - as part of a comprehensive development scheme, which would result in making more agricultural land available not only for Arabs, but for settlement of Jews. This is borne out by the passages marked in paragraphs 9 and 10 of the report of the High Commissioner's interview on 12th February with representatives of the Jewish Agency.*

* Enclosure II in No. 3 in 75072/35.

Past

Past attempts at solution of the problem.

7. It will be convenient at this stage to indicate briefly the action which has been taken and the proposals that have been made in past years to solve the double problem under discussion:-

(a) <u>Land speculation.</u>

* Para. 2.

As noted above*, apart from the shortlived Land Transfer Ordinance of 1920, no steps have been taken to check land speculation. This aspect of the problem has naturally assumed importance only intermittently. There was a shortlived land boom in 1925-26 followed by a period of depression in which Jewish unemployment caused a certain amount of trouble and expense to the Jewish Agency, but, as far as I can ascertain, no restrictive action was taken or contemplated by the Government. After the disturbances of 1929 Sir John Hope-Simpson reported generally on the land question and the solution which he recommended, viz., a comprehensive development scheme which would have involved Government control for many years over dispositions of land throughout the country, would, if it had been adopted, have provided adequate safeguards against land speculation.

Speculation began again a year or two ago in the urban areas of Tel-Aviv and Haifa and a year ago a Rent Restriction Ordinance was introduced in these two towns. Speculation has since spread to the rural areas, including the hill districts, in which Jewish land purchases had hitherto been negligible, and a

dangerous

dangerous land boom is now in full swing.

(b) <u>Protection of the Arab smallholder</u>.

As already noted, the Land Transfer Ordinance of 1920 required Government approval (i.e., either by the District Commissioner, in the case of small areas, or the High Commissioner, in the case of larger areas) of all dispositions of land, and stipulated that approval should not be given unless the owner retained an area sufficient for the maintenance of himself and his family. This provision was, however, repealed in 1921.

8. Sir John Hope-Simpson's investigations clarified the situation and, in the light of a careful calculation of the total amount of cultivable land in relation to the numbers and prospective increase of the Arab rural population, emphasised the serious dangers arising out of unrestricted purchase of land by the Jews. Sir John Hope-Simpson indicated a constructive solution of the problem, viz., a Government controlled scheme of development covering the whole country, by means of which the land might be put into condition for intensive methods of agriculture, and which by reducing the amount of land required for an individual holding, would make more land available both for Arabs and Jews. Sir J. Hope-Simpson made it clear that such a scheme would involve years of work and would cost many millions of pounds and that, while the scheme was being worked out, it would be essential that Government should have complete control over dispositions of land in order that the harmony of the scheme might not be jeopardised.

9. The main principles of the Hope-Simpson scheme

scheme were adopted in the White Paper of 1930 but, mainly for financial reasons, the scope of the scheme was restricted. A development a loan of 2½ million pounds only was proposed and it was expected that this would allow of the resettlement of the "displaced" Arabs and possibly for the settlement of a small number of Jewish families in addition.

10. Mr. French was appointed Director of Development for the purpose of working out the details of such a scheme but, in view of the increasing financial stringency in this country, it was decided shortly after Mr. French's appointment to reduce expenditure still further to one million pounds.

11. Eventually it was decided (see Cabinet memorandum of 1st February, 1933*) to abandon any idea of a comprehensive development scheme in view of the uncertainty of world economic conditions and financial stringency at home; and to confine action to the raising of a loan of 2 million pounds to cover the cost of resettling the 889 families of "displaced" Arabs and certain urgent public works. It was decided to restrict land legislation to certain necessary amendments of the Protection of Cultivators Ordinance in the interests of tenant cultivators and to take no action for the present to prevent owner-occupiers from selling their land. This decision was in conformity with the decision of the Director of Development not to register owner-occupiers as "landless" Arabs.

12. It may be noted here that Mr. French, in his reports, recommended the enactment of two Ordinances, one the Occupancy Tenants Ordinance to protect tenants and

* C.P.16 (33) - copy under No.2 in 17272/1/33.

and the other, the Homestead Protection Ordinance, which would prevent an owner-occupier or occupancy-tenant from parting with a minimum "homestead area". The object of ~~the former~~ Ordinance was secured by the new Protection of Cultivators Ordinance, to which reference has already been made, and, in accordance with the decision not to legislate in the case of owner-occupiers, the Homestead Protection Ordinance was not adopted.

Sir Arthur Wauchope's proposal.

13. Early in 1933 when the Secretary of State visited Palestine, the High Commissioner indicated that he had changed his views as to the necessity for protecting the Arab smallholder and thought that such action might soon be necessary. The Secretary of State thought that legislation of this nature might be difficult to justify and said that he would probably find it necessary to consult the Cabinet and that he would require some reasonable estimate of the amount of land which the proposed legislation would withhold from the market.

* (3) in 75072/35.

14. In his despatch of 22nd February, 1935,* Sir Arthur Wauchope gives a general outline of his proposal, which is to re-enact, subject to various modifications, some of the provisions of the Land Transfer Ordinance of 1920. A copy of the Ordinance is enclosed in the High Commissioner's despatch.

15. It will be seen from the preamble that the object of the restrictive provisions of the Ordinance

of

of 1920 was twofold, (1) to prevent speculative dealings in land and (2) to protect the present occupants.

16. For this purpose the control of all dispositions of immovable property was placed in the hands of District Governors (as regards areas not exceeding 300 dunums in the case of agricultural land and 30 dunums in the case of urban land) and in the hands of the High Commissioner (as regards larger areas). Apart from this general control, the Ordinance contained provisions specifically directed against (1) land speculation and (2) eviction of the present occupants.

17. As to (1), the chief restrictions were

(a) that the purchaser must be resident in Palestine;

(b) that he must not obtain an area exceeding £3,000 in value, or larger than 300 dunums (agricultural) and 30 dunums (urban), except in such special cases as might be approved by the High Commissioner himself;

(c) that the purchaser must himself cultivate or develop the land immediately;

(d) that approval of a disposition might be withheld if the land had been sold or otherwise disposed of within a year and the seller failed to give a satisfactory reason for wishing again to dispose of it.

18. As to (2), the chief provision was that approval for a disposition of land would not be given unless

unless the District Governors were satisfied that in the case of agricultural land either the person transferring the property, if he were in possession, or the tenant in occupancy, if the property were leased, would retain sufficient land in the district or elsewhere for the maintenance of himself and his family.

19. The Ordinance provided that every disposition, to which the consent of the Administration had not been obtained, should be null and void, and that, if any person entered into possession of such land or permitted the other party to enter into possession, he should be liable to a fine not exceeding one-fourth of the property.

20. The other provisions of the Ordinance are either irrelevant to our present purpose or of little importance.

21. The High Commissioner's despatch contains only the barest outline of the new legislation which he has in mind. He devotes little attention to the question of preventing land speculation and his main object is clearly to secure a modicum of protection for the small Arab landowner. In this connection, his proposals may be summarised as follows:-

(a) The new Ordinance should apply to the whole of Palestine except

    (i) the Beersheba Sub-district;

    (ii) urban areas; and

    (iii) land already planted with citrus.

The grounds for these exceptions are given in the despatch.

    (i) The grounds for exclusion of Beersheba are

are not exactly convincing but there is little doubt
that the High Commissioner's hope is by this means to
lessen Jewish opposition, since it is known that the
Jewish organisations are planning schemes of
colonisation in that sub-district.

(ii) The exclusion of urban areas makes it
perfectly clear that the High Commissioner is not at
the moment concerning himself to any extent with the
problem of land speculation, which is even more acute
in the urban areas than in the country.

(iii) The reason for the exclusion of land already
planted with citrus is not clearly stated, but it is
probable that very little, if any, of such land is
in the hands of small Arab owners.

(b) The sanction of the District Commissioner
should be required for transactions in property up
to a maximum area of 1,000 dunums, but that the High
Commissioner (compare Section 8 of the 1920 Ordinance)
should have discretion to sanction larger transactions
for special purposes. Paragraph 8(d) of the despatch
is somewhat difficult to understand, but I take it
to mean that the Ordinance will be so worded as to
make it clear that the District Commissioner or the
High Commissioner will invariably approve transactions
provided that the condition as to the retention of
a "subsistence area" is fulfilled.

(c) The District Commissioners should be empowered
to sanction purchases by <u>Jewish national bodies</u> without
any limit of area, provided that the transactions
otherwise comply with the terms of the Ordinance.

22.

22. As regards land speculation the High Commissioner's only suggestion is (paragraph 8(c)) that provision should be made for the imposition of some penalty, probably in the form of a tax, on persons who, having acquired land under the condition that they intend to cultivate or develop the land immediately, fail to do so. It may be assumed that the High Commissioner has no intention at present of re-introducing the other provisions against land speculation which appeared in the Ordinance of 1920 (see para. 17 above).

Possible criticism of High Commissioner's proposal.

23. It has been noted above that the High Commissioner's despatch is almost entirely confined to the question of the protection of the small Arab landowner and it is only necessary to consider possible criticisms of his proposal under that head.

A. <u>Jewish criticism</u>.

The Jews have always fought against any purely negative restrictions on the purchase of land, and the justice of their contention in this respect was practically admitted in the Prime Minister's letter of 1931, in which the Prime Minister was at pains to refute the contention that the White Paper of 1930 implied the intention to prohibit the acquisition of additional land by the Jews. Paragraph 13 of the Prime Minister's letter contains the following:-

"The

"The statement of policy of His Majesty's Government did not imply the prohibition of acquisition of additional land by Jews. It contains no such prohibition, nor is any such intended. What it does contemplate is such <u>temporary</u> control of land, disposition and transfers as may be necessary not to impair the harmony and effectiveness of the scheme of land settlement to be undertaken."

The following passage appears in paragraph 12:-

"In giving effect to the policy of land settlement .... it is necessary .... that there should exist some <u>centralised control of transactions</u> relating to the acquisition and transfer of land during such interim period as may probably be necessary to place the development scheme upon a sure foundation. The power contemplated is regulative and not prohibitory, although it does involve a power to prevent transactions which are inconsistent with the tenure of the scheme.......... <u>The centralised control will take effect as from such a date only as the authority charged with the duty of carrying out the policy of land development shall begin to operate.</u> The High Commissioner will, pending the establishment of such centralised control, have full powers to take all steps necessary to protect the tenancy and occupancy rights, including the rights of squatters throughout Palestine."

24. Though

24. Though the control which the High Commissioner now contemplates is limited to agricultural areas (excluding planted citrus lands and the Beersheba Sub-district) and although it is proposed that the single purpose of the control shall be to ensure that the owner retains a "subsistence area", it seems probable that the Jews will resist the proposed measure on principle, except as a concomitant of a development scheme, taking their stand on the wording of the Prime Minister's letter. The marked passages in paragraphs 9 and 10 of the record of the High Commissioner's interview with the Jewish Agency* confirm this view.

* Enclosure IV.

25. It will, I think, be very difficult to answer any such contention, both because of its essential reasonableness (and as to this the Jews can invoke Sir John Hope-Simpson) and because of the undertakings given in the Prime Minister's letter. As to the Prime Minister's letter, in the first draft of the Cabinet memorandum of 1933* an attempt was made to justify legislation for the protection of the small owner (which was at that time contemplated) as consistent with the Prime Minister's letter, but the suggested defence is almost too subtle for practical use, and, if the High Commissioner's proposal is to be adopted, there seems to be no alternative to admitting that it goes beyond the Prime Minister's letter. This will be difficult to justify

* Appendix I.C. of No. 3 in 97072/32 Secret.

justify since the problem with which we are dealing is of long standing and is really inherent in the present policy, whereby the expansion of the Jewish national home is limited merely by the Government's control over immigration; immigration is determined by economic absorptive capacity; economic absorptive capacity is calculated by/unemployment returns and labour vacancies; and the Government imposes no <u>territorial</u> limitation on the expansion of the Jewish national home either by controlling land purchase or by marking out definite areas for Jewish and Arab development.

26. The only justification for taking action now (viz., control of land transfers without a development scheme) which the Prime Minister said would not be taken in 1931, is not that a new problem has arisen, but that the necessity for dealing with an old problem has become more pressing owing to the recent acceleration of Jewish immigration and land purchase.

27. Such a defence does not, however, answer the contention that the most effective way of dealing with the problem (and one that would do justice to the mandatory rights of both Jews and Arabs) is a Government control/development scheme on the lines advocated by Sir John Hope-Simpson. In 1932 the decision (after consultation of the French reports) not to proceed with the development scheme contemplated in the White Paper of 1930 was influenced by three main

main considerations:-

 (a) The financial position in this country.

 (b) The world depression which involved the risk that no markets would be found for the increased production which the development scheme would imply.*

 (c) The financial position of Palestine which, though improving, was still uncertain.

* Mr. French stressed this difficulty in his reports.

28. As to (a) and (c), the financial position of Palestine has now so far improved that it would probably be possible to embark upon a development scheme without assistance from Imperial funds, although this would necessitate the retardation of the numerous public works which are now in progress in Palestine or are in contemplation.

29. The difficulty (b) still remains, but could be met by a careful regulation of the speed of development under Government control. It must be remembered that Sir John Hope-Simpson contemplated that his development scheme would involve "years of work" (page 143) during which it would be essential that Government should have complete control over dispositions of land. Such control, however, as an essential part of a development policy could, however, as Sir J. Hope-Simpson saw clearly, be defended against the criticism which Jews and their supporters in this country would certainly make against a merely negative control (e.g. by formation of "Arab reserves", or such reservation of "Arab homestead areas" as now contemplated or a complete prohibition of further

Jewish

Jewish land purchases). Such negative control involves to a greater or less extent the "crystallisation" of the Jewish national home which (the Jews maintain) would have such a deplorable psychological effect on world Jewry that contributions would cease and the Jewish national home would collapse.

3. B. <u>Arab criticism</u>.

It seems clear from the terms of the Mufti's memorandum of 27th December that the High Commissioner's proposal as regards the smallowners will by no means satisfy Arab opinion, which demands complete prohibition of further sales of land by Arabs to Jews. The Arabs will also maintain (and with some justice)

(a) that a measure to secure the retention of a homestead area by the smallowner is not enough, as no allowance is made for increase of population; and

(b) that (as maintained by the Arabs in the case of the Protection of Cultivators Ordinance) the proposed measure will be useless since the Jews will bribe the owners to abandon their homestead areas.

It might be possible to meet both these criticisms to some extent

(a) by requiring the owner to keep more than enough land for one family, and

(b) by placing all homestead areas under State control with a provision that, if not cultivated by the owner, they should revert to State ownership within a certain period. This would prevent the Jewish purchaser from entering upon the homestead area

if

if it were abandoned and might make it not worth while for him to attempt to bribe the owner to leave it.

31. To sum up:— If, as a matter of tactics, the High Commissioner (and he is the best judge) thinks that the situation will be eased by the proposed legislation for the protection of the Arab landowner, it would seem advisable to let him have his way, but the indications are

(i) that the Arabs will regard such legislation as inadequate and that the bitterness of Arab feeling will not be appreciably assuaged;

(ii) that the Jews will object to any such legislation except as part of a development scheme, and that, if they see that this legislation is inevitable, they will endeavour to steer discussion towards the scheme which the Jewish Agency adumbrated in 1930*, and which they outlined as follows:-

* see minutes on 97248/32.

"As an illustration of the methods for putting such a policy into effect, we would suggest the formation under the auspices of the Jewish Agency of a suitably equipped Irrigation and Settlement Company for the development on a comprehensive scale of intensive methods of cultivation on the holdings of Fellaheen who are willing to exchange part of their land for the irrigation and other improvement schemes carried out by the Company; the Palestine Administration to supervise that the value of loans so effected are in proper and economic

relation

relation to that of the land disposed of by the peasant, and generally to demand such safeguards as may be deemed necessary in the interests of the rural community as a whole, the surplus thus concentrated in the hands of the said Company to be used for Jewish close settlement."

This, of course, is not the kind of development scheme which was contemplated by Sir John Hope-Simpson and by His Majesty's Government in the White Paper of 1930 and would arouse intense Arab opposition.

(iii) That it will be difficult to defend the High Commissioner's proposal against responsible critics as a attempt to grapple with the problem, which is not a new one and was thoroughly ventilated in Sir John Hope-Simpson's report and in the White Paper of 1930.

9.07

THIS DOCUMENT IS THE PROPERTY OF HIS BRITANNIC MAJESTY'S GOVERNMENT

Printed for the Cabinet. January 1936.

SECRET.

Copy No. 59

C.P. 3 (36).

CABINET.

PALESTINE.

ARAB GRIEVANCES.

Memorandum by the Secretary of State for the Colonies.

I CIRCULATE as Appendices to this memorandum—

A memorandum submitted jointly by five Arab political parties in Palestine to the High Commissioner setting out their grievances against His Majesty's Government and their demands for measures to be taken to safeguard the interests of the Arab community. (Appendix I.)

Three despatches in which Sir Arthur Wauchope comments on the general situation in Palestine and on the demands made by the Arabs in their memorandum. (Appendices II, III and IV.)

At the interview on the 25th November, 1935, when the Arab leaders submitted their memorandum, they informed the High Commissioner that, unless they received a reply to their memorandum which could be generally regarded as giving satisfaction to their requests, they would lose all influence with their followers, extreme and irresponsible counsels would prevail and the political situation would rapidly deteriorate. The High Commissioner has himself emphasized the importance of receiving at the earliest possible moment such a reply as will enable him to give some satisfaction to the Arab leaders, as he thinks that they are right in saying that otherwise they will lose such influence as they now possess, and that the possibility will then disappear of alleviating the present situation by means of the measures which the High Commissioner recommends should be taken.

2. The leaders of the Arab parties have arranged to meet again on the 15th January, and, unless they can be sufficiently reassured as to the attitude and intentions of His Majesty's Government, the High Commissioner considers that there is every indication that trouble will occur at some time after the date of that meeting. Though he does not at present fear riots on a large scale, Sir Arthur Wauchope thinks it right to say that in the present state of tension untoward incidents might cause considerable disturbances.

3. The principal demands made by the Arab leaders in their memorandum fall under three heads.

(a) "*The establishment of a democratic government in the country in accordance with the terms of the Covenant of the League of Nations and in execution of the second part of Article 2 of the Palestine Mandate.*"

4. As to this, I am circulating to the Cabinet a separate memorandum dealing with the proposals for setting up a Legislative Council in Palestine.

[12550] B

(b) *That Jewish immigration should be stopped immediately.*

5. Clearly no such demand can be entertained, but it is a fact that the economic future of Palestine is becoming more and more obscure and the difficulty of forecasting the consequences of the remarkable increase in recent years in Jewish immigration is enhanced by the present uncertainty as regards the international situation. In Sir Arthur Wauchope's opinion, it is necessary on economic grounds alone that there should be some slowing down in the pace of Jewish immigration, which has risen from about 30,000 in 1933 to about 60,000 in 1935. The High Commissioner has accordingly felt it necessary to aim at a total immigration for 1936 of about 44,000, although this figure may, in his opinion, well prove too high if even a small economic set-back should occur. He has, in consequence, decided to authorize a labour schedule (*i.e.*, for wage-earners) for the current half-year ending the 31st March next of 3,250 immigration certificates. Application by the Jewish Agency for this schedule had been considerably delayed owing to the temporary economic dislocation and unemployment arising from the bank panic last autumn but 1,000 certificates on account of this schedule were issued in advance during November last.

6. The High Commissioner also proposes to impose certain restrictions on the immigration of dependants in order to check the inflow of unselected and unskilled immigrants, who would be among the first to suffer unemployment in the event of any economic set-back.

7. A third measure which Sir Arthur Wauchope has in mind is to increase from £1,000 to £2,000 the qualifying capital, the possession of which enables an immigrant to enter the country without any quota restriction. Sir Arthur Wauchope considers that, owing to the abnormally high cost of land and the rise in rents and labour charges, an immigrant cannot now count upon an assured prospect of permanent establishment in the country with so small a capital as £1,000. On this point I informed him by telegraph on the 2nd January that I approved of his discussing the proposal with the local representatives of the Jewish Agency, and that while I was disposed to agree with his proposal, I should prefer not to take any final decision pending receipt of a further report from him after his discussion with representatives of the Agency.

(c) *The prohibition by law of the transfer of Arab lands to Jews.*

8. Leaving aside the political motives which have led to this demand, the High Commissioner, who has been feeling anxiety on the subject for some time past, has reached the conclusion that an economic situation is rapidly being created by the progressive transfer of agricultural land from Arab to Jewish hands, which, if no remedy is applied, will lead to very undesirable consequences.

9. Measures have already been taken to prevent agricultural tenants from being evicted when the estates of which their holdings form a part change ownership. There are, however, now strong indications that the Jews are to an increasing extent buying land in comparatively small plots from owners who cultivate their own land. The Arab agriculturist is notoriously improvident and tends, after squandering the purchase money of his land, to seek employment in the towns. Under present economic conditions no serious ill-effects of this tendency are yet visible, but, unless there should be some fundamental change of Jewish policy, the process of land purchase may be expected to continue, if it is not checked, until practically the whole of the agricultural land of the country which it is profitable for the Jews to buy has passed into Jewish hands, with the exception of the citrus estates of relatively large Arab landowners, with the result that the urban population will be increased by many thousands of Arabs seeking employment as wage-earners who would constitute a serious social and economic problem in the event of any considerable check to the possibly abnormal prosperity which the country is at present enjoying.

10. The High Commissioner urges that it is the duty of Government under the Mandate to take some positive action which will have the effect of protecting the small Arab landowner, and he recommends that he should be authorised to

enact legislation to that end. He proposes that this legislation should not apply to—

(a) The Beersheba Sub-District, where land is comparatively plentiful and the population comparatively scanty;
(b) Urban areas;
(c) Land already planted with citrus.

But as regards the rest of Palestine he proposes that no landowner should be permitted to sell any of his land unless he retains a minimum area sufficient to afford him and his family a means of subsistence. This minimum area would be inalienable and would revert to Government should the owner-occupier for any reason desert his holding and cease to cultivate it.

11. Information is not yet available as to the extent to which such a restriction would limit the further purchase of agricultural land by the Jews, as the minimum subsistence area will naturally vary in extent from one locality to another and the details of the scheme have yet to be worked out. It would, however, I think, be wise to assume that the imposition of such a restriction would result in withholding from the market a very considerable proportion of agricultural land at present in Arab ownership.

12. In any event the High Commissioner's proposals will be strongly attacked by the Jews as imposing an artificial check upon the development of the Jewish National Home, and it may even be contended that to do so would be a violation of the terms of the letter written to Dr. Weizmann by Mr. Ramsay MacDonald, as Prime Minister, on the 13th February, 1931. Apart, however, from the fact that important areas of Palestine would be expressly excepted from the scope of the proposed legislation, it must be borne in mind that Mr. Ramsay MacDonald's assurances were given with specific reference to the policy of land settlement and development referred to in the White Paper of October 1930. In fact, the whole letter is described in the opening paragraph as " the authoritative interpretation of the White Paper on the matters with which this letter deals." In the relevant paragraphs of his letter Mr. Ramsay MacDonald was concerned to reassure the Jews on one special point, viz., that such a policy of land settlement would not be used as an excuse for imposing for an ulterior purpose restrictions upon land transactions which would be more than what was required for the purposes of carrying out that policy. His assurances could not be interpreted as debarring His Majesty's Government indefinitely from taking any action which, even if no development or resettlement were in view, might be considered necessary in the general interests of Palestine at some future date and in the face of developments which had not then assumed any serious prominence.

13. It will be observed that the High Commissioner's proposal introduces an entirely new principle. The legislation which has been enacted to protect tenants can be justified by the practice at home; whereas legislation to protect owners against themselves is an entire innovation. But the answer given by Sir Arthur Wauchope is that the Mandate demands that he should protect the interests of all sections of the community, and he believes that this proposal is necessary in order to do so.

(Initialled) J. H. T.

*Colonial Office, Downing Street,
January 10, 1936.*

APPENDIX 1.

Translation of the Arab Memorandum handed to the High Commissioner for Palestine on November 25, 1935.

His Excellency the High Commissioner,
Government Offices, Jerusalem.

Your Excellency,

THE British Government announced recently, through its Representative at the League of Nations, that it was prepared to use all the forces at its disposal in order to uphold the Covenant of the League of Nations. It has expressed its eagerness before the public opinion to protect the independence of Abyssinia and its preparedness to defend that independence, in furtherance of the cause of right and justice, as an act of support to weak nations which have been the object of aggression. It even expressed its willingness to embark, if necessary, on any adventure in defence of the principles of humanity which are represented in the League of Nations.

But in Palestine, the contrary has been the case. Here the British Government disregarded the pledges which were made to the Arabs, did not take the Covenant of the League of Nations into account and overlooked the principles of humanity which are based on justice and equity. It exceeds every limit in depriving the Arabs of Palestine of the right of independence and trespasses upon their economical and administrative rights in order to facilitate the establishment of a National Home for the Jews.

It will be recalled that the British Government undertook in 1915, through its Representative, Sir Henry McMahon, to recognize and support the independence of Arab countries, including Palestine, within the limits which were laid down at the time by the late King (then Sherif) Hussain, in his capacity as representative of the Arabs, in consideration for the heavy blood which was shed by the Arabs, including Palestinian Arabs, during the Great War on the side of the Allies.

The Great War did not come to an end except after the Allies have acknowledged for all nations the principle of self-determination as was announced recently by His Majesty's Secretary of State for Foreign Affairs before the League of Nations. In the case of Palestine, however, Great Britain not only failed to apply this principle but completely ignored it in furtherance of the establishment of the National Home for the Jews.

Even if we disregard all these factors and take into consideration the Covenant of the League of Nations, for the maintenance of which His Majesty's Government has expressed its preparedness to make every sacrifice, it will appear, beyond doubt, that as regards Palestine, His Majesty's Government has dishonestly infringed that Covenant. Article 22 of the Covenant recognized the independence of such countries which formerly belonged to the Turkish Empire subject to a temporary Mandate in the form of advice and assistance to be rendered by the Mandatory until such time as these countries, within which Palestine was included, are able to stand alone. The British Government, however, failed to apply this express provision, on the ground that it was inconsistent with the Balfour Declaration of 1917, which is, in itself, repugnant to the Article of the Covenant quoted above. That Declaration should have been abrogated by virtue of Article 19 of the Covenant, under which members of the League severally accepted the Covenant as abrogating all obligations or understandings *inter se* which are inconsistent with its terms. On the contrary, the British Government has gone as far as to trespass on the rights of the Arabs which were fully safeguarded, both in the Balfour Declaration and in the Mandate and which were interpreted by the Mandatory Power, through

5

Sir Herbert Samuel, the ardent Zionist, in its Report on the Administration of Palestine for 1920-21 in the following terms:—

"The measures to foster the well-being of the Arabs should be precisely those which we should adopt in Palestine if there were no Zionist question and if there had been no Balfour Declaration."

He also added:—

"In a word, the degree to which Jewish national aspiration can be fulfilled in Palestine is conditioned by the rights of the present inhabitants."

Taking the present form of Government which exists in Palestine, it will be found that it consists of a British Government which is under the Mandate of another British Government in London. There does not exist in the country any form of independence of whatever nature, the establishment of which is required by the Covenant of the League of Nations and the terms of the Balfour Declaration which restrain the British Government, in the application of the Declaration, from doing anything which may prejudice the rights of the Arabs and from taking any step which may be inconsistent with their interest.

For the last eighteen years the Arabs have been demanding a fair and equitable treatment. They entertained the hope that His Majesty's Government will ultimately realize the futility of its policy and its consequences and will abandon such policy. But all these hopes were frustrated as this wrong policy is still applied, injustice is still meted out to the people and justice and equity are persistently ignored or violated. The present form of Government may serve as the best example. After all this long period that has already passed, the inhabitants of the country have no effective say in the Administration which is maintained, as it does by the bayonets of the Mandatory Government, irrespective of the will of the people and in a manner inconsistent with their interests. In these circumstances, while not recognizing the Mandate which was imposed upon us, we demand the establishment of a democratic Government in the country in accordance with the terms of the Covenant of the League of Nations and in execution of the second part of Article 2 of the Palestine Mandate.

Lands.

Sir John Hope Simpson, the British Expert, who was delegated by the British Government in 1930 to investigate into Immigration, Land Settlement and Development, and whose views were corroborated by Mr. Lewis French in his report for 1931, calculated the lot-viable for an Arab family at 130 dunums. He found out that the cultivable land which was in possession of the Arabs at the time (*i.e.*, 1930) would not afford an average lot in excess of 90 dunums. Since that time, the number of the Arab population has increased by not less than 150,000 and the area of land in possession of the Arabs decreased, through acquisition by the Jews, by not less than 600,000; thus the area of the average holding of an Arab family was greatly reduced.

As the best illustration of the precarious position of the Arabs, notwithstanding the insufficiency of the land in their possession, the letter which Mr. Hankin, a Jewish Land Expert and agent of the Palestine Land Development Company, addressed to Mr. French in July 1930 may be quoted. Mr. Hankin admitted this fact in the following terms:—

". . . . but we have possibility of acquiring 100,000 dunums without having to make any settlement for the tenants, since the acquisition of such an area will not cause harm to anybody and will not oust anybody from his land; only after this area has been acquired we shall have to see to a proper settlement for the tenants. . . . ."

Since that express admission was made, an additional area of 600,000 dunums was acquired by the Jews. It will be seen that taking the admission of the Jews themselves Government is under a duty to stop any further transfer of lands from the Arabs to Jews.

Any person who studies the conditions of Palestine and the speedy developments which are taking place whereby the Arabs are continually dispossessed of their land and Arab villages supplanted by Jewish Settlements (the names of some of which were published at occasions in the Palestine Gazette, while the names of others were deliberately not published) will come to the conclusion that the destiny of the Arab people of Palestine, as a whole, would not be dissimilar to that of the inhabitants of these villages who were dispossessed of their land and whose villages were supplanted by Jewish Settlements in which the Arabs have no traces.

The acquisition of such large areas of land by Jews and the eviction of the people therefrom does not only prejudicially affect the owners of the lands who are displaced; it also destructively affects the neighbouring Arab towns which, before the eviction of the inhabitants of the villages, are usually flourishing and exchange with the neighbouring villagers the sale of all kinds of goods, commodities and trade and live in co-operation with one another. Nazareth may be quoted as an example. Most of the places of business in this town were closed and its trade became stagnant as soon as the Jews acquired the plain of Esdraelon and its villages, evicted the Arab inhabitants therefrom and established for themselves special markets from which the Arabs derive no benefit.

It is the practice of Jewish organizations to create the lands which they acquire as a trust to be held as the inalienable property of the Jewish people. They impose on the cultivator a condition not to employ on the land but Jewish labour, failing which he will be liable to various penalties. These facts were confirmed, by evidence, by Sir John Hope Simpson in his Report and admitted by the Jewish Agency.

That this is the case is shown by paragraph 19 of the White Paper, 1930, which reads, in part :—

". . . . Moreover, the effect of Jewish colonization on the existing population is very intimately affected by the conditions on which the various Jewish bodies hold, utilize and lease their land. It is provided by the Constitution of the Enlarged Jewish Agency, signed at Zurich on the 14th August, 1929 (Article 3 (*d*) and (*e*)), that the land acquired shall be held as the 'inalienable property of the Jewish people,' and that in 'all the works or undertakings carried out or furthered by the Agency, it shall be deemed to be a matter of principle that Jewish labour shall be employed.' Moreover, by Article 23 of the draft lease, which it is proposed to execute in respect of all holdings granted by the Jewish National Fund, the lessee undertakes to execute all works connected with the cultivation of the holdings only with Jewish labour."

Under the circumstances described above, every plot of land in Palestine which is transferred to Jewish bodies is definitely extra-territorialized. It ceases to be land from which the Arab can gain any advantage either now or at any time in the future, nor can he ever hope to cultivate it, but he is deprived for ever from employment on that land and from purchasing or acquiring it at any time. It follows, therefore, that if alienation of Arab lands continues and the Jews were able to acquire the largest part or all of the lands of Palestine, that will definitely mean that Palestine, as a whole, would be alienated for ever and the Arab people will not be able, under the stringent conditions laid down by Jewish bodies, either to reacquire any part of such land or to derive any advantage therefrom through employment or otherwise.

It will appear from the above that the position of the Arabs in Palestine, from the land point of view, is very precarious and threatened with danger. Any person who carefully studies this situation will necessarily come to the conclusion that the question of land in Palestine is governed by an oppressive and premeditated policy which will result, sooner or later, in the expropriation of the Arabs from their lands, in their dispersion, and in the undermining of their national structure in order to instal on their ruins a national home for the Jews. It is a matter of surprise that Government should have failed to enforce the recommendations of the Commissions of Enquiry and British experts who were delegated by the Mandatory Government to enquire into the land problem, although they have all shown, at least implicitly, that the Arabs were facing such a danger. Failure of Government to enforce these recommendations shows that it follows a laid down policy which is calculated to annihilate the Arabs and to expropriate them, for ever, from their country.

This situation prompts us to strongly assert the demand which has been repeatedly made that a law be issued prohibiting the transfer of Arab lands to Jews, and that a further law be made, similar to the Five Feddans Law of Egypt, which should also be made applicable to transactions between Arabs themselves.

7

Immigration.

The British Government declared its intention, in the White Paper of 1922, to regulate immigration so that—
  (i) Immigration will not exceed the economic absorptive capacity of the country.
  (ii) Immigrants will not become a burden on the country as a whole.
  (iii) Immigrants will not deprive any of the existing population of his employment.

The number of immigrants who entered Palestine in that year (*i.e.*, 1922) amounted to 6,341, but by 1925 their number reached the high figure of 33,000, on the assumption that such number of immigrants was not in excess of the economic capacity of the country. But the crisis which prevailed in the country in 1926 and the following years has shown that this assumption was unfounded. Sir John Campbell, an acknowledged authority on economics, who was delegated by the Zionist organization to report on the economic conditions in Palestine, stated in his report that the crisis of 1927 and 1928 was due " to the fact that immigrants have come into Palestine in excess of the economic absorptive power of the country." Again, in the Annual Report on the Administration of Palestine for 1928, it was stated that—

"Palestine still suffered . . . . from the repercussions of the uneconomic immigration of 1925. . . . ."

Referring to the period between 1922–29, during which period the annual average of Jewish immigrants was 8,000 only, the Parliamentary Commission of Enquiry of 1929 confirmed in its report that—

" . . . . there is incontestable evidence that in the matter of immigration, there has been a serious departure . . . . from the doctrine accepted . . . . in 1922, that immigration should be regulated by the economic capacity of the country to absorb new arrivals."

In its recommendations the Commission said—

"Immigration should be reviewed with the object of preventing a repetition of the excessive immigration of 1925 and 1926."

But notwithstanding all this evidence, which proves beyond any doubt the futility of the policy which was adopted during that period during which the average number of Jewish immigrants was not more than 8,000 per year, the Palestine Government, acting again under the assumption that the economic capacity of the country can absorb new immigrants, opened the gates of the country, before the immigrants, to the extent that the number of immigrants who were admitted last year was 42,359, exclusive of the illicit immigrants, which according to the statement made by His Excellency the High Commissioner in a speech which he made at Nablus, in 1933, is not much less than that of legal immigrants. The admission of such a large number of immigrants will not only place the country in a difficult position as a result of the wrongful policy of Government, but is inconsistent with rules (i) and (ii), quoted above, which were laid down by the British Government in 1922 for the purpose of regulating immigration.

Furthermore, the attitude taken by Jewish immigrants in compelling Arab labourers through their pickets and organizations to leave their employment in Jewish Settlements and places is sufficient to show that such immigration has resulted in the violation of rule (ii) referred to above.

This immigration is not only in contravention of the doctrines laid down in the White Paper of 1922, but is also inconsistent with Article 6 of the Mandate, which imposes that the "administration of Palestine, while ensuring that the rights and position of other sections of the population are not prejudiced, shall facilitate Jewish immigration under suitable conditions." This provision means that not only the economic and administrative rights of the original inhabitants should not be prejudiced, but also their general position as constituting the overwhelming majority of the population. Indeed, Government statistics show that this "Arab majority" is being continually affected by the increase of Jewish immigration, and, should immigration be not stopped, it will disappear altogether.

8

The difficulty of the present position and the bad consequences which may ensue in future may be illustrated by the statement contained in the Report on the Census of Palestine, 1931. This is a scientific and economic fact which has no bearing on politics. It was stated in that Report that—

"Without these proportionate increases in imported invisible value (foreign contributions) and in internal production of special supplies, surplus to the internal requirements of the country, and so available for sale abroad, it is difficult to see how the rate of increase of subsistence for the population is to keep pace with the growth of the population.

"It is, therefore, of interest to imagine Palestine as maintaining a population at its present rates of increase, but linked to the world only by its small export trade and by its large imports of value . . . . before the population overtakes its means of subsistence."

It may be observed in this connection that the Policy which has been applied by Government in recent years with regard to immigration is calculated to accelerate the prevalence of such a difficult situation.

There is another proof which shows the leniency of Government and its desire to overcrowd the country with Jewish immigrants in order to enable them to become the majority of the population. Government has failed, until now, to take any action with regard to the 6,000 Jews who entered the country in connection with the Macabiad, and, although they delivered their passports to Government and paid the necessary deposits, they remained in the country and failed to leave it until now. We understand that the passports of these persons are still in the Departments of Police and Immigration, who appear to have failed to discover their countries of origin and to repatriate them.

In these circumstances, we demand—
(1) That Jewish immigration be immediately stopped, and that a committee be formed of the competent elements to study the absorptive capacity of the country and to lay down a principle for immigration, as is the case in most countries of the world.
(2) That a law be made requiring every lawful resident in Palestine to hold an identity card to be issued by Government, and to produce such card on demand by any officer of Government in order to ascertain whether or not he was lawfully admitted to Palestine.
(3) That effective immediate investigations be made into the question of immigrants who illicitly entered the country or who entered on valid endorsements for a limited period, but remained in the country.

Effect of Immigration on Public Morality.

This immigration has enabled vagabonds and outcasts to enter Palestine, the Holy Land, the land of peace and the birthplace of religions, and to spread in this country their strange doctrines and destructive practices in a manner which reflects on the sanctity of this country. This country is not used to such frightful incidents which daily emanate from Jewish centres, such as the organized acts of brigandage, fraud and forgery, in which some Jewish officers either take a direct part or are responsible for their commission or concealment. There is no doubt that Your Excellency shares our view that this immigration has enabled Communists and Bolsheviks to propagate and disseminate their doctrines not only in Palestine, but to use Palestine as a centre for their activities amongst the Arabs in all parts of the Near East. The manner in which the settlers live in some of the Jewish settlements such as Ain Harod and other settlements is a clear indication that the Jews, headed by the Socialist Party, which has overpowered all the other Jewish Parties, intend, at the end, to overflow this country with subversive doctrines which are inconsistent with religious principles and doctrines of morality.

We take this opportunity to draw Your Excellency's attention to that strange spirit which the Jews propagate amongst the population, and in which they encourage the violation of the law, the defeat of public authorities and the escape of the requirements of the law. The best example which would prove this view is the manner in which they secure the illegal admission of immigrants and thereafter oppose the Police Authorities, whenever they seek the arrest of such immigrants. Individuals as well as bodies co-operate in concealing all such

9

immigrants, as was the case with those persons who entered Palestine as travellers in connection with the Macabiad. which took place at the beginning of this year. and remained in the country, as was admitted by the Department of Immigration. We also wish to refer, on this occasion, to the smuggling of arms and ammunition by Jews which has taken place for some time and which has recently been carried out on a larger scale, challenging as they did the authority of Government and threatening the lives of the Arabs.

In order that a check be put to such activities, we persistently demand that Government should apply the Ordinance which it enacted to meet such cases, such as the Criminal Law (Seditious Offences) Ordinance and the Prevention of Crimes Ordinance, the application of which has hitherto been restricted to the Arabs in unjustifiable cases.

Conclusion.

The Arabs have entertained great hopes when His Excellency Sir Arthur Grenfell Wauchope was appointed as High Commissioner about four years ago. They expected that His Excellency will embark on the application of the reports and recommendations of the various Commissions of Enquiry without any discrimination and in such an equitable manner as may be dictated by his military honour. Unfortunately, their hopes were not realised, for during all these four years of his office, His Excellency continually spoke of self-government, but never fulfilled anything. He opened the gates of the country before Jewish immigration, utterly ignoring the previous experience of the Government and its painful consequences. He facilitated, during that period, the admission of a large number of Jewish immigrants, which exceeds the number which was admitted by his predecessors during fourteen years, and enabled the Jews, during his short time of office, to acquire land which is larger in area than the land acquired by them since the British Occupation. and in so doing he ignored the recommendations of commissions and experts on these matters.

For that reason, we feel ourselves compelled. in our capacity as representatives of the various Arab Parties which represent the Palestine Arab Nation, to express our deepest regret at the frustration of the hopes which we entertained and the non-realization of our expectations and hopes which we had in His Excellency, and at the loss of the confidence of the Arabs who have reached a state of despondency through Your Excellency's policy, although they were inclined to co-operate with you in such a manner as will protect all their rights had they seen a keen desire towards that end on Your Excellency's part.

With highest respects.

(Signed) MOHAMMAD ISHAQ BUDEIRI.
On behalf of the Islah Party.

(Signed) RAGHEB NASHASHIBI.
President, the National Defence Party.

(Signed) ABDULLATIF SALAH.
President. National Block.

(Signed) JAMAL HUSSEINI,
President, Palestine Arab Party.

(Signed) YACOUB GHUSSAIN.
President, Executive Committee. Arab Youngmen Congress.

November 25. 1935.

APPENDIX II.

Secret Despatch from the High Commissioner for Palestine to the Secretary of State for the Colonies, dated December 7, 1935.

(Secret.)
Reference No. CF/409/35.
Sir,   December 7, 1935.

    1. I HAVE the honour to enclose for your consideration a memorandum* signed by Ragheb Nashashibi, President, The National Defence Party, Mohammad Ishaq Budeiri, on behalf of the Islah Party, Jamal Husseini, President, Palestine Arab Party, Abdullatif Salah, President, National Block, and Yacoub Ghussain, President, Executive Committee, Arab Youngmen Congress.

    2. This memorandum was presented to me at the interview which I granted these gentlemen at their request on the 25th November, shortly after my return to Palestine. I enclose also a record† of the interview. I have dealt fully in my despatch, Secret, " A," of the 7th December,‡ with the political situation which forms the background of the memorandum. I have also indicated the lines of a reply to the three principal demands in the memorandum. I will not, therefore, recapitulate them here. But I emphasise the importance of receiving from you at the earliest moment possible such a reply as will enable me to give some satisfaction to the Arab leaders, since I think they are right in saying that otherwise they will lose such influence as they now possess and that the possibility of alleviating the present situation by means of the moderate measures suggested by me will disappear.

    3. As regards the standing of the gentlemen who have signed the memorandum enclosed with this despatch, Ragheb Bey Nashashibi and Jamal Eff. Husseini are well known to the Colonial Office. These two gentlemen are representative of two important sections of political opinion. But the five signatories represent the five active Arab political parties and they are generally representative of informed Arab political opinion in Palestine. It is unlikely that their present association together for a common purpose will last long. I mention this point particularly because, when I discussed the Legislative Council with a number of individuals in the early part of this year, I emphasised the necessity of creating an Arab committee which could be regarded as representing the collective opinions of the community, so that there might be some single Arab body with which I could discuss the proposals for a Legislative Council. The present situation has temporarily brought into existence such a' body, though with other motives and for other purposes. This situation is unlikely to last long and may not recur. I feel, therefore, that the present opportunity should not be missed since there appears to be a chance of effecting a *détente* in the situation. The alternative is an increasing tenseness in the situation punctuated by sporadic disturbances of the peace.

                                   I have, &c.
            (Signed)   A. G. WAUCHOPE,
                            High Commissioner for Palestine.

---

* Enclosure I (printed as Appendix I).
† Enclosure II (not printed).
‡ Printed as Appendix III.

11

APPENDIX III.

Secret Despatch from the High Commissioner for Palestine to the Secretary of State for the Colonies, dated December 7, 1935.

(Secret. A.)
Reference No. CF/409/35.
Sir,   December 7, 1935.

IN my telegram to the Secretary of State of the 15th November dealing with the possible reduction in strength of the British garrison in Palestine, I stated that there had been signs during the last few months that the general feeling among Arabs had become definitely more hostile to Government and that the leaders spoke in public of the necessity for Arabs to take what they termed firm action to obtain redress of their wrongs.

During the last few weeks there have been no signs in the press or elsewhere of any lessening of this resentment, which the leaders of the five parties state is stronger now than it ever has been in Palestine. This statement is an exaggeration, but that the feeling of antagonism is strong is true.

At the same time, the leaders of the five Arab parties told me at the interview which I gave them on the 25th November that, unless they received a reply to their memorandum which could be generally regarded as giving satisfaction to their requests, they would lose all influence with their followers; extreme and irresponsible counsels would prevail and the political situation would rapidly deteriorate.

Though I do not fear riots on a large scale. I think it right to say that in the present state of tension untoward incidents might cause considerable disturbances.

Arab Parties are now discussing a boycott of Government, resignation of Arab employees, non-payment of taxes and closure of Mosques. I do not anticipate that these proposals will materialise; but requests to hold Arab demonstrations are now being received, and I think such action as strikes is not unlikely.

2. It would be well if I were to try to diagnose the causes of this hostility.

In the first place, as I have reported before, the Arabs have, or imagine they have, three separate and fundamental grievances against Government.

The first is that the Arabs believe that a promise was made that an independent Arab State would be formed after the last war, an Arab State which would include Palestine.

The second cause of resentment is due to the Balfour Declaration and its results.

The third grievance is the neglect of Government to "encourage local autonomy."

3. The first is strongly felt by the Effendi class; but the second, that the Jew is "eating up the land," is felt in every town and village in Palestine, and year by year with increasing strength.

My reply that the fellah now earns a higher wage has little effect. About one-fifth of Arab villagers are already landless. Village communities are well aware that they have sold, or their neighbours have sold, large sections of their land to Jews and that they have not permanently benefited by the transaction. The money has gone, the shortage of land has increased.) Their fear that the process will continue till the bulk of the land is gone is genuine.

The sense of injury formerly directed against the Jew is now against the Government, which permits the Jew with little restriction to enter the country, and with less restriction to buy land.

4. The Arabs have consistently refused to recognise the Balfour Declaration, and consistently opposed all steps that the Palestine Government have taken to "secure the establishment of a Jewish National Home."

5. As regards the third grievance, certain steps well known to you have, in fact, been taken in the direction of encouraging local autonomy during the last few years.

Provided that a Legislative Council is now established in accordance with our pledges. I consider that this grievance will cease to have foundation in fact.

[12550]

D

6. On the subject of the first two grievances I have consistently adopted the attitude that I have no knowledge of any promise having been given for the formation of an independent Arab State in Palestine, and that as High Commissioner I fully accept the Balfour Declaration and the obligations of the Mandate; and consequently it is part of my policy to facilitate " the establishment in Palestine of a national home for the Jewish people, it being clearly understood that nothing should be done which might prejudice the civil and religious rights of existing non-Jewish communities in Palestine."

7. We may look upon these three grievances as imaginary, but to the Arabs they are real, and are the cause of a widespread belief that they have been unjustly treated. To this sense of injustice must now be added a genuine feeling of fear that the Jews will succeed in establishing themselves in such large numbers that in the not distant future they will gain economic and political control over the whole country.

Accepting the fact that, rightly or wrongly, the Arabs believe in this double injustice, we cannot be surprised that there exists a latent feeling of hostility towards the Mandatory Power. Nor can we be surprised if untoward events, or even trivial incidents of friction between groups of the two races, cause spasmodic outbursts of disturbance, or a general increase of tension among the Arab population.

The existing tension is illustrated by the recent incident described in my despatch Secret " C " of the 30th November, on the activities of an armed band in the Jenin area. The leader of the gang deliberately shot a policeman, yet he and his accomplices have been acclaimed by many Arab leaders and by the whole Arabic Press as martyrs and heroes, bravely sacrificing themselves in the cause of national and religious independence.

8. This increase of ill-directed national feeling has been brought about recently by three principal contributory causes.

The first of these had its origin in the feeling of general uneasiness that existed this autumn in the Eastern Mediterranean, when some Arabs of cloudy mind and lively imagination pictured themselves leading non-existent armies in the cause of Arab freedom and Jewish expulsion. When realization came that these expectations would not be fulfilled and that the full authority of the Mandatory Power would be maintained, naturally enough there arose a feeling of reaction, disappointment and even bitterness.

9. The second cause was due to the discovery of illegal importation of arms. About the time of this reaction a large quantity of hidden arms was discovered to have been imported into Jaffa Port. This consignment was universally believed by Arabs to have been destined certainly for Jews and probably for the *Haganaa* organisation.

That consignments of arms have previously been imported for Jewish organisations has long been suspected by me, and long been believed in by Arabs. Consequently, when this consignment was discovered, and the culprits could not be found, feelings of anger, resentment and fear spread through the Arab population. This feeling of fear has been enhanced by the fact that a number of recent Jewish immigrants have acted very aggressively towards individual Arabs, over half a dozen offenders in such attacks having been convicted in the last few months in Tel-Aviv alone.

I do not suggest that Arab villagers expect an attack from Jews. I do state that Arabs are beginning to feel that when disturbances occur the Jews will be well armed and the Arabs will not.

10. The third cause which has contributed to the increase of political tension is the recent disturbances in Egypt which have reacted adversely upon Arab public opinion in Palestine.

11. The main reason, however, of this increased feeling of resentment is to be found in the fact that the results of Government's help in establishing the National Home grow more apparent each year and consequently more odious to the Arab people.

Arabs often quote the fact that the Jewish population in Palestine has increased from 57,000 in 1919 to 320,000 in 1935, and has increased its ownership of land from 643,000 dunums in 1919 to 1,300,000 dunums in 1935. And this figure includes some of the most valuable urban and rural property in Palestine.

Such are the fundamental and immediate causes of Arab resentment towards Government.

13

12. In December 1933 I wrote to the Secretary of State that the widening breach between Arabs and British would not remain stationary; either we find means of bringing ruler and ruled more in sympathy, or hostility will grow deeper and more permanent each year.

By improving the material condition of the fellah and by carrying out our pledge as to a Legislative Council I hoped to achieve this object, and I remain hopeful. But goodwill is of slow growth and the Legislative Council not yet in being.

13. In my despatch Secret of the 7th December, which goes by the same mail as this one, I have enclosed a memorandum signed by the leaders of the five Arab parties, together with an account of an interview which I gave them on the 25th November.

The three main demands of the Arab leaders, as set forth in this memorandum, are the complete cessation of Jewish immigration, the prohibition of all sales of land, and local self-government.

The last demand, in my opinion, will be fairly met by the establishment of a Legislative Council.

To accept the first two demands would cause grave injustice to the Jews, but both questions require consideration.

14. With regard to immigration, until the end of 1934 I considered that the number of immigrants corresponded, so far as I could judge, with the absorptive capacity of the country.

In 1933 we admitted roughly 30,000 Jewish immigrants; in 1934 roughly 42,000 Jewish immigrants. The Commissioner for Migration estimates now that the total for 1935 will exceed our expectations and will amount to fully 60,000.

This figure is, in my opinion, beyond the absorptive capacity of the country, and I am addressing you separately on measures I suggest to reduce the total immigration, at any rate for the present.

Already signs are appearing which suggest that the limits of the present absorptive capacity of Palestine are being approached. The normal stationary figure of Jewish unemployment of 1,600 has risen to 4,500–5,000. After the orange-picking season an additional 2,000 will have to be absorbed into the labour market.

15. As regards sale of land, I placed a memorandum on this subject before the Colonial Office last October.

I consider some measure is needed not to prevent Jews from acquiring land, but to help Arab small holders, in view of the ever-increasing sale of land, to preserve a subsistence area. I shall be glad to hear if you approve the principle submitted in the memorandum mentioned above, in which case I would prepare more detailed proposals after discussion with Jewish and Arab leaders.

16. The establishment of a Legislative Council, a reduction in the excess number of immigrants admitted in 1934, a measure to give protection to small landowners, and an ordinance at present in draft to promote closer co-operation between Government and village communities, will all tend to check the growing antagonism felt to-day by so many Arabs towards the Mandatory Power.

17. I need hardly add that I do not urge these measures on account of Arab ill-feeling or resentment; I do so because I consider that to carry out our double duty under the Mandate, these measures, which were not necessary a few years ago, are now needed under changed conditions. This is the attitude which I have constantly maintained and, subject to your approval, I shall continue steadfastly to maintain as I consider in continuity of policy lies our chief hope of inducing both Arab and Jew to accept the limitations imposed on us by the double duty laid on us by the Mandate—" What cannot be eschewed needs must be embraced." The measures I suggest involve or imply no change in policy; on the contrary owing to changing conditions they are called for to enable Government to maintain the principles underlying its policy of the past four years.

18. Among these " Thoughts on Present Discontents " I have not referred to any Jewish grievances. I think none are grave, and none are considered very serious even by the Agency. They dislike the idea of a Legislative Council, but they realise Government must fulfil definite pledges, and that our present proposals will not injure the National Home as they first feared. They ask always for freer immigration, but they know that during the last four years the number of immigrants admitted has exceeded all expectation. They ask that a higher proportion of Jews should be employed on Public Works and in the

[12550]

D 2

14

Police, but they know that excessive high wages during the past two years has made this impossible.

As Doctor Weizmann recently said, the situation of Jews in Europe compels the Agency " always to ask and ask again for more." But they realise how much Government has done and is doing to help forward the National Home.

Jew and Arab much as they trouble one another—and often their rulers—possess fine qualities, though some of these run to excess. Acquisitiveness in the one, and an idiosyncrasy for Nationalism in the other.

I have, &c.

(Signed) A. G. WAUCHOPE.
High Commissioner for Palestine.

APPENDIX IV.

Secret Despatch from the High Commissioner for Palestine to the Secretary of State for the Colonies, dated December 21, 1935.

(Secret.)
Reference No. CF/444/35.
Sir, December 21, 1935.

I HAVE the honour to transmit to you for your information the accompanying copy of a special report which has been submitted to Government by the Deputy Inspector-General, Criminal Investigation Department, on the present political situation in Palestine.

2. It will be seen from this report that the political situation has further deteriorated since my despatch, Secret A of the 7th December,* was written, and that there is additional reason for Government to apprehend that it must be prepared to meet some form of hostile expression or demonstration in the near future.

I believe this deterioration to be due in part to the illogical attitude Arabs here have taken as to the granting of the 1923 Constitution immediately after the riots in Cairo. They argue that attention will only be paid to their demands after demonstrations and acts of civil disobedience.

3. I am not apprehensive of any immediate disorders, but there is every indication of the occurrence of trouble some time after the meeting of the Arab leaders which has been called for the 15th January, 1936. In these circumstances it will be helpful for me to be in possession of your reply to my Secret despatch before that date, and I trust that you will find it possible to send the answering despatch in time.

One development in the situation which causes me particular concern and regret is that resentment against Government is beginning to spread among many villages in Palestine. While I personally receive a good welcome in every village which I visit, it is true that feelings are being roused by the large number of immigrants admitted this last year, and the constant and increasing sale of land.

4. I have the following comments to offer on the suggestions put forward in paragraph 11 of Mr. Rice's report :—

(a) A general, though unofficial, warning was addressed to the Press by the Press Officer a week or so ago. While such warnings have little perceptible or immediate effect, the Press Officer continues to do everything possible to exercise a moderating influence on individual editors. It may be mentioned that the Arabic newspaper *Al Difaa* was recently suspended for a month on account of an article commending the example of the Egyptian riots.

(b) It would not be practicable to put into effect any condition that speeches made at public meetings should not be inflammatory or anti-British in tone.

* Appendix III.

15

(c) It would be possible to refuse permission for those who took part in the recent meeting at Jaffa to hold political meetings elsewhere. The effect of such prohibition would, however, in fact be negligible, since the persons in question would no doubt arrange to appear and to make speeches at meetings organized by persons who were not present at the Jaffa meeting.

(d) I agree that a warning should be addressed to Mohammad Ali Taher, who is a notorious agitator of Egyptian antecedents at present on a short visit to Palestine, but there are so many other active political agitators that I have some doubt whether a warning addressed to a single individual would have much practical effect.

I am causing immediate enquiries to be made as to the names and activities of political agitators who are in the same position as Ali Taher, and I shall consider this question further when a report on those enquiries has been received.

I have, &c.
(Signed) A. G. WAUCHOPE,
High Commissioner for Palestine.

(No. 36/G/S.)   *Headquarters, The Palestine Police Force,*
(Secret.)   *(Criminal Investigation Department),*
Sir,   *P.O.B. 850, Jerusalem, December 14, 1935.*

Subject: Special Report on Political Situation.

I CONSIDER that it is necessary to inform you that there are a number of indications which suggest that the political situation shows signs of deteriorating, and that within the fairly near future some form of expression or demonstration against Government must be expected.

Lt.-Col. Peake, Officer Commanding, Arab Legion, recently informed me that the Arabs in Transjordan are, for the first time in his experience, becoming politically-minded regarding affairs in Palestine. It is his opinion that the Transjordan Arabs believe disorders to be imminent.

2. I am addressing you separately regarding the meeting held in Jaffa by various Arab politicians on the 9th instant, when speeches were definitely inciting and anti-Government. The tone of the press has probably been worse recently than it has been for a considerable time. I have addressed District Superintendents of Police and Deputy District Superintendents, and I am informed by them that the situation and the attitude of Arabs generally, particularly politicians, must be regarded with considerable seriousness. I am requesting these Officers to keep me immediately informed of any improvement or deterioration in the situation.

3. Recent developments in Egypt are the subject of popular discussion and the fact that disorders resulted in the achievement of some of their aspirations as far as the politicians are concerned, is being cited as a reason why disorders should be promoted in Palestine. There are reasons to support a report that the fellahin are becoming interested, to say the least of it, in what politicians describe as "the Arab Cause."

4. The late Sheikh Izzel Din-el-Kassam, the destruction of whose gang was reported to the Secretary of State in the High Commissioner's despatch Secret (C) of the 30th November, 1935, is continually referred to, together with his deceased followers, as "martyrs," and their action in "dying for their religion and Cause" is generally praised. Nuh Ibrahim, a poet of Haifa, has been visiting villages in the Tulkarm area praising the deceased and distributing their photographs.

5. A noticeable feature is the development of what are known as Young Men's Groups. Since the partial strike held on the 13th November, and more particularly since the decision of the all-party representatives to defer decision on the future course of action until the 15th January, independent young men

16

groups have increased their activities. They have acquired followers and have established closer co-operation amongst them.

These independent groups consist of:—

(a) Akram Zueitar, and his followers in Nablus. Their success in the partial strike on the 13th November principally, won for them the support of other political elements in Nablus.
(b) Hamdi Husseini, Hashem-el-Sabie and others in Jaffa, whose connections with the Revolutionary Youth Committee of Qalqilya has been referred to before, and who have now secured the collaboration of Michel Mitri, leader of the Arab Labour Society of Jaffa.
(c) Ibrahim Shanti; in contact with certain leaders of the Istiqlal.
(d) Salim Abdel Rahman and other leaders of Abu Obeida and other scout groups in Tulkarm area.
(e) Atef Nouralla and his following in Haifa.

6. They have certain followers in Jerusalem who are of lesser importance, as Tahsin Kamal, ex-Police Officer, and Shukri Kutteineh, besides the group which Osman Kassem is endeavouring to attract to *Al Liwa*, which newspaper has opened its columns for Hamdi Husseini and Akram Zueitar and their inciting articles. Nimer Odeh, who recently resigned from the Department of Education, is on the staff of the paper.

7. These groups are supported by certain leaders of the Istiqlal Party, principally Izzet Darwazeh of the Moslem Supreme Council, and Ajjaj Nweihed, who does not seem at present to have any obvious means of livelihood.

8. It is obvious that it is the intention of these combined groups:—

(a) To direct political agitation against the British authorities, and not against Zionism. This is clear from their writings and speeches.
(b) To force the party leaders to adopt some firm decision at the Nablus meeting on the 15th January, such as non-co-operation, non-payment of taxes, demonstrations, &c.
(c) To stimulate agitation and public feeling until the meeting on the 15th January. It was for this purpose the meeting was held in Jaffa on the 9th inst.
(d) Subsequently to create disorders.

9. It will be observed that Hamdi Husseini, Akram Zueitar and Ibrahim-el-Shanti are engaged in a press campaign of the most virulent nature urging non-co-operation, violence (though in veiled terms), the resignation of Arab Government officials, boycott of official receptions and eulogizing acts of Izzel Din-el-Kassam, imprisonment in the national cause and immortalizing the memory of "martyrs." Sheikh Abdel Khader Muzaffar (Muzghar) visited Nablus on the 12th, and in Abdel Latif Salah's house informed a private meeting that the public expected active measures and that Arabs should welcome imprisonment for their actions. Abdel Latif Salah is reported to have said he was prepared to carry out the wishes of the people.

10. I have received information from a reliable source, which is confirmed, that recently in the North certain Moslem ladies of the upper class were being visited by other ladies from another portion of Palestine, as is customary during Ramadan, and were discussing the situation when one made a statement that a secret plan was afoot whereby in the near future sudden and simultaneous disorders would occur. It is, I consider, unlikely that anything untoward is to be expected until after the feasts of Ramadan. The 5th January is nominated as the 40th day after the death of the late Sheikh Izzel Din-el-Kassam and some of his followers. This date and period will need to be carefully watched, as must the proposed all-party meeting to be held at Nablus on the 15th January.

11. I have the honour to offer the following suggestions:—

(a) That the Arabic press should be given a general warning couched in emphatic terms to improve their tone, and to refrain from further incitement.
(b) That the question of further public meetings similar to that held at Jaffa on the 9th inst., be permitted only on sufficiently strict conditions so as to prevent speeches of an inciting and anti-British nature.

17

(c) The question to be considered of refusing permission for similar meetings to be held by the same persons as were responsible for the meeting in Jaffa.
(d) That Mohamed Ali Taher be warned that if he does not cease political agitation in this country, he will not be permitted any further facilities to return here, once he leaves.
(e) That if it is possible favourably to reply to any of the petitions of the Arab leaders which have already been submitted to Government, that such be done as early as possible, so to placate the small remaining portion of the Arab population, which is yet not anti-Government.

I have, &c.
(Signed)   H. P. RICE,
Deputy Inspector-General C.I.D.

The Chief Secretary,
 Government Offices,
  Jerusalem.

o

9.08

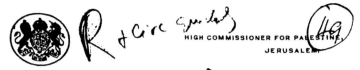

HIGH COMMISSIONER FOR PALESTINE,
JERUSALEM

May, 1936.

My dear Parkinson,

------ I enclose, for your information, a memorandum which I have had prepared on the subject of the proposed land sales restrictions, including a brief history of the situation prior to the time when I put forward the present proposals, and a note of the objections which have been voiced since the intention to apply some restrictions was announced.

I shall be glad to have as early as possible your comments on the memorandum as I propose, if you have no objection, to communicate a copy of it privately to the Jewish Agency with whom we have promised to have full discussions as to all details. I will write further as to our discussions with Arab leaders on the same subject.

Yours, Arthur Wauchope

Brief on Government's Proposals for the
Protection of Small Owners by the Reservation
of Subsistence Areas.

History and Origins of Proposals.

It has been recognised from the Occupation that the development of the National Home by means of Jewish Immigration and Settlement on the land would sooner or later raise the question of "the present position" of the Arabs on the land, since the area of cultivable land in Palestine is limited and is wholly cultivated, whereas the population is increasing rapidly both naturally and by immigration. Between the Transfer of Land Ordinances 1920-1921 and the Protection of Cultivators Ordinance 1933 the process of the displacement of tenants and cultivators from the land went on practically unchecked, though it is only in the last three or four years that Jewish purchases have reached alarming proportions. The Shaw Commission reported in March, 1930, that the position arising from the dispossession of Arab tenants, as a result of the sale to Jews of the lands they were cultivating, had reached an acute stage. The Commission reached the conclusion that there was no alternative land to which persons evicted could remove and that in consequence a landless and discontented class, which was a potential danger to the country, was being created. They advised that unless some solution could be found to deal with this situation the question would remain a constant source of discontent and a potential cause of future disturbance. In the view of the Commission Palestine could not support a larger agricultural population than it carried in 1930, unless methods of farming were radically changed.

2./

- 2 -

2.   Following the Report of the Shaw Commission, H.M.G. sent Sir John Hope Simpson to Palestine in the Autumn of 1930 to examine on the spot the questions of immigration, land settlement and development. He summarised the situation in these words:

"It is the duty of the Administration, under the Mandate, to ensure that the position of the Arabs is not prejudiced by Jewish immigration. It is also its duty under the Mandate to encourage the close settlement of the Jews on the land, subject always to the former condition. It is only possible to reconcile these apparently conflicting duties by an active policy of agricultural development, having as its object close settlement on the land and intensive cultivation by both <u>Arabs</u> <u>and</u> <u>Jews</u>. To this end drastic action is necessary".

3.   Sir John Hope Simpson's principal recommendation for drastic action was that Government should undertake an Agricultural Development Scheme whereby the fellah's farming methods would be improved, so that he would be able to gain a reasonable livelihood from a smaller area of land than that which had previously been essential, and his holdings rearranged. By these two methods it would be possible to provide sufficient land for the Arab fellaheen as well as for additional Jewish settlement.

An essential feature of the Agricultural Development Scheme was that until the scheme was worked out the control of all disposition of land should rest with the authority in charge of the development. Transfers were only to be permitted in so far as they did not interfere with that scheme.

Apart from the specific Agricultural Development Scheme Sir John Hope Simpson made a large number of recommendations of a general nature for the economic

development/

- 5 -

development of Palestine.

4. Sir John Hope Simpson's main ideas were embodied in the White Paper of 1930. The Government were to provide by a loan of £P.2,500,000 for the Agricultural Development Scheme. But in the event, the economic and financial crisis of 1931 intervened and H.M.G. were obliged to abandon the project. At the same time, it was decided to go ahead with the recommendations of a general nature for the development of Palestine and, in fact, they have practically all been carried out or are in process of being carried out.

5. It is important to note at this point that when Sir Arthur Wauchope informed Mr. Arlosoroff, of the Executive of the Jewish Agency, on the 27th January, 1932, that Government was not proceeding with the Agricultural Development Scheme and that therefore the proposed restrictions on the sale of lands which had been an essential part of that scheme would not be proceeded with, he made it clear that Government did not thereby bind itself to refrain from all restrictions on the sale of lands in any circumstances.

6. One other important result of Sir John Hope Simpson's report and the White Paper was an investigation into the number of 'landless Arabs' as specially defined in this way:

AR 1933 p.9

> "Arabs who have been displaced from the land which they occupied in consequence of those lands having passed into Jewish hands, and who have failed to obtain other holdings on which to establish themselves or equally satisfactory occupation, subject to the following exceptions:
> (1) Persons who have themselves sold their land, that is, owners who of their own free will have sold their lands;

(2)/

- 4 -

(2) Persons who own land elsewhere;

(3) Persons who have found and are now cultivating as tenants land other than that from which they were displaced;

(4) Persons who obtained land after the sale of the land from which they were displaced, but have since ceased to cultivate it on account of poverty or other reasons;

(5) Persons who were not cultivators at the time of the sale, for example, ploughmen and labourers."

The number of 'landless Arabs' as so defined was found to be 656. This number does not, of course, include those who did not come forward to make a claim. It also takes no account of those cultivators who, although displaced from the lands which they occupied owing to those lands having passed into Jewish hands, are not covered by the foregoing definition: of these the principal category comprises individuals who obtained industrial employment in the towns and who would, in the event of any severe industrial set-back, lose their new means of livelihood and have no possibility of resuming their former agricultural occupations.

7. The last important consequence of Sir John Hope Simpson's Report and the White Paper to be mentioned here was the introduction in 1933 of the Protection of Cultivators Ordinance. The object of this Ordinance is to protect tenants from eviction from their holdings more especially where the ownership of the land is transferred. This Ordinance, which has been amended from time to time in the light of experience, is on the whole working well, and generally fulfilling the purpose for which it was enacted.

- 5 -

When this Ordinance was passed, careful consideration was given to the question whether it was necessary to protect small owners as well as tenants. It did not appear at the time to be necessary but the High Commissioner continued to watch the situation closely with a view to taking action in this direction, if the necessity should arise, in order to prevent serious consequences. In August 1934, the High Commissioner still considered that legislation to protect small owners was not necessary, though it might be required in the future. In February, 1935, the High Commissioner reported to the Secretary of State that the situation had in the meantime greatly changed owing to the greatly increased Jewish immigration which had taken place in the last two or three years combined with the fact that the Jews had largely increased funds at their disposal to make them to pay enhanced prices for the land which they wished to acquire. The High Commissioner had as a result formed the opinion that although there might be no immediate distress and little unemployment, the outlook was disquieting. The chief danger lay in the fact that although owners who sold their land were at the time finding employment otherwise, when employment became scarce they would join the ranks of the unemployed, and no longer having any land they would be unable to obtain a livelihood.

See para 3 of (31) in CF/15/35.

See para 4 of (31) in CF/15/35.

8. Before addressing the Secretary of State on the subject the High Commissioner had appointed a small Committee of Government officers to ascertain the facts as fully as possible and to consider possible remedies for the situation. His Excellency's report included tentative proposals for the introduction of legislation to prevent any landowner from selling the minimum area essential for his subsistence, and after correspondence

with/

- 6 -

with the Secretary of State these proposals were further elaborated in a memorandum sent to the High Commissioner in London in September, 1935.

The proposals may be summarised thus:

That legislation should be introduced to make it a condition of every disposition of rural land, including sale, mortgage, gift, dedication of wakf, and lease for more than three years, that the person making the disposition should retain ownership of the minimum area necessary for his subsistence (lot viable). The size of the subsistence area would depend upon the nature of the cultivation, and might be varied from time to time as the land is improved or its irrigation becomes possible. No restriction would be placed on the number of transactions to be allowed to each purchaser, or on the number to be allowed to each vendor provided that he retained the prescribed subsistence area, but sales of areas exceeding 1000 dunums would only be permitted as special cases at the discretion of the High Commissioner, who would also have the power to sanction the sale of a subsistence area in special cases. The following lands would be excluded from the operation of the legislation: all urban and town planning areas, the whole of the Beersheba sub-district and all land planted with citrus at the date of the enactment of the legislation. If the owner should desert his subsistence area, or otherwise fail to cultivate it, Government would have the right to resume after it had remained uncultivated for three years.

9. In their letter of the 25th November, 1935, the Arab leaders asked, among other things, for the complete stoppage of the sale of lands by Arabs to Jews. As a question of major policy, this request was referred by

the/

- 7 -

the High Commissioner to the Secretary of State who replied by telegram on the 16th January, 1936, that he approved in principle the proposal that the Palestine Government should take action on the lines recommended, namely that, except in the Beersheba sub-district, urban areas and land already planted with citrus, no landowner should be permitted to sell any of his land unless he retains a minimum area sufficient to afford a means of subsistence to himself and his family. The minimum area would be inalienable, and would revert to the Government if it ceased to be cultivated by the owner-occupier. The proposed legislation would be of general application so that sales of land to any person would be subject to restriction.

10. On the 8th February the High Commissioner decided to appoint a Committee to make close and detailed investigations into the problem and to make practical recommendations for the application of the principles approved by the Secretary of State.

11. The Committee, which is still pursuing its investigations, has already made the following preliminary recommendations:

(i) that in fixing the subsistence area use should be made of the classification of all rural lands into different categories for the purpose of the Rural Property Tax, and once the minimum subsistence area for each category is fixed it should not be varied. If at any time it is agreed that the category of any particular land has changed, the subsistence area appropriate to the new category would automatically be applied.

- 8 -

that the category of any particular land has changed, the subsistence area appropriate to the new category would automatically be applied. With the exception of land planted with bananas, and lands in categories below the lowest taxable category under the Rural Property Tax Ordinance, the subsistence area should be any holding upon which that tax to the amount of LP. 8 a year is payable. A separate criterion for banana plantations and land at present not taxable is being considered.

(ii) that with regard to the exclusion of land planted with citrus from the application of the proposed measures it will be necessary to provide careful safeguards to ensure that the citrus cultivation is genuine.

(iii) that the proposed measures should be applied to all sales pending at the time when the legislation is enacted. Provision should be made to protect a prospective vendor, who was thus prevented from fulfilling a contract to sell, from the penalty attaching to a breach of the contract, but where he is prevented only in part from fulfilling the contract the purchaser should be entitled to demand the completion of the contract to the extent possible.

(iv) that the proposed legislation should prescribe that contracts for the sale of land should be registered within 14 days of their conclusion, and should be invalid unless so registered. Registration should not be effected unless the prospective vendor was retaining a subsistence area.

(v) that provision should be made, in the case where the heirs of a deceased landowner inherit small parcels of land, to facilitate the consolidation of the parcels by permitting an heir who inherits a share less than a subsistence area to sell his share to a co-heir.

(vi) that some provision should be made to empower the District Commissioner to prepare and enforce a scheme to group a number of isolated subsistence areas into one consolidated block. Appeal against the District Commissioner's order would lie to the High Commissioner.

(vii)/

- 9 -

(vii) that the mortgage of a subsistence area should be allowed, but that the legislation should contain a provision that a subsistence area cannot be sold in execution.

(viii) that the lease of a subsistence area should be permitted without restriction up to a period of three years. The commutation of the rent into a lump sum should not be prohibited.

(ix) that the legislation should not interfere with the right of land-holding Companies to sell the lands which they have already bought.

(x) that as regards Musha' land, the registered owner of undivided shares should be allowed to sell them, and registered shares should be accepted as a subsistence area, subject to the same restrictions as in the case of divided lands.

(xi) that contracts for the sale of land should not be valid unless registered, and shall not be registered unless the vendor shows that he is retaining a subsistence area

(xii) that if a subsistence area escheats to Government on account of its abandonment by the owner-cultivator, the latter should, subject to certain conditions, have a right of pre-emption.

12. The following criticisms have been made by the Jews against the proposed legislation:

(i) <u>General</u>.

(a) The proposed legislation would be inconsistent with the statements made by the Prime Minister to Dr. Weizmann, in paragraphs 12 and 13 of his letter of the 13th January, 1931, to the effect that it would be necessary to have some centralised control of

land/

- 10 -

effectiveness of the scheme of land settlement to be undertaken. It is only as a part of such a development policy that the need for regulation can arise.

Note. On this point it is the view of His Majesty's Government that, apart from the fact that important areas of Palestine would be expressly excepted from the scope of the proposed legislation, Mr. Ramsay MacDonald's assurances were given with specific reference to the policy of land settlement and development referred to in the White Paper of October, 1930. In fact, the whole letter is described in the opening paragraph as "the authoritative interpretation of the White Paper on the matters with which this letter deals". In the relevant paragraphs of his letter Mr. MacDonald was concerned to reassure the Jews on one special point, namely, that such a policy of land settlement would not be used as an excuse for imposing for an ulterior purpose restrictions upon land transactions which would be more than what was required for the purposes of that policy. His assurances could not be interpreted as debarring His Majesty's Government indefinitely from taking any action which, even if no development or resettlement were in view, might be considered necessary in the general interests of Palestine at some future date and in the place of developments which had not then assumed any serious prominence.

(b)

- 11 -

(b) Under the Mandate the Government is under the obligation to encourage close settlement by Jews on the land, including State lands and waste lands not required for public purposes. The only important steps taken by Government in this direction were the lease of the Kabbara swamps to, and the assent to the acquisition of the Huleh Concession by, Jewish interests. Of all other State lands practically nothing has been set aside for Jewish settlement, and consequently the Jews have been compelled to buy land in the open market at a heavy price. The proposed restrictive legislation will create a new serious handicap, and will amount to a direct inversion of a fundamental provision of the Mandate.

Note. The lease of State lands to Jews is being proceeded with where possible, and Government has already leased, or is in process of leasing, 180,000 dunums. A survey of State and waste lands is now being undertaken, but the principal difficulty now is the fact that owing to the high prices given for land, the ownership of almost every dunum is disputed. These questions of ownership can only be decided in the course of land settlement. Assistance has been given indirectly to Jewish settlement by improvement of communications, increased security, and similar measures.

(c) /

- 12 -

(c) In the Mandate, the protection of the rights and position of the Arab population appears as ancillary to the promotion of Jewish immigration and settlement.

> Note. In paragraph 3 of his letter to Dr. Weizmann dated the 13th February, 1931, the Prime Minister made it clear that His Majesty's Government were resolved to give effect *in equal measure* to both parts of their undertaking, namely to the Jewish people on the one hand and to the non-Jewish population of Palestine on the other hand. In paragraph 15 of the same letter Mr. Ramsay MacDonald repeated that while His Majesty's Government have to be mindful of their obligations to facilitate Jewish immigration under suitable conditions and to encourage close settlement of Jews on the land, they have to be *equally mindful* of their duty to ensure that no prejudice results to the rights and position of the non-Jewish community.

(d) The measure will have a disastrous psychological effect. The Jewish people will feel it to be a slur on their good name, and non-Jews will interpret it as shewing that the Jews are an element against which the other sections of the population require protection.

> Note. There is no ground for regarding the measure as a slur on the good name of the Jewish people. The facts are that the amount of land is limited, and the

purchases/

- 13 -

purchases are increasing yearly beyond the rate of improvement of the land; consequently a measure of protection is necessary.

(ii) **Detailed.**

   (a) By rendering the subsistence area inalienable the proposed measure will make it impossible for the small holder to/mortgage credit. [raise]

       Note. The information so far received by the Committee is to the effect that the fellah generally obtains short-term credits on the security of his crops. Long-term loans for improvements will, it is hoped, be obtainable through co-operative societies as these develop; the conclusion of a long lease (see paragraph 11 (viii) of this note) would be another method of raising capital.

   (b) Two or more persons, burdened with small uneconomic plots, can, so long as there is a right of sale, reconstitute them into a single economic holding. The proposed legislation will impose an inevitable, endless and incurable partitioning.

       Note. Government does not intend to perpetuate uneconomic partitioning. As regards fragmentation on succession see paragraph 11 (v) of this note. In other cases it will be possible to invoke the High Commissioner's power to approve the sale of a subsistence area as a special case (see paragraph 11 (xi) of this note).

   (c) The exclusion of citrus land from the new

measure/

- 14 -

measure will constitute a direct and powerful inducement to concentrate on orange growing and neglect mixed and dairy farming, although Government for some time has been warning farmers against the dangers of monoculture and the difficulties of marketing an ever-increasing citrus crop.

> Note. The reason for excluding land planted with citrus from the proposed legislation is the fact that conditions in respect of such lands are entirely different from those prevailing in ordinary agricultural land, and the proposed measure would be inappropriate to them. Moreover, the exception will apply only to land planted with citrus at the time when the legislation is enacted, so that after that date there will be no special inducement to plant citrus.

15. (i) The proposals have been criticized in the Arabic Press in general terms, as not going far enough to safeguard Arab interests adequately. The comments appear to ignore the fact that while the proposed legislation is designed to safeguard the smallholder, agricultural tenants will continue to be protected by the Protection of Cultivators Ordinance.

(ii) In their interview with the High Commissioner on the 25th November, 1935, the representatives of the various Arab political parties made the following specific criticisms:

(a) that the problem is already acute and that such land as now remains in the hands of the Arabs may all be sold before the new legislation is enacted.

To this the High Commissioner replied that

he/

- 15 -

he is anxious to press on with the proposal and that there will be no avoidable delay, but that it is clear that it will take some months.

(b) that the Beersheba sub-district should be included in the proposed restrictions, particularly as the measure will not prevent the sale of surplus land.

The High Commissioner explained that conditions in the Beersheba sub-district are different from those in the densely populated areas. If an owner in the maritime plain sold his land he might not be able to purchase more land there, whereas a landowner in the Beersheba area could. His Excellency considered that the position in the Beersheba area is not acute, and that Government must proceed step by step.

(c) that if uncontrolled sales are allowed in the citrus belt the Jews will acquire all the best land and the Arabs would be left with nothing but the comparatively unproductive land in the hills.

The High Commissioner expressed the opinion that if protection were applied to the citrus belt it might upset the credit system of Palestine.

9.09

PALESTINE.

S E C R E T.

Reference No. CF/15/35.

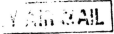

HIGH COMMISSIONER FOR PALESTINE,
JERUSALEM.

4 May, 1936.

Sir,

I have the honour to refer to your despatch Secret 2 of the 23rd January, 1936, and connected correspondence on the subject of the proposal for the restriction of land sales in Palestine, and to inform you that on the 8th February in Executive Council I decided to appoint a Committee, composed of the Chief Secretary as Chairman, and the Attorney General, the Treasurer, the Irrigation Adviser, the Commissioner for Lands and Surveys and the Development Officer as members, to erquire into the proposed measures and to make practic recommendations for the application of the principles which you have approved.

2. I now transmit herewith, for your consideration, two copies of the report of the Committee, with which I am in general agreement: but it is possible that after discussion with the Jewish Agency and Arab leaders, I may see fit to advise certain changes. Annexed to the report are the drafts of clauses which would give effect to the Committee's recommendations, but I do not propose to submit actual draft legislation until I have discussed the proposals with Jewish and Arab leaders.

3. If you see no objection, I propose to hand copies of the report and its annexures to the leaders as a basis of discussion. In order to avoid delay I shall be grateful if you will signify your approval of

this/

The Right Honourable J.H. Thomas, P.C., M.P.,
   His Majesty's Principal Secretary of State
                for the Colonies.

- 2 -

this course by telegraph.

                I have the honour to be,

                    Sir,

                Your most obedient,

                    humble servant,

Arthur Wauchope

                HIGH COMMISSIONER
                FOR PALESTINE.

REPORT OF COMMITTEE ON PROPOSED RESTRICTION OF LAND SALES.

Your Excellency,

A Committee, consisting of the Chief Secretary (Chairman), the Attorney General, the Treasurer, the Irrigation Adviser, the Commissioner for Lands and Surveys and the Development Officer was appointed, by Your Excellency's direction in Executive Council on the 8th February, 1956, to undertake an enquiry into the proposed measures for the restriction of sales of land and to make practical recommendations for the application of the principles approved by the Secretary of State.

2. These principles were enunciated in Your Excellency's statement to the Arab leaders on the 29th January, 1936, and may be summarised as follows:

That except in the Sub-District of Beersheba and in urban areas, and also except as regards land planted with citrus, no landowner should be permitted to sell any of his land unless he retains a minimum area sufficient to afford a means of subsistence to himself and his family, that this minimum area should be inalienable and should revert to Government if it ceases to be cultivated by the owner-occupier, and that the High Commissioner should have the power to approve the sale of a subsistence area if he is satisfied that this will be to the interest of the public good.

3. At its first meeting the Committee discussed a number of points which appeared to require careful consideration before detailed recommendations could be formulated for the application of the proposed measures, and reached a number of provisional conclusions, of which the principal were as follow:

HIS EXCELLENCY THE HIGH COMMISSIONER.

2.

(i) **Size of the subsistence area.** That in fixing the subsistence area use should be made of the classification of all rural lands into different categories for the purpose of the Rural Property Tax. This would avoid the necessity of carrying out a special investigation into the productivity of each parcel of land designated as a subsistence area by an intending vendor. Once the minimum subsistence area for each category is fixed it should not be varied, and if at any time it is agreed that the category of any particular land has changed, the subsistence area appropriate to the new category would automatically be applied.

(ii) **Citrus land.** That with regard to the exclusion of land planted with citrus from the application of the proposed measures it would be necessary to provide careful safeguards to ensure that the citrus cultivation is genuine.

(iii) **Pending sales.** That the proposed measures should be applied to all sales pending at the time when the legislation is enacted. It might be necessary to make some provision to protect a prospective vendor, who was thus prevented from fulfilling a contract to sell, from the penalty attaching to a breach of the contract.

(iv) **Unregistered sales.** That it might be necessary to prescribe special penalties for the conclusion of unregistered sales.

(v) **Succession.** That provision should be made, in the case where the heirs of a deceased landowner inherit small parcels of land, to facilitate the consolidation

3.

of the parcels by permitting an heir to sell his share to another member of the same family.

(vi) <u>Consolidation of subsistence areas into blocks</u>. That some provision should be made to allow the grouping of a number of subsistence areas into one consolidated block: it might be prescribed that if more than a certain proportion of the cultivators apply for such consolidation, and Government is satisfied that this would be to the benefit of the majority, all should be compelled to move to the consolidated block.

(vii) <u>Mortgages</u>. That it might be desirable to prohibit the mortgage of a subsistence area: existing mortgages of course would not be interfered with. Alternatively the legislation might provide that a subsistence area shall not be sold in execution.

(viii) <u>Leases</u>. That the lease of a subsistence area should be permitted up to a certain maximum period: longer leases might be concluded with the specific approval of Government in each case. The commutation of the rent into a lump sum should not be prohibited.

(ix) <u>Reversion of subsistence area if not cultivated</u>. That consideration should be given to the possibility of reserving to the village concerned a subsistence area which escheats to Government on account of non-cultivation.

4. Questions arising from these suggestions, and from the proposals generally, were further studied, in consultation

4.

with officers of the District Administration and non-officials with experience of land matters, by the Sub-Committee, consisting of the Attorney-General and the Development Officer, the appointment of which was decided upon by Your Excellency at the time the present Committee was appointed. The report of the Sub-Committee is annexed.

5.   This report has been considered by the full Committee which now submits the following further conclusions and recommendations for Your Excellency's consideration:

(i)   The Committee considers that the personal position of the prospective vendor should not be taken into account, and that the proposed legislation should provide that any person making a disposition of land should retain a subsistence area: this object would be achieved by preventing the registration of such transactions in the Land Registry, unless the Registrar was satisfied that this condition was complied with. The procedure suggested is that the person wishing to make the disposition should satisfy the officers of the District Administration that he is retaining a subsistence area; the Assistant District Commissioner would then issue to him a certificate to that effect; and the Registrar would register the disposition on production of the certificate.

In view of the fact that a number of persons who are registered owners of land no longer in fact own the land registered in their names it will be necessary to provide that the person making the disposition must show that he both owns and is the registered

5.

owner of the land which he is putting forward as a subsistence area.

In this connection the Committee proposes that the retention of a subsistence area in land planted with citrus, although such land is excluded from the application of the restrictions, should entitle the owner to sell his other land.

(ii) (a) With regard to the fixing of the subsistence area in relation to the class of the land, the Committee recommends that, with the exceptions noted in sub-paragraphs (b) and (c) below, the subsistence area should be any holding of land upon which Rural Property Tax to the amount of LP 2 a year is payable. The following table gives examples of the subsistence areas which would be required in different categories:

Category of land under R_ural Property Tax.	Description	Rate of Tax per dunum.	Subsistence Area.
5	1st grade irrigated land.	40 mils	50 dunums
8	1st grade ground crop land, etc.	25 mils	80 dunums
12	5th grade ground crop land, etc.	12 mils	166 dunums
15	6th grade ground crop land.	8 mils	250 dunums

(b) As regards lands in categories 1, 2 and 3, namely citrus (excluding Acre Sub-District), citrus (Acre Sub-District) and bananas, the Committee considers that the areas on which Rural Property Tax in the amount of LP 2

6.

would be payable, namely 2.42 dunums, 4.87 dunums and 3.57 dunums respectively, are inadequate as a subsistence area.

The Committee therefore recommends that in calculating the subsistence area for land of these categories, in accordance with the proposal in sub-paragraph (a) above, the tax payable should be deemed to be 200 mils a dunum instead of the tax actually payable under the Rural Property Tax Ordinance.

(c) It also appears to the Committee to be desirable that provision should be made for the acceptance as a subsistence area of an adequate holding of lands in categories below the lowest taxable category under the Rural Property Tax Ordinance, namely categories 14, 15 and 16.

For these categories the Committee recommends that the calculation of the subsistence area should be based on a notional tax of 5 mils a dunum, although it must be expected that in the less productive lands of these categories a holding which at this rate would pay tax of an amount of LP.2 would not always provide the owner with adequate subsistence.

(iii) In regard to musha' land the Committee recommends that, subject to the same restrictions as in the case of divided lands, the registered owner of undivided shares should be permitted to sell them, and registered shares of musha' land should be accepted as a subsistence area. Although an owner of undivided shares may have difficulty in bringing the register up to date, the suggested procedure appears preferable to a total prohibition of transactions in musha' land.

7.

(iv) The Committee has considered the fact that there are many contracts for sale of land or of shares of undivided land, which are tantamount to unregistered sales, particularly as in the course of land settlement such contracts are accepted as evidence of change of ownership, enabling the property to be registered in the name of the purchaser.

The Committee recommends that the proposed legislation should prescribe that no contract for the sale of any land in the area to which the restrictions are to be applied, or any share or interest therein, made after the enactment of the legislation, should be valid unless registered within fourteen days of its making, and that it should not be registered unless the vendor shows that he is possessed of a subsistence area. Further that at the date of the registration of the actual transfer, or of the acceptance of the purchaser as the owner at land settlement, the vendor must still be possessed of a subsistence area.

A provision of this nature is essential to prevent the sale of subsistence areas through the production of contracts at land settlement. In addition it will be of great advantage to Government to have information regarding these unregistered sales. It may also assist in checking speculation. The Committee proposes that the registration should be effected at the Land Registries, and is giving consideration to the departmental machinery which will be necessary and the form of register which should be adopted. The latter would be prescribed by Rules under the proposed legislation.

8.

The prescription regarding the registration of contracts would not apply to contracts entered into prior to the date of the enactment of the proposed legislation, but all dispositions brought before the Land Registry for registration after that date would be subject to the proviso regarding the retention of a subsistence area. Consequently it will be necessary to provide that if a prospective vendor is prevented by the legislation from fulfilling a contract to sell he should not be liable for damages for breach of the contract, if he refunds any deposit paid. But if he is prevented only in part from fulfilling the contract the purchaser should be entitled to demand the completion of the contract to the extent that this is not rendered impossible by the legislation.

(v) In the earlier discussions on the subject of the proposed legislation it was suggested that the dispositions to which the restrictions would apply should include a mortgage.

The Committee now recommends that no restriction should be placed on the mortgaging of land, but that the position of the smallholder in this respect should be safeguarded by a provision that upon a sale by way of execution arising from a mortgage or other debt, a subsistence area is to be retained for the judgment debtor. It would be for the prospective lender to decide whether he will take the risk of lending money on a mortgage knowing that he cannot execute on the borrower's land without leaving him a subsistence area.

9.

(vi) As regards leases, the Committee recommends that the present provision of the Law, to the effect that leases for three years or less need not be registered, should not be changed, so that an owner of agricultural land could lease it for not more than three years, even though he did not retain other land as a subsistence area. But in order to prevent a lessee entering into an unregistered lease combined with a contract that the unregistered lease would be renewed from time to time the Committee proposes that the new legislation should include a provision that no contract to grant or to renew a lease of land which shall not become operative within three months of its making shall be a binding agreement.

(vii) With regard to the reversion to Government of any subsistence area which ceases to be cultivated by the owner cultivator the Committee understands that the legislation must give effect to the terms of the High Commissioner's statement to the Arab leaders on the 29th January, 1936, but observes that it must not debar the owner-cultivator from leasing his subsistence area in accordance with the proposals in the preceding subsection of this report. The Committee recommends that when a subsistence area thus reverts to Government the High Commissioner should have discretion to reassign it to the former owner, on payment of any taxes due in respect of the area, or to direct that it should be used for a public purpose or for the benefit of the village.

(viii) The provisions of the Law of Succession which provide for the division of an estate between the heirs of the deceased owner, when applied in conjunction with

10.

the proposed enforced retention of a subsistence area, present difficulty since by successive inheritances the share of each heir would become less, until each was absurdly small.

The Committee therefore recommends that an heir who inherits a share which is less than a subsistence area should be allowed to sell his share to a co-heir. This will enable small shares to be combined into an economic holding.

(ix) Under the proposed legislation it will be possible for purchases of land to be made from a number of owners of adjacent land, each of whom will retain a subsistence area. There may well be circumstances in which it will be found in the public interest to group together the subsistence areas in order to avoid a number of isolated holdings.

The Committee consequently recommends that the proposed legislation should contain a provision empowering the District Commissioner, on application being made to him, to prepare and, after due notification, to enforce a scheme for the exchange of such land as may be necessary in order to group together isolated holdings. If in any case it were decided that compensation should be paid to the owner of the holding in respect of his compulsory transfer to a new holding, such compensation would be paid by the person applying for the grouping.

The Committee also proposes that the legislation should provide for an appeal to the High Commissioner-in-Council from the District Commissioner's Order for the application of such a scheme, and suggests in addition that an administrative instruction should

11.

be issued to District Commissioners to the effect that they should not execute any such scheme without the prior sanction of Government.

6. In order to facilitate consideration of the foregoing recommendations, the Committee has annexed hereto a number of clauses which would give effect to its recommendations.

     We have the honour to be,
     Your Excellency's
     obedient servants,

    (Signed) J. Hathorn Hall

     CHAIRMAN.

(Signed) H. H. Trusted ⎫
" W. J. Johnson ⎬ MEMBERS.
" D. G. Harris ⎪
" F. J. Salmon ⎪
" L. Andrews ⎭

1st May, 1936.

REPORT OF SUB-COMMITTEE APPOINTED TO ENQUIRE INTO PROPOSALS TO RESTRICT SALES OF LAND.

We have discussed the question with the three District Commissioners, most of the Assistant District Commissioners, a number of District Officers, Bank Managers, villagers and others. We have not discussed the matter with any non-official Jews. In the course of these discussions and in discussions between ourselves, a number of aspects of the problem have presented themselves. The matter has also been discussed with Mr. Stubbs, and the chaotic state of the land law and land tenure greatly increase the difficulties.

2. The proposed legislation might take the form of providing that upon **every** sale a portion of **the land sold** should be retained. In the case of the holder of one piece of land who was selling it, there would be no great objection to this, but in the case of a man owning several pieces of land selling only one of them, or of a man selling part only of one piece of land it might well be argued that the object of the law was not to insure that the cultivator retained the holding, which on economic and political grounds can be defended, but to prevent the sale of land to the Jews.

3. We feel that great difficulty would be experienced if the personal position of the actual vendor had to be taken into account, e.g. if the Ordinance referred to sales by actual cultivators, vendors would cease to be cultivators and become labourers or builders before they sold; if the Ordinance referred to sales by persons who have actually cultivated for a fixed period, if the period was short, vendors would stop cultivating

2.

for the required period, or if long, a judicial enquiry would have to be held to ascertain the facts. Similarly references to other permanent means of livelihood might require lengthy investigations.

4. Assuming the law is to be of general application, it seems doubtful if it can do more than provide that any person selling or leasing land, should retain a subsistence area not necessarily being part of the land sold or leased. If this is accepted, the easiest way to achieve the desired result would seem to be to prevent the registration of certain transactions in the Land Registry, unless that Department was satisfied that at the date of registration the vendor or lessor had other unencumbered land registered in his name, similar provisions being made in connection with execution of judgments by the court in the case of mortgages and otherwise.

According to Mr. Stubbs there are, however, a certain number of persons who are registered as owners who no longer in fact own the land registered in their names, it would therefore seem necessary to provide that the vendor or lessor owns land of which he is registered as the owner.

5. All the persons with whom we discussed the matter were in favour of a law such as had been generally outlined in His Excellency's statement.

6. We attempted to obtain from officers with local experience and others, an estimate, based on practical knowledge, of what area should be regarded as a subsistence area. Estimates varied from 100 to 270 dunums for non-irrigated land, and were about 50 dunums for irrigated land, or 60 to 70 dunums if the land was partly irrigated and

3.

partly not irrigated. Naturally the land must vary according to local conditions, but a fair average estimate of non-irrigated land from the information we obtained would seem to be about 150 dunums.

7. The general opinion was that the categories in the schedule to the Rural Property Tax Ordinance, 1935, would form a useful basis for deciding upon the number of dunums to be regarded as a subsistence area for various classes of land. The District Commissioner, Jerusalem District, suggested that this might be carried a step further and that any holding of land upon which that tax to the amount of two pounds was payable, might be regarded as a subsistence area e.g.

Category	Description	Rate of Tax.	Holding represented by payment of £P.2.
3	bananas	560 mils	3½ dunums
5	1st grade irrigated land.	40 mils	50 dunums
8	1st grade ground crop land, etc.	25 mils	80 dunums
12	5th grade ground crop land, etc.	12 mils	166 dunums
13	6th grade ground crop land, etc.	8 mils	250 dunums

It may be noted that under this system the last three categories in the schedule on which no tax is paid, could never amount to a subsistence holding, but as they pay no tax, presumably, on the principle that they produce little or no profit, this would seem not unreasonable. If necessary, special cases of land in this category could be dealt with under the power which it is suggested should be vested in the High Commissioner to deal with exceptional cases.

8. Land held in musha'a tenure presents considerable difficulties. From our enquiries it would seem that in

4.

practice the incidence of this tenure varies in different villages and that in the majority of cases the land registers are not up to date, in most cases such land being registered in the names of holders as at some fifty or sixty years ago. Moreover, in some cases a proportion of the shares is in fact held by an effendi and the remainder by the fellaheen.

The officials and others with whom we discussed the matter were of opinion that until partition had taken place and the actual land of the individual holders had thus been ascertained, it would be difficult to regulate the sale of musha'a holdings.

On the assumption that a sale is not to be registered unless the vendor satisfies the Land Registry that he has other land amounting to a subsistence area, we are concerned with musha'a land from two angles, i.e. actual sales and musha'a holdings put forward as subsistence areas. In the latter case it may be easy for a vendor to show that he has cultivated land and in fact paid tax upon it, but in either case, we think that in practice it will be difficult for him to show that he is the registered owner of shares owing to the registers not being up to date, and that in many cases it will be difficult for him to bring the registers up to date.

Most of the officials with whom we discussed the question were of opinion that it would be better to exclude musha'a holdings from the operation of the Ordinance and to prohibit any dealing in musha'a until settlement, with which we agree, but we realize that there might be considerable objections to this and we are of opinion that the most satisfactory course would be to

5.

provide for sales by the registered owners of shares and to regard registered shares as a subsistence area.

Until the registers are brought up to date, there cannot be any registration of the transfer of shares, but there may be, as there have been in the past, contracts for the sale of shares which are produced by the purchaser under such contracts at subsequent land settlement. These are generally referred to by the Land Registry as "unofficial sales" and by the settlement officers as "renunciations".

To deal with this difficulty, we suggest that the Ordinance might provide that no contract for the sale of any land or any share or interest therein made after the commencement of the Ordinance be valid unless registered within fourteen days of the making thereof, and that it shall not be registered unless the vendor showed that he was possessed of a subsistence area, and it will be necessary to provide that at the date of the registration of the actual transfer or of the acceptance of the purchaser as the owner at land settlement, the vendor is still possessed of a subsistence area.

Mr. Stubbs felt some doubt if the contract should be registered but we are inclined to think that it would be well to discuss the making of such contracts. Mr. Stubbs was of opinion that these unofficial sales should not be accepted at settlement as apart from other considerations they defraud the revenue of fees on transfer but we are not satisfied that that is a consideration with which we are presently concerned.

9. We were informed that except to some extent in the neighbourhood of Jaffa, the ordinary cultivator does not raise money on mortgage but obtains the ordinary annual

6.

working capital required on the security of the crop, his personal security or collective guarantee. We are of opinion that the argument that a mortgage of a subsistence area or a part thereof should be allowed in order to facilitate development is largely theoretical, for example, the Agricultural Mortgage Company has not so far advanced more than one pound per dunum upon ordinary cereal land. Assuming, therefore, that a subsistence area is, say, one hundred or one hundred and fifty dunums, the total amount that the owner could raise on the whole holding would probably not be enough for permanent improvements. Assuming, however, that the Ordinance takes the form of providing that upon a sale by way of execution arising from a mortgage or other debt, a subsistence area is to be retained for the judgment debtor there would appear to be no need to provide in terms that a subsistence area could not be mortgaged, leaving it to the prospective lender to decide whether it is worth his while to lend money on mortgage knowing that he cannot execute on the borrower's land without leaving him a subsistence area.

10. In order to combat any attempt to avoid the provisions of the Ordinance, it has been suggested that leases should not be registered unless the lessor showed that he had a subsistence area. At present, leases for less than three years need not be registered, and if this provision is allowed to remain, any owner of land could lease it for not more than three years, although he might have no other land amounting to a subsistence area. We see no great objection to this if the Ordinance provides that no contract to renew or to grant a lease of land which shall not become operative within, say, three months of the date of making shall be a binding agreement. This

7.

should prevent lessees entering under an unregistered lease plus a contract that the unregistered lease would be renewed from time to time.

The power to lease for short terms would in some measure meet one of the criticisms, i.e. that a non-cultivator who became possessed of land, which owing to the operation of the Ordinance he was unable to sell, was being unfairly treated.

It may be argued that so long as the Protection of Cultivators Ordinance is in operation, a tenant, even under an unregistered lease, would obtain a certain security of tenure, but we think it hardly likely that organised changes in the holding of land would take place on the security of that Ordinance alone.

We are of opinion that if short term leases were allowed it is most unlikely that any appreciable amount of land would remain uncultivated. In practice, the absentee owner generally arranges with a relative or friend in the village to cultivate during his absence, and we are doubtful if it is necessary to legislate with reference to uncultivated land and that it might be sufficient to rely upon the somewhat obscure provisions of the existing law as to mahloul.

11. The provisions of the Law of Succession which provide for the dividing of an estate upon the death of the owner, present an obvious criticism of the proposed law. So long as the shares of the heirs amount to or exceed a subsistence area, they are in the same position as anybody else, and presumably, the ordinary provision of the law should apply to them. If the shares of the heirs are less than a subsistence area, it is an obvious argument that they

8.

cannot themselves theoretically live on those shares and in process of time the position becomes absurd. It is suggested, therefore, that an heir who inherits a share less than a subsistence area should be allowed to sell his share to a co-heir. The theoretical objection to this is that the shares of the heirs might be transferred to one of their number and sold less that one heir's subsistence area and the proceeds divided among the other heirs, for example, ten heirs inherit ninety dunums each, the land is transferred to one of them who then becomes possessed of nine hundred dunums. He might then sell eight hundred dunums, retaining a subsistence area for himself of one hundred dunums, and the purchase price might be divided. It is difficult to see how this could be avoided, but it would in practice only apply to small estates and is probably a lesser evil than insisting upon the retention of a diminishing share being less than a subsistence area.

12.   On the assumption that in the future purchases of land may be made from a number of owners of adjacent land each of whom may retain a subsistence area, we discussed with the officers of the District Administration the desirability of grouping together the subsistence areas in order to avoid a number of isolated holdings particularly when the owners are Arabs scattered amongst land owned by Jews. With the exception of the Acting District Commissioner, Northern District, everyone was of opinion that it was desirable and most officers were of opinion that it was necessary, on the grounds of public security and convenience, that such holdings should be grouped. We suggest therefore that the legislation should contain some provision to effect this. It is not, however, altogether easy to work out. If the grouping depends upon the wish of the majority of persons concerned, the recalcitrant owner will exploit the situation to his own advantage and probably receive

9.

in practice a greater sum than the owner who is amenable to a reasonable suggestion. On the other hand, it would seem undesirable to move owners by force. We suggest that the District Commissioner be given power to carry out a scheme and that it will have to be left to the District Administration to do so as tactfully as possible.

(Signed) H.H. Trusted.
L. Andrews.

27.3.36.

Interpretation. CLAUSE A.

In this Ordinance, the expression "land to which this Ordinance applies" means land other than

(a) land of category 4 in the schedule to the Rural Property Tax Ordinance, 1935, and land of categories 1 or 2 in that schedule which belonged to either of those categories at the date of the coming into operation of this Ordinance;

(b) land in the Beersheba Sub-District;

(c) land within any municipal area or town planning area;

(d) land which is exempted from the provisions of this Ordinance by an order of the High Commissioner-in-Council under section D of this Ordinance.

"Court" means any civil or religious court competent to deal with actions concerning land as well as any land court;

"Director" means the Director of Land Registration;

"Disposition" means a sale, gift, dedication of wakf of every description, and any other disposition of immovable property, except a devise by will or a lease for a term not exceeding three years, and includes a lease containing an option by virtue of which the term may exceed three years;

"Land" includes houses, buildings and things permanently fixed in the land.

"Subsistence Area" means unencumbered land or a share of such land upon which respectively rural property tax of an amount of not less than two pounds per annum is payable under the provisions of the Rural Property Tax Ordinance, 1935, not being land of category 4 in the schedule to that Ordinance:

Provided that for the purpose of this definition the tax on land of categories 1, 2 and 3 in the schedule

2.

to the Rural Property Tax Ordinance, 1935, shall be deemed to be payable at the rate of 200 mils per dunum and rural property tax at the rate of 5 mils per dunum shall be deemed to be payable on land of categories 14, 15 and 16 in that schedule.

Certain dispositions not to be registered.

CLAUSE B.

(1) No disposition of any land to which this Ordinance applies or any share of any such land shall be registered in the Land Registry unless the person wishing to make such disposition shall prove to the satisfaction of the Director that he owns and is the registered owner of a subsistence area.

(2) The provisions of this section shall not apply to the disposition of any land by

(a) His Majesty or any of His Majesty's Principal Secretaries of State;

(b) the High Commissioner or the Government of Palestine;

(c) any religious body or institution;

(d) any corporate body;

(e) an heir under the provisions of section 10 of this Ordinance.

(3) The Director may require any person wishing to make any disposition of any land to which this Ordinance applies to support such application by affidavits by himself and any other person.

(4) Any person

(a) who knowingly makes any false statement in any affidavit made for the purposes of this section; or

(b) who knowingly uses for the purposes of this section any affidavit containing any false statement;

shall be liable to imprisonment for seven years.

Contracts made before the commencement of this Ordinance.

CLAUSE C.

Where owing to the provisions of this Ordinance any contract made before the commencement thereof cannot be completed in whole or in part, notwithstanding anything contained in such contract, no damages shall be recoverable in any court in respect of any such non-completion.

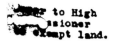
Power to High Commissioner to exempt land.

CLAUSE D.

The High Commissioner-in-Council may by Order, if in his opinion it is in the public interest so to do, exempt any land to which this Ordinance would otherwise apply from the provisions of this Ordinance.

Certain contracts to be registered.

CLAUSE E.

(1)   No contract made after the commencement of this Ordinance to sell any land to which this Ordinance applies or any share of such land or to renounce any interest in such land or in any share thereof shall be valid wholly or in part for any purpose unless such contract is attested before a notary public and registered in the Land Registry within fourteen days of the making thereof.

No such contract shall be registered unless the Director is satisfied that the person agreeing to sell or renounce thereunder owns and is the registered owner of a subsistence area.

(2)   Notwithstanding the provisions of Sub-Section (1) thereof, the provisions of section B of this Ordinance shall apply to any disposition of any land in respect of which any such contract is made.

(3)   No claim based upon or arising out of any such contract shall be admitted by any Settlement Officer under the Land Settlement Ordinance, 1928, unless such contract has been attested and registered in accordance with the provisions of sub-section (1) hereof and such officer is satisfied that the person agreeing to sell or renounce under such contract owns and is the registered owner of a subsistence area.

(4)   The registration of any contract under the provisions of sub-section (1) hereof shall not constitute any encumbrance or charge upon the land to which such contract refers and such contract shall not be deemed to be valid or binding contract by reason only of such registration.

Restriction on execution.

CLAUSE F.

Notwithstanding anything contained in any other law or Ordinance, no order for the sale of land to which this Ordinance applies or of a share of such land shall be made in the execution of any judgment or in satisfaction of any mortgage unless the judge or execution officer is satisfied that the judgment debtor owns and is the registered owner of a subsistence area:

Provided that the provisions of this section shall not apply to any judgment or order made in respect of a mortgage made and registered before the commencement of this Ordinance:

Provided also that nothing in this section shall be deemed to derogate from the power of any court or execution officer with regard to land other than land to which this Ordinance applies or to order the retention by any judgment debtor of any land in excess of a subsistence area.

Protection and division of bankrupt's property.

CLAUSE G.

Where under the provisions of any bankruptcy law in force a bankrupt is to retain land necessary for his support and that of his dependants, the land so retained shall not be less than a subsistence area.

Certain contracts concerning leases to be invalid.

CLAUSE H.

No contract for the grant of any lease for a term of less than three years or for the renewal of any lease of any land to which this Ordinance applies whereunder such grant or renewal does not become operative within three months of the making thereof shall be valid or binding in whole or in part for any purpose.

[illegible]es between [illegible]irs.

CLAUSE I.

Where under the provisions of any law of succession in force in Palestine any heir becomes entitled to any share of any land and such share is less than a subsistence area, such heir may dispose of such share to any co-heir of his and the provisions of section B of this Ordinance shall not apply to such disposition.

District Commissioner to group holdings in certain cases.

CLAUSE J.

(1) Where within the lands of any village or adjacent villages there are situated any number of holdings of land all or some of which are separated from the others and the District Commissioner <u>upon application being made to him</u> is of opinion that such holdings or some of them should be grouped together he may prepare a scheme for the exchange of such land as may be necessary either with or without compensation payable by the applicant.

Such scheme shall be exhibited in the village or villages for not less than fourteen days whereafter the District Commissioner shall hear and determine any objections thereto.

If there are no objections or where such objections have been heard and determined the District Commissioner shall order that such scheme shall apply whereupon such scheme shall have the force of law and any magistrate may issue any orders of eviction as may be necessary to enforce such scheme.

(2) Any person aggrieved by the order of the District Commissioner may within fourteen days of the date thereof appeal to the High Commissioner-in-Council whose decision shall be final. Where any such appeal is made no steps shall be taken to enforce the order of the District Commissioner until the decision of the High Commissioner-in-Council shall have been given.

and to which this Ordinance applies which remains uncultivated by the owner, etc.

CLAUSE K.

(1) Where any land to which this Ordinance applies shall be uncultivated by the owner or any kinsman of his or by any tenant of the owner for a period of three consecutive years, such land shall become vested in the High Commissioner who may at his discretion

> (a) reassign such land to the owner or his heirs upon the payment of all taxes due (if any) in respect thereof;
>
> (b) direct that such land may be used for any purpose for the benefit of the public or of the village in the lands of which such land is situated.

(2) The provisions of the Ottoman Land Law as to mahlul shall no longer apply to any land to which this section applies.

Power of High Commissioner to make rules.

CLAUSE L.

The High Commissioner may from time to time make rules under the provisions of section 16 of the Transfer of Land Ordinance, 1920 (as amended by the Transfer of Land (Amendment) Ordinance, 1929) and the provisions of that section shall be deemed to apply to this Ordinance as though it were enacted therein <u>mutatis</u> <u>mutandis</u>.

9.10

CF/15/35.
SECRET.

HIGH COMMISSIONER FOR PALESTINE,
JERUSALEM.

12 August, 1936.

Sir,

I have the honour to refer to your Secret despatch of the 6th July, 1936, regarding the proposals for the restriction of land sales in Palestine.

2. In consultation with the Committee which I appointed in February last to enquire into those proposals I have studied the memorandum which was enclosed in the despatch under reference and I submit the following observations on the different points raised therein (the references are those quoted in the memorandum):

(i) I, (11(i)). The minimum subsistence area has been calculated on the basis of a man and a family of four persons. Since the early days of the Palestine Administration this has been the accepted figure for an average family, and this estimate was borne out by the results of the 1931 Census.

It is for consideration whether the existing schedule to the Rural Property Tax Ordinance, setting out the rates of tax per dunum for each category of land, should not form a schedule to the proposed legislation for the restriction of land sales. If at any future date the rates of Rural Property tax were varied for reasons that the average yield or financial return from a dunum of land of one or more of the

categories/

The Right Honourable W.G.A. Ormsby-Gore, P.C., M.P.,
His Majesty's Principal Secretary of State
for the Colonies.

- 2 -

categories had changed, the amount of Rural Property tax taken as the basis of the subsistence area would of course remain unchanged. If, however, the rate of Rural Property tax for a dunum of land of one or more of the categories were varied for reasons unconnected with the average yield or financial return, the amount of Rural Property tax taken as the basis of the subsistence area might of course have to be changed in respect of the categories affected.

(ii) I, (11(v)). I am advised that it would be impracticable to enact legislation making it compulsory for an owner of a subsistence area to nominate his heir to such an area. This would run counter to the Jewish, as well as the Moslem, law of inheritance. It is believed that the danger of continued partition, on inheritance, into uneconomic units is much less than might be expected. The object of the recommendation of the Committee is to make sale between co-heirs permissible in respect of a subsistence area, in exception to the proposed general prohibition of the sale of such an area. My advisers assure me that up to the present the existing inheritance laws, which have been operating in this country for many years, have not resulted in uneconomic fractionisation.

(iii) I, (11(vi)). I do not think it advisable that the District Commissioner should be bound by the majority opinion of the owners of the holdings concerned. The draft clause J was purposely framed in general terms, so that the District Commissioner, in preparing a scheme and in hearing objections, might be guided by the general merits of the case. The phrase "upon application being made to him" in the draft clause was intended to cover the initiation of a scheme by

Government/

- 3 -

Government through any appropriate Department. It is agreed that the wording of the clause does not make this clear and I therefore now suggest that the words "upon application being made to him" should be omitted.

(iv) I, (11(vii)). The practical effect of the proposal is correctly set out in the memorandum. Although the draft clauses do not in terms prohibit the mortgaging of a subsistence area such a mortgage would in fact be impossible, since the sale of the subsistence area in satisfaction of a mortgage is prohibited by clause F.

(v) I, (11(x)). Musha' land is land held in common by a number of owners (often all the landowners of a village) each of whose holdings is expressed as a fraction of the whole of the land involved. No individual has a permanent right to a particular piece of the land, each man's share being defined anew on the ground every year or two years, according to local custom. Such undivided shares are regularly bought and sold. Consequently, while it would be impossible for an owner of a share in musha' land to cite a particular registered parcel as his permanent subsistence area, it is considered that provided he is the registered owner of a share on which Rural Property Tax to an amount of £P.2 is payable, this share may be accepted as a subsistence area (enabling him to sell any other land which he may possess) although it does not constitute a specifically registered parcel of land, and the areas of the different categories of land which comprise it may vary from time to time.

(vi) II, (12(ii)(a)). The criticism is valid. If the owner of no more than a subsistence area is unable to mortgage his holding he will be unable to obtain sufficient capital for any substantial development. It is not

believed/

- 4 -

believed, however, that any harmful result will ensue as even at present it is impossible for a small holder to raise any appreciable sum on his holding. The Agricultural Mortgage Company, for example, makes advances on agricultural land at the rate of only about £P.1 to £P.2 a dunum, which is much too small for substantial development.

(vii) III. The suggestion that the village rather than the individual should be made the unit in any scheme for the preservation of subsistence areas is certainly attractive at first sight. But the practical difficulties in giving effect to this suggestion would be, I fear, almost insuperable.

For example it is the common practice of villagers in one village to own and cultivate lands in another village, and consequently the consolidation of village lands and their declaration as the inalienable property of the persons dwelling in the village would involve the exchange or transfer of individual holdings on a large scale, and such a process would be strongly resisted.

Moreover, in fact, there is little prospect that a number of small isolated subsistence areas will be created, scattered throughout alienated lands. The position is rather the reverse. From such facts as are available it is already clear that under the suggested legislation very few parcels would be available for sale in the hill villages, and that even in villages in the plain the amount of land which could be sold would be relatively small. Even if the alienated parcels were grouped under the provisions of draft clause J, they would, in the majority of cases, form a comparatively small block surrounded by a much larger

area/

- 5 -

area of subsistence areas, and such blocks would in many cases not be attractive to Jewish potential purchasers.

3. In reconsidering the proposals in the light of the memorandum enclosed in your despatch under reference, the opportunity has been taken to review certain of the draft clauses annexed to the Committee's Report, and I now suggest the following further modifications:

(i) Clause E(i). It is conceivable that when a contract is produced for registration the examination of the vendor's claim to own a subsistence area might require more than fourteen days. I therefore propose that the words "and registered in the Land Registry within fourteen days of the making thereof." should be replaced by the words "and is submitted for registration in the Land Registry within fourteen days of the making thereof and is subsequently registered.".

(ii) Clause E(ii). For "thereof" read "hereof".

(iii) Clause K(i). It has been pointed out that the introduction of a new term "kinsman", which has no precise significance, may give rise to difficulty. A comprehensive definition of the term heir is given in the Ottoman Law of Succession, and I therefore recommend that the words "or any kinsman of his" should be replaced by the words "or by any person or the spouse of any person capable of becoming his heir within the meaning of the Ottoman Provisional Law relating to the succession to immovable property dated 3 Rabi ul Awal, 1331".

4. In paragraph 4 of your despatch under reference you advert to my proposal that I should begin discussion of the proposed measures with Arab and Jewish leaders when the time

appeared/

- 6 -

appeared favourable. Since I made my recommendation the Arabs have adopted a much more uncompromising attitude generally, and I consider that there would be no advantage in attempting to discuss these proposals with them at present. There is consequently nothing to be gained in opening discussions with the Jewish leaders. Unless, therefore, there is an early improvement in the general situation, I see little prospect of discussing the matter usefully with either party prior to the arrival of the Royal Commission.

                I have the honour to be,

                      Sir,

                    Your most obedient,

                        humble servant,

Arthur Wauchope
HIGH COMMISSIONER
FOR PALESTINE.

9.11

CONFIDENTIAL.
SECRET

Memorandum regarding Mr. Ramsay MacDonald's letter to Dr. Weizmann of the 13th February, 1931, with special reference to its bearing upon the proposals recently approved in principle for restricting the sale of land in certain areas of Palestine.

The publication as a White Paper in October 1930 of the statement of policy regarding Palestine (Cmd. 3692) led to a storm of protest from the Jews throughout the world and to organized pressure upon His Majesty's Government both in Parliament and outside to induce them to modify that statement, which was represented as inconsistent with the spirit of the Balfour Declaration and of the Mandate and as gravely injurious to the interests of the Jewish National Home in Palestine. His Majesty's Government viewed the political situation created by this campaign with such gravity that on the 6th November, 1930, the Cabinet decided to appoint a Cabinet Committee to consider the Palestine situation, with the co-operation of the Lord Advocate of Scotland as regards the juridical aspects of the question. This Committee was also to get into touch with the Jewish representatives and to make recommendations as to the attitude to be taken up by the Government in view of the reception of the recently issued White Paper.

(5) on 77339/1/30.

The Committee consisted of
    The Secretary of State for Foreign Affairs
        (Mr. Henderson)
    The Secretary of State for the Colonies
        (Lord Passfield)
    The First Lord of the Admiralty
        (Mr. Alexander)

Enclosures in (42) and (43) on 77050/30/ Part D.

The Committee and the Lord Advocate were furnished by the Colonial Office with a summary of the principal criticisms and misrepresentations to which

the

the White Paper had been subjected by the Jews, together with Departmental comments in defence of the White Paper on the various points attacked. On the basis of this material the Lord Advocate drafted a memorandum for the use of the Cabinet Committee in explaining the situation to the Jewish representatives and in endeavouring to remove the misapprehensions and to allay the fears which had been expressed. Before communication to the Cabinet Committee the Lord Advocate's memorandum was considered in draft both in the Foreign Office and in the Colonial Office and certain modifications were made in consultation with the Lord Advocate himself.

(54) on 77050/30/ Part D.

It was decided by the Cabinet Committee that the Lord Advocate's memorandum should be converted, with certain further modifications, into the draft of a letter addressed to Dr. Weizmann. This was accordingly done and a copy of the draft letter was sent to Dr. Weizmann under cover of a personal letter from Mr. Henderson on the 29th November, 1930.

See (65) on 77050/30/ Part D.

In the meantime meetings had taken place between the Cabinet Committee and the Jewish leaders including Dr. Weizmann. There were six of these meetings: the first was held on the 17th November, 1930, and the last on the 12th February, 1931. In the intervals of these meetings between the Cabinet Committee and the Jewish leaders various discussions took place between on the one side the Lord Advocate and representatives of the Colonial Office, Foreign Office and Treasury, and on the other side representatives of the Jewish Agency.

(4) on 77050/1/30.
(6) on 87050/5/31.

Great

Great pressure was exerted by the Jews to induce His Majesty's Government to accept modifications of the wording of the draft letter to Dr. Weizmann designed to attenuate as far as possible the meaning to be attached to various passages in the White Paper to which objection was felt by the Jews, and so impressed were His Majesty's Government with the importance of going as far as possible to meet Jewish wishes in this respect that they felt obliged to disregard the strong protests received from Sir John Chancellor, then High Commissioner for Palestine, and, after prolonged discussion with the Departmental representatives, very considerable concessions were made as regards the wording of the draft letter. The draft as finally agreed by the Cabinet Committee was circulated to the Cabinet by the Secretary of State for Foreign Affairs on the 30th January, 1931, in a memorandum suggesting the desirability of the Prime Minister signing the letter as the head of the Government after its approval by the Cabinet. This letter was accordingly signed by Mr. Ramsay MacDonald and sent to Dr. Weizmann on the 13th February, 1931.

The object of the letter was stated in the first paragraph of the letter to be to remove certain misconceptions and misunderstandings which had arisen as to the policy of His Majesty's Government with regard to Palestine as set forth in the White Paper, and it was stated that the letter "will fall to be read as the authoritative interpretation of the White Paper on the matters with which this letter deals". Among those matters was the question of land settlement and the proposals in the White Paper for agricultural development and

and the control by the authority in charge of development of all dispositions of land.

The passages dealing with these subjects in the White Paper and the authoritative interpretation placed upon them by the relevant passages of the letter to Dr. Weizmann will be dealt with later. It appears, however, desirable in the first place to give a short explanation of the reasons why these proposals were made in the White Paper.

The conclusion reached by Sir John Hope Simpson, as the result of the investigation which he was commissioned to undertake, was :-

(1) that at the time of his report, August 1930, with the present methods of Arab cultivation, there was no margin of land available for agricultural settlement by new immigrants with the exception of such undeveloped land as various Jewish organizations held in reserve;

(2) that the only way to carry out the twofold obligation of His Majesty's Government under the Mandate and so to enable more Jews to be settled on the land, without prejudice to the rights and position of the Arabs, was an active policy of agricultural development having as its object close settlement on the land and intensive cultivation by both Arabs and Jews.

(Cmd 3686) In his report no estimate of the amount of money which would be required to carry out his recommendations in full was given by Sir John Hope Simpson. It is understood that this estimate was excluded at the

express

express request of the Secretary of State, Lord Passfield.

On the receipt of Sir John Hope Simpson's report a draft statement of policy based in general terms upon the recommendations of Sir John Hope Simpson was considered, together with his report, by the Cabinet Committee on Palestine policy. That Committee approved the draft statement in principle and subsequently appointed an expert Sub-Committee to consider the financial aspects of the recommendations embodied in it. That Committee, which was presided over by Sir Basil Blackett, included Sir John Campbell and Departmental representatives of the Treasury and the Colonial Office, and had the benefit of Sir John Hope Simpson's assistance in their deliberations.

In the course of discussion it became clear that Sir John Hope Simpson's estimate of the full cost of his scheme might amount to as much as £8,000,000. For this expenditure it was estimated that 10,000 Arab families and 20,000 Jewish families could be settled on the land on the assumption that the settlement of the Jewish families was carried out at the same cost per family as the Arabs. The figure of 10,000 Arab families represented a rough estimate given orally by Sir John Hope Simpson of the number of Arab families who had been dispossessed of their holdings as a result of the manner in which the policy of the Balfour Declaration and the Mandate had hitherto been applied.

The report of the Expert Sub-Committee was considered by the Cabinet Committee with the assistance of Sir John Hope Simpson, who attended by invitation.

The

See Cabinet Conclusion in (6) on 77050/c/30

The report of the Cabinet Committee to the Cabinet contained the following conclusions and recommendations:-

(1) That His Majesty's Government are morally bound to see that provision is made for the dispossessed Arabs. No financial obligation, however, of any kind rests on the Government in regard to the settlement of Jews on the land for the purpose of the Jewish National Home.

(2) That Jewish organizations should be permitted to proceed at their own expense with the development and settlement of reserved land (i.e. land already bought but not yet settled). At the then rate of Jewish settlement this reserved land was expected to be sufficient to meet all Jewish requirements over the next five years.

(3) That to guard against the contingency of demands for further expenditure when the funds now contemplated were exhausted the Palestine Administration should take immediate steps

(a) to provide by means of legislation that during the next five years no further parcels of land shall be acquired by Jewish organizations in order to give time for the assimilation of the landless Arabs. (These were assumed on Sir John Hope Simpson's rough estimate to amount to 10,000 families);

(b) to restrict the immigration of Jews to such numbers as can be settled on the reserved land or can confidently be expected to be absorbed into industrial occupation.

(4) That statutory provision should be made as to occupancy rights to safeguard the position of Arab occupants on the reserved lands.

(5) That the dispossessed Arab families should be resettled at a gross estimated cost of
£2,500,000

£2,500,000 in all, but that it should be stated in any public announcement that the money was being provided for the development of land primarily for the resettlement of landless Arabs, but that the settlement of Jews was not excluded from consideration.

(6) That legislation should be introduced to authorize His Majesty's Government to guarantee a loan for the above purpose.

(7) That provision should be made from British funds for the interest and sinking fund charges for the first five years.

(8) That the draft statement of policy amended in accordance with the proposals contained in the report should be approved and its publication authorized simultaneously with the Hope Simpson report.

The Cabinet considered the above report of their Committee on the 24th September, 1930, and after considerable discussion agreed to approve the report of the Cabinet Committee as well as the publication simultaneously of the Hope Simpson report and of the draft statement of policy "which will be revised in accordance with the recommendations of the Cabinet Committee".

The net result of these important decisions was that the draft statement of policy, which had originally been framed on the assumption that the full programme of development envisaged by Sir John Hope Simpson would be adopted despite the inevitable heavy expenditure (attention to which was drawn in the

Departmental

Departmental minutes at the time when the draft was framed), had now to be remodelled so as to harmonize with the decision to incur expenditure which was estimated to suffice only for the resettlement of 10,000 dispossessed Arab families; although it was decided that in any public announcement regarding the provision of money for land development it should be stated that it was primarily for the settlement of landless Arabs but that the settlement of Jews was not excluded from consideration.

The resultant situation was a difficult one. The whole point of Sir John Hope Simpson's recommendations was that, in view of the situation which had arisen, the only way in which it was possible to carry out the obligations of His Majesty's Government with regard to the Jewish National Home, at any rate in so far as it involved the acquisition and colonization of land, was by a scheme of intensive development which, while setting right the prejudice which had already occurred in regard to the rights and position of certain classes of landless Arabs, would give eventual scope for the settlement of a large number of Jewish families on the land. The number was estimated in paragraph 16 of Sir John Hope Simpson's confidential letter of the 18th August, 1930, to Lord Passfield as "not less than 20,000 families. It might well be 40,000".

Sir John Hope Simpson had reason to suppose, from private conversations which he had had with leading Jews, that such a scheme would go far towards satisfying the more moderate Zionists that His Majesty's Government were not guilty of the charge of "crystallizing" the Jewish National Home at the stage then reached.

It

It was not clear, however, how the actual provision of £2½ million could of itself result in any material extension of Jewish land settlement if Sir John Hope Simpson's estimate was correct as to the number of dispossessed Arabs and the cost of resettlement. At the same time, it was necessary, in view of the Cabinet conclusions, to hold out some hope that the settlement of Jews would not be excluded from consideration.

/As a matter of fact, when the question of resettling dispossessed Arabs was actively taken up, it was discovered that the number of families which were qualified to be registered as displaced Arabs, in the sense in which "landless Arabs" was authoritatively interpreted in paragraph 9 of the Prime Minister's letter to Dr. Weizmann of the 13th February, 1931, was only about 650, although the estimate given in his report by Mr. French for the cost of resettlement per family was considerably higher than the provisional figure suggested by Sir John Hope Simpson. At the time, however, when the final decisions of the Cabinet were taken, there was no reason to suppose that Sir John Hope Simpson had so greatly over-estimated the number of dispossessed Arabs, although it should be borne in mind that in his estimate he included Arabs who had owned the land which they cultivated as well as Arab tenants; but when compiling the register of displaced Arabs it was decided to disqualify owner-cultivators./

It was obvious that the various restrictions envisaged by the Government's intended policy as regards immigration, and in particular as regards the control of land transactions, would be far more distasteful to the Jews and far less easy to justify in the light of the

positive

positive obligation on His Majesty's Government to encourage close settlement by Jews on the land, now that it had been decided to confine development expenditure to a £2½ million loan. The amendment of the draft statement of policy was therefore far from easy and attention was drawn in Departmental minutes to the unsatisfactory result when the revised draft was submitted for final approval.

It will, I think, be clear from the foregoing account that there were considerable grounds for Jewish uneasiness, if not for the extreme interpretation placed upon the intentions of His Majesty's Government in the attacks levied by the Jews upon the White Paper. Moreover, the somewhat ambiguous position in which His Majesty's Government found themselves with regard to the recommendations of Sir John Hope Simpson made the task of justifying the policy in the White Paper and reassuring Jewish opinion a peculiarly difficult one.

To revert now to the text of the Prime Minister's letter to Dr. Weizmann of the 13th February, 1931. As already stated, a draft of this letter was sent by Mr. Henderson to Dr. Weizmann on the 29th November, and it was first discussed by the Cabinet

(12) on 77050/1/30.

Committee and the Jewish leaders at their third meeting, which took place on the 5th December, 1930. Pages 9-12 of the minutes of the meeting deal with the discussion on land transfers. As will be seen from those minutes, the terms of the draft letter were not dealt with in detail and the discussion turned upon the powers to be conferred upon the proposed Development Commission and the objections

felt

felt by the Jews to certain draft Ordinances for the control of land transfers which had been submitted by the High Commissioner to the Jewish Agency in Palestine for their observations. The point emphasized in the discussion was the objection felt to the proposal in the draft Ordinances that supreme power to veto land transactions should be placed in the hands of the High Commissioner.

The question was again referred to at the fourth meeting, which took place on the 19th December, 1930. At this meeting Dr. Weizmann took the view that questions regarding land were bound up with the question of the development scheme which would require extensive discussion. Mr. Henderson expressed the hope that he would be able to obtain from the Cabinet extended powers for the Committee to discuss this and other questions. At the fifth meeting, which took place on the 30th January, 1931, the final text of the draft letter was agreed with the Jewish representatives. There is nothing in the minutes of the meeting to indicate that any points relating to the control of land transfers were discussed at length. The reason for this was probably that the text of the draft letter had previously been exhaustively discussed by Jewish representatives with the Lord Advocate's Drafting Committee as explained above. On the 4th February the Cabinet considered the draft letter as agreed at the meeting of their Committee with the Jewish leaders on the 30th January and approved it.

The relevant portion of Mr. Ramsay MacDonald's letter to Dr. Weizmann is paragraphs 10-13. Annexed to this memorandum are -

(a)

(a) a copy of the ~~corresponding~~ relevant portion of the draft letter as sent to Dr. Weizmann on the 29th November, 1930; and

(b) a copy of the corresponding portion of the letter in its final form.

As will be seen, the first sub-paragraph of paragraph 10, the first four sentences of paragraph 12 and the whole of paragraph 13 follow closely the Lord Advocate's draft. The second sub-paragraph of paragraph 10 is an addition, paragraph 11 is in substitution for the first two sentences of paragraph 12 of the draft, and paragraph 14 of the draft has been omitted altogether. On the other hand, three sentences have been added to paragraph 12 in the final text to reassure the Jews regarding the nature of the control contemplated and the date from which it would come into force, and to make clear that the High Commissioner would, pending such centralized control, have powers to take the necessary steps to protect tenancy and occupancy rights.

I think that a study of the draft letter, of such discussions regarding it between the Cabinet Committee and the Jewish leaders as are recorded and of the final text will bear out the contention as set out in paragraph 12 of the memorandum circulated by Mr. Thomas to the Cabinet on the 10th January, 1936, (C.P. 3 (36)), viz., that the assurances in Mr. Ramsay MacDonald's letter are given with specific reference to the policy of land settlement and development referred to in the White Paper of October, 1930. In fact the whole letter is described in the opening paragraph as "the authoritative interpretation of the White Paper on the matters with which this letter deals". In the relevant paragraphs of his letter Mr. Ramsay MacDonald was concerned to reassure the

the Jews on one special point, viz., that such a policy of land settlement would not be used as an excuse for imposing for an ulterior purpose restrictions upon land transactions which would be more than what was required for the purposes of carrying out that policy. His assurances could not be interpreted as debarring His Majesty's Government indefinitely from taking any action which, even if no development or resettlement were in view, might be considered necessary in the general interests of Palestine at some future date and in the face of developments which had not then assumed any serious prominence.

See (1) on 75072/36. (*Colonel here*)

If, as is anticipated, Dr. Weizmann, on his arrival in this country, reverts to the charge that the High Commissioner's present proposals for restricting land sales in certain areas of Palestine are inconsistent with the assurances given in Mr. Ramsay MacDonald's letter, it seems clear that the primary argument in defence of the decision of the Cabinet to approve the High Commissioner's proposals in principle is that given immediately above. There are, however, certain other points which may be mentioned here as relevant to the consideration of the Government's defence. In the first place, various measures have been taken since the publication of the White Paper of October, 1930, with a view to promoting agricultural development, and in particular it may be said that all the measures mentioned in paragraph 24 of the White Paper and many others in addition have been introduced and developed during the last four years. It would not, however, be possible to contend that these measures constitute the extensive

scheme

scheme of development which in the White Paper and the Prime Minister's letter is stated as necessitating central control of land transactions, because the one measure of development recommended by Sir John Hope Simpson which would have necessitated the application of restrictions on the sale of land, viz., the acquisition by Government of tracts of land for development and close settlement, finds no place in the present programme of development of the Palestine Government.

While, however, this argument cannot be used, it could be pointed out to the Jewish Agency that the view indicated above as to the nature and scope of Mr. Ramsay MacDonald's assurances in February, 1931, is not an afterthought invented to justify the decision recently taken as regards restricting the sale of land. This is shown by the fact that Sir Arthur Wauchope, in his interview with Dr. Arlosoroff on the 27th January, 1932, made it clear to the Jewish Agency that His Majesty's Government did not bind themselves to abandon restrictions on land sales forever. If land sales had continued upon the same scale as obtained in 1931 and 1932 it is possible that no restrictions might now have been found necessary, but since that date Jewish purchases of land from Arabs have increased fourfold, and unfortunately the sale of land has outstripped development, and some restrictions, albeit much less drastic than those contemplated in the White Paper and in Mr. Ramsay MacDonald's letter, have become necessary in order to ensure that, in the words of Article 6 of the Mandate, the rights and position of other sections of the population are not prejudiced.

> See pages 8 and 12 of second enclosure to despatch at (18) on 97049/32.

In the next place there is a further point which might be made. It is true that owing to a change in the general financial situation the proposed resettlement and development loan of £2½ millions was dropped, but with it was dropped also any attempt to impose centralized control of land transactions except to the very limited extent to which this is involved in the protection given to "tenants" in the Protection of Cultivators Ordinance. This has left Jewish organizations free to acquire land & to settle upon it with the following results :-

According to the calculation made by Sir John Hope Simpson in Appendix 2 to his report (page 158 of Cmd. 3686), the Jewish agricultural population in the middle of 1930 was about 36,600. Of these, 18,300 were actually engaged in agricultural occupations.

According to the Jewish Agency's report for 1934 (page 8), during the five years 1930-34 the total net area acquired by Jews amounted to 155,900 dunums. To this must be added the Huleh Concession amounting to approximately 40,000 dunums together with 17,000 dunums of the lake itself.

On page 10 of the same report it is stated that at the date of the report the total number of Jewish settlements was 160 on an area of 1,300,000 dunums of agricultural land and with a population of 70,000. Of this total, 40,000 were occupied in agricultural work. This represents a very considerable increase on the agricultural side of the Jewish National Home, and it may be mentioned in this connection that in paragraph 10 of his confidential letter to Lord Passfield of the 13th

August

August, 1930, Sir John Hope Simpson says -

"I was informed by Mr. Hankin, the buyer of the Palestine Land Development Company, who purchases land not only for the Zionists but also for a considerable number of private persons and land companies, that after he has purchased another 100,000 dunums of land it will be impossible to acquire any more without making arrangements on the purchased property for the Arabs who had hitherto found their livelihood there."

There is one further point which may be mentioned. In paragraph 4 of his letter of the 23rd January to Sir Arthur Wauchope commenting on the proposed restriction on sales of land Mr. Shertok says -

"The Jewish national institutions have made it a matter of policy not to leave landless or otherwise unprovided for those Arabs who were previously deriving their livelihood from land acquired by them."

He goes on to say in paragraph 6 -

"In order to assist the fellah it is not enough to secure a tenure over a fixed area of land. It is essential to supply him with means to develop and fructify his land. Very often a smaller area with capital to develop it spells greater prosperity than a larger area without capital. .... So far the main source of such funds has been the sale of surplus Arab land to the Jews .... A measure which will check to a considerable extent the acquisition of land by the Jews will curtail to a

corresponding

corresponding extent the supply of capital for
the permanent improvement of the position of
the fellaheen."

It is difficult to follow this argument as the
whole object of the High Commissioner's proposals is
merely to prevent the complete extinction of the small
owner-occupier class of cultivator by making it impossible
for him to sell a minimum subsistence area. If he is
the owner of more than such an area it should be possible
for him to sell the surplus and, on Mr. Shertok's own
argument, to use the proceeds for improving the
cultivation of his subsistence area. If, however, as
may possibly be the case, the bulk of the owner-occupiers
left in the possession of land have at present little,
if anything, more than a bare subsistence area, then,
unless and until capital is forthcoming from some other
source than sale to enable a part of an extensively
cultivated subsistence area to be intensively cultivated,
thus releasing for sale the remainder, it is clear that
the Jews will be debarred from purchasing land over a
considerable area of Palestine. But at the same time,
if such is in fact found to be the position, it only
illustrates the serious situation with regard to the smallholder which has arisen and would be in itself a
justification of the High Commissioner's recommendations.

APPENDIX A.

Extract from draft letter
to Dr. Weizmann.

12. His Majesty's Government are also well aware that, as the Jewish Agency has emphasised, the congestion of the fellahin is more pronounced in the hill country than in the plains. But this circumstance does not absolve His Majesty's Government from the necessity of having regard to that congestion in framing a policy of land settlement best adapted, in conformity with the Mandate, to the close settlement by the Jews on the land. In framing a policy of land settlement it is essential that His Majesty's Government should take into consideration every circumstance that is relevant to the main purposes of the Mandate. The area of cultivable land, the possibilities of irrigation, the absorptive capacity of the country in relation to immigration are all elements pertinent to the issues to be elucidated, and the neglect of any one of them would be prejudicial to the formulation of a just and stable policy.

13. In giving effect to the policy of land settlement as contemplated in Article XI of the Mandate, it is necessary, if disorganisation is to be avoided, and if the policy is to have a chance to succeed, that there should exist some centralised control of all transactions relating to the acquisition and transfer of land during such interim period as may reasonably be necessary to place

the

the development scheme upon a sure foundation. The power contemplated is regulative, and not prohibitory, although it does involve a power to veto transactions which are inconsistent with the tenor of the general scheme. But the exercise of the power will be limited and in no respect arbitrary. In every case it will be conditioned by considerations as to how best to give effect to the purposes of the Mandate.

14. The colonisation operations of the Jewish organisations in respect of the land reserves at present held by them will continue without break. There would be close co-ordination between the Jewish Colonisation Agencies and the Administration of Palestine to secure that full effect is given to the purposes of the Mandate.

15. Further, the statement of policy of His Majesty's Government did not imply a prohibition of acquisition of additional land by Jews. It contains no such prohibition nor is any such intended. What it does contemplate is such temporary control of land disposition and transfers as may be necessary, not to impair the harmony and effectiveness of the scheme of land settlement to be undertaken. His Majesty's Government feels bound to point out, that they alone of the Governments which have been responsible for the administration of Palestine since the acceptance of the mandate, have declared their definite intention to initiate an active policy of development which it is believed will result in substantial and lasting benefit to the whole community of Palestine, both Jews and Arabs.

X   X

APPENDIX B.

Corresponding extract
from letter as sent.

x   x   x

10. In framing a policy of land settlement, it is essential that His Majesty's Government should take into consideration every circumstance that is relevant to the main purposes of the Mandate. The area of cultivable land, the possibilities of irrigation, the absorptive capacity of the country in relation to immigration are all elements pertinent to the issues to be elucidated, and the neglect of any one of them would be prejudicial to the formulation of a just and stable policy.

It is the intention of His Majesty's Government to institute an enquiry as soon as possible to ascertain, inter alia, what State and other lands are, or properly can be made, available for close settlement by Jews under reference to the obligation imposed upon the Mandatory by article 6 of the Mandate. This enquiry will be comprehensive in its scope, and will include the whole land resources of Palestine. In the conduct of the enquiry provision will be made for all interests, whether Jewish or Arab, making such representations as it may be desired to put forward.

11. The question of the congestion amongst the fellahin in the hill districts of Palestine is receiving the careful consideration of His Majesty's Government. It is contemplated that measures will be devised for the improvement and intensive development of the land, and for

bringing

bringing into cultivation areas which hitherto may have remained uncultivated, and thereby securing to the fellahin a better standard of living, without save in exceptional cases, having recourse to transfer.

12. In giving effect to the policy of land settlement, as contemplated in article 11 of the Mandate, it is necessary, if disorganization is to be avoided, and if the policy is to have a chance to succeed, that there should exist some centralised control of transactions relating to the acquisition and transfer of land during such interim period as may reasonably be necessary to place the development scheme upon a sure foundation. The power contemplated is regulative and not prohibitory, although it does involve a power to prevent transactions which are inconsistent with the tenor of the scheme. But the exercise of the power will be limited and in no respect arbitrary. In every case it will be conditioned by considerations as to how best to give effect to the purposes of the Mandate. Any control contemplated will be fenced with due safeguards to secure as little interference as possible with the free transfer of land. The centralised control will take effect as from such date only as the authority charged with the duty of carrying out the policy of land development shall begin to operate. The High Commissioner will, pending the establishment of such centralised control, have full powers to take all steps necessary to protect the tenancy and occupancy rights, including the rights of squatters, throughout Palestine.

13. Further, the statement of policy of His Majesty's Government did not imply a prohibition of acquisition of additional land by Jews. It contains no such prohibition,

nor

nor is any such intended. What it does contemplate is such temporary control of land disposition and transfers as may be necessary, not to impair the harmony and effectiveness of the scheme of land settlement to be undertaken. His Majesty's Government feel bound to point out that they alone of the Governments which have been responsible for the administration of Palestine since the acceptance of the Mandate have declared their definite intention to initiate an active policy of development which it is believed will result in substantial and lasting benefit to both Jews and Arabs.

9.12

S E C R E T.

Extract from Cabinet Paper C.P. 8 (36), January 1936.

x   x   x

<u>The prohibition by law of the transfer of Arab lands to Jews.</u>

Leaving aside the political motives which have led to this demand, the High Commissioner, who has been feeling anxiety on the subject for some time past, has reached the conclusion that an economic situation is rapidly being created by the progressive transfer of agricultural land from Arab to Jewish hands, which, if no remedy is applied, will lead to very undesirable consequences.

Measures have already been taken to prevent agricultural tenants from being evicted when the estates of which their holdings form a part change ownership. There are, however, now strong indications that the Jews are to an increasing extent buying land in comparatively small plots from owners who cultivate their own land. The Arab agriculturist is notoriously improvident and tends, after squandering the purchase money of his land, to seek employment in the towns. Under present economic conditions no serious ill-effects of this tendency are yet visible, but, unless there should be some fundamental change of Jewish policy, the process of land purchase may be expected to continue, if it is not checked, until practically the whole of the agricultural land of the country which it is profitable for the Jews to buy has passed into Jewish hands, with the exception of the citrus estates of relatively large Arab landowners, with the result that the urban

population

population will be increased by many thousands of Arabs seeking employment as wage-earners who would constitute a serious social and economic problem in the event of any considerable check to the possibly abnormal prosperity which the country is at present enjoying.

The High Commissioner urges that it is the duty of Government under the Mandate to take some positive action which will have the effect of protecting the small Arab landowner, and he recommends that he should be authorised to enact legislation to that end. He proposes that this legislation should not apply to -

(a) The Beersheba Sub-District, where land is comparatively plentiful and the population comparatively scanty;

(b) Urban areas;

(c) Land already planted with citrus.

But as regards the rest of Palestine he proposes that no landowner should be permitted to sell any of his land unless he retains a minimum area sufficient to afford him and his family a means of subsistence. This minimum area would be inalienable and would revert to Government should the owner-occupier for any reason desert his holding and cease to cultivate it.

Information is not yet available as to the extent to which such a restriction would limit the further purchase of agricultural land by the Jews, as the minimum subsistence area will naturally vary in extent from one locality to another and the details of the scheme have yet to be worked out. It would, however, I think, be wise to assume that the imposition of such a restriction would result in withholding from the market a very considerable proportion of agricultural land at present in Arab ownership.

In

In any event the High Commissioner's proposals will be strongly attacked by the Jews as imposing an artificial check upon the development of the Jewish National Home, and it may even be contended that to do so would be a violation of the terms of the letter written to Dr. Weizmann by Mr. Ramsay MacDonald, as Prime Minister, on the 13th February, 1931. Apart, however, from the fact that important areas of Palestine would be expressly excepted from the scope of the proposed legislation, it must be borne in mind that Mr. Ramsay MacDonald's assurances were given with specific reference to the policy of land settlement and development referred to in the White Paper of October 1930. In fact, the whole letter is described in the opening paragraph as "the authoritative interpretation of the White Paper on the matters with which this letter deals". In the relevant paragraphs of his letter Mr. Ramsay MacDonald was concerned to reassure the Jews on one special point, viz., that such a policy of land settlement would not be used as an excuse for imposing for an ulterior purpose restrictions upon land transactions which would be more than what was required for the purposes of carrying out that policy. His assurances could not be interpreted as debarring His Majesty's Government indefinitely from taking any action which, even if no development or resettlement were in view, might be considered necessary in the general interests of Palestine at some future date and in the face of developments which had not then assumed any serious prominence.

It will be observed that the High Commissioner's proposal introduces an entirely new principle. The legislation

legislation which has been enacted to protect tenants can be justified by the practice at home; whereas legislation to protect owners against themselves is an entire innovation. But the answer given by Sir Arthur Wauchope is that the Mandate demands that he should protect the interests of all sections of the community, and he believes that this proposal is necessary in order to do so.

9.13

Secretary of State.

You asked for a note on the references made by the Royal Commission to the compatibility of legislation controlling land transfers with Article 15 of the Mandate.

2. The Royal Commission's references to this question will be found in paragraphs 11-13 of Chapter IX of their Report. They pointed out that the chief problem in connection with the land lies in what is known as the "dual obligation". After quoting the relevant parts of Articles 2, 6, 11 and 15 of the Mandate, they go on to say -

"Whatever may be the proper construction of these articles, it seems clear that under the /Palestine_7 Order-in-Council quoted above the High Commissioner cannot enact a law that in certain areas land may not be sold to Jews. Nor could he reserve certain areas for Jewish settlements. Agrarian legislation, whether prohibitory or protective, must be of general and universal application, exceptions to which can be allowed by the Administration to meet racial requirements. This appears to us to be a subterfuge, and consequently an unsatisfactory arrangement.

As it stands at present, however, the Mandate in one article imposes a definite obligation as one of two main objects: yet another article is held to prevent the fulfilment of that obligation.

Here

2.

Here then, at the outset, we are faced by a fundamental difficulty. To quote the Shaw Commission:-

> 'In view of the obligation placed upon the Mandatory by Article 6 of the Mandate to 'encourage close settlement by Jews on the land' on the one hand and on the other to ensure 'that the rights and position of other sections of the population are not prejudiced' the solution of the land problem is obviously a difficult and delicate task, but some solution is essential in the interests of the whole population irrespective of creed and, unless one be found to deal with the situation that we have described, the question will remain a constant source of present discontent and a potential cause of future disturbance.'

If under the Mandate the Order in Council could be amended to empower the High Commissioner to prohibit the transfer of land in any particular area to Jews, a solution might be found. If this is not possible, we are of opinion that in this respect the Mandate should be amended. In any case such an amendment would be desirable to remove any doubts which may exist as to the power of the Mandatory in certain circumstances to carry out his main obligations."

5.3.40.

PALESTINE LAND TRANSFERS REGULATIONS.

Notes on Legal Aspects.

I. **Question.** Are Article 16 (d) of the Palestine (Amendment) Order-in-Council, 1939, and the Land Transfers Regulations of 28th February, 1940, made thereunder in conformity with the Palestine Mandate?

Answer. Yes. The Zionists have alleged that this legislation is inconsistent with -

(a) the Preamble and Article 2 of the Mandate, which in general make the Mandatory responsible for facilitating the establishment of the Jewish National Home;

(b) Article 6, which requires the Administration of Palestine to encourage, in co-operation with the Jewish agency referred to in Article 4, close settlement by Jews on the land, including State lands and waste lands not required for public purposes;

(c) Article 15, which lays down that no discrimination of any kind shall be made between the inhabitants of Palestine on the ground of race, religion or language.

The replies to these criticisms are as follows -

(a) The Preamble also requires the Mandatory Power to do nothing which might prejudice the civil and religious rights of existing
non-Jewish

2.

non-Jewish communities in Palestine, and Article 2 also requires the Mandatory Power to safeguard the civil and religious rights of all the inhabitants of Palestine.

(b) Article 6 also requires the Administration of Palestine to ensure that the rights and position of other sections of the population are not prejudiced.

The Land Transfers Regulations have been issued for the purpose of enabling His Majesty's Government and the Administration of Palestine to fulfil their obligations to the non-Jewish inhabitants of Palestine, as required by Articles 2 and 6.

(c) The reply to this point falls under three heads -

(i) The Order-in-Council of May, 1939, empowers the High Commissioner to issue regulations restricting or regulating transfers of land "from Arabs to Jews or to other persons not being Arabs; or from Jews to Arabs or to other persons not being Jews; or from Arabs or Jews to any bodies of persons corporate or unincorporate".

The Regulations, however, make no reference to "Jews". They provide merely for the prohibition or restriction of the transfer of land from Arabs to "persons not being Palestinian Arabs".

In form, therefore, the Regulations are not discriminatory as against Jews, and it

is

3.

is in any case worth noting that the discrimination applies not only to the Jew who will be unable to buy land in certain areas, but to the Arab who will be unable, as hitherto, to sell his land. This may, however, be regarded as a debating point.

(ii) It is by no means clear that Article 15 of the Mandate has any application except in connection with "freedom of conscience and the free exercise of all forms of worship", to which reference is made in the opening sentence of the Article.

(iii) The most effective reply and the one on which His Majesty's Government must rely is that even if the Land Regulations involve technical discrimination in the sense contemplated by Article 15 of the Mandate, the Mandatory Power is under an obligation to safeguard the civil rights of the non-Jewish communities (Preamble and Article 2) and to ensure that the rights and position of other sections of the population are not prejudiced (Article 6), and these general obligations are the governing factors.

II. Question. Does our land policy require the approval of the Council of the League?

Answer. No. The consent of the Council of the League is required (under Article 27 of the Mandate) for any modification of the terms of the Mandate, but in this case no such modification is

involved

4.

involved and our policy does not require the approval of the League Council. Apart from the requirements of Article 27, nothing in the Mandate or in international law imposes any obligation on His Majesty's Government to inform the Council of the League before taking any administrative or executive action in Palestine. In the ordinary course the policy and actions of the Mandatory Power and the Administration are set out in the Annual Report which is considered by the Permanent Mandates Commission. If the Permanent Mandates Commission take exception to any feature of the policy or to any action of the Mandatory Power or of the Administration, they may comment on the fact in their report to the League Council to which body the Permanent Mandates Commission acts in a purely advisory capacity. When the report of the Permanent Mandates Commission comes under the consideration of the League Council the Members of the Council have an opportunity of discussing with the representative of the Mandatory Power any criticism which may be made by the Permanent Mandates Commission.

In the present instance, however, since owing to the outbreak of war it was not possible for the League Council to hold their usual meeting in September for the purpose of discussing the report of the Permanent Mandates Commission on Palestine and other mandated territories,

5.

territories, His Majesty's Government thought it
right (as an exceptional procedure) to send copies
of the Regulations with an explanatory memorandum
to the Council of the League as well as to the
Permanent Mandates Commission in case any Member
of the Council might wish to ask that the Council
should be convened to discuss the position.

III. Question. Is the view expressed under II above
affected by the fact that in June last the
Permanent Mandates Commission by a majority of
four to three (four Members being absent) "did
not feel able to state that the policy of the
White Paper was in conformity with the Mandate,
any contrary conclusion appearing to them to be
ruled out by the very terms of the Mandate and
by the fundamental intentions of its authors".

Answer. No. The Permanent Mandates Commission,
as already recorded, is a purely advisory body
whose functions are (see Article 22 of the
Covenant) "to receive and examine the Annual
Reports of the Mandatories and to advise the
Council on all matters relating to the observance
of the Mandates". The Permanent Mandates
Commission has no special authority in the matter
of the <u>interpretation</u> of the Mandate and the only
provision affecting the interpretation of the
Mandate is to be found in Article 26, under which
"the Mandatory agrees that if any dispute whatever
should arise between the Mandatory and another
Member of the League of Nations relating to the

interpretation

6.

interpretation or the application of the provisions of the Mandate, such dispute, if it cannot be settled by negotiation, shall be submitted to the Permanent Court of International Justice provided for by Article 14 of the Covenant of the League of Nations".

The criticisms of the four Members of the Permanent Mandates Commission have not shaken His Majesty's Government in their conviction that the White Paper policy is in conformity with the Mandate, and His Majesty's Government have explained in detail why they are unable to agree with the four Members in the commentary which has been printed with the proceedings of the Thirty-sixth Session. It is there pointed out that the four Members who conclude that the land policy declared in the Command Paper is not in conformity with the Mandate in view of the obligation under Article 6 to encourage the close settlement of Jews on the land, omit to mention that in Article 6 this obligation is qualified by the requirement that the Administration should ensure "that the rights and position of other sections of the population are not prejudiced". The Council are also reminded that the Permanent Mandates Commission have in the past concurred in the view that "the obligations laid down by the Mandate in regard to the two sections of the population are of equal weight".

IV.

7.

IV. **Question.** Will His Majesty's Government invite the Council of the League to obtain an opinion from the Permanent Court of International Justice?

Answer. The answer must presumably be that, for reasons which were explained in His Majesty's Government's commentary on the Permanent Mandates Commission's report, His Majesty's Government remain of opinion that their policy is in conformity with the Palestine Mandate and that they see no reason to ask the League Council to take the action suggested.

V. **Question.** If the League Council should eventually find that the policy of the White Paper is not in conformity with the Mandate, will His Majesty's Government rescind the Land Regulations?

Answer. The answer might be that His Majesty's Government cannot conceive of any circumstances in which a majority of the Members of the Council might arrive at such a conclusion without at the same time agreeing to regularize the policy of the Mandatory Power by approving the necessary modification of the terms of the Mandate, and that His Majesty's Government is not prepared to indicate the line of action which it might pursue in circumstances of such remote possibility.

VI.

8.

VI. **Question.** Does not His Majesty's Government hold the Palestine Mandate from the League of Nations?

Answer. No. It was agreed by the Allied and Associated Powers that the Mandate for Palestine should be conferred on His Majesty's Government, and the only function of the League is to approve the terms of the Mandate which define the degree of authority and control to be exercised by the Mandatory. There can be no question of the League of Nations Council being in a position to deprive a Mandatory Power of its Mandate. The basis upon which a Mandate is held is that of agreement between (a) the principal Allied and Associated Powers, (b) the Council of the League, and (c) the Mandatory, and in the matter of the termination of a Mandate by agreement the Council of the League of Nations would have to be unanimous.

Therefore, so long as His Majesty's Government is on the Council it could not be dispossessed of the Palestine Mandate involuntarily. In the event of His Majesty's Government not having a seat on the Council, the consent of His Majesty's Government would in any case be necessary -

(a) quâ the Mandatory Power, and

(b) quâ one of the principal Allied and Associated Powers.

See Appendix 6 to Report of Sub-Committee of C.I.D. (C.M.G. 61 of June. 1936).

Section 10: Peel Commission

10.01

PALESTINE ROYAL COMMISSION

MEMORANDA PREPARED BY THE GOVERNMENT OF PALESTINE

Note.—The Minutes of Evidence heard by the Royal Commission at Public Sessions form a separate volume (*Colonial No.* 134).

Crown Copyright Reserved

LONDON
PRINTED AND PUBLISHED BY HIS MAJESTY'S STATIONERY OFFICE
To be purchased directly from H.M. STATIONERY OFFICE at the following addresses:
Adastral House, Kingsway, London, W.C.2; 120 George Street, Edinburgh 2;
26 York Street, Manchester 1; 1 St. Andrew's Crescent, Cardiff;
80 Chichester Street, Belfast;
or through any bookseller

1937

Price 9s. 0d. net

Colonial No. 133

S.O. Code No. 58-133

TABLE OF CONTENTS

Serial No.	TITLE	Page
1	Growth of population under the British Administration. Changes in composition and comparative effects of (a) Immigration and (b) Natural increase.	1
2	Regional distribution of population.	3
3	Numbers of immigrants annually by races.	8
4	Sources of immigration.	9
5	Allocation of immigration certificates	11
6	Aquisition of Palestinian citizenship.	13
7	Statistics of agricultural population, cultivable and uncultivable land in Palestine and area of land alienated to Jews.	15
8	Description of different kinds of land, and of agricultural production of each.	22
9	Description of measures being taken by Government (I) by education (II) by research (III) by irrigation (IV) by other means to improve productivity of different types of land and indication of extent to which (i) Arabs (ii) Jews benefit.	27
10	Description of various forms of ownership and tenure of land.	34
11	Description of the activities of the Department of Development in connection with the re-settlement of displaced Arab cultivators.	37
12	Description of land registration system.	38
13	Rural indebtedness.	41
14	Measures taken to provide agricultural credit.	45
15	Measures taken to encourage co-operation.	48
16	Account of system of land taxation and of effect of recent changes.	50
17	Description of measures adopted in Palestine to protect cultivators.	56
18	Co-operation of Jews and Arabs on various agricultural bodies.	58
19	The possibility of major irrigation projects in Palestine, including the Huleh reclamation scheme.	65
20	Development of the fisheries of Palestine.	68
21	Historical and descriptive account of system of Municipal and Local Councils, their composition and powers and extent to which they have functioned successfully, with note on racial co-operation in Local Government.	72
22	Account of representative institutions under the Ottoman Government.	80
23	Brief account of recent Legislative Council proposals and of their reception, including reference to the various 'pledges' and statements.	84
24	Constitution and finance of the Supreme Moslem Council.	94
25	Constitution and finance of Jewish Community.	101
26	Jewish affairs.	107
27	Description of the educational systems, Government, Jewish and Private, and method of allocation of Government Grants.	117
28	The educational organisation of the Va'ad Leumi, and the system of Government control.	128
29	Account of Government health services and comparison of benefits to (a) Arab (b) Jewish community.	130
30	Employment of Jews and Non-Jews in Government departments and on public works, with a note on Government regulations in regard to labour.	140
31	Position as regards use of the three official languages	148
32	Religious holidays (Jewish Sabbath. Moslem Friday) and Government respect for such religious matters.	152
33	Use of name 'Eretz-Israel'.	158
34	Principal activities of the Palestine Government since the establishment of the Civil Administration in respect of Railways, Posts and Telegraphs, Public Works and Harbours.	160
35	Industrial development of Palestine.	168
36	Cultivation of tobacco in Palestine.	184
37	Organisation and functions of the Chief Secretary's office.	189
38	State Domain.	190

MEMORANDA BY THE GOVERNMENT OF PALESTINE. 15

7. LAND STATISTICS.

MEMORANDUM No. 7.

STATISTICS OF AGRICULTURAL POPULATION, CULTIVABLE AND UNCULTIVABLE LAND IN PALESTINE AND AREA OF LAND ALIENATED TO JEWS.

1. AGRICULTURAL POPULATION.

In any country where a reliable census exists, the statistics resulting from the census are the most comprehensive and the most accurate data available regarding the composition of the population and the character of its activities. Thus the present enquiry as to the magnitude of the agricultural population of Palestine and its racial composition must take as its starting point the statistics obtained from the census of November, 1931.

2.—The first indispensable preliminary at the outset of any investigation of this kind is the clear definition of the subject with which the enquiry is to be concerned. In the present case, it would appear that the term "agricultural population", which might conceivably be defined in different ways, ought to be understood to be the grand total of all the earners whose chief occupation is agricultural or pastoral, together with their dependants. Those whose chief occupation at the date of the census was other than agricultural or pastoral cannot properly be regarded as part of the "agricultural population", even though they may add to their income from their chief source of livelihood some return, either in cash or in kind, from subsidiary agricultural activities. On the other hand, it would appear that the nomadic Beduin, who are in the main pastoral rather than agricultural in their pursuits but are vitally interested in the disposition of the lands of Palestine, should, for the purposes of the present enquiry, be included in the "agricultural population."

3.—The "agricultural population", as thus defined, is certainly smaller than the total rural population, with which it is sometimes confused. In Canada, the "farm population", which is equivalent to the "agricultural population", was found at the census of 1931 to be only about two-thirds of the whole rural population. In Eastern countries, however, a much higher percentage of "agricultural population" to total rural population is to be expected, since division of labour and specialization of function are much less prevalent in Oriental rural society, where the overwhelming majority of the residents of rural areas live on what they themselves produce. Thus, in 1931, the "agricultural population" of Palestine was no less than 89 per cent. of the total rural population, though it should be remembered in the consideration of the figures that the agricultural population included some agriculturists and receivers of rent living in urban communities, though just how many it is impossible to determine.

4.—The relation between the "agricultural population" and the total rural population of Palestine in 1931, by religious communities, was as follows:—

PALESTINE ROYAL COMMISSION.

7. LAND STATISTICS.

Total Rural Population of Palestine, aggregate Agricultural Population and proportion of the latter to the former as at the census of November, 1931.

	TOTAL RURAL POPULATION.	AGRICULTURAL POPULATION.	PERCENTAGE OF THE AGRICULTURAL POPULATION TO THE TOTAL RURAL POPULATION.
Moslems	571,637	526,225*	92.1
Jews	46,143	26,939	58.4
Christians	22,148	16,624	75.1
Others	8,602	7,928	92.2
TOTAL:	648,530	577,716*	89.2

*Includes 60,684 nomads.

5.—When the above figures are considered by communities, it is realised that both the rural population and the agricultural population of Palestine are overwhelmingly Moslem, no less than ten out of every eleven persons in the agricultural population being Moslems. As for the Jews, the relatively low percentage of agricultural population to total rural population shown in the table is partly accounted for by the fact that certain densely-peopled Jewish settlements with relatively large populations of an approximately urban character are regarded as rural areas; examples of such communities are Rehovot, Petah-Tiqva and Rishon le Tsiyon.

6.—The latest available estimate of the total rural population of Palestine by religious communities was at the middle of 1935, when the country was in a normal condition. That estimate is, by religions, as follows:—

Moslems	604,400
Jews	86,400
Christians	21,900
Others	9,400
Total rural population:	722,100

7.—On the assumption that the proportion of the agricultural population to the total rural population of each religious community was the same in 1935 as it was in 1931, the total agricultural population, defined as above, in each religious community, would be approximately as follows:—

Moslems	557,000
Jews	50,400
Christians	16,500
Others	8,700
Total agricultural population:	632,600

8.—The above assumption may be accepted as approximately correct in respect of the non-Jewish elements in the population, since these have not been materially affected by recent immigration. It would appear to be fairly near the truth in the case of the Jews also, but it has to be borne in mind that the total Jewish population approximately doubled in number between 1931 and 1935, and that a large number of the immigrating Jews are still in the early stages of their life in Palestine and can scarcely be described as permanently settled. 7,077 Jews whose previous occupation was agricultural entered Palestine between 1932 and the end of 1935, and brought with them an average of one and a half dependants, making a total addition of 17,700 persons to the Jewish agricultural population of 1931 through immigration. If these immigrating Jewish agriculturists are still engaged in agriculture, this would bring the Jewish agricultural population up to 44,639, exclusive of natural increase and of the Jews whose previous occupation was non-agricultural but who have turned to agriculture in Palestine. In view of the strenuous efforts of the Jewish authorities to plant more Jews upon the land, it may be concluded that the Jewish agricultural population at the present time is nearly if not quite 50,000.

9.—A table is attached, as Appendix I, showing the distribution of the agricultural population by religion and by specific occupation as in 1931. It is not possible to make an estimate of the present distribution of the agricultural population by specific occupation, but it may be observed that citrus and other fruit growing and market-gardening are undoubtedly relatively more important in providing occupation for the agricultural population than they were in 1931.

II. AREAS OF CULTIVABLE AND UNCULTIVABLE LAND.

10.—The Fiscal Survey of Palestine, made on the 1 to 10,000 scale for the purposes of the application of the Rural Property Tax, has been completed in respect of all but Beersheba Sub-district, and the 1 to 2,500 scale survey, made for Land Settlement purposes, covers about 10 per cent. of the area included in the Fiscal Survey. It is, therefore, possible to estimate the area of the country and the proportion which may be regarded as cultivable with more accuracy than has previously been the case.

11.—Palestine, which is nearly half as large again as Wales, has a total area of about 27,009,000 dunums or 10,400 square miles (1 dunum = 1,000 square metres = about ¼ acre).

12.—A precise computation of the area is not, however, possible owing to:—

(a) the frequent changes in the course of the River Jordan, between the Sea of Galilee and the Dead Sea, the Jordan forming part of the frontier between Palestine and Trans-Jordan;

(b) the frontier with Trans-Jordan between the southern end of the Dead Sea and the Gulf of Akaba not being surveyed. This, however, only affects the area of Beersheba Sub-district, which is mainly uncultivable.

MEMORANDA BY THE GOVERNMENT OF PALESTINE.

7. LAND STATISTICS.

13.—The area may be sub-divided as follows:

	Dunums.	Dunums.
(a) Total land area excluding Beersheba Sub-district.	13,742,000*	
(b) Beersheba Sub-district.	12,577,000 (approx.)	
Total Land Area		26,319,000
(c) Dead Sea (one half)	525,000 (approx.)	
(d) Sea of Galilee	165,000	
Total Water Area		690,000
Grand Total		27,009,000

Urban Areas.

14.—The areas to which the Urban Property Tax Ordinances, 1928-35, have been applied amount to 101,691 dunums and include all towns controlled by Municipal Councils and the more important village and settlement "built-on" areas where Local Councils function.

Cultivable Areas.

15.—The term "cultivable land" is held to cover land which is actually under cultivation or which can be brought under cultivation by the application of the labour and financial resources of the average Palestinian cultivator. It includes land planted, although often sparsely, with olive trees and comprises the area included in the Rural Property Tax Categories 1 to 15, excepting village or settlement "built-on" areas (Category 4.).

16.—The Land Area may be further sub-divided as follows:—

(a) *Land Area, excluding Beersheba Sub-district:*

	Dunums.	Dunums.
Cultivable (excluding Citrus)	6,885,000	
Citrus (1934)	235,000	
Village & Settlement 'Built-on' Areas	29,000	
Forest	695,000	
Uncultivable	5,797,000	
Total Rural lands:		13,641,000
to which may be added Urban Areas extending to 100,771 dunums, say		101,000
Total Land Area (excluding Beersheba Sub-district):		13,742,000
Total Land Area (excluding Beersheba Sub-district):		13,742,000

(b) *Beersheba Sub-district:*

	Dunums.	Dunums.
Cultivable	1,640,000	
Uncultivable	10,936,000	
Total Rural Lands		12,576,000
to which may be added Beersheba Urban Area which extends to 920 dunums, say		1,000
Total Land Area Beersheba Sub-district:		12,577,000
Grand Total of Land Area:		26,319,000

* Includes Lake Huleh which covers about 14,000 dunums.

17.—These figures may be summarised as follows:

	Dunums.
Cultivable Area	8,760,000
Village & Settlement 'Built-on' Areas	29,000
Uncultivable (including Forest)	17,428,000
Total Rural Lands	26,217,000
Urban Areas	102,000
Grand Total of Land Area:	26,319,000

Source of the figures for the cultivable area.

(a) *Beersheba Sub-district.*

18.—Except in the case of the urban area, Beersheba Sub-district has not been surveyed and, as cultivation depends on an uncertain and capricious rainfall, any estimate of the cultivable area is largely a matter of guess-work. The figure supplied to Sir John Hope Simpson was 1,500,000 dunums and a later estimate gives 1,640,000 dunums, which is the figure now accepted.

(b) *Palestine, excluding Beersheba Sub-district.*

19.—(i) The whole of this area, with the exception of a comparatively small portion of the uncultivated and uncultivable wilderness of Judaea, has been surveyed and mapped on the scale of 1 to 10,000, while the areas "settled" under the Land Settlement Ordinances 1928-36, which cover about 10 per cent. of the whole, have been surveyed and mapped on a scale of 1 to 2,500.

(ii) When the fiscal survey for the rural property tax was made, plantations were surveyed and shown on the 1 to 2,500 scale block plan or the 1 to 10,000 scale village map and at the same time the cultivable, uncultivable and forest lands were similarly indicated, together with buildings, roads, railways, threshing-floors, cemeteries and all physical features. Dates of planting and the percentages of cultivable land where patch cultivation existed were also shown.

(iii) From the field sheets, the areas were computed by parcel, plantation, etc., and showed the position as at the date of the survey. If a village was completely surveyed in 1929, the areas will reflect the state of affairs in that village or settlement at that time. This does not, however, apply to citrus, as a general revision of the citrus area was completed in 1934 on a scale of 1 to 20,000. Since the date of the survey, types of cultivation may have changed, but the cultivable area is unaffected unless land regarded as uncultivable has been developed by the employment of means not at the disposal of the average Palestinian cultivator.

(iv) Schedules were then compiled in respect of "settled" lands showing the classification of each parcel of land, and in non-settled areas schedules were prepared showing similar information according to blocks defined on the village maps.

PALESTINE ROYAL COMMISSION.

7. LAND STATISTICS.

(v) This information was summarized by village, Sub-district and, subsequently, for the whole of the rural lands of the country, exclusive of Beersheba Sub-district.

(vi) Previous estimates of the cultivable area have, in some cases, omitted land planted with olives for the reason that these trees are often scattered over rocky ground of which a considerable proportion is uncultivable. The present figures include land so planted as cultivable. Any over-estimate of the cultivable area caused by this is to some extent offset by the fact that

   (a) where scattered trees were found (below 20 per cent. of density) they were ignored, and

   (b) portions of village and settlement 'built-on' areas are cultivable and actually cultivated.

III. AREA ALIENATED TO JEWS.

20.—The area owned by Jews and Jewish concerns on the 31st December, 1935, was, according to Land Registry records, 1,317,000 dunums, which amounts to about 5 per cent. of the land area of the country.

This figure is based on the assumption that Jews and Jewish concerns at the end of 1920, when the Land Registers were opened, owned 650,000 dunums, a figure which was generally agreed to at the time.

To this area has been added the area of recorded acquisitions since that date up to the 31st December, 1935.

21.—It appears from page 113 of the Report of the Commission on the Palestine Disturbances, 1929, that Dr. Ruppin, of the Jewish Agency, stated that 1,200,000 Turkish dunums (1,103,160 metric dunums) were at the end of 1929 owned by Jews and Jewish concerns. If purchases from Arabs and others since that time are added, the total area so owned at the end of 1935 would be 1,332,000 dunums.

22.—Further to check these results, a scrutiny of the Rural Property Tax records has been carried out to ascertain the area owned by Jews and Jewish concerns within the area to which this tax has been applied, which excludes Urban Areas, Beersheba Sub-district and the Huleh lands in Safad Sub-district.

The figures were taken from the tax records in respect of the financial year 1935-36 and show the position at the 1st April, 1935.

The approximate area owned by Jews and Jewish organisations in urban areas appears to be 33,000 dunums out of the total area of 102,000 dunums. The figure was arrived at by estimating the percentage so owned in each urban assessment block.

It is probable that the method of ascertaining the extent of Jewish property, both in rural and urban areas, has tended to reduce the resultant area below the actual.

23.—In order to effect a comparison between the figures given in paragraphs 20 and 21 above and the estimate of Jewish owned land as on the 31st December, 1935, based on the Rural Property Tax records, certain additions have to be made to the figure obtained from the latter, as below:—

		Dunums.
Area in Jewish ownership extracted from Rural Property Tax records, as on the 1st April, 1935.		1,208,875
Area in Jewish ownership in Urban Areas.		33,000
Purchases in Beersheba Sub-district to the 31st December, 1935.		36,971
Area acquired throughout Palestine between the 1st April, 1935, and the 31st December, 1935, excluding Beersheba Sub-district.		
Purchases in 1935	48,355	
Less between the 1st January & the 31st March, 1935	18,901	29,454
		1,308,300

24.—These figures indicate that the area owned by Jews and Jewish organisations is between 1,310,000 and 1,330,000 dunums and that the records of the Land Registry may, therefore, be accepted.

25.—The recorded Jewish purchases of land for the first six months of the year 1936 cover an area of 14,782 dunums.

IV. STATE LAND HELD BY JEWS AND JEWISH CONCERNS.

26.—In addition to the area actually in Jewish ownership, certain State lands are held under concessions or leases. The list of these properties, which forms Appendix II to this memorandum, indicates that the area extends to some 180,000 dunums. It is estimated that not more than 20,000 dunums of this area are cultivable.

It will be observed that some of the areas included are held by Companies which cannot be regarded as entirely Jewish.

Negotiations are taking place involving the lease of a further area of about 30,000 dunums.

V. CULTIVABLE AREAS IN JEWISH OWNERSHIP.

27.—To arrive at the cultivable area in Jewish ownership, the area of approximately 33,000 dunums in urban areas must first be deducted from the total area of 1,317,000 dunums. This leaves an area of 1,284,000 dunums of rural lands.

By extracting from the Rural Property Tax records particulars of each area entered in the name of a Jew or Jewish organisation and noting the area and its category, it has been ascertained that some 22 per cent. of the area so owned is uncultivable. Applying this percentage to the rural area of 1,284,000 dunums, about 282,500 dunums are found to be uncultivable and 1,001,500 dunums cultivable. To the 1,001,500 dunums should be added the cultivable area of State land held under lease or concession, making a total cultivable area of approximately 1,021,500 dunums or about 12 per cent of the cultivable area of the country.

The cultivable area of the country remaining after deducting that held by Jews amounts to 7,738,500 dunums, which includes lands held by Arabs, Germans and others.

28.—Further investigations are being conducted with a view to a closer estimate being made of the area of land owned by Jews and it is possible that, as a result of these investigations, certain modifications may eventually have to be made in the figures quoted above.

APPENDIX I

AGRICULTURAL POPULATION OF PALESTINE:— NUMBER OF EARNERS AND THEIR DEPENDANTS IN ALL AGRICULTURAL AND PASTORAL OCCUPATIONS, IN THE SETTLED POPULATION OF PALESTINE (AND AMONG NOMADS) AT THE CENSUS OF 1931, BY RELIGIONS.

7. LAND STATISTICS.

		RENT OF AG. LAND	ORDINARY CULTIVATION	FARM SERVICE AND FIELD LABOUR	ORANGE GROWING	MARKET GARDENING & FRUIT ETC.	ANIMAL RAISING	SHEPHERDS AND HERDSMEN	OTHER	TOTAL
Moslems	Earners	5,027	63,190	20,077	2,000	7,430	2,947	4,942	580	115,193
	Dependants	12,559	234,571	61,947	5,357	20,271	8,495	5,815	1,333	350,348
	Total	17,586	297,761	91,024	7,357	27,701	11,442	10,757	1,913	465,541
Jews	Earners	10	3,669	2,582	1,691	3,754	78	24	545	12,263
	Dependants	14	5,370	1,718	3,092	3,511	175	34	742	14,656
	Total	24	9,039	4,300	4,712	7,265	253	58	1,287	26,939
Christians	Earners	236	2,376	512	186	812	79	44	47	4,292
	Dependants	482	7,783	962	415	2,351	201	62	76	12,332
	Total	718	10,159	1,474	601	3,163	280	106	123	16,624
Others	Earners	38	1,291	368	3	204	30	82	15	2,031
	Dependants	62	4,597	570	8	461	77	94	19	5,897
	Total	100	5,886	947	11	665	107	176	34	7,928
TOTAL SETTLED POPULATION	Earners	5,311	70,526	32,539	3,810	12,200	3,134	5,092	1,157	133,799
	Dependants	13,117	252,321	65,206	8,872	26,594	8,848	6,005	2,170	383,233
	Total	18,428	322,847	97,745	12,682	38,794	12,082	11,097	3,357	517,032
NOMAD POPULATION (MOSLEM)	Earners	—	11,506	1,749	—	—	—	3,962	—	17,217
	Dependants	—	36,339	5,940	—	—	—	1,888	—	43,467
	Total	—	47,845	6,989	—	—	—	5,850	—	60,684

PALESTINE ROYAL COMMISSION.

7. LAND STATISTICS.

APPENDIX II.
STATE DOMAINS LEASED TO JEWS.

State Domain No.	Town or Village	Area Dons. M2.	To whom leased	Period of Lease & Date of Commencement — No. of Years.	Period of Lease & Date of Commencement — As from.	Remarks.
Acre Sub-district:						
D/Acre/4	Rakavik-Damun	1,072.364	Asher Cucuy.	99	18.1.23	
Beersheba Sub-district:						
D/Beer/60	South of Dead Sea.	64,199.160	Palestine Potash Ltd.	70	1.5.34	
Haifa Sub-district:						
D/Hai/1	'Atlit	2,500.000	Concession to Palestine Jewish Colonization Association.	100	8.11.21	Agreement under revision. Area approximate.
D/Hai/18	Haifa, (Bassat Wadi Shiby, Zawara, and Caracol).	12.313	Keren Hayesod Ltd.	99	1.12.23	
D/Hai/63	Haifa, (Rushmiya).	2,086.283	Palestine Land Development Co.	99	8.8.34	
D/Hai/92	Haifa, (Ard el Ballan).	5.746	Palestine Jewish Colonization Association.	100	31.12.34	
D/Hai/103	Kabbara	3,793.000	Concession to Palestine Jewish Colonization Association.	100	8.11.21	Agreement under revision. Area approximate.
D/Hai/114	Caesarea	25,510.000	Concession to Palestine Jewish Colonization Association.	100	8.11.21	
D/Hai/119	Pardess Hanna (Birket el Batikh)	250.133	Palestine Jewish Colonization Association.	19	1.1.30	
D/Hai/145	Pardess Hanna (Ghabat Sherkass).	59.786	Palestine Jewish Colonization Association.	49	1.10.26	
D/Hai/146	Pardess Hanna (Ghabat Sherkass el Gharbiya).	27.620	Palestine Jewish Colonization Association.	49	1.10.26	
D/Hai/155	Haifa (Bat Galim).	6.664	Committee of Bat Galim Co-operative Ltd.	99	1.9.26	
D/Hai/177	Tantura (Bass esh Shamali).	786.000	Palestine Jewish Colonization Association.	49	1.4.30	
D/Hai/269	Jidru.	1,436.000	Keren Kayemeth Leisrael Ltd.	3	1.4.34	

MEMORANDA BY THE GOVERNMENT OF PALESTINE.

7. LAND STATISTICS.

State Domain No.	Town or Village	Area. Dons. M²	To whom leased	Period of lease & date of commencement. No. of years.	As from.	Remarks.
Affa Sub-District.						
)/Jaf/6	Tel-Aviv.	22.571	Town Council, Tel-Aviv.	90	1.4.23	
)/Jaf/62	Tel-Aviv.	50.286	Town Council, Tel-Aviv.	100	24.8.21	With option for further 50 years.
)/Jaf/63	Petah Tiqva (Basset Mulabbis).	1,558.478	Local Council, Petah Tiqva.	50	11.11.21	
)P/1/4	Yazur (Miqveh Israel).	2,486.853	Alliance Israelite Universelle, Paris.	Perpetual.		Held under Firman granted by the Sultan.
Jericho Sub-District.						
)/Jek/191	En Nabi Musa (Kallia).	966.109	T. G. Tullock, S. A. Van Vriesland & Ibrahim Haiboun.	49	25.6.31	
)/Jek/192	En Nabi Musa.	3,683.000	Palestine Potash Ltd.	72	1.7.32	
)/Jek/199	En Nabi Musa.	1,754.389	Palestine Potash Ltd.	72	21.12.32	
)/Jek/200	En Nabi Musa.	59.204	Palestine Potash Ltd.	70	25.1.34	
)/Jek/216	En Nabi Musa.	963.612	Palestine Potash Ltd.	68	1.1.36	
)/Jek/219	En Nabi Musa.	5,017.448	Palestine Potash Ltd.	75	1.1.30	
Jerusalem Sub-District.						
D/Jem/94	Jerusalem.	2.355	Menorah Club.	49	1.7.30	
D/Jem/160	Jerusalem.	2.286	Hadassah Women's Zionist Organization of America.	10	8.7.35	
Safad Sub-District.						
D/Saf/48	Aiyelet Hashahar (Dahnuneh & Mabarak).	717.100	The Agricultural Cooperative Labour Society.	50	1.10.21	
GP/6/1	Huleh.	56,940.000	Palestine Land Development Co.	Annual leases		Concession recently taken over from previous holders. An area not exceeding 15,772 dunums within the concession area is reserved for Arab cultivators.
	Miscellaneous Buildings at Safad.	0.146	Jewish tenants.			
Tiberias Sub-District.						
D/Tib/35	Samakh.	2.000	Israel Toister.	20	1.1.21	
D/Tib/45	Tiberias (Quarry).	5.003	Its-haq 'Efron.	20	1.6.30	
D/Tib/199	Samakh (Tell ed Duweir).	155.465	Palestine Electric Corporation Ltd.	70	1.3.27	
Tulkarm Sub-District.						
D/Tul/106	Nathanya.	114.084	Assigned by Hanotaiah Ltd. to Pardess Hagdud.	99	1.7.32	
	Total Area:	175,545.478				

PALESTINE ROYAL COMMISSION.

8. AGRICULTURAL PRODUCTION.

MEMORANDUM No. 8.

DESCRIPTION OF DIFFERENT KINDS OF LAND, AND OF AGRICULTURAL PRODUCTION OF EACH.

DESCRIPTION OF LANDS.

1—From an agricultural point of view, the lands of Palestine can be roughly divided into five categories, this division being based on type of soil, atmospheric conditions, rainfall, and availability of water.

(i) *Maritime Plain.*

The maritime plain stretches from the southern boundary of Palestine near Rafa to the northern boundary at Naqura. At its southern extremity its width is about 20 miles, but this width decreases until, at Mt. Carmel, it amounts to only a few hundred yards. North of Haifa it widens out again into the Acre plain.

The maritime plain is very fertile; it consists largely of sandy or sandy-loam soils interspersed with considerable areas of heavy land. In general, the more sandy lands skirt the coastal ridge, although patches of light land are to be found at considerable distances from the sea. To the north of Mt. Carmel much of the land is marshy and there are large stretches of heavy clay soils.

The maritime plain is intensively cultivated and includes what is known as the citrus belt. All citrus trees in this area are grown under irrigation. The value of land suitable for citrus has increased considerably in recent years and changes hands at about £P.15 to £P.30 per dunum, whereas the price of cereal lands, the value of which has also increased, varies from £P.2 to £P.5 per dunum or more. About 300,000 dunums are already under citrus cultivation and it is estimated that, within ten years, about 25 million boxes of fruit will be available for export as compared with an export of 7½ million boxes in 1934-35. Citrus cultivation is, of course, expensive. Whereas the outlay on cereal land, which occupies the greater part of the cultivated area of Palestine, involves little more than the cost of the seed and of a few cheap simple implements, the labour being usually supplied by the family, each dunum of citrus requires an outlay of about £P.75 per dunum up to the sixth year, and an annual maintenance charge of about £P.10 per dunum thereafter. The net returns, however, compensate for the greater expenditure, and a family should obtain from a full bearing citrus orchard of ten dunums the same net revenue as from a farm unit of a hundred dunums of cereal land.

(ii) *Inland Plains.*

The soils of the inland plains are mainly of heavy clay. They are very fertile and well suited to cereal and fodder production, fruits and vegetables being also profitably grown where wells have been sunk. The principal inland plains are:

(a) *Plain of Esdraelon.*

This is the triangular plain which extends from Haifa to Beisan, the soil of which is mainly of a heavy type. Vegetables, citrus and other fruit trees are grown in addition to cereals and fodders, wherever irrigation water is found.

(b) *Huleh Plain.*

This is the most northerly part of Palestine and lies to the east of the country, north of Lake Tiberias. The northern region of this plain is alluvial cultivable land, to the south of which there is a large marsh bordering Lake Huleh. The possibility of development in this area is dealt with in Memorandum No. 19.

(c) *Battouf Plain.*

This is one of the smaller inland plains and is located between two ranges of hills which extend from the south of the Acre Sub-district to Saffurieh in the Nazareth Sub-district. It is basin-shaped, is very fertile and is subject to inundation during seasons of heavy rain. Cereals and leguminous crops are the main products of this plain.

(d) *Sanour Plain.*

This plain, which is situated in the Jenin Sub-district, is about 5,000 dunums in extent and is also subject to flooding during periods of heavy rainfall. Its soil is of heavy loam, fertile and suitable for cereal growing.

(iii) *The Hills.*

A range of hills runs down the centre of the country extending from Mt. Carmel south-eastwards to Nablus, and thence in a southerly direction almost to Beersheba. In the north, beyond the plain of Esdraelon, the hills extend northwards from Nazareth to the Syrian mountain formation. The area comprises (a) the Galilean Hills (b) the Carmel range (c) the Samarian hills and (d) the Judaean hills. Many parts of the Galilean hills are of basaltic origin, while other parts and the whole of the southern hills are of limestone rocks in varying degrees of decomposition.

While cereal and leguminous crops are the main products of the hills, more and more of the area is annually being terraced and cultivated with fruit trees, such as olives, figs, vines and deciduous fruits. Where spring water is available, irrigated vegetables are grown in addition to those grown under dry culture.

Generally speaking, the western slopes of the hill ranges, which enjoy a fair rainfall, produce a good yield of crops, but on the eastern slopes overlooking the Jordan, where the rainfall is lower and irregular, the yield is both smaller and less certain.

(iv) *The Jordan Valley.*

This is a natural depression which lies between the central range of hills and the Jordan river. It starts slightly above sea level in the north

MEMORANDA BY THE GOVERNMENT OF PALESTINE.

8. AGRICULTURAL PRODUCTION.

and falls gradually to a depth of 1,300 ft. below sea level at the Dead Sea, the total length of the valley being about 160 kilometres.

Numerous springs in the foothills occur in the Jordan Valley. Where the water is sweet, it is utilized for irrigation purposes, and cereals, vegetables, bananas, and other tropical and sub-tropical fruits are grown. Citrus cultivation is extending at Jericho, but the main developments now taking place in the Jordan Valley are the extension of banana cultivation and the production of vegetables.

The land in the north of the Jordan Valley is very fertile, and is capable of further development.

(v) *Beersheba Plateau.*

This is the largest stretch of plain land in the country. The soil is of loess (wind-blown) formation, and supports little cultivation owing to the low rainfall. The principal crop is barley, wheat coming second.

The average rainfall is only about 6 inches per annum. If suitable underground water supplies could be found, very large areas could be placed under cultivation. Without irrigation, any material development of the area is impossible.

PASTURES AND GRAZING.

2—In Palestine, the rainy season is limited to the period from November to mid-April and consequently almost all the natural vegetation dries up in the hot and dry summer months. Grazing is practised on the uncultivated lands of the hill regions, in most forest reserves and on lands left fallow in the plains, but in such situations it is, for the most part, confined to the winter and spring months. In marshy tracts, on the banks of the Jordan and wherever perennial water is found, it is available also to a limited extent throughout the summer. Animals are usually grazed in the hills in winter and spring, being moved in summer to the plains to graze on the stubble left after harvest.

FOREST LANDS.

3—The deficiency of forests is one of the most striking features of the rural economy of Palestine and the remedying of this condition must inevitably be an important factor in any scheme for the improvement of the backward hill tracts. No exact data exist as to areas and growing stock, and determination will be difficult until land settlement operations have advanced into the hills. About 140,000 dunums, mainly in the Galilean Hills, are covered with scrub forest, consisting of oak, pine, arbutus and minor species. The area of natural high forest is negligible. Plantations of pine, eucalyptus, etc. cover some 30,000 dunums. In addition, there are over a million dunums of open scrub grazing grounds scattered throughout the hills which form potential forest areas.

Experimental plantation work has been carried out for a number of years, and a good start has been made on the provisional reservation of scrub areas, the so-called "Forest Reserves" totalling 740,000 dunums. These are being protected so far as possible pending land settlement. But very much larger areas will have to be brought under State control if cheap forest produce, including fodder, is to be made available, the water supply conserved and erosion prevented. In addition to the benefits which would accrue to agriculture from the proper management of such areas, they would provide a steady source of employment on lands at present derelict, eroded and barren. The only material now produced on these lands is a diminishing amount of charcoal and small timber, and a poor supply of fodder. The areas are at present overcut and overgrazed, with the result that general improvement is delayed. A separate Forest Department has recently been constituted and it is anticipated that the introduction of a proper system of control will ensure greatly increased production.

In the Forest Reserves, permits for grazing 68,000 head of stock are issued, but the ill-treated vegetation supports these animals for only a few months in the year. The annual cut is estimated roughly as 300,000 cubic feet, consisting of small timber and fuel, from which a revenue of £P.500 is obtained.

During 1935, in addition to the planting done in Forest Reserves, 180,000 fruit and forest trees were issued free from forest nurseries, to encourage horticulture and arboriculture.

PRODUCTION.

4—Cereal growing is the most important activity of the majority of Arab cultivators. The rotation system adopted varies from a two-year rotation, where cereal crops of wheat and barley are rotated with winter leguminous crops or with summer crops of dura (millet) and sesame, to a three-year rotation in which leguminous crops are normally introduced between the summer crops and the winter crops of cereals. In certain districts the winter cereal crops are sown in the dry, before the break of the rains, but in other areas sowing is delayed until the early rains have fallen. In districts with low rainfall, such as Beersheba and parts of the eastern ranges of the hills, little or no summer crops are grown and the land is left bare fallow during the second year of the rotation. Bare fallow is also adopted in areas where weeds are troublesome with the object of checking their excessive growth. In certain Jewish settlements, where cereal growing plays an important part in the agricultural system, a four-year course rotation has been adopted by the introduction of green manures or maize for the production of grain, green forage or silage. Wheat and barley are the chief cereal crops. Wheat is usually grown on the heavier types of soil, while barley is grown on the lighter soils, particularly in the south and in Beersheba, where not only is the rainfall much lower than in the north but the rainy season is also shorter. Winter leguminous crops consist of lentils, peas, beans and kersenneh (Vicia ervilia). Some vetch is also grown, but it is more usual to sow vetch with oats or barley as a hay or green fodder crop. Hay and fodder crops have been grown by Jewish settlements for several years, especially where dairy cattle are kept, and recently, as the result of propaganda by the Department of Agriculture and Fisheries, the growing of fodder crops has been taken up by Arab farmers also. Chick-peas are grown on the medium soils as a spring or early summer crop, mainly in the hills. Dura, sesame and melons constitute the main summer crops. Dura is grown in most districts; sesame is mostly grown in the north as its cultivation is a precarious matter, good yields being obtained only in years of abundant rainfall. Melons are grown in the lighter soils of the maritime plain, more especially in the south, in the Tulkarm-Khudera

PALESTINE ROYAL COMMISSION.

8. AGRICULTURAL PRODUCTION.

plain and in the Acre plain. Maize is grown in the Jewish and German settlements, both under irrigation and dry culture, for silage, green fodder and, to a limited extent, for grain. Its cultivation by Arab growers has, in the past, been limited to the Huleh area, but, owing to the Department's propaganda, it is now being taken up in other districts where conditions are favourable. Vegetable growing has recently developed extraordinarily well, and there has been a great advance in variety, quantity and quality. Good supplies of all kinds of European vegetables such as cabbages, cauliflowers, beans, peas, tomatoes, lettuce, carrots, beets, radishes, etc., are available during the winter and the early spring months. During the warmer summer months, beans, cucumbers, vegetable marrows, pumpkins, tomatoes, eggplants, peppers, ochras, etc., are abundant. All classes of farmers are now taking a keen interest in vegetable growing, for which there is an ever increasing demand in the towns. The quantity of potatoes imported increases year by year, although both the areas under potatoes and the yields of these areas are also increasing.

Tobacco cultivation is at present mainly confined to the hill villages of the Acre and Safad Sub-districts and the Carmel Range. The varieties are mainly Turkish and the yield, together with a small quantity of foreign leaf imported for blending, meets the local demand.

Citrus forms the principal export crop of the country. There were approximately 300,000 dunums of citrus trees under cultivation at the end of March, 1936, of which nearly two thirds have been planted during the last five years. About ten per cent. of the area is planted with grape-fruit and the balance with oranges. The orange trees are grown mainly on light soil, but grape-fruit budded on sour stock can thrive on heavy soil, and considerable areas are available for the further extension of citrus orchards, provided suitable water for irrigation can be procured. Marketing is likely to be a serious problem in the near future owing to the rapidly increasing crops.

Olive culture is, in many parts of the country, an important source of income for the Palestinian peasant and is the most valuable crop after citrus and wheat. The tree is well adapted to the difficult conditions of the barren rocky hills.

Apples, pears and quinces thrive in the mountains of Jerusalem, Samaria and Galilee, while grapes flourish at all elevations and in the light soils of the coastal plain. Stone fruits, such as apricots, plums and peaches, grow well both in the hills and on the plains and much attention is being paid to the extension of the culture of these fruits by the planting of better types. Fig trees are scattered throughout the countryside.

Bananas are grown under irrigation, mostly in Jericho but also in Beisan, Tiberias and Nablus, and to some extent along the coast.

5.—The following table shows the area and the production in 1935 of the principal crops:

	AREA IN DUNUMS	YIELD IN TONS
	(Estimates compiled from village note books)	
I. Cereals, Legumes & Oil Crops.		
Wheat	2,251,018	104,353
Barley	2,627,939	68,905
Lentils	82,693	2,696
Kersenneh	192,936	8,849
Maize	70,436	about 500 grain
		about 8,000 green fodder
Beans	32,564	1,489
Peas	2,548	225
Dura	1,004,977	46,136
Sesame	269,920	6,914
	6,535,031	248,066
II. Tobacco	22,232	1,032
III. Vegetables		
Tomatoes	32,246	17,286
Cucumbers	17,377	8,022
Potatoes	6,142	2,350
Other vegetables	about 60,000	about 28,000
	115,765	56,153
IV. Citrus Fruits		
Exports 1934-35	*Boxes*	
Oranges	6,507,995	
Lemons	30,058	
Grape-fruit	791,661	
Other	1,132	
Total exports	7,330,846	
Estimated local consumption	1,000,000	
Total	8,330,846	298,000	8,330,846 boxes

MEMORANDA BY THE GOVERNMENT OF PALESTINE.

8. AGRICULTURAL PRODUCTION.

	AREA—DUNUMS	YIELD—TONS
Other Fruits		
Olives	474,466	45,092
Melons & Water Melons	125,875	68,799
Grapes	149,450	28,818
Almonds	25,880	4,099
Figs	98,742	10,945
Apples	5,614	536
Pomegranates	2,419	824
Apricots	12,686	2,871
Pears	730	150
Peaches	1,182	379
Plums	769	171
Bananas	3,640	4,000
Total	901,453	166,984
II. *Fodder (for the Dairy Industry)* Estimate	100,000	
SUMMARY		
I. Cereals, Legumes & Oil crops	6,535,031	248,068
II. Tobacco	22,232	1,032
III. Vegetables	115,765	56,158
IV. Citrus Fruits	298,000	8,330,846 boxes
V. Other Fruits	901,453	166,984
VI. Fodder Crops	100,000	—
Dunums	7,972,481	472,242 tons & 8,330,846 boxes

6.—A summary, showing in tabular form the various kinds of land and the production of each kind, is attached as an Appendix to this memorandum.

APPENDIX

SUMMARY OF KINDS OF LAND AND PRODUCTION OF EACH KIND

8. AGRICULTURAL PRODUCTION.

Kind of Land	Main Crops Grown	Kind of Soil, etc.	Average Range of Rainfall	Availability of Water	Other Features
Maritime Plain.	Wheat, barley, legumes, durra, sesame, vegetables, maize, citrus and deciduous fruit trees.	Sand dunes, sandy loams, some patches of clayey soils.	300—400 mm. at Gaza-Majdal. 500—600 mm. at Jaffa-Haifa-Acre.	Water can be found in most places, at a depth from a few metres to 150 metres.	Citrus growing in the main branch. Other branches of intensive farming are vegetables and dairying. Poultry and bee-keeping are developing.
Inland plains.	Wheat, barley, legumes, durra, sesame, maize, some citrus, vines, olives and vegetables.	Mainly heavy clay interspersed with patches of light soils.	400—500 mm. in the Valley of Esdraelon. 500—600 mm. in the inner plains of the north.	Water can be found in most plains; but less certainly than in the maritime plains and at greater depths, usually from 50 to 150 metres. In the Huleh region irrigation water is abundant.	Fodders and vegetables are the main intensive branches. Table grapes and grape-fruits are grown profitably. Dairying and poultry are the chief branches of intensive farming in Jewish settlements.
The Hills.	Wheat, barley & legumes; a little durra and sesame. Olives, vines, figs and deciduous fruits are on the increase.	Mainly clayey loam.	400—600 mm. in the Judaean and Samarian hills. 500—700 mm. in the hills of the north.	Small springs can be found in certain localities.	Fruits are the main source of income; cereals are grown for local consumption of the hill population. Poultry and bee-keeping are also developing. Terracing would increase the area under cultivation.
The Jordan Valley.	Wheat, barley, legumes, vegetables, bananas and some citrus.	Alluvial clay loam.	100—400 mm.	Springs in the foot-hills are the main sources of irrigation. The Jordan river is little used owing to the high cost of lifting the water.	Tropical and sub-tropical fruits can be and are grown.
Beersheba Plateau	Mainly barley, a little wheat, durra and melons.	Deep loose soil. Calcareous clay loam.	150—200 mm.	Water resources not yet ascertained.	Large areas of land are available for cultivation if sweet water can be found.

MEMORANDA BY THE GOVERNMENT OF PALESTINE. 27

9. IMPROVEMENT OF PRODUCTIVITY.

MEMORANDUM No. 9.

DESCRIPTION OF MEASURES BEING TAKEN BY GOVERNMENT (I) BY EDUCATION (II) BY RESEARCH (III) BY IRRIGATION (IV) BY OTHER MEANS TO IMPROVE PRODUCTIVITY OF DIFFERENT TYPES OF LAND AND INDICATION OF EXTENT TO WHICH (i) ARABS (ii) JEWS BENEFIT.

(I) EDUCATION.

(a) *Agricultural Schools.*

Two Agricultural Schools were established by Government from a bequest of the late Sir Ellis Kadoorie, a philanthropic Jew from Shanghai. His bequest with interest accumulated to £P.7,000, the greater part of which was devoted to the construction of the schools; the balance was invested and yields an income of about £P.3,000 per annum, which is credited towards their annual maintenance.

The first school, for Arabs, was established at Tulkarm in 1931, and an additional wing was added from funds provided from the private purse of the present High Commissioner so that there is now accommodation for 70 residential students.

The second school, for Jews, was established at Mt. Tabor in 1934, with accommodation for 50 residential students, and married quarters were later added from a further donation from Sir Elly Kadoorie, the brother of the original donor.

The object of these schools is to provide practical courses of agriculture in all its branches, supplemented by lectures in elementary agricultural and allied sciences, so that when the students return to their lands they may not only develop their own farms, but encourage the adoption of improved farm practices; and it is hoped that their farms will serve as models to the neighbouring villages and settlements.

At the Tulkarm School, ten students who complete their two-year course in agriculture are selected annually to receive a third year's training in pedagogy, with a view to their appointment as teachers in rural schools so as to give an agricultural bias to education. 35 such students have been trained since the inception of the scheme in 1933.

There is a tendency among the students from the Tulkarm School to seek Government employment, but it is clear that, apart from those trained as rural teachers, only a small proportion can be absorbed into the public service.

In addition to these two schools, which receive an annual subvention from Government to the extent of about £P.3,500 each, there are several private schools, mainly Jewish, supported by Jewish institutions. They are listed below, the number of students and the annual expenditure and revenue being shown, where this information is available:—

NAME OF SCHOOL.	No. of Students		Annual Expenditure on		Annual Revenue	
	Boys	Girls	School	Farm	School Fees	Sale of Farm Products.
			£P.	£P.	£P.	£P.
Alliance Israélite Agricultural School, Mikveh Israel.	244		15,509	16,692	10,259	19,543
The Canadian Hadassah Agricultural School for Girls at Nahalal. (W.I.Z.O.)†		100	5,100	3,086	2,150	3,350
Children's Farm, Ben Shemen.	80	51	7,300	2,798	4,500	2,890
Children's Village, Meir Shfeya	60	50	5,993	1,044		1,630
Girls Training Farm, Ayanoth. (W.I.Z.O.)†		70	3,000	3,000	300	2,700
Agricultural Secondary School, Hardess Hanna. (In course of completion)	29		Not yet known as the school is not yet working with a full number of students or staff, and dormitory, class-rooms, and laboratory, etc. not yet completed.			
TOTAL.	413	276				

† Women's International Zionist Organisation.

PALESTINE ROYAL COMMISSION.

9. IMPROVEMENT OF PRODUCTIVITY.

There are three private Arab (Christian Catholic) schools, where agricultural training is provided, as follows:—

Name of School	No. of Students		Annual Expenditure on		Annual Revenue	
	Boys	Girls	School	Farm	School Fees	Sale of Farm Products
			£P.	£P.	£P.	£P.
Salesian Agricultural School of Beit Jemal.	71	—	1,276	2,558	Nil	3,780
Orphelinat Agricole des Pères Trappists, Latrun.	16	—	—	—	—	—
Agricultural School, Rafaat.	32	—	—	—	—	—
TOTAL	119	—	—	—	—	—

In other words, apart from the 120 students in the two Government Agricultural Schools, there are 639 students, of whom 276 are girls, in private Jewish Agricultural Schools, and 119 students in private Arab Christian (Catholic) schools; thus in all, 928 students are receiving agricultural education.

Government assistance to private agricultural schools takes the form of per capita grants amounting in all to about £P.300 per annum, the largest grant being £P.100 per annum to the Mikveh Israel School, which is the oldest and largest agricultural school in Palestine.

Besides these agricultural schools proper, there are several other Jewish orphanages, schools or nurseries which have agricultural or horticultural sections or branches, maintaining fruit and forest nurseries, vegetable gardens and some cows and poultry; these are not yet sufficiently important in the agricultural sense to merit the status of "agricultural schools" although they are doing very useful educational work. They are supported entirely by contributions from Jewish sources.

(b) *School Gardens.*

2.—Apart from these schools, there are 192 Arab village school gardens which are supervised by the Department of Education, 86 being under trained agricultural teachers, and about 100 gardens attached to Jewish schools. The Department of Agriculture issues supplies of improved seed, plants, fruit trees and vegetables to these schools, and lends them simple implements where possible.

(c) *Demonstrations and Extension work.*

3.—A large proportion of the officers of the Department of Agriculture make regular visits to the villages and settlements in order to encourage the rural population to adopt improved farming practices. These officers advise farmers on systems of rotation, introduction of new crops and vegetables, the application of organic manure and fertilizers, the care, management and feeding of animals and poultry, the necessity for growing more fodder crops and making silage to supplement the feeding rations of animals, the treatment of diseases and pests, etc., and issue improved seed, vegetable seedlings, fruit trees, bud-wood, pedigree poultry, etc., to the farmers whom they visit.

37 demonstration farms or plots have been laid down in co-operation with progressive farmers. The plots are usually about 75 dunums in extent and are designed to demonstrate to the neighbouring villages and settlements improved rotation systems, new crops such as forage and potatoes, the better results obtained from improved and graded seed, the higher yields obtained by the application of fertilisers, and generally the benefits which would accrue by the adoption of improved methods of tillage.

To improve and stimulate poultry and bee-keeping in Arab villages, ten District Poultry Stations and Apiaries have been established. These stations serve as demonstration centres for Arab poultry and bee-keepers of the surrounding areas. Hatching eggs, day-old chicks and six weeks old pullets and cockerels are sold from these stations at reasonable prices to villagers, and instruction in poultry keeping is given by touring personnel. To improve the fowls in villages, over 3,000 cockerels between 8 and 12 weeks old were distributed recently in different villages in exchange for local birds. The results of this grading scheme have been very promising in certain villages where pure bred cockerels have been used during the last two years. To encourage and establish modern bee-keeping in villages, Government issues frame hives with full equipment on the "hire-purchase" system and 2,100 bee hives have thus been issued during the last three years. Special instructors frequently visit those Arab bee-keepers to whom frame hives have been issued and advise and instruct them, step by step, on the management of bees kept in modern hives.

Entomological Officers give advice on the methods of combating and controlling pests and diseases, and demonstrate the use of spraying and dusting machines which are also lent to farmers. The latter are also given small initial quantities of insecticides free of charge and citrus trees are fumigated compulsorily (about 140 000 each year during the past three years) under the Plant Protection Ordinance, to check the spread of scale insects which would otherwise reduce the yields of the trees and render the fruit unmarketable.

(d) *Agricultural and Horticultural Stations.*

4.—There are six Agricultural Stations, at Faradiyeh, Acre, Beisan, Jericho, Ain Arrub and

MEMORANDA BY THE GOVERNMENT OF PALESTINE.

9. IMPROVEMENT OF PRODUCTIVITY.

Majdal. These stations are so sited as to embrace all the different climatic conditions of the country.

Comparative experiments are carried out to ascertain the most remunerative crops to grow, and the best methods of cultivation. Selected seed is raised in considerable quantities, and distributed to farmers with a view to improving both the quantity and quality of their crops. The practical results obtained at these stations form the basis of the work of a staff of inspectors, who constantly tour the villages and settlements for the purpose of demonstrating improved agricultural practices. These officers encourage the use of selected seed and improved vegetable seedlings from the agricultural stations, and educate the farming population in the cultivation of new crops and fodder plants.

Both Arabs and Jews benefit from this work, although, in practice, it has been customary to devote more attention to the Arab villages, partly because of their more backward condition and partly because the Jewish Agency have their own Research and Experimental Stations with an Extension Staff which advises Jewish farmers.

There are nine Horticultural Stations, three in the hills at Farradiyeh, Nablus and Ain Arrub; three in the plains at Majdal, Sarafand and Acre; and three in the Jordan Valley, below sea level, at Jericho, Farwana and Beisan. The staff of these stations are frequently consulted by the general public, and meetings are occasionally held at them.

Twenty nine horticultural demonstration plots throughout the countryside serve as a practical means of educating the people in methods of fruit culture and the best kinds of fruit trees to grow. Recently, the general public have been kept in closer touch with this work by means of the Palestine Broadcasting Service, the Department of Agriculture's monthly Agricultural Supplement, and occasional leaflets.

Arabs and Jews have equal opportunities of benefiting from the educational work undertaken.

(e) *Education in regard to Animal Husbandry.*

5.—Every effort is made to induce stock-owners to report promptly the occurrence of any disease of a contagious or infectious nature. Veterinary Officers, who are in constant touch with the farmers, explain to them the nature and symptoms of scheduled diseases and how diseased animals should be isolated pending the arrival of a Government Veterinary Officer, and make every endeavour, by demonstration and persuasion, to overcome the ignorance of villagers of disease control and their apathy towards it. The Jewish settlers, however, are more cognisant of the necessity for suppression and control of animal contagious diseases. In order to convince stock-owners of the benefits which they can derive from disease control measures, the results of preventive and curative treatment in respect of each disease are demonstrated to them. For example, dipping demonstrations are carried out to show the benefits of regular dipping of stock. Animals exposed to anthrax infection are vaccinated free of charge to prove the efficacy of vaccination.

Except in the case of ploughing animals, the Arab farmer does not hand-feed his animals when grazing is scarce, but leaves them to subsist on whatever they can find. His female stock are served at random, mostly by inferior sires, and, as a result, the local breeds of animals have degenerated. Touring staff consequently explain the necessity for and advantages of rational feeding. To demonstrate the value of using good sires, Government grants premiums to owners of bulls and jackasses which are selected and approved as stud sires by Veterinary Officers, provided the owners agree to allow villagers to use them gratis. In villages where a premium bull or jackass is provided, all other male bovines and jackasses are castrated. The progeny of these selected sires is, of course, better than that of scrub male stock and thus the fellah gradually learns the benefit of selecting his reproducing stock and of eliminating scrub and unprofitable animals.

Poultry and Bee Instructors tour villages and settlements and educate villagers in the proper feeding and management of poultry and bees. Special fortnightly courses in bee-keeping are held at the Central Acre Poultry Station and Apiary. These courses are well attended by Arab and Jewish bee-keepers. In addition, practical courses in poultry and bee-keeping of three months duration are held at Acre, all the year round, and they are well attended by Arab and Jewish students.

(II) RESEARCH.

A. FIELD CROPS AND VEGETABLES.

6.—Research or experiments at Government Agricultural Stations are confined to the practical problems of finding means to obtain higher yields and better quality of crops. The work comprises the following branches.

(a) *Improvement of yields and quality of cereals and leguminous crops.*

7.—This class of research takes the form of:—

(a) comparative trial plots of the various local varieties;

(b) elimination of the unsuitable types or strains;

(c) field selection of the best seed within the type;

(d) the introduction of varieties or types from other countries.

Of the numerous varieties tried, a limited number has been selected for propagation. Varieties have been determined which possess specified properties, such as those most suitable for early and late sowings, those most resistant to "rust", those best suited for areas where the rainfall is low, or those having the shortest period of growth. Large quantities of these seeds are now being grown at Government Stations and issued to co-operative seed farmers, who, in turn, disseminate them in their village or in the surrounding villages.

Among the varieties introduced from elsewhere are wheats which produce white flour, as distinct from the dark coloured flour produced by the local hard varieties.

(b) *Improvement and Extension of Vegetable Production.*

8.—Comparative trials of improved varieties of vegetables have been carried out. The varieties most suitable to local conditions have been determined and seed or seedlings of the same are issued to vegetable growers and village schools

9. IMPROVEMENT OF PRODUCTIVITY.

in large quantities. Thus the local inferior varieties of vegetables are gradually being replaced by improved varieties from elsewhere.

(c) Crop Rotational Experiments.

9.—These are carried out by the introduction of green manuring, leguminous crops, and cultivated fallow instead of the bare fallow normally practised by farmers. It has been found that, through a rational rotation, productivity can be considerably increased, especially in lands where yields have fallen to the lowest limit of fertility.

(d) Irrigation and Duty of Water Experiments.

10.—These have been carried out at such stations as Acre, Sarafand, Beisan and Jericho, where crops and vegetables are normally grown under irrigation in the vicinity. The object is to ascertain the most economical use of water, the optimum quantities of water required for the various crops, the period of irrigation, etc. Experiments have been made at Beisan to determine the effect on citrus growth of water of various salinities, three different springs being utilised for the purpose. A large scale investigation into the respective merits of the "furrow" and "basin" systems of irrigating citrus has also recently been carried out in a private grove by two officers of the Department of Development working in conjunction with the owner of the grove, and a comprehensive report has been published describing the results obtained.

(e) Manurial Experiments.

11.—These are carried out mainly with artificial fertilisers to determine the optimum quantities to be applied, and the conditions under which different kinds of fertilisers should be applied.

(f) Dates of Sowing Experiments.

12.—These are to determine the most suitable periods for sowing the various varieties of cereals and vegetables, having regard to the different conditions experienced in different parts of the country.

(g) Methods of Cultivation Experiments.

13.—These are to determine the advantages of the use of modern implements and ploughs, harrows, cultivators, etc. over the local primitive implements in use, under certain conditions. Depth of ploughing and sowing, and the dates of various cultural operations are also studied.

14.—Although Arabs and Jews are able to benefit equally from this research, it is probable that, in practice, the Arabs benefit more, since the methods of the Jewish farmers are more advanced and their special requirements are met to some extent by the more specialised work being done by the Research Station of the Jewish Agency. Consequently the Jewish farmers, being more progressive and their farming being generally on a higher level, do not stand in the same need of advice. The research at Government Agricultural Stations necessarily envisages, in the main, the problems of the bulk of the farming community.

B. FRUITS.

15.—Research work in horticulture is primarily confined to investigations as to types of tree crops and methods of cultivation suited to the different altitudes and soil conditions of the country.

Generally, stone fruits and vines do well under hill and plain conditions, while pears, apples and olives are more suited to the hills. Citrus can only be grown successfully in the plains; and dates, bananas and other sub-tropicals in the Jordan Valley.

Jews and Arabs have an equal opportunity to benefit from research work of this kind, except as regards the economic survey of the citrus groves of the Acre Sub-district which is now being made and as regards olive culture, both of which are mainly in the hands of Arabs.

C. THE CONTROL OF PESTS AND DISEASES WHICH ATTACK CROPS, FRUITS AND VEGETABLES.

16.—Unless the pests and diseases which affect crops, fruits, and vegetables were controlled, heavy losses would be incurred annually by farmers and fruit growers. In some cases empiric methods of control can be adopted; but in most cases it is necessary to evolve, after research and experiment, the most efficacious methods of combating pests and diseases under local conditions.

The life histories of injurious insects and the use of insecticides are therefore being studied in the Government entomological laboratories at Jerusalem, Sarafand, Acre and Tiberias.

Arabs and Jews alike benefit from the results of this research.

D. ANIMAL HUSBANDRY.

17.—A Veterinary Laboratory has been established by Government to diagnose disease, to prepare vaccines and sera for use in the field and to investigate local diseases the causes of which are unknown.

Cross breeding experiments with pure-bred Karakul rams and native ewes are being carried out at the Acre Stock Farm with the object of ascertaining the possibility of producing highpriced lamb skins and at the same time maintaining the average milk yield of producing ewes. Results to date are encouraging and, provided the experiments are successful, sheep raisers will be encouraged and assisted to produce such skins on a sufficiently large scale to establish an industry in the production of Karakul fur skins.

At the Government Poultry Station at Acre, various experiments and investigations are conducted in connection with local problems affecting the poultry and bee industries.

Arabs and Jews benefit alike from such research.

E. RESEARCH BY JEWISH INSTITUTIONS.

18.—The more advanced and intensive state of Jewish farming generally has resulted in the creation of special problems which have to some extent been met by the creation of special research organisations controlled by various Jewish Institutions. The oldest of these organisations is the research section of the Miqveh Israel Agricultural School, founded in 1870, which enjoys a high reputation and has on its staff some very experienced and enthusiastic workers. The Palestine Jewish Colonisation Association (Edmond de Rothschild Foundation) also carries out agricultural research, as does also the Hebrew University in its departments of Botany, Geology and Zoology and in its Laboratory of Soil Science. But the most systematic and comprehensive research has been concentrated at the Rehovoth Station of the Jewish Agency. As this Station not only possesses the necessary land, buildings and equipment but also employs a large staff of specialists, it was decided some years ago that, in order to

MEMORANDA BY THE GOVERNMENT OF PALESTINE.

9. IMPROVEMENT OF PRODUCTIVITY.

obviate over-lapping and duplication of effort and resources, certain essential research which ought normally to be undertaken by Government but which would require the engagement of specialised research workers, the acquisition of more land, the erection of buildings, and the purchase of special equipment and apparatus, could be more economically carried out by the Research Station of the Jewish Agency under a system of Government grants-in-aid.

In 1935-36 the following Government grants were made, and are being continued in 1936-37, to the Jewish Agency's Research Stations and the Hebrew University for approved schemes:—

	£P.
Grant for citrus research.	3,000
Grant for Experimental Fruit growing at Hillside Station, Kiryat Anavim.	300
Grant for Intensive Farming Experiments.	300
Grant for Field and Garden Experiments.	1,200
Grant for Animal Nutrition.	500
Grant for Mycological Investigations.	350
Grant for Irrigated Fruit Trees Experiments at Gevah.	200
Grant for Non-irrigated Fruit Trees Experiments at Gevat.	300
Grant for Studies in Rural Economics.	400
GRANTS TO THE HEBREW UNIVERSITY.	
For Spirochaetosis Research	180
For field mice investigations.	200
Total:	£P. 6,930

The conditions of the grant of £P. 3,000 per annum for citrus research for 5 years are:—

(a) That Arab growers and cultivators be given the same facilities as Jews in obtaining data in their own language, and in having access to and making use of the Research Station, by arrangement of visits and otherwise.

(b) That all results of general interest be published in the three official languages.

(c) That the Jewish Agency undertake in writing to spend £P. 5,000 a year, in addition to the Government subvention, so long as that subvention is received.

(d) That there be an Advisory Committee, including an Arab member and such number of Government representatives as will ensure that Government shall have an adequate voice in the formulation of the programme of research from time to time in the manner best devised to benefit all sections of citriculturists.

(e) That the Jewish Agency keep separate accounts of expenditure charged to the Government subvention.

(f) That the Research Station advise, as far as possible, on specific enquiries referred to it through the Government Department by citriculturists.

The programme of research must in any case include experiments

(i) as to the possibility of developing activities in which citrus culls are utilised; and

(ii) in methods of controlling rot diseases in citrus fruits; and mycological investigations.

(g) That detailed estimates of expenditure of the grant of £P. 3,000 be submitted to and approved by Government annually at the commencement of the financial year; and the accounts of expenditure from the grant be subject to Government audit.

The conditions attaching to payment of the other grants are similar except for the provision in paragraph (d) relating to a special Advisory Committee for Citrus Research.

III. IRRIGATION.

19.—The possibility of the construction of major projects for the purpose of ensuring the most effective use of the water supplies available in the country is discussed in Memorandum No. 19, where the conclusion is reached that these possibilities are strictly limited and that springs and wells are likely to remain the main sources of irrigation supply in the future, as they have been in the past.

A. SPRINGS.

Government Irrigation Systems.

20.—There are only two Government irrigation systems dependent on springs, one drawing its supply from the Ain es Sultan near Jericho and the other from the Ain el Josak near Beisan. The former system supplies water to the experimental station at Jericho and irrigates a considerable area of State Domain land in the vicinity, which is leased to Arab cultivators. By the provision of concrete channels and properly designed outlets the distribution of the water has been much improved and the resulting economy has enabled the area irrigated from the spring to be greatly extended. The latter system feeds the Beisan settlement for landless Arabs, which is described in Memorandum No. 11. The spring was cleaned out and new channels, some concrete and some earth, were constructed with the result that both the settlement and the land below it are now assured of a good and constant supply of water.

B. WELLS.

(a) Well boring by Government.

21.—Irrigation from wells is a matter which, in Palestine, rests entirely in private hands, but Government has undertaken a small amount of exploratory work with a view to demonstrating the existence or otherwise of water in out of the way areas and is now contemplating legislation to enable it to control well sinking to some extent so as to prevent an excessive drain on the subsoil supplies

Since 1930, four boring plants have been purchased by Government. They have been used

9. IMPROVEMENT OF PRODUCTIVITY.

partly for exploratory purposes and partly in connection with the provision of water supplies for villages and urban areas. Altogether eighteen bore holes have been sunk. In nine instances sweet water was discovered, in three (including the only two bores sunk in the Beersheba Sub-district) the water was too saline for use, in two no water was found and work is still in progress in the case of the remaining four. It is intended, as soon as a suitable plant can be made available for the purpose, to make further trials in the vicinity of Beersheba in the hope of discovering fresh water in that area.

(b) Sub-soil water survey.

22.—There is, of course, always a danger that, as more and more wells are sunk, an excessive drain may be imposed upon the sub-soil water supplies. In order to secure a datum for future observations, Government has recently caused a survey of underground water levels to be made in those portions of Palestine where well irrigation is most intense. A network of levels was first spread over the surface of the country and the depth to water measured in many hundreds of wells; from these observations the levels of the underground water were calculated. This survey has just been completed and the results are now being tabulated and mapped. A number of control stations have also been established throughout the area, at which fluctuations in the sub-soil water level are regularly noted and the water tested for salinity.

IV. OTHER MEANS.

A. FIELD CROPS, VEGETABLES AND FRUITS.

(a) Issue of Improved Seed.

23.—It has been the practice, for several years past, to raise at Agricultural Stations and distribute to cultivators improved seed of proved and tested strains of wheat and barley to suit the soil and climatic conditions of each locality. The seed is sold to farmers at market rates, but issued gratis in deserving cases.

Oats, vetch and maize seeds are also raised at Agricultural Stations and distributed gratis to farmers for producing hay in order to supplement the feeding rations of animals in dry seasons. This new practice is now spreading among Arab farmers. Maize growing under dry cultivation has also been introduced into Arab villages. The maize is fed green, and is also made into silage.

In 1933-34, 46 tons of selected seed of wheat, barley, oats, maize and legumes were so issued and in 1934-35, 113 tons; in 1935-36, however, only 53 tons were issued owing to crop failures as a result of drought. In consequence, Government purchased in 1935 120 tons of wheat and 23 tons of barley in various localities from farmers whose crops were raised from improved seed originally issued from Government Agricultural Stations; this seed was cleaned and graded for re-issue to other farmers at cost price, in order to continue the policy of replacing poor seed-grain by improved seed throughout the country.

(b) Vegetables.

24.—To meet the increasing demand for vegetables in the towns, the Department has introduced improved varieties of vegetable seeds from the United Kingdom and the Continent. After testing, large quantities of vegetable seedlings and seed are raised and distributed to growers.

In 1934-35, 500,000 seedlings and 200 kilogrammes of seed were distributed gratis, and in 1935-36 750,000 seedlings and 138 kilogrammes of seed were so issued.

(c) Potato Seed.

25.—Prior to 1930, very small quantities of potatoes were raised in this country. After trials with various imported varieties of potato seed, it was established that potatoes can be grown successfully in Palestine. To stimulate the development of this crop, the Department imported 56 tons of seed potatoes from Ireland in 1934 and 140 tons in 1935, for sale to farmers at cost price. Government also encouraged the growing of this crop by increasing the import duty in 1934 on imported potatoes from £P. 1 to £P. 3 per ton during the main harvesting season of April to mid-July. In consequence, production has increased to about 7,000 tons in 1936, which compares with a production of under 1,000 tons five years ago. About 20,000 tons of potatoes would have to be grown locally to meet the present local requirements; in 1935 potatoes were imported to the extent of 15,774 tons.

(d) Tomatoes.

26.—Early in 1936, Government doubled the import duty on imported tomatoes from £P. 2 to. £P. 4 per ton to protect this vegetable, the cultivation of which has extended considerably. Production has increased from 7,000 tons in 1931 to 17,000 tons in 1935.

(e) Inspection of Plants.

27.—All imports of plants are inspected by Plant Inspectors under the Plant Protection Ordinance, in order to prevent the introduction of injurious pests and diseases from abroad. 9,069 consignments of imported plants, fruits, vegetables and seeds were so inspected in 1934-35, and 9,553 consignments in 1935-36.

(f) Locusts.

28.—Palestine was invaded by locusts in 1928, 1929 and 1930, and campaigns were then organised by the Entomological Service; equipment and labour for this purpose were provided by Government with exceptionally satisfactory results. The damage done by locusts was negligible, as they were destroyed as they settled on the boundaries of Palestine and in Trans-Jordan. The laying-places were marked, and the eggs and hoppers were then destroyed. Thus the country was saved from the very severe damage which was the rule before the war, when locusts periodically invaded the country and met with relatively little or ineffective resistance.

Large supplies of anti-locust equipment are now held in store, in readiness for future invasions. A Locust Destruction Ordinance was prepared and published in 1932 to enable prompt and efficacious measures to be taken in the future.

(g) Grading of Seed.

29.—Twenty five small portable grading machines have been purchased and are used in the villages for the elimination of injurious weed seeds and the grading of the seed grain, with the result that villages are not only enabled to obtain higher prices from millers for their grain, but thereby procure better seed for re-sowing in the following season. These machines are transferred to different villages throughout the country in order to demonstrate the value of eliminating weeds and grading seed.

9. IMPROVEMENT OF PRODUCTIVITY.

(h) Government Plant Nurseries.

30.—Government Plant Nurseries for distribution of fruit trees are maintained at Acre, Farradiya, Majdal, Nablus and Jerusalem.

The number of trees distributed by sale or free during the 1935-36 season was as follows:—

SALES

	Vines	Trees	Citrus
Arabs	15,127	17,121	17,843
Jews	37,439	8,613	460
	52,566	25,734	18,303

FREE ISSUES

	Vines	Trees	Citrus
Horticultural Stations.	6,889	13,348	8,270
Military & Police	200	471	—
Schools	4,555	1,182	—
Public	720	55	—
	12,364	15,056	8,270

In addition, 12,000 stocks of apple, pear, quince and stone fruits, 1,000 fig cuttings, 2,500 olive suckers, 2,500 vine cuttings, and 13,500 banana suckers were distributed to villagers of the Nablus Sub-district who had suffered loss during the floods of February, 1935. A large number of fruit buds were also distributed to private nurseries.

(i) Private Plant Nurseries.

31.—Government controls the output of a good type of plant from private nurseries by means of rules made under the Plant Protection Ordinance. The object is to ensure that the plants are true to type and free from pests and diseases before they are distributed in the country. Of the 187 nurseries which have applied for registration, 177 are Jewish, 6 are German and 4 Arab.

(j) Fruit Inspection.

32.—Government indirectly improves the quality of the citrus export crop by means of the Fruit Inspection Service, which operates under the Fruit Export Ordinance. For this purpose a staff of one Chief Fruit Inspector, three Fruit Inspectors, and three Assistant Fruit Inspectors, are employed, together with a large temporary staff during the export season. In the off-season, the permanent staff visit the citrus groves and advise owners as to control of pests and diseases.

B. ANIMAL HUSBANDRY.

33.—In 1934, there were in Palestine, in round figures, 135,000 cattle, 188,000 sheep, 381,000 goats, 16,500 horses, 7,500 mules, 76,000 donkeys and 32,000 camels, making a total of 836,000 animals, and over 1,500,000 poultry. It is considered, however, that the actual numbers are greater as some animals were not returned by their owners. The value of this stock, based on average market prices, is about five million pounds.

(a) Quarantine-prevention of the introduction of stock diseases.

34.—With the attempt to improve the quality of livestock must be combined protection against epidemics which might be introduced from adjacent territories and from overseas. This involves carefully designed measures and constant vigilance, as the land frontiers are passable and fordable by livestock at innumerable places, especially during the dry season, and natural features do not assist frontier patrols to the extent necessary to prevent entirely the smuggling of animals, which is greatly encouraged by the local heavy demands for food animals.

To prevent the introduction of epidemics, a chain of fourteen land frontier quarantine stations, situated at the main points of entry of livestock into Palestine from adjacent territories, has been established. At Haifa, another quarantine station, which is the largest of all, deals with animals imported from overseas. Imported stock are detained in quarantine for varying periods under regulations which prescribe also the conditions under which different classes of livestock may be imported by sea and land routes into Palestine from different countries. Personnel stationed at frontier quarantine stations patrol the frontiers with the object of preventing the illicit importation of livestock.

Imports of livestock in 1935-36 were as follows:—

42,188 cattle, 317,117 sheep, 139,413 goats, 3,420 equines, 17,264 camels and 1,985,930 head of poultry.

Due to the efficacy of quarantine, Palestine has been free from major epizootic diseases for the past ten years.

From this freedom of disease both Arab and Jewish stock-owners benefit alike.

(b) Control and suppression of animal diseases in the country.

35.—It would be unwise to improve livestock and increase its productivity unless, at the same time, adequate machinery were provided to control and suppress endemic animal diseases, as it is well known that improved breeds are more susceptible to disease. Without such machinery, the work of years might be reduced to naught in a few days by a sweeping epidemic. In order, therefore, to protect the flocks and herds of the country, a staff of qualified veterinary surgeons is employed to deal promptly and effectively with any epizootic disease which may suddenly appear, and to control and eradicate gradually the more serious endemic animal diseases.

Cattle Plague (Rinderpest) which occurred ten years ago was successfully eradicated with negligible losses to farmers, while under the Turkish régime this plague caused considerable losses every two or three years.

Good progress has and is being made in the suppression of endemic diseases. From this veterinary service Arabs and Jews benefit alike.

(c) Improvement of livestock.

36.—Every encouragement is given to villagers to improve their local livestock. Little permanent improvement can, however, be expected until greater attention is paid to the feeding of village stock. Endeavours are being made to improve natural pastures and to educate fellaheen to raise fodder crops.

PALESTINE ROYAL COMMISSION.

9. IMPROVEMENT OF PRODUCTIVITY.

Inferior and scrub male livestock is being castrated and selected Government sires are being distributed during the breeding seasons for use by fellaheen.

The Government Stock Farm established at Acre maintains a small herd of Lebanese cows, a selected flock of native sheep and a herd of Damascus and Syrian goats, for the production of suitable bulls, rams and bucks which are either lent or sold to villagers for improvement of their animals.

Mules are much in demand but, unfortunately, few are bred in the country and consequently large numbers are imported annually. To encourage mule breeding, Government jackasses are distributed in the districts for stud purposes. The present jackasses are, however, not up to standard and it is the intention of Government to improve the position by the purchase in due course of Cyprian and Catalonian donkey mares and stallions for the Stock Farm.

A good mule cannot be bred by using a poor quality mare. It is necessary consequently to improve the horse of the country. Government at present maintains two Arab stallions for stud purposes but this is insufficient. It is intended to purchase additional stallions for district stud purposes and mares from which to breed suitable sires as and when funds become available.

Two Guernsey bulls were imported last year by Government and lent to settlements for experimental crossing with grade cows with the object of ascertaining the value of the cross.

An official Milk Recorder was appointed by Government for the first Milk Recording Society in the country which was formed on the 1st October, 1934. Over 1,400 cows are recorded by this Society which embraces 20 Jewish settlements situated in the Jordan Valley, Nouris Block and Affula-Nahalal Block.

(d) Poultry and bee-keeping industries.

37.—The Government Poultry Station at Acre maintains flocks of pure bred hens of the Leghorn, Sussex, Australorp, Rhode Island Red and Wyandotte breeds and imports annually fresh birds of these breeds to maintain the purity of the breeds. Hatching eggs of the Leghorn breed particularly maintained at Acre are much sought after in settlements and over 29,000 were sold last breeding season as well as 1,800 pullets and cockerels.

10. OWNERSHIP AND TENURE OF LAND.

Sugar, free of import duty to the amount of 10 kilogrammes per hive, is issued to bee-keepers during years when the honey crop is poor, to encourage them to feed their bees to the full extent necessary. 190 tons were so distributed last year.

C. AFFORESTATION.

38.—It has been felt, for some considerable time, that a more progressive forest policy is necessary in Palestine, and such a policy is now in process of formation. This, if adopted, will provide for measures to increase the productivity of the lands to be acquired and protected by afforestation and of the neighbouring lands which now suffer periodically from the effects of erosion and drought. Certain areas will be set aside for the supply of much needed forest produce, such as timber, firewood, charcoal and tanning materials. Other forests will be maintained on steep slopes to prevent erosion. On other areas fodder from selected specimens of scrub will be systematically controlled so long as the hill villages are in need of it. When the demand for fodder in any locality ceases, such fodder lands will be turned into productive forests or orchards, as may be found advisable. These results can only follow the adoption and steady maintenance of a forward forest policy. Some of the hill areas are as backward as any in the Mediterranean region, and no real progress in agriculture can be effected in such places without corresponding progress in forestry.

The main benefits of such a policy would be enjoyed by the whole country, irrespective of race, but particular advantage would accrue to the Arabs who inhabit the hill villages. They would enjoy employment in afforestation and auxiliary work; their animal husbandry would be improved by the establishment of the managed fodder areas; the "Village Forests" would supply them with cheap forest produce; and, eventually, the utilisation operations in the main forests, and the industries dependent on them, would be of great benefit to the villages in question.

MEMORANDUM No. 10.

DESCRIPTION OF VARIOUS FORMS OF OWNERSHIP AND TENURE OF LAND.

The Palestine Order in Council of the 1st September, 1922, is the supreme authority for the laws now in force in Palestine. Article 46 of the Order runs as follows:—

"The jurisdiction of the Civil Courts shall be exercised in conformity with the Ottoman Law in force in Palestine on November 1st, 1914, and such later Ottoman Laws as have been or may be declared to be in force by Public Notice, and such Orders in Council, Ordinances and regulations as are in force in Palestine at the date of the commencement of this Order or may hereafter be applied or enacted...".

2.—It follows that immovable property in Palestine is governed by the Ottoman Law in force on the 1st November, 1914, as amended by local legislation.

3.—The Ottoman Laws still remain the guiding authority under which matters relating to immovable property are considered and administered by Government and in the Courts. The foundation of the statute law governing the tenure of land in Palestine is the Ottoman Land Code 1274 A.H. (1858 A.D.). The Ottoman Civil Code (the Mejelle) also contains important provisions relating to interests in land.

4.—The Land Code recognizes five land tenures:—

(1) Mulk.
(2) Miri.
(3) Waqf.
(4) Metruke.
(5) Mewat.

10. OWNERSHIP AND TENURE OF LAND.

This memorandum deals briefly with these in the order in which they appear in the Code.

5.—MULK.

(a) The word Mulk means "property". It refers alike to movable and immovable property. Mulk land is held in undiluted ownership assimilated to that of chattels, the fee-simple being vested in the owner. Article 1192 of the Mejelle provides that "every man can deal as he likes with his mulk".

(b) The Ottoman Land Code does not apply to Mulk. In matters of personal status such as wills, succession and the creation of Waqf (Trust) it is governed by religious law. In other matters such as mortgage, lease and sale in execution of debts it is subject to the civil law. The owner enjoys absolute freedom of disposition, including devise by will. On intestacy it is distributed by the Religious Court of the Community to which the deceased belonged in accordance with the law of that Community. If no Religious Court exists, or if the heirs elect to have recourse to the Civil Courts, it is distributed by the District Court in accordance with the Civil Law. Foreigners may invoke the national law. Land of Mulk tenure is almost entirely limited to building sites in towns and villages. In Palestine there is little, if any, agricultural land of this category.

6.—MIRI.

(a) The term Miri is derived from "Emir", a Prince, and was land which was within the gift of the Ruler. For practical purposes it now means land of which the fee-simple is vested in the State and over which heritable and assignable rights of occupancy in perpetuity are enjoyed by the holder. The right of occupancy is, however, subject to certain conditions, the principal of which is the maintenance of continuous cultivation so that the State may at all times derive revenue in the form of a tithe. The tithe has now been replaced by a land tax.

(b) Prior to 1331 A.H. (1912 A.D.) considerable restrictions were imposed on the use of Miri; the soil could not be used for brick making and the planting of vineyards and orchards, and the erection of houses or farm buildings or enclosures were prohibited unless with the consent of Government. In 1331 A. H. Ottoman legislation conferred on the holder power to use the land for any purpose he wished provided that he registered in the Land Registry, and with the taxation authorities, any buildings, trees or other accretions to the land.

(c) Freedom of disposition is permitted, provided the land is not made the subject of a testamentary gift nor can any Waqf (Trust) be created in respect of it. On the death of the holder it devolves according to the statute law and not in accordance with the law of the Religious Community of the deceased, as is the case with Mulk. If Miri remains unproductive for three consecutive years without lawful excuse as, for instance, flooding or the absence of the holder on military service, it reverts to the State. The possessor may, however, redeem it on payment of its unimproved capital value. In practice liability to forfeiture rarely occurs. There has been only one instance since the inception of the British Administration. As there is no power of testamentary disposition it reverts to the State on failure of heirs. The determination of the heirs and the distribution among them are matters within the jurisdiction of the Civil Courts or the Religious Courts of the various communities according as the heirs may elect, provided that the distribution in all cases is in accordance with the Civil Law.

(d) If Miri in a given village is sold to a person who is not an inhabitant of that village, any inhabitant who is in need of land may claim priority of purchase at any time within one year of the sale.

If the trees or buildings on Miri belong to a person other than the owner of the land, the owner of the former has a prior right of purchase.

(e) In many Miri villages a custom of joint ownership known as Masha'a is practised. The village (or localities in it) is owned by large numbers of persons in undivided shares, the interest of each being expressed in a fraction, of which the denominator may consist of, say, eight or ten figures, whilst the nominator represents the individual share. No person owns a specific piece of land. Periodically—usually every two years to suit the crop rotation — the elders of the village allot a fresh piece of land in satisfaction of a share. For one period it may be good land, for the next indifferent, for the next bad, and so on. Consequently no one has any inducement to improve his land, as the fruits of his industry would be reaped by his successor in occupation. The system of Masha'a is being broken up by the partition of areas by land settlement and survey. Further, Government has a number of officers who are constantly touring the villages placing expert assistance and guidance at the disposal of the cultivators as to the best method of breaking up Masha'a.

(f) A novel provision limiting the acquisition of land by companies is contained in Section 15 of the Companies Ordinance, 1929, which reads:—

(1) "The Registrar (of Companies) shall not register any Company which has as its object or one of its objects the acquisition and development of land generally unless such Company produces a certificate under the hand of the High Commissioner empowering it to hold land generally.

(2) The High Commissioner may at any time, and shall, if he is satisfied that the Company is not cultivating or developing land acquired by it, revoke a certificate enabling the Company to hold lands generally; and thereupon the Company may be wound up by the Court. Provided that before such certificate is revoked the High Commissioner shall give the Company notice in writing of his intention and shall afford the Company an opportunity of being heard in opposition to the revocation".

PALESTINE ROYAL COMMISSION.

10. Ownership and Tenure of Land.

(g) In 1921 the prohibition against sale in execution of a mortgage was repealed, and it was provided that a mortgagee desiring to realise his security in the event of default must apply to the President of the District Court for an order of sale. The Transfer of Land Ordinance, No. 2 of 1921, Section 1(2) provides:—

"...The President may order postponement of the sale if he is satisfied:—

(a) that the debtor has reasonable prospects of payment if given time; or

(b) that having regard to all the circumstances of the case, including the needs of the creditor, it would involve undue hardship to sell the property of the debtor".

If an order for sale is made, the property is submitted for sale by public auction.

7.—Waqf.

(a) Waqf is land some right over which has been dedicated to a pious object. It approximates to the Trust of English Equity. Strictly speaking, Waqf is an Islamic institution but it has been adopted by most of the other Religious Communities in Palestine.

Every object which tends to the good of mankind, individually or collectively, is a pious purpose. The latter expression includes provision for one's children or kindred.

The Moslem jurist, Sayed Emir Aly, states that "where a property is made Waqf the proprietary right of the grantor is divested and it remains henceforth in the implied ownership of the Almighty. The usufruct only is applied for the benefit of human beings and the subject of the dedication becomes inalienable and non-heritable in perpetuity".

(b) The Courts of the Moslem, Jewish and the several Christian Communities have exclusive jurisdiction over any case concerning the constitution or internal administration of a Waqf or religious endowment constituted before the Religious Court of the Community.

The Moslem Courts have no jurisdiction over Waqfs constituted before them prior to the war where the object of the dedication is non-Moslem. Such Waqfs now fall within the purview of the Rabbinical Court or of the appropriate Christian Court. In the case of those communities not represented by a Religious Court, the matter falls within the jurisdiction of the Civil Courts. Waqfs are administered in accordance with the wishes of the donor as expressed in the Waqfieh (Deed of Trust) by Mutawallis (Trustees) nominated by the dedicator or, in default, by the appropriate Court.

Moslem Waqfs previously administered direct by the Ottoman Ministry of Waqf are now administered by the Supreme Moslem Council.

(c) For practical purposes Waqf is divided into two categories: True Waqf and Untrue Waqf.

(d) Only Mulk can be dedicated as True Waqf. It is therefore almost entirely limited to buildings and building sites in the towns or villages. In this category the actual property itself is dedicated.

(e) Untrue Waqf arises chiefly where the tithe payable on Miri land has been dedicated and consecrated by Government to a particular object. The land is not affected. In a large number of villages in Palestine the tithe has been so dedicated by the Ottoman Government.

Since the abolition of tithe and the substitution of a land tax, an agreement has been reached between Government and the Supreme Moslem Council by which an annual sum is paid to the latter in lieu of the tithe. The land is not affected by the dedication of the tithe and continues to be governed by the Civil Law.

8.—Metroukeh.

Metroukeh is common public land, such as highways, market sites, village threshing floors, watering places and areas assigned as common grazing grounds. There are few, if any, such assigned areas in Palestine. Nor are there any noteworthy incidents attached to the tenure. Legislation is about to be enacted which will enable the High Commissioner to change the category of Metroukeh where the land in question is required for public purposes, provided that equally satisfactory common rights in respect of communications, etc. are provided in the place of those afforded by the land of which the category is thus changed.

9.—Mewat.

Mewat is dead or unreclaimed land. Typical examples are the coastal sand dunes, the eastern slope of the Judaean hills towards the Jordan Valley and the forest areas in the hills of Hebron. Mewat is State Domain.

Where Mewat is set aside as a forest reserve, existing beneficial practices, such as grazing or collection of firewood, are permitted subject to safeguards for the preservation of the forest. The High Commissioner may grant permission to revive Mewat on such terms as he deems fit.

10.—This memorandum is necessarily a review of the main points of a system of land tenure having its roots in a distant past and conforming in general character to the Moslem Religious Law as modified by custom. It makes no pretence at being a discussion of many of the finer and somewhat obscure incidents and rights attaching to the tenures.

MEMORANDA BY THE GOVERNMENT OF PALESTINE.

11. LANDLESS ARABS.

MEMORANDUM No. 11.

DESCRIPTION OF THE ACTIVITIES OF THE DEPARTMENT OF DEVELOPMENT IN CONNECTION WITH THE RE-SETTLEMENT OF DISPLACED ARAB CULTIVATORS.

GENERAL.

Sir John Hope Simpson, in Chapter 11 of his Report of 1930 on Immigration, Land Settlement and Development in Palestine (Command Paper No. 3686), recommended that the development of the land could best be ensured by the appointment of a Development Commission invested with the necessary powers. As a result of this recommendation, Mr. Lewis French, C.I.E., C.B.E., was deputed by His Majesty's Government in 1931 to investigate and report on the problems pertaining to Development and Land Settlement in Palestine.

2. Mr. French was appointed Director of Development with the following duties:—

(i) To prepare a register of "landless Arabs".

(ii) To draw up a scheme for re-settling such Arabs.

(iii) To ascertain what State and other lands could be made available for close settlement by Jews with reference to the obligation imposed upon the Mandatory by Article 6 of the Mandate.

(iv) To report on the improvement and intensive development of land in the hills in order to secure to the fellaheen a better standard of living without, save in exceptional cases, having recourse to transfer.

(v) To report on the feasibility and advisability of providing credits for Arab cultivators and Jewish settlers, and if so, the best methods of achieving this purpose.

(vi) To put forward proposals for draining, irrigating and otherwise reclaiming land not at present cultivated or cultivated only to a limited extent.

Mr. French presented a Report in December, 1931, and a Supplementary Report in April, 1932.*

3.—The Arab Executive and the Jewish Agency were both invited to nominate one member each to assist Mr. French in an advisory capacity, but no progress was made with these appointments. Before Mr. French reached the country, the Arab Executive had made it plain that they would have nothing to do with the Development Scheme. They declined to enter into any discussions on the subject unless Government assented to their condition that such a scheme should not be based on the principles embodied in the letter addressed by the Prime Minister to Dr. Weizmann. The Jews, on their part, took no effective steps to appoint a representative.

4.—The first duty of the Director of Development was to ascertain the number of "landless Arabs" in Palestine and to make a register of them. "Landless Arabs" had been defined as "such Arabs as could be shown to have been displaced from the lands which they occupied in consequence of the lands falling into Jewish hands and who had not obtained other holdings on which they could establish themselves or other

* Reports on Agricultural Development and Land Settlement in Palestine by Lewis French, C.I.E., C.B.E. (Crown Agents for the Colonies).

equally satisfactory occupation". The Director, in preparing the Register, was given the assistance of a Legal Assessor whose duty it was to scrutinise claims and advise him as to the sufficiency of evidence in each case before the claim was admitted.

5.—As a first step to obtaining particulars of displacement, the District Authorities were asked to ascertain in what villages displacement of Arab cultivators had occurred and to see that, if claims were made, some *prima facie* evidence was forthcoming which satisfied the conditions prescribed in the preceding paragraph.

6.—The following categories of Arabs, though in fact landless, were not considered:—

(1) Persons who owned land other than that sold which they cultivated as tenants.

(2) Persons who had found land other than that from which they were displaced and were now cultivating it as tenants.

(3) Persons who, subsequent to the sale of the land from which they were displaced, obtained other land but, on account of poverty or other reasons, had since ceased to cultivate it.

(4) Persons who, at the time of sale, were not cultivators, such as labourers and ploughmen.

(5) Persons who had themselves sold their land to Jews.

(6) Persons who, although landless, had obtained equally satisfactory occupation.

Consequently, up to the 1st January, 1936, although 3,271 applications for re-settlement had been received from landless Arabs, only 664 had been admitted to the Register while 2,607 had been disallowed.

7.—The policy of His Majesty's Government as formulated in 1930, after the presentation of Sir John Hope Simpson's Report, contemplated the initiation of a comprehensive development scheme to be financed from a guaranteed loan of £P.2,500,000, and that, during the first years of that scheme, provision should be made from British votes of such annual amounts as might be required to meet the interest and sinking fund charges upon the loan. But in January, 1932, the Secretary of State intimated that conditions had changed in the interim, and that it could not be assumed that it would be found practicable to make £P.2,500,000 available for development purposes.

8.—The Director of Development left Palestine in June, 1932, and the Department of Development was reorganized and placed in the charge of the present Development Officer. This Officer was instructed to draw up schemes for the re-settlement of the displaced Arab cultivators admitted to the Register, which schemes were to be financed from a sum of £P.250,000 made available for the purpose as an advance against the proposed £2,500,000 loan.

9.—As suitable State Domain lands were not available, land on which to settle the displaced cultivators on the Register had to be purchased from private owners. An area of 17,868 dunums

PALESTINE ROYAL COMMISSION.

11. LANDLESS ARABS.

was accordingly purchased in the Beisan and Jenin Sub-districts at a cost of £P.72,240. It was calculated that this area would provide subsistence areas for some 400 families.

THE CASE OF THE WADI HAWARITH ARABS.

10.—The first landless Arabs to be dealt with were the Wadi Hawarith Arabs, whose landlord had disposed of his land to the Jewish National Fund. Judgment for their eviction had already been passed as early as the end of 1929, and it became imperative to find other land to which they could move. Government thereupon undertook the reclamation and deep ploughing of some 10,000 dunums of the land which it had purchased in the Beisan Sub-district, with a view to settling these Arabs upon it, and by the 31st of August, 1933, the major portion of the area was ready for occupation. On being evicted from the Wadi Hawarith, the Arabs, however, refused to settle on the lands prepared for them on the grounds that they were used neither to the climate nor to irrigated cultivation; their settlement in the Beisan Sub-district had accordingly to be abandoned.

11.—In view of this refusal, the possibility of making other arrangements for the settlement of the tribe on land lying in the vicinity of the Wadi Hawarith was investigated. The Northern Section of the Wadi Hawarith Arabs, comprising 90 families, was accordingly settled on a State Domain in the Tulkarm Sub-district known as Basset Sheikh Muhammad. This area consisted mainly of swampy land bordered by sand dunes and is 1,571 dunums in extent. After it had been drained and deep ploughed, the land was allotted equally among the ninety families. The Southern Section, numbering 109 families, are now camped on an area of 240 dunums taken over from the Jewish National Fund in exchange for a parcel of State Domain. The Arabs are cultivating, on lease, land in the neighbouring Wadi Qabbani and elsewhere.

THE ARAB ZUBEID OF THE SAFAD SUB-DISTRICT.

12.—These Arabs, numbering some 68 families, having been evicted from their camping grounds, Government authorized the provision for them of a new camping site in the Safad Sub-district near an area of land, the owner of which was willing to allow them to cultivate it. This site, which was the property of the Palestine Jewish Colonisation Association, was received in exchange for a neighbouring parcel of State Domain of which the Association had already a long term lease.

12. LAND REGISTRATION SYSTEM.

The Arab Zubeid were given a loan of £P.100; they have settled permanently on the new site and some of them have already built houses there, although in the past they had been tent-dwelling nomads.

OTHER RE-SETTLEMENT SCHEMES.

13.—In addition to the Arabs of Wadi Hawarith and Arab Zubeid, some 80 families, evicted from different parts of the country, expressed their willingness to take up land under Government's schemes, and for these families two settlements were started in 1934, one in the Beisan Sub-district and one in the Jenin Sub-district.

14.—The Beisan Scheme covers an area of 1,515 dunums of irrigated land, of which 1,200 dunums have been divided among 40 settlers at the rate of 30 dunums per family. The settlers have been provided with accommodation for themselves and for their animals and a system of irrigation has been laid out. On their arrival, they were provided with recoverable advances to enable them to make a fair start. The settlers are undoubtedly enjoying better conditions since they have been re-settled than they ever experienced in the past.

15.—Some 4,000 dunums are covered by the Jenin Scheme and the settlers, who have been provided with 80 dunums each, the land being unirrigated, are satisfactorily cultivating their allotments. As in the case of the Beisan Scheme, the settlers in Jenin were also granted loans, which are gradually being recovered.

16.—Up to the present, as stated in paragraph 6, only 664 families have substantiated claims to be included in the Register of landless Arabs, and of these some 347 families have been provided for by Government as under:—

Wadi Hawarith:	
Northern Section	90
Southern Section	109
Arab Zubeid	68
Jenin Scheme	40
Beisan Scheme	40
	347

None of the other registered Arabs have been prepared to take up holdings upon Government estates. That only a small number of Arabs has so far come forward to take up the land offered them is due to the fact that, prior to the present disturbances, there was plenty of employment to be found in the towns and neighbouring orange groves.

MEMORANDUM No. 12.

DESCRIPTION OF LAND REGISTRATION SYSTEM

Following the enactment of the Ottoman Land Code 1274 A.H. (1858 A.D.), the provisions of which are dealt with in Memorandum No. 10, the Turkish Government passed the Land Registration Law 1275 A.H. (1858 A.D.).

2.—Prior to these dates land was held by virtue of Sultanic decrees, grants made by conquerors of various areas, judgments of both Civil and Moslem Courts, orders of administrative authorities and deeds of sale executed before the Moslem Courts. Encroachment on unoccupied land belonging to the State and various other unauthorised methods accounted for large holdings. Land acquired by lawful means (such as grant from a competent authority) was, in theory at least, reported to Constantinople, where an effort was made to maintain a series of registers known as the Daftar Hakani (Imperial Land Registers).

3.—Subsequent to the coming into operation of the Land Registration Law 1275 (1858), the Turkish authorities proceeded to organize local

MEMORANDA BY THE GOVERNMENT OF PALESTINE.

12. LAND REGISTRATION SYSTEM.

Land Registries in various parts of the then Ottoman Empire. The real object appears to have been the collection of tithe and taxes. The Land Registries in Palestine were apparently opened between the years 1284 (1867) and 1290 (1873). The procedure was that a Yuklama (roll call) was held in each village. Claims submitted were subjected to a casual investigation and successful claimants had their rights recorded in the registers. The law required that all future dealings should be recorded in both the land and taxation registers, but it was soon apparent to the cultivators that the registers were being used as a means of identifying properties for the purpose of taxation and of disclosing the existence of persons subject to military conscription. For these reasons, only a small proportion of transactions was recorded, and these chiefly concerned elderly persons, females, foreigners and those sufficiently influential to be able to avoid military service. As an index of owners, the registers therefore became hopelessly incomplete. Nor was there any survey. Areas were sometimes expressed in the quantity of seed required to sow them, or in dunums (quarter acres) the number of which was arrived at by the merest guess. In other instances areas were entirely omitted. There was a loose verbal description of the boundaries by reference to the name of adjoining owners or physical features. The law provided that all land within given boundaries was the property of the recorded owner and that no regard was to be had to expressed areas. The result was that, in order to avoid taxation, a person owning some hundreds of dunums had them recorded as an area of, say, ten or twenty dunums. In effect the register, in so far as it functioned at all, was a record of transactions between persons and not one of transactions with reference to adequately defined plots of land. State Domain, the property of the Sultan in his capacity as Caliph, was not recorded.

4.—The result was that, at the time of the occupation of Palestine by the allied forces in 1917 and 1918, the authorities succeeded to thirteen District Land Registries, the records of which were in a state of complete chaos as regards names of owners, areas and correct definition of the land affected. To add further to the confusion, the Turkish Army in the course of its retreat had removed many of the records to Damascus, Adana, and other towns in the interior of Turkey. Many of these archives have not been recovered. The Ottoman Land Registry records, incomplete as they are, still constitute the basis of a large number of claims to real rights in Palestine.

5.—After the occupation of Palestine the military authorities closed the Land Registries, prohibited transactions in immovable property and restrained the Courts from ordering the sale of land in execution of mortgages.

6.—In 1919 Judge Williamson, then Registrar General in the Sudan, was invited to initiate a new system of Land Registration in Palestine. He devised a set of registers and a series of forms, and in 1920 legislation was passed repealing the prohibition imposed by the military authorities, establishing a Land Registry and providing that no disposition of immovable property should be valid unless recorded in the Registry. "Disposition" was defined as "Sale, mortgage, gift, dedication of waqf (trust) of every description and every other disposition of immovable property except a lease for a term not exceeding three years. It includes transfer of mortgage and a lease containing an option by virtue of which the term may exceed three years". The Registries opened on the 1st October, 1920.

7.—The procedure of registration of all dispositions between living persons is identical. In every case the parties submit to the Registrar of Lands within whose district the property is situated a petition seeking the approval of Government. The petition is accompanied by documents in support of title and by a certificate from the Mukhtar (headman) of the village or quarter stating that the grantor is the owner of the right being disposed of and setting out the situation, boundaries and description of the property.

The land is, when necessary, surveyed by a Government Surveyor or a private licensed surveyor.

The petition is entered in a petition book and the title is then investigated. If the grantor has a good title the file is passed to the Revenue Officer to ensure that there are no outstanding Government taxes. On the return of the file to the Registry with a certificate that all taxes have been paid, the Registrar, or the Advocate of the parties, prepares the necessary document evidencing the transaction (sale, mortgage, lease, etc.). The documents are then read over and explained to the parties and signed before the Registrar who attests the due execution thereof.

Ad valorem fees, based on a percentage of the consideration, are paid and the documents are then passed for inscription in the Register. The original of every document is retained in the Registry. Where the transaction is for a limited interest, such as a lease or mortgage, the counterparts are handed to the parties entitled to them. In the case of an absolute disposition, such as succession or sale, certificates of registration are issued to the registered owners.

Transmission of intestate estates of deceased persons is registered on production of a certificate of succession from the competent Court and evidence of the identity of the heirs. Bequests are registered on production of probate or letters of administration. Provision exists for the appointment of guardians of persons under disability and for the sanction of the Courts in dealing with the interests of such persons.

Matters of personal status in relation to property are complicated by the fact that there is a multiplicity of Religious Courts having jurisdiction.

8.—The system of registration, as initiated by Judge Williamson, is defective owing to the absence of a cadastral survey rigorously maintained to date whereby the parcels of land affected are accurately defined on a plan on which it is related to all contiguous plots and to a national framework of triangulation. That it enjoys a large measure of public confidence is, however, shown by the increasingly large number of transactions recorded.

The system may be described as a combination of a register of deeds and a register of transactions.

9.—So far, reference has been made to the system of registration inherited from the Turks and to that initiated by Judge Williamson. There remains yet a third, which is intended to supersede these two.

PALESTINE ROYAL COMMISSION.

12. LAND REGISTRATION SYSTEM.

10.—Acting on the recommendations made by Sir Ernest Dowson in 1926, Government decided, in 1927, to introduce registration of title based on the Torrens System in use in Australia.

11.—The first pre-requisite to such a system is a cadastral survey linked to a series of triangulation points forming a national framework to which can be related the precise position of any given parcel of land. A second pre-requisite is quasi-judicial investigation, carried out on the spot, to determine the category, ownership and existence of every right in land.

12.—To provide for this, the organization of the Survey Department was enlarged and a temporary Department of Land Settlement was organized, which has since been absorbed in the Department of Lands and Surveys. Legislation was enacted providing for land settlement and for the introduction of a new system of registration. This was designed to overcome the anomalies and deficiencies of the existing systems and to set up an orderly system of registration of title to land and registrable interests in land, based on numbered parcels in numbered registration blocks, each area being correctly measured, definitely defined in relation to adjoining land and tied to a triangulation point.

13.—Under this procedure, a survey party delimits the external boundaries of a village and divides the lands into a number of blocks, each consisting, so far as is possible, of land of equal value. These blocks serve as fiscal units for land taxation and as registration blocks for the new system. Assistant Settlement Officers, having no judicial powers, in consultation with the Village Settlement Committee and adjoining owners, then determine the limits of individual areas, the owners of those areas and other registrable rights (such as leases or mortgages) affecting them.

Plans are then prepared and, on these, boundary disputes, if any, are indicated. Schedules of Claims are prepared showing the names of claimants to all areas by reference to the block and parcel numbers shown on the plan, and the nature of the interest claimed. Disputes are shown as such. These Schedules of Claims and maps are posted up in the village. At a given date they are revised to eliminate errors and to give effect to agreements which have been arrived at in disputed claims.

After the lapse of a prescribed period a Settlement Officer, invested with judicial powers, visits the village and proceeds to determine disputes. If they are numerous or likely to be protracted he may direct the posting of a Schedule of Decisions showing all the undisputed parcels and those in respect of which disputes have been determined. At the expiration of thirty days this Schedule of Decisions is served on the Land Registry for inscription in the new registers, of which they form the basis. An appeal from the decision of the Settlement Officer lies to the Land Court, and, on a point of law, to the Court of Appeal. Settlement operations have been applied to 1,858,788 dunums of which 1,364,631 had been completed on December 31st, 1935.

14.—The new Register is loose leaf in form. It omits all reference to boundaries or other verbal description. Land is described by reference to block and parcel numbers and the plan is deemed to be conclusive evidence of area and boundaries. The completion of a transaction under this system is much simpler than it was under the other systems. Names and interests recorded in the Register are deemed to be conclusive without further investigation. Documents are submitted to a critical scrutiny to ensure that they comply with the law, that they create or convey a registrable interest, that the parties are competent and that the transaction is otherwise in order. Alleged interests not entered in the register are disregarded. Registration under the system does not affect tenure or other legal incidents attaching to the interest recorded. The office routine approximates to, but is simpler than, that of unsettled villages.

The Registers and other books used since 1920 are kept in English. Forms intended for submission to the Land Registry and documents evidencing transactions may be in any one of the official languages. Turkish is necessarily largely used.

15.—There is no guarantee of indefeasibility of title. Article 3 of the Law of Disposition 1331 (1912) in speaking of title deeds issued by the Land Registry says:

"Formal title deeds are valid and executory. The Civil Moslem Courts shall give judgment on these deeds and their registration without further proof. A formal title deed shall not be annulled except by judgment of a Court based on lawful reasons."

Registration made in pursuance of land settlement can be voided only on the ground of fraud.

"The legal value of an entry in the Land Registers and of the corresponding certificate of registration has been examined in a number of cases before the Palestine Courts which appears to justify the view that such entry gives more than a merely prima facie title and is conclusive evidence of ownership in the absence of fraud" (Goadby and Doukhan; Land Law of Palestine, p. 308).

16.—Evidence of confidence in the value of registration in the Land Registry is indicated by the increasingly large number of transactions, a record of which is given in the Appendix to this memorandum, which covers the period from the reopening of the Registries on the 1st October, 1920 to the 31st December, 1935.

17.—Land settlement and the consequent registration of title has been warmly welcomed by all sections of the population, whose only criticism is that progress has not been more rapid. For the first time a definite record of title based on accurate survey and a clear record of other registrable rights have been established. The existence of unreclaimed or other forms of State Domain has been disclosed. The feeling of security which derives from a clear record of good title has promoted development in areas where stagnation had long prevailed. In settled villages there is a marked absence of those breaches of the peace which previously occurred with alarming frequency and which had their origin in land disputes.

MEMORANDA BY THE GOVERNMENT OF PALESTINE.

12. LAND REGISTRATION SYSTEM.　　　　　　　　13. RURAL INDEBTEDNESS.

APPENDIX

STATEMENT OF REVENUE COLLECTED AND NUMBER OF TRANSACTIONS COMPLETED FROM THE 1st OCTOBER, 1920 TO THE 31st DECEMBER, 1935.

Year	Revenue £P.	No. of Transactions
1920 (October-December)	4,928	469
1921	38,913	3,361
1922	56,978	5,117
1923	41,834	6,514
1924	41.222	7,113
1925	113,165	10,761
1926	82,998	11,821
1927	57,233	9,655
1928	65,720	11,643
1929	68,247	11,290
1930	69,550	13,315
1931	74,245	14,263
1932	97,876	18,392
1933	206,124	28,293
1934	330,481	36,555
1935	455,146	49,133

MEMORANDUM No. 13.

RURAL INDEBTEDNESS.

A. ARAB RURAL INDEBTEDNESS.

It is necessary to define, at the outset, the term "indebtedness" as used in this portion of the memorandum. The term includes only the unproductive debts of the fellah to professional money-lenders and traders, on which usurious rates of interest are usually paid. It does not include debts to Government on account of taxation, debts to banks or to Government on account of agricultural loans of the nature referred to in Memorandum No. 14, or debts secured by mortgages on land or charges on crops or stock or both. All the above are, or should be, productive debt, but what is here in question is the unproductive debt of the fellah. The security which money-lenders and traders hold in respect of such debt is usually in the form of promissory notes drawn up so as to conceal the exact nature of the transaction and often showing the borrower as having received a larger sum than has actually been paid to him.

2.—It has long been recognised that indebtedness is no new thing in Palestine. It is generally alleged that the Palestinian fellah is born in debt, lives in debt and dies in debt. It is also contended that for many generations, and indeed centuries, his life has been made miserable by the pressure of his creditors and that his moral and material progress has been severely handicapped by the burden of his debts and by the cruel rate of interest paid by him.

3.—Yet the story of the fellah's indebtedness is but imperfectly known. No full enquiry has ever been made to determine the amounts, origins and other salient aspects of this indebtedness so that all current statements and opinions must be conjectural only and at best no more than matters of speculation.

4.—The only serious attempt to investigate this problem was made by a Committee appointed by the Government in 1930 to enquire into the economic condition of agriculturists. This Committee, under the chairmanship of Mr. W. J. Johnson, C.M.G., O.B.E., at the time Deputy Treasurer, investigated the position of 21,000 fellah families (about 26% of the total number of families engaged in agriculture) inhabiting 104 villages (about 12% of the total number of villages) and cultivating an area of 1,250,000 dunums (about 10% of the total cultivable area). The findings of the Committee were based on estimates given by the villages in answer to a questionnaire. No documentary evidence was either called for or produced.

5.—The following are quotations from the report of the Committee touching upon the subject of the fellah's indebtedness:—

Para. 57. This total (i.e. the estimated annual cost of living) takes no cognisance of debt, which works out on the estimates given by villagers to some £P.27 per family. Even the interest at the rate of 30%, which cannot be regarded as unusual, would amount to £P.8 per annum.

Para. 60. We may now turn to the financial situation of the Arab farmer. In the absence of reliable data, it has been difficult to check the information provided in the answers to the questionnaire. But whatever may be thought of individual items, it is the view of the Committee that, up till the middle of 1929, the net income of the average agricultural family has been between £P.25 and £P.30, and that the family has contrived to live on this income. It is clear, however, that there must have been many families less favourably situated, who have been obliged either to lower their standard of living or to fall into debt. The figures quoted for debt indicate that recourse has

PALESTINE ROYAL COMMISSION.

13. RURAL INDEBTEDNESS.

often been had to the latter alternative. Part of this debt is doubtless due to improvidence and extravagance, but the bulk of it must have gone to pay for costs of production, cost of living, and part payment of capital and of interest on previous debts. Little of it appears to have been devoted to capital improvement. If the average debt of the 21,066 families is uniform over the whole country, the total debt amounts to some £P.2,000,000. It is interesting to note that the security for such a debt would be covered by the sum of the values of the annual produce of the country and of the agricultural stock. The position appears to have been similar before the War, except that the sums involved were much smaller. During the War and for a few years after it, prices were very high. The farmer as a rule seems to have cleared off his debts and to have become comparatively prosperous. His standard of living improved accordingly. Unfortunately, he came to look upon the abnormal war-time prices as normal, and when prices began to fall to their natural level, it took time for him to adjust his outlook or his standard of living to meet the changed conditions. Consequently, he began again to borrow, and more heavily than before, while the money-lender was improvident enough to advance unduly large sums. Whenever the time came for repayment the farmer was unable to pay more than a fraction of the amount due, and was obliged to renew the bulk of the loan at an exorbitant rate of interest. A rate of 30 per cent. per annum is perhaps the commonest but 50 per cent. for three months is not unusual. The result is that many farmers now owe sums that are quite beyond their capacity to pay. In justice to the money-lender, it must be recognized that, in default of other sources of credit, he has performed a certain service to agriculture; and that, from an economic standpoint, the inadequate security for his loans justified relatively high rates of interest. For many of the transactions of money-lenders, however, no justification can be offered.

Para. 82. The Committee hesitates to recommend the provision by Government aid of credit facilities for agriculturists, since it has been shown that the average farmer is hardly in a position to repay any loan from net profits. There are, however, farmers with incomes sufficiently above the average to leave a margin for repayments, who need advances to tide them over to the next harvest, or to enable them to improve their land. There are others who, though their incomes do not for the moment leave any margin for repayment, could increase their incomes sufficiently to permit of repayment if they could find the necessary funds for improving their cultivation or to free themselves from a burden of debt at high interest. These classes would benefit by credit facilities, but as a rule only their fellow-villagers would be in a position to know if they were suitable persons to receive loans. We recommend therefore that Government should provide credit facilities, but that loans should normally be given through the medium of a village group of a co-operative nature, which would be responsible for the issue, control and repayment of the loans. Apart from the issue of loans for agricultural purposes, we see no objection to the issue through these groups of loans for the repayment of loans from money-lenders at usurious rates, provided that adequate security is offered for such loans. It is essential that loans for improvement should be for comparatively long periods and at a low rate of interest. It would sometimes be necessary to require as a condition for a loan that the borrower should undertake prescribed improvements to his land of a nature to enable him to repay the loan in due course. We therefore recommend that the Government should take steps to organise co-operative groups for dealing with village loans and to finance these groups. Care should of course be taken to avoid competition with local banks and other credit institutions.

6.—The conclusions of the Committee were, in brief, that the indebtedness of all the fellahin amounted to £P.2,000,000, representing an average of £P.27 per family, and that the average rate of interest paid on this debt was 30 per cent.

7.—Evidence from other sources, such as District Authorities and Government Departments concerned with village work (Education, Agriculture, Land and Co-operative Societies), tended to support the figures of the Committee although they may have differed slightly in details. Thus figures collected by the Registrar of Co-operative Societies in 11 villages among 190 members of Co-operative societies showed an average indebtedness of £P.19 and an average rate of interest of 20%. But since members of the Co-operative Societies are usually recruited from among wealthier fellahin, a lower rate of indebtedness and better conditions of borrowing are not unnatural consequences. Again Mr. Strickland, who followed up the enquiry of the Committee, suggested that the average indebtedness per fellah family was £P.20. In general, however, the figures of the Committee may be regarded as the most authoritative available in spite of their inherent uncertainty.

8.—Approaching these figures from a somewhat different angle, the Committee concluded that the volume of the individual fellah's indebtedness represented the full value of his annual income from crops and agricultural stock, or in other words, of his temporary wealth. His wealth was accordingly encumbered to the full, leaving him no surplus which could serve as security for credit where such was required to improve his farming so as to bring about an increase in the value of his annual produce.

9.—It is of interest to compare the figures and conclusions of the Committee with the short-term indebtedness of small holders in two other countries :—

	Average indebtedness per farmer with holding of 100 dunums.	Ratio of indebtedness to value of annual produce.
England	£P.15	1 : 20
U. S. A.	£P.94	1 : 6
Palestine Fellah	£P.27	1 : 1

MEMORANDA BY THE GOVERNMENT OF PALESTINE.

13. RURAL INDEBTEDNESS.

10.—Before deciding the measures necessary in order to relieve the fellah of his burden, the Government, in accordance with the recommendation made in paragraph 82 of the Johnson Committee's report, invited Mr. C.F. Strickland of the Indian Civil Service to advise on the methods to be adopted for the introduction of co-operation in Arab villages. Mr. Strickland studied the problem on the spot and submitted his report at the end of 1930.

11.—His first and most important conclusion was that "the amount of (the fellah's) debt is not only burdensome and such as to hamper any attempt at progressive agriculture but no small percentage of the cultivators are entirely insolvent and neither co-operative credit nor any form of State loans can place them on a solvent footing if the whole nominal claim of their creditors is to be paid".

12.—The recommendations of Mr. Strickland were, briefly, first, the formation of primary credit societies on the Raifeisen system in Arab villages; secondly, the appointment of a trained Registrar and staff; thirdly, legislation for settlement of debts through special tribunals; fourthly, short-term loans from Government for working expenses; fifthly, long-term credit through certain agencies for repayment of old debts and for development; sixthly, restrictions on sales of land, etc. in execution; seventhly, amendment of the law regarding imprisonment for debt; eighthly, the extension of the Law of Bankruptcy to farmers; and, ninthly, the imposition of penalties for usury.

13.—Government has taken action on most of these recommendations. The first and second proposals were accepted in their entirety and, since 1933, a number of co-operative societies have been established with satisfactory results in Arab villages under the supervision of a trained Registrar, although they have not yet reached the stage of attacking the fundamental problem of the indebtedness of their members. The fourth proposal was accepted and carried out in a slightly modified form. In addition to a sum of £P.189,934 advanced by Government in the form of short-term loans to cultivators during the years 1930-36, the Short Term Crop Loans Security Ordinance, 1935, has been passed to enable approved banks and companies to extend short-term credit and seasonal loans against the security of the crop. The fifth proposal has also been carried into partial effect. A sum of £P.50,000 has been allocated by Government for development loans in the hills and an Agricultural Mortgage Company has been constituted. A detailed description of Government's activities in this field will be found in Memorandum No. 14. The seventh proposal was accepted and the necessary legislation embodied in amendments of the Imprisonment for Debt Ordinances of 1931 and 1932, a line being drawn between honest and dishonest debtors by disallowing arbitrary imprisonment and providing that the Execution Officer must satisfy himself that the judgment debtor is in a position to pay. The eighth proposal has been met by the new Bankruptcy Ordinance of 1936 which extends the law of bankruptcy to every kind of debtor including cultivator debtors. Prior to its enactment only merchants could be declared bankrupt. The ninth proposal regarding usury has been embodied in the Usurious Loans Ordinance of 1934, which imposes a duty upon the Courts when trying a claim in which debts are concerned to raise certain issues regarding the interest charged thereon.

In pursuance of the sixth proposal, Government is considering the insertion of a suitable clause in the Civil Procedure (Execution of Judgments) Ordinance to secure that, if the debtor is a farmer, so much of his land shall be exempted from sale in execution as, in the opinion of the Court, is necessary for the support of himself and his family. This amendment has not yet been enacted, but in the meantime the Judiciary may use their powers under the Ottoman Law of Execution to afford the necessary protection to the cultivator against the rapacity of money-lenders.

14.—There remains only the third proposal, in which legislation is recommended for the settlement of debts by special tribunals. In 1933, Mr. Strickland amplified his recommendations of 1930 and submitted a general scheme for the summary relief of indebted cultivators. This scheme visualizes an arrangement under which, on the issue of an execution warrant against a debtor, the debtor would be able to apply for summary relief, which would involve, in the first place, the reduction of his debts to fair and non-usurious figures and, in the second, the reduction of the fair debts to an amount which the debtor could pay over a term of years. The necessary extent of these reductions was to be determined on the basis of a non-judicial enquiry by the District Authorities. The scheme has received careful consideration by Government but the difficulties in the way are manifold, not the least of them being to reduce the proposal to terms which, while permitting of elasticity of application, will not be so vague as to lead to abuse. Moreover, the success of the scheme propounded by Mr. Strickland depends to a large extent on stabilising the character of the Arab cultivator, since without such stabilisation there is little hope of freeing him permanently from the debt which he has learned to regard as inevitable.

15.—An alternative proposal for the summary relief of indebted cultivators, based on an issue of bonds guaranteed by Government, was considered but rejected on the ground that it would be unwise for Government to become a large creditor of cultivators.

16.—The measures undertaken by Government, coupled with the general increase in agricultural production which Palestine has witnessed in recent years and the consequent increase in the temporary wealth of the fellah, have undoubtedly afforded the latter substantial permanent advantages, despite several crop failures due to drought, involving the provision of relief works and reduction or remission of taxes in distressed areas. The benefits conferred upon the rural population by the Imprisonment for Debt Ordinance of 1931 and the Usurious Loans Ordinance of 1934 are becoming more and more apparent. Money-lenders have circumscribed their activities and the fellahin can turn to other sources of credit on equitable terms, such as Barclay's Bank (D.C. & O.), the Agricultural Mortgage Company of Palestine Ltd. and the Arab Agricultural Bank.

There has thus been a mitigation of the burden of debt under which farmers had laboured for many years past; and to this improvement the provision of relief works and the remission of rural taxation by Government have contributed not a little. In the Northern District alone it is said that the debts of the cultivators have been reduced by at least 60 per cent. in the course of the last five years.

PALESTINE ROYAL COMMISSION.

13. RURAL INDEBTEDNESS.

B. JEWISH RURAL INDEBTEDNESS.

17.—No inquiry has ever been made to ascertain the extent of Jewish rural indebtedness as defined in paragraph 1 of this memorandum. The most that can be given in connection with the Jewish settlements is an approximation of the total indebtedness of the Jewish cultivator, the term being defined so as to include all debts whether productive or not. Such an approximation is afforded by the figures in the Appendix annexed.

18.—The investigation upon which these figures are based covered 160 Jewish settlements with a total area of 563,190 dunums, of which 373,871 dunums are cultivated. Of this area, 106,993 dunums are under citrus and the balance under other crops. The settlements to which the investigation related contained about 66 per cent. of the total Jewish citrus area and about 75 per cent. of the total Jewish agricultural population.

The area in the 160 settlements in question was cultivated as follows:—

Under cereals	225,385 dunums
Under citrus	106,993 dunums
Under other plantations	30,801 dunums
Under various crops	10,692 dunums
Total	373,871 dunums

These settlements support an agricultural population of 37,803 persons, exclusive of agricultural labourers.

19.—It was found impossible to obtain separate figures, in the case of Jewish settlements, for mortgage or long-term debts and seasonal or short-term debts, but the distribution of the indebtedness between these two categories of debt can be estimated by reference to the means at the disposal of the two organisations from which short-term credit is usually obtained, namely, the Central Bank of Co-operative Institutions in Palestine, Ltd., and the Rural Credit Co-operative Societies. On this basis it would appear that, of a total indebtedness of £P.4,497,882, £P.1,145,197 represents short-term credit while £P.3,352,685 represents mortgage or long-term loans.

Long term credit is supplied by the various Jewish national institutions, the Palestine Jewish Colonization Association, Banks and private persons.

20.—The data used in the investigation were collected by two different methods. In 91 settlements, most of which are registered as co-operative societies, the figures produced were supported by audit reports. Elsewhere it was necessary to obtain the best information possible from the village committees and the Va'adim Haklaim, the committees in charge of agricultural matters, which exist in nearly all Jewish settlements. In the latter case the figures for total indebtedness may not be fully reliable. The average Jewish cultivator, like anyone else similarly situated, is as a rule reluctant to divulge his full indebtedness; on the other hand, certain of the more well-to-do cultivators are by no means averse from being pitied as debtors. Even in areas where land settlement operations have been completed and the mortgage debts of every cultivator are common knowledge, there will inevitably be understatement by some and exaggeration by others of other forms of indebtedness. The committees have consequently had to make assumptions and allowances for the correctness of which, in many cases, proof is not forthcoming.

21.—Another factor which militates against accuracy in the figures is the fact that the basis of computation differs from settlement to settlement. Where, for example, a settlement is situated on land belonging to the Jewish National Fund, the value of the land is excluded from the settlement's indebtedness. Again, debts due to national Jewish organizations have in certain cases been remitted on various grounds and the measure of indebtedness has been thus arbitrarily reduced. In consequence, any figures presented must necessarily be accepted with considerable reserve.

22.—As is to be expected, the individual indebtedness of the cultivator is greatest in those areas where citrus forms the major part of the cultivation, since a citrus grove necessitates heavy capital investments which are usually beyond the cultivator's normal means and must therefore be raised by credit. The Appendix to this memorandum distinguishes between the various settlements according to the percentage of the cultivated area which is planted with citrus. As will be seen from the Appendix, the total indebtedness of the 160 settlements is estimated at £P.4,497,882 representing £P.286 per earner or £P.12 per dunum of cultivated land.

23.—In view of the collective nature of some of the settlements, the tables refer to earners and dependents and not to families or to individual holdings. This collectivism also explains the apparent paucity of dependents since women are not treated as dependents in the collective settlements.

APPENDIX.

Percentage of citrus cultivation to total cultivation	Number of settlements	Cultivated area	Area under citrus	Number of earners	Number of dependents	Total indebtedness	Indebtedness per dunum cultivated	per earner
		dunums	dunums			£P.	£P.	£P.
Over 50 per cent.	54	120,933	98,830	4,994	11,746	2,878,897	23.8	576.5
20—50 per cent.	11	7,210	2,521	1,492	743	151,704	21.0	101.7
10—20 per cent.	7	41,474	1,460	1,151	2,860	135,151	3.3	117.4
Under 10 per cent.	88	204,254	4,182	8,084	6,733	1,332,130	6.4	164.7
Total	160	373,871	106,993	15,721	22,082	4,497,882	12	286

MEMORANDA BY THE GOVERNMENT OF PALESTINE.

14. AGRICULTURAL CREDIT.

MEMORANDUM No. 14.

MEASURES TAKEN TO PROVIDE AGRICULTURAL CREDIT.

Under the Ottoman Régime, agricultural credit was made available by the Ottoman Agricultural Bank, a semi-official institution which succeeded the former Caisses d'Utilité Publique in 1898. Its capital was made up from the assets of the Caisses d'Utilité Publique and of the receipts from an additional 1%, subsequently reduced to $\frac{1}{2}$%, on the tithe, which increased the rate to $12\frac{1}{2}$%. This additional $\frac{1}{2}$% on the tithe was to cease when the capital of the Bank reached £T.10,000,000. The Government of Palestine collected the tithe at $12\frac{1}{2}$% and carried the whole amount to revenue, but in 1925, it restored the tithe to 10%. The primary object of the Bank was to afford seasonal credit to cultivators and thus to avoid their having recourse to usurers. Loans were secured by mortgages on immovable property or other suitable security. In certain cases long term loans were also issued by the Bank, and on transfer of the securities held by usurers the Bank liquidated the debts of borrowers. The rate of interest charged by the Bank was 6% and it also collected an initial charge of 1% to cover administrative expenses.

The Ottoman Agricultural Bank had thirteen Agencies operating in Palestine at the time when the territory was occupied, all of which were accommodated in Government offices, but its records were, for the most part, removed before the British occupation. The liquidation of the assets of the Bank was entrusted to the Public Custodian of Enemy Property, who proceeded to reconstruct the accounts from whatever documentary evidence was available. The net amount realised from the liquidation has amounted to date to approximately £P.20,000, and approval has been obtained to utilise this sum for the issue of loans to Arab Co-operative Credit Societies whenever credit facilities from commercial sources are not obtainable. Loans so issued may not exceed £P.500 each and the term of these loans varies between three and five years.

2.—During the war the credit which the Ottoman Agricultural Bank afforded ceased, and the agricultural activities of Palestine received a definite set back. The country was depleted of its stock of animals. Many of the forests and even olive trees had been felled and used as fuel for the railway and other purposes. The Turkish Army requisitioned whatever grain was available and, in cases in which payment was made, it was effected in much depreciated Turkish paper currency. Many of the orange groves in the plains around Jaffa were destroyed owing to the owners' inability to water the grove on account of the lack of fuel for driving the pumps. Military conscription, banishment and epidemics had all had disastrous effects on the agricultural condition of the country at the time of its occupation.

Mule Loans 1918.

3.—This deplorable condition engaged the attention of the British Military Administration of the country, and as early as 1918 authority was given for the issue of what were then termed "Mule Loans." These loans took the form of sales on credit of Army mules which were no longer serviceable for military purposes but which could be used for ploughing and general agricultural work. Interest was charged at the rate of 6% on the outstanding balance of the purchase price; the terms of payment were in no way onerous and in certain cases the period of the loan extended over as much as 5 years. In 1921, a balance of £P.8,590 was still outstanding and, after the settlement of the accounts between the Military and Civil Administrations, this outstanding balance was transferred to the group known as "Agricultural Loans 1919-1923." Many of the mules, however, never became acclimatized to their new conditions of life and a number of them died shortly after their purchase by the cultivators. It therefore became necessary in many cases to remit whatever balance was outstanding. These remissions are included in the amounts shown in paragraph 8 as having been remitted in respect of the Agricultural Loans 1919-1923.

Agricultural Loans 1919-1923.

4.—It was soon realised that credit in cash would in any case be necessary to restore in some degree the condition of agriculture, and an agreement was reached in 1919 between the Military Administration and the Anglo-Egyptian Bank Ltd., now amalgamated in Barclays Bank (Dominion, Colonial & Overseas), whereby the Bank undertook to advance, as and when required, a sum not exceeding, without special agreement, £E.500,000 for the issue by the Administration, on its responsibility, of loans to cultivators. The Bank charged interest at the rate of 6% per annum on amounts withdrawn by the Administration and the latter charged borrowers interest at the rate of $6\frac{1}{2}$% on instalments repaid on due date. The rate of interest on instalments which fell in arrear was raised to 9% as a penal measure calculated to act as an incentive to prompt payment as instalments fell due. These arrangements were continued by the Civil Administration until the year 1923, when loans to cultivators were suspended owing partly to financial stringency and partly to the reluctance of the Bank to make further advances to the Administration without a guarantee from His Majesty's Government. During the period 1919 to 1923, loans in Egyptian currency to the equivalent of £P.576,319 were made to cultivators. Sums collected were transferred periodically to the Bank, and in January, 1928, Government paid the balance outstanding at that date and retained the subsequent collections. This course was dictated by considerations of economy, since the Bank charged interest at 6% whereas Government's surplus balance was invested in London at an average rate of 4%. Of the total amount advanced, £P.545,426 has been recovered, £P.18,033 has been written off as a measure of relief owing to the inability of the cultivators to pay, and a balance of £P.12,860 is still outstanding.

Beersheba Loans 1927.

5.—In consequence of a severe drought in 1927 in the Beersheba Sub-district and the consequent failure of the crops, it was found necessary to issue loans to Bedu cultivators in the Sub-district for the purchase of seed and the replacement of livestock. The total amount issued was £P.19,980 and these loans have been repaid with the exception of a sum of £P.547 which was written off.

PALESTINE ROYAL COMMISSION.

14. AGRICULTURAL CREDIT.

Seed Loans 1928.

6.—In 1928, the crops failed almost completely in the Northern District and here again it became necessary to offer cultivators some help, as it was feared that otherwise many would be forced to resort to money lenders and obtain the credit necessary at usurious rates of interest, and that others, who were unable to do so, would leave their land fallow. A sum was set aside for the issue of short term loans at 5% interest. Very few of the loans issued exceeded £P.10, the total sum advanced amounting to £P.19,366. A sum of £P.7,892 has been repaid and £P.6,448 written off as irrecoverable owing to the poverty of borrowers. On the 31st March, 1936, the balance outstanding was £P.5,026.

Loans after 1928.

7.—Ever since 1930 it has been necessary to issue loans annually to cultivators in order to provide them with the short term credit necessary for cultivation. The rate of interest was reduced from 6½% to 5%, except in the case of the 1935-36 loans which were issued at 9% interest, the rate at which Co-operative Credit Societies lend to their members. In most cases the loans issued are recoverable in two equal annual instalments after the crop is harvested. Few of these loans exceeded £P.10 in amount and it was thought that an annual instalment varying between £P.2 and £P.5 would not prove to be too heavy a charge on the gross income of the borrower. In 1933-34 the drought was so severe that, in addition to agricultural loans issued in that year, it was found necessary to issue fodder loans to the extent of £P.20,720. In this case individual loans did not exceed £P.5 and they were all to be repaid within one year from the date of issue together with interest at the rate of 5%.

The total amount of loans issued during the period 1930-31 to 1935-36 amounted to £P.189,934 of which £P.40,665 have been recovered leaving a balance of £P.149,269.

Summary of Loans issued by Government.

8.—The table appended shows, in summarised form, the total amount of loans issued since 1919, the recoveries effected to the 31st March, 1936, the total remissions granted and the balance outstanding. The greater portion of the amount outstanding is in respect of instalments overdue.

	Total Loans Issued	Recoveries to 31.3.36	Amounts written off to 31.3.36	Balance outstanding at 31.3.36
	£P.	£P.	£P.	£P.
Loans issued from 1919-1923	576,319	545,426	18,033	12,860
Beersheba Loans 1927	19,980	19,433	547	—
Northern District Loans 1928	19,366	7,892	6,448	5,026
£P.	615,665	572,751	25,028	17,886
Loans issued after 1928, as under:—				
Agricultural Loans issued in 1930	29,980	7,692	--	22,288
Agricultural Loans issued in 1931	17,137	12,070	—	5,067
Agricultural Loans issued in 1932-33	53,537	17,416	—	36,121
Agricultural Loans issued in 1933-34	57,259	3,064	—	54,195
Fodder Loans issued in 1933-34	20,720	406	—	20,314
Agricultural Loans issued in 1934-35	6,313	17	--	6,296
Agricultural Loans issued in 1935-36	4,988	—		4,988
£P.	189,934	40,665		149,269
Total Loans issued by Government £P.	805,599	613,416	25,028	167,155

Seasonal Credit by Barclays Bank (D. C. & O.) since 1933.

9.—In 1933 an arrangement was made with Barclays Bank (D.C. & O.) for the issue of seasonal credit to cultivators. The Bank had been issuing such loans in Nazareth and it was found that no undue risk attended the operations. The Bank agreed to extend this class of business to its branches already established in towns which served as rural centres, but it was unable, owing to the scarcity of other business, to open branches in other rural areas. It was, therefore, agreed that Government would help the Bank in establishing new branches for the purpose by making a grant of £P.500 per annum for a period of three years in respect of each branch specially opened with the approval of Government for the issue of short term seasonal loans. The branches which existed at the time this arrangement was made were those at Nazareth, Acre and Nablus, and further branches have since been established at Hebron and Gaza. Arrangements have been made for opening a new branch at Ramle, but owing to the present disturbances the matter is in abeyance for the time being. The amount issued in loans in 1935-36 approximated £P.230,000, repayable in instalments which fall due at varying dates between the middle of September and the end of December, 1936.

14. AGRICULTURAL CREDIT.

10.—Barclays Bank had agreed to issue seasonal credit at 8% but, in order not to impede the development of Co-operative Societies, and at the instance of the Registrar of those Societies, the Bank agreed to adopt a rate of 6% for loans issued to Co-operative Credit Societies. These societies lend the money so borrowed to their members at the rate of 9%, utilising the difference between 6% and 9% to cover what little expense they incur and to form the nucleus of the Societies' own funds. It was necessary in the circumstances for Barclays Bank to charge individual borrowers interest at the same rate as that charged by Co-operative Societies to their members.

11.—In order to facilitate the issue of these loans by the offer of a better security, Government has enacted an Ordinance entitled the Short Term Crop Loans (Security) Ordinance, 1935. This Ordinance follows closely the terms of Section 26 of the Co-operative Societies Ordinance, 1933. Under its provisions, an "approved" Company or Bank may take a charge on the crops of a borrower whether the crop is or is not in existence at the time the charge is created. The Ordinance also provides for a simple procedure for the registration of such charges by the District Officer in favour of an approved company for a nominal fee. Adequate penalties are provided against fraudulent disposition of the crop charged, these penalties being intended to act as deterrents.

Long Term Development Loans by the Agricultural Mortgage Company of Palestine, Ltd.

12.—In 1933, negotiations began for the establishment of a financial institution having for its object the issue of long term development loans mainly for agricultural purposes. Negotiations were long and difficult, particularly as it was desired that the institution should serve the interests of agriculture generally. After lengthy discussions between the promoters and Government an agreement was reached and the Agricultural Mortgage Company of Palestine, Ltd. has now been established, its main object being the issue of long term development loans secured on first mortgage of immovable property. The General Manager has been instructed that he should, so far as possible, secure that 75% of the total loans issued shall be for agricultural development.

13.—The Board of Directors of the Company is constituted as follows:—

The Rt. Hon. LORD GREENWOOD, P.C., K.C., (Chairman),
   Government Director.

The Rt. Hon. VISCOUNT GOSCHEN, G.C.I.E.,
   Ottoman Bank.

SIR ROBERT WALEY-COHEN, K.B.E.,
   Palestine Corporation Limited.

GEORGE W. REYNOLDS, Esq.,
   Guardian Assurance Company.

HARRY SACHER, Esq.,
   Anglo-Palestine Bank Limited.

PAUL SINGER, Esq.,
   Palestine Economic Corporation of New York.

HERBERT L M. TRITTON, Esq.,
   Barclays Bank (D.C. and O.)

14.—In order to assist in the formation of the Company, Government has advanced to the Company a sum of £P.150,000 to constitute a Guarantee Fund as an additional security to bond holders and to meet any loss up to a maximum of £P.25,000 which the Company may sustain, owing to the operation of the Protection of Cultivators Ordinance, 1933, on the realisation of the mortgages accepted by the Company during the first five years from the date of the agreement. The Company is under an obligation to restore the Guarantee Fund to its original amount from profits whenever the amount of the profits is more than sufficient to pay a dividend of 6% to shareholders. The amount advanced by Government earns interest at a variable rate depending on the profits of the Company and the dividends declared. If the profits of the Company are not sufficient to pay a dividend of 6% and interest on the advance at 6%, the Government receives the difference between the profits of the Company and dividends at 6%. When the profits of the Company are sufficient to pay 6% in dividends and 6% on the advance, Government will receive interest at the rate of 6%; and when the profits are more than sufficient for this purpose and a dividend of more than 6% is declared, the interest on the advance will be at the same rate as the dividends on the paid-up share capital. During the first 10 years of the Company, however, no interest will be paid to Government in respect of the advance unless a dividend is declared exceeding 6%, in which case interest will be payable at the same rate as the declared dividend. On the termination of 25 years from the date of the agreement with the Company, Government is to be allotted shares in the Company at par to the full extent of the sum advanced. The nominal value of the shares allotted to Government will constitute the Guarantee Fund. In effect, therefore, after the twenty-fifth year, Government will share in the profits of the Company in respect of its holding *pari passu* with other share-holders.

Government also agreed to pay to the Company an amount equal to the registration fees under the Companies Ordinance, 1929. The amount so paid amounted to £P.4,045. In order to facilitate the operations of the Company, Government has under consideration the enactment of legislation whereby the Company will be free from the restriction in the Ottoman Law limiting the total amount of interest recoverable on any loan to the amount of the principal, irrespective of the term for which the loan is contracted. On the other hand, Government has the right to nominate the Chairman of the Board of Directors and also to maintain a nominee on the Local Committee which assists the General Manager in an advisory capacity. The appointment of the General Manager must also be approved by Government.

15.—The Company commenced business on the 16th July, 1935. Owing to the present unsettled condition of the country it has not been possible for it to operate on any large scale. Of a total of approximately 320 applications received, the Company has so far issued 47 loans for a total amount of £P.42,680 or an average of approximately £P.900 per loan. The term of these loans varies between 5 years and 20 years, and the interest charged is 8%. Loans to individuals may not exceed £P.2,000 each, while loans to groups, whether Co-operative Societies or corporate bodies, may be as high as £P.5,000. The longest term for which the Company may lend is 20 years. The Company is still too young for it to be possible to forecast the benefits which will accrue from its activities to the agricultural development of the country, but it is hoped that the availability of long term credit will assist materially towards this end.

PALESTINE ROYAL COMMISSION.

14. AGRICULTURAL CREDIT.

Long Term Development Loans by Government.

16.—It should be pointed out that, owing to insecurity of title in the hill districts which have not as yet been subjected to land settlement, the Agricultural Mortgage Company has limited its activities to the plains. In order to provide long term credit facilities for development of the hill districts, Government has set aside a sum of £P.50,000 for the issue of long term development loans in these districts. A scheme has been worked out to utilise this sum as a revolving credit under the management of a Board of Civil Servants. Applications for loans so far received far exceed the sum of £P.50,000 but, owing to the present disturbances, no loans have yet been issued.

17.—It has not been possible in this memorandum to specify the regional and racial distribution of loans. The memorandum is concerned solely with agricultural credit afforded by Government or furthered by its endeavour and co-operation. This limitation leaves out of account large sources of credit, mainly Jewish, so that the result of an attempt to classify the credit made available by Government or through Government activities would be misleading. In any case, there are no records from which the information could be extracted. Moreover, the credit available through Barclays Bank (D.C. & O.) in respect of short term seasonal loans and through the Agricultural Mortgage Company of Palestine, Ltd. in respect of long term development loans is not restricted either regionally or racially although, as stated previously, the last named Company's operations do not extend to the hill districts. Furthermore, Arab credit institutions and Jewish financial establishments are open for general business and are not precluded from giving credit to members of the other community.

15. CO-OPERATION.

MEMORANDUM No. 15.

MEASURES TAKEN TO ENCOURAGE CO-OPERATION.

In a much changed and still changing country like Palestine, inhabited by a population which shows perhaps more variety of type, way of life and culture than is to be found in any other country of its size, it is not unnatural that co-operation as practised should present certain unusual features and a large variety.

2.—A short description of these features is given below.

3.—Co-operation in Palestine is not a unified movement and has no political banners. With very few exceptions it is run on racial lines. It is composed of independent societies organised for a large diversity of purposes. The bulk of the members of these societies are not at present much concerned about the social mission of co-operation but are fully alive to its high economic value. Co-operation is not looked upon as a social experiment and has no organised opposition to encounter. Its economic success does not depend on any great ideals or on any financial privileges from Government. Business efficiency, community of interests and loyalty of members are its mainstay. The movement has no central organisations and is consequently guilty of some proceedings which are definitely unco-operative.

4.—In comparison with co-operative movements in Europe or other more highly civilised States, where traditional, regional and religious loyalties are great factors, where the creeds of political parties are accepted standards and where opposition by vested interests has to be faced in every corner of the economic field, co-operation in Palestine assumes a more satisfactory, if also a more prosaic, aspect. It also stands in complete contrast to those co-operative movements to which the State is called upon to give financial as well as moral support.

5.—In Palestine no such demands are made on Government. Here Government's task is of two different kinds which do not, however, clash. As regards Jewish co-operation, Government is expected, on the one hand, to recognise that it is a self-reliant and vigorous force, which has nearly 150,000 adherents and a movement of capital of about £P.10,000,000 and which, owing to its economic importance in every field of activity, must have adequate consideration and care, up to date legislation and such protection as will ensure its proper exercise in an atmosphere of complete freedom. On the other hand it is the task of Government to take such steps as will purify the movement and correct the errors which have been allowed to creep in through lack of unified guidance and as a result of the circumstances which dominate all pioneer communities.

6.—It can confidently be claimed that Government has achieved a large measure of success in carrying out these tasks. The relations between Jewish societies and Government have been very cordial. An Advisory Committee composed of outstanding Jewish co-operators has been co-operating with the Registrar in all matters affecting the control of Jewish societies. New legislation, passed in 1933 and 1934, while leaving to the Registrar many options and full freedom of action, gave societies the much needed control over their members, simplified the procedure governing liquidations and amalgamations, exempted shares or interests of members in the capital of societies from attachment by any Court of Justice and set up machinery for the creation of charges on present or future assets of societies and of their members, thereby providing societies with the means of obtaining credit facilities which are not available to other bodies. The new legislation also accorded recognition to audit unions and in the course of 1933 five such unions were formed and 280 societies (out of a total of 740 societies) have voluntarily taken up affiliation with them. The unions, though mainly concerned with the audit of the accounts of affiliated societies, are at the same time fulfilling the functions of guiding bodies in as much as they are exercising their influence to eliminate overlapping and waste and to secure avoidance of harmful competition between their associated societies. It is noteworthy that the sectarian spirit, which is markedly absent in the primary societies, comes to full expression in these audit unions, four out of the five unions being labour unions while the fifth controls the larger urban and rural credit societies in which membership is not confined to any particular political or social creed.

MEMORANDA BY THE GOVERNMENT OF PALESTINE.

15. CO-OPERATION.

7.—As regards Arab societies, Government has a more active task, namely, that of co-operative training and guidance in the early stages of their development. Co-operative training implies two distinct problems, first, the education of the members of co-operative societies and, secondly, the education of the staff which they employ.

8.—Government entered upon this task in accordance with a plan devised by an expert on co-operation (Mr. Strickland of the Indian Civil Service) who visited Palestine in 1930 and again in 1933, and submitted full reports and recommendations.

9.—In the course of 1933, 1934 and 1935, more than 200 Arab villages (out of a total of 800 villages) have been initiated in co-operative practices; in 60 villages primary societies have actually been started with considerable success, and in 1936, preparations have been made for the formation of 60 additional societies.

10.—Popular pamphlets on the advantages and practices of co-operation have been widely circulated and numerous meetings have been addressed by the Registrar and his Arab Assistant in villages, town centres and Government schools. Government has also printed and sold at cost price Arabic account ledgers and other commercial books and forms required in the management of primary societies. A staff of Arab field organisers has been trained at Head Quarters and stationed in outlying Sub-districts for the purpose of keeping in close touch with the staff of the newly formed societies and for propaganda purposes in new villages.

11.—The manner in which co-operation has been taking root in Arab villages has justified the expectations formed. The villagers have not been slow in realising its advantages and possibilities and the individual members have shown much loyalty and ample intelligence in the management of their societies. In the three years under review not one overdue debt has been recorded and as a matter of fact most repayments have been made in advance of due dates. For the time being and for several years to come, Government proposes to concentrate on the formation of primary village societies of the Raifeisen type similar to those already in existence and its programme aims at a society in every village of suitable size or in groups of smaller villages. Arab public opinion has welcomed Government initiative in this direction, and the Press has occasionally reported favourably on the efforts of the Registrar and his staff.

12.—Co-operation in Arab urban centres, and the introduction of marketing and producing societies, is to be the second and more advanced stage of the programme.

13.—As stated above, none of the Palestine societies is financed by Government. Arab societies obtain their credits from Barclays Bank at a low rate of interest (6 per cent. as compared with 9 per cent. which is the normal rate for advances to individual or group borrowers), while Jewish societies rely mostly on their own financing institutions.

14.—The following statement gives a vivid illustration of the large variety of Palestine co-operation. Societies in Palestine are conveniently grouped under 7 main groups and 21 sub-groups; yet even this rich classification does not exhaust their variety and in every group it is necessary to provide for a miscellaneous sub-group to include those types of societies which cannot be brought under any defined sub-group.

CLASSIFICATION OF SOCIETIES AND DESCRIPTION OF THEIR DIVERSE ACTIVITIES.

Group A. *Credit and Thrift Societies.*

Sub-group —

(a) Rural Credit and Thrift Societies on the Raifeisen model with unlimited liability.

(b) Rural Credit and Thrift Societies on the Shulze Delitch model with limited liability.

(c) Urban Co-operative Banks.

(d) Thrift and Provident Societies.

Group B. *Agricultural Societies.*

Sub-group —

(a) Collective Settlements.
(common ownership of land, buildings and stock, common purse).

(b) General Agricultural Societies.
(joint purchase and sale of agricultural requirements, joint cultivation of certain crops, joint irrigation, joint ownership of agricultural machinery, joint borrowing).

(c) Co-operative dairies.
(cattle owned individually, dairy products sold jointly).

(d) Irrigation societies.
(joint ownership of wells, installation and plant).

(e) Societies for marketing of special products.
(citrus fruit, almonds, vegetables).

(f) Societies for processing and marketing of special products.
(citrus by-products, wine).

(g) Central Marketing Societies.
(for marketing agricultural products of Sub-groups (a) and (b)).

(h) Cattle Insurance and Veterinary Service Societies.
(mutual insurance of stock and provision of veterinary service).

(i) Miscellaneous Agricultural Associations.
(Central settlement societies, societies for stock improvement etc., joint packing houses).

Group C. *Labour Co-partnerships.*

Sub-group —

(a) Producers Societies.
(workers in metals, wood, leather, cloth, stone, cement, fibres, mechanics and fitters, printers and publishers).

(b) Service Societies.
(transport of passengers and goods, delivery and distribution services, bakeries, restaurant keepers, butcheries, laundries, well drillers, deep ploughers, building contractors).

(c) Professional Associations.
(co-operative clinics, schools, theatrical performers, ritual killers and meat dressers).

(d) Miscellaneous Societies.
(association of retailers, lighter owners, green grocers, etc.)

Group D. *Consumers Societies and their Central Supply Societies.*

PALESTINE ROYAL COMMISSION.

15. CO-OPERATION.

Group E. Housing Societies.

Sub-group —

(a) Societies for development of suburbs. (building clubs).

(b) Societies for public services in suburbs. (supply of water, light, watchmen, transportation and public institutions)

(c) Communal Houses.
(societies constructing apartments and flats or separate houses for their members, raising loans jointly and maintaining public institutions).

(d) Miscellaneous Building Societies. (development of commercial centres, seaside resorts, etc.).

Group F. Mutual Insurance Societies.

Group G. General Purpose Societies.

(mutual aid societies for diverse purposes of farmers, labourers and immigrants from certain countries).

16. LAND TAXATION.

15.—The societies themselves are as varied as the movement and the buildings in which they are housed, and the conditions under which their business is transacted, are as varied as the societies. At one end of the scale are to be found the humble stores housed in old corrugated iron huts, relics of the days of the military occupation, small workshops with primitive tools and hand contrivances, insignificant small societies of drivers of horse drawn vehicles or lorries and the drab offices of small credit societies. At the other end are the marble-faced co-operative restaurants with capped and aproned waitresses, magnificent brick factories and packing houses, the latest type of buses replete with every comfort (six transport societies carry as many as 50 million passengers per annum) and the luxurious offices of the Co-operative Banks. Yet in all this variety there is nothing strange; in the process of development such diversity is only natural.

MEMORANDUM No. 16.

ACCOUNT OF SYSTEM OF LAND TAXATION AND OF EFFECT OF RECENT CHANGES.

THE OLD SYSTEM.

At the time of the British Occupation in 1918 the taxes on or directly affecting immovable property were:—

(a) The House and Land Tax (Werko);

(b) The Roofed Property Tax (Musaqqafat), levied only in Haifa, Acre and Shefa 'Amr;

(c) The Tithe;

(d) The Animal Tax.

(a) *The House and Land Tax (Werko).*

2.—The House and Land Tax was levied on immovable property of every description, Mulk or Miri, whether Waqf or not,* and was governed by the Ottoman Law of 1886 and various vizierial circulars.

3.—The tax was based on the capital value and was variable by Imperial Irade. The rate of tax on Miri (rural) land was 4 per mil., on Mulk (town) land 10 per mil., and on built-on properties from 4 to 10 per mil., according to their kind or value. Mulk land paid a higher rate of tax than Miri but tithe was not payable in respect of it, while payable on Miri land.

4.—Additions aggregating 41 per cent. of the above assessments on buildings and 56 per cent. on land were levied from time to time by Ottoman Decrees and continued to be collected after the Occupation, except on buildings and lands re-assessed since 1919. Immovable property registered in the name of corporate bodies was subject to an additional tax, varying from ½ to 1 per mil. of its assessed value, but this was abolished as from the 1st April, 1933.

---

* For a definition of these terms see Memorandum No. 10. Description of various forms of ownership and tenure of land.

5.—The Werko tax had many defects, among which were:—

(a) It was not based on a survey such as would enable each property to be identified;

(b) There had been no general re-assessment or revision for about 25 years;

(c) Some of the records had been destroyed, lost or taken away by the retreating Turks;

(d) When, after the re-opening of the Land Registries in 1920, a land transaction occurred, the Werko became payable on the basis of the transfer price or a valuation made at the time, whereas properties not the subject of such transactions continued to be taxed on the old assessment. This led to unequal distribution of the incidence of the tax, even though the additions of 41 per cent. on buildings and 56 per cent. on lands were no longer payable when such re-assessments were made. As most of the purchases of large areas were made by Jewish institutions, it followed that the Jews were the principal sufferers from the increased assessments;

(e) The absence of reliable records of those liable to pay the tax and of the property on which it was payable rendered its collection difficult.

6.—Many of the Tax Collectors who had been in the employ of the Ottoman Government were, however, available, and these officers knew the aggregate amount of Werko payable by the inhabitants of a village. This sum was then distributed by the village elders, who provided lists of the persons liable and of the amounts payable by them.

7.—The following statement shows the assessment of House and Land Tax and of Musaqqafat

MEMORANDA BY THE GOVERNMENT OF PALESTINE.

16. LAND TAXATION.

Tax (including the Municipal share) in respect of the years from 1918-19 to 1928:—

Year	£P.
1918-19	£P.126,757
1919-20	144,765
1920-21	146,977
1921-22	151,465
1922-23	164,950
1923-24	172,717
1924-25	182,270
1925-26	194,012
1926-27	219,127
1927-28	231,997
1928-29	238,850

(b) The "Roofed Property" Tax (Musaqqafat).

8.—The Musaqqafat Tax was applied by the Civil Administration in 1921 in Haifa, Acre and Shefa 'Amr. The Ottoman Law of 1910 provided for the levy of this tax on built property within Municipal areas at the rate of 12½ per cent. of the annual value. This rate combined both the Government and the Municipal taxes on built property and was payable by the owner. It replaced the Werko on built property but not on vacant land. The tax was originally collected at the rate of 8½ per cent. of the annual value but, with effect from the 1st April, 1926, in the case of Haifa and Acre, and from the 1st April, 1928, in the case of Shefa 'Amr, the rate was raised to 11 per cent. The tax was collected by Government, by whom 3½ per cent. was retained, 5 per cent., and later 7½ per cent. being paid to the Municipality concerned.

9.—It was realised that, failing a general reassessment of immovable property and with the existence of different methods of taxation in Palestine, the incidence of the taxes levied under two distinct Ottoman Laws could never be fairly distributed. Consequently throughout Palestine, except in the Beersheba Sub-district and the Huleh lands in Safad Sub-district, the Werko and Musaqqafat Taxes have gradually been replaced, in urban areas by the Urban Property Tax and in rural lands by the Rural Property Tax.

(c) The Tithe.

10.—Moslem law treated all land in private hands as subject either to payment of tithe or tribute. The tithe represented the share of the Sovereign, or of the community as a whole, in the produce of the soil. It was not, of course, peculiarly a Moslem institution, but occurs in widely separated countries. Tribute was not exacted, but tithe was, in principle, still payable by all private owners. Its collection was governed by the Ottoman Tithes Regulations, 1871-1905.

11.—The tithe, as its name indicates, was supposed to be equal to one-tenth of the produce. The original tithe had, however, been increased from time to time by the Ottoman Government for revenue purposes and at the time of the Occupation it was collected at the rate of 12½ per cent. of the gross yield of the land. Crops were assessed on the threshing floor or in the field and the tithe was collected from the cultivators.

12.—The tithe, under the Ottoman Régime, was not collected directly through Government Agency; but was farmed out by public auction usually to influential persons of means who were able to provide adequate security. This practice was open to abuse and was therefore discontinued after the British Occupation but it was early realised that this form of taxation was defective, and by the Tithe Reduction Ordinance of 1925, all additional percentages were abolished and the tithe on all crops and other produce was reduced to 10 per cent.

13.—The annual estimation of crops was troublesome, open to abuse and also a handicap to the cultivator in the disposal of his crop, though it had the advantage of varying the incidence annually according to the crop produced in a bad or good year. Consequently, with a view to alleviating the situation, the Commutation of Tithes Ordinance was enacted and from 1928 was applied gradually to the whole country.

14.—While the Government collected the tithe in respect of the whole country, in the case of certain lands of the Waqf (religious foundation) Category the tithe was payable to the administrators of the Waqf.

15.—The commuted tithe for a village, settlement or tribe was a fixed aggregate amount paid annually. It corresponded to the average amount of tithe that had been paid by the village during the four years immediately preceding the application of the Ordinance to it, and was distributed by village committees under official supervision on the basis of the productivity in cereals (or fruit trees) of the land.

16.—The Exemption from Tithe Ordinance, 1929, provides for the exemption from tithe of the produce of any land utilized for the purpose of agricultural instruction or research.

17.—Remissions were granted as below from time to time under Section 18 of the Commutation of Tithes Ordinance owing to the destruction or failure of crops or to a fall in prices. No remission was granted, however, on the commuted tithe in respect of areas planted with citrus trees.

1930—50 per cent. of the tithe was remitted by reason of a fall in the price of agricultural produce and of the failure of the harvest, and a variable remission of the balance was granted in respect of lands of which the crops were destroyed or damaged by locusts, field mice or drought. These remissions amounted to £P.113,670.

1931—Similar remissions were granted amounting to a total of £P.150,258.

1932-33—The tax year was changed from the calendar year to the financial year (1st April to 31st March). A general remission of 25 per cent. was granted, in addition to variable percentages where individual villages suffered from partial or complete failure of winter and summer crops. The amount of these remissions totalled £P.111,542.

During the year, remissions amounting to £P.54,163 were granted in respect of arrears of tithe due prior to 1930.

1933-34—A total remission of tithe on summer crops and a remission of 25 per cent. of the winter tithe assessment were granted. In addition, variable percentages were remitted in respect of the balance of the winter tithe assessment in individual villages. These remissions amounted to about £P.193,500.

PALESTINE ROYAL COMMISSION.

16. LAND TAXATION.

1934-35—Similar remissions were granted as in 1932-33, totalling £P.130,731.

1935-36—50 per cent. of the tithe in Beersheba Sub-district was remitted on account of drought. No remission was granted in respect of the Huleh lands which was the only other area to which the Commutation of Tithes Ordinance was still applicable.

18.—The following statement shows the tax payable in the year 1934-35:—

(a) Commuted Tithe payable in respect of 1934-35, the last year of its general application to the whole country

	£P.	£P.
Treasury Share	223,061	
Waqf Share	40,777	263,838
(b) Less remissions granted		
Treasury Share	114,122	
Waqf Share	16,609	130,731
(c) Net amount payable:		133,107
(d) As compared with the ordinary tithe payable in 1925-26		326,410

19.—Commuted tithe is still payable in the Beersheba Sub-district and in the Huleh area in the Safad Sub-district, but elsewhere it has been replaced by the Rural or Urban Property Taxes.

(d) *The Animal Tax.*

20.—The Animal Tax is imposed per capita once annually; it is governed by the Animal Tax Law of 1905 and is levied at the following rates:

Sheep and goats	48 mils.
Camels & buffaloes	120 mils.
Pigs	90 mils.

Camels and buffaloes used solely for ploughing are exempt from the tax. Double taxes are charged on all animals not declared by the owners at the time of enumeration.

21.—The following is a statement of the total amounts payable during the years 1931-32 to 1935-36:—

1931-32	£P.41,515
1932-33	39,475
1933-34	37,117
1934-35	8,090
1935-36	32,138

Note:—Remissions totalling £P.23,366 were granted in 1934 on account of death of cattle due to drought.

THE NEW SYSTEM.

22.—As previously stated, with the exception of the Animal Tax, which is still collected throughout Palestine, and the House and Land Tax (Werko) and Tithe, which is still payable in Beersheba Sub-district and in respect of the Huleh lands, the taxation system has been revised and the previous taxes have recently been replaced by:—

(a) The Urban Property Tax.

(b) The Rural Property Tax.

23.—Government has been in negotiation with the Supreme Moslem Council and the Waqf authorities concerned with a view to the payment of a fixed sum annually in lieu of the share of the tithe previously paid in respect of waqf lands.

(a) *The Urban Property Tax.*

24.—The Urban Property Tax Ordinance, 1928, was introduced with a view to the simplification and replacement of previous forms of taxation in urban areas, and was applied town by town by order of the High Commissioner.

25.—The urban boundary having been determined on a plan, the area is divided into blocks and parcels and each parcel is dealt with as a unit. The tax has been applied to the following towns as from the date indicated:—

From 1st April, 1929 —
   Jerusalem, Jaffa (including Tel-Aviv & Sarona), Gaza, Beisan, Tulkarm, Ramle, Lydda.

From 1st April 1930 —
   Tiberias, Nablus.

From 1st April 1931 —
   Nazareth, Beersheba, Safad, Jenin, Hebron, Bethlehem, Beit-Jala, Ramallah.

From 1st April 1932 —
   Haifa, Acre.

From 1st April 1933 —
   Rishon le Tsiyon, Rehovot, Petah Tiqva, Majdal.

From 1st April 1934 —
   Shefa 'Amr, Khan Yunis.

From 1st April 1935 —
   Hadera, Ramat Gan, Beit-Sahur.

26.—The tax is payable by the reputed owner and is a percentage of the net annual value of land and buildings within the boundaries of the urban area, the rate being determined annually by order of the High Commissioner.

27.—The net annual value is arrived at by deducting a percentage varying from 20 to $33\frac{1}{3}$ per cent. for repairs and other charges from the gross annual value which is based on the rent or estimated rent. In the case of vacant land the net annual value is deemed to be six per cent. of the estimated capital value.

28.—The valuations are made by assessment committees, consisting of two official and two non-official members. An Official Inspector may examine the work of an assessment committee and request a committee to revise the valuation. Valuation Lists are posted and the reputed owner has a right of objection and appeal against the valuation.

29.—The Ordinance provides for the following categories on which different rates may be imposed:—

(a) All house property except house property constructed and used solely for the purpose of an industrial undertaking in which mechanically driven machinery is used;

(b) House property constructed and used for the purpose of an industrial undertaking in which mechanically driven machinery is used; and

MEMORANDA BY THE GOVERNMENT OF PALESTINE.

16. LAND TAXATION.

(c) Land which is not the site of house property.

30.—The maximum rate of the tax was, originally, 10 per cent. but was raised to 15 per cent. as from the 1st April, 1931, while the actual rate is determined by the High Commissioner annually.

31.—The following have been the rates in force since the promulgation of the Ordinance:

Financial Year.	House Property.	Industrial Establishments.	Land.
1929-1930	9%	6%	7%
1930-1931	9%	6%	7%
1931-1932	12%	8%	8½%
1932-1933	15%	10%	10%
1933-1934	15%	10%	10%
1934-1935	12½%	10%	10%
1935-1936	10%	10%	10%

Until the 31st of March, 1935, the following taxes were payable in addition to the Urban Property Tax:—

(a) Commuted Tithe — on vacant land;

(b) Muqata'a — on waqf land upon which buildings had been erected; and

(c) Ijara Zamin — on land planted with ornamental trees.

32.—Exemption is granted in the following cases: —

(a) Properties, such as ecclesiastical institutions, which formerly enjoyed exemption in respect of house and land tax;

(b) House Property, occupied by the registered owner, with a net annual value less than the sums specified by order, which in no case shall exceed £P.20.

The following shows the limit of exemption specified in the order in respect of each urban area:—

£P.20 — Jerusalem, Jaffa, Haifa.

£P.13 — Tulkarm, Tiberias, Nablus.

£P.10 — Acre.

£P. 7 — Beisan, Gaza, Ramle, Lydda, Nazareth, Beersheba, Safad, Jenin, Hebron, Bethlehem, Petah Tiqva, Rishon le Tsiyon, Rehovot, Ramat Gan, Hadera, Majdal.

£P. 4 — Beit Jala, Ramallah, Khan Yunis, Shefa 'Amr.

(c) Newly constructed house property, which receives exemption for three years. This privilege has recently been extended to additions to house property.

The High Commissioner may remit wholly or in part the tax on playing fields and open spaces accessible to the public, and on property on which building is prohibited or restricted under town planning schemes.

33.—The Ordinance also provides for annual revision where the net annual value of property has increased or decreased by 20 per cent. or more since the last assessment and in certain other circumstances, and for quinquennial revaluation.

34.—The House and Land Tax (Werko) and Badal el Ushr, which was a tax levied on the actual site of miri land on which a building had been erected, which were replaced in urban areas by the Urban Property Tax, amounted in urban areas to £P.118,962, to which should be added a sum of about £P.2,682 being the commuted tithe which was also payable annually on cultivated land within urban areas until the 31st March, 1935, making a total of £P.121,644.

35.—As indicated in paragraph 25 above, the Urban Property Tax was originally applied to the various urban areas in the country in different years. The following statement shows the total of the original assessments in each area in the first year of the application of the tax as compared with the assessments for the financial year 1935-36:—

	First year of application of Urban Property Tax Ordinance		1935-36.	
(1) Urban Property Tax Gross assessment:				
(a) House Property	£P.123,103		£P.281,084	
(b) Industrial Establishments	1,562		2,994	
(c) Land	33,294	£P.167,959	73,571	£P.357,649
(2) Less Exemptions		8,876		104,722
(3) Net amount payable		£P.159,083		£P.252,927

PALESTINE ROYAL COMMISSION.

16. LAND TAXATION.

(b) *The Rural Property Tax.*

36.—The Rural Property Tax Ordinance, 1935, was introduced in view of the inequitable incidence of the old system of taxation on agricultural land, and was applied as from the 1st April, 1935, to all the rural lands of Palestine except Beersheba Sub-district and the Huleh lands of Safad Sub-district.

37.—Plans were prepared of all villages and settlements, showing the boundaries of each and the areas planted with fruit trees, cultivable and uncultivable land, etc.

38.—Each village and settlement was visited by official valuers, who, after consultation with those concerned, divided the village into blocks of land of a similar ground crop productivity value, and determined the category of productivity in which each block should be placed. At the same time the "built-on" village area was demarcated on the plan.

39.—The Rural Property Tax is a tax per dunum at varying rates, on categories arranged according to estimated productivity of the soil; and the rates bear some relation to the net annual yield. The tax is payable by reputed owners. The schedule of categories and rates paid thereon is set out below:—

Category	Description.	Rate of tax per dunum. Mils.
1	Citrus (excluding Acre Sub-district)	825
2	Citrus (Acre Sub-district)	410
3	Bananas	560
4	Village built-on area or reserved therefor	160
5	1st Grade Irrigated Land and *1st Grade Fruit Plantation	40
6	2nd Grade Irrigated Land and *2nd Grade Fruit Plantation	35
7	3rd Grade Irrigated Land and *3rd Grade Fruit Plantation	30
8	1st Grade ground crop land 4th Grade Irrigated Land and *4th Grade Fruit Plantation	25
9	2nd Grade Ground Crop Land 5th Grade Irrigated Land and *5th Grade Fruit Plantation	20
10	3rd Grade Ground Crop Land 6th Grade Irrigated Land and *6th Grade Fruit Plantation	18
11	4th Grade Ground Crop Land 7th Grade Irrigated Land and *7th Grade Fruit Plantation	15
12	5th Grade Ground Crop Land 8th Grade Irrigated Land and *8th Grade Fruit Plantation	12
13	6th Grade Ground Crop Land 9th Grade Irrigated Land and *9th Grade Fruit Plantation	
14	7th Grade Ground Crop Land and 10th Grade Irrigated Land	Nil.
15	8th Grade Ground Crop Land	Nil.
16	Forest, planted and indigenous, and uncultivable land	Nil.

* Other than Citrus and Bananas.

40.—The rates of tax per dunum approximate to 10 per cent. of the estimated net annual value of the several categories of land, except in the case of citrus land, where it is approximately 12 per cent. Moreover the last three categories of land are exempted from the payment of the tax on the ground of their low net annual yield.

16. LAND TAXATION.

41.—The Official Valuer prepares a roll in respect of each village or settlement, showing the area and category of the land in each block. Objections and appeals having been decided, the amount of tax payable is computed.

42.—The District Officer, in areas settled under the Land Settlement Ordinances, 1928-36, and Village Distribution Committees in non-settled villages or settlements, distribute the tax and prepare Distribution Lists showing each parcel, its owner and category and the tax thereon. Objections and appeals having been dealt with, this becomes the Tax Distribution List in force for the year.

43.—Buildings are not assessed as such unless they are industrial buildings of a net annual value exceeding £P.20. A Valuation List of such buildings is prepared by an Official Valuer which is subject to objection and appeal. The net annual value is arrived at by deducting one-third from the gross annual or full rental value. On the net annual value a tax, prescribed annually by order, is payable at a rate not exceeding 15 per cent. The rate of tax for the financial year 1935-36 was fixed at 10 per cent.

44.—Provision is made in the Ordinance for annual supplementary rolls where changes of category have occurred and for a redistribution of the tax when necessary. Supplementary valuation lists in respect of industrial buildings are also provided for. The same provisions regarding objections and appeals are applicable to the supplementary as to the original rolls or lists.

45.—Whenever the High Commissioner-in-Council is satisfied that it is proper so to do, having regard to any emergency affecting Palestine or any area or part of an area which is due to unavoidable natural causes or to such a fall in the value of crops as to make the grant of relief expedient, he may, with the approval of the Secretary of State:—

(i) postpone payment of the tax;

(ii) reduce the rates set out in the Schedule;

(iii) both postpone payment and reduce the rates set out in the Schedule.

Provision is also made to enable the High Commissioner-in-Council, on or after the 31st March, 1938, to vary the categories or rates set out in the Schedule to the Ordinance, or both, provided that the varied Schedule shall remain in force for a period of not less than five years.

46.—Owners who develop their land or erect industrial buildings are required to notify the District Officer in order that the category of the land may be amended, but in such cases owners are not required to pay tax at the higher rate for the following varying periods:—

(1) Land previously regarded as "uncultivable" brought under cultivation — 6 years.

(2) Land newly planted with bananas — 2 years.

(3) Land newly planted with citrus — 6 years.

(4) Land newly planted with any fruit tree other than citrus — 10 years.

Newly constructed industrial buildings or additions thereto are entitled to three years' exemption from the commencement of the year following completion.

Exemption is also provided for the owner of land who was enjoying exemption from:

(1) House and Land Tax or Tithe;

(2) Tithes on vineyards grafted on American stock, for the remainder of the period of exemption previously allowed.

The High Commissioner may remit the tax wholly or in part on land being used as a threshing-floor or cemetery and, where plantations or crops are destroyed, exemption may be given from the tax for the remainder of the year.

47.—Owing to exceptionally severe Khamsin (east) winds in the spring of 1935, many growers of citrus suffered considerable losses of crop, and the exportable crop was reduced from an anticipated eight million boxes to less than six million. In consequence of this the High Commissioner, with the approval of the Secretary of State, authorised reductions in the rate of Rural Property Tax on groves in seriously affected areas in respect of the tax year 1935-36, involving a waiver of about £P.16,500. The percentage reductions were as follows:—

Sub-district

Jaffa	— 25%
Ramle	— 30%
Gaza	— 30%
Tulkarm	— 30%
Haifa	— Nil.
Nablus	— Nil.
Jenin	— 30%
Tiberias	— 25%
Nazareth	— 25%
Safad	— Nil.
Beisan	— Nil.
Jericho	— 25%
Acre	— 25%

48.—It would serve no useful purpose to compare the assessment of the Tithe and the House and Land Tax in rural areas with the assessment of the Rural Property Tax which replaced them, as large remissions were made owing to the inability of tax-payers to pay. It is estimated, however, that the assessment of the Rural Property Tax is approximately one-half that of the Tithe and the House and Land Tax in rural areas.

PALESTINE ROYAL COMMISSION.

17. PROTECTION OF CULTIVATORS.

MEMORANDUM No. 17.

DESCRIPTION OF MEASURES ADOPTED IN PALESTINE TO PROTECT CULTIVATORS.

In September, 1920, the High Commissioner, Sir Herbert Samuel, enacted the Transfer of Land Ordinance, which contained a Section empowering the Governor of a District to withhold his consent to any transfer of land until he was satisfied that, in the case of leased agricultural land, the tenant in occupation retained sufficient land in the district or elsewhere for the maintenance of himself and his family.

2.—This provision was altered in 1921 when the Ordinance was amended. Under the amendment, Government's consent was required to every disposition of immovable property; such consent was to be given by the Director of Lands and communicated to the Registrar of the District, who was to satisfy himself, before the disposition was registered, that any tenant of agricultural land affected by the disposition retained an adequate subsistence area elsewhere. In executive instructions issued to the officers concerned, the Government explained that, while desirous to promote in every possible way the closer settlement of the country, it was at the same time anxious that the interests of the present tenants and occupants of land, whether Government property or private property, should be properly protected. It was therefore considered necessary on the one hand to take steps to prevent the eviction of tenants by the landlords on a sale of land, and on the other to secure for those who had exercised customary rights of cultivation and grazing, without full legal title, a sufficient area for the maintenance of their families.

3.—Unfortunately, the Ordinance proved unworkable; the purchasers paid the tenants to decamp and the latter had thus usually left the land before the transaction was brought to the Land Registry.

4.—The Ordinances of 1920 and 1921 remained in force until the 31st July, 1929, when they were replaced by the Protection of Cultivators Ordinance. This Ordinance provided for the payment of compensation, both for disturbance and for improvements effected by them, to tenants who received a valid notice to quit the holding of which they had been in occupation. It further provided for the constitution of Boards to decide disputes as to whether or not compensation for disturbance or improvement was payable, and as to the amount of any such compensation. The previous requirement, that a cultivator must retain a subsistence area elsewhere, found no place in the new Ordinance. It also made no provision for sub-tenants, and this fact furnished a loop-hole for evasion. In one case, for example, the owner of a village, in order to free himself of his tenants, let the lands of the village to a brother land-owner; he then commenced proceedings in the Magistrate's Court for the ejectment of some forty cultivators on the ground that they were not his tenants but those of the new lessee. His application was successful, as the Magistrate had no alternative but to find that there was no longer any contract of tenancy between the defendants and the owner of the land; the ejectment of the cultivators was therefore ordered. This loop-hole was closed in 1932 by the enactment of the Protection of Cultivators (Amendment) Ordinance, No. 1, in which a tenant was defined so as to include a sub-tenant.

5.—During the period during which the Land Transfer Ordinances of 1920 and 1921 and the Protection of Cultivators Ordinances of 1929 and 1932 were in force, a large number of cultivators were displaced from the land, and in 1933 a Tribunal appointed for the purpose found that some 664 families had been unable to obtain other holdings on which they could establish themselves, or to find other equally satisfactory occupation. Where the land passed into Jewish possession, the extent of displacement varied with the policy of the purchasing body. Certain of these aimed not only at acquiring ownership but at ensuring that the work required on the land should, so far as possible, be performed by Jews; the official land-purchasing agency of the Zionist Organization, the Jewish National Fund, went further and insisted that it should be performed by Jews only. Where such policies were adopted, not only was the landlord changed, but the tenants, and practically all the wage-earning class dependent on the land, were compelled to move also.

6.—Policies of this kind were not, however, universal. Certain private Jewish bodies, such as the Palestine Jewish Colonization Association and Hanotaiah Limited, afforded employment to the tenants displaced by their operations, who, in many cases, are now earning a better livelihood than previously. Since the British occupation of Palestine, the lands of some 22 Arab villages in the Northern District with a population at the Census of 1922 of 5,138 persons have passed into Jewish hands. In the Southern District, no large displacement of Arabs has taken place.

7.—On his arrival in Palestine, Sir Arthur Wauchope made a particular study of the peculiar problems relating to agricultural development in the country. As a result, he decided that it was essential, on financial, political and economic grounds, to take action to check the process of displacement of Arab cultivators, and, on the 31st of August, 1933, a new Protection of Cultivators Ordinance was enacted for this purpose.

8.—This legislation, which repealed the Protection of Cultivators Ordinance of 1929, the three amending Ordinances of 1931 and 1932 and the "Extension" Ordinance of 1933, which provided for a tenancy of two years before a tenant obtained protection and for monetary compensation for eviction, was so drafted as to cause as little interference as possible with the economic life of the country. It creates a "statutory tenant" and provides that any such tenant, who has occupied and cultivated a holding for a period of not less than one year, shall not, provided that he has paid his rent and that he has not grossly neglected his holding, be ejected therefrom unless he has been provided with a subsistence area approved by the High Commissioner. Such subsistence area is to be, so far as possible, in the vicinity of the land from which he has been displaced.

9.—Prior to the enactment of this Ordinance, all disputes as to whether a cultivator was a tenant or not had, in the first instance, to be referred to the Courts, a somewhat lengthy and expensive procedure. In order to overcome this difficulty, it was laid down, in Section 19 of the Ordinance of 1933, that any dispute:

17. PROTECTION OF CULTIVATORS.

(a) as to whether any person is a statutory tenant of a holding, or

(b) as to the length of time that any statutory tenant has occupied and cultivated a holding, or

(c) as to whether any person is the landlord of a holding, or

(d) as to whether any person has exercised continuously any practice of grazing or watering animals or cutting wood or reeds or other beneficial occupation of a similar character by right, custom, usage or sufferance,

should be referred to a Special Commission to be appointed by the High Commissioner, the Chairman being a British Judicial Officer. It was also provided that any person aggrieved by the decision of any such Commission might appeal to the High Commissioner-in-Council, whose decision was to be final, no appeal lying therefrom to any Court.

10.—As the immediate result of the enactment of this Ordinance, a considerable number of disputes were put forward for settlement. The Commission mentioned in the preceding paragraph/ was, however, never set up. Objection was raised in certain quarters to a British Judicial Officer acting as Chairman of a Commission on which he might be outvoted by laymen and doubts were further expressed whether Government was empowered to set up any authority, other than the Courts established for the purpose under the Palestine Order in Council, to decide rights in land. There was thus delay in putting the provisions of the legislation into effect, with the result that the public began to lose faith in the Ordinance, and it was found impossible to protect the genuine tenant or the honest landlord. To remedy this state of affairs, the Protection of Cultivators (Amendment) Ordinance was enacted on the 3rd February, 1934, and the Principal Ordinance was amended so as to give the High Commissioner power to appoint one or more Commissions, consisting respectively of not less than two persons, to adjudicate on disputes, an appeal on a point of law lying to the Land Court by leave of that Court by case stated.

11.—Commissions have been set up in each District to investigate disputes submitted under Section 19 of the Principal Ordinance. These Commissions began to sit on the 7th February, 1934, on which date 87 disputes were awaiting investigation in the Southern District, and 48 cases in the Northern District. In the course of these sittings, additional cases were presented for investigation and up to the 31st July, 1936, the number of disputes preferred was as follows:—

	Jerusalem District	Northern District	Southern District
Number of disputes submitted	34	856	906
Number decided	34	656	797
Number adjourned	—	50	28
Number still to be investigated		150	81
Appeals applied for	1	68	33

The number of disputes listed does not show the actual number of individual claimants nor the actual number of landlords concerned. Claimants varied from one to seventy-two in individual disputes.

12.—In an endeavour further to ensure that villagers were made aware of their rights under the Ordinance, the High Commissioner directed that District Officers should be instructed that, when an intending sale of land was brought to their notice, they should at once proceed to the village and inform all concerned of the protection afforded to them by the Ordinance.

13. But little use has been made of the Ordinance in the hills, as is evidenced by the fact that thirty-four disputes only have been submitted in the Jerusalem District. In the Northern District also, with few exceptions, the claims submitted have been in respect of lands in the plains. Two claims only have been received under Section 18 of the Ordinance, i. e. claims based on the exercise of a practice of grazing or watering animals or the cutting of wood or reeds, etc. In neither case could the claimants substantiate their claims, nor could any record of their having paid animal tax be found in the Government registers.

14.—The present Ordinance is undoubtedly effective in preventing tenants, who would otherwise be liable to eviction on payment of compensation, from being ejected from the land, although many tenants find it difficult to refuse the offer of ready cash as compensation for giving up their rights and vacating their holdings. As the usual period of tenancy is somewhat less than one year, a period of nine to ten months sufficing for the cultivation and harvesting of the winter and summer crops, Government has recently published an Amending Bill extending the rights and liabilities of the principal Ordinance to any statutory tenant who cultivates a holding for a period of one year or for a period necessary to raise a winter and a summer crop. A new section is also being inserted to provide for the restoration to their holdings of displaced statutory tenants and empowering Special Commissions, in certain circumstances, to dismiss the claims of any person to the rights of a statutory tenant, where they are satisfied that he already possesses or retains elsewhere sufficient land for his maintenance.

Annexures:—

Protection of Cultivators Ordinance, No. 37 of 1933.

Protection of Cultivators (Amendment) Ordinance, No. 7 of 1934.

Protection of Cultivators (Amendment) Bill, 1936.

PALESTINE ROYAL COMMISSION.

38. STATE DOMAIN.

MEMORANDUM No. 38.

STATE DOMAIN.

It is admitted that the position in regard to State properties is far from satisfactory and to appreciate the position it is necessary to give a short account of how land in Palestine comes to be recorded in Government ownership.

2.—A description of the various forms of ownership and tenure of land is given in Memorandum No. 10, from which it will be seen that, while Government has a nominal overlordship over land, private individuals and corporations, etc. have registrable rights over much of the country.

3.—The principal classes of property are:

(a) Mulk, which is usually within towns and is similar to the English freehold;

(b) Miri, which covers most of the cultivable area of the country and is held under title deed so long as it is cultivated and there are heirs to succeed;

(c) Mewat, which is waste land, unregistered, and is the property of the State.

4.—In certain circumstances, if Miri land is uncultivated for three years, or there are no heirs on the death of a registered owner, Government can declare it Mahlul (vacant). The declaration of land as Mahlul owing to failure to cultivate has not, generally speaking, been enforced either during the Ottoman régime or since the Occupation.

5.—At the time of the British Occupation, the only areas which were known to be Government property were those registered as such; these comprised lands which had been

(a) previously recorded as the property of Sultan Abdul Hamid;

(b) recorded as Mahlul (vacant) land;

(c) confiscated owing to the non-payment of dues to the Ottoman Government; and

(d) acquired by the Ottoman Government.

Lands under (c) comprised small areas held for the most part as guarantees from tax-farmers, in respect of which redemption has been allowed, while those included under (d) were only of small extent.

In all these cases, however, there were rarely any plans and the description of the boundaries in the records was often incomprehensible and could not be followed on the ground. Cases of disputed boundaries are, consequently, frequent.

6.—Mewat (waste) lands were not registered or recorded in any way and their location and boundaries were, therefore, unknown. Since the Occupation, endeavours have been made to regularize the position and to register unrecorded Mahlul and Mewat land in the name of Government.

The Mahlul Land Ordinance, 1920, and the Mewat Land Ordinance, 1921, were promulgated with the intention of protecting the rights of the State in these lands.

The Mahlul Land Ordinance required persons who had taken possession of land which, owing to failure of heirs or non-cultivation, became Mahlul (vacant) to inform the Government. No notifications were submitted under this Ordinance.

The Mewat Land Ordinance required any person who had cultivated such waste land without authority to submit a notification and apply for a title deed. Following this legislation Commissions were appointed to deal with applications under this Ordinance.

Under the Woods and Forests Ordinance, 1920, a public notice dated the 10th November, 1921, was published constituting Commissions to demarcate Government lands. Certain areas were demarcated under this notice and were later declared forest reserves.

These efforts were not, however, very successful owing to the counter-claims which could not be decided without recourse to the Courts and to the lack, at the time, of a suitable survey. As a general rule, wherever there is a proposal to utilize one of these areas for any purpose, adverse claims are made and interminable litigation ensues.

7.—It was the usual practice during the Ottoman régime for the areas in title deeds to be very much underestimated and, as plans were not insisted upon, the Ottoman Law (Section 47 of the Ottoman Land Code) provided that the boundaries indicated in the title deeds should be accepted and not the area. The boundaries of properties recorded in the Turkish registrations were often vague and applications for the correction of boundaries and areas are frequent. Plans passed by the Survey Department are now insisted upon and such applications are carefully scrutinized to see that there is no encroachment upon State Domain.

8.—Land Settlement is the only satisfactory process for the definition of the boundaries of State lands and until this is carried out the position must remain unsatisfactory.

Except for three villages in hilly regions, which are being dealt with as special cases, settlement is so far only being carried out in the plains.

While it is considered uneconomical to resort to sporadic settlement operations, priority is given whenever possible to areas in which the State is interested.

9.—The area of Mewat land throughout the country is unknown but it may amount to something considerable in the aggregate, made up of uncultivated land, sand dunes and scattered rocky patches.

It may, however, be found that villagers have established grazing or other rights over these lands and that, owing to the size and scattered nature of the lands adjudicated to Government, much of the area will be of little or no value for development purposes.

When the claim of the State to Mewat land is confirmed, it is registered in the name of the

MEMORANDA BY THE GOVERNMENT OF PALESTINE.

38. STATE DOMAIN.

High Commissioner for the time being in trust for the Government of Palestine as Miri land and is then available for disposal.

10.—Government also acquires land from time to time by purchase for specific purposes. The area so acquired since the Occupation is about 19,500 dunums. It comprises land for civil air ports, agricultural stations, settlement of landless Arabs and small areas reserved for schools, police stations, and other Government purposes.

11.—Land is also acquired by purchase or lease for His Majesty's Forces, power to do this being provided under the Acquisition of Land for the Army and Air Force Ordinance, 1925. Such lands when acquired are vested in the High Commissioner on behalf of His Britannic Majesty's Principal Secretary of State for War or the President of the Air Council. A policy of leasing land for this purpose has been adopted, though many of the areas have been occupied for many years.

12.—Sales of State Domains are now comparatively rare as it is the policy of Government to grant long term leases of any extensive area available in order that development may be assured and any benefit due to rising values may be secured to Government. It is usual to insert in such leases provision for re-assessment of the rent at stated intervals.

13.—The approximate extent of known State Domain is 1,036,000 dunums, but this is subject to adjustment and the area is sometimes extended as decisions are given under the Land Settlement Ordinances. To this area might reasonably be added about 227,600 dunums of Sand Dunes which are being claimed at Land Settlement. A plan* has been prepared showing the larger State properties in red, and their areas are set out in Appendix I. The plan and schedule do not include the land allotted under the Ghor Mudawwara Land Agreement, 1921, but include the Sand Dunes being claimed at Land Settlement. Forest Reserves which have been demarcated and surveyed are shown on the plan coloured green while those declared forest reserves which are not yet demarcated or surveyed are indicated hachured green.

14.—Of the 1,036,000 dunums of State Domain, 382,886 dunums are within the areas subject to the Ghor Mudawwara Agreement, 1921. The total area is distributed as follows:—

Allotted to Transferees:

(a) Irrigable land	112,552 duns.	
(b) Non-irrigable land	129,396 duns.	
(c) Land allotted for the use of villagers	2,048 duns.	
	243,996 duns.	

Unallotted:

(d) including roads, railways, etc.	138,890 duns.	
	382,836 duns.	

The allotted areas can no longer be considered as State property, as, according to clause 16 of the Ghor Mudawwara Land Agreement, dated the 19th November, 1921, the person to whom land is allotted is to be regarded as the owner. Government's interest in the allotted areas is restricted to the collection of the transfer price and to the remote possibility of the resumption of possession in the event of the failure of a transferee to pay the purchase price. Government has re-purchased from transferees land amounting to 11,547 dunums for the settlement of landless Arabs on this area. Of the unallotted land mentioned above, about 6,000 dunums are used for public purposes such as roads, railways, streams, etc. A brief history of these lands is attached as Appendix II together with a schedule of unallotted lands.

15.—Appendix III shows 156,303 dunums of land held by Arabs, under what must be regarded as hereditary and assignable tenure of a similar nature to the Beisan Lands. These are for the most part properties which were recorded at one time in the name of the Sultan Abdul Hamid but were taken over by the Ottoman Government at the time of his deposition in 1909 and have been regarded as Government property since the British Occupation.

Until the application of the Rural Property Tax Ordinance, 1935, rental tithe (the equivalent of the tithe) was collected in addition to the tithe. House and Land Tax (Werko) was not paid by the cultivators. Since the Tithe and Werko were replaced by the Rural Property Tax an additional sum, equal to the amount of this tax, is collected by way of rent.

Certain of these properties have been dealt with under the Land Settlement Ordinances, 1927-35; these are shown separately in Appendix III and extend to a total area of 66,754 dunums. In the case of the villages of Jaladiya, Kaufakha, Muharraqa, Rafah, Qazaza and Sajad, the Settlement Officers decided that the lands were Government property over which the cultivators had registrable hereditary and assignable rights; the Land Court, however, sitting as a Court of Appeal, confirmed the Government's ownership but ruled that the cultivators' rights were not registrable.

No policy has as yet been decided upon in regard to these lands and it is not known whether any part of them can be regarded as available for development as they are occupied by tenants of long standing.

16.—Appendix IV shows State lands which are held by Arabs with particulars of the term of occupation in each case. The total area amounts to 143,645 dunums.

17.—A list of the State lands held by Jews is attached as Appendix V and indicates the length of the term of the lease or concession in each case. The area is shown as being 175,545 dunums. It will be observed that some of the areas included are held by companies which cannot be regarded as entirely Jewish.

18.—Appendix VI comprises properties extending to 29,290 dunums in respect of which negotiations for lease are being carried out with Jewish organizations.

19.—An area of approximately 2,258 dunums is leased or under negotiation for lease to non-Arab and non-Jewish bodies, such as Oil Companies.

20.—State and other properties occupied by Government and His Majesty's Forces total 81,700 dunums. A considerable part of this is covered by roads and railways but large areas are also

---

*Not printed.

PALESTINE ROYAL COMMISSION.

38. STATE DOMAIN.

occupied by Forests, Aerodromes, and Agricultural Stations. A number of small properties scattered over the country within and outside towns comprising the sites of Government and other buildings are also included in this area. The Haifa Harbour (Reclaimed Area) Estate is also included as most of the area is used for Government purposes. A separate note on this Estate is attached as Appendix IX.

21.—Appendix VII includes recently settled lands which may be regarded as available and the use to which they are to be put is under consideration. They total an area of 147,295 dunums.

22.—Appendix VIII comprises 67,328 dunums of non-settled land which Government has not yet disposed of in any way. It is for the most part uncultivable land and its disposal is complicated by boundary and ownership disputes.

23.—Memorandum 3C*, which deals with the development of forestry, refers in paragraph 3 to an area of about 739,000 dunums which, by 1935, had been declared Forest Reserve. Of this area 17,079 dunums, which are included in paragraph 20 above, are known to be State Domain. After land settlement it is hoped that much of the declared forest reserves will, subject to rights of grazing, wood cutting etc., be found to be Government property.

*Not included in this volume.

24.—The position of State Domain may be summarised as follows:—

	Dunums.	
(a) Ghor Mudawwara Land Agreement: Allotted to Arabs less area purchased	232,449	
(b) Area held by Arabs with hereditary and assignable interests	156,303	
(c) Area held by Arabs on lease etc.	143,645	532,397
(d) Area held by Jews	175,545	
(e) Area under negotiation with Jewish organizations	29,290	204,835
(f) Area leased etc. to other bodies		2,258
(g) Area owned and occupied by Government and the Forces, including roads, etc.		81,700
(h) Settled area available	147,295	
(j) Non-settled area available	67,328	214,623
		1,035,813
(k) Sand dunes being claimed at Land Settlement		227,684
Total:		1,263,497

APPENDIX I.

STATE DOMAIN.

Schedule showing the larger Properties.

Serial No.	State Domain No.	Name of Property	Sub-district	Area Dunums.
1	GP/6/1	Hula Concession	Safad.	56,940
2	D/Saf/1	Jazair, Alma.	Safad.	788
3	D/Saf/48	Dahnuneh & Mubarak	Safad.	674
4	D/Saf/5	Mansura	Safad.	2,500
5	D/Saf/74	Meis	Safad.	87
6	D/Saf/18	Jish	Safad.	238
7	D/Saf/113	Ash Shuna	Safad.	208
8	LD/3/4	Agricultural Station, Kafr Inan.	Acre.	400
9	LD/3/4/1	Agricultural Station, Faradiya.	Safad.	103
10	D/Tib/1	Hittin	Tiberias.	362
11	GP/12/1	Tiberias	Tiberias.	3,345
12	D/Tib/224	Al Hamme Baths	Tiberias.	204
13	D/Tib/176	Delhamiya	Tiberias.	344
14	SD/25/2	Beisan lands.	Beisan	72,664
15	D/Beis/737	Tel Esh Shok	Beisan	3,189
16	D/Naz/10	Kaukab	Nazareth	2,472
17	D/Acre/67	Ras en Nakura Frontier Station.	Acre	44
18	D/Acre/104	Nahr Sand Dunes.	Acre	129
19	D/Acre/112	Tob Alti	Acre	2,761
20	D/Acre/4	Rakayek	Acre	1,072
21	D/Acre/5	Na'amin River Swamps.	Acre	7,587
22	D/Acre/319	Acre Sand Dunes	Acre	1,903
23	D/Hai/311	Haifa Bay Sand Dunes	Haifa	1,400
24	D/Hai/310	Railway Workshops	Haifa	525
25	D/Hai/142	Haifa Air Port	Haifa	594
26	D/Hai/159	Military Grazing Land, Haifa	Haifa	507
27	HRA/1/1	Haifa Harbour (Reclaimed Area) Estate.	Haifa	600
28	D/Hai/141	Es Sa'adeh	Haifa	165
29	D/Hai/63	Rushmiya	Haifa	2,086
30	D/Hai/139	Farsh Iskandar	Haifa	743

MEMORANDA BY THE GOVERNMENT OF PALESTINE.

38. STATE DOMAIN.

Serial No.	State Domain No.	Name of Property	Sub-district	Area Dunums.
31	SD/3/2	Khureiba Lands.	Haifa	4,068
32	D/Hai/168	Abu Zureik	Haifa	772
33	D/Jen/6	Zalafa & Tel ed Dahab	Jenin	8,638
34	GP/7/2	Muqeibila	Jenin	4,293
35	D/Jen/8	Deir Ghazaleh	Jenin	5,301
36	GP/7/1	Beit Qad	Jenin	2,095
37	D/Hai/11	Atlit	Haifa	3,200
38	D/Hai/15	El Burj—Tantura	Haifa	920
39	D/Hai/103	Kabara	Haifa	3,793
40	D/Hai/114	Qisariya	Haifa	25,793
41	D/Hai/145	Cherqas Swamps	Haifa	658
42	D/Tul/32	Wadi Hawareth	Tulkarm	1,058
43	D/Tul/107	Agricultural School, Tulkarm.	Tulkarm	532
44	D/Naz/23	Agricultural School, Kefar Tavor.	Nazareth	2,176
45	D/Naz/11	Arab Subeih	Nazareth	2,920
46	D/Nab/37	Tubas Lands.	Nablus	67,380
47	GP/11/1	Ghor el Fari'a	Nablus	65,350
48	D/Nab/35	Aqrabaniya & Mazraat Hamra.	Nablus	25,721
49	D/Nab/2	Bassat el Yaraki	Nablus	2,500
50	D/Jek/182	Jericho Jiftlik	Jericho	41,743
51	D/Jek/177	Es Suweid, Juhayyir, Hajla & Fashkha lands.	Jericho	50,965
52	D/Jek/191	"Kallia"	Jericho	966
53	D/Jek/192	Palestine Potash Concession (North)	Jericho	10,778
54	D/Beer/60	Palestine Potash Concession (South)	Beersheba	64,199
55	D/Jem/65	'Anata.	Jerusalem	20,112
56	LV/1/40	Broadcasting Station (Bira)	Ramallah	60
57	D/Jem/2	Mount Scopus Police Camp.	Jerusalem	47
58	D/Jem/144	Government House.	Jerusalem	177
59	D/Jem/147	Talavera Barracks.	Jerusalem	127
60	D/Jem/131	Hospital Sites.	Jerusalem	210
61	D/Jem/96	Qaryat el Inab.	Jerusalem	230
62	LV/1/39	Jerusalem Water Supply Pumping Stations.	Jerusalem	317
63	D/Jaf/63	Basset el Mulabbis, Petah Tiqva.	Jaffa	1,621
64	GP/1/13	Sheikh Muwannis Sand Dunes.	Jaffa	785
65	GP/1/4	Miqveh Yisrael Agricultural School.	Jaffa	2,467
66	D/Jaf/99	Jaffa Sand Dunes.	Jaffa	402
67	D/Jaf/99	South Jaffa Sand Dunes.	Jaffa	5,650
68	GP/2/35	Rishon Sand Dunes.	Jaffa	18,940
69	GP/1/1	Beit Dajan Sand Dunes.	Jaffa	2,386
70	AC/9/1	Lydda Air Port.	Ramle	1,580
71	GP/2/21	Ramle Aerodrome.	Ramle	549
72	GP/2/1	Mughar.	Ramle	906
73	LV/1/49	Beit 'Ummar Horticultural Station.	Hebron	297
74	GP/3/37	Majdal Agricultural Station.	Gaza	600
75	GP/3/37	Sand Dunes.	Gaza	69,000
76	GP/3/1	Khan Yunis Sand Dunes.	Gaza	7,969
77	GP/2/18 & GP/2/44	Qazaza & Sajad.	Ramle	6,574
78	GP/3/26	Jaladiya.	Gaza	4,214
79	D/Heb/7	Zeita.	Hebron	5,632
80	GP/3/8	Muharraqa.	Gaza	4,628
81	GP/3/19	Kaufakha.	Gaza	3,279
82	GP/3/20	Rafah.	Gaza	23,875
83	D/Heb/3	Tel-Arad	Hebron	42,361
84	D/Beer/53	Nakhbar el Baghel, Beersheba.	Beersheba	1,314
85	GP/4/14	Pardess Hanna.	Haifa	728
86	D/Tul/24	Deir el Ghusun.	Tulkarm	389
87	D/Tul/60	Basset Zeita	Tulkarm	177
88	D/Tul/30	Qaqun	Tulkarm	935
89	D/Tul/106	Kafr Sur Sand Dunes.	Tulkarm	6,598
90	D/Jem/113	Kafr Ishwa'	Ramallah	184
91	D/Jem/110	Deir esh Sheikh & Beit 'Itab.	Jerusalem	4,353
92	D/Beer/55 & 58 H.	Auja Hafir.	Beersheba	657
93	D/Jem/143	Allar	Bethlehem	368
94	D/Jem/—	Al Khadr	Bethlehem	138
95	D/Heb/23	Beit Nattif	Hebron	637
96	GP/2/59	Sand Dunes.	Gaza	129,883
97	D/Ram/17	Jarisha	Ramle	468
98	GP/2/13	Sarafand Horticultural Station	Ramle	150
99	D/Saf/82	Hunin.	Safad	148
100	D/Naz/14	Ein Mahil—Sartaba.	Nazareth	1,589
				939,180

PALESTINE ROYAL COMMISSION.

38. STATE DOMAIN.

APPENDIX II.

BEISAN LANDS.

Up to the late sixties of the last century the Beisan lands were apparently occupied by cultivators who held no recorded title. Owing to the activity of marauding tribes from east of the Jordan, lack of public security, poor harvests and other reasons, the area was abandoned. In 1870, the Ottoman Authorities appointed a Commission to report upon the area. In 1872, the Sublime Porte directed that the lands of the villages affected were to be put up for sale by public auction. They were either bought by Sultan Abdul Hamid or instructions were received from Constantinople to register them in his name. By this time many of the occupants had returned, others were admitted, and when the State took over the properties on the deposition of the Sultan in 1909 the occupiers became State tenants on a customary unwritten tenure, under which they paid a rental tithe of 10% of the gross produce. This was the position at the time of the Occupation.

In 1921 the occupants pressed for a return of the areas to them, alleging that they had been ousted by force. Sir Herbert Samuel, then High Commissioner, called for a report and accepted a recommendation that the areas, in possession of the occupants should be returned to them on payment of 150 Egyptian Piastres (approximately £.1.10.3) per dunum for irrigable land and 125 Egyptian Piastres (approximately £.1.5.1) per dunum for non-irrigable land, payable in instalments, with interest, over a period of 15 years.

A demarcation Commission presided over by a British Officer allotted the areas, which were surveyed and registered in the names of transferees with an encumbrance in favour of Government to secure the unpaid balances and interest.

In view of the inability of the transferees to meet their obligations, the price of the non-irrigable land was reduced from 125 Egyptian Piastres (£.1.5.1) to 800 mils (16/-) per dunum and the interest reduced from 6½% to 3½% per annum.

The price of the irrigable land was not reduced but the interest was reduced to 3½%.

SCHEDULE OF UNALLOTTED LANDS.

VILLAGE.	Roads, Railways, Streams etc. Dunums.	Other unallotted land Dunums.	TOTAL. Dunums.	REMARKS.
'Arida, Al	49	170	219	
Ashrafiya	123	77	210	
Bashatiwa	352	3,700	4,052	
Bawati, Al	41	3,616	3,657	
Beisan	985	4,472	5,457	
Bira	22	1,978	2,000	
Danna	23	1,207	1,230	
Farwana	41	954	995	
Fatur	21	—	21	
Ghazzawiya	114	3,847	3,961	
Hamidiya	232	4,480	4,712	
Hamra, Al	36	622	658	
Jabbul	219	9,897	10,116	
Jisr el Majami'	6	177	183	
Kafra	183	1,594	1,777	
Kafr Misr	162	3,910	4,072	
Kaukab el Hawa	70	3,780	3,850	
Khuneizir, Al	74	68	142	
Masil el Jizl	39	3,227	3,266	
Murassas, Al	359	1,097	1,456	
Safa, Es	13	1,909	1,922	
Sakhina	153	198	351	
Samiriya	27	372	399	
Sirin	252	11,314	11,566	
Tall esh Shok	262	105	367	
Tira, Et	89	3,058	3,147	
Umm 'Ajra	19	1,420	1,429	
Yubla	149	1,224	1,373	
Zara'a	32	29	61	
Samakh	412	479	891	
Ghor el Fara'	1,439	63,911	65,350	
	5,998	132,892	138,890	

NOTE:—The other unallotted land includes Antiquity Sites amounting in all to about 1,600 dunums in area.

MEMORANDA BY THE GOVERNMENT OF PALESTINE.

38. STATE DOMAIN.

APPENDIX III.

STATE DOMAIN.

LAND OCCUPIED BY ARABS WITH CULTIVATION RIGHTS.

State Domain No.	Village	Sub-District.	Area Dunums.	Remarks.
SETTLED LANDS:				
GP/2/18	Qazaza	Ramle.	3,893	Rent paid on basis of Rural Property Tax.
GP/2/44	Sajad	Ramle.	2,682	— do —
GP/3/8	Muharraqa	Gaza.	4,756	— do —
GP/3/76	Jaladiya	Gaza.	4,288	— do —
GP/3/19	Kaufakha	Gaza.	8,455	— do —
GP/3/20	Rafah	Gaza.	24,746	— do —
D/Beis/736	Ashrafiya	Beisan.	4,143	Occupied by "Landless Arabs".
D/Beis/737	Tell esh Shok	Beisan.	3,189	— do —
D/Beis/738	El Mafraq, Beisan	Beisan.	451	Being exchanged for land in Tell esh Shok.
D/Beis/739	Es Samiriya	Beisan.	628	Occupied by "Landless Arabs".
D/Beis/740	Ghazzawiya	Beisan.	1,527	— do —
D/Beis/741	Umm 'Ajra	Beisan.	1,083	— do —
D/Beis/742	Es Safa	Beisan.	526	— do —
GP/7/1	Beit Qad	Jenin.	2,094	— do —
GP/7/2	Muqeibila	Jenin.	4,293	— do —
	Total settled lands:		66,754	
NON-SETTLED LANDS:				
D/Heb/7	Zeita	Hebron.	5,632	Rent paid on basis of Rural Property Tax.
D/Jek/182	Jericho	Jericho.	36,367	— do —
D/Jen/5	Zalafa	Jenin.	3,516	— do —
D/Jen/6	Tell edh Dhabab	Jenin.	5,120	— do —
D/Jen/7	Deir Ghazzale	Jenin.	5,301	— do —
D/Nab/34	Ard el Firush	Nablus.	25,721	— do —
D/Naz/10	Kaukab	Nazareth.	2,472	State Domain is 3/24 undivided shares of the village. Rent paid on basis of Rural Property Tax.
D/Naz/11	Arab Sbeih	Nazareth.	2,920	Rent paid on basis of Rural Property Tax.
D/Saf/5	Mansurat el Kheit	Safad.	2,500	Rent paid on basis of Rural Property Tax.
	Total non-settled lands:		89,549	
	Total area occupied:		156,303	

PALESTINE ROYAL COMMISSION:

38. STATE DOMAIN.

APPENDIX IV.

STATE DOMAINS HELD BY ARABS.

State Domain No.	Town or Village	Area Dums. M2	Held by	Term and Date of Commencement — No. of years	Term and Date of Commencement — as from	Remarks
Acre Sub-District:						
D/Acre/81	Bassa	3.677	Mukhlis Jabbur Sima'an Arab cultivators	2	1.10.35	
D/Acre/82	'Arraba	21.144	„	„	„	
	Miscellaneous Shops and Buildings	7.153	Arab tenants	annual lease		
Beersheba Sub-District:						
D/Beer/58. H	Auja Hafir Flour Mill	13.035	Heirs of Daoud Eff. Khalil el Khatib	49	1.1.29	
D/Beer/25	Khirbet el Maliya, Beersheba.	176.188	Arab cultivators	annual lease		
Bethlehem Sub-District:						
D/Jek/176	'Ein Feshka	946.879*	Ahmad Khalaf Arab cultivators	„		State Domain is ⅓ share of 14.694 dunums.
D/Jem/69	Beit Safafa	3.673		„		
Gaza Sub-District:						
D/Gaz/22	Zeitun Quarter, Gaza.	3.677	Abdul Mu'ti Mabruk	3	1.10.34	
D/Gaz/23	Daraj Quarter, Gaza.	30.854	Yusef eff. el Sayegh	2	1.10.36	
D/Gaz/53	Kh. Khisas.	5.527	Zaneh Salem Abu Hassan	3	1.1.36	
D/Gaz/58	Gaza	47.600	Arab cultivator.	annual lease		
Haifa Sub-District:						
D/Hai/25-32	Hudeidun, Pardess Hanna.	570.000*	Arab cultivators	annual lease		Ownership disputed.
D/Hai/59	Bassatin er Ramel, Haifa.	3.103	Bassila Jabbour	99	1.4.25	
D/Hai/143	Miscellaneous Buildings & Building Sites.	282.816 / 3.058	Sa'id Khamis & partners Arab tenants	annual lease		
Hebron Sub-District:						
D/Heb/1	Beit Jibrin	208.350*	Arab cultivators	annual lease		
D/Heb/8	Tel 'Arad	42,361.000*	Arab villagers of nearby villages	two agricultural seasons		The State Domain is an undivided share of the village lands.

*Owing to lack of accurate surveys and disputes in regard to boundaries, the areas marked with an asterisk must be regarded as very approximate.

MEMORANDA BY THE GOVERNMENT OF PALESTINE.

38. STATE DOMAIN.

State Domain No.	Town or Village	Area Duns. M2	Held by	Term and Date of Commencement — No. of years	Term and Date of Commencement — as from	Remarks
JAFFA SUB-DISTRICT:						
GP/1/5	Jarisha	0.028	Mahmud Hasan Hajaj	annual lease		Area leased is half share of a building.
JERICHO SUB-DISTRICT:						
D/Jek/157	Zor el Jisr, Jericho	71.618	George Kattan	49	1.12.24	
D/Jek/169	Jericho	9.230	Joseph Albina	3	28.6.34	
D/Jek/181	Allenby Bridge, Jericho	167.473	George Kattan	49	1.12.25	
D/Jek/198	Deir Hajla, En Nabi Musa	94.800	Saba Zedan and partners	3	15.6.34	
JERUSALEM SUB-DISTRICT:						
D/Jem/165	'Anata	20,112.000*	Arab cultivators			Ownership disputed.
NABLUS SUB-DISTRICT:						
D/Nab/2	Basset el Yaraki	2,500.000*	Faiz ibn Kassem al Malik Kahin Taufiq es Samiri	annual lease		State Domain is 6/24 shares of 64.352 dunums.
D/Nab/4	Burin	16.088		,, ,,		Ownership disputed.
D/Nab/37	Tubas	67,380.000*	Arab cultivators of Tubas village	—		State Domain is a share of a number of scattered parcels of land.
D/Nab/65	'Immatin	14.937	Arab cultivators	annual lease		
D/Nab/74	Kafr Qaddum	3.216	— do —	,, ,,		do.
	Miscellaneous Buildings in Nablus.	0.307	Arab tenants	,, ,,		
NAZARETH SUB-DISTRICT:						
D/Naz/10	Kaukab	2,472.000*	Arab cultivators of Kaukab			State Domain is an undivided share of village lands.
RAMLE SUB-DISTRICT:						
GP/2/8	Lydda	36.794	Hafiz Abdul Hafiz	annual lease		
SAFAD SUB-DISTRICT:						
D/Saf/1	Jazair, Alma	786.000*	'Ammar Hussein	20	1.11.26	
D/Saf/10	Taitaba	18.000	Ahmad Selim	annual lease		
D/Saf/11	Taitaba	24.000	Muhammad Musa Abdul Latif	,, ,,		

*Owing to lack of accurate surveys and disputes in regard to boundaries, the areas marked with an asterisk must be regarded as very approximate.

38. STATE DOMAIN.

State Domain No.	Town or Village	Area Dugs. M2	Held by	Term and Date of Commencement.		Remarks.
				No. of years.	as from	
D/Saf/17	Dhahiriya et Tahta.	22.250	Mahmud Mustafa Ibrahim.	annual lease		
D/Saf/18	Jish	238.095*	Arab cultivators.	,, ,,		State Domain is an undivided share of 6 duuums.
D/Saf/36	Safad	7.362	Arab cultivators.	,, ,,		State Domain is an undivided share of a number of scattered parcels.
D/Saf/39	Safad	3.750	Arab cultivators.	,, ,,		
D/Saf/57	Kihaniya	27.928	Arab cultivators.	,, ,,		do.
D/Saf/74	Meis al Jabal	87.385	Arab cultivators.	,, ,,		
D/Saf/82	Hunin	139.964*	Muhammad Salman Tahmaz.	,, ,,		
	Miscellaneous Buildings in Safad town.	0.110	Arab tenants.	annual lease		
TIBERIAS SUB-DISTRICT:						
D/Tib/2	Nimrin	27.579	Muhammad el Bakir.	annual lease		
D/Tib/4	Migdal, Ard esh Shawahit.	630.500*	Muhammad el Ajaj.	,, ,,		
D/Tib/14	Tiberias	27.579	Khalaf ed Deeb.	,, ,,		
D/Tib/15	Tiberias	29.417	— do —	,, ,,		
D/Tib/16	Tiberias	27.579	— do —	,, ,,		
D/Tib/17	Tiberias	27.579	— do —	,, ,,		
D/Tib/19	Tiberias	27.579	Husni Eff. el 'Ali	,, ,,		
D/Tib/21	Tiberias	90.000	Husni Eff. el 'Ali	,, ,,		
D/Tib/23	Tiberias	45.000	Arab cultivators.	,, ,,		Disputed.
D/Tib/33	Kafr Sabt	2,757.900*	Muhammad Sa'diyeh.	,, ,,		
D/Tib/60	Tiberias	6.895	— do —	annual lease		
D/Tib/61	Tiberias-	7.354	— do —	,, ,,		
D/Tib/70	Tiberias	16.547	— do —	,, ,,		
D/Tib/71	Tiberias	16.547	Yunis es Sabi'	,, ,,		
D/Tib/98	Hittin	253.055*	Arab cultivators.	,, ,,		
D/Tib/175	Dalhamiya	347.477*	Arab cultivators.	,, ,,		
D/Tib/197	'Ubeidiya	32.727	Suleiman Bey Nassif.	31	30.12.30	
D/Tib/224	El Hamna	204.260				Ownership disputed.
TULKARM SUB-DISTRICT:						
D/Tul/26	Deir el Ghusun	45.965	Muhammad Radi Husein 'Omar	annual lease		
D/Tul/70	Taiyiba el Fauqa	1.379	Hassan Suleiman Baransi	,, ,,		
D/Tul/71	Taiyiba el Fauqa	3.677	— do —	,, ,,		
D/Tul/76	Zeita	4.596	Ahmad Muhammad Nimer.			

*Owing to lack of accurate surveys and disputes in regard to boundaries, the areas marked with an asterisk must be regarded as very approximate.

38. STATE DOMAIN.

State Domain No.	Town or Village	Area Duns. M2	Held by	Term and Date of Commencement — No. of years.	Term and Date of Commencement — as from	Remarks
D/Tul/77	Zeita	7.354	Ahmad Muhammad Nimer	annual lease		
D/Tul/110	Kafr Saba	61.170	Assad Abdul Qader.	" "		
GP/5/5	Jaljulya	3.366	Abdul Karim Jaiyusi.	" "		
GP/5/12	Kafr Saba	5.399	Sharif Daoud Mahmud.	" "		
GP/5/17	'Attil	13.180	Ahmad Mohd. Nimer Abu Mana'.	" "		
	Total Area:	143,644.729				

APPENDIX V.

STATE DOMAIN HELD BY JEWS.

State Domain No.	Town or Village	Area Duns. M2	Held by	Term and Date of Commencement — No. of years.	Term and Date of Commencement — as from	Remarks
ACRE SUB-DISTRICT:						
D/Acre/4	Rakayik — Damun	1,072.364	Asher Cucuy	99	18.1.23	
BEERSHEBA SUB-DISTRICT:						
D/Beer/60	South of Dead Sea	64,199.160	Palestine Potash Ltd.	70	1.6.34	
HAIFA SUB-DISTRICT:						
D/Hai/1	'Atlit	2,500.000	Concession to Palestine Jewish Colonization Association.	100	8.11.21	
D/Hai/18	Haifa (Basset Wadi Shiby, Zawara, and Caracol)	12.313	Keren Hayesod Ltd.	99	1.12.23	
D/Hai/63	Haifa (Rushmiya)	2,086.283	Palestine Land Development Co.	99	8.8.34	Agreement under revision. Area approximate.
D/Hai/92	Haifa (Ard el Ballan)	5.746	Palestine Jewish Colonization Association.	100	31.12.34	

38. STATE DOMAIN.

State Domain No.	Town or Village.	Area Duns. M2	Held by	Term and Date of Commencement.		Remarks.
				No. of years.	as from	
D/Hai/103	Kabbara	3,793.000	Concession to Palestine Jewish Colonization Association.	100	8.11.21	Agreement under revision. Area approximate.
D/Hai/114	Caesarea	25,510.000	Concession to Palestine Jewish Colonization Association.	100	8.11.21	
D/Hai/119	Pardess Hanna (Birket el Batikh)	250.133	Palestine Jewish Colonization Association.	49	1.1.30	
D/Hai/146	Pardess Hanna (Ghabat Sherkass)	59.786	Palestine Jewish Colonization Association.	49	1.10.26	
D/Hai/146	Pardess Hanna (Ghabat Sherkass el Gharbiya)	27.620	— do —	49	1.10.26	
D/Hai/155	Haifa (Bat Galim)	6.684	Committee of Bat Galim Co-operative Ltd.	99	1.9.26	
D/Hai/177	Tantura (Bass esh Shamali)	786.000	Palestine Jewish Colonization Association.	49	1.4.30	
D/Hai/269	Jidru	1,436.000	Keren Kayemeth Leisrael Ltd.	3	1.4.34	
Jaffa Sub-District:						
D/Jaf/6	Tel-Aviv	22.571	Town Council, Tel-Aviv.	99	1.4.23	
D/Jaf/62	Tel-Aviv	50.286	Town Council, Tel-Aviv.	100	24.8.21	
D/Jaf/63	Petah Tiqva (Basset Mulabbis)	1,558.478	Local Council, Petah-Tiqva.	50	11.11.21	With option for further 50 years.
GP/1/4	Yazur (Miqve Israel)	2,486.853	Alliance Israelite Universelle, Paris.	Perpetual.		Held under Firman granted by the Sultan.
Jericho Sub-District:						
D/Jek/191	En Nabi Musa (Kallia)	966.109	T. G. Tullock, S.A. Van Vriesland and Ibrahim Hazboun.	49	25.6.31	
D/Jek/192	En Nabi Musa	3,683.000	Palestine Potash Ltd.	72	1.7.32	
D/Jek/199	En Nabi Musa	1,754.389	— do —	72	21.12.32	
D/Jek/200	En Nabi Musa	59.204	— do —	70	25.1.34	
D/Jek/216	En Nabi Musa	263.612	— do —	68	1.1.36	
D/Jek/219	En Nabi Musa	5,017.448	— do —	75	1.1.30	

38. STATE DOMAIN.

State Domain No.	Town or Village	Area Duns. M²	Held by	Term and Date of Commencement		Remarks
				No. of years	as from	
JERUSALEM SUB-DISTRICT:						
D/Jem/94	Jerusalem	2.355	Menorah Club	49	1.7.30	
D/Jem/160	Jerusalem	2.286	Hadassah Women's Zionist Organization of America.	10	8.7.35	
SAFAD SUB-DISTRICT:						
D/Saf/46	Aiyelet Hashabar (Dahnuneh and Mabarak)	717.100	The Agricultural Co-operative Labour Society	50	1.10.21	Concession recently taken over from previous holders. An area not exceeding 15,772 dunums within the concession area is reserved for Arab cultivators.
GP/6/1	Huleh	56,940.000	Palestine Land Development Co.			
	Miscellaneous Buildings at Safad.	0.146	Jewish tenants.	annual leases.		
TIBERIAS SUB-DISTRICT:						
D/Tib/35	Samakh	2.000	Israel Toister	20	1.1.21	
D/Tib/45	Tiberias (Quarry)	5.003	Itshaq 'Efron	20	1.6.36	
D/Tib/199	Samakh (Tell ed Duweir)	155.465	Palestine Electric Corporation Ltd.	70	1.3.27	
TULKARM SUB-DISTRICT:						
D/Tul/106	Nathanya	114.084	Assigned by Hanote'a Ltd. to Pardess Hagdud.	99	1.7.32	
	Total Area:	175,545.478				

PALESTINE ROYAL COMMISSION.

38. STATE DOMAIN.

APPENDIX VI.

STATE DOMAINS PROPOSED TO BE LEASED TO JEWS.

State Domain No.	Town or Village.	Area Dubs. M²	Proposed to be Leased to	Remarks.
Haifa Sub-District:				
D/Hai/309	Haifa (sand dunes)	1,700.000	Keren Kayemeth Leisrael Ltd. and Haifa Bay Development Company.	Area approximate.
Jaffa Sub-District:				
D/Jaf/3	Tel-Aviv	92.180	The Municipal Council, Tel-Aviv.	
D/Jaf/99	Jaffa (Bassa)	402.382	Shikun Workers Housing Co. Ltd.	
SD/12/(3)	Hertseliya	34.056	Hertseliya Seashore Development Co.	
SD/12/(5)	Tel-Aviv	255.000	Lt. Col. F.H. Kisch.	
GP/1/(3)	Beit Dajan	1,083.121	Keren Kayemeth Leisrael Ltd.	Area subject to adjustment.
GP/1/1(4)	Beit Dajan	708.849	Palestine Land Development Co.	
GP/1/1(6)	Beit Dajan	594.350	— do —	
GP/1/13(9)	Sheikh Muwannis	720.941	Housing of Jewish Battalion Former Members.	
GP/1/20(5)	El Haram	192.331	Agricultural Cooperative Society Ltd. Hertseliya.	
GP/2/35	Rishon le Tsiyon (Sand Dunes)	21,000.000	Keren Kayemeth Leisrael Ltd.	Area approximate.
Ramle Sub-District:				
GP/2/1(1)	Mughar	806.594	Keren Kayemeth Leisrael Ltd.	
Jericho Sub-District:				
SD/19(12)	Jericho	1,700.000	Palestine Potash Ltd.	Part of D/Jek/178. Area approximate.
	Total Area:	29,289.804		

38. STATE DOMAIN.

APPENDIX VII.

"SETTLED" LAND NOT YET DISPOSED OF.

State Domain No.	Town or Village.	Area. Dunums.	Remarks.
Beisan Sub-District:			
SD/25/2	Unallotted land in Beisan Sub-District.	68,502	Unallotted under the Ghor Mudawwara Land Agreement, 1921. For the most part uncultivable.
Gaza Sub-District:			
GP/3/1	Khan Yunis	10,855	Sand Dunes.
GP/3/1	Khan Yunis	118	14 plots of sandy land.
GP/3/3	Beit Hanun	1,421	40 plots of rocky land.
GP/3/29	Deir el Balah	573	Sand Dunes.
GP/2/23	Beit Daras	112	14 plots.
	Miscellaneous plots	37	
Haifa Sub-District:			
GP/4/14	Pardess Hanna	482	Redemption by former owners being considered.
Jaffa Sub-District:			
GP/1/4	Yazur	27	Subject to a post-settlement claim to ownership.
GP/11/12	Petah Tiqva	23	Subject to rights of owners whose whereabouts are unknown.
Nablus Sub-District:			
GP/11/1	Ghor el Fara' unallotted land.	63,911	Unallotted under the Ghor Mudawwara Land Agreement, 1921. For the most part uncultivable.
Ramle Sub-District:			
GP/2/11	Idhnibba	157	Proposal for long term lease to villagers now under consideration.
GP/2/1	Mughar	100	Lease of this area to an Arab being considered.
GP/2/25	Majdal Yaba	22	3 plots.
GP/2/25	Majdal Yaba	54	Land around the head waters of the River 'Auja.
	Miscellaneous scattered plots.	83	
Tiberias Sub-District:			
SD/25/5	Samakh. Unallotted land.	479	Unallotted under the Ghor Mudawwara Land Agreement, 1921. Land along the bank of the River Yarmuk.
Tulkarm Sub-District:			
GP/5/18	Qalansuwa.	88	Sand dunes.
GP/5/18	Qalansuwa.	251	To be used for "landless" Arabs.
	Total:	147,295	

PALESTINE ROYAL COMMISSION.

38. State Domain.

APPENDIX VIII.

NON-SETTLED LAND NOT YET DISPOSED OF.

State Domain No.	Town or Village	Area Dunums.	Remarks.
Acre Sub-District:			
D/Acre/5	Damun Swamps	3,065	Marsh. Boundaries encroached upon.
D/Acre/100	Shawabit, Manshiya.	518	Ownership disputed. Decision given to grant part on payment of Bedl Misl.
D/Acre/104	En Nahr	129	Sand Dunes.
	Miscellaneous plots	91	Scattered areas.
Beersheba Sub-District:			
D/Beer/23	Wadi Beersheba	59	Ownership disputed.
D/Beer/53 & 54.	Nakhbar al Bagble, Beersheba.	847	Ownership disputed.
D/Beer/57	Sawakhne, Beersheba.	25	Steep uncultivable land.
D/Beer/58	'Auja Hafir	644	Historical Site.
D/Beer/59	Beersheba—Hakuk Braiki	36	Uncultivable land in the Wadi el Bahr.
	Miscellaneous plots	53	
Beisan Sub-District:			
D/Beis/732	Shatta	508	Rocky land.
Bethlehem Sub-District:			
D/Jem/143	'Allar		Uncultivable land adjoining a Forest Reserve. Claimed as State Domain.
Gaza Sub-District:			
	Miscellaneous plots		Small scattered areas of sandy land.

MEMORANDA BY THE GOVERNMENT OF PALESTINE.

38. STATE DOMAIN.

State Domain No.	Town or Village.	Area. Dunums.	Remarks.
Haifa Sub-District:			
D/Hai/1	'Atlit	919	Part to be used for Arab squatters. Boundaries disputed.
D/Hai/16	Kufrin	63	Government share in 7 scattered parcels.
D/Hai/136	Tell Abu Madwara	257	Ownership disputed.
D/Hai/137	Wadi Kafr Sanu', Tira.	144	Ownership disputed. Earmarked for Exchange.
D/Hai/139	Farsh Iskandar, Tira.	743	Ownership disputed.
D/Hai/149	El Mafka, Tira.	69	Ownership disputed.
D/Hai/153	Bir 'Amir, Tira.	41	To be granted on payment of Bedl-Misl.
D/Hai/159	River Qishon, Haifa.	360	Comprise beds of Wadis, etc. now filled in. Absorbed in adjoining parcels.
D/Hai/159(10)	Old Military Grazing Ground, Haifa.	146	Ownership disputed. Cut up by Town Planning Scheme.
D/Hai/164	Safet Siyah, Haifa.	180	Uncultivable land.
D/Hai/167	Kbleileh, Haifa.	225	Ownership disputed.
D/Hai/216	Shefa 'Amr	80	⅓ share of a number of scattered parcels.
LD/61	Shefa 'Amr	1,677	To be used as Forest Reserve.
D/Hai/271	'Ein el Faraj — Tira.	41	Rocky land.
D/Hai/305	Ras Wadi Abdullah, Tira.	71	Ownership disputed. Earmarked for Exchange.
D/Hai/306	Ras Wadi Abdullah, Tira.	14	Ownership disputed.
D/Hai/307	Farsh en Nahli — Tira.	36	Rocky land.
SD/23/1	Na'amin River Marshes.	4,522	Now under Land Settlement. Boundaries undetermined.
	Miscellaneous building sites and scattered parcels.	205	The ownership of a number of parcels is disputed.
Jaffa Sub-District:			
	Miscellaneous building sites		
Jenin Sub-District:			
D/Jen/9	El Barid		Ownership disputed.
Jericho Sub-District:			
D/Jek/81	En Nabi Musa	48,318	Salt lands adjoining the Dead Sea. Boundaries disputed.
D/Jem/96	Qaryat Inab	230	Uncultivable land.
D/Jem/110	Deir esh Sheikh	448	Uncultivable land adjoining Forest Reserve. Claimed as State Domain.
D/Jem/112	Deir esh Sheikh	279	— do —
D/Jem/135	Deir esh Sheikh	37	— do —
	Miscellaneous building sites, etc.	48	

38. STATE DOMAIN.

State Domain No.	Town or Village	Area Dunums.	Remarks.
Nazareth Sub-District:			
D/Naz/18	Nazareth, Ard el Majoud		Part used as a Stone Quarry.
Ramle Sub-District:			
	Miscellaneous plots		
Safad Sub-District:			
D/Saf/113	Esh Shuna	208	Ownership disputed.
	Miscellaneous plots	16	
Tiberias Sub-District:			
D/Tib/32	Kafr Sabt	222	Ownership disputed.
D/Tib/34	Mughar	115	Uncultivable land adjoining a Forest Reserve. Claimed as State Domain.
D/Tib/—	Tiberias	598	Some 94 scattered parcels. Now under Land Settlement.
Tulkarm Sub-District:			
D/Tul/12	El Wa'ara — Tulkarm	37	Earmarked for public purposes.
D/Tul/14 to 22	Kafr Saba	18	9 small parcels. Now under Land Settlement. Redemption by former owner under consideration.
D/Tul/24	Deir el Ghusun	79	Ownership disputed.
D/Tul/28	Deir el Ghusun	264	Ownership disputed.
D/Tul/60	Basset Qazaza — Zeita	177	Swamp. Ownership disputed.
D/Tul/109	Ard Tushan — Kafr Jammal	37	Uncultivable land.
D/Tul/112	Tulkarm	23	Uncultivable land.
	Miscellaneous plots.	3	
		67,328	

MEMORANDA BY THE GOVERNMENT OF PALESTINE.

38. STATE DOMAIN.

APPENDIX IX.

HAIFA HARBOUR (RECLAIMED AREA) ESTATE.

By the construction of the Harbour at Haifa a considerable area of land was reclaimed from the sea and this, together with adjacent Government owned property, now forms the Haifa Harbour (Reclaimed Area) Estate which extends in all to about six hundred dunums.

The requirements of the Harbour and the provision of adequate clearance and transit facilities were considered to be of paramount importance; suitable areas were allocated for these purposes and are now under the control of the Department of Customs, Excise and Trade and the Palestine Railways, respectively. There then remained an area of some one hundred and thirty dunums immediately available for general and commercial development.

A town planning parcellation scheme, in which the principal considerations were the amenities of the port and town of Haifa, provided a zone for warehouses and stores, a central square in which are to be situated the new passenger railway station and the General Post Office, and a thirty metre wide shopping thoroughfare which traverses the south side of the Estate. From the Kingsway there are at present two main approaches to the Harbour. Another road provides access to the warehouse zone.

Certain plots are set aside for municipal purposes, one being for a vegetable and milk market, while at the eastern entrance to the harbour a Sailors' Home has been constructed by the British Sailors' Society.

Towards the end of 1934, twenty-three plots in the warehouse zone, all but one of which have facilities for railway sidings, with a total area of 21 dunums 425 square metres, were offered for lease by auction. The lease offered was for a term of 75 years, at the expiry of which the building would revert to Government. The accepted bids totalled £P.7,410 per annum, equivalent to an average rent of about 350 mils per square metre per annum. The remaining plots in the warehouse zone, extending to about 10 dunums, were retained.

A second auction was held in June, 1935, at which 47 plots were offered, with a total area of about 19 dunums. These plots were intended principally for the erection of shop and office buildings. The lease was for a similar term to that of the warehouse plots. All the plots offered were taken up, with the exception of a site which was reserved for the erection of an hotel. The accepted bids totalled £P.22,647 per annum or an average of about £P.1.445 mils per square metre per annum.

It was considered desirable that the buildings fronting on Kingsway should have a uniform facade, and the lessees were accordingly required to adhere to a design which has been prepared on behalf of Government by Mr. A. Clifford Holliday, M. Arch., F.R.I.B.A. It is anticipated that, when the buildings are completed and occupied, Haifa will have a shopping street inferior to none in the Near East.

The height of shop and office buildings with a frontage to Kingsway is generally 25 metres, and along Harbour Street 18.75 metres, while the maximum height of buildings in the warehouse zone is 17.50 metres.

Fifteen of the warehouse buildings have been completed and others are nearing completion. Since the date of the last auction development on the Estate has proceeded rapidly and building is in progress on the majority of the shop and office sites and on the new railway station.

It is anticipated that, by the middle of 1937, three floors of the buildings on all the shop and office sites which have been leased will be erected while many will be completed up to the maximum permissible height.

A water supply has been provided and the sewerage and drainage systems have been completed. The street lighting of Kingsway is in operation, whilst a scheme for the lighting of the rest of the leased area is in preparation.

There is still a further area to the west of Plumer Square which will eventually be laid out for development and leased to the public but the date when this will be available is dependent upon the completion of the Harbour.

10.02

FOR OFFICIAL USE ONLY.

MEMORANDA

PREPARED BY

THE GOVERNMENT OF PALESTINE

FOR THE USE OF

THE PALESTINE ROYAL COMMISSION

VOLUME 2

PRINTED AT THE GOVERNMENT PRINTING PRESS, JERUSALEM.

TABLE OF CONTENTS

Serial No.	TITLE	Page
1C	Memorandum on immigration legislation and system of control.	1
2C	Determination of Labour Schedules, with a brief account of each quota since 1929 and (so far as the records show) of the considerations on which the estimate of economic absorptive capacity on each occasion was based.	7
3C	Development of forestry.	16
4C	Relative contributions of Arabs and Jews to revenue and benefits derived by each race from expenditure.	20
5C	Note on the system of determining changes in the Customs Tariff with some account of the more important recent changes, and their effect on the interests of the different races.	25
6C	Note on 'normal' revenue and expenditure with special reference to the possibilities of increasing the expenditure on 'social' services.	39
7C	Colonial Development Fund.	50

3 C. DEVELOPMENT OF FORESTRY.

MEMORANDUM No. 3 C.
DEVELOPMENT OF FORESTRY.

A. HISTORICAL.

The forestry activities of the Government up to 1925 were summarised as follows in Sir Herbert Samuel's Report on the Administration of Palestine, 1920-1925:—

"With respect to afforestation, the work of the Department has been severely restricted by the inadequacy of its budget, but it has demarcated certain uncultivated State lands as protected forest areas; it has fostered regrowth from the stumps still existing in the destroyed forests, has planted about a million trees, and, through the nurseries it maintains, has facilitated plantation by others. Altogether four to five million timber and fruit trees have been planted in these years in Palestine. The Department has conducted successful experiments also in the planting of grasses and trees on sand dunes — a matter of great importance, for the line of dunes along the coast is slowly advancing inland; it has already overwhelmed a considerable area of cultivated land, and, unless stopped by planting, will certainly prove fatal to the adjoining cultivation."

2.—The Forestry Section of the Department of Agriculture was established in 1920 with one qualified forest officer who was also Deputy Director of the Department. At first its chief function was the protection, by a system of licensing, of valuable trees in private properties which in the circumstances of the time were specially liable to be prematurely felled for fuel. It soon became evident that the protection of the remaining forest land in the country was of even greater importance. The demand for agricultural land had become intensified by the fact that large areas of steeply sloping ground had been rendered useless by soil erosion. This demand for new land had resulted in the destruction of forest vegetation, except on small plots of remote and rocky ground. An Ordinance was passed in 1926, authorising the establishment of forest reserves, to include uncultivated land which was not clearly private property. It was intended that investigation by Land Settlement Officers should, within a few years, clear up all questions of title, whereafter such land as was proved to be private property was to be excluded from the reserves. The remainder was then to be declared State Forest and brought under proper management.

3.—By 1935, 739 square kilometres of forest reserve had been declared. Unfortunately, the difficulties encountered by Land Settlement Officers delayed the termination of the temporary arrangement referred to in the last paragraph.

4.—The condition of both soil and vegetation in the forest reserves is most unsatisfactory, since the reservation did not attempt to terminate the over-grazing and over-cutting, which had reduced them to their desolate state. As a result, though the rapid clearing and cultivation of the land has been checked, the vegetation in many cases shows no improvement. It has not been found possible to check the demands of right-holders for grazing and forest produce far in excess of the growth capacity of the land.

5.—Very little silvicultural information was available for the first afforestation operations, which were therefore mainly of an experimental nature. Owing to the local importance of sand-fixation, the first plantations were, for the most part, established on the sand dunes. Of an approximate total of 500,000 dunums of sand dunes, 44,000 dunums have been declared forest reserves, of which 12,000 dunums, at Acre, are now being alienated to private interests. In all, 3,000 dunums of sand dunes were planted. Attention was then turned to the hills, and 13,000 dunums of plantations have been established, mainly near Nazareth and Hebron. In addition to the local species, many varieties of exotics have been tried but with no striking success, the local pines remaining the standard plantation trees. Nursery technique has improved, and the annual production of plants averages about 1,200,000, of which some 200,000 are issued annually gratis to institutions and private individuals.

6.—It was not until 1930 that a Horticultural Section was set up in the Department of Agriculture, and, until that date, the Forestry Section was forced to include the care of fruit trees in its nurseries and operations. As a result, the propagation of the hardier fruit trees, and even of ornamental shrubs, is usually regarded locally as falling within the province of forestry.

7.—The progress of forestry was undoubtedly retarded by the fact that, until 1929, the only qualified forest officer was overwhelmed with agricultural administration, while his staff had received no training in the technical side of their duties. Much work was, however, done in such routine matters as the issue of licences for private properties and the prevention of encroachment, while the nursery staff and the men engaged in plantation work acquired a certain degree of technical knowledge.

8.—In 1929, a qualified Palestinian officer was added to the Forest Service, but he was kept busy with administrative work and was consequently unable to give any training to the staff, many of whom were uneducated and even illiterate.

9.—By 1933, the unsatisfactory condition of much of the hill country of Palestine had aroused general interest, and the need for re-afforestation was widely admitted. It was by then agreed:—

(a) that the area of forest was seriously deficient;

(b) that the condition of the existing forests was extremely bad;

(c) that in the hill country agriculture and rural life were adversely affected by the entire lack of good forests;

(d) that the country was suffering seriously from soil erosion, waste of water, and lack of forest produce;

(e) that it was necessary to embark without delay on a vigorous policy of afforestation.

10.—The aims towards which a forest policy must be directed were summarised as follows:—

(a) To re-afforest hilly and waste lands in order to conserve water supplies, to prevent

MEMORANDA BY THE GOVERNMENT OF PALESTINE.

3 C. DEVELOPMENT OF FORESTRY.

soil erosion and denudation, and to afford shelter and protection to adjoining crops and orchards;

(b) to curtail the encroachment of sand dunes; and

(c) to bring into economic use land not suited to agriculture and horticulture by the production of timber, fuel and other forest products.

11.—In addition, it was clear that the Forestry Service would be expected to provide fodder in large quantities and to encourage the growth of hardy fruit trees. In view of the importance of the measures to be taken, it was resolved to establish a separate Department of Forests and to increase the Palestinian staff by the addition of two fully qualified officers.

12.—The Department, which was officially formed on April 1st, 1936, consists of 4 qualified officers who are members of the Colonial Forest Service, 20 junior classified officers, and 58 other ranks. A copy of the first year's estimates as originally proposed is attached as an Appendix to this memorandum.

B. THE NEED FOR AFFORESTATION.

13.—The natural cover of the hills of Palestine was originally a forest which varied in height and composition with the various climatic zones of the country. The demands of the early population for agricultural land were met by the gradual clearing of the natural vegetation. There is reason to believe that when man was, in ancient days, less completely master of his environment, his tendency was to cultivate only the land nearest to his village, and to graze his animals in the close vicinity. The wild beasts, and in troublous times the bandits and cattle thieves, thus befriended the forests, and by concentrating the cultivation, forced the peasants to perfect the art of terracing to make the most of their village areas. Later, however, wide disturbances and the decay of agriculture allowed the terraces to fall into disrepair, and when the population began to increase again, agriculture was more extensive and less skilful. The forest and scrub growth was cleared and slopes were cultivated without terraces; as soon as an area had been denuded of soil by this process, it was abandoned, and another plot cleaned, cultivated and finally ruined.

14.—Under the conditions obtaining in Palestine, planned rural development would permit the cultivation of certain areas, while, quite apart from the need for a sustained supply of forest produce, other areas would be maintained as forests. The latter would include:—

(a) Steep slopes where clearing would expose the soil to erosion, to the detriment of the slope itself and the lands below.

(b) Catchment areas of rivers and important water supplies. The maintenance of the bed of a stream is of great importance, while erosion at the sources leads to flooding, destruction of bridges and other works, scouring of riverside fields, silting and consequent shifting of the bed in the lower reaches, silting of reservoirs, and general dislocation of the ordered life of the valley.

(c) Sand dunes and other exposed areas of light soil where the action of wind may imitate the damage done by water on steep slopes.

15.—All these considerations have been neglected in Palestine, with the result that soil and water have been wasted and what were fertile slopes have become rocky and barren. The damage which has been done cannot soon be repaired, but further deterioration can be prevented and a gradual improvement maintained by the acquisition, afforestation and management of considerable areas, mostly in the hills.

16.—The afforestation of slopes and catchment areas would result in the checking of erosion and the accumulation of soil, the lessening of floods and the improvement of summer springs. In consequence, the surface of the valley, which is now in comparatively rapid movement, would be allowed to weather and consolidate, a much greater percentage would be cultivable, damage done to bridges, roads and railways would be minimised, and a larger population supported in greater comfort.

17.—The afforestation of the slopes would be accompanied by increased employment and production in the hill country. While a few plots of cultivation would have to be taken over, and larger areas of ruined grazing land afforested, the actual formation, tending and management of the plantations would afford a great deal of employment. Further, provision could be made for the supply of fodder for the better breeds of domestic animals which the Department of Agriculture is endeavouring to introduce in the villages. Forest products of the most essential types would be supplied more cheaply and plentifully for village use.

C. FOREST POLICY UNDER CONSIDERATION.

18.—A report on forest policy has recently been received from the Conservator of Forests, and is under consideration.

19.—After references to past history and the present position, the report describes certain conditions upon which the success of afforestation operations will depend.

(a) *Conditions of Success.*

20.—Technical difficulties of some complexity can be overcome by intelligent methods. But a free hand in all technical matters is considered essential. The afforestation and management of the areas dedicated to forestry should not be subject to any action which would interfere with continuity of management. Rights and servitudes should be settled, valued and terminated.

21.—It must not be expected that land under treatment can be opened to grazing except when managed with that object. Vegetation can be used for producing mutton and milk, or it can be allowed to grow into timber. In Palestine it is impracticable to produce both on one area. Further, on a steep denuded slope where disturbance of any kind retards the desired improvement of vegetation and accumulation of soil, grazing cannot be permitted.

22.—Security of tenure is essential. The land must be held by Government in clear title, and there should be no normal possibility of Government action to alienate forest land or put it to other uses.

23.—The absence of these conditions has frequently militated against success in the past, and should not be allowed to interfere with the larger operations contemplated for the future.

(b) *Afforestation and Closure.*

24.—Afforestation is an urgent necessity, and should be continued on a moderate scale; but a

PALESTINE ROYAL COMMISSION.

3 C. DEVELOPMENT OF FORESTRY.

big increase at the moment is deprecated because the staff is untrained, silvicultural technique needs to be further developed, preliminary survey and classification is required, and the shape, distribution and ownership of the forest reserves are all unsatisfactory.

25.—In addition to the continuance of planting, the closure of considerable areas is recommended, to allow them to rest and to improve what vegetation now exists, as a necessary preliminary to more intensive afforestation.

(c) *Land Settlement.*

26.—An acceleration of land settlement in the areas which need afforestation is strongly urged, as satisfactory forestry is impossible without clear title, and no land should be brought under treatment unless it is State Domain beyond dispute.

(d) *Land Acquisition.*

27.—Out of a total land area of 26,000 square kilometres, some 16,000 square kilometres are described as fit for afforestation or cultivation. It is believed that only about 200 square kilometres will be revealed as "valuable scrub forest and plantations", that no natural high forest exists, and that a further 1,200 square kilometres retains some forest characteristics, but has been ruined by overgrazing, over-cutting and other misuse. Thus of the non-desert area of the country, only 1.25 per cent. is forest, compared with 15 per cent. in Germany which is regarded as normal in this respect. The forest reserves, while totalling 739 square kilometres, are described in the report as "strips and tatters of land", mere relics from which almost every plot of good soil has been picked out and cultivated. Their irregular shape and the length of their boundaries would make protection and management economically impossible. Further they are so weighed down with grazing rights, timber and firewood rights and servitudes, that successful forestry would be out of the question.

28.—The need is reiterated for substantial blocks of land, with reasonably straight boundaries and free from all rights and servitudes, and considerable land acquisitions are shown to be necessary. Additional areas will be needed to straighten out the boundaries of the present forest reserves, and the cultivated plots within the reserves must be taken over. In addition, larger areas where afforestation is needed must be acquired.

(e) *Objects of Management.*

29.—It is emphasised that land under the Department will not be lost to the community, but usefully employed, and that increasing population makes it more important to allocate land to forestry. The areas under management will be classified as Forest Lands, Fodder Lands and Protected Lands.

30.—"Forest Lands" will be divided into three categories:—

(i) Production Forests on the best and most accessible land, supplying timber and firewood to towns, industries and the countryside.

(ii) Village Forests, supplying small forest produce to nearby communities.

(iii) Protection Forests, maintained to prevent erosion and conserve water, mainly on steep slopes and catchment areas.

An approximate estimate of 1,000 square kilometres is given for these Forest Lands.

31.—"Fodder Lands", also estimated at about 1,000 square kilometres, should be protected and managed with due regard to the improvement of the soil and the prevention of erosion, but with the main object of growing fodder, for controlled grazing as long as it is necessary but in due course for the hand-feeding of well-bred stock in the adjacent villages.

32.—"Protected Lands" to the extent of about 250 square kilometres where erosion is a danger, and mainly in the vicinity of the forests, should be terraced, planted with hardy fruit trees, and leased at low rents, with strict upkeep conditions, so conserving soil and water, producing fruit and giving employment.

(f) *Ways and Means.*

33.—The impossibility of benefitting equally every individual and village is mentioned in the report, but the claim is made that the community will profit greatly and that no injustice will be done. The aim indeed should be the benefit of the community as a whole.

34.—The acquisition of land and the extinction of rights is discussed, and the gradual nature of the change emphasised. The area available for grazing has been estimated at 5,000 square kilometres and the improvement of the managed grazing grounds should offset the loss of fodder on the Forest Lands and Protected Lands which must be closed to grazing. "The aim of the whole scheme is the amelioration of the condition of the backward hill country", which will benefit the whole community, and the hill villagers most of all.

(g) *Financial Aspect.*

35.—The cost of the scheme is discussed, and shown to vary with several factors:—

(a) The amount of work undertaken in any financial year.

(b) The total area of land which it is found necessary eventually to control.

(c) The degree of benevolence with which Government decides to treat their tenants in terraced Protected Lands, Grazing Lands and Village Forests. If rents and fees are raised, the net cost of the scheme will be less.

(d) The level at which Government decides to fix timber and fuel prices. This decision will be more remote but most important.

(e) The amount of compensation paid on expropriation of what is at present mainly ruined, almost useless, land.

36.—Several schemes are described to show the probable course of future operations.

37.—The report concludes as follows:—

"It is thus clear that, while it is essential to have a long-term forest land policy, and to approve continuous action towards a considered goal, there will be, by the approval of this policy, no actual commitments in any given year or period. The amounts to be allotted annually to forestry will be the subject of further consideration, but whatever they may be, their expenditure will produce the best possible results only if a long-term policy has previously been approved".

MEMORANDA BY THE GOVERNMENT OF PALESTINE.

3 C. DEVELOPMENT OF FORESTRY.

ENCLOSURE I.

Items	1936/37	DETAILS OF EXPENDITURE	Estimates 1936/37
			£P.
		XIV. DEPARTMENT OF FORESTS.	
		A. Personal Emoluments.	
1	1	Conservator of Forests £P.800—25—1,000	1,000
2		Expatriation Allowance at £P.100 p.a.	100
5	3	**Assistant Conservator of Forests, £P.300—12—420—10—430—15—550	853
6	2	*Forest Surveyors £P.160—8—276	392
7	2	Assistant Forest Surveyors £P.60—6—168	128
8	1	Forest Ranger £P.288—12—360	288
9	4	***Forest Rangers £P.180—8—276	846
10	8	*Forest Rangers £P.60—6—168	1,079
11	48	Forest Guards:	3,240
		30 Mounted at £P.5—7 p.m.	
		18 Unmounted at £P.4—6 p.m.	
12	2	Forest Nursery Superintendents £P.60—6—168	201
15	10	Forest Gardeners at £P.5 to £P.7 p.m.	720
16	1	*Sylvicultural Assistant £P.60—6—168	168
17	8	****Officers of the General Clerical Service.	1,105
18		Stenography Allowance	36
20		Messengers and Cleaners	117
21		Cost of Living Allowance	606
		Total Personal Emoluments	10,879
		B. Other Charges.	
22		Transport and Travelling	4,415
23		Railway Fares and Freight	350
24		Telegrams, Telephones and Postage	180
25		Lighting and Heating	30
26		Uniforms	484
27		Forage	50
28		Upkeep of Library and Records	15
29		Upkeep of Forest Nurseries	2,300
30		Rent of Forest Nurseries	10
31		Demarcation of Forests	180
32		Sylvicultural Research	100
34		Afforestation	10,300
35		Departmental Extraction of Forest Produce	100
36		Grafting of Wild Carob Trees in Forest Reserves.	600
37		Firearms and Ammunition	65
38		Contribution to Imperial Forestry Institute	35
39		Draught Animals, Carts and Harness	5
40		Contingencies	30
		Total Other Charges.	19,249
		Special Expenditure.	
41		Camp Equipment	20
42		Typewriters	120
44		Training of Assistant Conservator of Forests	304
45		Training of Forest Rangers	41
46		Research on Soil Erosion	500
47		Road-side Planting	300
48		Distribution of Olive Suckers	100
50		Grant towards planting the Mount of Olives	1,000
		Total Special Expenditure	2,385
		Total { Personel Emoluments / Other Charges / Special Expenditure }	10,879 / 19,249 / 2,385
		TOTAL DEPARTMENT OF FORESTS	32,513

* Pensionable.
** One only pensionable.
*** Two only pensionable.
**** Four only pensionable.

10.03

PALESTINE ROYAL COMMISSION

MINUTES OF EVIDENCE HEARD AT PUBLIC SESSIONS
(with Index)

Note :—The Memoranda supplied by the Government of Palestine for the use of the Royal Commission are published in a separate volume (Colonial No. 133), price 9s. 0d. net.

Crown Copyright Reserved

LONDON
PRINTED AND PUBLISHED BY HIS MAJESTY'S STATIONERY OFFICE
To be purchased directly from H.M. STATIONERY OFFICE at the following addresses:
Adastral House, Kingsway, London, W.C.2; 120 George Street, Edinburgh 2;
26 York Street, Manchester 1; 1 St. Andrew's Crescent, Cardiff;
80 Chichester Street, Belfast;
or through any bookseller
1937
Price £1 15s. 0d. net

Colonial No. 134

IV

I.

SPEECH BY HIS EXCELLENCY GENERAL SIR ARTHUR WAUCHOPE, G.C.M.G., K.C.B., C.I.E., D.S.O., HIGH COMMISSIONER FOR PALESTINE AND TRANS-JORDAN.

As a general rule, the significant dates in a country's history come to be discerned only in after years. At the time they often pass unnoticed. Now and again, however, an event occurs of such importance that it can be recognized at once as a historical landmark. I feel that the 12th of November, 1936, will stand out as such a date in the history of Palestine. To-day the Royal Commission enters upon its labours.

A Royal Commission is the highest form of inquiry known in the British Empire. It is of its nature impartial, independent and uncontrolled by the Government of the day; its duty is to report on the questions committed to it in any sense that may seem to be just and right. Its responsibilities are vast, and only a body of men of the eminence of those who, at much personal sacrifice, have accepted service on the Palestine Royal Commission could fittingly be called upon to discharge them.

I welcome the Chairman and Members of the Commission and I gladly acknowledge the debt which we owe them for coming to Palestine to undertake this inquiry. No one knows better than I the difficulties of the task which confronts them; but I have every confidence that, with their collective wisdom, wide experience and great authority, they will succeed in pointing the way to a just and equitable solution of the problems which beset this country.

I wish them God speed in their labours; I trust that they will receive every help from all sections of the population so that they may have the advantage of learning at first hand the different aspects of every question in dispute; and I humbly pray and believe that their recommendations may provide the foundation for lasting peace and contentment in this land.

II.

SPEECH BY THE RIGHT HONOURABLE EARL PEEL, G.C.S.I., G.B.E.

On behalf of my colleagues and myself, may I thank Your Excellency very warmly for the most kind words with which you have received us ? May we also thank all those who have come here to-day to welcome us at the outset of our enquiry ? May I lay stress upon those words " the outset of our enquiry " ? We were most anxious to begin our task here in Palestine with minds as free as possible from any prepossession and from all preconceived ideas. We bring, I believe, each of us some contribution of experience derived from one sphere or another of public life : but we were determined that, as regards views and judgments on the affairs of Palestine, we should apply minds fresh and impartial to the problems before us. We therefore heard no evidence before we left London and our only meeting was devoted to discussions of procedure and other points of detail. When our departure from London was delayed, we again considered this question, but in spite of the loss of time we came again to the same conclusion.

But we have been by no means inactive. We were appointed by His Majesty the King as long ago as August last. We have had, therefore, time to acquire some knowledge of the elementary facts of the situation in Palestine and of the machinery of government and of policies on which we may expect to hear evidence. The Government of Palestine and its officers have been of the greatest possible assistance in these requirements. They have answered very fully our rather onerous requests for facts and figures, and we should like to express, through Your Excellency, our keen sense of gratitude to your officers for the fullness and lucidity of the papers with which we have been supplied and for the figures, statistics and descriptions of administrative detail which we have studied. They have saved us an immense amount of labour and have lightened the burden of our enquiry. They have given us a framework which makes it far more easy for us to appreciate the evidence which will be laid before us.

Let me refer to one point of procedure. The question of whether we should hold our sittings in public or in private has been before us. We have decided that in an enquiry of this importance it would be wiser to hold our sittings as far as possible in public, but we recognize that there may be witnesses whom it would be proper to hear in private and that, in many cases, the witnesses themselves may prefer to give their evidence or part of their evidence in a similar manner.

You have heard the terms of reference approved by His Majesty. We are " to ascertain the underlying causes of the disturbances which broke out in Palestine in the middle of April." You will note the words " underlying causes." It does not appear to be necessary, therefore, to enquire into the detailed course of events in the last six or seven months. If there are claims and counter-claims arising out of these events, they are matters for the Courts or for the Administration, but we have to deal, I believe, with wider issues.

Official Reports and Memoranda, Part IV

PALESTINE ROYAL COMMISSION

Notes of Evidence taken on Tuesday, 24th November, 1936

SEVENTH MEETING (Public)

Present:

The Rt. Hon. Earl PEEL, G.C.S.I., G.B.E. *(Chairman).*

The Rt. Hon. Sir HORACE GEORGE MONTAGU RUMBOLD, Bt., G.C.B., G.C.M.G., M.V.O. *(Vice-Chairman).*
Sir EGBERT LAURIE LUCAS HAMMOND, K.C.S.I., C.B.E.

Sir WILLIAM MORRIS CARTER, C.B.E.
Sir HAROLD MORRIS, M.B.E., K.C.
Professor REGINALD COUPLAND, C.I.E.

Mr. J. M. MARTIN *(Secretary).*

In Attendance:

Mr. P. G. HEATHCOAT-AMORY.

Witnesses:

Mr. D. G. HARRIS, C.S.I., C.I.E., Irrigation Adviser (Commissioner on Special Duty).
Colonel F. J. SALMON, M.C., Commissioner for Lands and Surveys.

Mr. L. Y. ANDREWS, O.B.E., Development Officer (Assistant Commissioner on Special Duty).
Mr. M. C. BENNETT, Assistant Director, Department of Lands and Surveys.

Evidence of Mr. D. G. HARRIS, C.S.I., C.I.E., Colonel F. J. SALMON, M.C., Mr. L. Y. ANDREWS, O.B.E., and Mr. M. C. BENNETT.

338. *Chairman:* We were going to consider certain questions connected with the land and we have the benefit of the advice of four witnesses. Perhaps you will kindly give your names and positions for the purpose of the note?—My name is D. G. Harris, and I am Irrigation Adviser.—My name is L. Andrews, and I am the Development Officer.—My name is F. J. Salmon, Commissioner for Lands and Survey.—My name is M. C. Bennett, and I am an Assistant Director in the Department of Lands and Surveys.

339. I wish to ask a few general questions first. Shall I ask them from you, Colonel Salmon?— *(Colonel Salmon):* If you please.

340. I have here a paper supplied by the Palestine Government which gives the area and ownership by the rural property tax categories on the 1st April, 1935. There are a few general questions I want to ask on that. You give there the total area of cultivable land which you work out at 7,097,000 dunums —I am leaving out the hundreds for the moment. The other figure is what is called category 16 (forests and uncultivable land), 6,417,000 dunums, and then with roads you get a total of 13,583,000 dunums. You follow me so far?—Yes.

341. Do those figures include the Beersheba sub-district as well?—That is excluded in those figures.

342. That is excluded both as regards cultivable and uncultivable land?—Yes.

343. Therefore just for the moment we are dealing with the land of Palestine less——?—Less the Beersheba sub-district, Huleh and urban areas.

344. That is quite clear?—Yes.

345. You give in this paper the area owned by Arabs, Jews, state domain and Germans. May I bring you for a moment to the column for state domain and villages. The total there for cultivable land is 93,000 dunums and, including roads and forests and uncultivable land, 179,758 dunums. Does that represent the whole of the state domain land?—Not the whole of the state domain.

346. It is very important that we should ascertain what is the total land which the state can dispose of as its own. Is that figure of 179,000 complete?—Mr. Bennett worked out those figures and he got them from the rural property tax returns.

347. The rural property tax returns are for the purpose of taxation. I am talking of state land. That is not taxed, is it?—No, unless leased.

348. I want to know whether the Commission can rely upon this figure of 179,000 as being a complete statement of all the state domain land?— *(Mr. Bennett):* No, Sir. I would rather not use this as a statement of all state domain land, because it only applies to what we obtained from the rural property tax records.

349. Then can you tell me what is your figure for the state domain lands?—We estimate that we have 1,100,000 dunums approximately of state domain land.

350. What relation does that figure of 1,100,000 bear to this figure of 179,000 state domain land? —This, as you see, includes also roads and various other lands, such as wadis.

351. I see that, but I am much more interested in what is excluded than what is included, because it is far larger?—We estimate that the approximate area of known state domain is 1,100,000 dunums, but this is being constantly extended by the fact that at land settlement we ascertain additional state domain of which we have no prior knowledge.

352. Will you explain that statement? I do not quite understand it. It is very fortunate to discover things you did not know you had, but it is rather remarkable. How does that come about? — *(Colonel Salmon):* At present there are, for instance, big areas down the coast, of sand dunes. We think, or we did think, most of that was state domain. When the Settlement Officer comes to make his decisions there are many claims. Very often these claims are substantiated and we find the area is not state domain, but private, so we do not know how much of these sand dunes and how much of the other areas which we thought were state domain will be finally settled as such.

353. Are these mainly the sand dunes?—Mainly the sand dunes, but there are other areas.

354. The 1,100,000 includes the 179,000, does it not?—*(Mr. Bennett):* Yes.

355. It does include it?—The 179,758 dunums is included in the 1,100,000.

356. As I thought. Then why was this particular figure of 179,000 as it were cut out and shown as being state domain? Why did it get this preference, as it were?—Because this statement was obtained from the rural property tax records for a certain purpose. We were not then trying to get the total area of state domain. We were trying to divide an area which appears in certain records among certain people.

357. Then we will go a little more fully later into what that figure of 1,100,000 state domain is.

[1936.] Mr. D. G. HARRIS, C.S.I., C.I.E., Colonel F. J. [Continued.
SALMON, M.C., Mr. L. Y. ANDREWS, O.B.E., and Mr. M. C. BENNETT.

you say it is disputable and largely an ... Is that so?—Yes. ...this paper you have classified the land ... ories?—Yes. ...you have given the respective area in ... category. We are talking now of ...able land owned by Arabs, Jews, ... the state?—Yes. ... in the first category the holdings of ... Jews are approximately equal. That is ... that is so, that is citrus. ... In the next category the Arabs have ... and nobody else has anything?— ... in Acre sub-district. ... that is classified as No. 2?—Yes. ...you tell me how this very elaborate ... is arrived at? It is divided into 16 ... rather 15, is it not, because that in ... ribed generally as uncultivable?—Yes. It ... as you know, that the old forms of ... were unsuitable and, after considerable in... ... and consideration, it was decided to ... what is called a land tax, though perhaps ... strictly a land tax, in place of both the ... in rural areas. We decided that we should ... the land into categories and eventually ... fixed tax on each category. The cate... ... determined taking them down the list ... citrus, No. 2 citrus Acre sub-district—— ... do not think you need go through the whole ... you can refer probably to a paper show... ... names. My question was simply as to ... by which it was done, the machinery ... it was carried out?—How it was actually ... the ground? ... you have 16 categories. My question ... you do it, who did it?—I suppose ... I did. ... that is a very good answer. Then nobody ... us better than you can how you did it? ... went round to each village with the map ... had already been prepared by the Survey ... ment, the map showing on it the boundaries ... village and the various names of localities ... the village. ... Sir Laurie Hammond: Can we have a look ... of those maps? (Map produced.)—This is a ... of Bir Zeit, a hill village. ... What is the scale?—One to 10,000. ... Chairman: What is this?—This is the fiscal ... map, 1/10,000 scale, which we were given ... Survey Department before we went out on ... the land to inspect. It had previously been ... up into localities and on it was shown the ... of the land; as to whether it was planted or ... ted; whether it was cultivable or not cul-

... That is done by the Survey Department?— ... (Salmon): The surveyor in the field had to ... It was his estimation of how much culti... ... there was. ... Can a surveyor judge whether land is cul... ... uncultivable? Anyhow he did it, he did ... (Mr. Bennett): He did his best and we ... can. ... You believe he can?—Yes. Each planta... ... divided up separately to show what it con-

... Laurie Hammond: What do you mean ... plantation "exactly?—Land planted with ...

... You refer to fruit trees when you say " plan... ... Yes. Localities are divided up to show ... they are planted with olives and/or vines ... they may be planted with. Against ... shown the percentage of trees within each ... percentage, being based on a schedule ob... ... the time from the Department of Agri... ... and agreed with them to show what can

be regarded as 100 per cent. trees. For instance, in the case of olives 100 per cent. trees was 13 trees per dunum.

375. *Chairman*: That is the best that is possible? —That is the best possible.

376. In the circumstances?—In respect of each area which was planted with olives this percentage of trees was estimated by measurement and by counting the number of trees approximately to the dunum. The result is shown as a percentage in relation to 100 per cent. In this particular area it shows olives 90 per cent. In places where trees were under 20 per cent. they were ignored; that is to say, in the case of olives if there were only two trees per dunum or something like that, they were ignored. Having got to the village with this map we checked in certain cases the areas. Of course, we could not check the whole. That was done and we accepted it as the general rule, checking only in certain instances just to satisfy ourselves. Having got to the village we then catechised the cultivators at a meeting in the village in regard to the nature of their lands to arrive principally at the ground crop category of their areas, based all the time on their locality names, which they all know well. We would obtain from them the general opinion of their own properties by this questioning, to ascertain which was the best area in their village for ordinary cereal growing and by that means we would find which localities were of a similar category, which were the best, which the second best, the third best, fourth best and so on, thereby placing the cereal land in the categories shown on the list.

377. We talk about localities, which is rather a large name. Those are quite small areas, are they not?—I forget offhand.

378. What is the area of it?—About 2,000 dunums.

379. Each of these patches?—The localities vary in size enormously, but they might be 200 dunums.

380. I only want to get the order of magnitude? —About 200 dunums, but they vary enormously. We simply took the village by itself and arrived at the various grades of land in it for ground crop purposes. Then of course we had our own ideas as to the categories throughout the country, starting at the best downward. We then went to the next village and did the same there and found out how the one village compared with the other in the cultivators' own estimation and in ours. We classified them then in their categories by comparison with the other lands in the country, thereby arriving at the category of this particular village's best land, scaling it down in accordance with the crop yields into the lower categories.

381. Have you done the whole of the rural area in this way?—The whole of the country. In the case of the Jewish settlements, in practically all cases, I think we can say all, we consulted the organisation which happened to be in charge of that particular settlement, but otherwise we catechised the people on the spot.

382. How long did that take, roughly?—From 1928 to 1935.

383. Six or seven years, and of course, revisions are going on?—We do not think that the category changes of land under ground crops. Plantations are the only things that change and we revise them by an adjustment. In 1934, a revision was carried out of citrus cultivation.

384. All these figures for the different classifications and categories of land owned by Arabs, Jews, Germans and so on, were they compiled at the time this survey was going on?—No. That particular schedule was compiled in great haste for the High Commissioner and was actually compiled from information obtained over the telephone from district authorities and they were not given a very fair opportunity of producing an accurate statement. They confirmed it as well as they could afterwards

[Original copy is very poor quality.]

PALESTINE ROYAL COMMISSION

24 November, 1936.] Mr. D. G. HARRIS, C.S.I., C.I$_{\cdot}$E., Colonel F. J. SALMON, M.C., Mr. L. Y. ANDREWS, O.B.E., and Mr. M. C. BENNETT. [*Continued.*

in writing, but it was all done very quickly. They were really endeavouring to obtain from the distribution lists the area and the categories owned by Jews, to do which they went through the distribution lists and looked for Jewish names and put these parcels in their various categories and then added up the area.

385. *Sir Morris Carter*: When was this compiled?—It was done comparatively recently, probably about August.

386. *Sir Laurie Hammond*: This map does not represent any land settlement operations? It was done for fiscal purposes?—Yes, for fiscal purposes only.

387. Then questions of ownership or tenancy do not come in?—No, except boundaries. Wherever possible when it goes to settlement they endeavour to adhere to these boundaries which show the boundaries of land of the same category.

388. *Chairman*: This list must be regarded as not strictly accurate. You must allow a certain discount on it?—I should not like to guarantee it as absolutely accurate.

389. There is another paper I want to ask you about—this memorandum of land purchased by Jews from non-Jews from 1920 to the 31st August, 1936. That gives a total of 682,800 odd dunums purchased between 1920 and 1936 and the value of the purchase price is about £7,731,000. Have you an accurate record of all those purchases and sales of land and the prices paid for them during those years? Are they estimates or are they accurate information supplied by purchasers or sellers?—(*Colonel Salmon*): They come from the Land Registry and are reasonably accurate. The value has to be estimated.

390. The 7¾ millions is an estimate?—That is an estimate.

391. According to what you know in different districts is roughly the price?—When you transfer a piece of land you have to give your statement of the value and the transfer fees are charged on the sale price, but the valuation can be varied by the Land Registry official if he thinks you have been under-estimating.

392. Then this should be the value put on it by the Land Registry official, not the actual money paid?—That is so—agreed by the Land Registry official.

393. *Chairman*: As corrected possibly by the value put on it by the purchasers?—I think it is usually the value of the purchaser puts on it as the sale price, but it is checked by the Land Registry officer and if he sees any reason to do so he alters it.

394. These figures showing the land purchased by Jews from non-Jews, are they ascertained by the names?—By the names.

395. And that you think is a correct figure for the actual area, although the money may be to some extent an estimate, is that so?—There may be a few slight errors where transactions have taken place on an old title deed and there has not been a re-survey.

396. There is a discrepancy, it may be unimportant, as to the land held by the Jews. In the paper showing the ownership of land on the 1st April, 1935, by rural property tax categories it amounted to 1,208,000 dunums?—(*Mr. Bennett*): Yes.

397. Here the figure is—dunums of land purchased by Jews from non-Jews 682,800 and the Government note says that the land in possession of Jews prior to the date of Occupation was 650,000 dunums?—Yes.

398. If you add those two figures together, they are substantially more than the figure given in the list of ownership by property tax categories?—Yes. I think I can explain that. The area in Jewish ownership extracted from the rural property tax lists is 1,208,000 dunums and then there are areas in urban areas which are owned by Jews to be added to that.

399. It is the land owned by Jews in urban areas that makes the difference, is it?—Yes, and purchases in the Beersheba district up to a certain date.

400. We were leaving out Beersheba because we understood that all these figures were less the Beersheba figures?—No, the Land Registry figure includes Beersheba. There are also other areas which we have to add to that in order to bring it up to the same date, that is to say, this statement is up to 1st April, 1935, and therefore we have to add purchases from 1st April, 1935, to the end of the year. When we have done all that, we get an area of 1,308,000 dunums, which does not quite coincide with the Land Registry figure for Jewish acquisitions, which is 1,317,000 dunums up to the end of 1935.

401. Anyhow, what is the last figure you have got?—The Land Registry figure, which we believe is the most reliable, is 1,317,000 dunums up to the end of 1935 or 1,333,000 dunums at 31st August, 1936.

402. *Sir Morris Carter*: Could you say what amount of land in Beersheba is included in this total area?—36,971 dunums.

403. *Sir Laurie Hammond*: That is land purchased by Jews in Beersheba?—Purchased in Beersheba District up to 31st December, 1935.

404. *Sir Morris Carter*: And that, of course, does not include land on which they have got options or contracts?—No, we know nothing about that.

405. *Sir Laurie Hammond*: That is land for which the purchase money has been paid?—That is their own arrangement, of course.

406. Which is registered?—Which is registered.

407. And for which the deed of sale has been registered in your Registry?—Yes.

408. *Chairman*: There is one point which applies to the rest of the problem and upon which I would like your view, this question of subsistence areas. We have heard a good deal about these subsistence areas and how much land it takes for a man to live upon or make a living. Do you attach any importance, or much importance, to these figures of subsistence areas? Can you get an accurate figure?—No, we certainly cannot. (*Colonel Salmon*): Not so far at any rate. (*Mr. Bennett*): We have carried out, or tried to carry out, an investigation during the summer based on the Rural Property Tax and I think Mr. Harris is probably in a better position than I am to say something about that, beyond the fact that we in our office actually made the sort by entering up the details from our Rural Property Tax records on to cards so that they could be sorted to ascertain what might be the average holding in the country. Those figures were then passed to the Statistical Department and they have been working on them ever since and, in fact, they still are, but I think there are certain figures which Mr. Harris has at the moment and which he would probably give you better than I can.

409. Would you like to answer that rather difficult question, Mr. Harris?—(*Mr. Harris*): The main difficulty which arises in dealing with subsistence areas is to determine to what extent a man is living on his holding. The investigation, which was made village by village and which covered rather more than one-third of Palestine, showed that about 35 per cent. of the holdings in Palestine are under five dunums in extent. It is perfectly certain that no one can live on that area and that consequently a very large proportion of the rural population of Palestine is actually doing something else besides agriculture. In these particular cases it would appear that the main occupation is non-agricultural. If, however, one excludes all holdings of five dunums and less, so as not to vitiate the averages, and if one also excludes all holdings

[*November*, 1936.] Mr. D. G. HARRIS, C.S.I., C.I.E., Colonel F. J. SALMON, M.C., Mr. L. Y. ANDREWS, O.B.E., and Mr. M. C. BENNETT. [*Continued.*

... dunums, that is to say, all the larger ... which there are not very many, the ... area of cultivable land, in the holdings be- ... five dunums and 500 dunums in extent, is ... dunums.
... That is a fact?—It is a fact as regards the ... which we have tested. I am afraid there ... an uncertain factor, namely, that the sort was ... by villages. That is to say, if a man owns ... plots of land in a certain village, the five ... have been added together and the total of ... five plots taken as his holding. It is possible ... he may also hold land in another village, ... it has been impossible in the time available ... to take this point into consideration. To do that, ... would require a proper agricultural census. In ... respects, the figure is reasonably reliable, ... having been derived from a plot to plot sort of ... village.
411. Having arrived at that figure of an average ... 33 dunums, what inferences can you draw from ... it?—I think the only inference is that a very large ... number of the agricultural population have a sub- ... sidiary means of subsistence, since this area of ... 33 dunums does not agree with our experience of ... what is necessary for a man to live on if he is ... doing nothing but agriculture.
412. And this figure of 33 dunums is only an ... average covering the five different classes of land? ... covering the whole cultivable land.
413. So that it would not appear that it is a ... very helpful figure as regards ascertaining what ... would be the minimum necessary for a man to ... obtain a living on in the different classes of land? ... —No. We have got figures in rather more detail. ... If one takes categories 1 to 3, which comprise citrus ... and bananas, and categories 5 to 8, which are ... mostly fruit plantations, the average holding comes ... out at about 19 dunums. If you take all the ... categories together, cultivable and uncultivable, it ... comes to 43 dunums, so those are really what one ... might call the two limits.
414. It would appear to be rather difficult to ... found any practical conclusion upon those figures?— ... I think it is quite impossible to found any practical ... conclusion on it.
415. The object, I presume, was to try and draw ... some inference as to how many persons you could ... settle on certain areas of land?—Yes, but I do not ... think the figures we have got have given us any ... information on that point. Where we are very ... handicapped at the moment is by the fact that the ... last Census, which took place in 1931, is altogether ... out of date. Things have changed greatly since ... then. At that time there was an occupational ... census, which showed how many agriculturists had ... other means of livelihood, but owing to the develop- ... ment which has taken place since then one cannot ... apply those figures to the present time. We are ... suffering very badly from the need of a new Census.
416. I suppose, in pursuit of the ideal figure, ... you did gain valuable information as to the areas ... in which different people were living and you drew ... the inference that a good many people must be ... living a double life, as it were, both subsistence from ... the land and from some other occupation?—Yes.
417. That was of value I take it?—Yes.
418. You said that the first four or five categories ... roughly represented fruit growing?—I said one to ... eight.
419. And from eight onwards they represent ... roughly cereals?—Yes; I would mention again that ... this figure of 33 dunums represents holdings in a ... single village only and that if you included the ... land which a man may hold in other villages you ... might get a somewhat larger area. I do not think, ... however, that it would materially affect the figure.
420. I wanted to ask one more general question— ... I do not know to which of you gentlemen I should ... address it, perhaps to none. I do not know whether ... it is possible for you to give us merely an outline of what has been done or aimed at being done under Article 6 of the Mandate? You know the words very well, " to encourage in co-operation with the Jewish Agency close settlement by Jews on the land, including state lands and waste lands not required for public purposes." Would it be possible for you to give an outline of the policy on that?—I think so. Generally speaking, the whole policy of the Government of Palestine has been directed towards facilitating close settlement, although it may not always have involved actual agricultural work. I might instance the construction of roads by Government and the help given towards the construction of roads by local agency in rural areas, and in the citrus belt. There has also been a great deal of swamp reclamation, which has been undertaken largely in the interest of the health of the areas in which close settlement is in progress. There is, for example, the Birkat Ramadan drainage scheme, which you visited, and the Wadi Rubin drainage scheme below Jaffa. A great deal of swamp clearance has been done in the Beisan area, where close settlement is now being undertaken. I do not think I need enumerate them all; there are seven or eight such schemes.
421. Anyhow you have translated those words into a certain policy and that policy has been really the reclamation of land as a preliminary to close settlement. You have considered that that is facilitating close settlement, is that so?—That is the view we have taken on the subject.
422. Is there any other branch of activity connected with that?—Yes. There are the general agricultural and veterinary services of Government, which are intended to improve agriculture; there are demonstration plots and horticultural stations, and there is the annual grant which is made every year to various Jewish organisations for experimental work. Last year a grant of some £6,500 was made to the Jewish Agency's research stations, which includes £3,000 earmarked for citrus research. Government has also financed the Agricultural Mortgage Company to the extent of about £150,000, the object being to admit of mortgages being given to landowners for the further development of their land. Finally, a very important matter, there is the very large expenditure which Government has incurred on public security. This is largely necessitated by the existence of close settlement; but for that factor, the expenditure on public security would be very much less.
423. *Sir Morris Carter*: Does the reduction of taxation on land come into it?—I had not mentioned that as its effect is rather more indirect. I think it could be taken as coming into it.
424. *Chairman*: It is a transfer of the burden of taxation from cultivators and landowners to other people?—Yes. Mr. Andrews points out that it did not affect the Jew nearly so much as it affected the Arab.
425. You mean that it affected the Arab more?— The Arab benefited more.
426. Because he was cultivating a larger percentage of the cereal lands?—Yes.
427. *Sir Laurie Hammond*: I have seen in some of the papers a statement as to how far you had got in survey and settlement. As to the trigonometrical survey, you have done the whole country?—(*Colonel Salmon*): Yes, except in the Beersheba district.
428. In settlement, if I remember the figure correctly, you have done about one-tenth?— Actually I find now that we have done a bit more, we have done very nearly one-sixth.
429. All in the plain districts, I believe?—Almost all in the plain districts. We have done a very few villages in the hills for special purposes.
430. Exactly what do your settlement operations consist in? Can you tell us that?—It starts off with the survey.
431. Making of the maps?—Making the maps And it may be of interest to mention that no

good settlement can be carried out without a good survey and no good detailed survey can be carried out without a good triangulation framework. That was done by my predecessor and it was done very well. Palestine, I think will be one of the few countries which will not be beset with troubles about overlaps of boundaries, because the framework is really reliable. It is also well marked, which is an important matter, because if the marks disappear you have to do the whole thing over again. The process of settlement is roughly this. The triangulation having been done previously, a settlement survey party goes out to the field—usually about five surveyors with one surveyor in charge. They camp on the spot and go out and make what is called a croquis, that is, a rough sketch of the village, and for doing that these rural property tax maps were very useful as we could use them as a basis.

432. You made them?—We made them originally for rural property tax purposes and we found them very useful in settlement. The surveyor has got all these localities shown and he can sketch on the 1/10,000 plans, roughly, his boundaries. He goes out with the villagers and they are supposed to define their own boundaries with angle irons which they supply themselves at their own expense. He does, really, a little bit of settlement himself, because there are always a number of small disputes as to exactly where the boundary is. If you went out and saw the surveyor doing this work you might think there was a riot on, because there is a tremendous lot of shouting and argument, but really it is a fairly peaceful business and after wasting a great deal of time they decide where so-and-so's angle iron is to go in. Those angle irons are then sketched out on the croquis. The surveyors then go out with their croquis, which show them roughly where angle irons are, and they make an accurate detailed survey of the whole village and record the names of the claimants. They do not actually call them claimants, because that happens afterwards in land settlement, they call them reputed owners. They do not go into the matter of the claim, but they simply take the name of the man who says, "This is my land." Having made that survey of course there is no plan yet, but the work is all recorded in field books. The field books are sent in to the head office of the survey and plans are prepared. Those plans are then sent to the field again with another party called an examination party and they are thoroughly checked on the ground; the actual lengths of the boundaries are measured. The officer in charge of that party checks them again, and that is called the final examination.

433. What is the officer in charge of that party? Is he an assistant settlement officer?—An officer of the survey department just the same as the man who did the original survey—a Grade "N" or "O" surveyor. The plans are then sent to the Survey Office and the areas of the parcels are computed and listed. Against the parcel you have the number, the area, and the reputed owner. The plans with these lists of reputed owners are then handed over to the Settlement Branch. A Palestinian assistant settlement officer goes out and actually camps in the village and starts the process of recording claims. It is all done legally. Notices are posted and the claimants have to come forward and present their claims. The assistant settlement officer is supposed to visit every parcel in the village to make certain that the boundaries are clear and to discuss with the claimants any discrepancies that may occur. He then makes out a list of the claimants and also a list showing the parcels where there are several claimants, in other words, where there are disputes. Where there is no dispute the matter is simple. The lists of undisputed claims are examined by the British settlement officer, who signs them and ultimately they appear in the Schedule of Rights. Where there are disputes the British settlement officer has to hear them as cases, and here there is a matter of special interest, I think. In the Hope Simpson Report the decisions of the settlement officers are referred to as quasi-judicial. If you look at the Settlement Ordinance you will find that the word "court" is not mentioned and that the expression "judicial proceedings" is only mentioned once. The Ordinance gave settlement officers certain powers, and it was supposed that they would deal with the work in a summary way. But things have now changed: the cases they have to try have become more complicated. They have to deal with arguments involving not only the ownership of the land but the land category under the Ottoman Law. I believe you have had a memorandum explaining these different categories. The claimants are very often represented by counsel; very large numbers of witnesses sometimes have to be heard and long judgments given in writing. Perhaps the legal members of the Royal Commission might like to see some of those judgments. It may give them an idea of the sort of work the settlement officers have to do.

434. You think they would like to read judgments?—It would give them an idea of the sort of disputes that occur. Some of them, of course, are very simple. Sometimes you will get a judgment in about four lines; sometimes it is a question of 19 pages. It might help to show the difficulties that occur.

435. *Sir Laurie Hammond*: Actually what they are doing is they are deciding title suits?—Yes, deciding title.

436. It is not a question only of ownership or possession, but they go into the question of title?—They go into the question of title. Appeals to the Land Court are not very frequent, and there are very few reversals of settlement officers' decisions, so their work is good. Of course, as the value of the land has gone up so has the number of claimants and a good deal of time is wasted in going into shadowy claims. Although the people who put up frivolous claims are penalised by having to pay the costs we still have to deal with a good many of them. In the last year or so we have started an experiment which has been rather successful. Although the assistant settlement officer has in theory nothing to do with the decision of disputes (he deals simply with undisputed claims) we have appointed a certain number of them, calling them amicable settlement officers, to go round to the people who are disputing claims in an endeavour to get them to settle the business without its going to the settlement officer's court; and that has met with quite considerable success. It is very important, because it speeds up settlement considerably. There is a great deal of delay, sometimes, in these settlement cases. Another thing the settlement officer can do, which helps a good deal in the development of the country, is to prescribe minima, that is to say that he will not consider parcels of land below a certain size, either 1-dunum, ½-dunum or ¼-dunum according to the class of land, nor will he accept parcels in long strips that are too narrow. Usually anything under 5-metres in width is not accepted. He can also straighten out boundaries, either by give and take, or, if it is absolutely essential, he can arrange for compensation if some party loses a small part of their land in the course of straightening. He deals with the alignment of roads and also means of access. When he has finished his work he signs the Schedule of Rights and that goes to the Land Registration Branch, where the parcels are registered.

437. At the end of his work is there a preliminary publication and then a final publication?—Yes, it is all published and posted in the village and there is plenty of time for anybody to object.

24 *November*, 1936.]   Mr. D. G. HARRIS, C.S.I., C.I.E., Colonel F. J.   [*Continued.*
SALMON, M.C., Mr. L. Y. ANDREWS, O.B.E., and Mr. M. C. BENNETT.

438. What interval of time is there between the preliminary and the final?—I must look that up in the Land Settlement Ordinance.

439. What I want to get at is this. When these various stages have been accomplished, possibly there has been a dispute and it has been settled by the settlement officer or arranged amicably by one of the other people, then what does the man in the field get? Do you give him a certificate of possession or of ownership?—Yes, he can get a *kushan*. He does not get it from the settlement officer; it has to be prepared by the Land Registration Branch.

440. But he will get it from them?—The Land Registration Branch deals with all transfers of land, before settlement and after settlement, but during settlement the books are closed except for very special cases when the settlement officers authorises them.

441. Once your proceedings are over you hand over the recorded results to the Land Registration Department?—To the Land Registration Branch.

442. And then, if a man wants to show that he has got the title to that bit of land he has to go to them to get a copy of the entry in the Register?—He can be given a copy of it at any time.

443. He would have to pay for it, I suppose? He would have to pay the fees and so on?—I do not consider he actually pays for the *kushan* or registration, but he has to pay the settlement officer's fees and for the survey.

444. He has to pay the cost of the survey?—Yes.

445. All this must take a long time, does it not?—I am afraid it does.

446. The settlement of a title dispute must be a very long business?—It is sometimes.

447. When did your settlement proceedings begin?—At the end of 1927.

448. You have had eight seasons?—Yes. We started with three settlement officers. I pressed for an increase last year and I have now got five. We are trying various methods of speeding up, including, as I told you, the recently introduced system of amicable settlement.

449. You began in the cold weather of 1927?—Yes.

450. I suppose this year you have not been able to do anything at all, you have shut down your settlement operations, have you not?—It has not been entirely bad for settlement, because we had got behindhand in a good deal of clerical work, and the preparation of cases for the settlement Courts, and that work continued during the disturbances. The settlement officers themselves were all taken back to the district administration for special duty. The survey went on for quite a long time. It was rather remarkable how they were able to continue. With Jews and Arabs very often in the same camp, each looked after the other, but finally we had to withdraw them from the field, except in a few cases.

451. When the settlement officer makes a final settlement of the disputed claim, does he go out to the village?—Yes.

452. And stays there?—He does not stay there. The country is so small that that is not necessary. Some of his cases he tries in the town; it suits the people because they have their advocates there.

453. Let us get down to the figures. You have had eight seasons?—Yes.

454. In the course of that time you have been able to settle?—1,364,631 dunums.

455. That is, actually settled and in the registration office?—Actually settled, and that comes to about one-sixth of the cultivable area outside Beersheba.

456. What is the total area outside Beersheba?—7,815,000 dunums, cultivable land plus forest.

457. We have it here somewhere—total land area excluding the Beersheba sub-district 13,742,000 dunums, but you are only dealing with the cultivable area?—The cultivable area. I am including in those 7,815,000 dunums the forest areas, because we have to settle them.

458. Lay out the boundaries so that they can be preserved?—It is more than that. We may not find that they are all state domain when it comes to settlement.

459. There may be disputes of title. How much did you say was the total cultivable area?—I think I am right in saying 7,815,000 dunums, but that includes the forests. We have surveyed about one-third of that now—2,458,954 dunums.

460. You have surveyed the whole country in regard to cultivable or non-cultivable?—The surveyed area is practically all cultivable; it is so far all in the plains, and includes the sand dunes, which of course, are sometimes cultivated.*

461. You have had a survey in the hills too, have you not?—I am only speaking of the settlement survey. That does include about three hill villages that we have settled or are settling for special purposes. One of them is quite close to Jerusalem.

462. You call it settling when you have a map of a particular size?—1/2,500, which is about the same as the 25 in. map at home, is the usual scale for settlement surveys.

463. It will take you some time before you are able to finish the settlement of the land so that your Land Registers and everything will be absolutely up to date?—I am afraid it will take a very long time.

464. It will take how long? Thirty or forty years?—It is very difficult to estimate. We did hope when settlement started that we should get along quickly, when we had finished with the plains and got into the hills, where the value of the land is very much less, but we are beginning to find that the claimants in the hills are probably just as many, if not more, than in the plains. Rock areas, which you can do very little with, we thought would be left as waste land and would be state domain, but people are putting in claims to them now because they hope that some day they will be developed, perhaps towns built on them and it is worth while claiming them. In addition to that the actual survey work in the hills is much more expensive and more difficult than in the plains and we have not yet devised the proper method of doing it. My surveyors have been trained in the same way and equipped with the same instruments as the Survey of Egypt, where methods are designed for survey work in the plains, and when they go up into the hills we shall have to train them to use other methods.

465. Aerial survey is no good to you?—On an aerial photograph you cannot see the small angle iron which is what you are looking for in the survey for claims.

466. Do I gather that the land that has been settled is all in the plains area?—Practically all in the plains.

467. And in the plains area how much more is there to be settled?—I shall have to work out that figure.

468. Perhaps you would let us know that?—Yes, I can give it to you afterwards.† Here is another

---

* In a letter dated the 11th December, 1936, the Commissioner for Lands and Surveys stated that the surveyed area, exclusive of sand dunes, was 2,331,000 dunums.

† In a letter dated the 11th December, 1936, the Commissioner for Lands and Surveys stated that the approximate areas of the plain areas, excluding sand dunes, were as follows :—

Coastal	2,928,300
Acre	315,900
Esdraelon	351,100
Jezreel	64,800
	3,660,100
Settled area (excluding sand dunes)...	1,352,196
Leaving to be settled	2,307,904

PALESTINE ROYAL COMMISSION

24 November, 1936.] Mr. D. G. HARRIS, C.S.I., C.I.E., Colonel F. J. SALMON, M.C., Mr. L. Y. ANDREWS, O.B.E., and Mr. M. C. BENNETT. [*Continued.*

thing you asked for: the Schedule of Rights at the end of settlement has to be posted for 15 days.
469. And after that it is final?—Yes. You can appeal only for two reasons (1) if there has been fraud, and (2) if one of the claimants was abroad and was unable to submit his claim.
470. Now we come back to the question of close settlement. Exactly what do you understand by close settlement? Let us put it this way. Can you give me the total Jewish population?—(*Mr. Harris*): The latest estimate of the total Jewish population in 1936 is 370,000.
471. Can you say how many of those are on the land?—The estimate—and, of course, it is only an estimate because there has been no Census since 1931 and we have had to make a good many assumptions in getting at the figures—the estimate is that the rural population amounts to 86,000 and the agricultural population, which excludes people living in the rural areas who are not engaged in agriculture, amounts to approximately 50,000.
472. I may take it roughly that out of that 370,000, 50,000 only were engaged in the close settlement of the land?—Yes.
473. What percentage is that?—About 14 per cent.
474. *Sir Morris Carter*: Will those figures be materially affected by that big Jewish settlement which is going to become urban, near Tel-Aviv?—You refer to Petah Tiqva. It is difficult to say, as we are dealing entirely with conclusions drawn from the figures for the last Census, but actually they should not be altered because, whether Petah Tikvah is recorded as an urban or a rural area, its agricultural population, if properly counted, should remain the same.
475. And they will be actually on the land?—Yes.
476. *Chairman*: And the difference between 50,000 and 86,000 are, though not actually working on the land, connected with industries or businesses which are closely connected with the land? They might be repairing cart wheels and so on?—Not altogether. The reason for the very large difference is that at the last Census such places as Rehovot and Petah Tiqva were regarded as rural areas and the 86,000 includes the total population of those places. There are in them a number of factories making furniture and so forth which have no connection with the agricultural population.
477. *Sir Laurie Hammond*: Up to date we may say that about 14 per cent. of the Jewish population—and that, of course, includes people who were here before the Occupation—have managed to get on to the land?—Yes.
478. Presumably in close settlement?—Yes.
479. How much more land is there available for that purpose? That is the real problem, is it not?—Yes.
480. We get some figures in memorandum B (a). Roughly you might say 7,000,000 dunums of cultivable area outside the Beersheba district?—Yes. The cultivable land, exclusive of Beersheba, is 7,120,000 dunums, to the best of our knowledge.
481. *Chairman*: That is a slight addition to the figure given in the paper showing the areas on the 1st April, 1935?—Yes.
482. *Sir Laurie Hammond*: That made it 7,097,000 dunums?—Yes. I think I can explain that small difference; it is because the figure which I have given includes the Huleh area. The figure which you quote is based on the rural property tax records; rural property tax has not been introduced in the Huleh area and that may account for any small difference.
483. Taking it as 7,000,000 dunums for this purpose, how much of that, do we know, has been already taken up and is under cultivation, or how much of it is occupied, we will say? It has all been surveyed for the rural property tax?—Yes. I think the figures you have before you will give the facts.

484. Here you show so much for the Arabs, so much for the Jews and so much for Germans and then state domain. In your appendix II to memorandum B (a) you show state domains leased to Jews as 178,982 dunums?—I may perhaps mention that that figure is slightly in dispute as to one or two of its component items. The general order will not be affected but the figure cannot be vouched for as absolutely accurate. The statement shows the actual amount of state domain of which leases have been given to various Jewish bodies or organisations.
485. Do they come into "land held by the Jews" in your statement of the 1st April, 1935?—A very large amount of the land in question is uncultivable. Only about 20,000 dunums are cultivable.
Sir Laurie Hammond: I take it this state domain land which is shown as leased to Jewish Companies and others is not included in the statement of ownership calculated on the rural property tax?
486. *Sir Morris Carter*: Except in so far as it is cultivable?—(*Mr. Bennett*): It would be included as long as it falls within the area. We have the amount of that which is known to be leased to Jewish bodies, but it includes a number of areas such as areas south of Beersheba which is certainly not included in the rural property tax area.
487. The land leased to the Palestine Potash Company?—Yes, and furthermore it includes a lot of land which is uncultivable.
488. It includes Huleh?—It includes Huleh, which is not included in the rural property tax.
489. Are you in a position to tell us how much land there is still which you might say is available for further development?—As far as state domain is concerned one can roughly say there is no cultivable land available.
490. Am I right in assuming that the Development Commissioner has bought up any state domain now cultivable for the purpose of settling dispossessed Arabs?—(*Mr. Andrews*): Any state domain that can be used has been taken and used.
491. And earmarked for that purpose?—Yes.
492. And we can take it there is no state domain available?—(*Mr. Bennett*): Not cultivable. You know our definition of cultivable?
493. *Chairman*: I think we might have it?—"The term ' cultivable ' land is held to cover land which is actually under cultivation or which can be brought under cultivation by the application of labour and the financial resources of the average Palestinian cultivator. It includes land planted although often sparsely with olive trees and comprises the area included in the rural property tax categories one to fifteen, except village or settlement built on areas ".
494. It does not say anything about the application of water?—It may be, of course, by expending sums which we consider the ordinary Palestinian cultivator is not able to provide that it might become cultivable.
495. *Sir Morris Carter*: What does " the ordinary Palestinian cultivator " mean? Does that include an average between the richest Jew and the poorest Arab?—It certainly does not include the richest Jew. It includes the ordinary Arab cultivator.
496. Only Arab, not the resources of the Jews?—No, not the resources of the Jews.
497. So the word Arab ought to appear here?—It might be more correct if it did.
Chairman: The word " average " does not mean anything.
Sir Morris Carter: Average Arab.
Chairman: An average Arab? There is no such thing is there?
498. *Sir Laurie Hammond*: You mentioned just now about the distinction between agricultural and rural. Exactly what do you understand here by cultivator? For instance I think you call the *haratheen* a cultivator?—(*Mr. Andrews*): He is the man who ploughs.

MINUTES OF EVIDENCE

24 *November*, 1936.]   Mr. D. G. HARRIS, C.S.I., C.I.E., Colonel F. J.   [*Continued.*
SALMON, M.C., Mr. L. Y. ANDREWS, O.B.E., and Mr. M. C. BENNETT.

499. He is a hired labourer. Do you include him as a cultivator in your agricultural population?—Yes.

500. If an effendi sells his land to a Jew, and he has been working his land with hired labour, those people will lose their employment. Would you call them cultivators?—I have called them farm labourers.

501. Has any endeavour been made to try and get land upon which they can settle?—No.

502. That has been the object of most of the Indian land settlement—to get the man who actually digs the ground on to the ground, so to speak, but they are regarded as a separate class to the tenants?—Yes. They were not included in the landless Arab inquiry.

503. And they are not included—what I am trying to get at now is the categories of the population, agricultural and rural—are they included in agricultural or rural?—(*Mr. Harris*): I have not got the census details, but they would almost certainly be regarded as agricultural population, being people who derive their income from agriculture.

504. There is one more question I should like to put to Colonel Salmon. When you are carrying out your settlement operations they are very long and rather difficult, but you continually send away your people for special inquiries? That is to say, some big settlement has been started and they want the land surveyed and settled there?—(*Colonel Salmon*): For settlement and survey to be done economically it should sweep right across the country, but it has been necessary to take up this sporadic work. I have always resisted it, but some of it becomes essential and has to be done.

505. But it comes at fairly frequent intervals?—It has become more and more frequent.

506. That is due to immigration?—I do not think it is that. We never carry out sporadic settlement for any private interests. It is only for public interests. Two of the recent cases were because there were violent disputes and we were afraid there would be a breach of the peace, so we got on with the settlement as fast as we could. There is a case up at Ataroth landing ground. There is an area there which has been leased by the R.A.F. They do not know to whom to pay the money for the lease and we are settling the village.

507. I read in some of the papers that some big Jewish colonisation scheme was started and your department was asked to go and lay out the boundaries and survey and settle the land. That is not so?—Unless there is some special reason we do not go out of our ordinary programme.

508. The Administration never ask you to do so?—They may have asked us but we have not done it.

509. What about the urban areas?—That is a different thing altogether. They are primarily surveyed for the urban property tax.

510. That falls on your department?—We are responsible for the general direction of Urban Taxation. For the Land Registration branch we do some sporadic surveys in cases where no dispute or land settlement is involved, but these registration surveys are usually done by private licensed surveyors, whose work, however, has to be checked in the field by our surveyors.

511. What about urban surveys such as Tel Aviv?—We do all those. We have just finished a large scale survey at Tel Aviv, Jaffa is finished, Haifa is nearly finished, Jerusalem is nearly finished.

512. And that has been done with the present staff or do you have additional staff for that purpose?—It is all done with the present staff. I have 134 surveyors and of those I suppose not more than 80 or 90 are actually on settlement work, others are doing land registration surveys. There are a couple of levelling parties establishing accurate levels all over the country for water resources survey. There are land registration surveyors who are surveying boundaries for the purpose of transfer of title to land; there are numbers of them in towns working on the urban property tax surveys.

513. You have not finished the whole of the plain area yet?—We are still working on that.

514. How much of the plain area have you done?—I will let you have those figures. We have done well over half of it. Esdraelon we consider a plain area and we are just starting that now. I have sent a settlement survey party up close to Jenin. They are going to work from the south northwards. In the Acre plain we have surveyed a few odd pieces for special purposes and although I should like to get on with that area now I have to avoid it because the cases are so complicated and I should simply fill my settlement offices with files of cases they cannot deal with. I want to get on somewhere where settlement, I hope, will be a bit simpler.

515. In any event it must take a very long time?—I think so unless we can devise some quicker method of doing it. I have thought very hard, I have had many conferences with my settlement officers, but I have not thought out anything yet for speeding up the process.

516. It is not possible that you can do it by regarding so-and-so as in possession, it may be disputed or undisputed possession, and then refer the parties to the civil courts?—The courts would have so many cases that they could not deal with them. We are, practically, taking over a lot of the work of the land courts. The public count on us and we are trying to get their title to the land. Until they get a more or less indefeasible title they cannot develop it properly.

517. Your department has a certain amount to do with the water survey?—Yes, largely because we have the administrative facilities for dealing with parties in the field. We undertook the water resources survey, really, for the Department of Development.

518. How far have you got with that?—What we wanted to do was first of all to get information about all the wells and springs in the plains. That is finished. We have made a survey of the whole of the Plain of Esdraelon and the whole of the coastal plain, visited all the wells, tested the salinity of the water, found out figures about pumping the amount of water available, and the height of the water table. We are still carrying on now with a system of accurate levels. Our trouble was that we had no good levelling in the country and could not establish the height of the water table. Precise levelling is being carried out all over the country, not only for water resources purposes, but in order to have accurate levels from which engineering schemes could be designed for roads, water supply, irrigation, etc.

519. And from the results of these inquiries are you able to say whether there is a chance of large development?—(*Mr. Harris*): It is impossible to say at present, because the survey was only finished three months ago and we are at present engaged on tabulating the results. All I can say is that, so far as I can see at present, there is no sign of any exhaustion of the sub-soil water table in the coastal plain, except in one or two minor cases.

520. Have you any hopes that more land will become cultivable as a result of these inquiries?—It is bound to. Anybody can put down wells in their own land and, so far as we can see, the sinking of wells can continue without danger. There is no obvious evidence that the coastal plain water is being overdrawn.

521. Sir *Horace Rumbold*: I should like to ask a question relevant to what has been said. You gave a figure of 1,100,000 dunums as the total of state domains, subject to readjustment as land settlement proceeds?—Yes.

PALESTINE ROYAL COMMISSION

24 *November,* 1936.]   Mr. D. G. HARRIS, C.S.I., C.I.E., Colonel F. J.   [*Continued.*
SALMON, M.C., Mr. L. Y. ANDREWS, O.B.E., and Mr. M. C. BENNETT.

522. Would the sand dunes upon which Tel Aviv has been built be considered from your point of view as uncultivable?—Yes.

523. We understood that there is a scheme for buying some sand dunes near Gaza to develop. I suppose, a town or village there?—I think I am correct in saying that that project has fallen through for the time being.

524. But still the fact remains, that that land upon which Tel Aviv has been built would have been considered uncultivable?—Yes.

525. Out of the uncultivable portion of state domains there would be a certain amount available for Jews if they chose to build another town on the same lines?—Yes.

526. *Sir Morris Carter*: I am afraid I do not quite understand this. It is stated that the state domains are 179,758 dunums. Then you mentioned a figure of 1,100,000 dunums. I do not quite follow what the difference is?—(*Mr. Bennett*): The state domain of 179,000?

Sir Morris Carter: We have got that figure in this statement of area ownership by rural property categories. 179,758 dunums includes the total cultivable land and the forest and uncultivable land and the roads.

527. *Chairman*: What I understood was that the 179,000 dunums, whether cultivable or uncultivable, were entirely state domains. The very large figure was land cultivable or uncultivable as to which the ownership was disputed, but they might be state domains?—Yes, in that statement from the rural property tax you have got, as you see, the cultivable area as shown and there is the other figure of uncultivable and then roads. Much of the uncultivable we believe is actually state domain, but it is claimed as privately owned or much of it is claimed as privately owned and our 1,100,000 dunums, or much of that area, is included in this 6,417,000 dunums, which is the total of the uncultivable land in the rural property tax areas. This uncultivable land under the heading of state domain is only part of what we believe is state domain.

528. *Chairman*: Am I right in this, that extra amount representing the difference between 179,000 and 1,100,000 is contained somewhere in those 6,417,000 dunums?—Of the uncultivable land, yes.

529. And therefore must be deducted in some form or other from the uncultivable land in the possession of Jews or Arabs, is that so?—Yes, that is so.

Sir Morris Carter: Mainly Arabs?
Chairman: The Arabs must be the largest holders in that category.

530. *Professor Coupland*: On this question of what you call, I think, a water survey, your survey was an examination of existing water supplies? —(*Colonel Salmon*): It was.

531. And their yield of water and the character of the water?—Yes.

532. It is a different procedure to discover what further water supplies may be available. Your survey has nothing to do with that?—No, the Public Works Department deal with that.

533. Is it at this session that we should ask and, if so, who shall I ask as to what has been done to discover what new sources of water there are in Palestine?—Mr. Harris can answer that. He has been on the Committee.

534. And that question can be put at this session? —(*Mr. Harris.*) I have no objection to answering it to the best of my ability.

535. I should like an account of what has been done to discover water in this country?—The answer must be very little. In the year 1931. Government got out a boring plant for doing experimental borings. That was supplemented in 1933 by a second small plant and since then two more plants, one last year and one this year, have been purchased.

536. Nothing before 1931?—Nothing before 1931 and only two up to March of last year. These boring plants have been used to a certain extent for exploration purposes. They made two bore holes in the Beersheba sub-district and another one is now being sunk there; they have also been used in three or four other cases for the same type of exploratory work. Altogether, I think we have made five exploratory bore holes plus one at present being made.

537. Six exploratory bore holes have been made in Palestine since 1931?—I think that is a correct statement. For the rest, these machines have been in constant demand for villages which have no water at all and which consequently suffer from drought, for Jewish settlements, for town water supplies and so forth, and they have not been used primarily for exploratory purposes. When one could be spared from dealing with immediate needs it has been put on to exploratory work.

538. In those cases you knew there was water there and you supplied the plant?—Generally speaking, yes, although in some cases bores have been sunk in settlements or villages which have failed to produce water. In other cases, existing wells had gone dry and we have bored them deeper.

539. What is the cost of boring apparatus? We saw one the other day in the Beersheba area?—The cost varies according to the depth to which they are designed to bore. You can say from £1,000 to £1,500.

540. I take it there is a considerable further expenditure in the way of staff?—It costs anything up to £2,000 or £2,500 per annum to run such a plant.

541. To run one plant?—To run one plant.

542. From the amount of exploration that has been done, which as you say is relatively very small, have you formed any opinion as to sources of water supply, the possible future sources of water supply?—I think not; there have not been sufficient data.

543. How much more borehole exploration is required in order to obtain a fairly safe estimate as to the water possibilities?—A very great amount. Over the coastal plain as a whole we have an enormous amount of information and from that it is possible, subject to the uncertainty always adherent in conclusions as to water resources derived from rainfall, height of water table and so forth, to draw reasonable deductions.

544. Because it has been settled largely and you know the wells nearby have produced similar results?—We can examine a well here and a well there, knowing what the pumps are pumping out and noting the effect. From such examination we can tell to some extent what further development is possible. But when you take an enormous area like the Beersheba sub-district you would, in order to get any clear knowledge of the water conditions there, require a very large number of wells at frequent intervals, more especially as the problem is a very complicated one owing to the fact that you have saline water on the one hand and fresh water on the other and nobody knows where fresh and saline water, respectively, will be found.

545. You have a line of fresh water quite close to the sea. You have an impression there whether a well which is sunk is likely or may yield fresh water?—Yes.

546. *Sir Harold Morris*: Would you mind just checking that amount. One boring plant in 1931? —Yes.

547. Supplemented by another in 1933?—Yes

548. I did not get the time of the two more?— One in March, 1935, and one in February this year

549. Those four boring plants have made six exploratory boreholes since the time of the first one?— Six exploratory boreholes, but they have done a good deal more than that. They have made six exploratory boreholes, five boreholes in connection with town

MINUTES OF EVIDENCE

24 *November*, 1936.] Mr. D. G. HARRIS, C.S.I., C.I.E., Colonel F. J. SALMON, M.C., Mr. L. Y. ANDREWS, O.B.E., and Mr. M. C. BENNETT. [*Continued*

supplies, at Hebron, Haifa and Tulkarm, four boreholes in Jewish settlements, one in an Arab village and one in a German settlement. The number of exploratory boreholes made should actually be seven, not six.

550. Now may I go back to the exploratory for a moment. Have all those been done in south or northern Palestine?—In both.

551. Can you give me how many in Beersheba roughly?—Three; two have been completed, one is now being bored.

552. And so far as those in Beersheba are concerned have you been able to get any kind of estimate as to whether you can get fresh water? —No, we found salt water in both cases.

553. What about your tests in the northern half? —Some of them have been satisfactory. In fact, I think there have mainly been successful.

554. Whereabouts have they been?—They have generally been along the Jenin-Nablus road and out beyond, between Jenin and Nazareth; also in the Jordan Valley.

555. Apart from what the Government has done in exploratory boreholes and trying to find water, have you heard of any commercial enterprise on the same lines?—Yes, there are several enterprises in this country which do this well boring and can be employed by anybody who wants it done.

556. Have they done any exploratory boring as far as you know?—Not so far as I know. I am now speaking without the book, but Mr. Andrews tells me they did some exploratory boring at Yavniel and found water which they did not know was there before.

557. *Chairman*: Where is that?—(*Mr. Andrews*): In the Tiberias sub-district, not far from the Horns of Hattin.

558. Did they find fresh water?—Yes, a large supply. There are others; that is the one I know of.

559. *Chairman*: I want to get, if I can, a little closer to that question of what these state domains are. All we have so far is this, that there is a number of dunums belonging to the State amounting to 179,000. Then we have another figure which is described as an estimate of 1,100,000 dunums and when I ask whether that is contained in the statement of area ownership by rural property categories I am told it is somewhere buried among the 6,417,000 of uncultivable land and forests and that may belong to Arabs and Jews, probably to Arabs because they hold six millions of that land as against 250,000 held by the Jews. Further we were told there was some dispute about title, but even so, even if there is a dispute about title, I do not understand why we cannot be told any more about it. Is there no accurate figure given for that? If there is, it must be known where these dunums are?— (*Mr. Bennett*): May I make a general statement?

560. You see my difficulty?—I do, and I appreciate it. It is a difficult problem altogether I am afraid. The Government exercises a general overlordship of all land throughout Palestine. There is what we call the *mulk* category of land, which is practically equivalent to our freehold in England, over which we have very little say at all; but the majority of the land, principally the rural land, is of the *miri* category, over which people are given rights of cultivation and practical ownership so long as they cultivate it and so long as they have heirs to succeed. Then there are other categories, but the other principal category is *mewat*, which is dead land or land which is waste and which is regarded as Government land in the more strict sense of the word. The *miri* land, which, as I say, is held under title deed, can revert to the State if it is uncultivated for three years and after certain processes are carried through, but this is practically a dead letter. It is only in the rarest instances that it has been taken over by the state for that reason, but a few areas do come to us by failure of heirs, in which case it is registered as Government property. At the time of the British occupation the only areas which we really had any real knowledge of were those actually registered. These consisted of areas which were or had previously been in the ownership of the Sultan Abdul Hamid and were eventually transferred to the Turkish Treasury and were therefore Government property at the time of the occupation; lands which had reverted for failure of heirs and similar reasons, lands which had been confiscated from time to time by the Government owing to failure of payment of dues and such like and areas granted to or purchased by Government. Those were the only areas which at the time of the occupation we can say we had any knowledge of at all and these were very difficult to trace in many cases owing to the fact that there were practically no plans available and the registration in almost every case was vague: the description of boundaries were also bad. *Mewat* lands throughout the country were not registered and we were consequently unaware of their actual location. In a few cases we have carried on investigations since the occupation and a few areas have since been registered as Government property, but the majority of these *mewat* areas we have no sure knowledge of. The only way satisfactorily to find out where they are is to carry out land settlement. Land settlement is gradually progressing and as these areas are discovered they are duly recorded as Government property and then they are available for development if they are suitable. Now the approximate area of known state domains at the present time is, as I have said, somewhere about 1,100,000 dunums——

561. Of known state domains?—Yes. This is being constantly extended, as I say, as land settlement progresses. I think there is no doubt about that. We think there will be considerably more eventually.

562. That being so, there may be a considerable amount more land available for settlement?—Yes, but it is not what we regard as cultivable land under our definition. This land is not cultivable land.

563. Not under that particular definition, but it may be cultivable under a wider definition?—It might be with considerable expenditure. It is largely sand dune areas and that sort of thing.

564. I am still rather in a difficulty, because if you do not know exactly where this land is and so on I do not understand how you can pronounce whether it is cultivable or uncultivable?—(*Mr. Andrews*): Here is a map of state domain lands, which may help you. (*Map produced*.)

565. Thank you, that is very useful. Does that give the 1,100,000 dunums?—(*Mr. Andrews*): I do not think it does cover it all. (*Mr. Andrews*): It covers most of it. (*Mr. Bennett*): It covers the big areas, but not the isolated areas all over the country.

566. Roughly speaking, what would that cover in area?—It is the same as is included in Sir John Hope Simpson's report.

567. That is very largely in the Jordan Valley? —The area shown on the map covers about 970,000 dunums.

568. That is a very substantial amount of it. Is it possible to make any general statement about that area for settlement purposes?—(*Mr. Andrews*): Quite a lot of it is sand dunes and a lot of it is in the Jordan Valley, which is very, very salty land which would require a lot of money to sweeten it.

569. What I meant was, is it possible to give us figures, even though rather approximate figures, of the amount of land included in this 1,100,000 dunums which could be deemed in any sense or in a general sense as cultivable?—(*Mr. Bennett*): I should not like to say about cultivable. I can tell you approximately what part of it is leased. About 700,000 dunums are leased.

C 3

PALESTINE ROYAL COMMISSION

24 November, 1936.] Mr. D. G. HARRIS, C.S.I., C.I.E., Colonel F. J. [Continued.
SALMON, M.C., Mr. L. Y. ANDREWS, O.B.E., and Mr. M. C. BENNETT.

570. Are leased to cultivators?—Are leased to cultivators, leased to Jewish organisations and to Arabs.

571. But are these yearly leases, are they long leases?—There are various types of leases. It includes the Beisan area, which, as you know, is granted to the Arabs and they are in process of purchasing it under an agreement. If we take this area separately, they have an agreement under which they can purchase the area over a period of 10 years.

572. There is this word in the Mandate about including state lands. Unless we know what that is, it is impossible to know whether there is anything left for closer settlement. It is not quite helpful enough to say that here are these areas, some are leased, some not leased. Do not the Government know a little more clearly than that which of those lands are available?—We know we have approximately 1,100,000 dunums, of which 700,000 dunums are leased under some arrangement with cultivators or tenants.

573. All that is so very vague. It makes such an immense difference with land. You say you have 10,000 acres, but have you any land for settlement? To say it has been leased means nothing. I might have leased it for 21 years or for life, or for one year. We must really get something a little more definite than that. If you cannot give it to us now I will send in some questions to be answered after consideration, if you cannot answer straight off. You have told us about the 700,000. I wanted to press it, because obviously that general information is not of very much use and if you could give us something a little more definite, not now, but we will send you some questions about it?—I can only speak very generally. These areas are leased under various terms. There are 520,000 dunums occupied by Arabs under various types of agreements and 180,000 leased to Jews.

574. That is another figure we have not had until now. The figure for the Arabs is what?—520,000 dunums.

575. Would you say the rest of it in your judgment is uncultivable according to your standard?—Yes, 300,000 dunums are uncultivable.

576. That means to say the economic effort to make them cultivable would be very expensive?—I consider it would be expensive. It is mainly sand dune and such like.

577. We may ask you one or two questions to get that clearer. There is only one other thing I wanted to know. Looking down this list it shows how much of the land is owned by Arabs or Jews; it does not tell you anything about the occupying tenant. I suppose in many cases it might be occupied and worked by either Jew or Arab as the case, might be and the figures of occupation would be rather different from the figures of ownership?—(Colonel Salmon): I do not think they would be very different. If it has been purchased by the Jews, the Jews would be working it.

578. Jews might be working it, but not the same person who owned it. These dunums owned by Jews are owned probably by various Associations as well as by individuals and both would be leased to other persons?—Yes.

579. And would that apply to the Arabs or would the Arabs more likely be working their own?—They would more likely be working their own.

580. Sir Morris Carter: This 520,000 dunums was the figure you gave as being the land that is leased. Does that pay no taxes?—Mr. Bennett: Yes, it pays taxes.

581. It is included in these figures of the area covered by the rural property tax, is it?—Yes, it is certainly included in those figures.

582. Therefore the 520,000 dunums are included in the figure of 6,000,000 for Arabs and 930,000 for Jews, is it?—Yes, it comes under one of the three

583. If it is state domain and is unleased then it will not pay any tax, will it?—No, it will not.

584. Therefore, it must come under the first two columns, or the German column?—Perhaps it is not quite correct to say that. In the rural property tax, from which this is taken, the owner is liable to be taxed, but in certain cases, state domain for instance, the tenant pays the tax.

585. But the tenant is included in these figures of ownership?—Under those three columns, yes.

586. Chairman: I want to make it quite clear. Some of those religious trusts do not pay rural property tax, do they? Am I right in thinking that they do not pay rural property tax, but make a payment in lieu?—Under the Ordinance there are certain exemptions.

587. What I wanted to get at was this, whether all these figures include land held by religious trusts, whether Arab or Jew, because if they did not pay rural property tax, as I believe in some cases they do not, but technically pay something in lieu of it, they would not appear in this list of ownerships?—Yes, they would appear.

588. And we should have to add their areas?—They would appear in that list because there is no question of exemption arising under that list.

589. Do you mean to say all the land held by all religious trusts in the country will appear in this list?—Yes.

590. Sir Morris Carter: In regard to the sinking of wells, can you tell us the cost of the two wells which have been sunk in the Beersheba area, so as to get some sort of idea of how much it would cost to bore?—(Mr. Harris): Bore No. 1 in Beersheba cost £1,994; it was 1,170 feet deep. Bore No. 2, which was 375 feet deep, only cost £300. I may add, in regard to the first one, that of that £1,994, about £330 represented the cost of casing which was left in the bore.

591. To get any practical knowledge of the water possibilities of the Beersheba area, roughly how many wells do you think you would have to sink before you could come to any conclusion?—That is a very difficult question.

592. What I am trying to get at is, is it going to cost tens of thousands or hundreds of thousands?—Tens of thousands certainly and possibly more.

593. Sir Laurie Hammond: Might I put one question to Colonel Salmon. How far are you progressing with regard to these Masha'a villages, the ones that are held in co-partnership?—(Colonel Salmon): In the course of settlement most of those areas are partitioned. We made an attempt last year to do some partitioning in advance of settlement, but it was not very successful. Unless the whole of the people were willing, we had no power to do it and there were very few villages which were done. My predecessor tried to produce some legislation to make those partitions final, but the scheme was not very successful and there were so few villages that agreed to advance partition of them that it was not worth while carrying on with it.

594. In 1923 56 per cent. of the land in the villages was Masha'a land and in 1929 that had gone down to 46 per cent., so that 10 per cent. had been partitioned?—Yes.

595. How much further have you got since then?—It is very difficult to say. I should have to look that up. There are various methods of dividing Masha'a land. One is at land settlement. Another is where it has been done in the course of sales and transfer of land, and then there are the areas where an assistant settlement officer did a little advance partition.

596. Do you think you could extract those figures to give us an idea of how far you have got?—Yes, I could do it; in time. Outside settlement areas it might take a long time; it would mean going through the Land Registers to find out what had been partitioned, but I think we could do it.

MINUTES OF EVIDENCE

24 *November*, 1936.]   Mr. D. G. HARRIS, C.S.I., C.I.E., Colonel F. J.   [*Continued.*
SALMON, M.C., Mr. L. Y. ANDREWS, O.B.E., and Mr. M. C. BENNETT.

Chairman: I think we might go on to the next subject, the question of the re-settlement of displaced Arab cultivators.

597. *Sir Horace Rumbold*: Landless Arabs have been defined as such Arabs as can be shown to have been displaced from the lands which they occupied in consequence of the lands falling into Jewish hands and who have not obtained other holdings upon which they could establish themselves or other equally satisfactory occupations. Apparently a Register was opened and eventually only 664 families substantiated claims to be included in the Register of Landless Arabs and of those some 347 families have been provided for by the Government in various places. First of all, I would like to know what has happened, what accounts for the difference between the 664 families who proved their claims and the 347 families who have actually been settled?—(*Mr. Andrews*): What has happened to the 300 odd families? They are working in towns, most of them.

598. Would they have had a possibility of being settled on the land and have rejected that possibility?—They were given the opportunity to settle on the land and they rejected it for the time being, for various reasons which they gave. Some of them would not come because they said they were not going to come on to land unless they were given the title deeds for it, and we do not give title deeds; we settle landless Arabs as tenants of Government. Others said that they were contented where they were at the moment and were not in distress. Others said they could not live on the land offered because the climate was not healthy. Others said that they wanted to be resettled on the land from which they had been displaced. Those are the sort of excuses they gave.

599. When you said that they said the climate was not healthy, was that malarial swamps?—No, that was in regard to land in the Beisan sub-district, where there are no swamps.

600. *Chairman*: What is the particular unhealthiness in that area?—It is below sea level, and the actual land is close to the Jewish colony of Beth Alfa, which is the most prosperous colony in the district.

601. There is no malaria, or anything of that sort? They did not show any evidence of unhealthiness due to malaria or anything of that kind? —No. They were really thinking back to the old days when Beisan was unhealthy. At the beginning of the Occupation Beisan was a very malarious spot, but Government carried out a lot of work there and it is now a very healthy spot. However, the Arabs would not go there. The land is in the Beisan sub-district.

602. *Sir Horace Rumbold*: And the 347 families who have been settled are contented with their present lot, as far as you know?—Most of them. There are about 20 families who are not contented.

603. Why?—Because they were displaced from the land about 10 years before they were put back by us and in the meantime they had been living in the town of Nazareth, where they had become used to town life and so did not like going back on to the land. They came out for a time and when they found that they had to work harder than they anticipated they gradually drifted back into Nazareth, where they are working as stone dressers and using their camels for carrying goods, and so on

604. That deals with the families who have substantiated their claim to be regarded as landless, but there were four categories of Arabs who were exempted from this claim. In the first category are persons who have been displaced in consequence of the purchase of the land by non-Jews?—Yes.

605. What is the difference between that and the definition of landless Arab which I read out before? —The difference is that the one gets settled back on the land at the expense of the State and the other does not, as he does not come within the definition.

Under the definition he must be displaced as a result of the sale of land to Jews.

606. They have been displaced in consequence of purchases by non-Jews?—Yes.

607. What has happened to them?—I have not been able to follow all of them, but of those claims submitted it would have made a difference of 73 additional people who would have been admitted to the Register.

608. Only 73?—That is all.

609. 73 families?—73 families out of the number of claims submitted.

610. I suppose the figure of 3,271 applications for re-settlement includes those four categories?—Yes, anybody in those four categories who put in an application for re-settlement is included in that figure of 3,000 odd.

611. The second category includes persons who at the time of the sale to Jews were not tenant cultivators, e.g., owners who habitually let their lands, ploughmen and persons who, from debt or bad seasons or other causes, had ceased to be cultivators and had become labourers, etc.?—Yes, they were people who had been living in a village and had left some time before the land was actually sold to the Jews. Those people then came along and put in applications to be admitted to the Register, but they were not considered.

612. The third category, persons who were able to obtain other lands after the sale, but subsequently gave up cultivating owing to bad seasons or for some other reason, you would consider that they were not really very serious claims?—They were people who came away: they had a number of animals and a certain amount of money. They went away and after having cultivated for five or six years actually became landless not as a result of the sale of their lands to Jews, but as a result of Acts of God. They came up against bad seasons and were not able to carry on.

613. Finally, persons who had obtained employment of a fairly permanent nature, would that be in the towns?—In the towns. Quite a number of them went to the towns. We took as fairly permanent employment a man who had been working for the same employer for several years and had become more or less an expert in, say, cement brick making. Quite a number of them went to Haifa and have become quite expert cement brick makers. A number of them have gone to the Nesher Cement Company and have been employed there for a number of years. Those people, I consider, are in fairly permanent employment.

614. You told us that the 73 families would cover all four categories?—All four categories of the people who applied.

615. Although there were 3,271 applications?— That is right, and of the people who applied and who would have been admitted to the list out of those four categories of people, 73 families would have been admitted to the list as landless Arabs if there had not been these four provisos.

616. Can you explain the difference between the figure of 73 and the big figure of 3,271 which is about 3,200 more?—Yes.

617. What were they?—Many of them put in applications when they were not tenants. They were ploughmen. Many of them had found other land. Some of them were shopkeepers in the villages and were not tenants, and others were people who had actually bought land with the compensation they had received.

618. And who had no claim to be settled in other areas?—No. May I add this? All this was gone into by the Legal Assessor attached to the Department. He went into every claim. He went out and met the people in the various centres and he decided whether or not a man was legally entitled to be included in the register. The register was made up from his investigations.

PALESTINE ROYAL COMMISSION

24 *November*, 1936.]   Mr. D. G. HARRIS, C.S.I., C.I.E., Colonel F. J.   [*Continued.*
SALMON, M.C., Mr. L. Y. ANDREWS, O.B.E., and Mr. M. C. BENNETT.

619. So that the landless Arabs are, or were, a very small class, and you have now reduced them to something like 300 hundred families who have not been settled?—That is correct.

620. And who do not want to be, who are not keen to be settled?—Who are not keen to be settled.

621. *Chairman*: There are only one or two small points I would like to put to you on this. I see you are talking of the Wadi Hawarith Arabs and you say that the southern section, numbering 109 families, are now camped in an area of 240 dunums taken over from the Jewish National Fund in exchange?—Yes.

622. What does that mean, camped?—It means that they refused to go to Beisan, where a large area of land had been prepared for them and an irrigation system laid down. They said they would not move from where they were then camped, and an arrangement was made with the Jewish National Fund who wanted a piece of state domain land in another area, whereby the Fund were given that piece of state domain land in exchange for the piece of land on which the Wadi Hawarith Arabs southern section are now camped. This camp site is next to a wadi, a piece of land where the Arabs are able to lease land and where they are now cultivating for an Arab.

623. Do you mean that a number of those 109 families have got leases?—They have got leases or they are working in Jewish colonies or they are employed in supplying manure or bringing coarse sand from the seashore for building purposes.

624. They have got occupations?—They have got occupations, yes.

625. What does "camping" mean? That they have no stone houses?—No, they live in tents.

626. That is, they are temporarily camped there?—No, they move round within those 240 dunums.

627. A limited migration within that area?—They can go outside if they want to and go elsewhere, but that area is known as the Wadi Hawarith camping site.

628. What I want to know is this. You consider that your responsibility for them has been discharged, do you?—Yes.

629. Because you offered them some land which you anyhow considered good and which they refused on climatic grounds and because they did not understand irrigation?—That is right.

630. And now they are settled, or camped, to use your expression, there and have got occupations?—Yes.

631. So that they have not drifted to the towns, any of them?—No, they have not drifted to the towns. Of course, they always have lived in hair tents; they are bedouin, as we call them.

632. Originally Mr. French, who was responsible for this question of settlement, was to have been assisted by some nominated members from the Arab Executive and the Jewish Agency?—That is right.

633. And neither of those bodies wished to assist in this work?—The Arabs definitely did not want to assist. The Jews were ready to appoint someone if an Arab had come forward.

634. So that fell through?—That fell through.

635. *Sir Harold Morris*: Would you mind turning to the memorandum describing the activities of the Department of Development. You say in paragraph 6 that only 664 had been admitted to the register, while 2,607 had been disallowed. If you deduct 73 from that it gives you 2,534?—Yes.

636. Were they all disallowed simply because their claims could not be substantiated?—That is correct.

637. Because, for instance, some of them had been ploughmen and had not been tenants?—Some of them, yes.

638. Roughly how many would there be in that category?—That I cannot say. I could let you know after making inquiry.

639. It is such a large proportion who apply and are disallowed for reasons which are not given and only 73 who are disallowed for reasons which are given, the four reasons given?—Yes.

640. Does it mean that a number of people made claims which it was obvious could not be substantiated?—Quite a number did, yes. If you like I could get you out a statement on that point.

641. I imagined that the figure of 2,607 was related to those four categories, but it is not so at all?—No. I am afraid I misled you there. The figure of 73 refers to the one category "(4)", "persons who had obtained employment of a fairly permanent nature."

642. I was rather thinking that categories (1), (2) and (3) might be larger numbers altogether?—That is right.

643. Would you like to go through that again and give us some details as to how the figure of 2,607 works out?—Certainly.

644. *Sir Laurie Hammond*: On this point there was one thing I did not quite understand. In 1920 I think you had your Land Transfer Ordinance, by which land was not to be transferred without the consent of the High Commissioner?—Yes.

645. And that was found to be quite useless?—That is right.

646. And nothing was done till your Ordinance of 1929?—Until our Ordinance of 1933.

647. You had a new Ordinance in 1929, did you not?—There was a new Ordinance in 1929.

648. Which tried to remedy matters?—Yes.

649. Taking those years 1920 to 1929, over 400,000 dunums of land were sold to Jews?—Yes.

650. And we have it on record that there was no protection whatever then for the Arabs who were displaced?—Yes.

651. What has happened to all those people?—They are included in this 3,000 odd. All those people put in claims.

652. *Professor Coupland*: Retrospectively?—Yes.

653. *Sir Laurie Hammond*: Were their claims regarded as time barred?—No, there was no time bar.

654. What has happened to them?—Some of them went into other villages where they obtained other land and others went into towns.

655. The Shaw Commission recorded the following opinion: "In the past, persons dispossessed have in many cases been absorbed in the neighbouring villages"?—That is right.

656. "We were, however, told that this process, though it may have been possible four or five years ago, is no longer possible to-day; the point of absorption has been reached. The plain facts of the case are, so we are advised, that there is no further land available which can be occupied by new immigrants without displacing the present population"?—Yes.

657. That was what the Shaw Commission arrived at in 1930?—Yes, but you have to remember that there has been a large increase in the planting of orange groves both by Arabs and Jews and the growth of the towns since Sir John Hope Simpson was out here. Some of them have doubled and trebled, and with their accompanying industries have provided sources of employment which did not exist before. Lots of these people have gone into the towns and have obtained employment in the towns.

658. And there has been a transfer from extensive cultivation to intensive cultivation in the citrus groves?—That is correct.

659. And that has occupied some of them?—It has taken a lot of people, yes.

660. *Chairman*: I want to ask you one general question about that. We have seen the small figures you have given us as to the number of Arabs displaced from the land and we have also had some figures showing the large amount of land that had been acquired by Jews up to 1936. When

24 *November*, 1936.] Mr. D. G. HARRIS, C.S.I., C.I.E., Colonel F. J. SALMON, M.C., Mr. L. Y. ANDREWS, O.B.E., and Mr. M. C. BENNETT. [*Continued.*

the Jews acquired that land apparently the Arabs, or a great many of them at any rate, must have remained on as cultivators; otherwise the number of displacements would have been far greater. Is that a correct inference?—No. The figures I give are the figures of people who have come to Government and said, " We have been displaced." It may not be the figure of the total number of people who were displaced.

661. Very well, then you say there may have been and probably was another number of persons who were displaced when the Jews acquired land held by Arabs? Is that so?—That is correct.

662. But you have no record of that?—No, we have no record of that.

663. And so far as you know, no complaints have been made of that by the Arabs?—No. In fact, we had a very good " scout round " to get people to put in applications and we were accused at the time of forcing people to put in applications unnecessarily.

664. What is the proper inference to draw? You say I am wrong in thinking that a good many Arabs were not displaced. You think they were displaced but they apparently made no representations or complaints to Government? You have no record of that?—No, we have no record of that.

665. What happened to them? Did they go into the towns?—They must have gone into the towns or else have been employed in other agricultural industries or in orange groves or other places.

666. It is clear that the comparatively small figures you are dealing with do not bear much relation to the question of the number of those who may have been displaced by these large purchases of land by Jews. Is that right?—I would not say that it may not be a couple of thousand out, but that is about all. I should think, as far as I can see.

667. Those Arabs who came before you and made claims were comparatively late comers, as it were, and their claims did not go back very far in years? —Yes, the claims went back and anybody who was displaced since 1920 could have put a claim in.

668. Since 1920? Then can you explain to me why there were so comparatively few complaints and applications?—The only answer I can give is that there were not so many people displaced as we imagined. Many of these tenants had very large areas. In the plains of Esdraelon, Jezreel and Acre I think the Jewish purchase was about 400,000 dunums and we had 700 claims from that large area. The average holding was over 300 dunums per tenant.

669. You think it is partly due to the fact that the holdings were much larger?—Yes.

10.04

218

CHAPTER IX.

THE LAND.

1.—The first problem: the dual obligation.

1. There are three main problems connected with the land in Palestine:—

(1) The fulfilment of the instructions in the Mandate regarding "close settlement by Jews on the land", combined with the obligation of safeguarding "the rights and position of other sections of the population."

(2) The area available for cultivation by residents or immigrants, due allowance being made not only for waste land, but for that required for afforestation or grazing and the means by which it may best be developed in the interests of both races.

(3) The extent to which extensive can be replaced by intensive cultivation and the water resources in Palestine can be developed.

In connection with these problems, we have also to consider certain grievances put forward by Arabs and Jews.

2. In examining all these questions we follow a well-beaten track. We have had the advantage of reading many earlier reports of various committees and experts. There have been no less than twelve such enquiries, apart from committees appointed to discuss agrarian legislation, which have dealt *inter alia* with the land, proprietary rights and tenancy, and also with irrigation. The series commenced in 1920, when a travelling Land Commission was appointed to advise on the registration, control, and the closer settlement of State Domains. Two other committees were appointed to discover and demarcate vacant and escheated lands.

3. They were hampered by the absence of any previous survey, or any record of boundaries. They were also regarded with suspicion by the Arabs. Thus in 1920 the Transfer of Land Ordinance was enacted, requiring the consent of Government to all dispositions of immovable property and forbidding alienation to others than residents in Palestine. This protective legislation, it was stated by the Commission of Enquiry which reported on the riots of 1921(*) was regarded by the Arabs as having been introduced to keep down the price of land, and to throw land which was in the market into the hands of Jews at a low price. Throughout all these investigations, and indeed throughout our present enquiry, the absence of final and reliable

---

* Page 51 above.

data, coupled with the deep-seated mistrust of the Arabs, has added to the difficulty of an already difficult problem. The striking fact to-day is that, after all these reports, covering a period of fifteen years, the Palestine Government are unable to state with any degree of accuracy how much land they hold either as State Domains or as waste land.

4. In 1923 a Commission was appointed by the High Commissioner to examine the system of ownership known as *masha'a*, under which the whole of the property in a village is held in common, the individual shares being revised and divided every two years, an obvious bar to any agricultural development. There can be no incentive to plant trees or even to manure the land when ownership is to be transferred at an early date. The endeavours to replace joint by individual ownership involve very lengthy negotiations, and are one of the causes of delay. In 1923, 56 per cent. of the villages were *masha'a* : in 1930, 46 per cent. It is believed that many villages are *masha'a* in name, but are actually cultivated as individual parcels. The system, however, can be invoked for purposes of delay or litigation. In 1930 it was reported that, though this Committee had " made certain radical proposals, including the recommendation that legislation should be introduced empowering the executive authorities to enforce partition, nothing had been done." We endorse this criticism. Since then, efforts, partially successful, have been made to effect amicable partition, but it appears evident that, in certain areas, the Arabs regard this system of tenancy, destructive as it is of all development, as a safeguard against alienation, and that the Administration have been reluctant for political reasons to abolish it by legislation. It is being broken up gradually by the partition of areas as the land comes under settlement operations after cadastral survey. Further, Government have a number of officers who are constantly touring the villages, placing expert assistance and guidance at the disposal of the cultivators as to the best method of breaking up *masha'a*.

Where it has been proved to be to the benefit of both Arabs and Jews that the land should be parcellated into individual ownership, we consider that the Land Expropriation Ordinance might be used with advantage.

5. In 1924 Sir Ernest Dowson, late Financial Adviser and Director-General of Surveys to the Government of Egypt, was engaged to report on the co-ordination of the Survey, Land and Finance Departments, and to prepare a scheme of land settlement operations with a view to obtaining an accurate record of rights. A programme for this was issued in 1926.

6. At the beginning of 1927 Lord Plumer appointed a Committee, under the Chairmanship of the Attorney-General and

Chapter IX.   220

with the Commissioner of Lands as one of its members, to consider (1) whether legislation for the protection of tenants from evictions would be effective and beneficial; (2) if such legislation is considered effective and beneficial, to report what form it should take. We discuss the resultant legislation later on. In 1928 experts were appointed by the Joint Palestine Survey Commision. They included Sir John Campbell, a retired Indian Civilian with special experience in land administration in India. Among other matters they discussed the financial condition of Jewish settlements.

7. In 1930 a Commission under the Chairmanship of Sir Walter Shaw, reporting on the disturbances of the previous year, dealt very fully with the land problem. As a result of their recommendations, Sir John Hope Simpson, visited Palestine and made a thorough investigation into all questions connected with land and its possible development.

At the same time the High Commissioner had appointed a committee to enquire into the economic condition of agriculturists and the fiscal measures of Government in relation thereto, whose findings were used by Sir John Hope Simpson. Another Commission, under Sir Samuel O'Donnell, reported on the revenue, expenditure and general organization of the Palestine Administration, and examined the procedure for land settlement and the registration of titles.

8. In 1932 Mr. Lewis French, of the Indian Civil Service, submitted two comprehensive reports on agricultural development and land settlement. Mr. C. F. Strickland also reported in 1931 and again in 1933 on the co-operative movement, designed to relieve the *fellah* of his heavy burden of debt. In 1933 Government voted £6,000 to enable a hydrographic survey to be undertaken.

9. Lastly, it has to be remembered that every year the Permanent Mandates Commission issued enquiries which usually contained references to the land policy of the Administration. Each annual report of the Administration contains full replies to these references.

10. To all these enquiries and reports we are much indebted. Some of the proposals made have not been carried out: others must take many years to bear fruit. The statistics and conclusions derived from them in some of the reports have been challenged as inaccurate and unreliable. Though in some cases the lapse of time has justified the criticism, the general principles enunciated have not in our opinion been materially impaired. They may be shortly stated as follows:—

(1) Unless there is a marked change in the methods of cultivation, the land in Palestine is unable to support a large increase in the population.

(2) Any such change must necessarily be a very slow process spread over many years, and depends largely on the extension of education in the Arab villages.

(3) The general indebtedness of the *fellaheen* is a serious hindrance to the desired progress.

(4) It is on the extension of irrigation, combined with the regularized control of the water resources of the country by Government, that reliance must mainly be placed for any marked increase in the productivity of the land.

(5) The accurate recording of all rights in every parcel of land after a field to field survey is essential.

(6) There is already congestion on the land in the hill districts.

11. The chief problem in connection with the land lies in what is known as the " dual obligation ".

Under Article 6 of the Mandate " the Administration of Palestine, while ensuring that the rights and position of other sections of the population are not prejudiced . . . shall encourage, in co-operation with the Jewish agency . . . close settlement by Jews on the land, including State lands and waste lands not required for public purposes ".

Under Article 11, " the Administration of Palestine shall take all necessary measures to safeguard the interests of the community in connection with the development of the country . . . It shall introduce a land system appropriate to the needs of the country, having regard, among other things, to the desirability of promoting the close settlement and intensive cultivation of the land ".

Article 17 (1) (*a*) of the Palestine Order in Council, as amended in 1923, contains the proviso that " No Ordinance shall be promulgated . . . which shall tend to discriminate in any way between the inhabitants of Palestine on the ground of race, religion, or language ".

Article 2 of the Mandate also places on the Mandatory responsibility for " safeguarding the civil and religious rights of all the inhabitants of Palestine, irrespective of race and religion ", while under Article 15 " no discrimination of any kind shall be made between the inhabitants of Palestine on the ground of race, religion or language ". Even if it is held that Article 15 refers only to matters connected with religion, freedom of conscience and education, Article 2, it is contended, prohibits any legislation which discriminates between persons of different races or religions.

12. Whatever may be the proper construction of these articles, it seems clear that under the Order in Council quoted above the High Commissioner cannot enact a law that in certain areas land

Chapter IX.

222

may not be sold to Jews. Nor could he reserve certain areas for Jewish settlements. Agrarian legislation, whether prohibitory or protective, must be of general and universal application, exceptions to which can be allowed by the Administration to meet racial requirements. This appears to us to be a subterfuge, and consequently an unsatisfactory arrangement.

As it stands at present, however, the Mandate in one article imposes a definite obligation as one of two main objects: yet another article is held to prevent the fulfilment of that obligation.

13. Here then, at the outset, we are faced by a fundamental difficulty. To quote the Shaw Commission:—

> "In view of the obligation placed upon the Mandatory by Article 6 of the Mandate to 'encourage close settlement by Jews on the land' on the one hand and on the other to ensure 'that the rights and position of other sections of the population are not prejudiced' the solution of the land problem is obviously a difficult and delicate task; but some solution is essential in the interests of the whole population irrespective of creed and, unless one be found to deal with the situation that we have described, the question will remain a constant source of present discontent and a potential cause of future disturbance."

If under the Mandate the Order in Council could be amended to empower the High Commissioner to prohibit the transfer of land in any particular area to Jews, a solution might be found. If this is not possible, we are of opinion that in this respect the Mandate should be amended. In any case such an amendment would be desirable to remove any doubts which may exist as to the power of the Mandatory in certain circumstances to carry out his main obligations.

14. As a result, presumably, of these restrictions, the Transfer of Land Ordinance, 1920, required that the consent of the Government should be obtained to *all* dispositions of immovable property; it prohibited the transfer of land to " others than residents in Palestine ".

The Land Transfer Ordinance of 1921, while repeating the necessity for the consent of Government to any disposition of immovable property, added, in Section 8 (1), a proviso that such consent should only be given after the Director of Lands was " satisfied that any tenant in occupation will retain sufficient land in the district or elsewhere for the maintenance of himself and his family ".

These Ordinances failed to achieve their purpose of safeguarding Arab tenants and cultivating owners. They proved in fact to be unworkable. Neither vendor nor purchaser applied for the consent of Government to the transaction. Owners and tenants took the money for purchase or compensation and departed. The change in ownership was not discovered till some months later.

15. These Ordinances were therefore replaced in 1929 by the Protection of Cultivators Ordinance, which provided for the payment of compensation, both for disturbance and for improvements effected by them, to tenants who received a valid notice to quit the holding of which they had been in occupation. It further provided for the constitution of Boards to decide disputes as to whether or not compensation for disturbance or improvement was payable, and as to the amount of any such compensation. The previous requirement, that a cultivator must retain a subsistence area elsewhere, found no place in the new Ordinance. It also made no provision for sub-tenants, and this fact furnished a loop-hole for evasion. Lastly, as pointed out by Sir John Hope Simpson in 1930, what eminently required was not compensation for disturbance, but a provision against disturbance.

16. This led to the Protection of Cultivators (Amendment) Ordinance, No. 1 of 1932, in which a tenant was so defined as to include a sub-tenant, and in 1933 a new Ordinance, No. 37, was enacted under the same title in a further endeavour to check the process of displacement of Arab cultivators. This again had to be amended in 1934. Under this Ordinance the High Commissioner could appoint one or more Commissions to adjudicate on disputes as to whether a cultivator was or was not a " statutory tenant ", as to who was landlord, and whether any person had exercised continuously " any practice of grazing or watering animals or cutting wood or reeds or other beneficial occupation ". An amending Bill has recently been published extending the rights and liabilities of the principal Ordinance to any statutory tenant who cultivates a holding for one year or " for a period necessary to raise two successive crops ". A new clause provides for the restoration to their holdings of displaced statutory tenants, and empowers special Commissions in certain circumstances to dismiss the claims of any person to the rights of a statutory tenant, where they are satisfied that he already possesses or retains elsewhere sufficient land for his maintenance.

17. In addition to the Protection of Cultivators Ordinances, in 1932 and 1934 the Land Disputes (Possession) Ordinances were enacted. The intention was to empower the District Commissioner to hold a summary enquiry into any dispute regarding land, water or grazing rights etc. which was likely to cause a breach of the peace, and to decide which party should be entitled to possession, or to exercise certain rights.

All these " protective " Ordinances have been the subject of criticism and protest by the Jews, with which we shall deal later.

Chapter IX.   224

18. In 1920 an Ordinance enacted that illegal occupiers of land which had become vacant through death or abandonment of cultivation (known as *mahlul*) were to notify Government under penalty of fine. The same year a Survey Ordinance was passed to facilitate entry into properties, and in 1921 preliminary triangulation began as the first step towards the ultimate cadastral survey and settlement of ownership. The same year saw the enactment of three Ordinances, one constituting Land Courts to determine rights in land, settle land disputes and demarcate State Lands, another prohibiting an increase in rents, and the third to protect State Lands (*Mewat*) from encroachment. It was not, however, till 1926, after the appointment of Sir E. Dowson as Commissioner of Lands that land settlement operations began in earnest, and a programme for land survey and settlement was drawn up.

19. In 1926 the Correction of Land Registers Ordinance was enacted, introducing a unified system for the registration of land. In 1927 the tithes payable on holdings of land and collected in kind were commuted for a fixed money payment based upon averages and allotted by a village Assessment Committee.

20. In 1930, as a result of the recommendations of the Shaw Commission, Sir John Hope Simpson (to whose findings we have referred above in paragraphs 4 and 7) made a thorough investigation of the land problem in Palestine, arriving at conclusions as to the land available for the settlement of Jews, and submitted recommendations for development, including the acceleration of survey and land settlement, and the improvement of agriculture. While several of the statistics and conclusions based thereon have been challenged before us and some require modification, his Report still remains an excellent and comprehensive appreciation of the agrarian position in Palestine at the time of his inquiry. It is unfortunate that his proposal for a Development Commission on which both Arab and Jew would be represented was not accepted by either.

21. In 1933 the Co-operative Societies Ordinance was enacted to facilitate the formation of Rural Co-operative Credit Societies, while the Land Law (Amendment) Ordinance gave the High Commissioner power to declare land which had become vacant (*Mahlul*) to be public land and auction it to prospective cultivators.

22. In 1935 a Rural Property Tax Ordinance was introduced, substituting a single simplified tax in place of the Turkish Tithe and House and Land Tax (*Werko*). This effected a large reduction, in some cases up to 70 per cent., in the taxes payable by the peasantry, in the hope of so encouraging agricultural developments.

Chapter IX.

23. The above summary of legislative activity shows the efforts made by the Administration to fulfil their obligations under Article 11 in circumstances of singular difficulty, not rendered any easier by the unavoidable pressure of the Jews for land purchase and consequent land speculation, and sadly hampered by the political outbreaks and consequent lack of funds, since revenue which might have been available for large schemes of development was diverted to expenditure on public security. And, largely as a result, so it appears to us, of these difficulties, we have not now, after 15 years' administration of Palestine by the Mandatory Power, been presented with a really final and reliable statement either of the waste lands, the Government Domains, or of the cultivable area. Nor will this be possible until the survey and land settlement operations are concluded.

24. Whatever may be the cultivable area of Palestine, a matter we discuss later on, it is at least certain that it is limited and in a large measure already in use. The systems of cultivation may be improved. It may be possible in certain localities to replace extensive by intensive cultivation. An active policy of agricultural development having this as its object must, even allowing for the utmost activity on the part of Government, take many years before its fulfilment can provide land for close settlement for both Jews and Arabs. There appears at present to be little hope of responsive co-operation on the part of the Arabs. It is feared that during this long period the further displacement of Arabs from the land may intensify political discontent, as evidenced by the demand now made by the Arabs for a complete stoppage of the sale of land to the Jews.

It is, therefore, considered necessary by the Administration to protect the Arab against himself, not by prohibiting sales, but by making it a condition of every disposition of rural land, including sale, mortgage, gift, dedication of *waqf*, and lease for more than three years, that the person making the disposition should retain ownership of the minimum area necessary for his subsistence (*lot viable*). The size of the subsistence area would depend upon the nature of the cultivation, and might be varied from time to time as the land was improved or its irrigation became possible. No restriction would be placed on the number of transactions to be allowed to each purchaser, or on the number to be allowed to each vendor, provided that he retained the prescribed subsistence area. The High Commissioner would have the power to sanction the sale of a subsistence area in special cases. The following lands would be excluded from the operation of the legislation:—all urban and town planning areas, the whole of the Beersheba Sub-District and all land planted with citrus at the date of the enactment of the legislation. If the owner should desert his subsistence area, or otherwise fail to cultivate it, Government would have the right to

Chapter IX. 226

resume ownership after it had remained uncultivated for three years. It is proposed to introduce legislation to this effect.

25. We are doubtful whether any committee or any individual could satisfactorily prescribe at any given time a minimum subsistence area, even if based on the fertility of the soil as displayed in the various categories of the Rural Property Tax Ordinance. In support of this we may instance the case of the Beisan land.* Secondly, any such legislation would in practice be difficult to enforce. It relies on the present land registry system, which we consider unsatisfactory and over-centralized. Thirdly, it is not clear that it makes any allowance for the natural increase of population. Fourthly, it appears to be based on the assumption that the price received for the land sold, apart from the *lot viable* retained for the cultivator and his family, will not only free him from debt, but also enable him to adopt intensive cultivation, a process only possible, so far as is at present known, in the maritime and plain areas. Even there, the small cultivator would depend for the cultivation of his reduced plot of land on the sharing of a water supply with his neighbours. Lastly, it would result in the retention of a number of small Arab holdings in an area most of which would be held by Jews. It would thus provide a fruitful source of friction in the matter of water rights, access or grazing.

26. We recommend elsewhere that survey and settlement operations should be completed with the utmost despatch. Until this has been done and their completion has provided both vendor and purchaser with an accurate and reliable record of rights and there is suitable rural official machinery to maintain it, we would welcome the definite prohibition of the sale of isolated and comparatively small plots of rural land to Jews. We would prefer larger schemes for the rearrangement of proprietorship under Government supervision, both during their introduction and subsequent development, carrying with it the consolidation of holdings, recourse being had, if necessary, to the Land Expropriation Ordinance. The case of Caesarea sand dunes, dealt with below, is an illustration of the need for this procedure. In this way we believe it should be possible to ensure an equitable distribution to Arabs and Jews alike, such as is now in contemplation in the case of the Lake Huleh area, providing subsistence for a larger number of Arabs than were on the land before the sale.† We would not exclude the possibility of combining a number of small holdings in such a scheme as would result in an area of not less than 500 dunums being available for distribution with a view to close settlement. Nor would there appear to be any valid objection to the sale, with the prior

---

* Paragraphs 126–133 below. † See paragraphs 120–125 below.

227   Chapter IX.

approval of the Government, of small holdings for the purpose of rounding off an estate or to facilitate irrigation, and the High Commissioner should retain powers to permit alienation in special cases, as has been proposed by Government in their Bill dealing with the possible sale of a subsistence area.*

27. The criticism has been made that the provision of Article 11 of the Mandate for the introduction of " a land system appropriate to the needs of the country, having regard, among other things, to the desirability of promoting the close settlement and intensive cultivation of the land " has not been implemented.

It is true that no new system has been introduced, no new land code has been enacted. The Ottoman Land Code has been retained, with all the difficulties involved in its various forms of ownership and tenure of land; several new laws have been passed to amend it, but it remains in essence the same complicated system, one which is not calculated to promote close settlement and intensive cultivation. Even with the amendments which it has been found possible to introduce, it cannot be deemed to be a satisfactory system in these respects, as will be seen from a perusal of this part of our Report. We may instance the difficulties with regard to *masha'a* and the Protection of Cultivators Ordinance.

To this extent the Jewish grievance appears to us to be justified.

28. We have above referred to the difficult conditions which the Mandatory Power had to face. The Land Registries had to be closed for a period, ownership was uncertain, the records incomplete and unreliable. The era of speculation which started when the Jews began to purchase land was a further complication. In 1932 there were 18,392 transactions in land, registration fees amounting to £97,876. In 1935 49,133 transactions were registered, at the cost of £455,146. Obviously the Department of Lands was fully occupied and had no time to devote to the codification of the land law.

29. The subject is one which seriously affects the proper development of the country. But the formulation of a land code which can absorb the existing system and adequately meet the needs of the Bedouin population on the one hand and an advanced urban and rural population on the other is an exceedingly difficult matter and one which the Attorney-General's Department has never had the necessary time to undertake. In our opinion, however, the time has now arrived at which the task should be undertaken. We recommend that a committee should be set up to deal with it, and should include, in addition to persons familiar with the present law and local

---
* See paragraph 24 above.

Chapter IX.   228

conditions, at least one person who is an expert in land law and has had experience in drafting agrarian legislation and of land administration elsewhere. We understand that this matter has more than once been the subject of consideration by the Palestine Government, which recognizes its importance and would probably welcome such action.

In the words used by Mr. Lewis French, we recommend that any such land code " should be framed on the broadcast and simplest lines possible, all minor details being left to rules and regulations ", which would presumably be published for criticism prior to adoption.

30. Before concluding this section, it is perhaps desirable to explain that " survey and settlement " are administrative operations distinct from, although essentially necessary to, the close settlement of Jews upon the land. The object of " survey and settlement " is the ascertainment of areas and boundaries, the preparation of maps to display them, and the compilation of a record of rights, which usually in the British Empire includes not merely a statement of the ownership of the land, but all the rights and easements connected with the use of the land, such as tenancies and sub-tenancies, grazing, fuel or irrigation rights. Often this record sets forth any fiscal obligations attaching to the land, whether revenue payable to the Government or rent payable to a landlord. In Palestine, however, there is at present no connection between rural property taxation and land settlement.

31. From any complete record of rights there should be compiled a register showing, village by village and plot by plot, the names of all owners and occupiers of land and their rights. The record should confer a presumptive title *contra mundum*, and if the land registers both locally and at headquarters are kept up to date, and mutations are systematically reported and recorded, it should be a simple matter for anyone to discover at once whether any person has or has not certain rights in any given plot in a village.

32. There are therefore two main branches in land settlement operations: first, the survey and mapping of land; secondly, the preparation of a record of rights, which may or may not include the fixing of rents as between proprietors and tenants, or the settlement of land revenue.

Before a land settlement survey can commence it is necessary to have a triangulated framework of fixed points, accurately determined and permanently marked. This was completed in Palestine, excluding Beersheba, in 1927. The next stage is a traverse survey by theodolite of a series of stations demarcated on the ground and the plotting of them on sheets, to serve as a framework on which the detailed or cadastral survey

229   Chapter IX.

may be made. Map No. 2 at the end of this Report shows the extent to which this has been accomplished in Palestine. The plans prepared for the settlement survey were on the scale of roughly 25 inches to the mile. It should be added that a fiscal survey was commenced in 1929 and completed in 1934, carried out by fairly rapid topographical methods on a smaller scale. All streams, roads, paths, and villages were surveyed, as well as the boundaries of the " localities " which were used as fiscal blocks. The large scale cadastral survey did not start till 1928. Towns and villages which came under the urban property tax had also to be surveyed, and every year fresh villages are added to the list. Triangulation survey has started in the Beersheba Sub-District.

33. The following statements show the progress made in survey and settlement. Survey commenced in 1927: settlement in 1928. There have been three breaks due to political disturbances, in 1929, 1933 and 1936.

COST OF SURVEY AND SETTLEMENT BUDGETARY PROVISION.

Year	Survey	Settlement	Total
	£	£	£
1927 (9 months)	32,453	—	32,453
1928	44,217	10,953	55,170
1929	43,494	23,410	66,904
1930	48,637	23,289	71,926
1931	49,410	24,893	74,303
1932 (3 months)	12,500	6,151	18,651
1932–33	51,039	25,183	76,222
1933–34	63,693	29,083	92,776
1934–35	67,933	30,088	98,021
1935–36	69,151	28,071	97,222
1936–37	68,332	35,065	103,397
£	550,859	236,186	787,045

The following figures show the progress of survey and settlement since 1927:—

Year	Area Surveyed Dunums	Area Settled Dunums
1927–1930	332,600	142,799
1931	149,485	138,387
1932	399,331	167,293
1933	424,600	334,139
1934	628,524	283,464
1935	360,660	298,549
1936	299,920	127,246
Total	2,595,120	1,491,877

Chapter IX.   230

The aggregate area of all land taxed under the Rural Property Tax Ordinance of 1935 is stated to be 13,592,306 dunums. Evidently, unless the operations can be expedited, completion of the settlement must take many years.

34. Land settlement in Palestine differs materially from that in the British Empire, notably in India. It has nothing to do with the settlement of land revenue, the fixation of rents, the fertility of the soil, or the recording of easements, but is restricted to judicial decisions, frequently in intricate cases demanding long judgments, of claims and title suits. The work is impeded by a large number of fictitious and frivolous claims, all of which have to be duly recorded, examined and decided. This procedure inevitably provokes and multiplies litigation, especially in a country where there has been a sudden and abnormal increase in land values. Whereas at first disputed claims were about 10 per cent. of the total submitted to Settlement Officers, there is now reported " a growing tendency to dispute every claim where there is a shadow of a case, and often where there is not ". Further delay is caused by the detachment of the staff to deal with special enquiries, like the water resources survey, or surveys of urban areas like Tel Aviv in connection with the urban property tax, or urgent cases where land disputes are, as at Beisan, likely to develop into riots on a large scale. We were informed that of 134 Surveyors not more than 80 or 90 were actually engaged on settlement work.

35. Two maps appended to this Report show the progress made with survey and land settlement to the end of 1936. Out of some 400 villages (outside Beersheba and the hill districts), the Land Settlement Ordinance has been applied to 160: the work has been finished in 107: in 31 villages disputes are under trial prior to completion of settlement: in 19, the final stage of investigation is in progress: in 3, preliminary field investigation has commenced. During the year 1936, owing to the disturbances, it was only found possible to settle 1,490 claims out of 9,333, leaving 7,843 disputes outstanding.

36. In the absence of a reliable record of rights for all the villages, instead of for one-quarter, it is evident that any statistics relating to the possession of land must be read as liable to considerable alteration when eventually settlement proceedings are completed. The need for their expedition is paramount. We recommend that steps should be taken to form three distinct settlement parties, one to deal with the southern and another with the northern area of the Maritime Plains, a third being available for special enquiries of the kind referred to above. It will probably take two years to train the staff, but once this has been accomplished, progress should

be rapid. We suggest for the consideration of the Palestine Government whether it might be possible to obtain the services of Settlement Officers and trained Surveyors with a knowledge of Arabic from India. In the meantime the necessary topographical survey can continue and large-scale maps can be prepared. It may be added that the work of the survey, as distinct from settlement, is excellent.

37. The present system of Land Courts appears to us to be contributory to delay. There are four District Courts, each composed of a British President and two Palestinian Judges. Jurisdiction is given to these Courts, composed of the President and one or more Judges of the District Court, to sit as a Land Court and to deal with questions of title to land. Such a Court also acts as Court of Appeal from the decisions of Magistrates in respect of recovery of land.

We should prefer two or, if necessary, three separate Land Courts, at any rate until the land survey and settlement operations have been completed. These Land Courts should deal with all possessory rights and easements as well as questions of title demarcation and should be able to issue mandatory injunctions or orders for specific performance. We are aware that in 1930 there were two special Land Courts, one at Jerusalem and one at Jaffa, and that the Financial Commission in 1931 recommended their abolition. That Commission held that " the distinction between Land Courts and the other Civil Courts rests admittedly on no principle and should be abolished. Land Courts were established because it was believed that cases relating to land were peculiarly difficult. It is now recognized that this is not so." Be that as it may, evidence was given before us to the effect that " the Land Courts are functioning very, very slowly, so that you are lucky if you get a case through in the Land Courts in two years." Further, we can discern no advantage in having two Judges to decide these cases. One Judge, a British officer with practical experience of Land Settlement, should be sufficient. There should be an appeal to the Supreme Court on a point of law.

38. Apart from the increase in the number of Settlement Officers and staff, advocated in paragraph 36 above, we consider that far more use should be made of the settlement procedure. It should not be limited as at present merely to ascertaining and settling disputes and claims. The aim should be the preparation of a reliable and accurate record of rights of the kind described in paragraph 30. With it should be combined a plot to-plot inquiry as to the fertility of the soil and the classification thereof in the appropriate category under the Rural Property Tax. The Settlement and Assistant Settlement Officers should camp in the villages where operations are in progress and hear all the claims and objections on the spot.

Chapter IX. 232

39. Assuming that traverse survey has been completed, the first stage in settlement proceedings would be the cadastral survey on the spot, the preparation of the draft record for attestation being undertaken during the recess, when maps are checked and examined, areas of villages and various plots therein extracted and the lists of interested parties, their rights and areas of plots prepared. The second year should see attestation or the inquiry into the draft record and the settlement and decision of disputes. This also should take place in the presence of all parties interested. Slips would be distributed to all persons believed to have rights in the land, landlords and tenants, showing the areas of all plots. Draft entries in the village register would be explained personally on the spot by the Assistant Settlement Officer, who would finally correct and attest them, after deciding all disputes as to status, possessory rights or easements. When attestation is completed the record of rights would be checked, corrected and prepared for draft publication, when one month should be allowed during which the record would be open to inspection. Any objections filed then should, after due notice of date of hearing, be tried summarily on the spot.

40. On the completion of these steps, the record of rights would be corrected and finally published, necessary certified extracts being given to all owners and tenants. The final record should then be sent to the Land Registry, where necessary entries should be made as regards all the various holdings, village by village. It should be provided, if necessary by legislation, that every entry in the record is to be presumed to be correct until it is proved by evidence to be incorrect. There should then be no difficulty in allowing the police to decide whether any given individual has any rights in the land or is a trespasser. The maintenance of the record by registering sanctioned mutations, i.e. transfers or dispositions of property registered by the Lands Department, may be difficult under existing circumstances in Palestine, where the village tax collector or *Mukhtar* does not always possess sufficient education. The remedy would seem to lie in the appointment, where necessary, of village Registrars, as advocated by Mr. Lewis French in 1931.

41. If exception is taken to these proposals on the grounds of expense, the reply must be that a contented tenantry and peasantry will in the end be much cheaper to govern, and that the absence of disputes regarding land, the prevention of trespass and the security of title conferred by these operations should conduce to the general prosperity and development of the country. Uncertainty regarding the land and rights therein creates disputes, encourages trespassers and promotes a feeling of insecurity, which in turn demands an ever larger police force

Chapter IX.

and results in increased litigation. In this matter of land settlement, i.e., the preparation for all the villages in the country of a reliable record of rights, the Administration, we consider, have not yet discharged their obligations under the Mandate.

2. The second problem: Cultivable area.

42. Remembering, then, that the settlement operations in five-sixths of the country may materially alter the present estimates as to ownership of land, it is now necessary to discuss the much debated problem as to how much of the land in Palestine is cultivable, and how production can be increased.

With the Sub-District of Beersheba we deal later. That is a separate problem depending, first, on the discovery of water and, secondly, on some arrangement which may induce the nomad Bedouins to adopt settled cultivation.

43. The following is an account by a Jewish eyewitness of the condition of the Maritime Plain in 1913. It was, we believe, at the time when it was written, a truthful and disinterested description.

The road leading from Gaza to the north was only a summer track suitable for transport by camels and carts. This track was dry and open for travel in the summer months only. In the rainy season it was impassable.

In the villages on both sides of the track and as far as the hills to the east no orange groves, orchards or vineyards were to be seen until one reached Yabna Village. Trees generally were a rare sight in these villages. . . . Nor were there any vegetable gardens to be seen in any of these villages except at Jora on the sea (Asqalan). In the Hawakir around the villages—small plots fenced around by cactus hedge—one could find in the winter green onions and in the summer cucumbers and water melons.

In all the villages dotting the plain between Gaza and Jaffa there was only one well in a village and in the smaller villages there were no wells at all. . . . Not in a single village in all this area was water used for irrigation. Water was scantily used for drinking purposes by man and beast.

Houses were all of mud. No windows were anywhere to be seen. The roofs were of caked mud. Every house was divided in two parts—one part slightly elevated above the other. The family lived in the elevated part while in the lower part the cattle were housed. The cattle were small and poor. So were the chickens.

The fields were sown with wheat, barley, kursena and lentils in the winter—and with dura and sesame in the summer. Fields used for summer crops one year were sown with winter crops the next year, and so in rotation. The ploughs used were of wood. European ploughs were not known in the whole area. Not a village could boast of a cart. Sowing was done by hand; harvesting by the scythe and threshing by animals. Fields were never manured.

The lands were all held in *masha'a* ownership. Every second year the fields were measured by stick and rope and distributed among the cultivators. Division of land always led to strife and bloodshed.

The yields were very poor. Wheat yield never exceeded 60 kgms. per dunum and barley about 100 kgms. per dunum. The wheat yield went to Government in payment of tithe and to the *effendi* in payment of interest on loans. The *fellah* himself made his bread from dura.

Chapter IX.   234

The sanitary conditions in the villages were horrible. Schools did not exist and the younger generation rolled about in the mud of the streets. The rate of infant mortality was very high. There was no medical service in any of the villages distant from a Jewish settlement. In passing a village one noticed a large number of blind, or half-blind persons. Malaria was rampant.

Starting from Yabna one could see in some villages several wells, some orange groves and vegetable fields under irrigation. In the neighbourhood of Wadi Rubin considerable quantities of vegetables, especially tomatoes, were grown. But the standing water in that *wadi* devastated the whole area, being a breeding place of malaria. At Wadi Hunein there were several orange groves belonging to *effendis*. Most of them were in a very neglected state. They were planted in irregular formation and irrigated in a very primitive manner. At Ramleh and Lydda old olive plantations and orchards of apricots and mulberries existed. At Beit Dajan, Yazur and Jaffa considerable areas were planted with orange trees. The quality of these groves was not superior to those of Wadi Hunein.

The entire area of orange groves owned by Arabs before the War was 20,000 dunums while the Jews owned 10,000 dunums. The export of oranges was as follows:—

	Cases.
1907	489,992
1908	418,835
1909	490,317
1910	628,013
1911	624,198
1912	803,620
1913	910,548

The area north of Jaffa as far as Hedera and Zichron Jacob, known as the Sharon, consisted of two distinctive parts divided by a line from south to north. The eastern part in the direction of the hills resembled in culture that of the Gaza-Jaffa area. There one could find many well populated villages with the little town of Tulkarm as their centre. The western part towards the sea was almost a desert. Sandy soil with numerous swampy stretches such as the Auja, Sidna Ali, Ramadan, Kabani and Hedera swamps and many other smaller swamps. The villages in this area were few and thinly populated. Many ruins of villages were scattered over the area as owing to the prevalence of malaria many villages were deserted by their inhabitants who migrated to the hills. The few patches in the western section which under cultivation produced Turmos in the winter and water melons in the summer. The rest was all covered by halfa and thorns.

44. The following figures as regards land areas were given us by the Palestine Government as their latest estimate, based on their definition of " cultivable land." This is held to cover land " which is actually under cultivation, or which can be brought under cultivation by the application of the labour and resources of the average Palestinian cultivator ".

The total area of Palestine is approximately 10,400 square miles or 27,009,000 dunums.

Excluding Beersheba, which has not been surveyed, but the area of which is estimated at 12,577,000 dunums, the *land area* of the remainder of Palestine is 13,742,000 dunums. This omits

235   Chapter IX.

the Dead Sea and the Sea of Galilee (690,000 dunums), but it includes the Lake of Huleh. The Administration regard 6,622,000 dunums as uncultivable, as being forest land, waste land, urban or village areas. They thus arrive at a total of 7,120,000 dunums as the " cultivable area ".

45. In their evidence before us the Jewish Agency did not give any definite figures as regards the total area and estimated cultivability. It is stated, however, in Mr. Granovsky's book *The Land Issue in Palestine* that " figures arrived at by the Jewish Agency experts show that the cultivable area of Palestine comprises, exclusive of the Beersheba Sub-District, 9,197,000 dunums, divided as follows: in the plains, 3,876,650 dunums; in the hill and mountain districts, 5,320,350 dunums ". Hence, taking the total land area of Palestine, excluding Beersheba, to be 13,742,000 dunums, " the uncultivable areas extend over 4,545,440 dunums ". These figures presumably include, as cultivable, forest areas, which are estimated by the Government at 695,000 dunums and are in their estimate excluded from the cultivable land, so that the net difference between the Government estimate of cultivable land and the Jewish figures is 1,382,000 dunums. We think that in arriving at these figures it is not improbable that the Jews have envisaged the expenditure, in making land cultivable, of an amount of capital which could not be justified on economic grounds.

Dr. Hexter said: " I cannot give an estimate, because I am convinced an estimate of mine might err in other directions, but my point is simply that in any development possibilities in this country one must go from one place to another literally to see what can be done "

46. We ourselves do not consider it possible at any given date to estimate with any accuracy how much land can be classed as " cultivable ". This must depend, as is generally recognized, on irrigation and the improved use of available water supplies, on the draining of marshy areas, and on the adoption of new methods of agriculture, more especially in the hills. These last in turn depend on the amount of capital available. The Arab peasant has at present neither the capital nor the education necessary for intensive cultivation. The Jew has. But the lack of these two essential requisites does not justify the expropriation of the Arab to make room for the richer and more enterprising colonist, even though the Arab's conservative methods, and in some cases his system of land tenure, may delay development. At a later stage we discuss the possibility of large scale development schemes.

47. All the estimates of cultivable land are challenged by the Jewish Agency mainly on two grounds. First, the definition adopted by the Palestine Government of " cultivable " land would exclude much land already brought under cultivation,

Chapter IX.   236

as well as land which can by appropriate methods of agriculture be cultivated. Secondly, sufficient allowance is not made for intensive cultivation, i.e. close settlement upon the land. This presupposes adequate irrigation, without which, except in a few specially favoured areas, intensive cultivation is impossible.

48. Dr. Maurice Hexter condemned the Palestine Government's definition of " cultivable land " because the figures, based on a fiscal survey, were necessarily falsified by the natural desire to evade the tax. They were compiled, he said, by surveyors unable to classify cultivability, and limited to recording areas actually under cultivation, omitting fallow lands.

The estimate of Government, he said:—

"excludes all or nearly all land not under cultivation; secondly, it excludes all or nearly all land requiring considerable capital outlay; thirdly, it excludes all land under water, such as Huleh; fourthly, it does not distinguish between quality and productivity of the soil; fifthly, the figures are still estimates; sixthly, their present basis seems to us no more final than the estimates which they displace; and, lastly, the definition is unrelated to realities, because it omits, as it shows by its very contents, technology, capital, education, skill and markets."

We notice, however, that the Jewish Agency, when complaining of the small amount of State lands placed at their disposal, included, amongst other deductions from the total, 22 per cent. as " uncultivable ". This was the average percentage arrived at by the Government on approximate figures obtained from Rural Property Tax records, and was based on their definition, now impugned, and on the enquiries of their surveyors, now discredited.

49. In criticism of the Government estimates of cultivable land, it was pointed out that the total area of land under cultivation is shown as much greater than the total area of cultivable land—on the face of it an obvious error and tending to show a serious underestimate of cultivable land. We have ascertained however, that this discrepancy is accounted for by the fact that the estimate of cultivated land is increased because the same areas of land may appear twice in the figures owing to their having two crops upon them, e.g., cereals planted between olives.

50. Dr. Hexter claimed that the definition underestimated the future possibilities of rural development in Palestine, and that the cultivable area could only be ascertained by a " detailed spot analysis ". He regarded this matter as of primary importance, since on the estimate of the land available for cultivation depended the admission of Jewish settlers, and because Sir John Hope Simpson's conclusion, based on this definition, was that there was " no margin of land available for agricultural settlement by new immigrants, with the

exception of such undeveloped land as the various Jewish Agencies hold in reserve ".

51. Dr. Hexter's own definition was as follows:—

" The word ' cultivable ' does not describe an inherent or absolute attribute of land which determines the use to which it can be put. ' Cultivability ' is not the independent determining factor, but is itself determined by the inter-action of the physical properties of the land (including availability of irrigation waters), and the economic factors of production which are applied to it and modify it. To what extent factors of production can be applied depends on the economic progress of the country as a whole, including possibilities of special products, and can only be forecasted from time to time. Land will be taken into cultivation or subjected to a more intensive or different form of cultivation as and when the supply of capital, labour, skill, and available markets warrant it. . . . For the purpose of determining whether particular land is cultivable, or whether, if cultivated, it is capable of more intensive cultivation, it is necessary to have an analysis of each particular project in relation to the particular area in question."

52. He realized that the determination of areas under his definition was " an extremely complicated process and a time-consuming process ", though he had already impressed on the Commission the fact that " we in our search for land have not time: we cannot wait ". Or as Dr. Ruppin put it:—

" It may be that we are impatient, but we are being pressed very much by the Jews who would like to settle here and who cannot settle here if the development activities are not carried out in rather quick tempo ".

And again:

" Generally what is important is the question of tempo, and the point of view from which you look at it. I have to look at it from the point of view of our desire to give as many Jews as possible the possibility of settling in agriculture. In the last 50 years we were concerned with the scarcity of land, and we understood that this scarcity could be overcome only by development, by intensification. My people are impatient. We have to be."

53. We are disposed to agree that no really satisfactory definition in advance can be found on which it would be safe to base an estimate as to the cultivable area. This must, we consider, and we hold this view also as regards the *lot viable* of the cultivator,* be discovered by experience, by a system of " trial and error " in the different parts of the country. But we consider that, until the contrary is proved by experience and practical experiment, the Administration will be wise in adhering to their own definition in so far as it relates to an increase of immigrants on the land. Until it has been *proved* that any particular area is capable of supporting further settlement, owing either to the discovery of irrigation facilities or to the application of new scientific methods, the present

---

* See paragraph 25.

Chapter IX. 238

position is such that, in the words of the Shaw Commission Report, " taking Palestine as a whole, the country cannot support a larger agricultural population than it at present carries, unless methods of farming undergo a radical change ". In other words, the economic absorptive capacity of the country appears to us to depend, so far as the land is concerned, not on the mere hope of extending cultivation by irrigation, but on the definitely ascertained existence of the various factors contained in the definition put forward by the Jewish Agency.

54. Before we discuss how best this object may be achieved, it is desirable to examine the complaint made by the Arabs that the Jews had already received too much land, thus creating a class of landless Arabs, and increasing " land-hunger ". Secondly, they complain that the Jews now hold nearly as much of the best land as the Arabs do, that classed in category 1 for the Rural Property Tax, although the rural population of the Jews at the census of 1931 was below 50,000, while the Arab rural population was about 590,000.

55. In the matter of land purchased by the Jews there was again a dispute as to the accuracy of the figures, since the statement prepared by the Administration included land acquired by Jews in pre-war days, and lands made over to companies, like the Palestine Potash Company, which are not entirely Jewish. In the matter of State Domains, for example, while the Government figures show a total of 175,545 dunums, the Jewish Agency claim that the amount which they have received for definitely Jewish ownership, since the Mandate, is only 82,605 dunums. The point does not appear to us to be one of primary importance, and depends chiefly on the method of calculation. While, for example, the Palestine Potash Company is not entirely Jewish, it is mainly Jewish and was, in fact, quoted as an instance of Jewish industrial enterprise. Similarly, whether land was obtained from the Turkish Government before the War or afterwards in fulfilment of an agreement made with that Government appears to us to be of less importance than the fact that such land is actually to-day in Jewish possession. For our present purpose we are prepared to accept the figures submitted by the Palestine Government showing each year since October, 1920, the land purchased by Jews. These total 682,865 dunums, of which some 36,971 dunums are in Beersheba, while pre-War holdings amounted to some 650,000, or a total of 1,332,865.

56. According to approximate figures prepared from the Rural Property Tax categories, Arabs hold 12,160,000 dunums, of which 6,037,000 are classed as cultivable, and Jews 1,208,000, with 939,000 dunums of cultivable land. In category 1 (Citrus), with a tax rate of 825 mils (16s. 6d.) per dunum, or £3 6s. per acre, Arabs hold 106,400 and Jews 102,000 dunums respectively.

Chapter IX.

57. The point at issue is whether, as a result of these purchases, the " rights and position " of the Arabs have or have not been prejudiced, or in other words, whether a considerable number of Arabs have been displaced by Jews and become landless. The Shaw Commission considered that this was likely to occur in the future. They reported:—

> "Any complete survey of the whole country must take a very considerable time. In the meantime the Palestine Government are confronted with the prospect of repetitions of the situation now existing at Wadi el Hawareth and of further calls upon the police to carry out evictions of large bodies of cultivators with no alternative land to which they can be moved or upon which they can settle. In the past, persons dispossessed have in many cases been absorbed in the neighbouring villages; we were, however, told that this process, though it may have been possible four or five years ago, is no longer possible to-day; the point of absorption has been reached. The plain facts of the case are, so we are advised, that there is no further land available which can be occupied by new immigrants without displacing the present population."

Sir John Hope Simpson recorded his opinion as follows:—

> "It is clear, however, that of the land which remains with the Government at the present time the area is exceedingly small, with the exception of tracts which, until developed, are required in their entirety for the maintenance of the Arabs already in occupation. It cannot be argued that Arabs should be dispossessed in order that the land should be made available for Jewish settlement. That would amount to a distinct breach of the provisions of Article 6 of the Mandate."

58. In the Statement of Policy issued by His Majesty's Government in 1930 it was stated:—

> "It appears that of the 86,980 rural Arab families in the villages, 29.4 per cent. are landless. It is not known how many of these are families who previously cultivated and have since lost their land. This is one point, among others, upon which, at present, it is not possible to speak with greater precision, but which will, it is hoped, be ascertained in the course of the Census which is to be taken next year."

Unfortunately, in the Census of 1931 this inquiry was never made. The proposal to hold a Census in 1936 was abandoned owing to the disturbances.

59. In 1931 Mr. Lewis French was appointed Director of Development, and one of his first duties was to prepare a register of " landless " Arabs and to draw up a scheme for resettling them.

In the inquiry which was the outcome of this instruction, the applications of Arabs, though in fact landless, were excluded if they came within any of the following categories:—

(1) Persons who owned land other than that sold which they cultivated as tenants.

Chapter IX.   240

(2) Persons who had found land other than that from which they were displaced and were now cultivating it as tenants.

(3) Persons who, subsequent to the sale of the land from which they were displaced, obtained other land but, on account of poverty or other reasons, had since ceased to cultivate it.

(4) Persons who, at the time of sale, were not cultivators, such as labourers and ploughmen.

(5) Persons who had themselves sold their land to Jews.

(6) Persons who, although landless, had obtained equally satisfactory occupation.

Some of the grounds of exclusion appear to us to be unduly restrictive: for example, sales by Arabs to Arab money-lenders with vacant possession and subsequent sales to Jews were not recorded, as coming within exception (5) above. We regret further that the inquiry should have been based on the registration only of those Arabs who had lost their land as tenants and cultivators and not also of those who had lost their occupation on it as hired labourers. The official total of " landless " Arabs is often misunderstood by those who are unaware of the limited definition of the term. It should be clear that this total can be regarded as representing only a portion of the displacement of Arab population resulting from Jewish land purchases.

60. Although 3,271 applications for resettlement were received from landless Arabs up to the 1st January, 1936, only 664 were admitted to the Register, 2,607 being disallowed. Government purchased lands at a cost of £72,240 for the resettlement of these proved displaced Arab cultivators, and at the time of our inquiry more than half of the 664 families had been provided with land. Some of the remainder declined the land offered them on the grounds that they were accustomed neither to the climate of the new area nor to irrigated cultivation.

61. The Jews also submitted evidence that they had made a careful enquiry into the matter of landless Arabs and they had discovered only 688 tenants who had been displaced by the land being sold over their heads; and that of these some 400 had found other land. This enquiry related to the period 1920 to 1930.

62. It has further to be remembered that the Jews, in their policy of creating an agricultural Jewish population, have restricted the employment of Arab labour on lands held by them. In February, 1935, an enquiry showed that in the Jewish-owned orange groves 40 per cent. of the labour was Jewish and 60 per cent. Arab. The position is now reversed and 60 per cent. of the labour is Jewish and 40 per cent. Arab. This is a subject of keen discussion between the Federation

241   Chapter IX.

of Jewish Labour and the Farmers' Federation. There has in fact been a movement to intimidate those Jewish farmers who employ Arab labour. Picketing in the post-war settlements in the Sharon was on such a scale as to require legislation— the Prevention of Intimidation Ordinance of 1927 (amended in 1936).

Though this policy has not increased the number of landless Arabs, it has reduced the field of employment for labourers and the means of livelihood of those cultivators who depend on work outside their holdings to obtain an adequate income.

63. The evidence we received from Government officers established the fact that up to 1930 or 1931 there was land available for displaced tenants, but that from 1932 onwards it has been extremely difficult for such people to find land. It is only right to say that the Jewish Agency disclaim any intention of displacing Arab cultivators. Thus Dr. Ruppin told us:—

> "There is no tendency on our part to oust Arab farmers from their holdings. The few cases where Arab tenants were displaced, which I mentioned yesterday, by Jewish purchases are negligible in comparison with the much bigger number of Arab farmers who have become landless by foreclosure of their holdings owing to debts to Arab creditors. Our aim is to improve agricultural methods, especially by irrigation, and to create new possibilities for settlement of Jews without prejudicing in any way the livelihood of the previous Arab cultivators. I am also of opinion that the Arab farmer will have a better income . . . from an irrigated and intensive farm of 20 dunums, than from 100 dunums of unirrigated land as it is in its present form. We accept, and have accepted since the time of Sir John Hope Simpson, the formula that in all cases of purchases of land by Jews the Arab cultivators should remain on the land and that their economic situation should not be worse, and I hope it will be better, than it was before. We agree to measures of control by the Government in respect of the fulfilment of these conditions, but in order to carry out a programme which will create new possibilities for Jewish settlement without doing harm to the Arabs, a much more active participation of the Government in the development activities is indispensable."

64. We welcome this statement of policy. As will be seen when we deal with the Huleh project, it has in fact suggested a practical proposal. We also are of opinion that up till now the Arab cultivator has benefited on the whole both from the work of British administration and from the presence of Jews in the country. Wages have gone up: the standard of living has improved: work on roads and buildings has been plentiful. In the Maritime Plains some Arabs have adopted improved methods of cultivation. But we are definitely of opinion that the greatest care must now be exercised to see that in the event of further sales of land by Arabs to Jews, the rights of any Arab tenant or cultivator in the land should be preserved. Further, we are of opinion that this alienation of

Chapter IX. 242

land should only be allowed where it is possible to replace extensive by intensive cultivation, which really means in the plains and not, at any rate at present, in the hills.

65. In the pre-war days conscription and malaria kept the Arab population low. It is now increasing rapidly. The Jewish Agency in their memorandum state: " Apart from more general considerations of a moral order, it is essential in the interests of the Jewish National Home that the *fellaheen* should be raised to a higher standard of life. On a long view, the Jewish village cannot prosper unless the Arab village prospers with it." We would endorse this statement, and add that in our opinion " a long view " means considering the interests of the next generation, or the effect of agrarian development 30 years hence, by which time the Moslem population will have more than doubled, if the present rate of increase is maintained. The shortage of land is, we consider, due less to the amount of land acquired by Jews than to the increase in the Arab population, as a result of the causes to which we have referred.

66. The Arab charge that the Jews have obtained too large a proportion of good land cannot be maintained. Much of the land now carrying orange groves was sand dunes or swamp and uncultivated when it was purchased. Though to-day, in the light of experience gained by Jewish energy and enterprise, the Arabs may denounce the vendors and regret the alienation of the land, there was at the time at least of the earlier sales little evidence that the owners possessed either the resources or training needed to develop the land. So far as the plains are concerned, we consider that, with due precautions, land may still be sold to Jews.

67. We have above referred to certain precautions which should be taken, by which we mean measures to protect the Arab cultivator. The legislation already enacted has been given above, where we noted that the Jews, who recognize the need for protective legislation, criticize the present Ordinances as failing to achieve their object, and as being actively harmful in promoting litigation and causing insecurity of tenure. We regard it as proved that recent alterations in the law relating to the protection of cultivators, and the machinery set up under the law, have led to grave abuse and to blackmailing claims by persons not entitled to protection under that law.

68. The Jews also complain of the difficulty in obtaining a proper title to land purchased. Even after it has been registered in their name they are not able to enforce their possessory rights. An instance will be found in the case of the land at Caesarea given below in Section 4 of this Chapter. To deal with

the complaints under this head in detail would necessitate setting them out *in extenso*, the consideration of the evidence involved, a discussion on the various interpretations put on the Ordinances by the Government, the Jews and the Courts and on the various powers which the latter could and should exercise, and by which of the Courts they could or should be exercised. In our opinion the expenditure of the time so required would be out of all proportion to the value of any detailed recommendations which we might make and which, moreover, would not, we feel, be made with such a full appreciation of the local conditions and of the land laws in Palestine as would be essential.

In addition, they are all matters which would form part of the subject which would be dealt with by the Committee on Land Legislation which we have recommended in paragraph 29 above.

69. As an example, we may mention the Protection of Cultivators Ordinance.

No objection is taken by the Jews to the general principles of the Ordinance, but they urge that as it stands, with its amendments, and with the methods under which is is administered, it affords too great an opportunity for bogus claims and puts a premium on trespassing, with the result that endless delays and great expense are incurred in resisting and buying off these claims before a clear title and undisputed possession of land can be obtained.

We are satisfied that serious delays do occur, but the question of whether the present difficulties in the way of a purchaser can be reduced while at the same time ensuring proper protection of the cultivator is a matter which will necessitate investigation and consideration by the Committee recommended by us, and also reorganization of the Courts and their procedure with a view to the speedier trial of land cases and to ensuring to a purchaser the possibility of establishing his title and of entering into possession with the minimum of delay.

Land settlement also enters into this question and where settlement has taken place on the land in issue, if our recommendations in Section 1 of this Chapter are accepted, and during land settlement operations officers record all easements affecting the land, the problem of dealing with trespassers will be simplified.

70. Other grievances advanced by the Jewish Agency appear to us to contain less just cause for complaint. The first relates to the " vanishing millions of dunums " owing, so it was alleged by the Jewish Agency, to the laxity or incompetence of the officers entrusted with the task of maintaining the Government's rights in the land. Dr. Bernard Joseph, a member of the Palestine Bar, who gave evidence on behalf of the Jewish Agency, referred us to the Government's Annual Report for 1920-1, in

Chapter IX.   244

which the figures of 942,000 dunums of State land and two to three million dunums of waste land " much of which is capable of improvement and productivity " are given.

71. At the present time the Government puts the approximate extent of State Domain at 1,036,000 dunums, to which, it is thought, might reasonably be added 227,600 dunums of sand dunes which are being claimed at Land Settlement. As regards *mewat*, or waste lands, the area throughout the country is unknown, but it may amount to something considerable in the aggregate, made up of uncultivated land, sand dunes and scattered rocky patches, over which it may be found, however, that villagers have established grazing or other rights. Owing to the size and scattered nature of the lands adjudicated to Government, much of the area, it is believed, will be of little or no value for development purposes.

72. At the time of the British Occupation the only areas which were known to be Government property were those which were registered as such. Waste lands were not registered or recorded in any way; their location and boundaries were unknown. Since the occupation, endeavours have been made to register unrecorded *mahlul* (vacant) and waste land in the name of the High Commissioner as *miri* land available for disposal.

73. Land Settlement, as we have pointed out in Section 1, is the only satisfactory process for the definition of the boundaries of State lands, and until it is carried out the position must remain unsatisfactory. Except for three villages in the hills, Settlement operations have so far been confined to the plains. If, however, the Land Settlement Department had dealt with State claims to public lands before undertaking the settlement of land held by private title, it would have postponed the latter for two or three years, and would have justified the criticism that Government, in their own interests ,had delayed the development of the more fertile area of the country, and close settlement upon the land.

74. Dr. Joseph declared that the shrinkage in the total area of State and waste lands was due to inadequate steps taken by Government to preserve its property, especially in earlier years. He stated that, in accordance with the Ottoman law, a man who had cultivated State land for ten years can come to the State and demand a title-deed to that property. He alleged the practice to be that a man came to the Land Registry, bringing with him a certificate signed by the *Mukhtar* of his village and two notables, to the effect that he had been working a piece of land contained within certain boundaries for the last ten years or more, that no notice of such claim was given to the Government, and that on the strength of this certificate the claimant was granted a title.

75. We made careful inquiries into this complaint and are satisfied that all such claims are subjected in the Land Registry to a most critical scrutiny, a survey being first made, including a report on the state of cultivation. The Registrar visits the property, and taxation records are searched to ascertain whether tithe or tax has been paid. The Inspector of Agriculture is then asked for a report, and if this report is not clear it is referred to the Chief Agricultural Officer for his views as to the period and state of cultivation. The allegation that such claims were readily granted in the earlier years is refuted by the number of actions instituted against Government to establish title refused by the Land Registry. In 1924, for example, 106 such cases were entered against Government.

76. We ascertained that the total area in respect of which titles have been granted by the Land Registry from the 1st October, 1920, to the 30th November, 1936, is 248,118 dunums. This figure includes claims by occupants against private property registered in the names of individuals and, although figures as to this are not available, it is considered probable that one-third of the above figure related to privately-owned land. It would seem, therefore, that not more than approximately 165,000 dunums of unregistered State land has been affected by claims of this nature, genuine or otherwise. A large area in Beersheba is included in this amount, as in that district there was no pre-war registration, although the same families had been in possession of land there for centuries. While admittedly the ascertainment and registration of Government ownership in land has been dilatory and even unsatisfactory, no useful purpose is served by exaggeration.

77. An equally groundless complaint was made that Government was not usually represented by competent lawyers in proceedings regarding the title of what might be State land. Actually we find that, though originally the Assistant Director of Lands personally represented Government in title suits, later on it was decided that this work should be done by the Attorney-General's Department, who employ officers who, though not admitted to practise as advocates, are fully qualified for the work, which is carefully watched by the Attorney-General and has been well reported on by the Judges before whom they appear. Since these cases have been transferred to the Government Advocate's branch, thirty-six cases have been decided: twenty-two cases have been won for the Government, two withdrawn at the request of the Director of Land Registration; one settled in Court by agreement and eleven lost. Such cases often turn on questions of fact as to occupation of land in the past, and Government is naturally at a disadvantage in such matters.

Chapter IX. 246

In view of these facts we consider that there is no substance in this complaint.

78. A third general charge brought against the Mandatory Power by the Jewish Agency is that Government has failed adequately to implement its obligations under Article 6 of the Mandate to make State and waste lands available for close settlement by Jews. The limited areas of State land leased to Jews were, it is said, for the most part either sand dunes or swamps which could only be put to use by a large expenditure on reclamation.

79. The general position with regard to State and waste lands has already been examined and stated. The bulk of the area claimed by Government as State Domain is, where cultivable, already occupied by Arab tenants. Expert advisers consider that there is already a scarcity of land in certain areas, notably the hill districts, for the indigenous population.

80. In this connection it has to be remembered that land placed by Government at the disposal of the Jewish National Fund becomes inalienable, in the same way as land acquired for a *Waqf* by the Supreme Moslem Council. Obviously in either case caution on the part of Government in dealing with such land is desirable. It is true that Government now only lease and do not sell State lands. But for practical purposes a long lease to the Jewish National Fund or to a *Waqf* estate may well be regarded as permanent alienation to one race, even though the terms on which the land may be held might many years later be altered.

81. We are of the opinion that, pending survey and land settlement, the Administration wisely refrained from handing over land which, in the light of fuller knowledge, they might find was essential for non-Jewish cultivators.

82. The Jews have, we think, a legitimate grievance in the failure of the Administration to arrange for the consolidation of holdings for the concentration of Arabs in one block. As stated above, we consider that recourse should be had, if necessary, to the Land Expropriation Ordinance and that scattered individual Arab holdings should not be allowed to interfere with the development of a scheme which has been proved to the satisfaction of Government beneficial to Jews and Arabs alike. The arguments for and against this procedure are given below in paragraphs 86-88.

83. The remaining grievances relate, first, to the inadequate steps taken to ascertain the resources of the country and the failure to establish irrigation schemes, a subject dealt with below in Section 3; secondly, to the dilatory proceedings of the Land Settlement Department. The second complaint, in our opinion, is justified. We have suggested the remedy in paragraphs 36-41

of this chapter. Lastly, the request is made that the Government should facilitate the settlement of the Beersheba area by, placing a large tract of land at the disposal of Jewish colonizing bodies, so that an organized effort might be made to discover water for irrigation purposes. With this object, it is suggested, Government should commence land settlement operations in the *Negeb* area.

84. It is obvious that at present Government cannot spare the staff for settlement operations in Beersheba. Far more urgent work in the Maritime Plains fully occupies their time. Further, the Beersheba question is a very difficult problem, which has not been fully examined and in regard to which we would, in view of the experience of the land settlement of the comparatively small area of Beisan, strongly deprecate haste. It appears to us that the first steps to be taken are to ascertain the attitude and desires of the Sheikhs of the various tribes, the rights enjoyed by the tribes, and their attitude towards changing a nomad life for one of settled cultivation. Haste has been a potent factor in creating the troubles in Palestine, and no useful purpose would be served by introducing Jewish immigrants into the Beersheba area until the Government were assured that they would be amicably received. In the meantime, we can see no objection to the Government or to the Jewish Agency exploring the possibilities of a fresh water supply in any part of that country. Any such action should be undertaken under the careful control of Government.

85. In view of the admitted fact that intensive cultivation of the soil is only possible if sufficient water is available at low cost, we referred to the Administration for consideration a proposal placed before us for the creation of special Public Utility Companies, rather on the lines of that suggested for Huleh (Section 4 below). Under this proposal comprehensive schemes of development in the interests of both the Arab and the Jewish communities could be undertaken under the close supervision of, and in active co-operation with, the Government. There would in such Companies be a Government director or directors, though not necessarily Government participation in the finance. The Company would undertake the discovery of sub-surface water resources, promote drainage, and rationalize the distribution of water. They would place their proposals, including their financial resources, before the Government, who would carefully examine both, obtain a report from their local officers as well as their experts on the condition of the land, its present occupants and the area which should be reserved for them. Government would also acquire the land, where the price had not been fixed by negotiation, under the Land Expropriation Ordinance, and take such steps as might be necessary to consolidate holdings. The Company, in return for its expenditure on the development

Chapter IX. 248

of the area, would be given a lease for such area as they might obtain, after the reasonable needs of present occupiers had been met, free of rent for 99 years, though the Rural Property Tax would still be payable and should be an increasing source of income to Government. Arabs would get their leases direct from Government: Jews from the Company. Government would, we suggest, retain control of the water rights, its distribution and price.

86. It is claimed that such a scheme would improve the lot of the Arab in the rationalization of his farm, and its crop rotation. By the consolidation of Arab holdings in the area, possibly in three or four blocks, chances of friction would be diminished, and irrigation more easily introduced. It should help to avert land speculation, and both Arab and Jew would benefit from the development of roads and, it is hoped in time, from co-operative marketing methods.

87. The Palestine Government, while recognizing that such a scheme would provide a place for additional Jewish settlers, doubt whether in the aggregate the position of present Arab owners and occupiers of the land would be improved. They foresee difficulties arising from various causes.

First, there is the deeply-rooted aversion which all Arab peasants have shown in the past to leaving the lands which they have cultivated for many generations. They would, it is believed, strongly object to a compulsory transfer, even from one part to another of the comparatively limited area envisaged in a scheme of this kind.

Secondly, the Arab cultivator finds it extremely difficult to change his methods of agriculture: to adapt himself to cultivation by irrigation. Even with the scientific example of his Jewish neighbours he would be unable to bring the land to its full productivity within many years. The change from dry farming and limited animal husbandry to intensive irrigation entails a complete change of the cultivator's habits, chief among which stands the fact that he would have to work all the year round, and that his farm would require daily attention instead of the leisurely annual disposal of cereal crops from dry farming.

Thirdly, the Palestine Government would have to assume, through its representative on the Board of Directors, direct responsibility for the welfare of each cultivator affected, in allocating to him a fixed area; a *lot viable*, sufficient for the maintenance of himself and his family, and impossible of enlargement if he fails to win a subsistence therefrom. Experience elsewhere, as at Beisan and also in Egypt, shows that in spite of continual help and supervision by Government only 60 per cent. of the tenants are even now beginning to appreciate the necessity for unremitting attention to their cultivation. Hence Government anticipate many calls for relief by way of remission of rent or taxation, and " at times by way of grants of seed and possibly of food or money ". It would induce a habit of dependence on Government.

Fourthly, they lay stress on the difficulty of determining the minimum area required by each existing owner or occupier, which once fixed could not be increased. If found to be definitely inadequate, it would be necessary to find land elsewhere, thus involving a second compulsory transfer of the cultivator concerned.

88. Apart from these practical difficulties, they regard the political considerations, in the present circumstances of Palestine, as of still greater importance. So far, it is urged, from meeting Arab demands to prevent the improvident landowner from selling his land to the Jews, this proposal contemplates the compulsory acquisition of Arab lands, in exchange for other lands on lease, the remainder to be handed over to Jewish organizations. Any such proposal would place in the hands of Arab agitators a weapon against which logical arguments as to the advantages of the scheme would be an ineffective defence.

89. We have already placed on record our conviction that the Arab's lack of capital and education does not justify his being deprived of land. We have also stated that we should welcome the definite prohibition of the sale of isolated and comparatively small plots of land to Jews. We assume that, in a scheme of the kind under consideration, there would, as is doubtless contemplated in the Government's proposals for the protection of small owners, be very careful and detailed enquiries before any land was acquired, any cultivator removed from his holding, or any *lot viable* determined.

90. The Protection of Cultivators Ordinance defines subsistence area as such land as will enable the statutory tenant to maintain his customary means of livelihood in an occupation with which he is familiar: the land must, as nearly as circumstances permit, be in the vicinity of the holding from which the tenant is ejected. " It is believed that the Ordinance will prevent the creation of further landless Arabs by the eviction of agricultural tenants without provision on the land for their subsistence, while at the same time it places no obstacle in the way of the buying and selling of land where the transfer of ownership will not adversely affect the tenant."

91. The acceptance of the first two arguments advanced by the Palestine Government against the proposal, namely the aversion of the peasant to change of location or method of agriculture, combined with his dislike of continuous work, means a sheer negation of progress, and would render it impossible for the Mandatory Power to fulfil its difficult obligation

Chapter IX. 250

to encourage close settlement on the land. We consider that the responsibility of Government for the displaced, and perhaps discontented, cultivator should be held to have been discharged if and when they are satisfied that he has been given land sufficient for his maintenance. We can discern no difficulties in this direction that might not arise under the proposals of the Palestine Government for the protection of small owners by the reservation of subsistence areas.

92. Nor should such a scheme, adequately supervised, increase the already existing tendency to the pauperization of the indigenous peasantry. Loans and remission of taxation have always been freely granted, as the following figures show.

In 1933, out of a demand in respect of a winter payment of tithe of £157,405, it was found that remissions amounting to £105,150 were inevitable.

In 1934 the total remissions amounted to £129,726, out of a total aggregate tithe assessment of £245,000, or 53 per cent.

In 1935 the following figures give the amount of Rural Property Tax due on the 1st April, 1935, the amount collected during the year 1935-6, and the amount outstanding:—

	£
Gross assessment at 1st April, 1935	222,276
Exemption granted under Section 6 of the Ordinance	53,650
Remissions granted during the year	14,058
Collected during the year	100,671
Outstanding on the 1st April, 1936	53,897

In 1935-6 repayments of agricultural loans totalled £7,259 and new loans for £6,562 were issued, leaving £168,943 outstanding.

In view of these figures before them, it is not surprising that the Palestine Government view with dismay anything likely to result in further claims upon their generosity.

93. The political difficulties form part of the general picture of the administration of the country, and we do not underrate them. But we cannot blind ourselves to the fact that, if the Mandate is to continue and the Mandatory Power is to discharge its obligation, the pace of progress must not be determined by factious agitators. Where, then, the following conditions are fulfilled,

(a) there is land available, and a general willingness to sell,

(b) it has been proved suitable for intensive cultivation, and

(c) satisfactory financial arrangements can be devised,

we do not think that such a scheme under Government supervision and control should be held up by calculated obstruction.

94. It is necessary, however, in order to prevent undue optimism, to state that in our opinion, *at present*, such areas are few, and, so far as we can see, are only to be found in the plains and not in the hill districts. In the north of the Huleh area, for example, the number of Arab cultivators is so large that it may not be possible to obtain spare land, especially if, as already noticed by us, account is taken of the natural increase in the population. But this should not preclude careful and detailed examination of any scheme, towards the preparation of which Government might help. Nor, if the necessary financial resources are provided by a Company, should Government hesitate to give every assistance even for a scheme which may not appear at the outset to be from the point of view of its promoters an economic proposition. We have dealt with this proposal at some length as illustrating the grave difficulties that attend any attempt to extend the cultivable area or productivity of the land in Palestine.

95. Such, we think, is the best policy that can be framed for dealing with the Land problem under the Mandate, or under a slightly amended form of it. But we wish to state definitely that in our opinion such a policy, though in the circumstances we consider it does justice to both Arabs and Jews, would not be accepted as just by either race nor remove the grievances they respectively entertain. The attitude of the Jews to the restrictions on land-purchase already proposed by the Palestine Government makes it more than probable that they would oppose the greater measure of restriction which our policy involves. The Arabs, for their part, have told us that no more land at all must be purchased by Jews. On neither side, therefore, would the adoption of our policy remove existing grievances.

3. The Third Problem: Irrigation.

96. This problem involves the proper conservation, control, development and utilization of all the water resources of the country. In Palestine there are four sources of irrigation to be considered—irrigation from rivers, from springs, from wells, and from reservoirs.

IRRIGATION FROM RIVERS.

97. There are only two rivers worthy of consideration in this connection, the Jordan and the Auja. The latter is no more than a small river from which irrigation can only be effected by pumping. A concession for this purpose has been granted to Mr. Rutenberg, the Managing Director of the Palestine Electric Corporation, who at present irrigates from it about 5,000 dunums of land and proposes to irrigate another 700 dunums. It seems probable that the surplus of water remaining will be required for the water supply of Tel Aviv, as there is no other adequate source available.

Chapter IX. 252

98. The Jordan is therefore the only potential source of river irrigation. It presents two possibilities—the Huleh scheme, which is considered in paragraphs 120 to 125 below, and the possibility of a canal from lower down the river. Down the river from Huleh, until a point some five miles below the Sea of Galilee is reached, any project of this nature is prevented by the Palestine Electric Corporation's concession, under which it would seem that nothing can be done in the way of drawing off water above these works which would diminish the supply to them. The canal would therefore have to take off at a point where the Jordan runs in a deep trough and would have to run through some 30 miles of cutting before the water could be brought on a level with the ground. The alternatives would be a very high dam, which would be very expensive and probably impracticable owing to the geological formation, and pumping, which would be ruled out by the expense: even when the water was brought on to the ground, further grave difficulties would arise owing to the configuration of the country, which would necessitate drains every 1,000 yards or so apart being constructed either under or above the canal to carry off flood water from the Judaean hills. The construction of such a canal therefore appears impracticable. The only other possibility of irrigation from the Jordan would be by pumping water at the points where it is required. It is very doubtful whether this would pay owing to the very great height the water would have to be pumped.

Thus the prospects of irrigation from the Jordan in existing conditions appear to be exceedingly doubtful, as the situation above described applies to the whole valley down to the Dead Sea.

IRRIGATION FROM SPRINGS.

99. There are a large number of springs in Palestine, especially in the Beisan plain, the Jordan valley, the Samarian and Judaean hills; but, apart from two small schemes in Beisan and Jericho which are fed from springs, nothing can be done by the Government in irrigating land by this means under the existing Ottoman law, under which the water in springs is the property of individuals, who can sell it as they please, with the consequence that nothing in the way of preventing waste is possible.

100. We consider that legislation vesting the surface water of the country in the High Commissioner is essential and we recommend that the amendment of the Palestine Order in Council which is necessary to enable this to be effected should be made without waiting for other amendments which may be desirable. Legislation of this nature has proved necessary in all countries where irrigation is of importance—in Australia, Canada, India

and the drier States of America. It should enable the Government to ensure in a large measure the economical use of spring water; but the additional area of land which can be irrigated in this way will be comparatively small.

IRRIGATION FROM WELLS.

101. Irrigation from wells is, and likely always to remain, the chief source of irrigation in Palestine. Wells are frequently being deepened and new wells sunk. In consequence the necessity of protecting existing well irrigation has been realized.

102. A complete survey of the coastal plain and the Plain of Esdraelon has been made and the water level in thousands of wells has been measured. At the present moment there is no reason to believe that there is any real diminution of the supply or any falling off in the level of the sub-soil water-table. But these dangers may arise at any time. It is therefore proposed to legislate, in the first place, in order to obviate the necessity for periodical surveys, by prescribing that well-owners must report at stated intervals the depth of the water in their wells and, secondly, if the water-table should in any case be found to be falling, to permit the Government to control the sinking of new, or the deepening of existing, wells, within prescribed areas.

IRRIGATION FROM RESERVOIRS.

103. Investigation by the Government into the possibilities of irrigation of this nature has only recently been started; up to date the results have been most disappointing. A search for satisfactory sites for reservoirs is being made, so far without success. Further investigations, which are proceeding, may lead to better results, but the outlook is not hopeful.

104. A gauging station was constructed near Jerusalem across the Wadi Suraa, which drains a large basin, and measurements of the amount of water running off the brim were taken. It was found that owing to the enormously absorptive character of the soil—a condition which applies to the whole country—99.5 per cent. of the rainfall was absorbed in the land as it fell, so that only $\frac{1}{2}$ of 1 per cent. ran down the Wadi.

105. In Beersheba a dam and reservoir were built. Only about 7 per cent. of the water falling in the large catchment area behind them passed into the reservoir formed by the dam, and at the end of the rains there remained in the reservoir only $\frac{1}{2}$ of 1 per cent. of the water which had fallen in the catchment area, the balance of the 7 per cent. having percolated away into the reservoir bed, which is simply the natural ground, the area being too large for anything in the nature of water-proofing to be effected.

Chapter IX.   254

106. From what has been written above it may be seen that the main sources of water for irrigation in Palestine are wells, which are increasing in number and size in the areas in which water is known to exist. The problem of close settlement of the land depends in the main on the discovery and development of water supplies for irrigation. As stated by Dr. Hexter, on behalf of the Jewish Agency, "The intensification of agriculture depends upon irrigation." Later in his evidence he endorsed a statement made by the Palestine Economic Corporation—"Intensive cultivation of the soil is only possible if sufficient water is available at low cost ". If water could be discovered in the Beersheba Sub-District enormous possibilities of development would be opened up, provided that such water could be brought into service at a reasonable cost. The Sub-District constitutes nearly half the total area of Palestine.

107. As Sir John Hope Simpson stated in his Report, " Given the possibility of irrigation there is practically an inexhaustible supply of cultivable land in the Beersheba area. Without irrigation, the country cannot be developed. Up to the present time there has been no organized attempt to ascertain whether there is or is not an artesian supply of water ".

108. Since the date of his Report it appears that very little has been done by Government to discover water in Palestine. In 1931 the Government obtained a boring plant for experimental purposes, another small plant was purchased in 1933, and in 1934 and 1935 another plant was bought in each year. These plants have been used to a certain extent for exploration purposes. In all, five purely exploratory boreholes have been completed, two of them in the Beersheba district, where work is proceeding on yet another. The plants have also been used for villages which had no water supply, in Jewish settlements where there was a drought, and for town water supplies.

109. The exploratory boreholes which have been made do not afford sufficient data upon which an opinion can be reached as to possible sources of water supply; much more work will have to be carried out before useful knowledge as regards the Beersheba district will be available. The problem is complicated by the existence of saline and fresh water in different parts of the district and it is not known which of the two is going to be found. In both the finished boreholes the water was salt.

110. The boring plants cost from £1,000 to £1,500 each according to the depth for which they are designed and the cost of running a plant varies between £2,000 and £2,500 per annum. The first borehole in Beersheba cost £1,994, being 1,170 ft. deep; the second cost £300, the depth being 375 ft.

111. We have received a considerable amount of evidence upon the subject of irrigation, both written and oral. The

255   Chapter IX.

Jewish experts have furnished calculations of the total amount of water available in Palestine and of the areas which could be irrigated. In their opinion the water resources in the country would be sufficient for the irrigation of at least 1,500,000 dunums of land, as compared with the 350,000 dunums at present irrigated, without taking into consideration the hill districts, in which irrigation is admittedly much more difficult, or the Beersheba area. One estimate for Palestine, excluding Beersheba and the south, puts the figure of irrigable land at 3,500,000 dunums, after allowing water for the civil and industrial needs of a population of 2,500,000 people.

112. We are not in a position to pronounce upon these estimates nor do we consider it in any way necessary for us to attempt to do so. Much work remains to be done before any reliable estimate can be made of the approximate quantity of water available and still more to ascertain how much can be brought into use as an economic proposition. There are large districts, including most of the hill country, in which irrigation would be so difficult, even in the improbable event of water being available, that these districts should, in our opinion, be omitted in any calculation of irrigable area.

113. The main difficulty in any comprehensive extension of irrigation in Palestine is not so much the inadequacy of the supply of water as the cost of making it available for use. If the expense is high the question arises as to what crops can be raised which will justify the expenditure. We are in no way suggesting that all possible steps should not be taken to increase the irrigated area of the country, a matter of vital importance to its development and to the realization of close settlement; but the difficulty remains of making any estimate of the area of land which can be irrigated on an economic basis.

114. Our recommendations (besides that in paragraph 100) are

(a) The transfer of those of the boring plants which are to be used for exploratory purposes from the Public Works Department to the Department of Development, in order that the control of all matters connected with irrigation may be in the hands of one Department.

(b) The purchase of further boring plant for exploratory work.

(c) The engagement of adequate staff—

(i) to secure the reasonably rapid development of the surface water of the country, and

(ii) to administer the Ordinance now in draft relating to wells, to maintain a continuous survey of sub-soil water conditions and to sink further bores for exploratory purposes.

Chapter IX. 256

4. Four Examples of Land Problems.

115. We give in some detail action taken by the Administration in four cases of settlement of land. These illustrate in the case of Birkat Ramadan successful co-operation; in that of Huleh a large project beneficial to both Jews and Arabs, which we were asked to examine and recommend: that of Beisan was instanced by the Jewish Agency as mistaken policy; while the case of Caesarea lands was quoted as showing the difficulties experienced by the Jews in obtaining possession of land, delivery of which was due under an agreement.

A.—BIRKAT RAMADAN.

116. In the Tulkarm Sub-District there were several Jewish settlements, Nathanya, Hertzelia, Tel Mond, Even Yehuda, Kadenia, as well as two Arab villages, Mesha and Umkhalid. All these were malaria-ridden owing to the marsh or swamp areas known as Birkat Ramadan and Bass um el Alaq. Much of the land originally acquired by Jewish bodies in rural areas was, according to Palestine standards, well-watered, and suitable, therefore, for close settlement with irrigation facilities, but at the same time malarious. In 1922 an Antimalarial Ordinance was enacted, placing on the owner or occupier the onus of carrying out any measures which might be prescribed by the Department of Public Health to prevent the breeding of mosquitoes and to provide such drainage as might be deemed necessary. The area which we are now considering was in fact offered to some of the Arabs displaced by Jewish purchasers but was declined by them. None of the registered " landless Arabs " were willing to settle in that locality.

117. Plans for the drainage of the swamps were drawn up in 1929, when it was discovered, as is not unusual in Palestine, that ownership was disputed, and it was decided to await the settlement operations, as a result of which, six years later in 1935, the lands were declared to be part of the *waqf* (dedicated land) of Khalil el Rahman, and should therefore be registered in the name of the Supreme Moslem Council as administrators of the *waqf*.

118. Action was not taken under the Antimalarial Ordinance of 1922, but negotiations were started by Government, and the Development Officer approached the Nathanya Seashore Development Company, who agreed to contribute £6,000 towards the cost of drainage. The Supreme Moslem Council, as administrators of the estate, agreed to pay £4,500, while the Government paid £7,500, making a total of £18,000. The work, which included the use of dynamite in cutting drainage canals, was visited by us and we were able to appreciate the marked improvement. A scheme for the economic exploitation of the water resources of this area has been drawn up by

the Irrigation Officer, to be administered by a Committee composed of the Development Officer, the Assistant District Commissioner and the *Mamour Awqaf*. Owing to the disturbances unhappily the Committee has been unable to function.

119. Thus an area of some 4,500 dunums, previously a source of malaria, has been turned into cultivable land which is also irrigable, at a cost of about £16 an acre. While the Jewish settlements benefit both in health and in the immediate capital appreciation of the value of their land, it appears to us that it is the proprietors, the Supreme Moslem Council, who derive the greatest benefit. And this land, it may be pointed out, is *waqf* property, and therefore inalienable. This is one of the few instances of that co-operation which in every enquiry has been reported to be so essential for future progress. It also illustrates the advisability of Government taking powers to control and regulate water-supplies to which we refer elsewhere.

B.—THE HULEH SCHEME.

120. Immediately below the Syrian border lies the Huleh basin, which, including a number of Arab villages and a large papyrus swamp draining south into Lake Huleh, is a triangular strip of land some 44 square miles in area. Just before the War, the Ottoman Government granted to two Beirut merchants a concession of the lower portion for the drainage of the lake and adjacent marshes, the project entailing the deepening of the River Jordan. In 1918 this concession was transferred to the Syro-Ottoman Agricultural Company, but very little work was done, and eventually in 1934 the Palestine Land Development Company, a Jewish Corporation, purchased the concession for £192,000. To the north of the concession area are the Arab villages referred to above. It is estimated that some four to five thousand Arabs are now living on this land as tenants of absentee landlords. This tract is intersected by the rivers and springs which form the head waters of the Jordan and is irrigated in a very haphazard manner by a network of small primitive canals. It is, owing to over-irrigation, now the most malarious tract in all Palestine. It might become one of the most fertile.

121. Sir John Hope Simpson reported in 1930:—

> "The Huleh area is all irrigable. The property might be a very valuable one and it is regrettable that the area owned by the Government therein has passed almost in its entirety out of the hands of the Government into the hands of a concessionaire . . . . The concession was originally made by the Turkish Government before the War, but was renewed by the Government of Palestine."
>
> "If the concession falls in, as is possible, it seems essential that the Government should retain the proprietary right in the area, for development purposes. . . . . . If the Huleh area should revert to the Government, a technical study should be made in order to ascertain the actual cost of the suggested drainage."

Chapter IX.   258

This enquiry was held, and negotiations with the new Concessionaires have now been completed. The consent of the Palestine Government was necessary to the transfer of the concession, and one of the conditions attached to it was the reservation within the concession area of 15,772 dunums for the Arab cultivators. Under the original concession 10,000 dunums were to be reserved.

122. When Messrs. Rendel, Palmer and Tritton were asked to prepare the scheme, they pointed out that it was necessary to examine the whole area of the Huleh basin, and not merely the concession area. Government agreed to extend the terms of reference to the Consulting Engineers, whose report estimates the approximate cost of the scheme at £933,000, allocating £222,600 of this to Government and £710,400 to the Concessionaires. The concession area comprises 18,568 dunums of cultivable land, 21,453 dunums of marshes, and 16,919 dunums of lake, or a total of 56,939 dunums. Apart from this, the land to the north of the concession, between the head works and the concession area, will be brought under controlled irrigation and drainage, while further north again there is the large area which, unless drained and controlled, will remain a source of malaria. If this can be included in the scheme, as appears to us to be essential, it is estimated that in all some 100,000 dunums of land will be benefited, of which two-thirds will be in Arab and one-third in Jewish ownership. The position now is that the Palestine Government have submitted the scheme to Your Majesty's Government in the hope of obtaining sanction to their share of the expenditure.

123. It appears to us that it is in large schemes of reclamation of this kind that the Mandatory Power can best fulfil its obligation of encouraging, " in co-operation with the Jewish Agency, ... close settlement by Jews on the land ". The sum proposed would be, we consider, a justifiable charge on public revenues for a scheme which eliminated malaria from an extensive tract, irrigated 60,000 dunums outside the concession and, inside it, after reserving 15,772 dunums to Arabs, provided 36,000 dunums for Jewish colonists. It was pointed out to us in evidence that, from the Jewish point of view, this was not " a money-making proposition ", and that the most that the various Jewish companies which may combine as a consortium to finance this large undertaking can hope for will be a repayment of the capital invested over a long period. We agree that it indicates what can be done in special districts to provide new areas for Jewish colonists, while at the same time benefiting and increasing the number of Arab cultivators. It is, however, right to point out that it commits the Palestine Government not only to heavy capital expenditure but to their share of the recurring charges necessary for maintenance of the irrigation system, and

259   Chapter IX.

further, unless the whole region to the north of the Huleh marsh is brought under anti-malarial operations and effective drainage, the scheme will be deprived of much of its value.

124. The net result, if the scheme comes to fruition, will be that land reserved for Arabs will cost Government some £13 an acre as against £110 per acre charged against the consortium. This means that to establish a Jewish family as colonists in this area, with buildings and the land prepared, will cost not less than £1,000. Expenditure on this scale is only possible in the exceptional circumstances which provide funds for the purpose. It is obvious that philanthropy and enthusiasm overrule the desire for profit usual in an ordinary commercial undertaking. We have no hesitation in commending the enterprise, even though the disregard of economic considerations does not diminish the difficulty experienced by the Administration in estimating " the purely economic " absorptive capacity of the country. It emphasizes the need for calculating the number of immigrants to be admitted for work on the land on the basis of ascertained facts, rather than on hopes, which may, or may not, be realized.

125. Should the scheme materialize, it is important that a careful record of rights should be prepared for all parties who have any interest in the land. In addition, it will be necessary for Government to control the irrigation, and limit in the initial settlement the rights to water to be exercised by any individual. The introduction of modern scientific means of collection and distribution of water should result in the irrigation of a considerably larger area of land, and also remove the malaria caused by water-logging. We have already referred to the necessity for legislation in this direction.

C.—BEISAN.

126. One of the legacies of the Ottoman Government was the Beisan area—the Bethshan referred to in the First Book of Samuel—dating back to 1870, when the Turkish Government appointed a Commission to enquire into the reasons why a large amount of arrears of crops and land taxes had accumulated. As a result, it was ordered that, with the exception of the land belonging to two Arab tribes, the whole area should be sold by public auction. Certain villages were purchased by Sultan Abdul Hamid: others were registered in his name. He subsequently also purchased the lands of the two excepted Arab tribes. When the British took over they found the tracts (we quote from the Report of Mr. Lewis French)

> " inhabited by fellahin who lived in mud hovels, suffered severely from the prevalent malaria and were of too low intelligence to be receptive of any suggestions for improvement of their housing, water supply or education. Large areas of their lands were uncultivated

Chapter IX.

260

and covered with weeds. There were no trees, no vegetables. The fellahín, if not themselves cattle thieves, were always ready to harbour these and other criminals. The individual plots of cultivation, such as it was, changed hands annually. There was little public security, and the fellahin's lot was an alternation of pillage and blackmail by their neighbours the Beduin . . . The Beduin, wild and lawless by nature, were constantly at feud with their neighbours on both sides of the Jordan, and raids and highway robberies formed their staple industry: while such cultivation as the Beduin were capable of filled in the intervals of more exciting occupation."

The lands were nominally *Jiftlik* or State Domains.

127. The Commission appointed in 1921 to examine the question of State Domains recommended that the tenants of Government *Jiftlik* areas should be given long-term leases, but these the cultivators in Beisan declined, partly fearing this might involve conscription for military service, partly because they refused to admit the legality of the ex-Sultan's despoliation. They organized a hostile demonstration. The land had never been surveyed: there had been no census, and the registry of lands gave no details as to the occupants. Computation of numbers and areas necessarily was guess-work. The Government decided that confirmation in the occupancy of these lands in this wild and unsettled locality should placate the seminomad Arabs who were at the time cultivating them. An agreement known as the Ghor-Mudawara (State Lands) Agreement was signed on the 19th November, 1921.

128. This agreement made a permanent settlement of the respective rights between the Government of Palestine and the cultivators of the land. Each applicant was allowed the area to which enquiries, made on such evidence as could be produced, showed him to be entitled on the ground that the family had exercised for 10 years or more cultivation rights. Where this was less than 150 dunums the allotment was increased to that area. If a family consisted of more than five individuals 30 additional dunums were to be transferred for each additional member. Under the agreement the transfer price to be paid to Government was 150 Egyptian piastres (£1 10s.) per dunum of irrigable land and 125 piastres (£1 5s.) per dunum of non-irrigable land, to be paid with the tithes, taken at 12½ per cent. of the produce, in 15 equal annual instalments. Interest was payable at the rate of 6½ per cent. per annum at the end of the fifth year on the instalments payable during the last 10 years. No disposition of the land except by mortgage to Government was to be made till the whole transfer price had been paid. The Supreme Court, however, in 1932 held that land in Beisan could be sold in execution of a decree obtained by a creditor. A Commission was appointed to demarcate the areas to be transferred and the land to be leased

for grazing, consisting of a representative of the Lands Department, a representative of the District Commissioner and two representatives of the transferees. In case of disagreement the members of the Commission were to appoint a fifth member.

129. The Commission started work in 1921 and took no less than 10 years to complete their task. In 1934 the terms had to be revised in accordance with the advice of another Committee in the light of experience gained. The price was reduced, and the period of payment was extended to a maximum of 30 years. The transferee was allowed on certain conditions to dispose of a portion of his holding to persons approved by Government, who had as their object intensive cultivation.

130. The lands as finally settled by the earlier Commission covered an area of over 90,000 acres. The irrigable area amounted to 112,552 dunums, non-irrigable to 129,696; 2,048 dunums were classed as common land, and 137,910 as unallotted waste. There were 2,614 transferees, some of whom were family groups or tribes. Some were resident in Trans-Jordan. The rights of absentee landlords were recognised. The enquiries of the second Committee showed that land speculation had begun and that 28,430 dunums of irrigable and 17,711 of non-irrigable land had been paid for and resold to outside interests.

131. Beisan is one of the few areas where irrigation from springs is possible. Under the present system of distribution and topography the water available will, it is estimated, irrigate only some 35 per cent. of the irrigable area at one time. Large tracts of land lie fallow under present methods of cultivation. Naturally the agreement has been subjected to severe criticism by the Jews, who considered that a unique opportunity of discharging the obligations under Article 6 of the Mandate was missed. They point out that Government had to pay £72,240 for the purchase of 17,868 dunums in the Beisan and Jenin Sub-Districts to be used for the settlement of displaced cultivators. Land, therefore, which Government had sold at £1 10s. or £1 5s. a dunum was resold to them at £4 and upwards. They have themselves purchased approximately 24,000 dunums, at an average price of over £4 10s.

132. Sir John Hope Simpson, while recognizing that " it was probably politically desirable that the lands covered by this Agreement should be settled with the Arab tenants who had undoubtedly enjoyed the use of the tract in the time of the Ottoman Government," at the same time pointed out that the agreement as modified in 1928 has

> " taken from the Government the control of a large area of fertile land, eminently suitable to development and for which there is ample water available for irrigation . . . The whole of the Beisan lands have been distributed, and large areas have already

been sold. Further large areas are in the market. The grant of the lands has led to land speculation on a considerable scale. The custom is that the vendor transfers to the vendee the liability for the price of the land still owing to the Government and in addition takes from him a sum varying from three to four pounds a dunum for land in the Jordan Valley. These proceedings invalidate the argument which was used to support the original agreement. It was made in order to provide the Arabs with a holding sufficient to maintain a decent standard of life, not to provide them with areas of land with which to speculate."

We associate ourselves with Sir John Hope Simpson's criticisms.

133. This case has been explained at some length as it shows, in our opinion, an error of judgment on the part of the Administration. The original agreement in 1921 was hastily made without sufficient examination. There was a disregard of possible development and unduly generous terms were given to Arabs, who were not in a position to take advantage of them, without sufficient safeguards against abuse. Dealt with on the lines of the Huleh scheme, the position to-day would be very different. Even now, at this late stage, it appears essential that Government should take over and regulate the water rights in this area, where close settlement is possible.

D.—CAESAREA.

134. There are three tracts of land near the seashore halfway between Tel Aviv and Haifa, known as Atlit, Kabbara and Caesarea. The Palestine Jewish Colonisation Association (commonly known as the P.I.C.A.) were promised a concession in 1914 of the marshes known as Kabbara and this concession, together with the sand-dunes of Caesarea, covered an area of 25,510 dunums or roughly 6,400 acres. The concession was confirmed by the Palestine Government by an agreement dated the 8th November, 1921. The Company was, however, unable to obtain possession of the Caesarea area as it was claimed jointly by Arabs in the vicinity, who maintained that they were proprietors of parts of the land and also had rights of grazing.

135. The Arabs refused to institute any action, and in 1928 (the seven years' interval was probably occupied by fruitless negotiations) Government filed a case in the Land Court claiming the land as waste or unreclaimed land (*mewat*). It was not till three years later that judgment was given. The two Judges of the Land Court differed and the case was referred to a third Judge. The upshot of the three judgments appears to be that the Arabs were declared entitled to 2,655 dunums and Government to 6,470 dunums of waste land. It is not possible from the judgments to discover the exact area affected by the judgments. One Judge dealt with an area of 9,000 dunums. Another referred to a claim of 32,000 dunums, and no decision was given as to grazing rights.

136. This case was brought to our notice by the Jewish Agency, not only as an instance of the law's delay and the difficulty of obtaining possession of land purchased, but as demonstrating the need for compulsory parcellation. It appears to us evident that the various plots assigned to the Arabs should, if necessary, be acquired by Government. The Arabs should be offered in exchange a consolidated plot of 2,655 dunums in order that the development of this large area near the sea may not be held up indefinitely.

137. This is one of the many cases in which the Administration patiently await land settlement proceedings. It is reported that, as regards the Kabbara area, land settlement has been completed, while the Atlit and Caesarea areas are being surveyed. The land settlement staff are fully occupied elsewhere in the regular settlement proceedings. This case therefore shows the need for a special staff, a peripatetic settlement party available for special inquiries. We are of opinion that in this case the Jews have legitimate cause for complaint.

5. Land in the Hill Districts.

138. It will be seen that the instances we have given (Birkat Ramadan, Huleh, Beisan, and Caesarea) relate to areas either in the plains or irrigable. As regards land in the hill districts, there is, unfortunately, very little chance of irrigation. Thus Dr. Ruppin, who suggested that another million and a-half dunums of land might be brought under irrigation, confined the area to the Maritime Plain, the Jordan Valley, the Vale of Esdraelon, and Galilee. When it was pointed out that this left out the hill districts, he stated that for them he had not yet any data.

139. Previous enquiries both by Sir John Hope Simpson and later by Mr. Lewis French have shown that there is considerable congestion of Arabs in the hills, and that the land is insufficient to meet all their requirements under their present system of agriculture. Even so, it is to be feared that the *fellaheen*, under their crushing load of debt, will offer lands for sale. Mr. French reported

"the absorption, gradual but inevitable, of the Arab peasant proprietor by the Arab *effendi* or capitalist landlord"

and

"the advance of the Jews, without such noticeable progress and development as in the coastal plains, but with similar results in reinforcing the claims of landless Arabs. Both facts need to be faced. Some form of protection for the small owner appears vital in order to ensure that the concentration of numerous smallholdings into the hands of large proprietors does not lead to the same evil as is anticipated from excessive expropriation by the Jews. In one Sub-District in the hilly tracts it is reported that in a decade no less than 30 per cent. of the land has passed from Arab peasants to Arab capitalists."

Chapter IX.

140. Sir John Hope Simpson held out the hope that it might be possible "to improve the method of cultivation of the Arab fellah in the dry tracts, and also to extend irrigation wherever that is possible, so that the fellah will be able to gain a reasonable livelihood from a smaller area of land than that which has been essential hitherto.". He further added that any scheme of development should provide for the settlement *both of Jews and of Arabs* on the developed area and should take into consideration the plans of colonisation of the Jewish agencies, in order that development by those agencies and by the Commission might be co-ordinated. It might well prove possible to combine two schemes of development in certain areas with mutual advantage and with considerable economy.

141. Dr. Ruppin in his evidence agreed that development was "the main thing necessary for Palestine", and he went on to show how this development might best take place. As regards the plain areas it depended on irrigation, but in dealing with the hills he could only hold out hopes of more intensive cultivation in the shape of mixed farming and the planting of fruit-trees.

142. The agricultural population in the hill districts is roughly Jewish 4,100, Arabs 355,000. There are some 25 Jewish settlements in the hills and the amount of land held by the Jews at present in the hills is 315,000 dunums. The hill districts were taken by Sir John Hope Simpson to be 6,144,000 dunums in area, of which 2,450,000 dunums might be cultivable. Quite apart from any question as to the reliability of these figures or the actual size of the cultivable area, the problem in the hills as regards the land is simply this. Is close settlement practicable? Can it be introduced to the mutual benefit of Arabs and Jews?

143. We visited two Jewish settlements in the hills, which were mentioned to us by several witnesses as being among their successful enterprises. The first was Atarot, some seven miles from Jerusalem, on which 24 agricultural families coming from Poland, Russia and Germany had been settled. The total area of this hilly land, certainly land which the ordinary observer would regard as unfertile if not uncultivable, was 1,700 dunums, of which some 750 dunums have up to date been brought under cultivation. Each settler has 15 dunums, slightly less than four acres. It is hoped eventually to accommodate 50 more families or a total of 74, which, allowing 15 dunums for each family, would absorb 1,110 dunums, apart from roads, forest, and absolutely uncultivable rock-land.

144. £4,200 was spent by the Jewish National Fund in purchasing land for this little colony before the War. Immigrants are expected to pay 2 per cent. on advances made to them. Apart from the cost of land it was estimated that nearly £600 was

265 Chapter IX.

necessary to provide the settler with a house, two cows, cowshed, chicken-run, fowls, implements, working capital, etc. £10,260 were advanced for 18 settlers. Others came and invested their own money. Thanks to the kind offices of Mr. Joshua Gordon, we were given a detailed inspection of the accounts and of the settlement. It appears that it was not till 1936 that a start was made in repaying the capital, but it was contended before us in evidence that this provided a refutation of the following criticism by Sir John Hope Simpson on the "uneconomic colony". In the case of the Zionist settlements he had reported that the system was

> "immensely costly. It demands very little from the settler himself. Indeed, however hard a settler may work and however desirous he may be to pay back sums that the fund expended on him, by no possibility can he arrive at that result. The debt which he owes cannot be repaid by any effort on his part. . . ."

And again,

> "It is undesirable from the point of view of ordinary morality that colonists should be allowed to benefit by the large expenditure which has been made for their settlement and yet to escape payment of the amount spent upon them. . . . If a strong, healthy and self-respecting peasantry is desired in the Jewish colonies in Palestine, it should be made quite clear to the settlers that they are under the obligation to repay the outlay which has been made on their behalf."

145. It will be seen that in the case of Atarot the total advances, including the cost of land, were £14,460. The Co-operative Society has also paid £2,600 for laying on water from the Jerusalem supply, on which the settlers pay a water-rate checked by meters. The mixed farming in the settlement depends chiefly on cows (fed on fodder purchased from the plains); these are Frisian, at an average cost of between £60 and £70, on which 11 per cent. is paid annually, 10 per cent. for insurance, 1 per cent. for treatment. It is calculated that each cow gives a profit of £2 per month. The farm also includes poultry and fruit trees. Poultry yield a small profit. The fruit trees are still in the experimental stage. On spare land vegetables are grown for the family. There is also a kindergarten school in which there are 42 children, the teachers being supplied by the Labour Federation. Medical attendance is supplied from the sick fund, to which the average payment is 3s. a month. Accident insurance costs 17s. a year and a special insurance fund of £1 14s. per year per family was created against the risk of being shot by Arabs. We regret to have to report that in this settlement there was one such claim.

146. The second settlement we visited was Kiriyat Anavim, which is some nine miles outside Jerusalem on the Jaffa road, with which it is connected by a track of about half a mile. The Jewish National Fund paid £11,406 for the land, totalling 4,151

Chapter IX. 266

dunums. 3,700 dunums were acquired during the years 1920-7 at an average of £2 5s. per dunum. For the land purchased in 1935 the price had risen to nearly £7. As regards the situation and soil, this settlement was more favourably placed than Atarot. The settlement is run on the communal principle. It was founded in 1920 with 40 members—men and women from Southern Russia and Galicia. In 1933, 40 immigrants from Poland joined the settlement and 20 from Germany in 1935. In 1936, 28 boys and girls from Germany were admitted for purposes of education and agricultural training. Of the 40 original members 32 have remained in the settlement to the present. There are now in the settlement 192 persons. Water is obtained from a well south of the main road which is pumped and stored in a reservoir in the centre of the settlement. There are also reservoirs for storing rain water. Some three years ago negotiations were concluded for buying water from one of the neighbouring Arab villages, a mile away; but owing to the disturbances this water could not be obtained, and an arrangement was made with Government for the supply to the settlement of water from the Jerusalem water system at 40 mils per cubic metre for drinking water, which is double the cost of water from local supplies.

147. The Palestine Foundation Fund (*Keren Hayesod*) invested in this settlement £20,593. This was subsequently revalued by a committee of experts and the debt of the settlement was reduced to £10,744, which is to be repaid by the settlement in the course of 40 years with interest at 2 per cent. Here again repayment of advances commenced only in 1936, 16 years after the start of the settlement.

148. The dairy-farming is extremely well managed. The settlement has a dairy containing a cooling room and a small laboratory for analysing the milk. Poultry farming, bee-hives and plantations of fruit-trees also contribute to the income. Food for cattle and poultry has to be bought, and the cost of water is an expensive item, but we were told that the net profit during the last five years was:—

	£
1930-31	444
1931-32	520
1932-33	528
1933-34	386
1934-35	361

The vines and fruit-trees which were first planted over 300 dunums of terrace lands failed, and by 1926 only 50 dunums of the vines and 10 dunums of the fruit-trees had survived. A new experimental orchard covering an area of 60 dunums was then planted with some 700 fruit-trees of 185 different varieties. It is supervised by the Agricultural Experimental Station of the

Jewish Agency. Here, as at Atarot, we noticed that even under skilled advice fruit-trees are still in the experimental stage. It has to be remembered that experience of fruit cultivation on a commercial scale is extremely limited, especially as regards deciduous fruits. The cows are imported from Holland, the poultry from America, queen bees from Italy. There are at present 103 Dutch and five Swiss cows. As at Atarot, there is no grazing and not even an exercise ground. Fear of disease prevents the farmers allowing the cows outside the farmyard.

149. Our impression, after seeing these two settlements, was that they were in every way a remarkable testimony to the enthusiastic energy not only of the immigrants but of those who financed and advised them. Land which under ordinary methods of cultivation would have given a precarious crop of cereals has been turned over to mixed farming; and, although these farms cannot be judged on any ordinary economic basis, they are a valuable feature in the Jewish colonization as affording a livelihood for settlers and training centres for young immigrants. It is obvious, however, that any development on these lines is quite beyond the financial resources of any Arab small proprietor.

150. Turning to Dr. Hexter's definition of cultivable land, success cannot be ascribed to the " interaction of the physical properties of the land, including availability of irrigation." It is true, however, that in these cases land was " subjected to a more intensive or different form of cultivation as and when the supply of capital, labour, skill and available markets warranted." It appears to us that many decades must pass before there will be the necessary supply of capital, labour and skill on the part of the Arabs.

151. The " active policy of development " advocated by the Jewish Agency contemplated generous loans to cultivators. Dr. Ruppin, for example, advocated planting the mountainous area with deciduous fruit-frees, and desired that Government should make loans to the farmers in the hills which they could start repaying after 15 years. In a subsequent letter he explained that what he suggested was " a mixed farm in which, in addition to cereal growing, poultry and bee-keeping, from 3 to 10 dunums should be planted with various fruit-trees and grapes . . . . Most of the farmers are so poor and so inactive that a powerful incentive is required to induce them to action. There are two such incentives: the first is to enable those who have a surplus of land to sell that surplus, or part of it, and to use the means so obtained for the planting of trees; and, second, to grant to those who have no surplus of land a loan equal to half the amount required for the planting and cultivation of trees until they reach the fruit-bearing stage." This would mean

Chapter IX.   268
adopting the financial system which we saw at work in these two settlements. Government would have to lend a very large sum of money either free of interest or at an extremely low rate on a speculative enterprise. It is admitted that both fruit-trees and cattle need constant scientific supervision, accompanied by a system of insurance in the case of the latter. On the plantation there would be no repayment of the money advanced for 15 years. Any proposal of this kind would, we feel sure, be heartily condemned by those Jewish witnesses who protested that revenues derived from Jewish sources were being spent on Arabs.

152. A further difficulty is that in the hill districts a large amount of land is held in village ownership under the *masha'a* system, and Dr. Ruppin himself noted that " under existing conditions of land tenure in the hill villages it is practically impossible for the farmer to sell part of his surplus land, since that land is either communal property or divided into tiny plots for which purchasers can either not be found at all or only at a very low price." He realized that it was essential to have these villages surveyed and settled as soon as possible. As we have already seen, many years must pass before this can take place.

153. Having regard to all the foregoing considerations and to the necessity of providing land for cultivators who may be dispossessed in order to meet the requirements of any adequate policy of afforestation, a subject with which we deal in a later Section, we are satisfied that there can be no expectation of finding accommodation for any large increase in the rural Arab population in the hills. We therefore have no hesitation in saying that at present, and indeed for many years to come, the Mandatory Power should not attempt to facilitate the close settlement of Jews in the hilly districts generally, though in the immediate neighbourhood of Jerusalem dairy and fruit farms might eventually prove self-supporting.

We have reached this conclusion quite independently of a consideration of the inadvisability on the grounds of security of scattered settlements of Jews in the midst of a hostile Arab population.

6. Agriculture.

154. The development of the Department of Agriculture has been remarkable. The expenditure in the year 1924-25 was £35,691; ten years later it was £147,286. The object was an active policy of agricultural development in the hope of facilitating the close settlement of Jews upon the land without prejudicing the position of the Arab. It was hoped that intensive would replace extensive cultivation, and that where an Arab

held fifty acres, thirty at any rate would be available for the Jewish immigrant. It is obvious that any such policy involves a radical change in the methods of cultivation by the *fellah.*

We were told by an official witness:—

"The view that the Arabs sell part of their land and spend the money in developing the other part of their land I do not think is consistent with the facts. Some years ago an enquiry was made into twelve villages which had sold a large portion of their land to the Jews and I think only in one or two villages was any improvement made."

155. We received evidence that the Jews themselves would welcome "a much more active participation by Government" in the attempt to improve the standard of the Arab farmers.

"More than half the soil of Palestine is in the hill country, in which I think there are big possibilities, not yet exploited, but the Government must assist the farmers by cheap loans. The farmer has no capital to invest for the cost of plantations: he must get help in the form of a long term cheap loan."

This witness also considered that the Agricultural Mortgage Bank could not meet indigenous requirements. The peasant who started a vineyard or an orchard would not be able to begin repayment of the capital expenditure till after fifteen years.

156. This statement was confirmed by an Arab witness who told us that while it was true that in the citrus-growing area many Arabs had adopted the improved method of cultivation introduced by Jews, several of them, owing to lack of capital, had become heavily embarrassed.

"The actual planting has all been done by borrowing. I know one village, Yebna; a few years ago I used to say 'Look at it—a model of prosperity', but they are about £120,000 in debt. I think thirty or forty, perhaps more, orange-groves are now being put up for sale at public auction."

157. It is frequently contended that the Arab has only to follow the example of the Jew to become prosperous. This is doubtless true of the relatively wealthy and enlightened Arab landowners who have developed citrus plantations in the Maritime Plain. But the case of the Arab cultivator is very different. Unless he can be provided with the same resources, in the shape of capital, continuous help and advice, he cannot possibly compete with the Jew. It is also clear that with the heavy expenditure on internal security, to which we refer elsewhere, it is impossible for Government to undertake the financial responsibility involved.

158. Meanwhile the Agricultural Department, with its six branches, Veterinary (animal husbandry), Agricultural (field and vegetable crops), Horticultural (fruit, etc.), Entomological, Fisheries, and Education and Research, is doing excellent work. It is aided by a General Agricultural Council consisting of six

Chapter IX.

270

Arabs, six Jews, three others and three Government officials. In the various Committees there was more sign of co-operation between Jew and Arab than in any other Department. It is unnecessary for us to give a detailed account of the departmental activities as displayed in the different agricultural stations, the improvement of cattle, seed selection, and village demonstration plots. In research it shares in the results obtained in the Jewish laboratories, a valuable privilege given in return for comparatively small grants-in-aid from Government.

159. Some results of the Department's enterprise are already apparent. Many Arabs now grow vegetables for the town markets; others find a new source of revenue in chicken farming and in apiaries. Inspectors distribute fruit trees and American vines and give advice on their cultivation. Veterinary Inspectors give instruction in animal husbandry and combat cattle disease. There are fifteen British experts in this Department, compared with a total District Administrative British staff of twelve. We were told that the Departmental officers were welcomed in the villages and that they were able to tour freely throughout the 1936 disturbances.

160. It is in no way a reflection on their efforts when we emphasize the need for time to show any results on a large scale. On one day we visited a village, Barriye, in the Ramleh Sub-District, towards the improvement of which Government had made a grant of £500. There were 80 families in this village, the population being some 400, who lived entirely on agriculture. The land cultivated by the village was 740 acres. Usually the villagers needed all the crops they grew, cereals, for their own sustenance and little was left for sale. In one respect this village had a unique advantage. It was one of the first villages to start bee-keeping and is now able to dispose of spare hives to other villages. The sale of bees and honey brings in an annual income of £1,000. At certain times of the year the bees have to be transported to other places, as, for example, orange-groves; hence a road connecting this village with the main road was necessary. The villagers gave their labour free, and a bridge over a stream, which filled during the rainy season, was being built from the Government grant of £500. The surplus will be devoted to an attempt to provide the village with drains, which were obviously needed, and to afforest a portion of the land. There was no school, though the villagers had subscribed £75 towards getting one: there was no room for the children in the neighbouring village school. Their methods of cultivation were primitive, the camel and the donkey being yoked together for purposes of ploughing. Farmyard manure was being collected in order that it might be stored for fuel. Irrigation was impossible, and the village was dependent on a capricious rainfall. Water was obtained in the summer from a

neighbouring village half-a-mile away. We were told that the villagers were short of land and that the surplus population had to go to the towns for work. Previously they had held land in an adjoining village which had been sold to Jews. The general impression we gained was that of congested poverty and ignorance, combined with an almost sub-conscious desire for village uplift.

161. The same afternoon we visited the remarkable laboratories at Rehovot developed under the personal supervision of Dr. Weizmann. Here we saw the latest developments in experimental research on strictly practical lines designed to improve the productive capacity of the soil, raise the standard of the products, and discover, if possible, marketable uses for by-products. Thus in plant-breeding experiments are being made to produce a tobacco free from nicotine. A new method is being applied to the problem of obtaining concentrated fruit juices without injuring the flavour or destroying the vitamin-content. The utilization of whey is being studied, and fermentative methods applied to the whey have given valuable results in the production of lactic acid. The conversion of technical proteins into a product which could serve as an easily digestible foodstuff is another experiment. In the pharmaceutical laboratory substances were in preparation which are expected to prove effective against the most serious of Near Eastern cattle diseases, namely, theileria. Soil analysis is being conducted by spectrographic methods.

162. We have referred in paragraph 7 of Chapter III to " the separation, almost, it might seem, by centuries ", of the Arab from the Jew. These two visits to the Arab village and the Jewish laboratory illustrate its meaning. Yet when the villager is sufficiently educated to appreciate the value of the discoveries of the laboratory the hoped-for assimilation of the races may begin. The idea still prevails in some quarters that Palestine is a fertile country, " a land of milk and honey ", whereas, for ten months out of the twelve it is in fact for the most part dry and barren. Crops can only be obtained by hard toil. Modern science may promote fertility. Whether in relieving the Arab peasant of his indebtedness by Co-operative Societies and Agricultural Banks, or in persuading him to irrigate his lands or to plant fruit-trees, several decades must pass before any marked change will be apparent.

7. Forests.

163. The fact has to be faced that there are to-day no real forests in Palestine and that if there is one country in the world in which afforestation is desirable that country is Palestine. A normal percentage of forest land compared with the total area of a country is said to be 15 per cent. In Palestine there are

Chapter IX. 272

only 76 square miles of scrub forest and plantations, out of some 6,250 square miles, which is the Government estimate of the land fit for cultivation or afforestation, of the total of 10,400 square miles of land area of Palestine, including Beersheba. In addition to this 76 square miles, there are a further 450 square miles which retain some forest characteristics, but they have been ruined by overgrazing, overcutting, and other misuse.

164. In ancient times the hills of Palestine were protected by forests, which in the course of centuries have been cleared by man in his search for agricultural land. As the population increased forests were cut down and the slopes cultivated without terraces. As soon as one area had been denuded of soil, it was abandoned and another plot cleared, cultivated and ultimately ruined. Finally, during the War large quantities of trees were felled, including olives, which were one of the main sources of revenue.

165. The result is that the hills are largely barren and rocky, and the soil which remains is being washed away by rainstorms. Overgrazing prevents the growth of any vegetation which might arrest the process of denudation. In the plains the country is also suffering seriously from the absence of trees and vegetation, which allows the sand-dunes along the coast to advance inland and cover areas which have hitherto been cultivable.

166. After the War the Administration began to take action in connection with forestry and the position in this connection was described in 1925 in Sir Herbert Samuel's Report on the Administration of Palestine, 1920-5, as follows:—

> "With respect to afforestation, the work of the Department has been severely restricted by the inadequacy of its budget, but it has demarcated certain uncultivated State lands as protected forest areas; it has fostered regrowth from the stumps still existing in the destroyed forests, has planted about a million trees, and, through the nurseries it maintains, has facilitated plantation by others. Altogether four to five million timber and fruit trees have been planted in these years in Palestine. The Department has conducted successful experiments also in the planting of grasses and trees on sand dunes—a matter of great importance, for the line of dunes along the coast is slowly advancing inland; it has already overwhelmed a considerable area of cultivated land, and, unless stopped by planting, will certainly prove fatal to the adjoining cultivation."

167. In 1920 the Forestry Section of the Department of Agriculture was established with one qualified Forest Officer, who was also Deputy Director of the Department and in that capacity was overwhelmed with agricultural administration until 1929. Moreover his staff had received no training in the technical side

---

* The figures and areas given in this section of the Report are approximate estimates.

273   Chapter IX.

of their duties. In the early years the main function of the Forestry Section was the protection of valuable trees on private property, which were liable to be prematurely felled for fuel.

168. It was soon however realized that the protection of the remaining forest land was of even greater importance, owing to the increased demand for agricultural land due to the fact that large areas of steeply sloping ground had been rendered useless by erosion. This demand resulted in the destruction of forest vegetation. Consequently in 1926 an Ordinance was passed authorizing the establishment of forest reserves to include uncultivated land which was not clearly private property. It was intended that investigation by Land Settlement Officers should, within a few years, clear up all questions of title, whereafter such land as was proved to be private property was to be excluded from the reserves and the remainder was to be declared State Forest and brought under proper management.

169. Up till the present time, although some 280 square miles have been notified as Forest Reserve, owing to the slowness of land settlement only a few square miles have been finally adjudicated as State Domain, and of these it has been found possible to gazette only 4,000 acres as "closed Forest Areas" in which no grazing or felling is allowed. Without closure and effective supervision by forest guards, to prevent grazing, no vegetation can grow, afforestation becomes impossible, and the land is denuded of soil. No improvement is possible where the goat—that "greatest enemy of prosperity"—is permitted to overrun the land.

170. The declaration of land as forest reserve had the effect of checking the rapid clearing and cultivation of the land, but it was not found possible to check the demands of holders of rights for grazing and forest produce far in excess of the growth capacity of the land, with the result that the condition of both soil and vegetation is most unsatisfactory.

171. As regards afforestation, owing to the local importance of sand fixation the first plantations were mainly on the sand-dunes, of which, out of an approximate total of 195 square miles, 17 square miles have been declared forest reserves, but of these 4½ square miles at Acre are being alienated to private interests. In all, 750 acres of sand-dunes were planted in the plains. Later, attention was turned to the hills, where five square miles of plantations have been established, mainly near Nazareth and Hebron, and the Government nurseries now produce an average of 1,200,000 plants, of which some 200,000 are issued annually gratis to institutions and private individuals.

172. In 1929 a qualified Palestinian officer was added to the Forest service, but he also was kept busy with administrative

Chapter IX.   274

work and unable to give any training to the staff. By 1933, the unsatisfactory condition of much of the hill country had aroused general interest, and the need for re-afforestation was widely admitted. It was recognized that the area of forest was seriously deficient and the existing forests were suffering from neglect, and that consequently it was necessary to embark without delay on a vigorous policy of afforestation, to remedy these defects and to curtail the encroachment of sand-dunes. This, further, would bring into economic use land not suited to agriculture and horticulture by the production of timber, fuel and other forest products, including large quantities of fodder.

173. In view of the importance of the measures to be taken, it was resolved to establish a separate Department of Forests with an increased staff. This Department was officially formed on the 1st April, 1935, and consists of four qualified officers, 20 junior officers and 58 other ranks, with a budget for 1936-7 of £32,513.

174. The Conservator of Forests has recently submitted a report on Forest Policy which is under consideration by the Government. In that report he states that afforestation is an urgent necessity and that it should be continued on a moderate scale, he does not recommend a large increase at the moment, because the staff is untrained, silvicultural technique needs to be further developed, preliminary survey and classification is required, and the shape, distribution and ownership of the forest reserves are all unsatisfactory. He recommends the closure of considerable areas to allow them to rest and in order to improve such vegetation as now exists, such action is a necessary preliminary to more intensive afforestation. He further strongly urges the acceleration of land settlement in order that it may be possible to bring suitable areas under management.

175. His proposals would necessitate considerable land acquisition by the Government. He recommends that lands under the control of his department should be divided into three categories:—

A. " Forest lands ", subdivided into Production Forests, Village Forests and Protection Forests, totalling in all about 390 square miles.

B. " Fodder Lands ", of about the same area.

C. " Protected Lands ", of about 97 square miles, in places where erosion is a danger, which should be terraced and planted with fruit trees.

176. If such an amount of land were placed under the control of the Forest Department, it would in all represent about 14 per cent. of the total area of 6,250 square miles which is estimated

by the Government as the extent of the land which is fit for cultivation and afforestation in Palestine, including Beersheba, but " Forest Lands " would only represent 6 to 7 per cent. of the total area, as compared with the area of forest land in Germany, which covers 15 per cent. of that country. The area of 390 square miles would be a minimum and would by no means supply the whole country with timber and fuel. It is emphasized that land under the Forest Department would not be lost to the community, but would be usefully employed.

177. Another scheme for afforestation on a much larger scale is contained in a Memorandum entitled " An Afforestation Scheme for Palestine " submitted to the Commission by Mr. Joseph Weitz, the Forestry Officer of the Jewish National Fund, in January of this year. In it, he considers that 97½ square miles of sand-dunes and 780 square miles in the hill country can and should be afforested. These areas compare with the 390 square miles of " Forest Lands " suggested in the Forest Policy Report, as the memorandum does not deal with " Fodder Lands " or " Protected Lands," on which under the Report fruit-trees would be planted.

178. Mr. Weitz states that since the War, only a little over 12 square miles have been afforested, whereas he considers that at least 15½ square miles should be planted every year with 6,500,000 forest and carob trees, the fruit of the latter being for forage purposes. He considers that this could be done if land were expropriated by the Government and leased to organizations and individuals prepared to afforest them at their own expense, but under Government control and restrictions; the Government themselves being left to afforest only 4 square miles each year.

179. We have mentioned these two proposals in order to show how great is the need for afforestation in Palestine in the opinion of experts. We fully realize the desirability of afforestation on a large scale and the advisability of a long-term policy on the subject. But, having regard to the conclusion which we have reached as to the scarcity of suitable land in the hills for the agricultural population, we cannot recommend a policy which involves expropriation of cultivators on a large scale, unless and until other cultivable land or satisfactory employment on the land can be found for them. That there is, however, in the aggregate a very large amount of land fit for afforestation but not for cultivation we have no doubt and, in any case, we strongly endorse a policy of (1) afforestation of steep hillsides to prevent erosion, (2) the prevention of grazing on land fit for afforestation, and (3) where practicable, the establishment of village forests for the benefit of the neighbouring cultivators.

Chapter IX. 276

8. Co-operative Societies.

180. In 1930 a Committee was appointed by the Palestine Government to inquire into the economic condition of agriculturists. They investigated the position of about a quarter of the total number of families engaged in agriculture, living in 104 villages (about 12 per cent. of the total number of villages) and cultivating an area of 1¼ million dunums, or about 10 per cent. of the total cultivable area. They found that the ordinary Arab family had contrived to live on a net annual income of between £25 and £30, but that there must have been many families who had been obliged either to lower their standard of living or to fall into debt. They estimated that the total debt of the agriculturists in the country might amount to some £2,000,000. For a few years after the War prices were very high, and the farmer seemed to have cleared off his debts and to have become comparatively prosperous, but when prices began to fall to their natural level he failed to adjust his outlook or standard of living to meet the changed conditions. Consequently, he began again to borrow more heavily than before at an exorbitant rate of interest. It was reported that " a rate of 30 per cent. per annum is perhaps the commonest, but 50 per cent. for three months is not unusual ".

181. The Committee recommended that Government should provide credit facilities, but that loans should normally be given through the medium of a village group of a co-operative nature, which would be responsible for the issue, control and repayment of loans.

182. Mr. C. F. Strickland, of the Indian Civil Service, came to Palestine to study the problem on the spot, and submitted a report at the end of 1930, in which he arrived at the conclusion that " the amount of the fellah's debt is not only burdensome and such as to hamper any attempt at progressive agriculture, but no small percentage of the cultivators are entirely insolvent. Neither co-operative credit nor any form of State loans can place them on a solvent footing if the whole normal claim of their creditors is to be paid." As a result of his recommendations, a trained Registrar was appointed with the necessary staff, a number of Co-operative Societies were established in Arab villages, short-term loans to cultivators during the years 1930-6 to the amount of £189,934 were advanced, and a Loan Security Ordinance, 1935, enabled approved banks and companies to extend short-term credit and seasonal loans against the security of the crop.

183. An amendment of the Imprisonment for Debt Ordinances of 1931 and 1932 disallowed arbitrary imprisonment and provided that the Execution Officer must satisfy himself that the judgment-debtor was in a position to pay. The

Usurious Loans Ordinance of 1934 imposed a duty upon the Courts, when trying a claim for debt, to raise certain issues regarding the interest charged. Lastly, a new Bankruptcy Ordinance of 1936 included cultivator debtors in the Law of Bankruptcy.

184. The Government found themselves unable to accept a proposal made by Mr. Strickland for the summary relief of indebted cultivators by the settlement of debts by special tribunals.

185. Mr. Strickland paid a second visit to Palestine in 1933, to advise as to the first practical steps to be taken for the formation of Arab societies and the improvement and promotion of the extensive Jewish co-operative movement already in existence. Largely on the basis of his recommendations a new Co-operative Societies Ordinance was enacted.

186. There has thus been a mitigation of the burden of debt under which farmers had laboured for many years past, and there has been considerable propaganda to encourage co-operation. Between 1933 and 1935 more than 200 Arab villages had been initiated in co-operative practice. In 60 villages Primary Societies had actually been successfully started, and preparations had been made to start 60 more in 1936.

187. As regards the Jewish population the case is very different. Here Sir John Hope Simpson reported that the co-operative movement had " not only been successfully launched amongst the Jewish population, but has already become a highly important economic factor in its daily life. On the whole, the Societies are extremely well managed. . . . There can be no doubt that the Co-operative Societies are doing magnificent work and are a valuable asset both to the villages and to the residents in the towns." He stated that the need of the Arab population for similar assistance was " desperately urgent ", and he pointed out the desirability of joint action between Jews and Arabs.

188. While there is little evidence at present to justify the hope that the co-operative movement may form the ground for mutual assistance and benefit as between Arab and Jew, Mr. Strickland has stressed the importance of an Arab co-operative movement as a means of strengthening the economic position of the Arabs, and thus removing or reducing their present belief, whether justified or not, that they are fighting against superior forces in the economic field. " If the Arabs ", he reports, " hold this belief, they will regard it as inevitable that their land should eventually pass out of their hands and will seek to meet the dangers not by an economic effort but by political and even violent action. If they felt themselves to be gaining ground economically, or at least so equipped that they could

Chapter IX.   278

hope to retain their present ground, they might divert much of their vigour into a campaign of self-improvement, social and economic, and the charge of neglect which is now brought (however unjustifiably) against the Palestine Administration would be excluded."

189. It is obvious that many years must pass before the Arab can hope that his Co-operative Societies can reach the standard necessary to give him confidence. Meanwhile, the measures taken by the Administration justify the hope that, given peaceful conditions, the indebtedness of the Arab peasant should gradually be reduced. It is desirable that the Registrar and his staff should inspect and advise both Jewish and Arab Societies. There are many difficult and specialized questions of co-operative principle and practice which frequently arise in connection with the Jewish Societies. Secondly, it is desirable to develop among the Arabs the urban as well as the rural, the social as well as the directly economic, types of Co-operative Society. It is not, as is so often assumed, the provision of facile credit which will improve the condition of the depressed cultivator, but his education in co-operative principles during a protracted and perhaps unpleasant course of discipline.

10.05

HIGH COMMISSIONER FOR PALESTINE,
JERUSALEM.

CONFIDENTIAL
REFERENCE NO.CF/326/37.

18 November, 1937.

Sir,

        I have the honour to refer to your despatch Confidential (6) of the 7th August, relating to the recommendations contained in the report of the Royal Commission on the subject of land legislation.

2.   Prior to the receipt of your despatch, the High Commissioner had appointed a Committee to examine and report on the issues arising out of the recommendations of the Royal Commission at paragraph 49(1) Chapter XXII of their report. (i.e. the recommendations for the "period of transition")

        A copy of the report of the Committee is enclosed herewith.

3.   Although I consider that the Committee did valuable work I was unable to accept their proposals for legislation because, as they point out, the proposals would inevitably conflict with the requirements of Article 17 of the Palestine Order in Council.

        Moreover, in the light of the Committee's report I am doubtful whether any legislation is necessary at least for the present. The Committee came to the conclusion, to which I may say that I and my advisers had already been leaning, that there did not appear to be any signs of any unusual movement for the purchase of land by Jews or Arabs. The fact seems to be that neither Jews nor Arabs are likely to embark on land transactions which they fear may prove a bad speculation. Indeed it seems to

THE RIGHT HONOURABLE W.G.A. ORMSBY-GORE, P.C., M.P.,
    HIS MAJESTY'S PRINCIPAL SECRETARY OF STATE
                  FOR THE COLONIES.

2.

be fully appreciated that persons who enter into transactions (after the publication of the Royal Commission's report) which might prejudice the partition scheme are not likely to be treated with consideration by the Government.

The Commissioner for Lands and Surveys confirms this view and considers that there is an absence of justification for the proposed legislation for the present.

4. Furthermore, I feel that in the present state of tension the promulgation of such legislation would be misinterpreted and might have an adverse effect on the proceedings of the Boundary Commission.

5. In these circumstances, I am of the opinion that the enactment of the proposed legislation might be deferred until there are definite signs that the complications which the Royal Commission anticipated might arise, are materialising.

If any such legislation is required the observations in the last sentence of paragraph 2 of your despatch under reference will be borne in mind.

6. As regards the appointment of an expert committee to draw up a comprehensive land code for the whole of Palestine, I share your view that consideration of this matter should be deferred until future political developments can be more clearly envisaged.

I have the honour to be,

Sir,

Your most obedient,
humble servant,

OFFICER ADMINISTERING THE GOVERNMENT.

ENCLOSURE.

SECRET

10th September, 1937.

CHIEF SECRETARY.

Sir,

    We have the honour to refer to your letter CF/326/37 dated 17th August 1937 in which we were appointed as a Committee with the following terms of reference:

> "1. To enquire into and report as to the measures that will be necessary to implement the recommendations of the Royal Commission that steps should be taken to prohibit the purchase of land by Jews within the Arab area (i.e. the area of the projected Arab State) or by Arabs within the Jewish area (i.e. the area of the projected Jewish State).
>
> 2. To enquire into and report as to what action if any should be taken by Government to deal with the situation that has arisen where negotiations for the purchase of land by Jews within the projected Arab State and by Arabs within the projected Jewish State had been entered into prior to the publication of the Royal Commission Report but which had not been concluded at the date of such publication.
>
> 3. To make such recommendations as they may think desirable in connection with matters not directly covered by the first and second term of reference but which may seem to them in the light of their investigations to be relevant to the issue generally."

    We have the honour now to submit our Report upon the enquiries made by us in those terms of reference.

1. **Introductory.**

  (1) With regard to recommendations of the Royal Commission that steps should be taken to prohibit the purchase of land by Jews within the projected Arab State and by Arabs within the Jewish State, we endeavoured to ascertain what actual purchases or contracts to purchase were going on in fact. This information was not easy to obtain. On the Arab side, terrorism and insecurity prevented frank speaking, and on the Jewish side, many of the more important

2.

men interested in land transactions were absent from the country.

(ii) We interviewed a very senior member of the directing staff of the Palestine Land Development Company and received very frank information, the veracity of which we have no reason to doubt. He told us that his Company had already purchased and registered over 40,000 dunums at Beersheba and that there were contracts for another 40,000. His Company were not at the moment making any new contracts since they were waiting for some permanent indication regarding the future.

Regarding Beisan, he stated that the areas still being purchased were not large or important. He did not think that the purchases by private persons, i.e., other than big groups, were important.

(iii) The information received from other sources all showed that, although owing to the economic distress, Arab owners in the Jaffa and Gaza districts were at present inclined to sell or mortgage either to Arab or to Jew, the purchasing was confined to individuals. The purchases of individuals are not generally of very large areas.

In the areas under Settlement, the sales to Jews are made:

(a) by an Arab occupant of unregistered land not contesting a Jewish claim to it so that the parcel is shown as undisputed; and

(b) by "renunciation" before the Settlement Officer of rights adjudged to the vendors by the Settlement Officer.

3.

The Committee found no confirmation of the reports that the Jews hoped by new purchases to influence the Boundary Commission.

(iv) The Committee came to the conclusion that there did not seem to exist at present any sign of a precipitate scramble to purchase by Jews in the Arab State or vice versa. Nevertheless, it might be a wise precaution to endeavour by legislation to restrict the majority of undisguised transfers from Arab to Jew in the Arab State and from Jew to Arab in the Jewish State. The Committee used the expression "majority" because it became abundantly clear to them that it is impossible to frame legislation which could deal with the problem with complete and infallible effectuality. In fact, the Committee were forced to the conclusion that any legislation can no more than impede the enlargement of the area in Jewish hands within the Arab State. It was not anticipated that there would in any event be a material increase of that in Arab hands within the Jewish State. It was decided that it was vain to hope that legislation, excepting the application of a kind of pre-emption as is suggested in paragraph 2(xv) below, might make smaller the area in the hands of the Jews and Arabs in the Arab and Jewish States respectively.

2. Proposed Legislation.

(i) Having come to this principal conclusion, the Committee proceeded to consider the general terms of the necessary legislation. They suggest that this should take the form of a special Ordinance, the execution of which should be made the responsibility of an officer to be designated in the Ordinance. This proposed Ordinance will, the Committee suggest, contain provisions

4.

to give effect to their recommendations in respect of both the first and second terms of reference.

(ii)   First of all, the legislation will inevitably conflict with the requirements of Article 17 of the Palestine Order-in-Council which prohibits legislation which tends to discriminate in any way between the inhabitants of Palestine on the ground of race, religion or language.

It is assumed therefore that this Article will be amended so as to enable the recommendations of the Royal Commission to be implemented.

It is of course possible that some foreign States might object to discrimination against their nationals even if they were Jews.

(iii)   With this assumption, it is necessary to define what is meant by a Jew and an Arab. There are difficulties in defining the former for the purposes of this Ordinance. Besides including all members of the Jewish Community who admit the jurisdiction of the Rabbinical Courts in matters of personal status in accordance with Article 53 of the Order-in-Council, the definition must also include all Jews of Hebrew race and faith, Palestinian or foreign who, for various reasons, may claim or may be considered not to be members of that community. It was not thought to be a function of this Committee to give a complete definition of what constitutes a Jew, but it is suggested that the Ordinance enacted for the purpose might empower the officer responsible for its operation in case of doubt to demand that a person who claims to be other than a Jew should prove to the satisfaction of that officer that he belongs to some other community or class of persons who could not be considered Jewish, or of Hebrew race or faith.

5.

In order to facilitate such enquiries, the Committee suggest that it should be considered whether every person entering the country could not be required to declare his religion and to name the local community in Palestine with which he considers himself in racial sympathy.

[margin note: Very difficult.]

(iv) As to the other side, namely, those who are to be prohibited from acquiring land in the Jewish State, the Committee thought that the simplest method of describing them would be by distinguishing them from the Jews, in the following or similar wording:

> "those who not being Jews as defined in the Ordinance are of Palestinian nationality".

It is realised that this would include persons of Armenian, Greek, Persian and other origin, besides those, who might, in the loose sense of the word, be termed Arabs.

(v) The proposed Ordinance will also have to provide for Companies, partnerships and other legal persons. Some companies, such as the Palestine Land Development Company, are frankly and purely Jewish. The Arab Agricultural Bank though some of its employees are Armenian, may be considered Arab. Some Jewish companies have Arab as well as Jewish Directors and there are of course partnerships between Jews and Arabs. The shares of a company might be owned tomorrow by persons other than those who own them today.

(vi) Both the Companies Ordinance and Partnerships Ordinance provide for the High Commissioner to issue certificates permitting the ownership of land. It might be considered rather drastic to amend these

6.

Ordinances in order to give the High Commissioner power to revoke all the certificates already issued and re-issue them with geographical restrictions according to whether they permitted the acquisition of land in either of the projected States.

Alternatively, it is suggested that the certificates of Palestinian companies only might, by an amendment of the Ordinances, be withdrawn and re-issued. Presumably there is no intention of prohibiting foreign companies from acquiring land unless these companies are obviously purely Jewish organizations. Such Jewish Companies might be separated by examining the list of those foreign companies to whom certificates have been issued.

(vii) The Committee suggest that the proposed Ordinance should empower the High Commissioner to define by Order in suitable manner the areas to which it would be applied. The areas would be classified as those it was thought might fall either

(a) in the projected Arab State; or
(b) in the projected Jewish State.

(viii) In (a), the Arab State, consent would not be given to any transaction which would result in a right or interest in land being registered in the name of any person who might be described according to the definition given in the proposed Ordinance as a Jew.

(ix) In (b), the Jewish State, consent would not be given in favour of any Palestinian national who was not a Jew within the meaning of the proposed Ordinance.

7.

(x) The proposed Ordinance should contain provision to permit transfers from Jew to Jew or non-Jew to non-Jew.

(xi) In the event of the Ordinances referred to in paragraph 2(vi) above being amended, then the proposed Ordinance should provide that in no part of Palestine would any company or other legal person who did not hold the special new High Commissioner's certificate for holding land in the particular area be allowed to become the registered owner of any right or interest.

(xii) It would have to be provided that nothing in the proposed Ordinance should be deemed to prevent registration in pursuance of a contract of transfer of which satisfactory evidence was shown to the officer operating the Ordinance that it was made before the date of the Ordinance. Similarly, nothing in the proposed Ordinance should be deemed to prevent a mortgagee becoming the owner of land which was mortgaged to him before the date of the Ordinance.

In the same connection, the proposed Ordinance would provide for existing leases to run their term or for renewal of leases in which there was a covenant of renewal.

(xiii) It would further have to be provided that nothing in the proposed Ordinance should prevent any undivided shares registered before the date of the Ordinance, being partitioned into parcels of land demarcated in accordance with the registered shares and registered in the name of the same owners.

(xiv) It would be necessary to provide that transfers of the prohibited kind should not, under the disguise of settlement operations, defeat the intention of the

8.

proposed Ordinance. Settlement Officers should be required to treat as null and void any renunciation between Arab and Jew which would conflict with the provisions of the Ordinance.

Settlement Officers should be required to investigate all undisputed claims to make sure that no transfer of the prohibited kind were disguised therein, even when no claim has been specifically made in the name of Government.

(xv) The Committee suggest that, when the boundaries of the two States are more clearly known and more permanently established, the doctrine of pre-emption which is familiar in the Mejelle and Ottoman Land Code, might be embodied in future legislation. Both the Mejelle and the Land Code admit the doctrine of "pre-emption" By the Shari'a law, a mulk owner has the right of re-purchasing, at the price actually paid, an immediately neighbouring mulk property sold to another. In the Land Code, any villager has the right of purchasing, at the present value, any miri lands in his village transferred to the inhabitant of another village. The Committee suggest that in the Jewish State, a Jew, and in the Arab State, an Arab should have a right of pre-emption, provided the right was exercised at the time of sale. For instance, if a Jew sold his lands in the Arab State to another Jew, an Arab may have the right, on payment of the actual consideration or the market value of becoming the registered owner of the property.

3. <u>Moratorium</u>.

With regard to representations which have been made to the Government by Advocate Seligman on behalf of certain unnamed clients and which are referred to in the second term of reference, the Committee's enquiries went

9.

to show that a moratorium was probably asked for to cover contracts amongst the Jews themselves and not between them and Arabs.

The Committee were of the opinion that if the proposed Ordinance contained the provisos mentioned above so that contracts made before its enactment were not interfered with; the need for a moratorium or any other action on the part of Government would not arise and financial questions amongst Jews would sort themselves out much more satisfactorily without Government intervention.

4. Settlement.

In the third term of reference the Committee suggest that District Commissioners might be empowered to prohibit the establishment of new Settlements by Jews in the Arab area and by non-Jews in the Jewish area where the District Commissioner is satisfied that such new settlements are calculated to prove a serious embarrassment to those responsible for security. These developments are considered changes in the status quo in a direction clearly thought undesirable by the Royal Commission.

We have the honour to be,
Sir,
Your obedient servants,

(Sgd.) R.F. Jardine   Chairman
(Sgd.) J. Pollock   Member
(Sgd.) R. Windham   Member

10.06

CONFIDENTIAL.

Bowyers Field,
Wrotham, Kent.
21st. June, 1938.

The Under-Secretary of State,
Colonial Office.

Sir,

Settlement and registration of title to land and associated fiscal reforms in Palestine.

Having been consulted two or three months ago on a matter affecting the future conduct of the above measures (customarily but ambiguously referred to as land settlement operations) I set myself to study carefully the Royal Commission's findings thereon as expressed in Chapter IX. Part I. of their report. This has taken me much longer than I expected, as it has necessitated reading a great many old papers and a good deal of thought. Moreover the issues raised extend to the whole field of this undertaking and are difficult to analyse and to present intelligibly in a readily digestible way. I now venture to submit the more important conclusions that appear to me to be indicated by the Royal Commission's findings, as read in the light of my earlier association with the general question, in the hope that these conclusions may be of service to you and to the Palestine Government in considering and implementing those findings.

2. The principal defects diagnosed by the Royal Commission and the more important causes to which they are attributed may be summarized as follows:-

(i) Failure to formulate a land code appropriate to the needs of the country and adapted to the economic requirements of both the primitive indigenous population and progressive immigrants. This is attributed to neither the Department of Lands nor the Attorney General's Department having had the time to give to this work.
(IX. 27-29).

(ii) Slow progress in the conduct of settlement of title and of other interests which is required to establish initially throughout the country an accurate record of all rights in every parcel of land after a field to field survey. This is attributed primarily to an unduly meticulous and over-legalistic procedure, due to judicially determined title having been sought, whereas a record of (an administratively determined) presumptive or possessory title opposable in the Courts would have been adequate. A secondary cause given is the diversion of officers engaged in the work to other duties.
(IX. 10 (5), 26, 31, 34-36, 40).

(iii) Defective nature of the resultant record in that it is limited to titles to ownership of land to the exclusion of other important interests and incidents of landed tenure, more particularly of land values, fiscal obligations, tenancy rights and easements. This is attributed primarily to the initial settlement having been restricted to judicial decisions and to there having been no connection between rural property taxation and settlement (of title). (IX. 30, 34, 38).

(iv) Lack of trustworthy statistical information regarding the land surface of the country. This is attributed largely to Jewish land pressure and consequent land speculation and to political outbreaks and consequent lack of funds. This defect is held to be irremediable until the operations of initial settlement (of title) are concluded (IX. 3, 23).

(v) Defective conduct of the (now) land register established to incorporate and maintain the fruits of the initial settlement of title. This is attributed to over-centralization and to lack of suitable rural machinery (IX. 25, 26, 31, 40). The Royal Commission also appear to have received the impression that the provision made in clauses 30 and 35 (inter alia) of the Land Settlement Ordinance for the routine embodiment of the results of settlement of title progressively in the new land register is imperfectly understood or applied.

The Royal Commission concludes its criticisms on the general subject with the verdict that "in this matter of land settlement, i.e. the preparation for all villages in the country of a reliable record of rights, the Administration, we consider, have not yet discharged their obligations under the Mandate" (IX. 4).

3. The necessity for the work arose from the chaotic state of land tenure and the prevailing ignorance both of private and of public rights to land which existed throughout the country. This necessity had been recognized by the Turks before the war, although it was accentuated afterwards by the obligation to provide a dependable basis for the implementation of the land policy prescribed by the mandate.

While no one is likely to question the Royal Commission's judgment regarding the paramount need for more expeditious completion of these long drawn out reforms, its diagnosis of the principal defects that have appeared, or the necessity for an effective overhaul of organization and procedure that is indicated, it appears to me that a number of detailed criticisms in the Report are occasioned by imperfect information or explanation, perhaps due to changes in individual officers during the long period covered by the initiation and application of the measures. It is also evident that the Royal Commission were concerned with major diagnosis and could not investigate exhaustively the detailed workings of operations which, however important, constituted but a small portion of the field of their vast and difficult inquiry.

In view, therefore, of my personal connection with the initial shaping of the measures during 1923-27 and of my close and continuous study of similar problems in a great many other countries during the last twenty years, I hope that I shall not appear lacking in the respect due to the dignity and authority of the Royal Commission if, in seeking to assist the achievement of their objectives, I suggest a reconsideration of a certain number of their detailed criticisms.

4. The field to be covered is so wide and complex that I have found considerable difficulty in presenting my conclusions in a clear and readily assimilable form. After various attempts I decided that it would be most convenient if I confined this letter to introductory remarks and explanations and presented my conclusions in the form of the two accompanying memoranda, which I have endeavoured to subdivide in a way which will simplify independent consideration of particular issues.

The first memorandum considers, under the heads cited, the remedy of the principal defects diagnosed by the Royal Commission:

    I. Revision and amendment of the land law.

    II. Acceleration of settlement of title.

    III. Associated fiscal measures.

    IV. Compilation of land statistics.

    V. Maintenance of the new land register.

Part V. has not yet been written, but shall follow.

The second memorandum reviews the history and organization of the work. For it appears to me that the major defects that have appeared in the conduct of the enterprise as a whole are essentially the fruits and symptoms of faulty organization which has its roots in the past: so that the lessons of that past require to be understood if the cause of these defects is to be effectively and finally removed.

5. The first step towards remedying these defects is to recognize their nature and effect as fully and objectively as possible. Firstly a failure, which has now extended over sixteen years, to put the land law of Palestine on to a clear, consistent and workable basis, without which the introduction of a land system appropriate to the needs of the country, that was enjoined by the mandate, was impossible. Secondly, acquiescence in a rate of progress of settlement of title, which postponed the completion of this work in the tiny territory concerned for another twenty or thirty years, that is until nearly half a century after the issue of the mandate. Thirdly, a seriously defective, and consequently ephemeral, maintenance of the basic record of rights to land that was being so slowly and laboriously constructed.

None of these were recondite effects and they manifestly menaced the whole utility of the associated operations.

Mistakes were naturally bound to be made and faults to appear in the initial years of such a difficult and complicated enterprise: but it would not ordinarily have required the machinery of a Royal Commission to demonstrate and press for the remedy of such palpable and lethal defects.

Various explanations of the failure to perceive and cure these defects locally as they appeared suggest themselves. From 1929 onwards Palestine has been subject repeatedly to the most serious unrest. Everyone who has been in any measure responsible for the conduct of public administration anywhere in times of grave political disturbance will know how imperatively the primary necessities of maintaining order, safeguarding life and promoting reconciliation impose disregard for all matters not of immediate vital concern, and particularly those of a long range character. Moreover the political disturbances in Palestine brought in their train an almost continuous succession of special inquiries, all demanding information about the rural population and the land. Necessary and beneficial in their wider aspects as these inquiries no doubt were, it was inevitable that, in conjunction with the direct demands made on all British Officers in times of more active disturbance, they should constantly interrupt concentration upon and introduce uncertainty into, the conduct of all important regular land operations. Settlement operations were consequently carried on, from their very inception in the field, under conditions that were most unfavourable to a timely discovery and early remedy of defects that in tretrospect appear so obvious.

6. It has, moreover, to be remembered that the Commissioner of Lands, who was in general charge of settlement operations, was also engaged during the period under consideration in the introduction throughout the 28 largest towns and the whole cultivated area of Palestine, of rational and equitable taxation in place of the capricious and indefensible remnants of old Turkish taxation on land and buildings that had persisted so long. He was concurrently responsible for the custody and administration of state lands throughout the country and for the conduct of the ex Ottoman Land Registry machinery pending its gradual replacement by the new register of title. And he was further charged with the duty of adviser to the Government in the large matter of framing its general land policy.

Under the most favourable circumstances this would have been a wide and exacting range of duties to discharge without giving some grounds for solid criticism. Under the difficult conditions that prevailed it would only, I think, have been possible for even the ablest and most devoted officer to do so, if he had full and well defined executive powers and a thoroughly adequate and appropriate organization at his command. Actually the powers of the Commissioner of Lands were ill defined in regard to important sections of his charge, while the organization at his command was inchoate and clumsy. These defects were the fruits of compromise between what appeared in principle desirable and what appeared in practice attainable in 1927; while it was expected that the embryo formation would evolve advantageously with changing circumstances under the stress of experience. This evolution was probably prevented by the distractions occasioned by political unrest which have already been mentioned. It may, however, be hoped that dominant considerations of a personal character which it was impossible to avoid in 1927, if the work was to get started at all, need not now prevent the considerable modifications that are needed to establish a suitable instrument to complete settlement and registration of title with the much greater dispatch and efficiency that will be needed to satisfy the requirements laid down by the Royal Commission. I have ventured to submit my own proposals to this end for consideration primarily in Memorandum II. and secondarily in Parts II. and V. of Memorandum I. accompanying, or following, this letter.

7. Stress has, and must properly continue to be, laid on the defects which have appeared in the application of the associated measures; because it is to the remedy of defects, not to the acclamation of successes, that attention has to be directed. But to preserve a just judgment alike of the services of the officers who have been responsible for the conduct and execution of the work and in planning remedial action now, it is,

------
*See Chief Secretary's Circular No.122 of the 30th.May 1928.

- 4 -

I suggest, important to recognize that no shadow of the searching criticisms made by the Royal Commission touches the quality of the results obtained in any phase of the initial settlement operations. It is not to be denied that neglect to simplify the land laws, tardiness in prosecuting reform generally, defective book-keeping of the results obtained, are capital failings in an enterprise which called so insistently for rapid and unimpeachable completion and subsequent maintenance: but it is on the other hand no light achievement, in the face of the disturbances that have racked Palestine, that the quality of the work done in the assessment of land and buildings for fiscal purposes throughout the whole country, in the definition and record of units of landed property by survey, and in the determination by Settlement Officers of the interests attaching to these units, has not been questioned. It was these effects about which the Government were so anxious when the work was being shaped and upon which its whole value depends. Indeed the most significant change that has occurred in the interval is that criticism, which then was directed to the feasibility or benefit of almost every detail of the measures that were adopted, is now virtually concentrated upon tardy or incomplete performance. But the best tribute to the quality of the day to day work done in the three associated settlement operations is that, however divided otherwise, all sections of the population have continued throughout to co-operate in the work to a remarkable degree and to press for its early extension to themselves. The importance is evident of not letting public confidence in the quality or suitability of the work to local requirements suffer in remedying the defects which the Royal Commission found.

8. In conclusion I should add that, in submitting my observations, I have written simply for the consideration of those responsible for the future conduct of the operations, who can weigh what I have said in the light of all existing circumstances. As I ceased a number of years ago to have any connection with the work I have very likely erred in important particulars on points of fact, but all the facts are readily verifiable by those on the spot. I also appreciate that many of my remarks may appear trite or my conclusions mistaken by those who have been responsible for the direction of affairs locally. It was not, however, possible to consult the latter on the innumerable details of the problem and it would have been tedious to qualify every statement.

I do not therefore pretend to be able after the lapse of time since I was in Palestine to appraise local issues properly; but such errors as I have made will be readily corrected by those on the spot or recently connected with the work, while it appeared to me that a completely independent approach to the Royal Commission's findings might have advantages.

I have to thank both Mr. A. Abramson, C.B.E., and Lieutenant Colonel Salmon, C.M.G., M.C., successive Commissioners of Lands in Palestine, for answering some questions. I shall be grateful if copies of this letter and of the accompanying memoranda may be sent to them for any corrections or comments they may think necessary.

I have generally avoided consideration of any reactions on the measures discussed of the political and territorial recommendations of the Royal Commission. But I have spared no pains to make this contribution to the solution of the present problem useful, for it seems so indisputably in the interest of all parties and of any future political units to press on steadily with these reforms as a united whole; since the future well-being of every part of the country, under whatsoever rule, cannot but be decisively assisted by any unravelling of the still persisting land tangle.

I have the honour to be,

Sir,

Your obedient servant,

(Signed) ERNEST M. DOWSON.

I. SS. 1-4. REVISION AND AMENDMENT OF THE LAND LAW.

1. The Royal Commission found a failure to formulate a land code appropriate to the needs of the country and adapted to the economic requirements of both the primitive indigenous population and progressive immigrants. This is attributed to neither the Department of Lands nor the Attorney General's Department having had the time to give to the work (ix.27-29).

It seems to have been overlooked that the Government recognized in 1926 that it was impossible for the regular services to combine with their current duties the heavy additional task of making a comprehensive revision and amendment of the land laws suited to present requirements. Dr. F.M.Goadby was accordingly invited early in that year to undertake the critically important and exacting preparatory study of the existing land law which was required as the foundation of the projected reform. Dr. Goadby was then occupying the part time post of Director of Legal Studies in Palestine, and had both the requisite leisure and the requisite preliminary knowledge of Muslim law and tradition. It was also arranged at Dr. Goadby's request that Mr. Doukhan, of the Lands Department, who had acquired valuable experience of the practical operation of the existing land laws in Palestine, should be available for reference and consultation. Excellent progress was reported by the Attorney General at a Conference held in Jerusalem on the 21st. February, 1927, by the High Commissioner (F.M.Lord Plumer) on the general subject of the associated reforms in preparation for an approaching visit by Sir John Shuckburgh to Palestine, as reference to the minutes of this Conference will show. A comprehensive explanatory statement of the existing land law, running into 400 pages, was issued for the guidance of Settlement Officers the same autumn. This was intended merely to be the first step, but the whole effort appears shortly afterwards to have been abandoned.

This seems to be a matter for the greatest regret, for the heaviest spade work had been done and another year's work should have seen the task substantially completed with the minimum disturbance of the regular public services. The progressive revision and amendment of the land laws during 1928 and 1929 would have increasingly simplified both initial settlement of title and the subsequent maintenance of the resultant new register, as the application of the amended law steadily displaced the uncertainties of the old. The cumulative effect this would have had on the facilitation, quality, speed and economy of settlement operations as a whole during the intervening decade cannot be readily exaggerated. Even now the broken threads could, I am confident, be picked up with little difficulty and the half finished work completed far more readily, rapidly and effectively with the assistance of the officer originally entrusted with the task than through the medium of any new agency, provided that officer could be persuaded to resume it and this course commended itself to the Government of Palestine generally and to the Attorney General in particular.

Nor does there seem much room for doubt that this effort is worth making. If arrangements could be initiated without delay and legislative processes were reasonably prompt, the major and most fruitful amendments at least could be law by this time next year to the immense benefit of every phase of the work. Throughout the proposed Arab areas this benefit, which could be extended to Transjordan, would be a lasting one, if the work was carried out with sympathy and understanding of Muslim conceptions, as it naturally would be. Throughout the proposed Jewish areas the benefit would also be solid, if transitional. For although it may be anticipated that the Jews will desire in due course to introduce a completely new body of land law into any areas coming under their jurisdiction, it would be shortsighted to reject on this account the early impetus which a prompt amendment of the existing land law would give to the speed and efficiency of settlement and registration of title in such areas, as well as the facilitation of any subsequent legislative reforms contemplated later therein by the Jews which the earlier disappearance of prevalent anomalies and ambiguities would promote.

2. It is not only within the sphere of settlement and registration of title that benefit would accrue. Thus the Royal Commission drew attention (ix.37) to the slow functioning of the Land Courts which have to hear and decide in their pristine tangles all actions concerning land in the still unsettled four-fifths of the country. The Royal Commission could discern no advantage in having two Judges to decide these cases (ix.37). While in Palestine between 1925 and 1927 I attended a number of Land Court cases and inquired of this among other matters. The explanation then given me was that two Judges were ordinarily needed, because few Britons had the mastery of the Ottoman Law and the Arabic language and few Palestinians the judicial independence and unassailable integrity that were required. So long as the existing obsolescences, omissions, inconsistencies and uncertainties of the current Ottoman land law are perpetuated they are bound to affect new cases and to continue to exert a serious drag on the despatch of all business in the Land Courts. The importance attached to these difficulties is signalized by the special provision in the Land Courts Ordinance directing the Court to have regard to equitable as well as to legal rights to land, or in otherwords to exercise their judgment as to what the law ought to be if it is uncertain or ambiguous. This provision has been in force now for seventeen years. Having regard to all the circumstances it can hardly be doubted that a fraction of the cost, effort and learning which has been expended during the above period in these and other Courts, on the interpretation of defects in the law, would have sufficed long ere this to have provided the country with a consistent body of land law appropriately amended to meet present day requirements.

3. But while the cumulative effect of the numerous defects in the current land law in hampering every branch of land reform is indisputably very great, I think that anyone who has been able to make a patient study of that law will agree that these defects are chiefly due to the principal elements never having been properly welded together. For it must be remembered that the Ottoman Land Code, which is ordinarily alone designated as the culprit, was promulgated eighty years ago and even when read with its associated legislation (as of course it must be) only constitutes one of the four principal elements in the existing land law of Palestine. The others are (i) the Majelle, the compilation of Muslim common law issued in sixteen books by successive Imperial Irades between 1870 and 1876, (ii) the post-revolutionary Ottoman land legislation issued for the most part in 1913, small in volume but of considerable importance, and (iii) post-war British legislation. Moreover an exaggerated impression of the current law's complexities is apt to be conveyed to those not nourished in it, by the unfamiliar Arabic terminology used, and the unfamiliar philosophy by which quite common concepts and practices are approached and expounded. The natural result is that the basis of Ottoman law is frequently blamed for effects for which it can hardly be justly held responsible. Thus the difficulties with regard to Mesha'a

and the Protection of Cultivators Ordinance appear to have been cited to the Royal Commission as instances of the maleficient effects of that law (ix.37). But mesha'a, or the periodic re-allotment of land held in common, is merely a primitive survival which lingers in other countries, for example India and even England. Far from being due to any provision of Ottoman land law, the practice is in specific contravention of that law, and would not have been in existence if that law had been enforced. Similarly the principal difficulty in protecting cultivators against disturbance has been the widespread absence of information regarding ownership and tenancies. Clandestine sales occurred and were accepted as valid (ix.14). If the land registers had been maintained as required, even by purely pre-war Ottoman law, the necessary information would have been available or readily obtainable upon the statutory application of any intended land transfer for registration. Under these conditions any provision thought proper against disturbance could have been readily enforced. Here again it was surely no adverse effect of Ottoman law, but a failure to implement it, (or alternatively to amend it promptly to facilitate such implementation) that has been the main obstacle to protecting cultivators against disturbance? Measures for the protection of tenants against disturbance are also a recent development in all countries. Little legislation contemporary with the Ottoman land code conforms to present views thereon. Moreover, its particular importance in Palestine was generated by the mandate; so that it is one of those features of reform arising out of modern conditions which, not unnaturally, required some specific constructive amendment of the pre-war Ottoman law.

4. It is not, of course, suggested that the Ottoman, or more correctly the Arab Muslim, basis of the current land laws of Palestine is ideal. But this presents, I think, far less impediment to expeditious and comprehensive reform to meet present day conditions than has been apprehended. However ideally desirable the introduction of a new land code framed on the broadest and simplest lines and leaving details to regulations may be (ix.29) the corresponding recent English reform shows how gradual the establishment of a sweeping simplification of a land law rooted in the history and traditions of a people must be. In Palestine, particularly, at the present time, consideration even of minor changes must pay careful and sympathetic regard to Muslim religious law and tradition, with which the land law is impregnated. This is not compatible with the introduction of a new land code confined to broad outlines and leaving all minor details to elastic regulation by a secular and foreign administration. It appears to me that the projected partition of the country precludes any real prospect of the establishment of any common ideal land code now, while the exacerbation of Muslim feeling that has occurred would make deeply suspect any proposal to introduce a land code of the character indicated. Surely it is prefeable to be content instead with the more modest objective of a prompt amendment of the land laws on lines acceptable to local Arab and Muslim sentiment. This would immensely facilitate the progress of all land reforms to the common advantage, prior to any partition; which appears to be the most important and most pressing need. And it would equip the Arab, Jewish and Mandatory territories alike, after partition with a marked advance on the current land law, which each could subsequently develop as it thought best.

II. §§. 5-18.   ACCELERATION OF SETTLEMENT OF TITLE.

5.   The Royal Commission found a paramount need to expedite settlement of title and other interests in land. The slow progress made hitherto is attributed primarily to an unduly meticulous and over legalistic procedure due to judicially determined title having been sought, whereas a settlement of presumptive or possessory title opposable in the Courts would have been sufficient. A secondary cause given is the diversion of officers engaged in the work to other duties. (ix. 10 (5), 26, 31, 34-36, 40).

Slow progress in the conduct of initial settlement of title hitherto cannot be disputed. In the eight and a half years active work considered by the Royal Commission (June 1928-1936) title to only 1,492 square kilometres of land was settled (ix. 33) out of an estimated total of about 7,120 square kilometres of cultivable land throughout the country excluding the Beersheba sub-district (ix. 44).* It is also undeniable that a settlement of possessory title can be effected more rapidly with the same resources than of absolute title. I myself recommended the former in 1923 for this reason. There was a good deal to be said for a rapid settlement of possessory title then, if provision was made (as proposed) to secure early maturity to absolute title by efflux of time of all titles not previously challenged in Court. But the Government consistently held that a settlement of immediately valid title was required. I felt, and still feel, that they were right; but a proportionately greater effort was necessitated. Whether this decision was right or wrong then, it appears to me that it would be clearly impolitic to reverse it now. For it would surely undermine all the confidence in the value of the work and the great measure of co-operation that has been slowly won, if, at this stage, after titles have been accorded for a fifth of the country on which (with rare exceptions) land can be safely sold and bought and loans securely and economically effected, a form of title is substituted for the remainder of the country which, even when associated with an efficient and up-to-date survey, does no more in the event of subsequent dispute than name the defendant in an action regarding the ownership of the land concerned? Moreover it is doubtful if the large measure of unchallenged maturity which possessory titles might have attained in 1923-29 could be recaptured now.

6.   As the Royal Commission recognize (ix.37) the limitation of the process of systematic settlement to possessory instead of judicially determined title would transfer that judicial determination in first instance to the already congested Land Courts in every case in which the Settlement Officer's administrative finding of possessory title was disputed. They accordingly recommend (i) an increase in the number of Land Courts to meet the increased

---

*This total includes some 244 square kilometres of State Domain (Jeftlik) allotted independently under the Beisan Agreement (ix.130).

volume of work that would be thrown on these Courts by the proposed change, and (ii) that this increase shall be accompanied by a limitation of the Land Court bench to a single Judge, a British Officer with practical experience of land settlement. The importance of these qualifications is evident, but they surely restrict the choice to existing or previous British Settlement Officers. So that the effect of the change might well be that the same men who previously had decided title finally in the capacity of Settlement Magistrates would now discharge substantially the same functions as Land Court Judges.

No doubt the cost, lessened accessibility, greater formality and slower working of the Land Courts would reduce the number of contested cases, particularly those affecting the poorer peasantry. But the reduction of cases by the withdrawal of facilities which the mass of small holders have grown to expect, could hardly fail to be misunderstood and resented. Actions in the Land Courts are moreover necessarily taken entirely at the instance of litigants in a sporadic way in respect alike of time and the location of the land affected. This tends to hamper rapid and economical territorial output and virtually preclude sittings in proximity to the land affected, a condition of the utmost importance in establishing facts about such land and in securing all material witnesses easily, quickly and cheaply, and with the least disturbance of their daily labours.

7. Originally the Government were most distrustful of the capacity of Settlement Officers to exercise any judicial functions. It was largely the manifest inability of the Land Courts to keep abreast, even with the stream of current land litigation, that persuaded the former to allow Settlement Officers to act as Settlement Magistrates at all. For the only practical alternative, if a settlement of absolute title was to be effected, was the creation of extra peripatetic Land Courts, which would have been much more costly. But it was then intended that Settlement Officers should always camp in the front line of field operations and decide disputed claims summarily on the spot as a part of their wider general functions. Comprehensive provision was made in the Land Settlement Ordinance for reference or appeal to the more experienced and judicially more competent Land Courts, to whom it was supposed that all the more complicated and difficult cases would go. Further appeal on points of law to the Court of Appeal was also provided.

It is clear from the Royal Commission's findings that circumstances prevented these intentions being realized. While with rapidly growing experience Settlement Officers learnt to discharge their judicial functions with ability and success, it appears that absorption in those functions has impelled them to withdraw from the active and pervasive control of field operations that was designed, and even to abandon residence in the villages among the working parties.

Among these circumstances evidently were (i) the continued congestion of the Land Courts with ordinary litigation (ix.37) which meant that as little additional work as possible must be thrown upon them, and (ii) the growing tendency to carry every dispute to a judicial decision (ix.34).

In the light of events it was evidently a serious misjudgment to expect a Settlement Officer to combine successfully the functions of Settlement Magistrate with those of pervasive field Settlement Officer. It is to this error that I primarily ascribe the tendency to dispute every claim in the Settlement Magistrates' Court, however frivolously. When the Land Settlement Ordinance was drafted it was considered that a Settlement Officer had adequate powers in conjunction with the Land Court to deal summarily with all frivolous or ill-founded disputes; or alternatively that those powers could be readily strengthened if necessary. But to enable such powers to be exercised justly and economically it was intended that all claims and objections should be thoroughly elucidated and sifted beforehand by preliminary field investigations carried out on the spot with the assistance of the village elders and interested parties. If such investigations are conducted patiently, understandingly and competently many disputes can be composed or exploded in the process, while the remainder are systematized and clarified. The reduction in volume and the simplification in character of the disputes requiring judicial decision that can be effected in this manner are very great; while the residue, broadly speaking, represents a genuine minimum of intractable cases which can only be settled justly and to the public satisfaction by judicial proceedings. At an early stage in the operations the desirability was recognized of utilizing Palestinian Officers as Assistant Settlement Officers to multiply the range and scope of the Settlement Officer's activities, among the more important of which was the conduct of these preliminary investigations. But the efficacy of these assistants was naturally largely determined by the degree to which the Settlement Officer himself participated in and controlled their work. But it has already appeared that circumstances precluded this to a critically injurious degree.

6. Great importance was attached in the original proposals to the development and utilization in these preliminary investigations of the Village Settlement Committee provided for in ss.13 and 14 of the Land Settlement Ordinance. The basis of all inquisition, definition and authoritative cataloguing of the possession, use and productivity of rural land in primitive countries must be some pooling and crystallization of local knowledge; since there is no other source from which the desired results can be derived. The compilation of Domesday Book through the agency of special Commissioners and local juries is an early English example of this very combination of Settlement Officers and Village Settlement Committees. Suitably constituted small village committees promised to be equally valuable instruments for a similar purpose in Palestine, as the benefits of settlement of title came to be appreciated and its procedure to be understood by village communities. The elders, indeed most of the members, of village communities are familiar with the claims and counterclaims to ownerships and other interests in land within every section of the village territory, as well as their origins and merits. Under the stimulus and direction of Settlement Officers it should be possible through the instrumentality of a well selected group of leading members of each village community to winnow claims and to locate the parcels of land affected progressively in each section of the village very effectively, before detail survey and settlement of title are commenced in a village at all. The immense facilities and acceleration of these conjoint operations that full and systematic use of this instrument offers is clear; but it appears that circumstances did not permit much use to be made of it. It is indeed evident that this would have entailed on Settlement Officers a degree of educative effort initially, and of continuous contact, encouragement and supervision subsequently, which was incompatible with the volume and character of the demands made upon these officers in their capacity as Settlement Magistrates.

9. Another important condition to be satisfied to secure rapid and economical working of settlement operations as a whole is the closest association between the complementary operations of cadastral survey and settlement of title. The two should indeed be interdependent processes, just as the two hands wash each other. If detail cadastral survey pushes appreciably ahead of settlement of title, an advance investigation into ostensible ownership must be made by the former to enable it to locate and record provisionally the property parcels which are then reported to exist. Considerable alteration in this advance parcellation of the land may be expected when settlement of title reaches the same block of territory if there has been any considerabl interval between the two phases of the work, both because (i) changes in the property mosaic due to amalgamations and sub-divisions of previous parcels occasioned by sales, inheritance, foreclosures etc., are unceasing throughout any country and because (ii) no property boundary can be authoritatively located unless and until the title of ownership on which all its particulars depend has also been authoritatively decided. On the other hand, if settlement of title pushes ahead of detail survey it has to devise makeshift substitutes to locate provisionally the property parcels which it settles and is held up thereby at every turn, Delay and waste of effort thus result every time these two complementary activities are allowed to get appreciably out of step.

Although the enormous difference of 1100 square kilometres between the area surveyed and the area settled by the end of 1936 (which is shown in the Table at the bottom of page 229 and Plate 3 of the Royal Commission's Report), exaggerates the gap between the advancing waves of the two processes, it is nevertheless evident that that gap was wastefully wide. A better co-ordinated effort might well have produced by that date, for the same aggregate expenditure of effort and funds, something more nearly approaching (a) 2000 instead of 1500 square kilometres of area settled and (b) 2100 instead of 2600 surveyed. So long as the two processes are conducted by separate organizations, however closely allied, it is impossible to have the complete freedom of adjustment between them which is necessary to secure effective and continuous synchronization. At the outset this separation appeared to be unavoidable, for various reasons which have ceased to be material. But although I have little personal knowledge of individual Survey Officers working in Palestine to-day, I am confident from experience elsewhere that a unification of the two processes should be feasible by now, after all the local experience that has been gained. Such a unification would involve a re-allocation of functions which could also be directed to remedy the other weaknesses in the conduct of settlement of title which have been previously indicated.

10. The re-allocation of functions which I recommend for consideration is as follows:

    (i) The conversion of the present, or other experienced, Settlement Officers into Settlement Magistrates exclusively discharging the judicial functions of these posts.

    (ii) The conduct of the remaining field processes of detail cadastral survey and settlement of title in conjunction under appropriate British Survey Officers, who would be conjointly nominated Settlement Officers without magisterial duties and given all the powers of existing Settlement Officers that are required for this purpose.

Under the latter arrangement all the assistant staff engaged in the field operations of settlement of title (that is those not requiring to be attached to Settlement Magistrates (as such) would come under the direction of the combined Survey and Settlement Officer within the area under his charge. This procedure was adopted in the execution of the Egyptian cadastral surveys, which were settlements of possessory title for fiscal purposes, with the results that (a) synchronization and co-ordination of the interdependent processes of detail cadastral survey and settlement of title was automatic and (b) the work swept forward steadily and rapidly as a consistent whole.

The re-allocation of functions suggested should not only unify the hitherto divided operations of detail cadastral survey and settlement of title similarly in Palestine, with commensurate effect in speed and economy of working; but it would also enable the new Settlement Officers to become the active and ubiquitous spearheads of settlement of title in the field, which the demands of their magisterial duties have precluded the present Settlement Officers from being. Concurrently the latter could then concentrate wholly on that essential and exacting portion of the common task, which they appear to have discharged with such general satisfaction and success qualitatively.

But if the whole tempo and efficiency of the operations of settlement of title are to be greatly increased in pursuance of the Royal Commission's recommendations, as is I think undoubtedly practicable, the mistake must clearly be avoided of seeking to remedy the error of overloading one category of officer by repeating the same error with another. While really rapid and economical working will not be attainable without organic unification of effort in the field, these effects will be jeopardized again, if the combined Survey and Settlement Officer becomes unduly absorbed in either of these associated activities. If I am substantially justified in the conclusions that I have drawn, there is a great deal of spade work still to be done in increasing the efficiency of the field operations as rapidly as possible, both in the administrative stages of settlement of title and in securing effective co-ordination between this aspect of the work and that of detail cadastral survey. This must be expected for some time to come to demand the primary attention of the conjoint Survey and Settlement Officer that I have suggested should be entrusted with general charge of field operations in a settlement area. If the officer is not in his turn to be overloaded he will require a more junior British Survey Officer as his lieutenant, to be occupied chiefly on the survey side at first, but increasingly in a general capacity.

11. Without prejudice to the increase in the number of settlement parties which the Royal Commission recommend (ix. 36), I am confident that the internal re-allocation of functions and strengthening of the British staff of existing Settlement parties that is suggested will yield far greater proportional effects, and these much more quickly, than any similar expenditure incurred in the establishment of new parties. But if this internal re-organization of existing settlement parties can be accompanied by an increase in the number of these parties, so much the better. The extent to which additional parties would yield useful results at an early date can only be gauged by those on the spot, as it would critically depend upon (i) the supply of

additional experienced local officers available to discharge the functions respectively of (a) Settlement Magistrates and (b) combined Survey and Settlement Officers, and (ii) the capacity of the enlarged Settlement Organization as a whole to push forward cadastral survey and settlement of title in effectively synchronized conjunction.

12. There is one further point that may perhaps be usefully mentioned. A year or two after settlement of title started steps were taken to relieve Settlement Officers in the field as far as possible of all routine clerical duties by the formation of a central clerical settlement office at Jaffa. This seemed to me in principle to be a sensible measure when I heard of it, while the Royal Commission's findings indubitably show that Settlement Officers have throughout been overburdened. It appears however from the 1936 Departmental Report that this office has been recently broken up and its work redistributed again to the various Settlement Officers. There must have been reasons for this which appeared to be good and sufficient at the time to those fully acquainted with the facts; but it may be worth reconsidering the matter now in connection with the implementation of the Royal Commission's findings.

13. It is now convenient to return to a consideration of the work of the Settlement Magistrates' Courts. It has already appeared that Settlement Officers have been charged with too wide a range of duties and that as settlement operations developed this has resulted (i) in the exercise of their functions as Settlement Magistrates having tended to absorb their energies to the detriment of their other duties, while (ii) the inadequate performance of their other duties reacted in turn to increase the demands made upon the Settlement Courts. These conclusions are not inconsistent with the strong impression received by the Royal Commission that the proceedings of Settlement Officers, when sitting as Magistrates, were as a rule unduly legalistic and protracted with a seriously retarding effect on the progress of settlement operations as a whole. This development should perhaps have been anticipated. The original apprehension of Government that Settlement Magistrates would act arbitrarily and without proper knowledge of, or regard for, law was well known to these officers. Again the omission to make the land law clear and consistent has perpetuated the number of occasions when the choice between hair-splitting and arbitrariness in some degree is inescapable. Under the circumstances a tendency to resort to the former, rather than the latter, was natural. It was also surely the better of the two. For injurious as has been the drag thereby exerted on the work as a whole yet, if a choice had to be made, it was better to win the confidence of the public and of the regular Courts by unduly meticulous work than to secure a larger output by superficial work.

But when all is said and done, there very rapidly comes a point under an admittedly defective law at which legal conscientiousness approaches legal quibbling and when the injustice of pursuing convolutions of the law at the cost alike of the general Palestinian taxpayer and of gravely retarding the settlement of land disputes throughout the remainder of the country is palpable.

14.   Emphasis is also laid by the Royal Commission on the necessity of hearing cases on the spot. (IX. 38). The importance of this cannot be too strongly stressed. It is only on the spot that there is any real assurance of being able to verify statements about the land with certainty, while it is in proximity of the land concerned that the most valuable witnesses - men who have been in touch with it and with the varying claims made to it from their childhood - are commonly to be found and can be most readily called as required.

Every one with experience of land cases knows the corrective effect of a visit to the land on even the most carefully tested second-hand information. The briefest visit to the site will explode misconceptions or the most plausible misrepresentations of fact in a way that nothing else will do. The mere hearing of a case in proximity to the land affected acts as a valuable deterrent against such misrepresentations, since their exposure is so greatly facilitated thereby. Moreover the peasant all over the world will speak more readily and frankly among his own fields than in the unfamiliar surroundings and alien atmosphere of a distant Court room.

15.   Delay in obtaining judgment in the case of a dispute about a particular parcel (or group of parcels) should not of course hold up the settlement and registration of title to contiguous parcels, provided there is material agreement about the positions of common boundaries. So that settlement and registration of title in cases that are decided without a judicial hearing (which should be something like four out of five) ought in principle to proceed independently, subject to some occasional later rectifications of boundaries when these abut on disputed parcels. But in practice any considerable honeycombing of the settled territory with parcels still sub judice soon become prohibitively uneconomical and disturbing to the orderly and rapid progress of the operations as a whole. It is, therefore, probably not going too far to say that the possibility of completing the present settlement of title with reasonable promptitude and at reasonable cost will depend upon the possibilities of effecting (i) a considerable reduction in the proportion and complexity of the cases that are brought to the Settlement Courts and (ii) a considerably more expeditious despatch of business therein.

A variety of recommendations have been made which should assist to achieve these ends: but if the early and rapid acceleration of general output that is aimed at is to be ensured, it is essential that punctual and informative statistics of progress in each branch of the work in each Settlement Area shall be continuously compiled and regularly presented to the Directing Officer and by him to Government. Only in this way can any failure to maintain speedy and properly co-ordinated progress be promptly detected and promptly cured. Since it appears that the practical limit to the speed of settlement operations as a whole is likely to continue to be set by the output of the Settlement Courts, the statistics of their cases will be among the most important for this purpose. These statistics should be designed to show inter alia (a) the proportionate demand made on the Courts and (b) their territorial output as well as the number and results of any appeals to Higher Courts. Territorial demand and output should be expressed by the number, the area and the value (as assessed for taxation) of the parcels of land affected. These returns should also classify separately cases concerning

(a) the proprietorship of parcels, (b) mortgages or analogous burdens and (c) other matters.

It is hoped to examine in an Appendix the important question of the character of title to land in principle, more fully than has been possible here.

III. §§.1b - 1e. ASSOCIATED FISCAL MEASURES.

16.
In Chapter ix. §.20 of the Royal Commission's Report it is said that there is at present no connection in Palestine between rural property taxation and land settlement. In §.34 it is said that land settlement in Palestine has nothing to do with the settlement of land revenue, the fixation of rents,* the fertility of the soil. In S.38 it is advocated that a plot to plot inquiry as to the fertility of the soil and its classification in the appropriate category under the rural property tax should form part of the procedure of settlement of title. These observations suggest that the object and character of the fiscal survey noted in §.32 was never fully explained to the Royal Commission.

When it was decided that the rapid completion of a combined programme of settlement of possessory title and assessment of land for fiscal purposes which I recommended in 1923 was precluded on financial grounds, I sought some alternative means of accelerating the introduction of land tax. In pursuance of this aim it was eventually agreed at the Conference held in Jerusalem on the 21st. February, 1927, which has been already mentioned, that a land survey on a scale of 1 : 10,000 should be pushed forward rapidly ahead of the 1 : 2,500 fully detailed cadastral survey which must proceed pari passu with the much slower march of settlement of title. This advance survey (christened topo-cadastral survey to denote its double function by the Director of Survey) was

> (a) to be accompanied by a definition of village boundaries, a sub-division of the land within those boundaries into fiscal blocks of approximately equal productive value, and the assessment (or classification) of these blocks for purposes of land tax (rural property tax) and,
>
> (b) to depict the village and fiscal block boundaries as well as all important topographical detail.

The execution of this survey was designed to satisfy four pressing needs without waiting until the much slower process of settlement and registration of title and ancillary cadastral survey was complete. These needs were:

> (i) to unify village areas within single continuous boundaries. Previously village lands were intermixed in a most haphazard way and disputes were endemic between villagers regarding the position and limits of such lands;
>
> (ii) to enable an equitably assessed land tax to be substituted as promptly as possible for the surviving remnants of Turkish tithe, werko and animal tax. This was to be secured by the subdivision of the lands of each village into the fiscal blocks already mentioned, throughout each of which land tax was to run at a uniform rate;

---

*Used no doubt in the sense common in Indian practice that land revenue was in principle a rent due to the ruler as ultimate owner of the soil.

(iii) to provide a trustworthy basis for statistics of the land surface of the country;

(iv) to provide an up-to-date and reliable series of maps of the country on an adequate scale for general public purposes.

17. The previous execution of this fiscal or topo-cadastral survey was also designed to play an important part in facilitating the subsequent operations of settlement and registration of title. Thus the officers responsible for making the preliminary arrangements were, no doubt, able to do so in the light of the reliable and detailed information furnished by the topo-cadastral map series. They found precisely defined unbroken village units accepted by the population, instead of a multitude of warring enclaves. And they also found each village area divided into convenient sections of uniform character (already described as fiscal blocks) which had been selected in consultation with the villagers and were familiar to them. Although initially selected as suitable units for land tax purposes, these fiscal blocks were also expressly designed and utilized (either integrally or by simple internal subdivision when unduly large) to form convenient "registration blocks", or small subdivisions required for purposes of cadastral survey and land registration. Civilized countries are normally divided into units of decreasing size, the smallest of which corresponds to the English parish or the Palestinian village; but in any closely settled and well developed territory these village units require to be further sub-divided to enable the complementary land survey and book-keeping sides of registration of title to be carried on easily and economically. These further sub-divisions are called cadastral or registration blocks. Each constitutes a stable territorial unit to which a self-contained section of the land register is devoted and within the perimeter of which property parcels can be conveniently reference-numbered and the effect of mutations in such parcels readily recorded.

18. . If this description has been clear it will be seen that the relations between the advanced operations associated with the fiscal or topo-cadastral survey and the subsequent operations of settlement and registration of title were as closely interlocked and interdependent as they well could be under the prescribed circumstances. Thus the limits of a fiscal block A. in any village should correspond exactly with those of one, two, or three coincident registration blocks. All the property parcels within these one, two or three registration blocks will be taxed at the iniform rate applying to fiscal block A. in proportion to the superficial areas of such parcels. There should therefore normally be no need to conduct a plot to plot inquiry in conjunction with settlement of title as suggested by the Royal Commission; because the process of assessment of the land for fiscal purposes was expressly carried out in advance, in order that the replacement of the survivals of Turkish taxation on land by more equitable methods should not have to await the more tardy progress of settlement of title. But although a very substantial instalment of fiscal reform was thus secured much earlier than would

otherwise have been practicable, the individual incidence of the reformed taxation was bound to remain imperfect until ultimately decided in the progress of settlement of title. In short settlement of title and the earlier fiscal operations were complementary and planned from the outset to be so.

The impression of complete dissociation between rural property taxation and settlement of title which the Royal Commission received, is I imagine to be attributed to these combined fiscal effects of the successive operations not having been embodied together systematically in the new Land Register as settlement of Title has proceeded. Special fiscal records have necessarily had to be constructed and maintained in advance of settlement of title, but as settlement of title progressed a single system of record should have been established for titles to land and all rights and obligations incident thereto. Not only are duplicate systems of record extravagant, but they inevitably breed confusion and error. If a register of title is properly maintained, it is a simple routine operation to prepare land tax lists from it regularly as required. If a register of title is defectively maintained in a country in which such a register is the lawful basis of all land titles, on what basis is a reliable and lawfully applicable land tax register to be constructed?

19.   These remarks do not of course apply to the assessment carried out in twenty-eight urban areas for purposes of urban property tax (see plate 2 Royal Commission's Report); but the unification of the tax and title records in these urban areas should have been for the most part even simpler. This arises from the facts (i) that urban properties must be individually assessed while (ii) from their nature they are ordinarily much more permanently and precisely defined on the ground than rural properties. In the process of urban assessment the "reputed owner" had to be identified and this should have accorded with the registered title holder if the latter was intelligibly recorded in the old land register. If not, the reputed owner stood in the position of the enjoyer of a possessory title. Thus the newly constructed urban tax registers constituted informal but comprehensive records of title to all urban properties, such title being judicially valid or purely possessory according to the circumstances of each case. To amend or convert the latter into the former is a relatively simple process if systematically pursued, whether by process of judicial settlement of title in due course or by recognizing maturity of title after a prescribed absence of opposition.

IV. §.20.   COMPILATION OF LAND STATISTICS.

Mention should also be made of the apparent omission to make any use of the topo-cadastral survey to provide trustworthy statistics of the land surface of the country to the absence of which the Royal Commission call particular attention (ix.3 and 23). The need has impressed all observers. The Royal Commission, it will be seen, apprehend that this defect is irremediable until the operations of settlement of title have been concluded. It is of course true that full and exact details of lawful ownership cannot be given until settlement of title has been completed throughout the country. Indeed these details will not even then be available unless in the meantime the land register has been maintained fully and correctly up to date under all relevant heads, which appears from the Royal Commission's findings to be doubtful. It may also be pertinent to ask whether any steps have been taken to compile and maintain these detailed statistics pari passu with the construction of the new register; for such compilation will be a lengthy and laborious task if left until the latter has been completed throughout the country.

But, while exact, up-to-date and detailed land statistics are one of the most valuable by-products of a comprehensive and efficient land register, it will be recognized that few countries have so far established such a register. England has not, France has not. Moreover, it is not the lack of detailed statistics of individual ownership and individual use of the land, which such a register could furnish, that is criticized by the Royal Commission and has been so much needed; but simply the lack of reliable returns of such primary data as the gross totals of the cultivable area, of the State Domain and of the waste or still unreclaimed land (mewat) in the country.

The reproach is serious that British Administration is ignorant of these figures after fifteen years application of a policy that critically depends upon them; and there should have been no occasion for it. For it would be difficult to conceive of a more trustworthy, a more convenient, or a more fruitful matrix for the production of the general statistics of the land surface of the country that have been required than the miniature of that land surface which the topo-cadastral map series should present. A systematic analysis of the area content of each sheet carried out in co-operation with various interested and specialist services as the survey proceeded would have provided progressively a classification of great trustworthiness and exactitude of the land surface of each village, of each district and eventually, of the whole country, excluding the Beersheba sub-district.

Since this survey has been successfully used as the basis of the land tax throughout the country, it must be assumed that it furnishes dependable information of the cultivated and cultivable land which is taxed, or, in other words is recognized a priori to be in private possession in each village, if not in each fiscal block. This information could also be readily classified racially. And it is to be supposed that as the survey proceeded the Director of Lands located in each village all cultivated or obviously cultivable land which he regarded as State Domain, if only for departmental information. Moreover, such land would otherwise tend to be taxed as in private possession and to pass into such possession. The depiction within the confines of each village (a) of the waste or still unreclaimed tracts (mewat) and (b) of the areas devoted to public or village use of some sort, (e.g. roads, railways, village sites, paths, threshing floors) were matters of routine survey, for the elucidation of which local or specialist assistance was readily available. No doubt uncertainties in classification would occur; but certainly nothing that, given industry and commonsense, would not be adequately interpretable both for fiscal and statistical purposes.

This analysis of the land surface of the country on the basis of the topo-cadastral sheets, and the resultant statistical compilation could still be made if, as I do not doubt, that survey was carried out upon the lines that were originally proposed; but the process would naturally be more laborious and costly than if it had been carried out in association with the field work.

10.07

CONFIDENTIAL.

Bowyers Field,
Wrotham, Kent,
16". August, 1938.

Dear Martin,

SETTLEMENT OF TITLE &C. re PALESTINE.

I am sending you herewith 5 copies of the second Memorandum mentioned in my official letter of the 21st. June last. Should you happen to need any further copies will you telephone to Miss Buchanan, Victoria 5537. An apology is due to Lloyd and yourself for having failed to let you have the Memorandum earlier. I found that my first draft was not either as clear or as conveniently arranged as it should have been.

The paper is a long one, but in view of my share in gettin the work going and the opportunities that have been missed of tackling it effectively during the last 20 years, I have felt under an uncomfortable obligation to summarize the whole story and to dig into its lessons to the best of my ability for those who are concerned with the problem to-day. The great difficulty has been to exclude nothing of importance while making the paper as easily assimilable by busy people as its complexity permits.

2. Three major mistakes appear to me to have been vitiated in the efforts made to carry out the work from 1919 onwards. Firstly, an omission to utilize properly the experience that wa available from the very start. Secondly an omission to revise the Ottoman land law, although the need to do so was recognized also at the outset. Thirdly, a failure to organize the work rationally either in 1919 or in 1927. For obvious reasons it is best to let the facts speak for themselves regarding the first. Attention was called to the second by the Royal Commission, although they clearly did not have the time or information to appreciate its full implications. The third, I think, naturally escaped them because they were concerned with effects, not with departmental machinery.

I have done my best to provide the basis for an independent objective judgment of these and other points. But in pursuance of previous conversations I think you would like me also to consider the re-organization of the work in relation to actual personnel. I will readily do so, as the practical results of changes, however desirable in principle, must depend in the last resort upon appropriate men being appointed to work them; but I hope it will be remembered that my knowledge of particular officers is very out of date and that proposals concerning them are intended to be suggestive only, and are made subject to the fullest reserve on this account and in reliance upon correction by those whose knowledge of such officers is more recent and goes deeper.

3. The primary need in the organization of the work (as I see it) is to combine unreservedly in a single service the conduct of (i) all branches of survey, (ii) settlement of title and of other interests in land, (iii) assessment of land for public purposes and (iv) land registration in its most catholic sense. These are all interdependent processes in the construction and maintenance of a national land record, which require specialist technical knowledge and experience for their united conduct; but are in no way necessarily (or

even advisedly) associated with any particular uses to which such a national land record may be put. Indeed if other services are to be associated with it (as is sometimes convenient administratively) it is preferable that they should be others of a metrological character (e.g. standardization of weights and measures, meteorlogical observations) than any sectional use of a record, the unbiased compilation and maintenance of which should be beyond suspicion.

In the light of earlier correspondence and discussions there seems no doubt that A.P. Mitchell is the best candidate for the direction of the above service. He should retain to the fullest extent that is politic and feasible, if only in advisory form, the effective control of similar operations in Transjordan. He should in my opinion drop the title of Commissioner of Lands and be given either that of Surveyor and Registrar General of Lands (Surveyor General in short) or Director of Survey and Land Registration. The former would be psychologically preferable and both he and the service as a whole will require all the prestige in the country they can be properly given.

4. I have still to let you have Part V. of my first Memorandum which is to consider the maintenance of the new land registers in a more satisfactory manner than hitherto; for although the Royal Commission are less precise in their criticisms of this side of the work their findings leave no room for uncertainty as to its gravely defective conduct. I have myself accordingly no doubt (i) that this branch of the work will require a thorough overhaul and probably considerable reconstruction and (ii) that this will need the concentrated attention of a competent, forceful and energetic officer specially assigned to this duty by the Land Records service. Mitchell will be too fully occupied with the general conduct of operations to do this himself. If Jardine is the man that he was, is still prepared to be bodily as well as mentally active, and will work happily in departmental subordination to Mitchell, it would be difficult to find a better man for the purpose. But it is essential that Jardine's subordination to Stubbs, which I believe still nominally continues, should be specifically terminated. I have always considered that the latter has exercised a dead hand over this branch of the work and, unless the Royal Commission have been seriously misled, this opinion seems to be amply confirmed. At the same time the separation between the technical and book-keeping sides of the new land records should be finally broken down so that Jardine's suggested duties should be those of an Administrator or Inspector of the offices of the Land Records service which are concerned with the maintenance of the new land register not those of a Director of a different service.

5. These comments of course apply only to the maintenance of the new land registers constructed in the course of initial cadastral survey and settlement, and not to the perpetuation of the ex-Ottoman registers in the areas not yet reached by settlement operations. As indicated in the accompanying memorandum there appears to me to be a good deal to be said for administering these independently of the new registers if a suitable officer can be found to entrust this work to. Such an officer should be under the direction of the Land Records service, since the location of the parcels of land, which entries in the ex-Ottoman registers purport to effect, should have been progressively improving and if this can only continue under the effective direction (however secured) of the

competent technical service. But the custody of the old
registers none the less affords an opportunity for valuable
service in a largely independent charge; and if such a charge
was constituted it would enable Jardine (or another) to concentrate completely on the more important and exacting task of
helping to establish and maintain the new record on a proper
footing.

Subject to certain important objections which may well
forbid it, Stubbs seems the obvious man to administer until
their extinction the old registers for the conduct of which he
has been primarily responsible since 1922. If his dignity
could be sufficiently safeguarded he might prefer this to early
retirement, while there cannot well be anyone (of comparable
status) whose knowledge of the tangles and obscurities of the
old register is as great. It may be doubted, however, whether
Stubbs would really take off his coat and wire in effectively
now to administer a gradually dying service. Another consideration that must be mentioned is the particular need for vigilance against corruption among subordinates in administering
records that depend so much upon personal interpretation. I
believe that some years ago allegations of corruption against the
service under his charge were investigated by a committee of
enquiry under Bowman's chairmanship and that there were grounds
for thinking that there was some substance in these charges. A
disappointed man, although willing to remain in the service,
might well be prone to neglect the active inspection and control
needed to prevent opportunities for corruption under the difficulties inherent in the nature of the old registers. Failing
Stubbs there may possibly be some other officer of ripe experience who could assume general control of the old registers
advantageously.

If no such appointment commends itself or proves feasible
it will probably be necessary to maintain the administrative
association between the old registers and the new; but the
radical difference between them points to the advisability of
treating each as a distinct problem in any case.

6. If the separation between (a) the Land Registries and
(b) the control of public lands should be approved, it would be
necessary also to consider what officer should be entrusted
with the latter. This would no doubt depend primarily upon the
possibilities still remaining open to this service. If the maintenance of existing departmental activity is considered sufficient an obvious possibility would be to let Stubbs carry on
as Controller of State lands.* If there is still thought to be
time to embark usefully upon a more extensive protection and
more active development of state lands it might be worth while
to entrust this to a Commissioner of Lands of status and functions on the altered lines suggested in the accompanying
memorandum and to appoint a man of larger calibre with the requisite qualifications and local knowledge for such a post.

7. I hope these rather discursive comments may be of
some assistance, read in conjunction with my two memoranda. I
will of course gladly come up and discuss any points further
at any time or with anyone if this seems likely to be helpful.
I will, as previously mentioned, send copies of the accompanying
memorandum confidentially also to Abramson and to Salmon for any
comments or corrections. As Jardine is at home I think it would
be useful to get his criticisms on the papers also if this is
permissable. He has been in the thick of it recently and is
both intelligent and practical.

*As an alternative to carrying on the ex Ottoman land regis[try].

I do not mind anybody seeing my letter of the 21st. June and the two memoranda that the C.O. and the Palestine Government consider it proper or advisable to show it to; but I shall not show the present letter to anyone and I suggest that it should not go beyond the C.O. and Battershill.

Yours sincerely,

Ernst m Dowson

CONFIDENTIAL.

MEMORANDUM II. reviewing the history of cadastral survey settlement of title and associated measures in Palestine between 1913 and 1936.

In studying the findings of the Royal Commission on the conduct of the above operations during 1928-36, as set forth in Chapter IX, Part I, of their Report, I found it necessary to review the origins of these operations fairly fully from 1913 onwards. As this review entailed a good deal of work and provides the basis for the corroboration or correction of the conclusions in my previous Memorandum, it seemed proper to summarize and put its more relevant portions on record in this Memorandum.

But it also appeared to me that the underlying cause of the major defects found by the Royal Commission was a faulty organization of the work, which had its roots in the earlier history mentioned. No enterprise of any magnitude can be free from mistakes and those that were made will be readily understood, if they were not in some respects indeed inevitable, at the time. But it is clearly desirable that they should be observed and considered now; for if the great acceleration of the work that is recommended by the Royal Commission is to be realized it will be necessary to facilitate its execution in every possible way.

I have presented the accompanying review as justly and objectively as I can; but it is necessarily selective for three reasons. Firstly because of the length and complexity of the full story. Secondly because no single individual can be cognisant of all the material facts in that story or fail in some respects to appraise, with proper judgment and detachment, even the issues with which he is familiar. Thirdly because the review is primarily directed to extract lessons on particular points. But I believe that in sum it will be found to be a faithful statement.

It should also be emphasized again that matters that may appear obvious enough in retrospect now, were frequently obscure in the days when Palestine was slowly emerging from the waste of war under a necessarily inexperienced administration, or could not be regarded in times of riot and disturbance, when it was an achievement to continue to do work of good quality at all.

I have endeavoured to subdivide the Memorandum as clearly and conveniently as possible under the following heads:-

	8.1.	Introduction.
I.	§§.2-6.	Situation inherited from the Turks, 1913-17.
II.	§§.7-10.	Initial British effort, 1918-23.
III.	§§.11-17.	Reconsideration of problem, 1923-27.
IV.	§§.18-20.	Recent progress, 1927-36.
V.	§§.21-27.	Lessons of earlier Egyptian experience, 1879-1906.
VI.	§§.28-end.	Conclusion.
	Appendix:	Copy of circular issued in May 1928, defining the relations between the Commissioner of Lands and the Departments of Land and of Survey.

Part V. which covers the period dealt with by the Royal Commission is largely a supplement to Memorandum I.

I have followed the Royal Commission in expressing output of settlement operations in square kilometres (thousands of dunums); but this necessarily ignores differences in conditions that may be important. If a more significant single measure is required, output is probably best expressed by the number of individual land parcels finally surveyed, settled and entered in the Land Register. But it is preferable to use several factors in conjunction (e.g. those given and one expressing the character of the terrain).

References to the Royal Commission's Report are preceded by the Chapter number ix. Other references if unexplained are to the Memorandum itself.

The technical aspects of cadastral survey are not touched on, because both this and my earlier memorandum are entirely directed to assist in remedying the defects found by the Royal Commission and the work of the survey was expressly commended. But it will be appreciated that the description given in the Royal Commission's Report of the technical methods used in the plains of Palestine would not be necessarily applicable elsewhere. Methods of cadastral survey must naturally be adapted to the character of the terrain, to the value of the land, and to the size and shape of the units in the prevailing parcellation.

I. §§. 2-6. SITUATION INHERITED FROM THE TURKS 1913-17.

2. The post-revolutionary Ottoman Government recognized before the war that land tenure and land taxation were chaotic both in law and in practice, in Palestine, as throughout the remainder of the Empire, and that this was seriously detrimental economically to the State as a whole and to the people individually. The compulsory registration of rights over immovable property had been embodied in Ottoman legislation for over half a century; and no person could legally hold immovable property in Palestine if not registered. None the less by far the greater part of the land was held unregistered in overt disregard of law; nor is this remarkable, because the Land Registry was commonly unable to provide from its records any dependable information of the extent or location of an ostensibly registered holding. This was the natural result: firstly of the enactment of the categorical a priori requirements of the Ottoman land registry laws without regard to their feasibility under the conditions that existed and with the agents that were available; and secondly of the maintenance of these laws on the statute book in the face of persistent failure. But even the best conceived and most efficient system of record could have done no more than reflect somewhat more accurately the confusion and disregard of the land laws proper that prevailed.

Recognizing these evils, the reformed Turkish Government made a resolute attempt to remedy them. This took shape in the issue of a series of provisional laws in 1913 designed (i) to amend progressively the Ottoman land laws proper and (ii) to place tenure and taxation of immovable property on to an intelligible and satisfactory basis throughout the Empire. Legislation in the first group constitutes an element in the existing land law of Palestine, as previously noted (Memorandum I. §.3.). It was intended to secure the second objective by a provisional law for the survey and registration of immovable property published on the 2nd. Rabi-el-Awal 1331 (February, 1913). This law provided comprehensively for (i) the fixing of village boundaries, (ii) the definition of property parcels by cadastral survey, (iii) the settlement and registration of title thereto, and (iv) the valuation of land and buildings with a view to the introduction of a land or immovable property tax in place of the existing jumble of rudimentary tithe, werko, musaqafat, animal tax and local impositions.

It will thus be seen that this law sought the same objectives that have been sought by British administration in the same field since the war and substantially in the same way; but it was too loose and doctrinaire an instrument to be successfully implemented textually under British administration, although the Turks, who would probably have interpreted it with greater elasticity, might have obtained useful results from it, if the war had not intervened.

3. In certain respects the passage of the war increased the difficulties of the comprehensive reform of land tenure that was required, while alleviating them in others; but it left the core of the problem unaffected. This was briefly to bring order out of a chaos which was too ancient and deep-seated to be materially aggravated even by the war; although that of course produced widespread detailed changes in occupation or abandonment, use or neglect, of land everywhere.

------

*A provisional Ottoman law was a law which was put into force provisionally before receiving formal ratification from the General Assembly in Constantinople.

D.

In short although every individual knot may have been altered during the war period, the general body of tangle was essentially no more and no less intractable than previously. Undue importance was also attached at first to the removal of documents by the retreating Turks and to the closing of the Land Registries in the early days of British Administration. The destruction or cessation of the activities of an untrustworthy land registry is probably more gain than loss. Indeed, as has been found elsewhere, registration may be commonly resorted to in such a registry, to give a false appearance of genuineness to fabricated documents.

The need for a comprehensive reform of land tenure and land taxation in Palestine was accordingly in no way the creation of the mandate. It was indeed in all essential particulars the same problem as confronted 'Iraq and Syria simultaneously, and had confronted Egypt much earlier, upon the separation of those territories from the Ottoman Empire. Doubtless the discharge of the dual obligation of the Mandate encountered its greatest problem in the possession of land; but this arose from the limited content of cultivable land available in a small and semi-arid country, not from there being any greater difficulty than in other similarly situated countries in reconciling and amending lawful and operative tenure so as to promote the economic development of the land. For the conditions which required to be established were the old and simple ones; clarity and security of tenure and related interests in land, equitable and unonerous taxation, freedom and incentive to develop the land to the greatest economic advantage, due protection of all cultivation against disturbance. The creation of these conditions was just as necessary to the indigenous cultivator - even mutatis mutandis to the cultivating Bedu' - as to the progressive immigrant, and depended fundamentally upon the same processes.

The establishment in Palestine of a national home for the Jewish people accentuated the urgency of the reform and imposed a higher standard of performance than might otherwise have been necessary; but basically the measures that were adopted were evoked by the economic needs of the land and the inhabitants, irrespective of creed or race, and would have been intrinsically just as necessary if the Balfour declaration had never been conceived. And although the requisite programme of reform was complex and formidable, this arose preponderantly from the mass of patient detailed labour by qualified workmen that was needed (i) to unravel the tangle of physical and paper possession, of genuine and spurious claims and (ii) to reconcile the inconsistencies and remove the obsolesences of the unstable amalgam of statutory and customary tenures that had been allowed to grow up and persist for so long.

4. To assess fairly the inheritance left by Turkish to British land administration in Palestine it is necessary, however, also to recognize that, although the welter of confusion in which land tenure and land taxation was found cannot be exaggerated, yet the strictures that have been commonly passed on the Ottoman land law are much less deserved. It has already been pointed out that mesha'a and the difficulty met with in protecting tenants, were the fruits of failure to apply that law not of viciousness in it (Memorandum I. §.3.). But the Royal Commission were impressed with the difficulties involved in the Ottoman land law's various forms of ownership and tenure of land and summed it up as being in essence a complicated system not calculated to promote close settlement and intensive cultivation (ix. 27). The undigested amalgam which has ruled so long as land law in Palestine, certainly

obstructs economic progress gravely. But a distinction should, I think, be drawn between the basic principles of the Ottoman land law and the effects of the failure, which has been previously indicated, to weld the main elements in the existing land law into a homogeneous whole and thus eliminate the obsolescences, obscurities, omissions and inconsistencies which at present so seriously impede its useful working. (Memorandum I. 3). Not only was the Arab Muslim basis of the Ottoman land law, which H. M. Government inherited, consecrated to the mass of the indigenous population by customary and religious sanctions, but it was also, I venture to think, intrinsically a suitable and adaptable instrument for that very promotion of closer settlement and intenser cultivation which the mandate enjoined.

5. It would not be possible to attempt any exposition of the law within the compass of the present note, even if I had the competence. Anyone seeking this should turn to the fruits of the preparatory study undertaken by Dr. Goadby with Mr. Doukhan's collaboration, which has already been mentioned (Memorandum I. 1.).* But the justification for the claims advanced may be indicated sufficiently for the immediate purpose, by a brief consideration of the nature of the much criticized five main categories into which land is divided under the Ottoman law. These five categories consist respectively of mulk, miri, muqufa (waqf), matruka and mewat lands.

Mulk means property. Muslim law makes little distinction between movable and immovable property. Everything that is owned, whether movable or immovable, is mulk. Immovables classified as mulk (i.e. property) are in the absolute (allodial) ownership of the proprietor. "Every man can deal as he likes with his mulk" (Majelle Art. 1192).Mulk land is practically confined to urban sites occupied by buildings and gardens, and constitutes a negligible fraction of the agricultural land in Palestine.

The vast majority of the cultivated land in Palestine is Miri land, which simply means land belonging to the State. Just as in England under feudal law all land was owned by the King and at best held of him in fee (i.e. as a heritable interest) on condition of military service, so in Palestine agricultural land in general is held in law of the State as a transferable, transmissible interest (known as tesarruf) on conditions of agricultural service. If the land so held suffers from agricultural neglect or failure of statutory succession, the land becomes "mahlul" (vacant) and the holder's interest is forfeited. The forfeiture is not harsh. The neglect must be a failure, not reasonably excusable, to cultivate for three years. An act of resumption by the State is required, while the dispossessed holder has specific rights of redemption. Succession is statutorily prescribed, since the successors are not, in Muslim law, heirs but beneficiaries of a gratuitous transmission regulated by civil law.

In England the feudal relation survives in theory only. In Palestine, as in a number of other Eastern countries, the

---

*Published for sale in revised form in 1935, with the permission of the Government, under the title of "The Land Law of Palestine".

principle is practised (so far as existing knowledge and machinery permits), that agricultural land ordinarily belongs to the State (or the Ruler) and is only held by private persons subject to cultivation being maintained and a share in the produce remitted. The conception of State lands being farmed, or otherwise exploited, directly by the State as such, does not seem, understandably enough, to have presented itself to the pre-revolutionary Ottoman legislator; but the Sultan held many estates under the generic name of the farms (jiftlik).* After the revolution these Estates were termed "mudawara" lands, because they were "turned over" to the State and treated as exploitable state domain; but this did not affect the statutory category of such lands, which were commonly miri although they may occasionally have been mulk.

Waqf land, as is well-known, is land dedicated in perpetuity to a pious purpose. Such pious foundations are broadly analogous in England to land vested in the Ecclesiastical or Charity Commissioners for religious or benevolent objects; but in Muslim law a pious purpose is much wider. Since a man can only dedicate his own property (mulk) as waqf, it is only mulk land that can be so dedicated. The general run of agricultural land, which is State land (miri), cannot be declared waqf by the holders. But in the course of time miri holders came to be authorised, with the express permission of the Sultan, to dedicate specific interests in the land to a pious purpose. This practice became known as a false waqf; but when a comprehensive dedication of interests was permitted the effect was little different to that of a true waqf, although in principle only a charge on the land was created.

Matruka land is land "left" for some public purpose, whether national (e.g. public roads) or local (e.g. a common village threshing floor).

Mewat land is the "dead" or rather "unvivified" land (i.e. waste or unreclaimed land) lying beyond earshot of any neighbouring villages, but over adjoining portions of which such villages may commonly exercise certain traditional rights of grazing, wood, water, &c. Mewat thus corresponds closely to the wild or forest land which used similarly to lie outside (foris) villages in England and over which similar rights were no less jealously claimed. It is authoritatively held that in law mewat land is no man's land, owned by no one - not even by the State - while still "dead"; but it may be "vivified" or reclaimed with the permission of the State and then becomes regular State land (miri).

6. This summary review of the five categories of land recognized by the Ottoman land law requires a great deal of qualification in detail; but it brings out certain important facts. Thus it will be seen that the five statutory categories of land are not bizarre doctrinaire conceptions, but reflect genuine practical differences which have close analogies in more familiar tenures. It will also

----

*Jiftlik in Turkish signifies "double", hence a yoke (of oxen) and hence a farm. See Goadby & Doukhan, Ch.v., p.62.

be seen that three of these categories are of negligible importance in relation to agricultural land. Mulk or absolute ownership is, with rare exceptions, limited to urban land. True pious foundations (waqf) are limited to mulk. Matruka, or land assigned for public purposes, comprises a minute portion of the land surface.

Mewat or wild land on the other hand cannot be owned by anyone, and it cannot be cultivated or exploited in any way without the permission of the Government. Moreover, both in law, as in fact, land ceases to be wild (mewat) if cultivated or otherwise exploited, and it then becomes in law regular State land (miri). Accordingly although mewat land constitutes (or did constitute) a potential reserve of cultivable land, no land in this category can be lawfully developed or even lawfully held by anyone.

Therefore, with rare exceptions, in the situation as inherited from the Turks and since maintained, all agricultural land throughout Palestine fell into the single category of miri or State land, the legal tenure of which afforded complete security to the genuine husbandman or other authorized user; but which, having regard to the closer settlement and intenser cultivation that was needed, possessed the supreme advantage of requiring those who failed to make reasonable use of the land to surrender it. No doubt such forfeiture was difficult to apply consistently and regularly in the absence of reliable maps and records, while redemption was too facile; but these were weaknesses which were curable. Further advantages in this tenure were (i) that succession was governed by the civil law, which made the task of removing the evils of excessive sub-division considerably less difficult, and (ii) that the land could not be dedicated in true waqf by the holder and could only be charged as false waqf with the permission of the State. Although the conditions of this tenure would have had to be applied with great discretion and consideration in any circumstances, and particularly in pursuance of the policy laid down in the mandate, yet the essential features of that tenure could hardly have been better adapted, if suitably clarified and amended, to promote the closer settlement and intenser cultivation of the soil by Arabs and Jews alike.

D

VI. §§. 7-10. INITIAL BRITISH EFFORT 1918-23.

7. The Military Administration established by H.M.G. in Palestine after the defeat of the Turks naturally endeavoured as far as circumstances permitted to maintain the laws in force and the executive usages of Government, to which the people were accustomed. In confirmation, legalization and definition of this course in the present connection, Article 46 of the Palestine Order in Council of the 10th. August 1922 laid down that immovable property in Palestine should remain governed by the Ottoman Laws in force on 1st. November 1914 subject to subsequent modification legally enacted. Since the conquest the operation of the Ottoman Law has been modified by local legislation, but it still remains the primary authority under which all matters relating to immovable property is considered and administered by the executive government and by the courts. Ottoman laws enacted after 1st. November 1914 have no force in Palestine unless expressly applied.

At the outset of the British occupation the position was so difficult that proclamations of the Chief Military Administrator (Major Gen. A.W.Money) dated 24th.June and 1st. November 1918 "for the better administration of justice" in Palestine expressly withheld from the Civil Courts the power to give judgments affecting the ownership of land or to order the sale of land in execution of a judgment or in satisfaction of a mortgage. They were followed by a proclamation dated 18th. November 1918, forbidding dispositions of immovable property as time was required to replace information removed by the Turks and to re-organize and re-establish the Land Registries. "This order" a competent observer briefly commented six months later was "entirely set aside by the people". It was, of course, as impossible to prevent dispositions of land by the mass of Palestinian landholders, large and small, as it was to halt Canute's sea.

8. The initiation of the first effort to deal with the problem constructively was marked by visits to Palestine in 1919, firstly by Mr. Williamson, the Director of Land Registries in the Sudan, and secondly by Mr. Sheppard, the Director of the Cadastral Survey in Egypt, to advise the Government.

In 1920 a standing Land Commission was set up, Mr. Ongley previously Registrar General of Lands in Cyprus was appointed Director of Land Registries in Palestine and Major Ley was appointed Director of Surveys. Mr. Ongley had had considerable experience of Ottoman land registry procedure and had published a special study of Ottoman land law. He re-opened the Land Registries in September of the same year under "The Transfer of Land Ordinance, 1920".

This ordinance contained no provisions either for clearing up the accumulated confusion or for the amendment of land registry methods, but contented itself with merely stating in the preamble that these registries had been re-established. The policy that inspired the Ordinance was explained in a note that was published with it. The general principle laid down was that all transactions (other than short leases) must be carried out through the Land Registry and must receive the consent of the Administration. The main reason for requiring registration was to secure some sort of record of transactions and to prevent fraud. The main reason for

- 8 -

requiring the consent of the Administration was to prevent speculation in land which would cause an excessive rise in prices and prevent development. No guarantee of title or of the validity of transactions was to be implied by the consent of the Administration or by registration. Transactions were only to be allowed if proof was supplied that the property would be immediately cultivated if it was agricultural, or immediately developed if it was urban, land. Further objects of administrative control were the protection of the small farmer in his holding by exercising a discriminative veto on sales, the limitation of acquisition of land by individual Palestinians, and the prevention of its acquisition by absentees from the country. Every disposition to which the written consent of the Administration had not been obtained was to be null and void, while contravention of the Ordinance entailed a liability to a fine up to a quarter of the value of the property concerned. "The Correction of Land Registries Ordinance 1920" was a complementary, but subordinate, measure.

The general aim of the Land Transfer Ordinance appears to have been the exercise of a close paternal control of all land transactions, while disclaiming all responsibility for the results. As already observed, this responsibility could not be discharged because the existing records were unreliable and incomplete and the methods of registration admittedly a failure; but these facts made the beneficial control aimed at equally impracticable. The advisability of the State attempting to exercise a detailed administrative control of all land transactions is very disputable; but such a control clearly requires reliable land records and an efficient land registry organization. It is difficult to understand how any experienced officer can have thought this Ordinance workable in the face of the complete breakdown of the land records which even the Turks themselves recognized to have occurred by 1913, and which was so palpable in 1918 that the land registries were kept closed by proclamation for another two years, in spite of the further accretion of occult, illegal, often irreconcilable, and even unintelligible, transactions that was bound to result. The need for an adjudication of existing titles was however recognized in the preamble of the Ordinance, which announced an intention to establish a Land Settlement Court in due course for this purpose.

As already noted, the Military Administration found it necessary when re-establishing the administration of Justice in the early days of the British Occupation to prohibit the Courts from ordering the sale of immovable property in execution of a judgment or in satisfaction of a mortgage and from giving any judgment deciding the ownership of land. "The Transfer of Land Ordinance 1920" re-affirmed these provisions but also provided (a) that the Courts could hear actions for the partition of land in accordance with the provisional Ottoman Law of the 14th. Muharram 1332 (December 1913) and (b) that the Legal Secretary might in special cases allow an action concerning the ownership of land to be heard.

On 4th. April 1921, "The Transfer of Land Ordinance No.2" restored to the regular Courts the power to order sales of immovable property in execution of judgment or in satisfaction of mortgages. On 8th. April the second disability was removed by

- 9 -

D

power being taken under "The Land Courts Ordinance 1921" to establish special Land Courts. Jurisdiction to decide rights to immovable property was not vested exclusively in the new Courts when formed. The power previously accorded Magistrates' Courts to hear actions concerning the possession or partition of land, and to the Legal Secretary in special cases to allow actions concerning ownership of land to be heard by a District Court, were retained.

In April 1922 Mr. Ongley was transferred to the Land Courts and replaced as Director of Land Registries by Mr. J. N. Stubbs, the direction of the Land Registries becoming associated with that of State lands on this appointment.

9. In reviewing the problem generally, the official report on the Palestine Administration for the period July 1920-December 1921 (p.109) found that "the chief weakness of the (existing) system (of land registration) lay in the fact that there was no cadastral or other survey, so that land could not be correctly described by reference either to area or boundaries." A little lower "the complicated nature of the Turkish land laws" was given as a second difficulty. In the same sentence the acceptance of Mr. Williamson's recommendations for the re-organization of the land registry offices was announced and three pages later the commencement in February 1921 of the cadastral survey of Palestine. Both Mr. Williamson and Mr. Sheppard were most competent advisers and provided a panel of advice on the problems submitted to them that could not have been readily bettered. It thus appeared in 1921 that the stage had been set, and the effective prosecution of the requisite reforms undertaken with great promptitude under the best auspices. Actually the Government was extremely uneasy as to the character and value of the work that was being done, as appears from a perusal of the contemporary files and the series of consultations with various officers who passed through Palestine during this time.

Upon my retirement from the Egyptian Government service in November 1923 I received a letter from the Chief Secretary (Sir Gilbert Clayton) expressing these doubts and formally inviting me to visit Palestine to assist Government to "review the situation as regards the programme of future work, the manner in which it should be carried out, and the re-organization of the machine by means of which it is to be done." My qualifications to advise on the problem were briefly that I had been (i) associated with the successful cadastral survey of Egypt carried out by Sir Henry Lyons under Lord Cromer's administration as a basis for the reassessment of land tax, (ii) Chairman of an Egyptian Government Commission, whose recommendations were adopted for the reform of the land registries and the establishment of registration of title to land in that country, and (iii) successively Under Secretary of State for Finance and Financial Adviser to the Egyptian Government.

10. I was only able to stay five days in Palestine; but the admirable arrangements made to facilitate my investigations and the glaring nature of the prevailing defects as illuminated by analogous earlier Egyptian experience (see Part V.) enabled me very readily to get a comprehensive grasp of the main elements in the situation in this time, which I have never had occasion to alter.

It should first of all be observed that in spite of the official announcement only a fleeting attention at most can have been given to Mr. Williamson's recommendations. I was never able to obtain a copy of his report and I was told that the forms he had drawn up had not proved satisfactory. I obtained a copy of Mr. Sheppard's report from him after my return to Egypt.

I found activities labelled "reorganization of the land registries" and "cadastral survey" in progress; but they were mysteries to all but the departments concerned. They implemented no approved Government policy and were governed by no appropriate legislation. In spite of the establishment of a competent Land Survey service two years earlier nothing whatsoever had been done to remedy the basic weakness of the Land Registries, which had been diagnosed in the Administration's report, namely inability to locate land that purported to be registered or to state its superficial area. The Director of the Land Registries admitted these defects with complete frankness and they were subsequently exemplified concretely by a series of tests on the ground. It is impossible to illustrate the former here but the table overleaf indicates the degree of the divergencies found between the areas of properties as recorded respectively in the land registers and in the tax registers and as measured on the ground after being located as closely as the available information and local inquiry permitted in each case. Even the Courts when requiring information about land commonly had recourse to incompetent persons and received for their guidance grossly inaccurate plans. The Land Survey were simultaneously conducting operations of a cadastral nature in the neighbourhood of Gaza which were quite useless, because they were unauthorized by law, were ignored by the Land Registry, and became obsolete before they were completed.

In short, the two services designed to clear up the land tangle - the Land Registry and the Land Survey - who should have been performing complementary operations day by day in the closest association with each other and with the Land Courts, were situated in different cities, worked in watertight compartments, even used discordant units, and undermined each other's utility by attempting to discharge each other's functions. It was accordingly not remarkable that not an acre of effective cadastral survey had been done, not a section of an effective register of title to land constructed. Two potentially valuable bodies had, however, been established; and although the Land Survey was still imperfectly organized and developed and had no knowledge or experience of cadastral work it was already a most promising technical instrument. Extremely useful investigations of various aspects of the general problem also had been undertaken by various special commissions, notably by the Land Commission, the Tithes Commission and the Mesha'a Commission. But while much good work of a preparatory character had been done, the general failure of this initial effort to establish a cadastral survey, put the Land Registries on to a sound basis, and clear up the land tangle was complete and undisguised.

- 11 -

COMPARATIVE TABLE of areas of certain properties as recorded in the Land and in the Tax Register and as located on the ground.

Reproduced from report submitted December 1925.

Property	Area in donums and square pics according to						Entries expressed % of measured area.	
	Land Reg.		Tax Reg.		Measurement.		Land Reg.	Tax Register.
1	31	0	3	0	5	139	610	60
2	2	0	0	900	0	348	1100	260
3	1	0	0	200	0	.244	670	82
4	15	0	8	800	6	726	230	130
5	25	0	2	100	2	664	1010	87
6	60	0	51	0	37	40	160	138
7	25	0	0	-1200	1	744	1670	52
8	27	0	1	-1200	26	626	101	6
9	25	0	1	-	0	1459	2800	110
10	1	0	0	-1200	0	1090	160	110
11	1	800	0	75	0	104	2400	75
12	28	0	-	-	6	302	450	-
13	15	0	1	800	2	634	625	63
14	108	0	42	800	11	190	9700	375
15	-	-	-	-	-	-	-	-
16	29	0	2	400	5	648	538	42
17	1	0	1	200	1	1426	53	60
18	37	0	-	-	5	482	700	-
19	76	800	12	0	9	1202	780	123
20	2	0	0	600	0	626	530	100
21	42	0	12	0	25	652	166	47
22	13	0	6	0	1	2(a)	1300	600
					3	766(b)	370	170
23	25	0	48	0	16	322	154	295
24	4	0	0	400	0	666	960	60
25	45	0	48	0	3	1027(a)	1240	1320
					6	301(b)	725	770
					20	529(c)	220	235
26	28	0	48	0	3	613	830	1410
27	20	0	25	800	10	548	194	245

N.B. 22 (a) and (b) and 25 (a), (b) and (c) represent various interpretations on the ground. The Table is expressed in the old (pre metric) donum on the doubtful assumptions that this is comparable throughout the two registry entries and that the relations of pic to donum are also constant. These uncertainties led the Survey to introduce the metre as their working unit and to the adoption of the present metric donum as the unit of area later.

D

III. §§.11-16. RECONSIDERATION OF PROBLEM 1923-27.

11. The principal needs of constructive reform in the general field of cadastral survey, settlement of title, and registration of title were evident, and I readily obtained all the detailed information on the existing position from the services immediately concerned. Indispensable guidance about particular local needs was given me by four officers of the District Administration, with whom I was expressly asked by the Chief Secretary to confer. These officers were Mr. A. Abramson, Colonel (now Sir Henry) Cox, Mr. J.E.F. Campbell and Mr. R.E.H. Crosbie. Mr. Abramson had previously been Chairman of the Land Commission and Director of the Land Department. They were all in close and continuous touch with the people and the countryside, spoke Arabic well, and had been associated with the work of the various commissions previously mentioned. They were united, clear and convincing as to the pressing necessity to put land tenure and land taxation on to a stable and equitable footing throughout the country and to terminate promptly the widespread evils of the tithe and other remnants of Turkish taxation and of mesha'a.

12. Owing to this ready and effective assistance I was able to submit my recommendations to the Government a month later in a report dated 7th. December, 1923. I will outline these as they constituted the basis of the measures ultimately adopted. The references are to the numbered sections of the report. The more important were briefly:-

   (i) Early revision of the existing land law to purge it of obsolescences, omissions and inconsistencies and to secure clarification and simplification (3, 11).

   (ii) Early formulation of suitable taxation of immovable property to replace the Turkish survivals of such taxation (ushr, musaqafat, werko) (11, 14, 23).

   (iii) Concurrent execution throughout the rural areas* of a combined measure of (a) settlement and registration of title to land, and (b) introduction of an equitably assessed and distributed land tax, based (c) upon appropriate and effective cadastral survey. (5, 13-20, 22).

   (iv) Settlement and registration of provisional or possessory title to be effected initially; but converted systematically into absolute title by (a) judicial proceedings if opposed within a prescribed period or (b) efflux of time otherwise. (13, 20)

   (v) Settlement of title and land tax assessment to be carried out in conjunction by appropriate settlement parties, headed by selected British officers, who spoke and read Arabic, had a good working knowledge of the land law, and were familiar with the viewpoints and customs of the people and with the conditions of the countryside (15).

---

*The expression "rural areas" here and hereafter, excludes the Beersheba sub-district.

- 13 -

These measures involved the disappearance of mesha'a and of the tithe, werko and other anomalies. These evils could not be justly and effectively terminated by independent processes.

(vi) Twelve of these parties to be established, any cost entailed which could not be covered from current budgetary revenues, to be met by a small loan, which might be put at a maximum of £500,000 spread over the period of the work. (6, 7, 16).

Early completion of these reforms appeared to me to be both politically and economically imperative, and also financially justifiable. I estimated from such data as were then available that it would take 18 years to complete the work from current revenues and with the existing agents; but believed that twelve quite modest settlement parties, if suitably constituted and directed, would be capable of doing so within the following six years. The first of these years (1924) would have had to be devoted to the considerable legislative, administrative and technical preparations that were still required. It was my opinion that any loan expenses would be fully and directly recouped from the saving of public rights in land of all categories; in economies in tax collection, police work and the administration of justice; and in the great stimulus to prosperity that would follow the establishment throughout the country of a secure and sensible land tenure and of regular and equitable taxation of land. The observations of the Royal Commission at the conclusion of Part I. of Chapter IX. appear relevant in this connection.

(vii) Systematic maintenance to date of the complementary cadastral survey and register of title after their initial completion in each village. It was specified that the register should be a comprehensive one and include fiscal data and other incidents of tenure (12, 13, 18, 22, 23).

(viii) Enactment of the requisite legislation to provide for the above, more particularly for:

(a) the necessary amendments to the land law and

(b) the initial establishment (by the processes of settlement of title) and

(c) subsequent maintenance of the register of title and complementary cadastral survey (3, 11, 13).

(ix) Reliable location and definition of land sporadically registered (in perpetuation of ex-Ottoman practice) in advance of systematic cadastral survey and settlement of title (10).

(x) The unified direction of the associated operations recommended in (iii) above on an approved general plan and time table, (16, 21-23).

(xi) Complete severance between (a) the conduct of these operations and (b) the custody of State domain and responsibility for land administration generally (21).

(xii) Investigation of the possibility of effecting the requisite parallel operations of settlement and registration of title and of re-assessment of immovable property within urban areas, through the agency of urban authorities on the basis of air photo mosaics, so as to enable as little effort as possible to be diverted from (what I judged to be) the politically and economically more important rural operations (24).

(xiii) A variety of other recommendations, chiefly of a technical nature, were also made which were for the most part adopted and call for no notice here (17, 25).

13. Most of these recommendations may appear obvious enough now, in the light of events during the intervening fourteen years and of the Royal Commission's recent criticisms; but to recapture the contemporary viewpoint it must be remembered that the Government approached the question in the disillusionment produced by the previous four years' abortive effort, which had appeared to be so well launched and promising. The financial situation of the country was also weak at the time and the Government, earnestly engaged in general retrenchment, were unable to entertain the idea of borrowing to expedite this particular programme of reform. Again, in marked contrast to the leading District Officers consulted, the officers of the Central Government generally were far from convinced at that time that the abolition of either the tithe or mesha' was desirable. Viewed from the capital there was an appearance of equity about the former and of village co-operation about the latter, the deceptive appeal of which evaporated very slowly. Objection was also felt to other features of my programme, more particularly (a) that the conduct of settlement of title and the associated measures should be severed from the control of State lands, and (b) that settlement should initially be limited to inscription of possessory title.

14. I was accordingly invited to visit Palestine again during the following winter 1924-25, and then made a detailed investigation in each part of the country of every branch of the composite problem and enquired into a number of related questions, such as the execution of the Beisan agreement, the demarcation and protection of State forests, the operation of the unofficial land registers kept by many Jewish colonies. The technical aspects of the cadastral operations that were suited to local conditions and needs were gone into very thoroughly with the Director of Survey, who utilized this period of reconsideration (1924-27) to such good purpose that this service was able to discharge its part of the common task with smoothness and efficiency when operations were resumed and to be the one branch of the work to be expressly commended by the Royal Commission recently.* The requirements of Land Registry reform were similarly gone into with the Director of Land Registries. The desirability of otherwise of abolishing the tithe and mesha'a, the most appropriate substitutes (provisional and ultimate) for the former, as well as innumerable other features of the projected measures were exhaustively discussed, which have since ceased to be matters of controversy and therefore call for no consideration here.

I accepted the view that a settlement of absolute title was desirable at the outset; while reference has been made separately to the reluctance of Government to entrust administrative officers with judicial powers for this purpose (Memorandum I, 7).

- 15 -

D

The Government maintained their objections to any recourse to a loan to secure early completion of the work, to recommendation (x) in executive form, and to recommendation (xi). The two latter were not objected to in principle, but because they were held not to be feasible or desirable for personal reasons.

These personal considerations were part of the legacy of the initial failure and their weight had to be recognized. They constituted in practice indeed the most serious obstacle of all to constructive reform; but affected recommendations (x) and (xi) differently. The principal difficulty in achieving the unified administrative and technical direction of the combined settlement operations that I recommended (x) was that there was no candidate, from within or without, who combined (a) the basic technical knowledge and experience that was required to shape and conduct the composite machine effectively with (b) the knowledge of local conditions and of the language as well as the standing with the people, the other members of the public service, and the Government that was needed to apply it successfully. The dilemma was inescapable and it came down to a choice between an outside candidate with the first set of qualifications and a local candidate without them. An additional impediment to the organic unification of effort that was required was the unfortunate location of the Land Survey Headquarters at Jaffa and the difficulty there proved to be of a transfer to the capital. A suitable outside candidate with the qualifications mentioned was in any case difficult to find and in fact there was remarkably general agreement from the start that Mr. Abramson was the best man to be entrusted with this difficult task, in spite of his lack of technical knowledge and previous experience of the various operations he would be required to unify. But the Director of Survey and the Director of Land Registries, while agreeing in principle as to the necessity of unified conduct of the requisite operations, had an understandable reluctance to be subordinated to an officer, however senior and well regarded, who lacked the technical qualifications of the one and the past association with a branch of the work of both. Everyone, and not least of all Mr. Abramson himself, had a natural sympathy with these feelings and sought means which would secure the effective co-ordination of these services with each other and with the other settlement operations, while preserving as fully as possible the status of these two officers in the concerted effort that was to be made to retrieve the earlier failure. It had to be recognized that neither officer could be justly held responsible for that failure which although largely occasioned no doubt by their lack of experience, was primarily due to absence of all competent higher direction.

The personal difficulty in adopting my recommendation that a complete severance should be effected between (a) the conduct of all settlement operations and (b) the custody of State domain and any responsibility for land administration (recommendation xi) was that the Land registries and the control of State domain had been under the united direction of Mr. J.N.Stubbs since he took over the former from Mr. Ongley in 1922 and the Government had great faith in him in both capacities.

- 16 -

Leaving these two important issues in suspense and subject to the modifications previously mentioned, I confirmed in all essentials the recommendations which I had made two years earlier, in a further report, submitted in December 1925, in the light of the further and fuller investigations that I had been requested to undertake. The most important new factors that had to be taken into account were:

(i) The abandonment of the prospect of a rapid completion of the work with the aid of a small loan.

(ii) The consequent necessity (inter alia) of providing some provisional reform of the taxation of land and buildings pending the much slower completion of the new land (and tax) register, that had now to be anticipated.

(iii) Recognition and utilization of the work done at Beisan and in some unofficial and irregular Jewish colony land registers, as parts of the general settlement operations.

The measures designed to secure (ii) have been previously explained. (Memorandum I. §§.16-18). Those designed to secure (iii) are outlined in §§.15-17 of this 1925 Report. Four other points newly emphasized in this report were the necessity (a) for timely and simple explanation of the intended measures to the people (§.10 covering memorandum), (b) for a periodic correlation between expenditure and results, (c) for a proper financial balance to be instituted and maintained between the various branches of the work (Report §.18) and (d) that the Central Government should give its earnest consideration to the problem itself, not simply in digesting reports, but in the detailed planning and execution of reform (Report §.11).

16. I was asked to pay two further visits to Palestine in the Spring of 1926 and the Winter 1926-27 for further discussions with the Government, during which the procedure for the reform of the taxation of immovable urban property was also investigated. The main outlines of the measures to be adopted for the conduct of settlement operations throughout the rural areas were at length crystallized at a Conference held in Jerusalem on the 21st. February, 1927 under the presidency of H.E. Field Marshal Lord Plumer, the High Commissioner, in anticipation of a visit by Sir John Shuckburgh to Palestine shortly afterwards. The minutes of this Conference are on record and are instructive on various points; but the effect of this formal meeting and of earlier discussions leading up to it was in general terms to authorize the measures that have been previously outlined, subject to the modifications that have already been indicated. Following this Conference it was decided (a) that selected British Administrative Officers having the qualifications already defined (§.12,v.) should be appointed as Settlement Officers and should exercise judicial functions in the performance of their duties, and (b) that a small but specialist organization should be established to plan and supervise the land assessment operations which, it will be remembered, were now to be conducted in advance. Fortunately suitable officers for this purpose were available on the spot and appear to have fully justified expectations. It was also agreed that a post of Commissioner of Lands should be created to unify the conduct of the various branches of the work and enable the Government to keep proper contact with it in future; but the exact nature of this officer's powers remained in debate for another year, being ultimately defined in Circular No.122 issued by the Chief Secretary on the 30th.May,1928. A copy of this circular appears as an appendix to this Memorandum.

- 17 -

I was not able to persuade the Government of the advisability of the severance that I recommended between the conduct of settlement operations and the custody of State lands; although it was agreed that the conjoint Director of Land Registries and of State Lands should in future be relieved of all responsibility for the conduct of litigation in connection with the latter which had diverted a great deal of his time and energy from his administrative and inspectorial duties, in both the above fields. (Minutes Jerusalem Conference 15).

17. The more important steps required to enable the programme that had been approved to be initiated were:

(i) To prepare and enact the necessary legislation. This fell under four heads:

    (a) Measures for the progressive amendment of the land law, which at that time appeared to be progressing most promisingly. (See S.1. Memorandum I.)

    (b) A measure to govern initial settlement and registration of title to land.

    (c) Measures to provide for the introduction of the taxation of immovable property and the assessment of such property for this purpose.

    (d) A new measure to govern the maintenance of the new register of title following its initial establishment under (b).

(ii) To select and appoint the staff required and give them adequate opportunities to learn their duties under representative working conditions.

(iii) In the light of these preliminary trials and of increasing experience to draw up the necessary programme and regulations for the detailed conduct of the work.

(iv) To acquire the requisite accommodation, equipment and stores.

(v) To explain the proposed operations to the local authorities, village elders, landholders and people, and to secure their goodwill and intelligent co-operation as fully as possible in advance.

IV. §§. 18-20. RECENT PROGRESS. 1927-36.

18.   The measure to govern settlement and initial registration of title to land (briefly entitled "The Land Settlement Ordinance" in due course) was drawn up in conformity with local requirements in the light of the practical experience gained in similar Egyptian operations and of careful studies of the Punjab Land Settlement Manuals, the Sudan Land Settlement Law, Swiss federal law and cantonal practice, and a recently received draft of a revised Malayan Law. The main provisions were formulated in three meetings with the Attorney General and the principal officers concerned, which were held in Jerusalem in June 1927 before my departure from Palestine.

The Statement of the Land Law of Palestine which, as already explained (Memorandum I. §. 1.), had been prepared by Dr. Goadby and Mr. Doukhan for the guidance of Settlement Officers was issued in the autumn of 1927.

The office of the newly appointed Commissioner of Lands (Mr. A. Abramson) was opened in Jerusalem in November. The following winter and spring were occupied in organizing the work, collecting and training staff, acquiring equipment, completing legislation and regulations for the conduct of the various inter-related operations, and in carefully explaining the object and nature of the projected operations to the rural population in advance.* The Commutation of Tithes Ordinance, an interim measure to alleviate some of the grosser objections to the tithe, was enacted in December 1927. The Land Settlement Ordinance was enacted in May 1928 and the Urban Property Tax Ordinance in July, 1928. The Rural Property Tax Ordinance, finally substituting a land tax for the tithe, was not enacted until January 1935, as its operation was dependent upon the completion of the fiscal survey and assessment explained in §§.16-19 of Memorandum I.

It had been contemplated at the Conference held on the 21st. February, 1927 that the preparation of an Ordinance to govern the maintenance of the new register of title should be deferred until a detailed application of the proposed new procedure had been thoroughly tested by the incorporation (a) of the Beisan Commission's land allotments and possibly (b) of the entries in the unofficial land registers of one of the Jewish colonies, both sets of records being concurrently and authoritatively brought up to date. (Minutes of Conference 16). I do not know whether this trial was subsequently made; but the preparation of the requisite ordinance to regulate the maintenance of the new land register in substitution for the old Turkish enactments on the subject does not appear to have been proceeded with.

---

*An Explanatory Note on Land Settlement was issued in the three languages, while the Department of Education gave most valuable assistance through the country schools.

19. There is no need to consider the operations of the fiscal survey and rural land assessment here, nor the corresponding operations in the urban areas, since no criticism of either appears to have been made. I am necessarily out of touch with the conduct of the technical operations of cadastral survey, but these happily call for no comment as they were expressly commended by the Royal Commission (ix. 36).

Settlement of title was begun by two settlement parties in June 1928, immediately after the enactment of the necessary ordinance, and naturally progressed slowly at first while both officers and people were acquiring experience and confidence and learning to co-operate. A third settlement party began work in May, 1930. In August, 1929, just as the first year's work had been completed and the operations were beginning to run smoothly and to gain speed, serious rioting broke out and has recurred at intervals since. When this has occurred settlement operations have been interfered with and the services of Settlement Officers have been utilized as special magistrates, etc. These interruptions were bound to retard the work out of all proportion to the time directly lost; since they upset arrangements, destroyed continuity and undermined the slowly won confidence and co-operation of the villagers. The successful discharge of the role of settlement officer among any simple rural population depends vitally upon such officer establishing a reputation for a sympathetic, indeed paternal, handling of their problems. It was consequently a severe handicap to the work of Settlement Officers in Palestine to be periodically diverted to duties which inevitably appeared unfeeling and severe to the indigenous rural population, from whom impartial detachment is too much to expect.

A second substantial, although less important drag on the progress of settlement operations was imposed by the periodic absences on leave abroad of settlement officers. Since the proceedings of the Settlement Officer's Court constituted the bottle neck of settlement operations, as has previously appeared, it follows that his unreplaced absence led to proportionately increased congestion. Activity, indeed clarification facilitating subsequent discharge, might continue inside the bottle; but outflow through the bottle neck was blocked during these absences, for there was no provision for a competent relief officer under the existing organization nor could such an officer be improvised.

20. As already noted two settlement parties began work in June, 1928 and a third in May 1930. If they had been able to work continuously they would have completed about 284 settlement-party months by the end of 1936. It appears that about 51 settlement-party months were directly lost by cessation of the work on account of disturbances and between the transfer of a settlement officer in 1932 to other duties and his replacement. Absences of Settlement Officers out of the country on leave appear to have occupied about 17 working months. The figures are crude, but the conclusion will not be far wrong that something like 212 effective settlement-party months were devoted to the conduct of settlement operations during the eight and a half years (mid 1928-1936) considered. This is equivalent to a direct loss through interruptions of about 25% of the output of the organization that was maintained. It is impossible to assess

quantitatively the total combined effect of this direct loss and of the indirect losses previously mentioned. Experienced officers will, however, probably agree that the output of the same organization might certainly have been doubled without change of procedure, if it had merely been in a position to concentrate effectively and continuously on its work. But it seems only reasonable to suppose that under these conditions the Government would have realized without any external inquiry that, admirable as was the quality of the results attained by the settlement operations in the field, these operations (a) were proceeding far too slowly and (b) were not being properly conserved. For it was indisputable that the land tangle left by the Turks choked the springs of progress throughout the country, whether in discharge of the special obligations of the mandate or of the more elementary one of promoting order and a common prosperity. It was also evident (i) that increased expedition in unravelling this tangle was called for, since no material progress in doing so had been made during the first decade of British administration in Palestine (1919-28) and also (ii) that the effort might be vitiated if the tangle was immediately to be allowed to grow again. Nor can it be doubted that improvements in both procedure and organization would have been progressively evolved and promptly applied if these effects had been appreciated earlier by the Government, as in times of less stress and anxiety they surely would have been.

But whatever may be the shortcomings in the volume, and in the conservation by the Land Registry, of the results obtained between 1928 and the present day, it has to be remembered that the devoted efforts of numerous officers, from the Commissioner of Lands downwards, during this very difficult period have provided Palestine with an organization for determining title which was entirely lacking in 1927 and which results show to be sound in its principal members, however defective in articulation and even in the discharge of certain functions. Such an organization cannot be improvised; and, since it exists, it should be practicable to remedy its weaknesses quickly and effectively, if this is resolved upon. Unfortunately it is also evident that for the time being the great measure of local confidence and local co-operation that was won by those conducting settlement operations between 1928 and 1936, in spite of epidemic disorder, may since have deteriorated or disappeared.

V. §§. 21-27. LESSONS OF EARLIER EGYPTIAN EXPERIENCE.

21. Reference has been made previously to the lessons that were available from Egypt's earlier analogous experience, and they appear to me to be still of value. The impact of Napoleon upon Egypt in 1798 and the recognition by the Porte of Mohammed Ali as Pasha of Egypt in 1906, mark the beginning of the slow severance of that country from the Ottoman Empire, which in Palestine's case occurred abruptly in 1917. Mohammed Ali took over from the Turk a more derelict country; a conglomeration of tenures and customary practices which had not been subjected even to the discipline of the partial codification attempted by the Turks later throughout the remainder of the Empire; land taxation of the same mediaeval type as was found in Palestine; an oppressed and starveling peasantry lacking incentive to improve the land they were yoked to; and a demonic river. He, and his successors until Ismail, looked upon Egypt as their personal estate; but they had the natural genius to remove many obsolete survivals and anomalies, to seek to bridle the river, and to introduce the culture of cotton.

But the economic regeneration of the country may, perhaps, be most justly dated from the appointment under the short-lived Anglo-French control, of an International Commission* which investigated the finances in 1878-79. Among other things that Commission recognized (i) the same need to put land tenure and land taxation on to a clear, secure and equitable basis as faced British administration in Palestine forty years later, and (ii) that this necessitated the execution of a cadastral survey and systematic record of title throughout the country.

22. The first attempt to execute this recommendation was instituted in 1879+. Outside of certain European countries the requirements of an effective cadastral survey were very little understood at that time: and it is consequently not altogether surprising that the successful execution of the requisite measures baffled Anglo-Egyptian administration for nineteen years. Nine years of abortive effort (1879-1888) were followed by four years of abandonment in despair (1888-1892). In the meantime the need was becoming increasingly imperative. The gradual extension and amelioration of cultivation, owing to the drastic improvement and reorganization of irrigation throughout the country, led to wide areas of land that were of the mewat category - barren and remote - being brought under cultivation without authorization or advice. The increasing resultant demands on the irrigation arteries and of public expenditure generally were thus accompanied by a wholesale loss of public land, not even mitigated by any corresponding increase in the land tax returns. A test survey to determine the loss of public land in a representative village was therefore made in 1891, which showed that about 12 square kilometres of mewat land had been filched in the confines of that village alone and also escaped land tax. Further tests confirmed the enormous loss of public land that was proceeding and led to the revival of the cadastral survey the following year, as it was evident that the settlement of public and of private claims to the ownership of land could only be pursued effectively and economically in conjunction. The next six years (1892-1898) were occupied in a very slow and defective cadastral survey of portions of the three northern provinces, during which the loss of public land and the gross inequities of the existing land taxation continued unabated elsewhere.

----

*Established by Khedivial Decree of the 27th. January 1878.

+By Khedivial Decree of 9th. February 1879.

By 1895 it was recognized that the long-standing failure to cope effectively with these evils must be terminated: and ten commissions, under Sir William Willcocks, were appointed to investigate the incidence of land taxation throughout the country. Systematic methods of assessment were formulated and the Capitulatory Powers consented to an aggregate annual remission of £216,000 in the land tax for ten years (1898-1907) so as to allow of a certain alleviation in the worst cases during this period; which they judged should be sufficient to complete the requisite cadastral survey and associated settlement of title, if these operations were intelligently conducted. Lord Cromer saw that a radical change in organization, direction and methods must be made: and in 1898, after careful consideration, he secured the appointment of Captain H.G.Lyons, R.E. (now Colonel Sir Henry Lyons, F.R.S.) under the conditions that the latter considered necessary to enable him to discharge the task. The effect was electrical. Futilities were abandoned, work in the three northern provinces was tidied up and completed; while thenceforward two provinces were done every year and the readjusted taxes published the following year. By the end of 1906 survey and settlement had been carried throughout the country and the readjustment of the taxes in the last two provinces was published by the end of 1907, the last year of the period of relief accorded by the Capitulatory Powers.

23. The attempt to execute the initial cadastral survey and accompanying settlement of title therefore extended over twenty-seven years, the results of which may be analysed as follows:-

1879-1888. Nine years of abortive effort.

1888-1892. Four years of abandonment in despair.

1892-1898. Six years of slow and defective revival yielding possibly 8,000 square kilometres of poor work, which had to be scrapped at the earliest opportunity.

1898-1906. Eight years of expeditious and rapidly improving operations yielding 23,500 square kilometres of work of the standard required.

This cadastral survey, as completed, gave the cultivated area of Egypt as approximately 31,500 square kilometres divided into 2¾ million holdings, of which 36% were under 2 dunums, 56% between 2 and 10 dunums, and 8% over 10 dunums.*

24. The outstanding feature of this protracted effort to carry out the measure recommended by the International Commission in 1878-79, and recognized continuously thereafter as an essential stone in the foundation of the country's economy and happiness, is the contrast between the ineffectiveness of the first nineteen years and the punctuality and magnitude of the output of work of a high standard during the last eight. The change was solely and exclusively due to the attainment of the objective during the earlier period having been left to the unco-ordinated efforts of unqualified bodies and pursued in a haphazard way; whereas in 1898 the associated operations of cadastral survey and settlement of title were, for the first time, (a) unified genuinely and completely, under (b) technically and administratively competent direction,

----

*Expressed in Palestinian metric dunums = 1000 square metres.

(c) pursuing a definite programme and (d) provided with adequate specialist staff and budgetary funds for the purpose.

The results testify sufficiently to the efficacy of the new policy and direction which, it will be noted, had to introduce efficiency without interrupting the work; but there was nothing mysterious or miraculous in the effects. Although developed with exceptional celerity, these effects were indeed such as would be expected from the substitution of competent, for incompetent, direction; and of sensible, for foolish, arrangements in any other branch of public activity.

25. The second important feature in Egyptian experience is the price that was paid for the great delay that occurred in carrying out the work. Although losses of public land similar in extent to those found in the first test carried out in 1891, probably only occurred in the outlying tracts of the delta and valley, these tracts were large; while it is not too much to say that in nearly every village throughout the country there was evidence of substantial, and often heavy, losses of public land which had become irretrievable through delay. Under conditions such as obtained in the early years of the British occupation of Egypt, as of Palestine, in which a considerable proportion of the land was undeveloped and in law belonged to the State, every year's delay in defining and asserting public rights was bound to result in heavy losses of those rights, if any striking economic revival was in progress, as in those countries during these periods. Probably the land lost on the confines of the single Egyptian village mentioned is worth fully a quarter of a million pounds to-day. It is by no means an extravagant assumption that if the cadastral survey and associated settlement of title could have been completed ten or fifteen years earlier in Egypt, the extent of public domain in the country would have been at least three or four times that eventually saved. The price paid in the maintenance of the gross inequities of the land tax for many additional years is incalculable; but this did not fall directly on the public purse, since the enormous evasions were balanced by fully as great extortions, chiefly from the peasantry who suffered most and were least able to resist them. The price paid in endemic village disorder, brigandage and misery; in lack of security and incentive to till the land; and in other indirect ways, instanced by the Palestine Royal Commission (ix.41) was probably the greatest of all.

26. The third feature in Egyptian experience that demands attention is the ephemeral character of the work. The cadastral survey in Egypt was conducted exclusively for purposes of settlement of possessory title and land tax assessment, not for purposes of settlement of absolute title for juridical and fiscal purposes combined, as in Palestine. This was of necessity, not of choice. The original intention of the 1878-79 International Commission may be presumed to have been the execution of a cadastral survey on the central European models familiar to the Commissioners. The desirability of establishing a proper register of title on the basis of the cadastral survey, in place of the grossly defective registries of deeds existing, was in any case recognized at an early date and was categorically recommended by a subsequent International Commission expressly appointed to investigate this subject in 1904-8 as the initial cadastral survey of the country was approaching completion.

The settlement of title, which had had perforce to be of a possessory character, could at that time have been converted into a settlement of absolute title comparatively readily, and the results embodied in a register of title to be systematically kept up to date thereafter in conjunction with the cadastral survey. But the consent of some fifteen Capitulatory Powers was then still required before any substantial reform could be effected in Egypt; and unfortunately the consent of two great Powers to these measures was withheld, for reasons totally unconnected with Egypt.

The results of the initial operations formed the basis of new fiscal registers for each village and were accorded great weight as evidence of title in the courts; but these results rapidly lost their value as both the survey and the settlement became obsolete under the cumulative effect of numerous changes in ownership and mutations in the property mosaic.

Upon the completion of the initial cadastral survey in 1906 it was found necessary to redo the indifferent work done in the northern provinces during 1892-98: but the failure to maintain the results of the subsequent work led to the latter having to be redone also and thus to a second, and in due course a third, cadastral survey and settlement of possessory title having to follow each other successively without a break. The absurdity and extravagance of repeated wholesale operations to clear up successive regrowths of confusion and uncertainty, instead of maintaining order when once achieved, is obvious and was, of course, recognized in Egypt. At the time of writing a series of combined cadastral survey and land registry offices are scattered about Egypt to keep work once done up to date thenceforward; but these belong to a later period of history than is now under consideration.

27. The more important lessons to be learnt from the experience of the initial cadastral survey and settlement of title in Egypt may therefore be summarized as follows:-

(i) The necessity of unifying the direction of the interrelated processes of cadastral survey, settlement of title and registration (or record) of title under a single technically and administratively competent officer.

(ii) The immense loss, direct and indirect, occasioned to the country by the protracted failure to complete the initial cadastral survey and associated operations.

(iii) The necessity of working to a definite programme if operations are to be both punctually and expeditiously completed.

(iv) The contingent necessity of providing adequate specialist staff and budgetary funds to enable this programme to be executed.

(v) The wastefulness and shortsightedness of not consolidating in some manner the fruits of initial cadastral survey and settlement in a juridically valid form.

(vi) The wastefulness and shortsightedness of not maintaining the resultant records punctually and faithfully in their fullest and most useful form when once made.

It will be appreciated that (iii) and (iv) are interdependent. Either the coat should be cut to fit the cloth or more cloth be paid for; but neither an indefinite, nor an unattainable, cost should be accepted.

VI. §§.28-end. CONCLUSION.

28. There is an evident similarity between the histories of the first cadastral survey and settlement of title of Egypt and Palestine respectively. The results obtained during different periods of the twenty-seven years that were taken to complete the former have been summarized earlier (§.23). The latter which is, of course, still incomplete was begun in February 1919 (§.9.)* The Royal Commission investigated the progress made by the end of 1936. The history of the whole effort during the intervening sixteen years broadly subdivides into the following three periods:

1921-23.	Three years of abortive effort.
1924-mid 1928.	Four and a half years of reconsideration and re-preparation.
Mid 1928-1936.	Eight and a half years revival resulting in 1,500 square kilometres of effective work (ix.33).

Fifteen hundred square kilometres represents approximately a fifth of the total cultivated area of Palestine which is estimated by the Government as about 7,120 square kilometres if the Beersheba sub-district is excluded (ix.44).

But while the period of failure and fruitlessness was more prolonged in Egypt, when recovery came there it was rapid and complete. In Palestine it was slow and partial. The most striking difference between the histories of the efforts in Egypt and Palestine successively, is in their aggregate of 23,300 and 1,500 square kilometres of effective output during the eight years 1898-1906 and 1928-36 respectively.

Palestine started with two great advantages over Egypt earlier. In Egypt, even in 1898, H.M.G. exercised at best a preponderant influence;+ in Palestine direct legislative and administrative power. Egypt had no comparable experience to draw upon; while Palestine had Egypt's and the Sudan's apposite experience at her very door and fully at her disposition from 1919 onwards. Having regard to these advantages and to the exceptional need to clear up quickly the chaotic conditions of land tenure and taxation that was imposed on Palestine by the addition of the obligations of the mandate to those of ordinary good custodianship that had prevailed in Egypt, it would have been reasonable to have expected in Palestine during 1928-36 at least a proportionately successful achievement in retrieving past failure as was made in the former during 1898-1906.

------

*When the Royal Commission state that the cadastral survey did not start until 1928 (ix.34) they refer to its revival.

+Egyptian Ministers were never the puppets they have commonly been represented to have been; while all important legislation had to secure the assent of all the Capitulatory Powers diplomatically, as well as of an Egyptian Assembly. "Egypt," Lord Cromer commented, "affords a unique example of a country well advanced on the road to civilization, which may be said to possess no general legislative system whatsoever." Modern Egypt, Ch.LII.

29. The Royal Commission attributed the meagreness of the output in Palestine during 1928-36 to that output having been governed by that of the Settlement Officers' Courts, which were congested, meticulous and slow. They concluded that the remedy was to abandon any judicial settlement of title. An attempt has been made earlier to study the effects of this course (Memorandum I.); but whatever views are held on the matter, it is indisputable, if output is to be increased to an adequate amount in the future, that the work must be released somehow or another from the grave limitation imposed on it in this way during 1928-36. Moreover, it is surely evident that the acceptance of this limitation on output for so long was a symptom of a deeper failure to perceive and cure a critical weakness, a sympton which would never have appeared if the work had been reasonably organized and a proper chain of decentralized responsibility for its conduct had existed. Any regular correlation of the periodic returns of the various stages of the work should have promptly revealed any tendency for any particular stage to delay output as a whole and cure should then have followed. For whatever may be considered to be the appropriate remedy for the delay occasioned by the congestion in the Settlement Officers' Courts, it was not very difficult to devise some effective remedy. Further, as has already been pointed out, this was not the only stage in the field operations that was seriously out of step (Memorandum I.8.9); while the Royal Commission also found that the construction and subsequent maintenance of the Register of Title intended to embody and perpetuate the fruits of these operations was unsatisfactory. Completer proof of defective co-ordination and unification of effort could hardly be found. The conclusion, in my opinion, points inescapably to the inability of the office of Commissioner of Lands as established, to discharge effectively the function of securing this co-ordination and unification of effort which it was expressly created to perform.

30. The protracted initial failure to carry out cadastral survey and settlement of title in Egypt, the completely abortive first attempt to do so in Palestine (1919-23), the lengthy discussions (1924-27) which prefaced the second attempt and the hesitation with which the latter was eventually launched, furnished plain warnings that these operations presented many difficulties and pitfalls. This consideration coupled with the time already lost (1919-28) emphasized the need to carry out the renewed operations in a manner which would give the greatest assurance of success. The conditions to be satisfied were neither onerous nor unusual. They were in brief (a) to establish an appropriate and well-balanced organization for the purpose in view, (b) working to an approved programme, (c) under the effective executive command of an officer, who (d) was in the confidence of the Central Government and in regular touch with it, and (e) able to concentrate exclusively on this task.

The purpose in view was the establishment and maintenance of a comprehensive combined clerical and technical record (Land Register and Cadastral Survey) which would show at any time the title to, and other interests in, every parcel of land in Palestine and also fiscal and other obligations arising therefrom. Closely associated technical, investigatory and assessment processes were needed to construct this record initially; but these are apt to divert attention from the more lasting requirements of the maintenance of this record when constructed. The latter depends primarily upon two factors (i) the punctual and effective concurrent maintenance to date of the basic cadastral survey, which records the existence, situation and extent of all the land parcels in the country at any moment and

(ii) the efficient book-keeping of all subsequent changes in the titles to these parcels, in other interests affecting them or in fiscal or other ancillary obligations arising therefrom. Provision is also needed for periodic or other reassessment of these land parcels (and immovables thereon).

To ensure success it was essential to combine under unified executive command in a well balanced but flexible organization all the various interdependent operations needed to secure these two related objectives: and there was surely ample experience to show that these conjoint operations constituted a sufficiently exacting task for an embryo organization under an officer without previous experience in this field, even if favourable internal conditions had continued to prevail in Palestine?

31. But the desire to perpetuate the previous amalgamation of the Land Registry with the administrative control of state lands prevented the establishment of the clear-cut organization that should, in my opinion, have been established; for while the Land Registry was an indispensable part of such an organization, the functions of the State Lands Department were completely extraneous to it. This would not have mattered seriously if the additional charge had been a minor one, but it constituted in its way fully as formidable a one as the principal objective of the organization. Accordingly instead of the officer in command of the new organization being able to concentrate all his energy and thought on his primary task he had to concern himself also with the very wide responsibilities attending the preservation and administration of state lands and in acting as the general consultant of the Government on matters of land policy as a whole. Even this would have mattered less if the discharge of the two main responsibilities with which the Commissioner of Lands was entrusted - viz. (i) the compilation and maintenance of the land record and (ii) the custody of state lands and advising on land policy generally - could have been clearly separated under two Assistants each concentrating on one branch: but this was, of course, incompatible with the perpetuation of the departmental association of the Land Registry and the Administration of State Lands under the Director of Lands.

32. Although it seems absurd to say so, I venture to think that this arose from the scope and importance of the duties attaching to the second of these two functions not having been sufficiently recognized in practice. It is difficult otherwise to understand how the policy was so tenaciously adhered to, of superposing this heavy responsibility upon the already sufficiently onerous one of retrieving past failure in the operations of cadastral survey, settlement of title and registration of title. Yet the responsibility for the custody of state lands and of advising on land administration generally was clearly very great. Among the problems that have occasioned the Government the most serious and protracted concern for many years have been those connected with the disposal, utilization or protection of state lands at Athlit, Beisan, Birket Ramadan, Caesarea, Huleh, along the whole coastal stretch of sand dunes, throughout the whole chain of actual or incipient state forests and in numerous lesser known places. These issues alone merited and would have amply repaid the concentrated and continuous attention of a well organized public lands administration under an experienced whole time director. Thus the Beisan operations were merely concerned with the allotment under specified conditions of about 242 square kilometres of recognized public domain (jiftlik) in peasant holdings, a proceeding which under a free and efficient public lands administration would not

have taken ten years or required constant consideration by the central Government. The other issues were equally susceptible in their respective ways to intelligent and sympathetic handling by such a service.

But the scope and potential value of an efficient public service that had been able to concentrate upon the custody and development of public land of all types throughout the whole country is perhaps best appreciated when it is realized what extensive stretches of the country at the termination of the war and for years afterwards were either mahlul (uncultivated and agriculturally forfeit) or mewat (wild) and thereby by accredited custom and in law properly public land in the general sense of that term. The protection, administration and development of all public domain (jiftlik), of all mahlul and of all mewat throughout the country would have been a supremely important public responsibility under ordinary conditions. Under the special obligations of the mandate its importance was proportionately enhanced.

33.   The Royal Commission dismisses as having little justification the complaint of the Jewish Agency that millions of dunums of state land vanished, owing to laxity or incompetence, especially during the early years of the administration (ix.70 et seq.). During 1924-27 I obtained the same impression as the Royal Commission of the care with which applications to register private claims were scrutinized and the defence of public rights conducted in court. But these were, I suggest, only the fringe of the matter. Everywhere I went I was offered testimony, and not least of all by the officials of the Land Registry and the State Lands Department itself that private rights were being steadily acquired over public land all over the country. The clandestine sales mentioned by the Royal Commission (ix.14) are an instance of such acquisitions being marketed. Indeed I think, as in Egypt earlier (§.25), that such losses were inevitable under the circumstances in the absence of all systematic stocktaking of public land: and, although their extent can only be guesswork, I have no doubt myself that they were in the aggregate considerable and important.

It appears also to have been suggested to the Royal Commission in mitigation of such losses that the only areas which were known to be public land were those that were registered as such (ix.72). But, as has already appeared, the boot was really on the other foot in that, with minor exceptions, all land in Palestine was public land of one form or another and it was only when private rights over such land were registered that these were lawfully valid. But impressive as these considerations are on paper, that impressiveness dwindles to truer proportions when the difficulty in interpreting the old registers is remembered and of locating the land which they purport to effect.

Accordingly, although it appears to me that a service that could have concentrated exclusively on the preservation, administration and development of public land, was needed from the outset and would have considerably reduced encroachments in important areas by constant perambulations and early assertion and defence of public rights, no comprehensive stocktaking of state land was practicable without systematic survey of some sort. The desirability and material advantage of completing that stocktaking rapidly was one of the grounds on which, in 1923, I urged the adoption of a programme to complete the cadastral survey and settlement of title within the following six years. But the Government's financial inability to seize that opportunity only made the utilization of the next the more important. The latter presented itself with the execution of the topo-cadastral or fiscal survey of the country carried out between 1928-36. Although that survey necessarily fell short of providing as complete a foundation as a full cadastral survey for the location of all public land in Palestine, it did provide a foundation on which a comprehensive and generally trustworthy location and record of all the more important areas of public land of all categories could have been completed by officers of the state lands department, working in conjunction with the survey and fiscal operations. But from the inability of the service even at the time of the Royal Commission's visit (ix.3) "to state with any degree of accuracy how much land they held either as State Domain or as waste land" (mewat), it certainly appears that this opportunity was insufficiently appreciated. If this was so, it must have been due to the vision of the combined Land Registry and State lands service having been limited to the possibilities of redressing the prevailing ignorance of the location and extent of public land by the completion of the register of title upon which that service was itself engaged, but which at the current rate of progress would clearly take a great many more years. No alive, well conducted independent State Lands Administration concentrating on its own duties could have failed to realize and take proper advantage of the unique opportunity which the passage of the topo-cadastral survey offered to put its own land record at least on a substantially sound basis throughout the whole country without waiting for the much slower advance of full settlement operations.

It consequently appears to me that the administrative association of the Land Registries and the custody of State Lands under the same Director is to be equally regretted in the interests of both the important public activities concerned.

It may be suggested that the Commissioner of Lands had finally been accorded executive command over the various services in his charge and that he was able to introduce any changes that he thought to be necessary in the distribution or organization of any part of the work. This may formally have been so; but it has to be recognized that the executive command of the Commissioner of Lands was rigidly restricted in fact particularly during the earlier years. His lack of technical knowledge made it inadvisable, as well as impracticable, for him to exercise any detailed control over the technical operations of the survey. The virtual absorption of Settlement Officers in judicial duties critically curtailed his freedom of command in the administrative conduct of settlement of title. And the Government's confidence in the efficiency of the departmental combination of Land Registry and State Lands Administration precluded any early and far-reaching changes there. Only in the sphere of land assessment could the Commissioner of Lands exercise genuine and unfettered executive command.

These restrictions were, of course, recognized when the post was established but I believed (i) that as the genuineness of the defects cited was established by experience these would be progressively remedied and (ii) that what started as a co-ordination of somewhat unsympathetic elements at the outset, would gradually evolve into a homogeneous organization, separating from the administration of State Lands and coming eventually under experienced technical direction. And I think that this belief was reasonable and that the alternative to launching the work in the form adopted in 1927 would only have been further debate and delay. What was unforeseen was the growth of endemic

- 31 -

[Original document is mis-numbered, having no para. 34.]

disturbance in Palestine which impeded normal healthy development in this as in other fields. It was the unfortunate combination of (as I hold) a defective initial organization with the development of conditions which precluded its cure under the impetus of experience that appears to me to have been the basic cause of the various weaknesses in the conduct of settlement and associated operations diagnosed by the Royal Commission and considered separately in my earlier memorandum.

35. For the most part it is better that I should leave the present review of past experience to speak for itself: but it may be convenient if I state briefly the principal points on which it appears to me that the conduct of the work as a whole requires to be reorganized if the various measures that have been suggested in my previous memorandum, or may otherwise be adopted for the remedy of the particular defects found by the Royal Commission are to yield their full results. The main needs under this head appear to me to be:

(i) To separate entirely (a) the custody and administration of public land from (b) the operations of cadastral survey, settlement of title, assessment of immovable property for public purposes, and registration of title to land and other interests and obligations thereto.

(ii) To unify as completely as possible under competent and experienced technical direction the second series of operations allowing the officer in charge all possible latitude in the organization and conduct of the work.

(iii) To lay down in consultation with that officer a definite programme of work to be aimed at annually until the whole country is completed or such portion of it as may be decided.

It may also be advisable in view of the seriously unsatisfactory nature of the maintenance of the new land register reported by the Royal Commission, (which presumably extends to the whole area settled since 1927) to appoint a suitable officer under such Director of Survey and Land Registries to be expressly charged with the duty of getting all the new land registers in this area into order and of inspecting them and all further new land registers regularly in future so as to ensure their proper maintenance.

This would render desirable the appointment of another officer to be responsible for the administration and conduct of all the old (ex Ottoman) Land Registers in advance of settlement of title. This would be a diminishing charge but also a very important one.

The subdivision of the Land Registry work in this way would be logical, and I think convenient, since the requirements of the two classes of land register are entirely different. The old land registers at best can only be based upon sporadic ad hoc or small scale survey. The new land registers are directly based upon systematic cadastral survey and the conduct of the two must be inter-dependent throughout. The conduct of the old land registers for a long time to come appear likely to require a personal knowledge, which is not easily come by, of past transactions and of the pitfalls of both the Ottoman law

- 32 -

and past registry expedients. The conduct of the new land registers no less clearly requires a capacity for organizing and maintaining an elastic system of record in conjunction with the cadastral survey much more efficiently than hitherto. The old registers are a makeshift and require to be administered as such to a considerable extent by personal judgment and knowledge. The new registers should be an orderly perpetuation of the cadastral survey and settlement of title and become virtually a self-running machine, all changes in parcellation being based upon standard mutation forms and all transfers or transmissions of rights on regular and properly attested documents. Legal difficulties will no doubt occur from time to time, but they should be few and of a nature best referred to trained legal opinion. It will, I think, be much easier to find an appropriate officer for each, than to administer them successfully as a homogeneous unit.

36. Some reference should be made to the secondary cause to which the Royal Commission attributed the slow progress in settlement operations in Palestine during 1928-36, which I omitted to consider in Memorandum I. This was the diversion of officers engaged on this work to other duties (ix.34). The Royal Commission were informed that out of 134 surveyors (on the rolls of the service) not more than 80 or 90 were engaged in settlement operations. It has, however, already been noted earlier that processes of survey (except possibly at the outset) were not a source of delay to the joint operations. It should also be recognized that however important the conduct of cadastral work may be in a country, it can never be the exclusive duty of any national survey. In all countries and under all circumstances there are bound to be unceasing demands on such a survey which can no more be gainsaid than those of a cadastral nature and may be even more imperative. The occasions for the diversions of survey staff mentioned by the Royal Commission indeed illustrate this. But there are also the other normal duties of a national survey to be considered among which may be cited the production of topographical and urban map series, precise spirit levelling for irrigation projects of a national character, etc., etc. Provision for needs of these kinds should be a normal matter in any national survey, nor does an allotment of staff to them of the proportions indicated appear to be extravagant.

But although the example cited by the Royal Commission may be unconvincing, experience elsewhere amply confirms the importance of their warning against diversions of effort, which I take to include dislocations of the approved programme of cadastral survey and settlement of title and consequent transfers of staff from such operations proceeding in one locality to new or accelerated work in another to meet sectional demands or apparent immediate advantages. The general programme should be planned with regard to the most rapid and advantageous completion of the work throughout the whole country, without consideration of sectional interests, and having been laid down should be steadily adhered to in the absence of reasons to modify it which are of a gravely compelling character capable of justification to the country at large.

Such changes of programme may be necessary occasionally; but they should be very jealously curtailed, as their deleterious effect on public confidence and on economy and rapidity of working is invariably much more serious than appears.

37. A few words should also be said concerning the Commissionership of Lands. The creation of this post was originally suggested simply to secure the co-ordination and, it was hoped, ultimately the organic unification of the operations of survey, settlement of title, assessment of land tax, and registration of title and of other interests in land. It was the decision to retain the earlier departmental combination of the Land Registry with the administration of State lands that necessitated the widening of the responsibilities of the Commissioner of Lands to include the latter also, and since its range had become thereby so extended, occasioned that office also to be charged with a general advisory duty to the Government on matters of land policy.

There was imperative need for an unified direction of settlement of title and associated operations. There was also, I think, a valuable part to be played by what may be called a genuine Commissioner of Lands. The responsibilities of the post as actually established, were too wide and its powers too indefinite to enable it to perform the former function successfully, as has already appeared. On the other hand, its sphere was too circumscribed and it was too occupied with the details of a particular series of operations to be able to discharge the functions of a genuine Commissioner of Lands properly.

It was at one time proposed that the Commissioner of Lands should have a seat on the Executive Council. This seemed to be a promising idea. The regular members of the Council had too many demands upon their time and energies to be able to devote the continuous consideration that was needed to the shaping and implementation of land policy. They were also too tied to Jerusalem to maintain the continuous personal contact with all parts and peoples of the country that was no less necessary. Moreover all Governments, indeed all dispersed undertakings, know the immense difficulty of maintaining effective connection and confidence between headquarters and local executive agents of all sorts. I have myself mentioned earlier (§.13) the reluctance that existed in 1923-25 at the Headquarters of Government to admit the evil effects of the tithe and of mesha'a in spite of both the unequivocal findings of careful local committees of enquiry and the undivided views of the ablest and most experienced District Officers on these matters. The Royal Commission found the same lack of touch of the central offices of the Government with the realities and difficulties of district administration generally and quoted as cogent the information given them that there was not a man in the secretariat who had been in the districts within the memory of man (vi.37). Interpretation of the realities and aims of the centre to the periphery is just as necessary, if less commonly emphasized. But this most important mutual contact and understanding can only be secured and maintained if it is specifically provided for in the regular machinery of government; and it is hardly fair to depend upon a secretariat, which is essentially a clerical body, to provide it.

In the important field of land policy as a whole invaluable service might have been performed in Palestine by an additional member of the Executive Council, who was able to speak Arabic well, was willing to tour the country indefatigably, possessed (or could win) the confidence of the people, and had the requisite authority, capacity, and knowledge to investigate and accommodate the programmes of the various public services that were concerned with the land and to interpret these to the Central

Government. The existence of such an officer might have spared the country many of the investigations (both by outside and inside agencies) to which it has been continuously subjected, or at least have greatly facilitated and accelerated them.

But the sphere of the Commissioner of Lands would have had to be considerably extended, so as to embrace all the public activities markedly concerned with the formulation and execution of land policy as a whole, if he was to keep the Government properly informed and advised on these matters. Those duties might - I think could - have been advantageously associated with the custody and administration of public lands, but must otherwise have been divorced from any direct responsibility for the conduct of particular departments. For to have performed his proposed larger functions as a special member of the Executive Council properly, such a Commissioner of Lands would have required (a) a large measure of freedom from all daily administrative responsibilities and (b) a position of unchallengeable impartiality in regard to the promotion of particular departmental activities.

Whether constitution of an office of such scope and status would be advantageous now, or whether a candidate of the requisite calibre, character and capacity could be found to fill it, are matters that can only be judged by those more cognisant than myself with existing conditions and future needs in Palestine. But I have no hesitation in saying (i) that the unification of the services concerned with settlement operations should be independent of any such appointment, and (ii) that if the office of Commissioner of Lands is retained its status and functions should be carefully reconsidered in the light of past experience and of the real weaknesses which it would be directed to remove.

(Signed) ERNEST M. DOWSON.

15th. August 1938.

Section 11: Anglo-American Committee of Enquiry, 1945-1946

11.01

A SURVEY OF PALESTINE

Prepared in December 1945 and January 1946

for the information of the

ANGLO-AMERICAN COMMITTEE OF INQUIRY.

VOLUME I.

PRINTED BY THE GOVERNMENT PRINTER, PALESTINE.

CHAPTER VIII.

LAND.

Section 1.
LAND TENURE IN PALESTINE.
Legislation and types of holding.

The land law in Palestine embraces the system of tenures inherited from the Ottoman regime, enriched by some amendments, mostly of a declaratory character, enacted since the British Occupation on the authority of the Palestine Orders-in-Council, 1922-1940. The Ottoman land law probably goes back to the ancient law of Jengis Khan, to which were assimilated previously existing tenures. Later, some of the principles of Muslim religious (shari'a) law were absorbed. A distinction was made between Muslim lands, or the lands under Arab suzerainty in the days of the Prophet, and the lands conquered since the beginning of Muslim expansion. The Muslim lands were allodial and the conquered lands were feudal. Palestine was conquered territory in the mind of the Ottoman rulers. The absolute ownership of land was vested in the State.

2. The Ottoman State continued the practice of the previous rulers of divesting itself of a temporary right of user conditional upon numerous feudal burdens. At first a direct grant of this right was made to feudal lords in consideration of military service. The lords had the lands cultivated by slaves. Later, military fiefs were abolished and the slaves became direct tenants from the State. Feudal burdens were gradually removed and a limited right of disposition was assimilated to the restricted right of user.

3. The land tenures of Ottoman law consist of various modes of user the features of which are set out in the Ottoman Land Code. Not all of these modes of user are actually found in Palestine. Most of the land is held under two distinct tenures commonly referred to as *mulk* and *miri*. *Mulk* means "property". The tenure called *mulk* is a private ownership tenure. Land so owned may be called "allodial" land. It is held in absolute ownership. The holder has almost unfettered freedom in regard to its use and disposition. *Miri* is a conditional usufruct tenure of land held

CHAPTER VIII.

by grant from the State. The holder or possessor is a usufructuary whose tenure resembles a leasehold, subject to certain limitations on the use and disposition of the land and to the payment of certain fees. The interest is indeterminate, assignable and hereditary. The extent of *mulk* or allodial lands in Palestine is limited, and is usually only found in the old cities or in garden areas. Rural land in this category is rare.

4. Although the State land tenure of Palestine is of feudal origin, comparisons with other feudal tenures which it resembles are misleading. The law and practices regulating land tenure in Palestine are far removed for instance from English land law which is also of feudal origin.

5. Palestine land law is rendered more difficult to understand by the difficulty of translating Ottoman legal terms into English. The terms *mulk* and *miri* have not an exact counterpart in English legal terminology. Their translation as "freehold" and "leasehold" or as "estate in fee simple" and "estate tail" is misleading. "Allodium" and "feodum" or "allodial land" and "feudal lands" are only nearer approximations. Similarly the terms "vacant" for *khali*, "communal profits-à-prendre" for *matruka murafaqa*, or "easements in common" for *matruka mahmiya*, as given in this note, must all be considered as terms suggested as giving a meaning nearest to the Turkish. It is essential to master the characteristics of the various categories in order to understand the land tenure of Palestine.

6. The Ottoman land law classifies land under five kinds or categories. These, with suggested approximate counterparts in English, are :—

    1. *Mulk*   = Private or allodial land;
    2. *Miri*   = State or feudal land;
    3. *Waqf*   = Land assured to pious foundations or revenue from land assured to pious foundations;
    4. *Matruka*   = Communal profits-à-prendre land or land subject to public easements in common;
    5. *Mewat*   = Dead or undeveloped land.

A more logical classification, based on the provisions of the law, would be in two main kinds, *mulk* and *miri*, with sub-divisions :—

  A. *Mulk* (Allodial or private land).
    1. *Mulk* (allodial land proper);
    2. *Waqf sahih* (allodial land in mortmain tenure).

CHAPTER VIII.

B. *Miri* (Feudal or State land).

1. *Miri khali* (vacant State land);
2. *Miri taht et tasarruf* (private usufruct State land);
3. *Miri matruka murafaqa* (communal profits-à-prendre State land).
4. *Miri matruka mahmiya* (common *easement or servitude* State land).

To these can be added two more categories :—

5. *Mahlul* (escheated State land) :
6. *Waqf gheir sahih* or *takhsisat waqf* or *miri mauquf* (usufruct State land of which the State revenues are assured to pious foundations).

7. The elements of land ownership under Ottoman land tenure are :—

1. The bare ownership (*raqaba*) :
2. The enjoyment or user (*tasarruf*);
3. The disposition (*ihala*).

In a general way the category indicates the mode of tenure, the amount of control which the State retains over the land, and the extent of the rights of user and disposition of which the State has divested itself in favour of private, communal or general public interests. These divested rights are lapsable, in which event they revert or escheat to the State. If the State retains a vestige of control, though it divests itself of the usufruct user and disposition rights, the land still remains State land. If the State divests itself of all its rights, the land becomes *mulk* (allodial land).

Mulk (allodial land proper).

8. *Mulk* (allodial) land proper assumes its character when all the three elements of the ownership are vested in the holder. The owner can use and dispose of his land freely and is not obliged to cultivate or use the land profitably (in contrast to the case of a usufructuary of State land). *Mulk* may be made *waqf* (mortmain) by dedication under the religious law to charitable purposes. Succession to *mulk* is laid down by the religious law. The owner may also devise it by will, subject to the rights of the legal heirs. Where there are no heirs and no outstanding debts, *mulk* property may be devised without interference from the State. Where an owner dies intestate and without heirs, *mulk* land escheats and becomes vacant State land. As the list of heirs

CHAPTER VIII.

entitled to succession under religious law is almost inexhaustible, this eventuality is remote. The law applicable to *mulk* proper is the Moslem religious law or the ecclesiastical law of the community of which the owner is a member.

Waqf sahih (mortmain land).

9. When *mulk* (allodial land proper) is dedicated to pious uses, it becomes *waqf sahih* (mortmain) land. The dedication may be by deed or by devise, and is irrevocable: the land must remain to the dedicated use in perpetuity. *Waqf* (mortmain) lands of the Moslem community are regulated by the Moslem religious law. These provisions are spread over several books on Moslem law. Commonly relied upon is Umar Hilmi's "A Gift to Posterity on the Laws of Evqaf". *Waqf* (mortmain) lands belonging to non-Moslem communities (whether or not originally constituted under Moslem religious law in Ottoman times) are regulated by the ecclesiastical laws of the respective communities.

Miri (State land).

10. State lands of all categories are regulated by the special Ottoman land laws known as :—

1. The Imperial Land Law of 1274 A.H.
2. The Land Law of 1275 A.H.
3. The Law as to *Miri* (usufruct title deeds) of 1326 A.H.

These were amended by laws generally referred to as the Provisional Land Laws enacted up to 1331 A.H. (1913 A.D.). The Ordinances enacted by the Government of Palestine have not greatly modified the Ottoman land tenure.

Khali (vacant land).

11. Vacant land is land which has not been allocated by the State to any interest and in respect of which it is safe to assume that there are no grants and no rights of private persons. So long as the land remains idle, the State may, if it so desires, allow inhabitants of the vicinity to graze or fell wood and draw water therefrom gratuitously. This would not legally create any right in favour of those using the land. Leave to exercise this *ex-gratia* user may be terminated by the State at any time, particularly if it intends to allocate the vacant land to some specified use. There may be forest laws aimed at preventing wastage of forests and soil erosion. Vacant lands used as pasturing and woodfelling grounds without being allocated to any particular community exclusively are to be distinguished from the *matruka murafaqa*

CHAPTER VIII.

(assigned communal profits-à-prendre) areas. A community has an exclusive right to profits-à-prendre user legally assigned to it.

Miri (usufruct land).

12. Land assumes the status of *miri* (usufruct) land when the *tasarruf* (usufruct) is allocated by the State to any private interest under grant (*ihala wa tafwidh*). The usufruct in State land comprises the rights of user and disposition with certain limitations. The grant of the usufruct may be express or presumed. It is express when it is embodied in a State deed of grant or in an official register. It is presumed as a "lost grant" (*haq el qarar*) from the incident of undisputed possession for a period of ten years or more, if the possessor can, in addition, establish legal origin, such as evidence of acquisition from a predecessor with a good title. Acquisitive prescription is foreign to Ottoman land tenure. In Palestine, because of historical events, by far the greatest number of grants are presumed. Most Ottoman registrations of *miri* (usufruct) titles existing in Palestine are based on a presumed or lost grant.

13. The grant of *miri* land is conditional on the payment of consideration to the State (with the exception of waste land revived with the prior leave of the State, in which case it is granted gratuitously). The consideration is two-fold. The first consideration consists of an "immediate payment" (*mu'ajala*), also called the "price of the land" (*tapu misl* or, shortly, *tapu*), and is sometimes referred to as the "fair price" (*badl misl*). The second consideration is referred to as the "deferred payment" (*mu-ajjala*) more commonly known as the annual tithe (*'ushr*). The immediate payment is a one-time payment made as an entrance fee. Under the Ottoman regime it was assessed by local experts on the basis of the fertility and situation of the land, i.e. on its economic value. The immediate payment is to-day assessed by a Commission and the Director of Land Settlement. The *mu-ajjala* (deferred payment) was a proportionate fee (originally paid in kind and later in money) on the annual produce of the land, basically a tenth or tithe, or its equivalent where the land was used for purposes other than crop raising. The Palestine Government has abolished the tithe, replacing it with land taxes based on the value of the land and having no relation to any produce.

14. The grant of the *tasarruf* (usufruct) is also, legally speaking, conditional on the land being maintained under effective cultivation or other profitable use. This was to ensure the collection of the tithe by the State. Originally *miri* (usufruct) lands were granted for ordinary seasonal grain cultivation. In 1913 A.D.

CHAPTER VIII.

the uses to which land could be put were extended to almost every use not repugnant to public policy, provided always that the prescribed taxes and land registry fees were paid and that the land was not alienated to *waqf* (mortmain) tenure by subterfuge, as had happened before.

15. A usufructuary may in his lifetime dispose of his usufruct right to other interests by transfer (*faragh*) on condition that he obtains the permission of the State and registers the transfer in the Land Registry. *Miri* land may be mortgaged and sold to satisfy a mortgage. The usufructuary may not in any way alienate his usufruct to *waqf* (mortmain) tenure. Usufruct land could, however, be converted into *mulk* (allodial) land if special leave was obtained from the head of the State.

16. The *tasarruf* (usufruct) automatically devolves by inheritance (*intiqal*) to statutory heirs in accordance with the special State Land Inheritance Law. It may not be devised by will. The absence of statutory heirs automatically terminates the grant of *miri* and the land becomes *mahlul* (option) land, i.e. subject, against payment, to re-grant to persons entitled to statutory options. In actual practice *mahlul* land rarely occurs in Palestine.

17. Co-sharers and those who jointly with the usufructuary enjoy servient rights of way and water easements have a right of priority to acquire the *miri* land against fair price (*badl misl*) whenever the usufructuary wishes to dispose of his rights to others.

18. If a person possesses *miri* land for more than ten years adversely to another, the latter is debarred from bringing an action for the recovery of the land because of the passage of time (*murur zaman*). This is based on the principle of "limitation of actions" but it does not necessarily destroy the right of the former usufructuary. It prevents him from asserting his rights through the court. It amounts to extinctive prescription. This rule originated from the time when there were no registrations of land, and gave the active possessors the benefit of the doubt as to legal acquisition.

19. Duly incorporated bodies (other than pious foundations constituted under religious law) have practically the same rights as private individuals in regard to the enjoyment of *tasarruf* (usufruct) in *miri* land. Ordinary trading companies may acquire land as may be required for their purposes. Companies dealing specifically with land must obtain a special licence from the High Commissioner.

20. *Miri* (usufruct) land may be held jointly by two or more co-sharers, so long as the shares are defined. There are two kinds

CHAPTER VIII.

of joint holding : ordinary partnership (*ishtirak*) and village or clan partnership (*musha'*). In the case of ordinary partnership the land need not necessarily be distributed for purposes of cultivation periodically. In the case of village or clan partnership the land is distributed periodically (usually once in two to four years) for cultivation, which means that a usufructuary cultivates sometimes in one locality and sometimes in another. This mode of tenure must be distinguished from the communal (*matruka*) tenure. Clan partnership applies strictly to usufruct land, that is for ordinary agricultural purposes, and each shareholder has a definite share which can be freely acquired or disposed of. As contrasted with this, communal tenure applies strictly to *matruka* (communal) land, that is for profits-à-prendre benefits only; secondly, the land is assigned to the community as a whole without specific shares for the beneficiaries, and cannot be disposed of by the members of the community either jointly or severally.

21. *Miri* (usufruct) land must be registered in the Land Registry. Owing to the failure of the Ottoman land registration machinery, a great deal of land of this nature is still held without registration or under imperfect and obsolete registration. Under the Land (Settlement of Title) Ordinance* an enquiry into existing titles has been conducted since 1928 with a view to registering all titles to land. A considerable part of Palestine has already been covered and registered under a new system, resembling that called the "Torrens" system (*vide* paragraph 29 of this chapter).

Matruka murafaqa (communal land).

22. Land is *matruka murafaqa* (communal land) when the profits-à-prendre user is assigned (*takhsis*) by the State to any specified communal interest. There is very little of such land in Palestine. The assignment of the profits-à-prendre user must in every case be express. In Turkish days the assignment was invariably conveyed by letters patent of assignment in the form of imperial rescript (*firman humayun*). Limitation of actions is not operative as regards communal land. Any accretions added to communal lands by squatters can be demolished.

Matruka mahmiya (common land).

23. *Matruka* (common) land is allocated by the State for the enjoyment of the public at large, possibly for a public right of way or of assembly. In practice, the allocation is presumed from immemorial user. The rules as to the duration of the user and as to the limitation of actions are the same as for communal lands.

---
* Drayton, Vol. II, page 853.

CHAPTER VIII.

Under Ottoman practice *matruka* (communal or common lands) were not registered in the Land Registries. Since the British Occupation the Land (Settlement of Title) Ordinance requires that all such land be registered at settlement.

Mahlul (option land).

24. Land assumes the status of *mahlul* land when existing usufruct grants over *miri* land lapse for any reason. Usufruct land does not directly escheat to the State, but is open to statutory options which must be exercised within prescribed times by persons of specified classes. If the option is exercised the grant is made against payment of the immediate consideration. Otherwise, the land is auctioned. Should the auction fail because the highest bid is insufficient, *mahlul* land reverts to the State and becomes vacant State land.

Waqf gheir sahih or *miri mauquf* or *takhsisat waqf* (quasi mortmain).

25. Land of this category is not *waqf* (mortmain) land in the true sense of the word. It is *miri* land of which the State revenues are dedicated to pious uses or the usufruct of which is dedicated to pious foundations. The ownership remains vested in the State. Quasi-mortmain land is held by private usufructuaries in the same way as any *miri* (usufruct) land proper. There are extensive areas of this nature in Palestine, mostly subject to the payment of the tithe by the Government to ancient imperial Moslem pious foundations instead of incorporating such tithe in the normal State budget. The Palestine Government, under an agreement with the Supreme Moslem Council, the authority controlling Moslem pious foundations, commuted the pious foundations tithes to a fixed sum payable annually to the Supreme Moslem Council for the purpose of the Moslem pious foundations.

Quasi-*mulk* (quasi-allodium).

26. Before 1913 A.D. accretions added to usufruct land (*miri*) were deemed the *mulk* (allodial) property of the usufructuary. Allodial accretions on usufruct land could, prior to 1913 A.D., be dedicated to *waqf* (mortmain). As the inheritance law applicable to *miri* land was different from the inheritance law applicable to *mulk* property, the land was deemed to follow the accretions for the purposes of devolution. Some *miri* land, though in theory State land, becomes in practice assimilated to *mulk* land. If the accretions disappeared, the land was deemed to have recovered its *miri* status. All accretions added to State land since 1913 A.D. follow

CHAPTER VIII.

the land, and the rules applicable to *miri* land are applied to the accretions as well.

Mewat (dead lands).

27. *Mewat* (dead lands) are unallocated or waste areas situated beyond the confines of inhabited regions which can only be rendered cultivable by special effort. Such land could be granted gratuitously to usufructuaries if revived with the State permission, as an inducement to controlled development of waste lands. Clandestine revival was penalised by the payment of a consideration. Nowadays, the development of "waste" land without prior leave from the State is legally a trespass. The conclusion is that *mewat* should have no significance and should be deemed undeveloped "vacant land" proper which cannot be possessed except by allocation from the State.

Section 2.
THE SETTLEMENT OF TITLE TO LAND.

28. The system of registration of land initiated in 1920, combined with the previous system inherited from the Turks, is described in section 3 of this chapter. That system is defective since it is not based on a cadastral survey rigorously kept up to date whereby the units of registration (parcels) are accurately defined on a plan on which they are related to all contiguous registration units, and to the national frame work of triangulation. The system may be described as a combination of a register of deeds and a register of transactions.

29. Acting on recommendations made by Sir Ernest Dowson (formerly Financial Adviser and Director-General of Surveys to the Government of Egypt, who was called in to advise), Government decided in 1927 to introduce registration of title based on the Torrens system in use in Australia and other parts of the British Empire. This is intended gradually to supersede the previous system. It involves :

(a) division of the land, by means of a cadastral survey, into units of registration called parcels according to the category and ownership. The survey is linked to a framework of triangulation points which is related to the precise position of each parcel; the parcels are grouped in units of survey, called blocks;

CHAPTER VIII.

(b) judicial investigation of all registerable rights in the parcel; and

(c) the recording in a new land register of the title and other registerable rights affecting the land concerned in a separate folio for each parcel; on this folio are subsequently recorded the successive incidents relating to the land comprised in the parcel.

To provide for this, the Land (Settlement of Title) Ordinance was enacted in 1928*.

30. Thus by "land settlement" is meant the examination of rights to land and the solution of disputes about the ownership, boundaries, category and other registerable rights in land, its cadastral survey for the purpose, and the eventual recording of the rights in Land Registers. *It must not be confused with the settlement of people on the land.*

31. The immediate purpose of the Land (Settlement of Title) Ordinance is to establish, at a comparatively low cost to the landowners, a clear and comprehensive record of registerable rights in the legal categories of land. The principal registerable rights are those of proprietorship, mortgages, leases for periods exceeding three years, and servitudes (usually rights of way). The record is based on plans of each block with its number and of the parcels with their numbers and areas in metric dunums and square metres.

Other aims served by the operations under the Land (Settlement of Title) Ordinance are the establishment of better records for taxation; the collection of increased fees on dispositions registered after settlement; better development from greater security of title and from the partition of land formerly held in common and periodically divided for the purpose of cultivation; increased public security through a decrease in the number of violent disputes about boundaries and possession based on claims to ownership; and the delimitation and registration of Government lands.

32. The principal stages of the operations under the Ordinance are these :—

I. After the High Commissioner has published an Order in the Palestine Gazette constituting a Settlement Area, a Settlement Officer publishes two notices in order to be in a position to proceed with the actual work of settlement in a given village. The first is a notice of intended settlement, the chief effect of which is to prevent the entering of fresh actions in the courts concerning

* Drayton, Vol. II, page 853, as amended in 1937, 1939, 1942 and 1944.

CHAPTER VIII.

rights to land in that village. The second notice is called the Settlement Notice; it gives the date for the actual commencement of work in the village.

II. Field officers under Assistant Settlement Officers, who work under the supervision of Settlement Officers, then proceed to examine the lands parcel by parcel and to record claims on special forms devised to give as complete information as possible about each parcel and the rights pertaining to it. The field officers at this stage of the work may use croquis or block plans provisionally prepared by the Survey Department. Officers of the Survey of Palestine, as may have been previously decided upon by the directors of the two Departments concerned, may be surveying the land at the same time. In the field work and in the recording of claims, the officers in the villages are assisted by Village Settlement Committees appointed under the provisions of the Ordinance.

III. After all claims have been recorded for a block or group of blocks, schedules of claims are prepared block by block and posted for a minimum period of fifteen days in order to give publicity and an opportunity for the submission of objections and additional claims.

IV. Officers in the field then send to the Settlement Officer the plans or croquis, claims, schedules of claims, and supporting documents, together with their own reports and observations, or, if there are not many difficult disputes, the Assistant Settlement Officer may retain them at his office in the village. The whole material is then examined and a draft schedule of decisions is prepared, which is used as the basis of an investigation in public by the Settlement Officer or his duly empowered assistant at a time notified to the public. At the public investigation the draft schedule of decisions and the plans are amended where necessary and the schedules of rights and final plans are based on them.

The procedure just described is applicable to blocks of land in which there are no disputes or very few disputes or none affecting boundaries. A dispute affecting a parcel or block boundary, unless the area itself is sufficiently large and of proper dimensions to form a separate parcel, must be settled before a final plan can be prepared. If the whole of a block or most of a block is in dispute, then a Settlement Officer or an Assistant Settlement Officer with judicial powers proceeds to deal with the matter in such number of actions as may be deemed necessary. Further public investigation may not be necessary although where many parcels and persons are concerned it is often desirable to make public a draft schedule of decisions as a precautionary measure against mistakes

CHAPTER VIII.

after or at the same time as the delivery of the judgment. Both administrative and judicial decisions at settlement are subject to appeal to the Supreme Court by leave of the Settlement Officer or of the Chief Justice.

Between the time when inspection is made on the ground and the beginning of the hearing of an action, and even afterwards, efforts are made by the Settlement Officers to persuade disputants to reach amicable settlements. Although the Ordinance provides for voluntary arbitration, litigants very seldom refer disputes to arbitration.

V. The last stage in the work of settlement is the posting of Schedules of Rights for thirty days, after which they are sent to the Registrar of Lands concerned for entering in the new registers. Copies are also sent to the District Officers for the collection of fees and to the Director of Land Settlement for use in connection with taxation of land and the care of Government lands. Final block plans are prepared by the Survey of Palestine on the basis of preliminary plans approved by the Settlement Officer. These are distributed in the same way as the Schedules of Rights.

In some instances a right in a given parcel may be entered in a Schedule of Rights as in dispute or not settled, in order that registration of the remaining rights in the block may not be delayed at settlement. The right in dispute or doubt is subsequently settled and is notified to all interested by amending order. If any change in the final plans is necessary, this is done in the form of a "mutation", i.e. a division or a combination of parcels or both, as may be necessary.

33. The title resulting from the completion of land settlement proceedings, though not a "fully guaranteed" title, is nevertheless almost indefeasible. The Ordinance provides that a registration as a result of settlement invalidates any right conflicting with that registration.

34. After the expiry of the appeal period, no appeal lies unless some new fact is established which could not have been within the knowledge of the interested party at an earlier date, or unless the claimant suffered prejudice because, owing to sickness, minority or absence, he was not able to bring the case to court before. After the completion of settlement the register can only be rectified on the ground of fraud, but even in this case the remedy may be one of compensation against the person responsible for the fraud if for any reason the entry in the register cannot be rectified.

CHAPTER VIII.

35. Land settlement has been warmly welcomed by all sections of the population. An almost indefeasible title, based on accurate survey, and a clear record of other registerable rights are established. The existence of unreclaimed or other forms of public Domain is disclosed. The feeling of security which derives from a good title has promoted development in areas where stagnation had long prevailed. In settled villages there is a marked absence of those violent breaches of the peace over land disputes which previously occurred with alarming frequency. The value of land with a settled title is invariably much higher than that the ownership of which is claimed on other less certain evidence.

36. In the eight years between the beginning of land settlement and the visit of the Royal Commission, 1,364,631 dunums were settled. The total area now settled (31st December, 1945), including the Ghor Mudawwara lands in the Beisan sub-District, is 4,808,458 dunums.

Section 3.

LAND REGISTRATION.

37. Following the enactment of the Ottoman Land Code, 1858, (see paragraph 3 of section 1 of this chapter) the Turkish Government passed the Land Registration Law, 1858. Prior to these dates land was held by virtue of Sultanic decrees, grants made by conquerors of various areas, judgments of both civil and Moslem religious courts, orders of administrative authorities and deeds of sale executed before the Moslem courts. Encroachment on unoccupied land belonging to the State and various other unauthorised methods accounted for large holdings. Land acquired by lawful means (such as grant from a competent authority) was, in theory at least, reported to Constantinople, where an effort was made to maintain a series of registers known as the *daftar khaqani* (imperial land registers).

38. Subsequent to the coming into operation of the Land Registration Law, 1858, the Turkish authorities proceeded to organize local land registries in various parts of the Ottoman Empire. The real object appears to have been the collection of tithe and taxes. The land registries in Palestine were apparently opened between the years 1867 and 1873. The procedure was that a *yuklama* (roll call) was held in each village. Claims submitted were subjected to a casual investigation and successful claimants

Chapter VIII.

had their rights recorded in the registers. The law required that all future dealings should be recorded in both the land and taxation registers, but it was soon apparent to the cultivators that the registers were being used as a means of identifying properties for the purpose of taxation and of disclosing the existence of persons subject to military conscription. For these reasons only a small proportion of transactions was recorded, and these chiefly concerned elderly persons, females, foreigners and those sufficiently influential to be able to avoid military service. As an index of owners, the registers therefore became hopelessly incomplete. Nor was there any survey. Areas were sometimes expressed in the quantity of seed required to sow them, or in dunums the number of which was arrived at by the merest guess. In other instances areas were entirely omitted. There was a loose verbal description of the boundaries by reference to the name of adjoining owners or physical features such as roads, streams or hills. The law provided that all land within given boundaries was the property of the recorded owner and that no regard was to be had to expressed areas. The result was that, in order to avoid taxation, a person owning some hundreds of dunums had them recorded as an area of, say, ten or twenty dunums. In effect the register, in so far as it functioned at all, was a record of transactions between persons and not one of transactions with reference to adequately defined plots of land. State Domain, the property of the Sultan in his capacity as Caliph, was not recorded.

39. The result was that, at the time of the occupation of Palestine by the allied forces in 1917 and 1918, the authorities succeeded to thirteen district land registries, the records of which were in a state of complete chaos as regards names of owners, areas and correct definition of the boundaries of the land affected. To add further to the confusion, the Turkish Army in the course of its retreat had removed many of the records to Damascus, Adana and towns in the interior of Turkey. Many of these archives have not been recovered. The Ottoman land registry records, incomplete as they are, still constitute the basis of a large number of claims to real rights in Palestine.

40. After the occupation of Palestine the military authority closed the land registries, prohibited transactions in immovable property and restrained the courts from ordering the sale of land in execution of mortages or judgments. In 1919 Judge Williamson, then Registrar-General in the Sudan, was invited to initiate a new system of land registration in Palestine. He devised a set of registers and a series of forms, and in 1920 legislation was passed repealing the prohibition imposed by the military

CHAPTER VIII.

authorities, establishing a land registry and providing that no disposition of immovable property should be valid unless recorded in the Land Registry, (the Land Transfer Ordinance, 1920)*. "Disposition" was defined as "a sale, mortgage, gift, dedication of *waqf* of every description, and every other disposition of immovable property, except a devise by will or a lease for a term not exceeding three years, and includes a transfer of mortgage and a lease containing an option by virtue of which the term may exceed three years". The registries opened on the 1st October, 1920.

41. The procedure of registration of all dispositions between living persons is identical. In every case the parties submit to the Registrar of Lands within whose district the property is situated a petition seeking the approval of Government. The petition is accompanied by all documents providing evidence as to title and by a certificate from the mukhtar (headman) of the village or quarter stating that the grantor is the owner of the right being disposed of and setting out the situation, boundaries and description of the property. The land is, when necessary, surveyed by a Government surveyor or a private licensed surveyor.

The petition is entered in a petition book and the title is then investigated. If the grantor establishes a good title the proposed transaction is communicated to the revenue officer to ensure that there are no outstanding Government taxes. On receipt by the Registry of a certificate that all taxes have been paid, the Registrar, or the advocate of the parties, prepares the necessary document in evidence of the transaction (sale, mortgage, lease, etc.). The documents are then read over and explained to the parties and signed before the Registrar who attests their due execution.

Ad valorem fees, based on a percentage of the value of the property (or of the amount of the loan or rental if the transaction is a mortgage or lease) are paid and the documents are then passed for inscription in the register. The original of every document is retained in the Registry. Where the transaction is for a limited interest, such as a lease or mortgage, the counterparts are handed to the parties entitled to them. In the case of an absolute disposition, such as succession or sale, certificates of registration are issued to the registered owners.

Transmission of intestate estates of deceased persons is registered on production of a certificate of succession from the competent court and evidence of the identity of the heirs. Bequests are

---

* Drayton, Vol. II, page 881.

CHAPTER VIII.

registered on production of probate or letters of administration. Provision exists for the appointment of guardians of persons under disability and for the sanction of the courts in dealing with the interests of such persons.

Matters of personal status in relation to property are complicated by the fact that there are eleven religious courts of different communities having jurisdiction.

42. The system of registration, as initiated by Judge Williamson, is defective owing to the absence of a cadastral survey, rigorously maintained to date, whereby the parcels of land affected are accurately defined on a plan on which it is related to all contiguous plots and to a national framework of triangulation. That it enjoys a large measure of public confidence is, however, shown by the increasingly large number of transactions recorded. The system may be described as a combination of a register of deeds and a register of transactions.

43. There is no guarantee of indefeasibility of title. Article 3 of the Ottoman Law of Disposition, in speaking of title deeds issued by the Land Registry says :—

> "Formal title deeds are valid and executory. The civil and Moslem courts shall give judgment on these deeds and their registration without further proof. A formal title deed shall not be annulled except by judgment of a court based on lawful reasons".

Registration made in pursuance of land settlement can be voided only on the ground of fraud.

> "The legal value of an entry in the land registers and of the corresponding certificate of registration has been examined in a number of cases before the Palestine courts which appears to justify the view that such entry gives more than a merely *prima facie* title and is conclusive evidence of ownership in the absence of fraud" (Goadby and Doukhan: Land Law of Palestine, p. 308).

44. Evidence of confidence in the value of registration in the Land Registry is indicated by the increasingly large number of transactions a record of which, covering the period from the reopening of the registries on the 1st October, 1920, to the 31st December, 1945, is given in paragraph 50 below.

45. So far, reference has been made to the system of registration inherited from the Turks and to that initiated by Judge Williamson. There remains yet a third, which is intended to supersede these two.

CHAPTER VIII.

46. As is explained in paragraph 29 above, Government decided, in 1927, to introduce registration of title based on the Torrens system in use in Australia and elsewhere. The first pre-requisite to such a system is a cadastral survey linked to a series of triangulation points forming a national framework to which can be related the precise position of any given parcel of land. A second prerequisite is quasi-judicial investigation, carried out on the spot, to determine the category, ownership and existence of all rights in land.

47. To provide for this, the organization of the Survey Department was enlarged and a Department of Land Settlement was established. Legislation was enacted providing for land settlement and for the introduction of a new system of registration. This was designed to overcome the anomalies and deficiencies of the existing systems and to set up an orderly system of registration of title to land and registerable interests in land, based on numbered parcels in numbered registration blocks, each area being correctly measured, precisely defined in relation to adjoining land and tied to a triangulation point. Survey and settlement operations (which are detailed in section 2 above) having been completed a Schedule of Rights is served upon the Land Registrars and its contents are inscribed in the registers and form evidence of all existing rights and the basis of all future transactions. The area registered under this system up to 31st December, 1945, is 4,424,834 dunums*.

48. The new register is loose leaf in form. It omits all reference to boundaries or other verbal description. Land is described by reference to block and parcel numbers and the plan is deemed to be conclusive evidence of area and boundaries. The completion of a transaction under this system is much simpler than it was under the other systems. Names and interests recorded in the register are deemed to be conclusive without further investigation. Documents are submitted to a critical scrutiny to ensure that they comply with the law, that they create or transfer a registerable interest, that the parties are competent and that the transaction is otherwise in order. Alleged interests not entered in the register are disregarded. Registration under the system does not affect tenure or other legal incidents attaching to the interest recorded. The registers and other books used since 1920 are kept in English. Forms intended for submission to the Land Registry and documents affording evidence of transactions may be in any one of the official languages. Constant reference to the old Turkish registers is still necessary.

---

* Does not include the ghor mudawwara lands.

Chapter VIII.

49. Registration of title based on land settlement has been warmly welcomed by all sections of the population, whose only criticism is that progress has not been more rapid. For the first time a definite record of title based on accurate survey and a clear record of other registerable rights have been established. The existence of unreclaimed or other forms of State Domain has been disclosed. The feeling of security which derives from a clear record of good title has prompted development in areas where stagnation had long prevailed. In settled villages there is a marked absence of those breaches of the peace which previously occurred with alarming frequency and which had their origin in land disputes.

50. Land Registry fees collected and the number of transactions completed from the 1st October, 1920, to the 31st December, 1945, are as follows :—

Year	Revenue £P.	Transactions
1920 (October-December)	4,928	469
1921	38,913	3,361
1922	56,973	5,117
1923	41,834	6,514
1924	41,222	7,113
1925	113,165	10,761
1926	82,998	11,821
1927	57,233	9,655
1928	65,720	11,643
1929	68,247	11,290
1930	69,550	13,315
1931	74,245	14,265
1932	97,876	18,392
1933	206,124	28,293
1934	330,481	36,555
1935	455,146	49,133
1936	219,687	36,101
1937	208,323	42,009
1938	142,381	30,574
1939	131,560	20,025
1940	180,673	28,267
1941	197,401	30,134
1942	377.806	37,061
1943	709,592	41,688
1944	668,336	36,384
1945	1,215,539	44,251
Totals £P.	5,855,953	584,191

CHAPTER VIII.

51. The increase in Land Registry revenue is primarily due to substantial rises in land values as the fees are, in most cases, *ad valorem* on the market value of the land affected. Interesting incidents of spectacular rises are afforded in the maritime plain where unimproved fertile land capable of irrigation with water obtainable at a reasonable depth, say, fifty metres, has risen from £P.5 to £P.40 per dunum in the last five years. Similar rises have taken place in buildings and building plots in Jerusalem, Haifa and Tel Aviv where vacant business sites in central positions have changed hands up to £P.100 per square metre. Substantial rises have also occurred in urban land ripe for building development in close vicinity to the larger towns where prices have advanced from £P.400 per dunum to £P.3000 per dunum during the past five years.

52. Between the opening of the Land Registries in October, 1920, and 31st December, 1945, Jews have purchased and registered a net area of 938,365 dunums. The assumption that they owned 650,000 dunums prior to October, 1920, is generally accepted. The total area now owned by them may, therefore, be put at about 1,588,000 dunums; this figure does not, however, include lands which are occupied by Jews, as legal tenants or otherwise, but of which the ownership is not registered in the Land Registries in the names of Jews. Table 1 at the end of this section shows the areas registered annually under Jewish ownership since October, 1920.

It should be explained that the Jewish National Fund (Keren Kayemeth Leisrael Ltd.) is prohibited by its statutes from selling any land, as all property is to be held in trust for the Jewish people*. The Hemnuta, which is a subsidiary of the Jewish National Fund, enjoys freedom of disposition and holds land which is intended for ultimate transfer to principals for whom the Fund is merely an agent or for exchange for consolidation or other purposes.

Table 2 shows the holdings of large Jewish land owners, being those holding 5000 dunums or more.

The areas owned by Jews (and shown as such in the Land Registries) in the three zones defined in the Land Transfers Regulations, 1940, are approximately as follows: in zone 'A', 409,000 dunums: in zone 'B', 560,000 dunums; and in the "free" zone, 620,000 dunums.

Areas given above are in respect of land owned by Jews and do not include areas leased by Jews from non-Jews.

---

* *Vide* Leviticus, XXV, 8, 23, 29-30.

CHAPTER VIII.

Table 1.

AREAS PURCHASED BY JEWS, 1920-1945.

Year		Dunums
Area owned before 1920 (estimated)		650,000
1920	=	1,048
1921	=	90,785
1922	=	39,359
1923	=	17,493
1924	=	44,765
1925	=	176,124
1926	=	38,978
1927	=	18,995
1928	=	21,515
1929	=	64,517
1930	=	19,365
1931	=	18,585
1932	=	18,893
1933	=	36,991
1934	=	62,114
1935	=	72,905
1936	=	18,146
1937	=	29,367
1938	=	27,280
1939	=	27,973
1940	=	22,481
1941	=	14,530
1942	=	18,810
1943	=	18,035
1944	=	8,311
1945 (estimated)	=	11.000
	TOTAL	1,588,365

CHAPTER VIII.

Table 2.

HOLDINGS OF LARGE JEWISH LAND OWNERS AS AT 31ST DECEMBER, 1945.

(in metric dunums).

	Jewish National Fund		Palestine Jewish Colonization Association		Palestine Land Development Co. Ltd.		Hemnuta Ltd.		Africa Palestine Investment Co. Ltd.		Bayside Land Corporation Ltd.		Palestine Kupat Am Bank Ltd.		Total
	in whole	in common	in whole	in common	in whole	in common	in whole	in common	in whole	in common	in whole	in common	in whole	in common	
GALILEE	272,000	49,600	128,800	8,900	2,200	—	—	200	—	—	—	—	—	—	451,700
HAIFA	112,600	—	60,800	—	6,000	200	—	—	9,900	—	8,500	—	6,300	2,100	206,400
SAMARIA	79,600	2,200	1,100	—	—	—	4,800	9,100	—	—	—	—	—	—	96,800
JERUSALEM	13,100	2,200	1,800	—	900	—	200	800	—	—	—	—	—	—	19,000
LYDDA	60,100	3,100	2,800	—	400	—	700	700	—	—	—	—	—	—	67,300
GAZA	63,400	2,200	—	—	—	—	—	—	—	—	—	—	—	—	65,600
TOTAL	600,800	59,300	189,800	8,900	9,500	200	5,700	10,800	9,900	—	8,500	—	6,300	2,100	906,800

Notes. (1) All areas have been taken to the nearest 100 dunums.
(2) Some areas are based on old records and will probably need revision when survey takes place.

Chapter VIII.

Section 4.

SYSTEMS OF LAND TAXATION.

53. The land taxation inherited from the Turkish regime consisted of :

(a) the A'shar (plural of 'ushr=a tenth) or the Tithes,

(b) the Vergo or House and Land Tax, and

(c) Musaqqafat, a tax on roofed buildings.

The Tithe:

54. Muslim law treated all land in private hands as subject to payment either of tithe or tribute. The tithe represented the share of the Sovereign, or of the community as a whole, in the produce of the soil. It was not, of course, peculiarly a Muslim institution. It occurs elsewhere in widely separated countries. Tribute was no longer being exacted by the Turks at the time of the British occupation but tithe was, in principle, still payable by all private owners.

The tithe, as its name indicates, was supposed to be equal to one-tenth of the produce. The original tithe had, however, been increased from time to time by the Ottoman Government for revenue purposes and at the time of the British occupation it was collected at the rate of 12½ per cent. of the gross yield of the land. Crops were assessed on the threshing floor or in the field and the tithe was collected from the cultivators.

The tithe, under the Ottoman regime, was frequently not collected directly through Government agency. It was farmed out by public auction usually to influential persons who were able to provide adequate security. This practice, being open to abuse, was discontinued after the British occupation. This was followed in 1925 by the abolition of all additional percentages and the reduction of the tithe on all crops and other produce to 10 per cent.

The annual estimation of crops fostered corruption and Government found it most cumbersome. To the cultivator it interfered with the disposal of his crop. Nevertheless it had the advantage of varying according to good or bad crops.

55. In 1928, as a measure of reform, Government began to apply an Ordinance for the "Commutation of Tithes". The commuted tithe for a village, settlement or tribe was a fixed aggregate amount paid annually. It was related to the average amount of tithe that had been paid by the village during the four

CHAPTER VIII.

years immediately preceding the application of the Ordinance to it, and was distributed by village committees under official supervision on the basis of the productivity of the land in cereals or fruit trees.

The produce of any land utilised for the purpose of agricultural instruction or research, was exempted from tithe and remissions were granted when there was destruction or failure of crops, or a fall in prices, except in the case of areas planted with citrus trees.

The following statement shows the commuted tithe payable in respect of 1934-35, the last year of its general application to the whole country:—

Treasury share	LP.223,061	
Waqf share	LP. 40,777	LP.263,838
Less remissions granted:—		
Treasury share	LP.114,122	
Waqf share	LP. 16,609	LP.130,731
Net amount payable:—		LP.133,107
Compare the ordinary tithe payable in 1925-26:—		LP.326,410

The House and Land Tax (*Vergo*):

56. The House and Land Tax was levied on immovable property of every description. It was based on the capital value and varied from 4 per thousand on *miri* (rural) land to 10 per thousand on *mulk* (town) land and from 4 to 10 per thousand on built-on properties. Immovable property registered in the name of corporate bodies was originally subject to an additional tax, varying from $\frac{1}{2}$ to 1 per thousand of its assessed value, but this was abolished in 1933. The House and Land Tax had many defects, since, in the absence of a survey, identification of each property was difficult; furthermore, at the time of the British occupation no general re-assessment had been carried out for 25 years and most of the records had been lost, destroyed or taken away by the Turks.

57. After the re-opening of the land registries in 1920, the House and Land Tax became payable on the basis of the transfer price or a valuation when properties were transferred, and consequently the tax on transferred properties became much heavier than on others. In the case of properties not the subject of transfers, reliance had to be placed on tax collectors who had been in the employ of the Ottoman Government and who knew what total House and Land Tax had been payable by the inhabitants of a village. The village elders provided lists of persons liable and of the amounts payable by them.

CHAPTER VIII.

The Tax on Roofed Buildings (*Musaqqafat*):

58. The *Musaqqafat* Tax was applied by the Civil Administration in 1921 in Haifa, Acre and Shefa 'Amr. This tax was, by an Ottoman law, levied on built property within municipal areas at the rate of 12½ per cent. of the annual value. This rate combined both the Government and the municipal taxes and was payable by the owner. It replaced the *Vergo* on built-on property but not on vacant land. The tax was first collected by the British authorities at the rate of 8½ per cent. of the annual value but, from 1926, the rate was raised to 11 per cent. The tax was collected by Government, by whom 3½ per cent. was retained, 5 per cent. (and later 7⅔ per cent.) being paid to the Municipality concerned.

59. The total assessments of House and Land Tax and of *Musaqqafat* Tax (including the municipal share) in respect of the years from 1918-19 to 1928-29 were :—

	£P.
1918—19	126,757
1919—20	144,765
1920—21	146,977
1921—22	151,465
1922—23	164,950
1923—24	172,717
1924—25	182,270
1925—26	194,012
1926—27	219,127
1927—28	231,997
1928—29	238,850

60. In an effort to secure better distribution of land taxation, the Urban and Rural Property Taxes were introduced in 1928 and 1935 respectively in replacement of the old Turkish taxes.

The Urban Property Tax:

61. The Urban Property Tax Ordinance, 1928 *, was applied town by town. There were amendments to improve procedure in 1940, 1942, 1944 and 1945. For the purpose of this tax, the land within the boundaries of the urban area is divided into blocks subdivided into parcels, the parcel being the unit for taxation. The tax is payable by the property owner and is a percentage of the

---

* Drayton, Vol. II, page 1512, repealed by the Urban Property Tax Ordinance, 1940, (Laws of 1940, Vol. I, page 275) which was amended by Ordinances No. 24 of 1942, (Laws of 1942, Vol. I, page 78), No. 10 of 1944, (Laws of 1944, Vol. I, page 30) and No. 7 of 1945, (Suppl. No. 1, page 45).

CHAPTER VIII.

net annual value of land and building. The rate is fixed annually by order. The net annual value is arrived at by deducting for repairs and other charges a percentage varying from 20 to 33⅓ per cent. from the gross annual value calculated from the rent of built-on property. In the case of vacant land the net annual value is six per cent. of the estimated capital value. The valuations are made by assessment committees, composed of two official and two non-official members. Official inspectors may examine the work of assessment committees and request the committees to revise the valuations. Valuation lists are posted and the owner has a right of objection and appeal against the valuation. There are measures for annual revision to cover cases where the net annual value of property has increased or decreased by 20 per cent. or more since the last assessment, and for quinquennial revaluation. The Ordinance differentiates between the following categories :—

(a) all house property except that used solely for the purpose of industrial undertakings in which mechanically-driven machinery is used;

(b) house property constructed and used for the purpose of industrial undertakings in which mechanically-driven machinery is used; and

(c) land which is not the site of house property.

The maximum rate of the tax was, originally, 10 per cent. but in 1931 it was raised to 15 per cent.

62. The following have been the rates in force since the promulgation of the Ordinance :—

Financial year	House property	Industrial establishments	Land
1929—1930	9 %	6%	7 %
1930—1931	9 %	6%	7 %
1931—1932	12 %	8%	8½%
1932—1933	15 %	10%	10 %
1933—1934	15 %	10%	10 %
1934—1935	12½%	10%	10 %
1935—1936 to 1941—1942	10 %	10%	10 %
1942—1943 to 1945—1946	10 %	15%	10 %

63. Provision now exists for exemption and remission of the tax as follows :—

(a) The whole or part of the tax for any year in respect of any house property the net annual value of which does not exceed

CHAPTER VIII.

a certain sum, if such remission is justified on grounds of extreme poverty.

(b) The whole or part of the tax on playing fields, open spaces accessible to the public, property on which buildings are prohibited or restricted under town planning schemes, and house property rendered unusable or uninhabitable by damage or destruction.

(c) Property of various descriptions, of which the main are State owned property, consulates, and property owned and used by religious, charitable or educational institutions.

Provision is also made for exemptions hitherto enjoyed by institutions or bodies by virtue of treaties and decrees or on other grounds and for the exemption of certain specific categories of property.

Rural Property Tax:

64. The Rural Property Tax Ordinance * was applied in 1935 to all the rural lands of Palestine except Beersheba sub-District and the Hula concession lands of Safad sub-District. In 1942, the Ordinance was improved by amendment and consolidation and in 1944 it was extended to the Hula concession area.

65. For the operation of this Ordinance, plans were prepared showing the boundaries of all villages and settlements, the boundaries and names of the various localities, the area planted with fruit trees and the cultivable and uncultivable land. Villages and settlements were divided by official valuers into blocks of land of a similar ground crop productivity value, and the category was determined in which each block should be placed. At the same time the built-on village area was demarcated on the plan.

66. The Rural Property Tax is a tax per dunum at varying rates on categories arranged according to the estimated productivity of the soil, and in some relation to the net annual yield. Generally the rates of tax per dunum approximate to 10 per cent. of a low estimated net annual value of the several categories of land. The last three categories were originally exempted from the payment of the tax on the ground of their low net annual yield. The tax is payable by the owner. Between 1935 and 1942 the tax was payable on the dunum, but in 1942 the tax became payable on the dunum or part thereof. The following schedule shows the original tax categories and basic rates and the amendments subsequently made to the basic rates :—

---

* Laws of 1935, Vol. I, page 1, repealed by the Rural Property Tax Ordinance, 1942, (Laws of 1942, Vol. I, page 11) which was amended by Ordinances No. 11 of 1944, (Laws of 1944, Vol. I, page 32) and No. 8 of 1945, (Suppl. No. 1, page 47).

CHAPTER VIII.

Category	Description	Rate of tax per dunum Mils	Amendments
1	Citrus (excluding Acre sub-District).	825	500 mils from 1.4.36 to 31.3.38. 400 mils from 1.4.38. Per dunum or part thereof as from 1.4.42.
2	Citrus (Acre sub-District).	410	50 mils from 1.4.36 to 31.3.38. 40 mils from 1.4.38. Per dunum or part thereof from 1.4.42.
3	Bananas	560	Per dunum or part thereof as from 1.4.42.
4	Village built-on areas or reserves thereof.	160	—
5	1st grade irrigated land and 1st grade fruit plantation.	40	Per dunum or part thereof as from 1.4.42.
6	2nd grade irrigated land and 2nd grade fruit plantation.	35	-do-
7	3rd grade irrigated land and 3rd grade fruit plantation.	30	-do-
8	1st grade ground crop land, 4th grade irrigated land and 4th grade fruit plantation.	25	-do-
9	2nd grade ground crop land, 5th grade irrigated land and 5th grade fruit plantation.	20	-do-
10	3rd grade ground crop land, 6th grade irrigated land and 6th grade fruit plantation.	18	-do-
11	4th grade ground crop land, 7th grade irrigated land and 7th grade fruit plantation.	15	-do-
12	5th grade ground crop land, 8th grade irrigated land and 8th grade fruit plantation.	12	-do-

CHAPTER VIII.

Category	Description	Rate of tax per dunum Mils	Amendments
13	6th grade ground crop land, 9th grade irrigated land and 9th grade fruit plantation.	8	Per dunum or part thereof as from 1.4.42.
14	7th grade ground crop land and 10th grade irrigated land.	Nil	4 mils per dunum or part thereof as from 1.4.44.
15	8th grade ground crop land.	Nil	2 mils per dunum or part thereof as from 1.4.44.
16	Forest, planted and indigenous, and uncultivated land.	Nil	
17	Fish ponds.		560 mils per dunum or part thereof as from 1.4.44.

67. The following is the procedure of assessment and demand. The official valuer, from information obtained by inspection, prepares, in respect of each survey block in a village or settlement, a roll showing the area and category of the land. Objections and appeals having been decided, the amount of tax payable is computed and the roll becomes final. In areas settled under the Land (Settlement of Title) Ordinance *, the official valuer and, in non-settled villages or settlements, a village distribution committee, prepare distribution lists showing each parcel, its owner and category and the tax thereon. Objections and appeals having been dealt with, this becomes the tax distribution list in force for the year. Buildings are not assessed as such unless they are industrial buildings of an annual value exceeding £P.20. A valuation list of taxable buildings, subject to objection and appeal, is prepared by an official valuer. The net annual value is calculated by deducting one-third from the gross annual or full rental value. On the net annual value a tax, prescribed annually by order, is payable at a rate not exceeding 15 per cent. The rate of tax during the period 1935-36 to 1941-42 was 10 per cent.; after April, 1942, the rate was 15 per cent. Provision is made in the Ordinance for annual supplementary rolls where there have been changes of category; for a redistribution of the tax when neces-

* Drayton, Vol. I, page 853.

CHAPTER VIII.

sary; and for supplementary valuation lists in respect of industrial buildings. Objections and appeals against the supplementary rolls are dealt with as if they were original rolls or lists.

68. Owners who develop their land or erect industrial buildings are required to notify Government in order that the category of land may be amended, but in such cases owners are not required to pay tax at the higher rate until the following varying periods have passed :—

(a) Land previously regarded as "uncultivable" brought under cultivation	6 years.
(b) Land newly planted with bananas	1 year.
(c) Land newly planted with citrus	6 years.
(d) Land newly planted with any fruit tree other than citrus and bananas	10 years.
(e) Top-worked citrus groves of not less than one dunum	4 years.

69. The High Commissioner has power to grant relief, by reducing the rates and by postponing or remitting payment, when he considers that such a course is necessitated by some unavoidable emergency or a fall in the value of crops. The High Commissioner may also remit the tax, wholly or in part, on land being used as a threshing-floor or cemetery and, where plantations or crops are destroyed, exemption may be given from the tax for the remainder of the year. As in the urban tax, property of various descriptions, of which the main categories are State owned property, consulates, and property owned and used by religious, charitable, or educational institutions, is exempted. Exemption hitherto enjoyed by institutions or bodies by virtue of treaties, firmans and decrees and the exemption of certain specific categories of property, are also provided for.

Severe *khamsin* (east) winds affected orange groves in the spring of 1935 and remissions of Rural Property Tax for the tax year 1935-36, involving £P.16,500, were authorised on this account. The tax on citrus (excluding Acre sub-District) was reduced for the year 1939-40 to 150 mils per dunum and since 1st April, 1940, the whole tax on citrus has been remitted annually throughout the country in view of the effects of the war on the industry.

70. As a war measure, in 1943-44 the rates of tax shown in paragraph 66 above were doubled, except in the case of citrus, and the total tax payable was, as a result, increased by about

Chapter VIII.

£P.111,000. As a further emergency measure the rates, again except those on citrus, were re-doubled in respect of the year 1944-45 and remained at the re-doubled rates, as follows, in 1945-46.

Category	Rates of tax Mils	
1	Nil	
2	Nil	
3	2,240	per dunum or part thereof.
4	640	per dunum.
5	160	per dunum or part thereof.
6	140	do.
7	120	do.
8	100	do.
9	80	do.
10	72	do.
11	60	do.
12	48	do.
13	32	do.
14	16	do.
15	8	do.
16	Nil	
17	2,240	do.

71. In 1944 amendments to the Urban and Rural Property Tax Ordinances enabled a penalty up to 20% to be imposed where these taxes were not paid within six months of the date upon which they first became due.

72. The receipts from direct taxes on land and house property during the financial year 1944-45 are as follows :—

	LP.
Urban property tax	680,398
Rural property tax	464,518
Tithes (Beersheba sub-District)	10,710
House and land tax (Beersheba sub-District).	1,722
LP.	1,157,348

CHAPTER VIII.
Section 5.
THE PUBLIC LANDS OF PALESTINE.

73. The public lands of Palestine are, according to the Palestine Orders-in-Council 1922-1940 *, all those lands which are subject to the control of the Government of Palestine by virtue of treaty, convention, agreement and succession, and all lands which are acquired for the public service or otherwise. Article 12 of the 1922 Order-in-Council requires that "All rights in or in relation to any public lands shall vest in and may be exercised by the High Commissioner for the time being in trust for the Government of Palestine". Article 13 enables the High Commissioner to make grants or leases of any public lands, or to permit such lands to be temporarily occupied on such terms or conditions as he may think fit, provided that the grant or disposition is in conformity with the existing law. The existing law in regard to land consists of the Ottoman Land Code and its subsidiary legislation, as amended by Ordinances promulgated by the High Commissioner.

74. The public lands of Palestine include lands varying greatly not only in physical characteristics, but also in the extent and nature of the ownership and control of Government in them. There are large areas in which the precise interest of the State has not yet been ascertained.

75. The tenures inherited from Ottoman legislation have been described in section 1 of this chapter. Property owned completely is called *mulk*. Muslim emperors and Turkish sultans of the past had made grants of land as *mulk*; and by the Ottoman Land Code, sites of houses in towns can be *mulk*; but generally speaking land privately owned is held on what Ottoman law called the *miri* tenure, which resembles a lease of indefinite duration, in which the rental, so to speak, is represented by the obligation to pay land taxes and land registry fees. When the *miri* interest is alienated, the ultimate ownership called *raqaba* is retained by the State. Most of the land owned by the State is registered as in the *miri* category but as the Government owns the *raqaba* as well, it might as well be called *mulk* except that perhaps this might cause complications when Government desired to alienate it by way of grant, sale or lease. The "owners" who hold land by *miri* tenure can only exercise such rights as can be shown to have been accorded to them by the State, and these rights are laid down in the Ottoman law. The right of succession to these rights is prescribed by law. Failure of successors brings the grant to an end and the land becomes *mahlul* and returns to the State. Theoretically, failure to cultivate also causes the

---
* *Vide* chapter IV.

Chapter VIII.

grant to lapse and the usufruct (*tasarruf*) to return to the State. In actual practice there is in Palestine little of this land (*miri mahlul*) which becomes part of the public domain by escheatment in this way; there is some Government land which was handed on as State Domain from the Turkish regime, as *mahlul*, but the circumstances in which it became *mahlul* are doubtful, and it appears that the expression *mahlul* may be used for any vacant public domain of the *miri* category. To avoid confusion, it is better to refer to all vacant public domain of this nature as unassigned State land.

76. Among the public domain of the *miri* category are the lands which the Ottoman Government took over from the Sultan Abdul Hamid after the revolution of 1908; these in turn were taken over by the Palestine Government. They are called *jiftlik* or *mudawwara*. Practically all of them were and are occupied to some extent by Arabs who claim rights based on many years presence on them.

77. Land which has not been granted or assigned to anyone and is consequently unregistered and which is distant from cultivation or habitation is called *mewat* i.e. dead land. The *mewat* lands are part of the public domain. When such lands are, during the course of operations of land settlement, found to be free from any private rights, they are registered as *miri* in the name of Government. It is frequently difficult to assume that there was in the past no grant, and consequently it is not safe to assume that all the empty lands south of Beersheba or east of Hebron, for instance, are *mewat*.

78. Under the Forest Ordinance * forest lands, which are not private property, can be proclaimed by the High Commissioner as forest reserves. On the assumption that there is no private property within these lands, and it has not been possible to make this assumption with complete certainty, they may be regarded as part of the *miri* or *mewat* lands of the State. When they come under the operations of the Land (Settlement of Title) Ordinance ** all these doubts are decided.

79. Another category of land described in section 1 of this chapter is that of *matruka*. This is common or communal land which is left for the general use of the public, or which is assigned for the inhabitants generally of some village or group of villages. The control of the Government over these lands is limited to that necessary to enable the public to benefit from them in the

---

* Drayton, Vol. I, page 710.
** Drayton, Vol. I, page 838.

CHAPTER VIII.

way intended. At land settlement, rivers, wadis and drainage channels have been registered in this category as lands controlled by Government on behalf of the community.

80. A considerable area of land is purchased or acquired (under the expropriation laws) by Government. This of course becomes the "private property" of the Government, although some, such as roads and irrigation channels, is devoted to the use of the community.

81. The account given above describes the various divisions of legal tenure in which public lands are controlled by the State. Land which, in the operation of the Land (Settlement of Title) Ordinance, is found to belong to the State is registered, in the phraseology used in the Order-in-Council, in the name of "the High Commissioner for the time being, in trust for the Government of Palestine". With the exception of the land referred to under paragraph 79 above as *matruka*, practically all such public lands are registered in the *miri* category; a few are registered as *mulk*.

82. The Royal Commission in 1937 found that a really final and reliable statement of the Government domains and waste lands would not be possible until the operations of the Land (Settlement of Title) Ordinance are concluded over the whole country.* Some 12,577 square kilometres lie in the deserts of Beersheba. It is possible that there may be private claims to over 2000 square kilometres which are cultivated from time to time. The remainder may be considered to be either *mewat* or empty *miri*. None of it has come under the operation of the Land (Settlement of Title) Ordinance. Excluding Beersheba, the remaining land area of Palestine is 13,743 square kilometres. Some 3000 of this is represented by the tract of mountainous wilderness east of Hebron, Jerusalem and Nablus. When this comes under settlement of title, a large part of it will doubtless be found to be empty State land. In the remaining 10,743 square kilometres the ownership of nearly 4,500 square kilometres has been settled and, of this, over 660 square kilometres has been found to be public land, the larger proportion unoccupied rocky or sandy land, wadis, etc. and areas reserved for forests or for village uses. The fiscal tax records show that out of the 10.743 square kilometres more than 7,000 are cultivated and may be assumed to contain a preponderance of private property; some will no doubt be found to be part of the village land. In addition to the area of 660 square kilometres "settled" as State Domain in Palestine, there is an area of 900 square kilometres in respect of

---
* Royal Commission's report, chapter IX, para 23.

CHAPTER VIII.

which there are certain records indicating that it is probably Government property. When the settlement of rights is complete, there is no doubt that this figure of 1,560 square kilometres (i.e. 660 plus 900) will be considerably increased, particularly as it includes land to be set aside for the communal use and development of the hill villages.

83. The following table shows to the nearest square kilometre the distribution of the 660 square kilometres of public lands in which the title has been settled under the Land (Settlement of Title) Ordinance :—

	Sq. kilometres
Railways, roads, wadis, rivers, etc.	112
Antiquity sites, forests allocated to the Forest Department and other public uses	93
Occupied by the Army	54
Occupied by Arabs on old tenancies	89
Leased to Arabs	25
Leased to Jews	95
Leased to others	3
Unoccupied rocky and marshy land	132
Unoccupied sandy land	33
Unoccupied arable land	24

Out of the figure of 24 square kilometres under the heading "unoccupied arable land", some is being disposed of by lease, and a good deal of it is hill village land awaiting development under special development schemes. A large part of the figure of 132 square kilometres of rocky and marshy land consists of hill-sides in the Beisan and Nablus sub-Districts and some of this is now the subject of study in connection with development schemes.

84. The 900 square kilometres of "unsettled" public land includes some 220 square kilometres of land occupied on lease, written or implied, 100 square kilometres of it to Jews and the rest to Arabs, the latter mostly tenants on *jiftlik* land; 600 square kilometres are allotted to Government departments, mostly for afforestation, and to the Army; the remaining 80 square kilometres consists mostly of the Jordan valley lands south of Jericho.

Chapter VIII.

Section 6.

STATE DOMAIN FOR THE RE-SETTLEMENT OF JEWISH EX-SERVICEMEN.

85. In May, 1944, the Jewish Agency put forward a request to Government that State Domain should be made available for the establishment of new agricultural settlements for demobilised soldiers. This request was considered by the High Commissioner, Sir Harold MacMichael, who decided that no Government support should be afforded to any scheme for the agricultural settlement of demobilised Jewish soldiers on land in zones A and B of the Land Transfers Regulations, 1940, (see section 7 of this chapter), unless such land was already in Jewish possession or was so situated that its transfer to Jewish possession would not infringe the principles of those regulations. It was agreed, however, that, if the Jewish Agency could show that any State Domain elsewhere could be used effectively for the settlement of Jewish demobilised soldiers, it should, if possible, be made available for that purpose. It was also decided that, as regards housing schemes, Government should do all in its power to make State Domain in the "free" zone of the Land Transfers Regulations available for any such schemes as were recommended by the Reconstruction Commissioner. Furthermore, it was decided that should it be that State Domain exceptionally suitable for housing schemes was not situated in the "free" zone, for example near Tel Aviv, Government would be justified in allotting such State Domain for a housing scheme even though situated in zone A.

86. These decisions were conveyed to the Jewish Agency in October, 1944, and at the same time a complete list of land in the "free" zone to which Government had a registered title was sent to them. A copy of this list was returned to Government by the Agency in November, 1944 after the Agency had marked thereon the properties which they considered might be suitable for the settlement of ex-soldiers. The total area of these properties amounted to some 42,500 dunums. A committee was thereupon appointed and charged with the detailed inspection of these properties and the duty of reporting as to their availability and suitability for the purpose in mind. A representative of the Director of Land Settlement was chairman of this committee and the members were representatives of the Departments of Agriculture and Forests and of the District Commissioner of the District in which the various parcels of land were situated. In the course of inspection of the lands the committee was accompanied by four representatives of the Jewish Agency's staff who pointed out the bound-

CHAPTER VIII.

aries of the land the Agency desired to have and explained the purposes for which the land was intended. The committee submitted their report in October, 1945. This report indicated that there is very little State Domain in the "free" zone which has not already been leased on long term and which can be made available immediately for the settlement of Jewish ex-servicemen. In the result it appears that the lands which it may be possible to offer the Jewish Agency are limited to certain areas in the Tulkarm sub-District, none of which exceeds a few hundred dunums in extent, and an area of about 6,000 dunums of sand dunes in Yibna village, Jaffa sub-District. The practicability of making these areas available is still under consideration.

Section 7.

THE LAND TRANSFERS REGULATIONS, 1940.

(a) The method of administration.

87. In paragraph 16 of the White Paper of May, 1939, it was stated that "the Administration of Palestine is required, under Article 6 of the Mandate, "while ensuring that the rights and position of other sections of the population are not prejudiced", to encourage "close settlement by Jews on the land......" and that the "reports of several expert Commissions have indicated that, owing to the natural growth of the Arab population and the steady sale in recent years of Arab land to Jews, there is now in certain areas no room for further transfers of Arab land, whilst in some other areas such transfers of land must be restricted if Arab cultivators are to maintain their existing standard of life and a considerable landless Arab population is not soon to be created". It was determined that "in these circumstances, the High Commissioner will be given general powers to prohibit and regulate transfers of land".

88. Under the Palestine (Amendment) Order-in-Council of 25th May, 1939 *, a new Article conferred on the High Commissioner these general powers. This Article reads as follows :

> "16D—(1) The High Commissioner may make regulations prohibiting, restricting or regulating transfers of land in Palestine or in any part thereof.
>
> (2) Without prejudice to the generality of the provisions of the foregoing paragraph, it is hereby declared that any such regulations may —

---

* Laws of 1939, Vol. II, page 459.

CHAPTER VIII.

(*a*) be made applicable only to transfers of land from Arabs to Jews or to other persons not being Arabs; or from Jews to Arabs or to other persons not being Jews; or from Arabs or Jews to any bodies of persons corporate or unincorporate;

(*b*) invalidate, or otherwise determine the effect of, any transfers made in contravention of the provisions of the regulations; and

(*c*) prescribe penalties for breach of the regulations.

(3) Regulations under this Article may provide that they shall take effect as from any date not being earlier than the 18th day of May, 1939.

(4) In this Article —
"land" includes water, buildings, trees and any interest in, or right in, to or over, land, water, buildings or trees.
"transfers" includes leases, mortgages, charges and other dispositions."

89. By the Land Transfers Regulations *, passed in February, 1940, to give effect to the policy mentioned in paragraph 87 above, the country was divided into three zones as follows :—

ZONE 'A', in which the transfer of land save to a Palestinian Arab is prohibited, except in case of a transfer made in execution of a judgment or order in satisfaction of a mortgage executed and registered before the 18th May, 1939, or delivered or made before the 28th February, 1940, or, with the High Commissioner's permission, for the purpose of consolidating holdings or of effecting the parcellation of *masha'a* or in cases where the land already belongs to a person who is not a Palestinian Arab and in certain other circumstances.

ZONE 'B', in which the transfer of land by a Palestinian Arab save to a Palestinian Arab is prohibited, except in the case of a transfer made in execution of a judgment or order in satisfaction of a mortgage executed and registered before the 18th May, 1939, or delivered or made before the 28th February, 1940, or with the specific approval of the High Commissioner which the High Commissioner may in his unfettered discretion grant or refuse.

"FREE" ZONE, in which no restriction is imposed.

90. For a precise demarcation of the three zones, attention is invited to the Schedule to the Regulations and to the relevant map. The areas of the three zones are approximately as follows:

Zone 'A':	16,680	square kilometres
Zone 'B':	8,348	" "
"Free" zone:	1,292	" "
Total	26,320	

* Laws of 1940, Vol. II, page 327.

CHAPTER VIII.

Broadly, zone 'A' includes the hill country as a whole, together with certain areas in the Jaffa sub-District and in the Gaza District including the northern part of Beersheba sub-District; it is in this zone that transfers to persons other than Palestinian Arabs is prohibited, save in exceptional circumstances for which provision is made under the Regulations. Zone 'B' includes the plains of Esdraelon and Jezreel; eastern Galilee; a stretch of the coastal plain south of Haifa; an area in the north-east of the Gaza District; and the southern part of the Beersheba sub-District. Transfers in zone 'B' are permitted subject to certain conditions announced when the Regulations were promulgated. These were that transfers by a Palestinian Arab to a person other than a Palestinian Arab would not ordinarily be granted unless the transfer could be shown to be either :

(i) for the purpose of consolidating, extending, or facilitating the irrigation of, holdings already in the possession of the transferee or of his community, the land to be transferred being contiguous to such holdings; or

(ii) for the purpose of enabling land held in undivided shares by the transferor and the transferee to be parcellated; or

(iii) the furtherance of some special scheme of development in the joint interests of both Arabs and Jews to which Government may have signified its approval.

The "free" zone includes the Haifa Bay area; the greater part of the coastal plain; an area south of Jaffa, the Jerusalem town planning area, and all municipal areas.

91. Applications for permission to effect transfers of land in zones 'A' and 'B' are submitted through the District Commissioner of the District in which the land is situated. The District Commissioner checks the particulars and, where the transfer purports to fulfil a condition stipulated in the Regulations or in the announcement regarding zone 'B', reviews the circumstances supporting this claim. He then makes his recommendation as to the advice to be proffered to the High Commissioner. Before the application is laid before the High Commissioner it is referred to a supervisory committee consisting of the Financial Secretary and the Director of Land Registration by whom it is scrutinized, with such assistance as may be required from the law officers, to ascertain if it is factually and legally in order and whether it satisfies the requirements of the Regulations. The committee advises whether the recommendations of the District Commissioner should be accepted or otherwise. The application is then submitted to the High Commissioner with these data and such other as may be added in the

CHAPTER VIII.

Chief Secretary's office and the High Commissioner records his decision.

(b) Statistics of applications made for transfer under the Regulations.

92. Since the inception of the Land Transfers Regulations in February, 1940, transfers of land from Arabs to non-Arabs have been approved by the High Commissioner in the total areas stated below. The figures are given in years calculated from February to February.

Zone	1940—41	1941—42	1942—43	1943—44	1944—45	1945—46 1st half	Total
	Dunums	Dunums	Dunums	Dunums	Dunums	Dunums	Dunums
A	318	333	890	600	215	158	2,514
B	4,494	5,860	293	45	34	151	10,877

The following land transfers have been registered in the Land Registries since February, 1941: they include the transfers approved by the High Commissioner under the Land Transfers Regulations as well as those completed through the processes of the courts:

Zone	1941—42	1942—43	1943—44	1944—45	1945—46 1st half
	Dunums	Dunums	Dunums	Dunums	Dunums
A	5,641	8,539	7,868	790	832
B	710	729	334	884	Nil

The discrepancy between the two tables is due to two factors:

(i) Certain transactions through processes of the courts are not affected by the Land Transfers Regulations, *vide* paragraph 89 above.

(ii) All transfers approved are not necessarily completed in the Land Registries.

93. Dealing first with zone A. the zone in which transfers by Arabs to non-Arabs are in general prohibited, an analysis of the applications received shows that of the 2,514 dunums of land for the transfer of which approval was granted —

(a) **946** dunums represented exchanges of properties and so resulted in no decrease in the gross area of land in Arab hands. These land exchanges are effected on a dunum for dunum

CHAPTER VIII.

basis and are designed to consolidate the land holdings of both Arabs and Jews.

(b) Transactions involving the transfer by way of sale of **924** dunums were approved on the ground that such transfers were necessary for the consolidation of existing Jewish holdings. In these cases the transfer of land by way of exchange on a dunum for dunum basis was impracticable.

(c) Permission was given to transfer **604** dunums of land relating to transactions which had been initiated *bona fide* in the Land Registries prior to the publication of the Regulations.

(d) Under clause (b) of the first proviso to Regulation 3, a total of **40** dunums were transferred to a cemetery board for the construction of a new cemetery for Jerusalem and to the Latin Patriarchate for the purpose of building a church, a convent, a boys' school, etc., in Jerusalem and Ramle.

94. Coming now to zone B, in which transfers from Arabs to non-Arabs are restricted, the analysis shows that of the 10,877 dunums of land for the transfer of which approval was granted —

(a) **1,430** dunums represented exchanges of properties and so resulted in no decrease in the gross area of land in Arab hands.

(b) Transactions involving the transfer by way of sale of **3,101** dunums were approved on the ground that such transfers were necessary for the consolidation of existing Jewish holdings.

(c) Permission was given to transfer **6,346** dunums of land relating to transactions which had been initiated *bona fide* in the Land Registries prior to the publication of the Regulations.

95. The following statement sets out the areas covered by applications made for the transfer of land under the Land Transfers Regulations which have been rejected by the High Commissioner since February, 1940, the date of the promulgation of these Regulations.

Zone	1940—41	1941—42	1942—43	1943—44	1944—45	1945—46 1st half	Total
	Dunums	Dunums	Dunums	Dunums	Dunums	Dunums	Dunums
A	5,255	321	5,885	949	204	80	12,694
B	—	364	10,592	11,394	9	5,685	28,044

96. Of the 12,694 dunums of land in zone A for the transfer of which approval was withheld—

CHAPTER VIII.

(a) 595 dunums related to State Domain lands. In this connection reference is invited to section (c) below;

(b) 12,081 dunums of land related to proposed transfers which could not be justified on any of the grounds mentioned in the Regulations, and

(c) an application to transfer 18 dunums of land by way of sale was rejected. It was, in this case, considered more feasible and in the spirit of the Regulations to effect the transfer by means of an exchange of land on a dunum for dunum basis.

97. In zone B, where transfers from Arabs to non-Arabs are restricted, all applications were rejected, as their approval could not be justified on any of the grounds mentioned in the explanatory statement which accompanied the publication of the Regulations (for the terms of which see paragraph 90 above). In one case, a proposed transfer involving a plot of land measuring 7 dunums, the refusal was based on the ground that the transfer ought properly to be effected by way of an exchange of land, not by sale.

98. Finally, the following transfers of land from Arab to Jewish interests have occurred in the "free" zone, where land purchases by Jews from Arabs are under no restriction—

1940—41	1941—42	1942—43	1943—44	1944—45	1945—46 1st half	TOTAL
Dunums	Dunums	Dunums	Dunums	Dunums	Dunums	Dunums
6,303	11,464	7,604	9,085	6,707	3,858	45,021

(c) **Application of the Regulations to State Domain.**

99. It was provided in regulation 8(b) of the Land Transfers Regulations that nothing in the Regulations shall be deemed "to apply to the transfer of any public land by or on behalf of the High Commissioner.................. in accordance with any law or Ordinance or otherwise".

100. The Jewish Agency has always considered that State Domain was specifically, and presumably with intent, excluded by regulation 8(b) from the operation of the Land Transfers Regulations and that, therefore, State Domain in zones A and B should be made available for the "close settlement by Jews on the land". This contention rests, however, upon a misinterpretation of the reasons underlying regulation 8(b). That regulation was inserted as an afterthought, because it was felt that, in its absence, Govment's hands might be unduly tied when dealing with special cases where no conflict of principle was involved. The particular

CHAPTER VIII.

case which gave rise to its insertion was that of Palestine Potash Limited : it was considered that in the absence of some such provision Government would be statutorily prevented from assigning State Domain in the Jordan valley for an extension of the potash works which was considered as likely to be necessary in the near future. But it was never intended that the general principles to be observed in the disposal of State Domain should be different from those governing the alienation of Arab land. As pointed out in paragraph 16 of the White Paper, quoted in paragraph 87 above, the reasons for the promulgation of the Regulations was the fact that there was already serious congestion in the Arab areas and that the Arab population was increasing at such a rate that it became double in the course of twenty-seven years. It was with a view to preventing, so far as possible, the further deterioration of Arab standards of living and the creation of a large landless Arab population that the alienation of further land to Jews in certain parts of Palestine was restricted. It appeared to the Palestine Government to be immaterial, in so far as the principles of the Regulations were concerned, whether the land in these restricted areas was State Domain or was owned by Arabs.

101. In view of the above considerations, the then High Commissioner, Sir Harold MacMichael, with the concurrence of the Executive Council, decided, early in 1941, that the power of transfer of public lands under regulation 8(b) would ordinarily only be exercised in cases in which the transfer would be permitted if it were from an Arab to a non-Arab. This decision was conveyed to the Jewish Agency in February, 1941.

102. In May, 1944, the Jewish Agency made enquiries as to the availability of State Domain for the establishment of new agricultural settlements for demobilized Jewish soldiers. This led to reconsideration, in June, 1944, by the High Commissioner in Executive Council of the question of the application of the Land Transfers Regulations to State Domain and it was decided that, with slight modification, the policy previously communicated to the Jewish Agency, i.e. that all transfers of State Domain must be considered in the light of the principles contained in those Regulations, should be adhered to. The modification was concerned with State Domain exceptionally suited for Jewish housing schemes situated in the restricted zones, for example near Tel Aviv; in such case it was agreed that Government would be justified in allotting such State Domain for a housing scheme.

103. In November, 1944, the Jewish Agency once more raised this general point of policy, again in connection with the resettlement of Jewish ex-servicemen. This led to consideration of

CHAPTER VIII.

the question *de novo* by Field-Marshal Lord Gort who, with the concurrence of the Executive Council, reached the conclusion that State Domain in zones A and B should not be made available for the agricultural settlement of Jewish ex-servicemen. This decision was yet again contested by the Jewish Agency in July, 1945, in an interview with the Officer Administering the Government, who subsequently informed them that it was not possible to modify the decision reached by Lord Gort.

104. The question of the availability of State Domain has been examined by Government in some detail and it has been shown that, although there are large areas of State Domain, it cannot be assumed that Government is in possession of extensive tracts of land which are lying idle. In fact, in respect both of land to which Government has a settled title and land claimed by Government as State Domain but still subject to settlement of title, there is very little that is not already put to some useful purpose. This fact is made clear by the following analysis of State Domain made at the end of 1943 :—

	Title settled*	Title not yet settled**
	dunums	dunums
(i) Lands used for public purposes, e.g. forests, railways, roads, etc.	219,695	619,858
(ii) Lands occupied under tenures deriving from the Ottoman regime	105,340	76,851
(iii) Leased to Jews for long periods	75,273	99,815
(iv) Leased to Jews for terms of less than 3 years	2,889	48
(v) Leased to Arabs for long periods	793	429
(vi) Leased to Arabs for terms of less than 3 years	17,591	44,931
(vii) Leased to others than Arabs or Jews	2,656	598
(viii) Earmarked for communal or public use	4,713	—
(ix) Uncultivable sand, marsh or rocks	167,429	—
(x) Unoccupied, including "paper" claims	—	84,699
(xi) Available for and offered on short term lease	20,082	—
	615,961	926,719

---

* i.e. registered in the name of the High Commissioner after land settlement of title.

** i.e. areas believed to be public land but which have not yet been registered after land settlement of title or have not yet come under land settlement.

CHAPTER VIII.

It will be seen from a comparison of items (iii) and (iv) with items (v) and (vi) that the Jews have a substantial advantage over the Arabs in the matter of leases of State Domain which was at the free disposal of Government. The occupiers of Government land under item (ii) are Arabs; their right to occupation derives from the Ottoman regime and has never been seriously in dispute; the figure of 105,340 dunums covers lands, such as the sandy wastes of Rafah, which, although within the areas of Arab occupation, include considerable patches of land at present uncultivable. Even taking the areas under item (ii) into account, however, the position, on the proportions of each community to the total population, is in favour of the Jews. The figure of 619,858 dunums under item (i) includes forest reserves and consequently may include land which is claimed by private persons and which at land settlement may be found not to belong to Government. Item (x) contains an assortment of claims not yet verified even as to area and locality; they derive from various vague Turkish registrations or old records left by the Turks. Item (ix) may appear to be a subject for experimental development, but if it had been possible to transform anything from this item to item (xi) that would have been done for revenue purposes. The figure of 167,429 includes 105,000 dunums of marshy or rocky land surveyed during the operations of the Ghor Mudawwara commission; some of this may be allocated for afforestation or grazing and some may in due course become the subject of development leases and, in the case of the Beisan lands, of schemes for the consolidation of holdings. The remainder is rocky land in the Nazareth and Ramle sub-districts or sand-dunes in the Gaza area. The figure of 20,082 dunums given in item (xi) represents the total area of lands which it was thought on 31st December, 1943 could be made available for lease; some of these lands have subsequently been leased, some offered for lease, while others are waiting treatment under development schemes; some are occupied on "implied" leases.

(d) Evasion of the Regulations.

105. In March, 1943 a number of allegations were made in the the press and elsewhere to the effect that the Land Transfers Regulations were being evaded, particularly in connection with transactions in the Gaza District. These allegations were investigated by the Committee on Land Transfers (whose Chairman at that time was Sir Douglas Harris) and that committee reported in May, 1943, that, as a result of their investigations, the following could be shown :—

CHAPTER VIII.

(a) That in one case advantage had been taken of a loophole in the Regulations in order to secure the transfer of Arab land in zone A to the Jewish National Fund. This loophole lies in the third proviso to regulation 3 which excludes from the ambit of the legislation transfers of land in satisfaction of a mortgage executed before the date of the White Paper or of a judgment of a court delivered before the date of the Regulations. In the case investigated it was shown that, although the Arab judgment debtor had been declared a debtor before the date of the Regulations, he had at that time been landless and had acquired land subsequently, long after the date of the Regulations; the land was then sold in execution of the judgment and bought by the Jewish National Fund. The proviso to the Regulations was never intended to cover land acquired by the judgment debtor subsequent to the date of the judgment; the failure to state this in the proviso constituted the loophole. No other similar case of evasion could be traced at that time. The committee stated that it would be easy to put a stop to transactions of this nature by an amendment to the Regulations but that, as it had been consistently held that it is undesirable to amend the Regulations unless and until loopholes are discovered so serious as to render this course essential, the committee did not consider that the single case cited established such essentiality.

(b) That in another case action by the Execution Officer in Tel Aviv resulted in the transfer from Arabs to Jews of a much larger area of Arab land in zone A than seemed to have been justified on the merits of the case. In this case a judgment was delivered in 1938 against an Arab of Gaza in favour of another Arab in the sum of £P.150. In 1941, upon application to the Execution Officer, an area of 624 dunums belonging to the judgment debtor was put to auction in satisfaction of this debt. The land was bought at this auction by the Jewish National Fund for £P.2,900.

(c) That in general, the extent to which evasions had taken place had been greatly exaggerated.

106. The considerations noticed under (b) above were brought to the attention of the Judiciary.

107. Following a question by Mr. Astor in the House of Commons in October, 1943, in which it was alleged that the Regulations were being evaded by the use of mortgage and foreclosure, a despatch was sent by the High Commissioner to the Secretary of State in December, 1943, forwarding the report of

CHAPTER VIII.

the Land Transfers Committee. Sir Harold MacMichael stated in that despatch that on the whole he was "satisfied that the Regulations, which are under constant scrutiny, are working well and call for no immediate tightening".

108. Allegations of evasion continued to be made by Arabs and, in March, 1945, a general political agitation for a tightening up of the Regulations was begun. Allegations of infringements were frequently made by the Arab press and publicly by Arab political leaders. The agitation led to pillory of Arab land brokers, one of whom was murdered in the streets of Jaffa. The Gaza area was again the principal field for accusations. The Arab leaders contented themselves in the main with vague accusations of a general nature that Government was doing nothing to prevent the evasions and at times even went so far as to hint that Government was conniving at them; they failed to quote specific cases of circumvention of the Regulations.

109. On the 14th April, 1945, Field Marshal Lord Gort gave an interview to five Arab leaders headed by Ahmad Hilmi Pasha (the chairman of the Umma Fund, an organisation established a few years ago as an Arab counterpart of the Jewish National Fund, for the collection of money for the purchase of land). The Arab leaders protested against alleged evasion of the Regulations, described in general terms the methods employed and suggested certain remedies. The High Commissioner assured the delegation that their proposals would receive careful examination. Lord Gort was of opinion, however, that Government should not be rushed into amendment of the law without being satisfied that there were real abuses on a substantial scale. He therefore decided to appoint an investigatory committee to go thoroughly into the allegations made. A committee was appointed accordingly on 2nd June, 1945, under the chairmanship of Mr. R. E. H. Crosbie, C.M.G., O.B.E., formerly a District Commissioner and now Chairman of the War Economic Advisory Committee. The committee contained only official members, of whom one was an Arab District Officer and another a Jewish District Officer. Their terms of reference were as follows :—

(i) To collate allegations made by members of the public in regard to transactions said to be in contravention of the Land Transfers Regulations, to investigate these transactions and to advise whether there have in fact been contraventions of the Regulations.

(ii) If there have in fact been contraventions, to report on the methods employed in contravention of the Regulations.

CHAPTER VIII.

(iii) To review the administration of the Land Transfers Regulations and to make recommendations in regard to any modifications which in the view of the committee would be likely to implement the purpose of the Regulations.

110. The committee submitted their report on 28th November, 1945. They stated that they had found no evidence of contraventions of the Regulations, but that there was evidence of their evasion. These evasions arose from :—

(a) the loophole in the third proviso to Regulation 3 (and the corresponding proviso to Regulation (4) to which reference is made in paragraph 105 (a) above; this relates to the free transfer of land made in execution of any judgment or order of a court, chief execution officer or land settlement officer in satisfaction of a mortgage executed and registered before 18th May, 1939, or delivered or made before 28th February, 1940;

(b) the procedure in the Execution Office under which, if adequate supervision is not exercised, an excessive area may be sold in satisfaction of a judgment or order; and

(c) the present procedure of land settlement under which full title to land may be obtained contrary to the intentions of the Regulations.

The committee recommended, in regard to (a), that the loophole should be stopped by amendment of the Regulations, in regard to (b), that the Chief Execution Officer should himself supervise any transfer to persons other than Palestinian Arabs of land situated in a restricted area and, in regard to (c), that steps should be taken by legislation to ensure that no prescriptive, equitable or possessory right to land should be given where legal right is debarred by the Regulations.

The committee also considered certain allegations that the spirit of the Regulations is being violated (1) through the practice of registration in the name of an Arab nominee of land purchased on behalf of Jews and usually occupied by them and (2) by purchase and possession of land by Jews without title. The committee were of opinion that the remedies for such violations of the spirit of the Regulations lie in the hands of the Arabs themselves; that it would be impracticable for Government to take steps which would prevent the use of Arab nominees; and that, since the Land Transfers Regulations are concerned only with title to land, questions of mere possession without title were outside their terms of reference.

111. The report of the committee is now under the consideration of Government.

Chapter VIII.

Section 8.

ADMINISTRATIVE PROBLEMS IN REGARD TO LAND HOLDINGS.

(a) Subsistence areas.

112. No question regarding the economic development of Palestine has been the subject of greater debate than that in regard to the determination of subsistence areas. The obvious importance of this question not only in relation to the resolution of the problem of absorptive capacity where immigration is concerned but also to the ability of the population to support a reasonable standard of existence has necessitated its study by successive commissions but no conclusions accepted as basic by all parties concerned have been formulated. As will be evident, the extent of the area required varies according to region, climate and availability of water and to the method of farming and standard of living assumed. There has been almost as great a divergence of opinion in regard to the total area of cultivable land in Palestine. This question is discussed in relation to particular areas and the possibility of extending irrigation in section 2 of chapter X. The Royal Commission, having examined a variety of opinions on the matter, recorded the view that "no really satisfactory definition in advance can be found on which it would be safe to base an estimate of the cultivable area. This must, we consider, and we hold this view also as regards the *lot viable* of the cultivator, be discovered by experience, by a system of 'trial and error' in the different parts of the country. But we consider that, until the contrary is proved by experience and practical experiment, the Administration will be wise in adhering to their own definition in so far as it relates to an increase of immigrants on the land". (Report, chapter IX, para. 53). The definition of "cultivable land" to which the Royal Commission referred is land which is already under cultivation, or which can be brought under cultivation by the application of the labour and resources of the average Palestinian cultivator.

113. Sir John Hope Simpson, who reported in 1930, quoted a number of opinions on the question of the *lot viable**. These may be summarised as follows :—

(a) Shaw Commission : "From evidence given before us it would appear that where the land is used for the purpose of

---

* Report on Immigration, Land Settlement and Development by Sir John Hope Simpson, C.I.E., pages 60—73.

CHAPTER VIII.

growing cereals the area which will provide a living for an Arab family varies from 100 to 150 dunums. No other figures were put forward from the Arab side, but Dr. Ruppin informed us that "the average area of a Jewish colonist in the old wheat growing colonies in lower Galilee is 250 dunums, in the Zionist settlement in the plain of Esdraelon with dairy farming it is 100 dunums, and in the coastal plain, where orange growing is the principal occupation, it is from ten to twenty dunums.

From the figures given by the experts who were appointed by the Joint Survey Commission and who visited Palestine in 1928, it would seem that the average Jewish holding of land in the Zionist colonies is to-day 130 dunums. These gentlemen found that few of the Jewish colonists were able to make a satisfactory living on their present holding. The experts were of opinion that in many districts the area of the average holding should be increased and we gather from their reports that, in their view, the area required varies from 160 dunums per family in good soil suitable for dairy farming to 320 dunums in the less productive of the cereal growing districts".

(b) "Key for the Settlement of Various Zones in Palestine". Ameliorated colonies on non-irrigated heavy soil, 200 to 250 dunums; improved farm of fixed system on a basis of dairying, 130 dunums; farm in process of improvement for reception of settlers, 140 to 150 dunums; heavy soil farm, entirely irrigated to support 8 cows, 25 dunums; farm in dry grain section with 10 dunums irrigated and four cows, 80 dunums.

(c) General Federation of Jewish Labour in respect of the grant of land for the settlement of Jewish ex-servicemen, 200 dunums for each settler. Mr. Ben Zvi, for the Federation, pointed out that the P.I.C.A. allowed 250 dunums for each family and that 200 dunums was the minimum that would suffice and this basis was accepted.

(d) Memorandum on "Land and Agricultural Development" by the Jewish Agency. The *lot viable* in the Emek, 100 to 150 dunums. Where water is available, the area can be reduced at the ratio of one dunum of irrigated soil to four or five dunums of dry soil. In the maritime plain irrigated areas suitable for oranges can be settled on the basis of one family to 15 dunums; if only partly suitable for oranges, one family to 22 dunums. In the Huleh area, 25 dunums of irrigated heavy soil or 22 dunums of irrigated soil. On the Beisan and Samakh lands an area of 86 dunums of unirrigated and 14 dunums of irrigated land is recommended.

CHAPTER VIII.

(e) Investigation of conditions at Bir Zeit (Jerusalem District). Of the cultivation, 27.4 per cent. consisted of olive groves, 8.2 per cent. of figs and other fruit trees, 17.8 per cent. of vines and 46.6 per cent. of cereals. The *lot viable* was 112 dunums and there were 115 families (out of a total of 180) in excess of the number which the village could actually support. The average indebtedness was about £P.39 per family.

114. Sir John Hope Simpson accordingly concluded that on unirrigated land the *lot viable* is not less than 130 dunums, unless command of considerable capital enabled the tenant to maintain a dairy herd of foreign or cross-bred animals, in which case in the richer tracts, the holding may possibly, but questionably, be reduced to 100 dunums. Where irrigation is available and where dairying is possible, the holding may be reduced to 40 dunums of which half is irrigable. Where plantations are established the *lot viable*, at the then current prices of oranges and bananas, might be placed at 15 to 20 dunums.

115. A number of schemes for improved mixed farms were analysed in "Planned Mixed Farming" by Professor Elazari-Volcani of the Jewish Agency Agricultural Research Station (1938). The sizes of farms contemplated were consolidated holdings of between 35 dunums irrigated and 50 dunums, the latter either irrigated by rotation or including 10 dunums of irrigated land. The estimated cash surplus was between £P.76 and £P.10 for the family.

116. In 1938, for the purposes of the Partition Commission, the Department of Agriculture calculated the area which might reasonably be regarded as a *lot viable* appropriate to each category of land as given in the Rural Property Tax Ordinance*. These areas were as set out on the next page.

The Partition Commission, while noting that lower estimates of a *lot viable* had in some cases been made, rejected the largely speculative assumptions on which the lower estimates had been founded and endorsed the Royal Commission's finding as recorded above "that, until the contrary is proved by experience and practical experiment, the Administration will be wise in adhering to their own definition" (Report of the Partition Commission, chapter VIII, para. 143).

---

* See section 4 of this chapter.

CHAPTER VIII.

Category	Description	Lot viable dunums
1	Citrus	10
3	Bananas	10
5	1st grade irrigated land and 1st grade fruit plantation	50
6	2nd grade irrigated land and 2nd grade fruit plantation	57
7	3rd grade irrigated land and 3rd grade fruit plantation	67
8	1st grade ground crop land, 4th grade irrigated land and 4th grade fruit plantation	80
9	2nd grade ground crop land, 5th grade irrigated land and 5th grade fruit plantation	100
10	3rd grade ground crop land, 6th grade irrigated land and 6th grade fruit plantation	111
11	4th grade ground crop land, 7th grade irrigated land and 7th grade fruit plantation	133
12	5th grade ground crop land, 8th grade irrigated land and 8th grade fruit plantation	167
13	6th grade ground crop land, 9th grade irrigated land and 9th grade fruit plantation	250
14	7th grade ground crop land (untaxable), 10th grade irrigated land	400
15	8th grade crop land (untaxable)	400
16	Uncultivable land	400

117. There are two factors of fundamental importance in the estimation of the *lot viable* neither of which have previously been investigated. These two factors relate to (1) the extent of fragmentation of holdings and farms and (2) the co-ownership in parcels of land. Throughout the Arab rural areas of Palestine extensive farming is the rule. One of the principal reasons for this extravagant use of the land in a country where land is scarce lies in the fragmentation of the holdings and co-ownership in the parcels. It is rarely that one encounters a family holding which consists of one continuous tract. In most cases a holding is composed of a number of scattered fragments or shares in various parcels.

118. A study carried out by the Department of Statistics in five typical cereal-growing villages revealed the prevalence of fragmentation and co-ownership over an area of approximately 25,000 dunums. The results are shown in the four following tables.

CHAPTER VIII.

Table 1.

FRAGMENTATION OF HOLDINGS OF RESIDENTS OF FIVE VILLAGES.

Gross size of holding (dunums)	No. of holdings composed of the following number of fragments						Total No. of holdings	Total No. of fragments	Area (dunums)	Number of fragments per holding	
	1—2	3—6	7—10	11—14	15—18	19+				Mean	Median
—5	90	4	5	3	2	—	104	241	282	2.3	1.0
6—10	41	27	5	14	2	—	89	416	687	4.7	3.0
11—20	30	60	22	11	21	5	149	1,051	2,208	7.1	5.0
21—40	9	50	22	36	14	30	161	1,880	4,738	11.7	10.0
41—60	1	12	24	23	10	7	77	920	3,861	11.9	11.0
61—80	1	5	6	11	9	12	44	674	3,045	15.3	13.5
81—120	—	4	10	13	9	5	41	553	4,214	13.5	13.0
121+	—	2	5	3	4	11	25	448	5,749	17.9	16.0
Total	172	164	99	114	71	70	690	6,183	24,784	9.0	9.0

Table 2.

FRAGMENTATION OF FAMILY HOLDINGS OF RESIDENTS OF FIVE VILLAGES.

Gross size of family holdings (dunums)	No. of family holdings composed of the following number of fragments						Total No. of family holdings	Total No. of fragments	Area (dunums)	Number of fragments per family holding	
	1—2	3—6	7—10	11—14	15—18	19+				Mean	Median
— 5	35	2	—	—	—	—	37	48	91	1.3	—
6— 10	16	11	1	—	—	—	28	79	229	2.8	—
11— 20	11	33	8	4	—	—	56	269	866	4.8	—
21— 40	4	37	18	17	5	8	89	820	2,718	9.2	—
41— 60	1	12	23	15	3	2	56	537	2,782	9.6	—
61— 80	1	2	7	13	7	13	43	682	2,985	15.9	—
81— 120	—	3	16	12	17	11	59	867	6,120	14.7	—
121+	—	1	7	10	5	20	43	803	8,993	18.7	—
Total	68	101	80	71	37	54	411	4,105	24,784	10.0	—

CHAPTER VIII.

Table 3.

FRAGMENTATION OF FARMS OF RESIDENTS OF FIVE VILLAGES.

Gross size of farm (dunums)	No. of farms composed of the following number of fragments						Total No. of farms	Total No. of fragments	Area (dunums)	Number of fragments per farm	
	1—2	3—6	7—10	11—14	15—18	19+				Mean	Median
— 5	40	7	3	—	—	—	50	106	115	2.1	—
6— 10	12	18	3	—	—	—	33	115	270	3.5	—
11— 20	9	21	7	1	—	—	38	173	563	4.6	—
21— 40	3	29	20	11	1	4	68	567	2,122	8.3	—
41— 60	1	15	19	9	3	3	50	467	2,483	9.3	—
61— 80	—	3	13	14	5	8	43	585	2,948	13.6	—
81—120	1	4	12	13	14	8	52	748	5,235	14.4	—
121+	—	4	17	12	6	30	69	1,402	13,380	20.3	—
Total	66	101	94	60	29	53	403	4,163	27,116	10.3	—

Table 4.

AVERAGE NUMBER OF CO-OWNERS PER PARCEL AND AVERAGE "FRACTIONAL SHARES"*.

Type of averages	Village					Total	
	A	B	C	D	E	Four villages A—D	Five villages A—E
1. Unweighted mean number of co-owners per parcel	3.3	2.9	1.7	3.5	2.2	3.0	2.7
2. Weighted mean number of co-owners per parcel	5.5	4.0	2.0	4.6	3.1	4.0	3.8
3. Unweighted mean "fractional share"	0.30	0.34	0.58	0.29	0.34	0.45	0.37

119. It will be noted that the number of fragments into which an individual holding is divided increases as the size of the holding increases. Thus, holdings of 6 to 10 dunums are composed, on the average, of 5 fragments. Holdings of 21 to 40 dunums are composed of 12 fragments while holdings of 81 to 120 dunums are composed of as many as 14 fragments. The average for all sizes of holdings is 9 fragments. In the case of *family* holdings the average number of fragments in holdings of 6 to 10 dunums amounts to 3; holdings of 21 to 40 dunums are composed of 9 fragments while holdings of 81 to 120 dunums are composed of almost 15 fragments. The average for all family holdings is 10 fragments. In the case of farms (i.e. areas operated by a family regardless of ownership) the average number of fragments is 3.3 fragments in the case of farms of 6 to 10 dunums, 8 fragments in the case of farms of 21 to 40 dunums, 14 fragments in the

---

* The fractional share in a parcel is the simple proportion of a parcel which is held by one co-owner (e.g. one-half, one-fifth etc.).

CHAPTER VIII.

case of farms of 81 to 120 dunums, while the average for all farms is 10 fragments.

120. The evils of fragmentation are increased by the dispersion of fragments. The extent of this is indicated very clearly in a sketch of one of the villages studied which is published in the General Monthly Bulletin of Current Statistics for December, 1945. In this sketch the dispersion of the holdings of 3 selected owners are shown by means of symbols. In these circumstances the mode of cultivation which is imposed on the *fellah* involves an extravagant use of land. In the exploitation of his scattered holding he is excluded from the advantages of mechanization and irrigation (even if water is available) while his freedom to use his land for plantations is seriously restricted. The economic exploitation of each fragment of holding is further impaired where co-ownership exists. It will be seen from table 4 that the average number of co-owners per parcel is three. There is little doubt that the existence of co-ownership hinders the proper development and utilization of the land. The division of ownership tends to destroy the incentive to improve the land.

121. The abnormal supply situation produced by the war and uncertainty as to the economic basis of much recent development makes a re-computation of formulas impracticable at this stage. The crude estimates of the area constituting a *lot viable* in any given category of land can be used, however, only as an index of primary application in assessing the question of congestion. They are naturally subject to running adjustment according to the extent to which the keeping of livestock is associated with cultivation as primary or secondary source of income. They are also subject to adjustment in relation to the development in agricultural centres of means of supplementing agricultural production by the development of other activities — local industries, for example, or accommodation for the holiday traffic. In other words, the "trial and error" method of assessing either the *lot viable* or the cultivable area which was sponsored by the Royal Commission forms the only satisfactory basis for firm conclusions. The two matters are not in such relations as to bring about the condition that a substantial change in one necessarily means a corresponding change in the other and a consequential increase in the agricultural population. The question of markets is of course here of fundamental importance. As the Partition Commission wrote (chapter VIII, page 130): "There is one other matter . . . . . which is relevant to all irrigation and land development schemes whether in the Jordan Valley or elsewhere in Palestine. It is the question of markets for the crops produced. If the rate charged for the water is sufficiently low to permit of holdings being devoted

CHAPTER VIII.

entirely to the cultivation of cereals, the question of markets is not of fundamental importance. But if the rate renders such a holding unprofitable and requires the adoption of mixed farming, including the growing of more expensive crops such as vegetables and fruit, markets are of vital importance". Again, in relation to the further development of the Gaza sub-district, they wrote (chapter VIII, para. 151) : "Even, however, if water should be made available in sufficient quantities, the process of change in land utilization would at best be a slow one, and great caution would have to be exercised if the farmer is to be given a chance of success under the new conditions. In particular, before it is decided to grow deciduous fruits on a large scale, more experience is needed of their cultivation in Palestine, of the possibility of controlling certain serious insect pests, and of the availability of markets."

122. By way of providing hypothetical data on which the problem of the *lot viable* as it exists to-day can be judged the following fully detailed illustrations are given. An attempt is made to define the different types and sizes of farms which it is estimated an Arab family of two adults and three children could manage and cultivate without employing any permanent hired labour. The farmers would, however, use outside labour at peak periods of demand at harvesting, following a practice which is customary in many peasant communities. Wherever possible farmers would use modern implements on a co-operative basis, or would hire them, for such operations as ploughing, harvesting hay crops, spraying and threshing.

123. The conditions of topography, soils and climate in Palestine are so very diverse that it is impossible to describe a system of farming which would be suitable for more than limited areas of the country. The following three different types of terrain (as distinguished from holding), representative of conditions over a large part of the country, are described :—

(a) A non-irrigated consolidated farm in the hills of the Jerusalem or Ramallah sub-district. The total surface area 95 dunums (23¾ acres).

(b) A consolidated farm in Jenin sub-district where water for irrigation is not available. Area 135 dunums (33¾ acres).

(c) A consolidated farm on heavy land in the plains where limited facilities for irrigation are available. Area 87 dunums (21¾ acres) including 12 dunums under irrigation.

It is emphasised that the areas alloted to each type of farm are not the areas at present available. They are the areas which it

Chapter VIII.

is judged could be cultivated by Arab farmers of reasonable intelligence who make the maximum use of their abilities while employing modern and improved methods of husbandry.

124. During the war years prices of vegetables, fruits, eggs and other intensive products have been very much higher in relation to the prices of the products from extensive farming. Pre-war prices are a more satisfactory basis for estimating the value of production and they have been used throughout these calculations. The prices given for the various commodities are the average prices which it is estimated the farmer would have received for his produce at not more than 20 kilometres from his village. They do not take into account forced sales at glut prices or exceptionally high prices for out-of-season produce.

125. No exact figures are available to determine the costs of production. The figures which are given are estimates based on knowledge of local conditions and various sources of information. Estimates of cost of production are given in the "Report of a Committee on the Economic Condition of Agriculturists in Palestine and the Fiscal Measures of Government in relation thereto" published in 1930; it is certain that if maximum yields are to be obtained and larger areas of intensive crops included in the rotation then the figure of £P.22 for the annual costs of production on 100 dunums of land planted to field crops is too low. A more reasonable estimate for field crops giving maximum yields on land farmed in an improved manner would be £P.55.000 per 100 dunums. The cost of production on irrigated lands is very much higher and should be estimated at £P.4 per dunum. The estimated costs of production do not include the cost of family labour.

126. No estimates have been made of the cost or standard of living of a farmer. After deducting the costs of production a figure is given showing the net income to the farmer from agricultural operations. Out of this figure of net income the farmer has to pay for all the food and clothing for his family, his personal expenses and his rent and taxes. In each case the yields from plantations are given as the yields which are obtained from fully matured trees. The cost of establishing plantation crops and maintaining them until they reach maturity has not been included; this is a heavy item of capital expenditure and especially in the case of olives.

127. The following is a summary of the areas, gross incomes, expenditure and net incomes on the three different types of farms of which details are given in Schedules A, B and C.

CHAPTER VIII.

Type of farm	Surface area Dunums	Gross income £P. Mils	Expenditure £P. Mils	Net income £P. Mils
1. Hill areas of Jerusalem or Ramallah	95	177.050	76.650	100.400
2. Non-irrigated farm in Jenin sub-district	135	207.600	103.750	103.850
3. Farm in inland plain	87 *	260.935	154.750	106.185

Schedule 'A'.

FAMILY FARM IN THE HILLS OF RAMALLAH OR JERUSALEM SUB-DISTRICT.

Surface area = 95 dunums.

1. *Division of surface area of 95 dunums.* Dunums
   (a) Uncultivable stony ground and rocks.   15
   (b) Uncultivable stony ground and rocks used for housing site, buildings, fuel plantation, etc.   5
   (c) Plantation crops   30
   (d) Annual crops   45

   Total surface area   95 dunums

2. *Stock and poultry.*
   2 selected baladi cows and 1 calf.
   2 tethered Damascus goats and 1 kid.
   20 *baladi* hens.
   1 mule.
   10 beehives.

3. *Yields and gross annual income at pre-war prices from crops.*

PLANTATION CROPS.

Crop	Area in dunums	Total yield in kgs.	Value in mils per kg.	Gross value £P. Mils
Olives	10	2,860 fruit = 700 oil	— 40	— 28.000
Figs	10	3,350 fresh = 2,000 dried	— 9	— 18.000
Table grapes	5	2,500	5	12.500
Apricots	3	2,100	8	16.800
Almonds	2	160	50	8.000
Total	30	—	—	83.300

* 12 dunums irrigated.

Chapter VIII.

Annual Crops.

Crop	Area in dunums	Total yield in kgs.	Value in mils per kgs.	Gross value £P. Mils
Winter Cereals				
Wheat	10	600	9	5.400
Barley	5	400	4	1.600
Winter legumes and hay				
Lentils	5	200	9	1.800
Broad beans	5	200	9	1.800
Vetch and oats hay	10	2,500	3½	8.750
Vegetables and green fodder				
Tomatoes	5	4,000	4	16.000
Pumpkins (fodder)	5	5,000	3	15.000
Total	45	—	—	50.350
Tibben straw from wheat, barley and lentils	—	1.300	1	1.300
				51.650

4. *Costs of production.*

Plantation Crops.

The following are the estimated costs of production of the plantation crops exclusive of labour. The expenditure is mainly for the costs of fertilizers, insecticides, and implements. The cost of ploughing does not include wages :—

Crop	Area in dunums	Annual expenditure in mils per dunum	Total annual expenditure £P. Mils
Olives	10	200	2.000
Figs	10	200	2.000
Table grapes	5	1,500	7.500
Apricots	3	1,050	3.150
Almonds	2	500	1.000
Ploughing	—	300	10.000
Total	30	—	25.650

Annual Crops.

The estimated cost of production in relation to yield of annual crops is 450 mils per dunum. The total annual costs of production on 45 dunums = £P.20.250.

CHAPTER VIII.

The following items are included in the cost of production :—

(i) Share of working animal.
(ii) Food for working animal.
(iii) Seeds.
(iv) Fertilizers and manure.
(v) Hired labour for harvesting.
(vi) Transport of crop to village.
(vii) Threshing.
(viii) Depreciation of implements.
(ix) Depreciation on marketing boxes and bags.

5. *Gross income from stock and poultry.*

(a) *Cattle.*
2 selected *baladi* cattle will give 800 litres milk per annum each if they are not worked and are given fodder in addition to the natural and stubble grazing available. Yield of cows milk = 1,600 litres at 11 mils = £P.17.600.

(b) *Goats.*
2 Damascus goats will give 400 litres of milk per annum each. Yield of goats milk = 800 litres at 11 mils per litre = £P.8.800.

(c) *Poultry.*
20 *baladi* hens will lay 1,600 eggs valued at 2 mils each = £P.3.200.

(d) *Bees.*
10 beehives will give an average of 15 kgs. of honey per hive valued at 50 mils per kg. = £P.7.500.

(e) *Sale of surplus stock.*
The annual gross income from the sale of surplus cattle and goats and the increases in value of animals is estimated at £P.5 per annum.

(f) *Total gross income from stock and poultry.*

	£P.
Cattle	17.600
Goats	8.800
Poultry	3.200
Bees	7.500
Sales	5.000
£P.	42.100

CHAPTER VIII.

6. *Expenditure on stock and poultry.*

Annual cost of food exclusive of grazing :—

	£P.
Cattle	11.500
Goats	9.000
Calves and kids	3.000
Poultry	Nil
Miscellaneous expenses including depreciation on byres and dairy utensils, veterinary attention, etc.	4.000
Upkeep of beehives and cost of sugar	3.250
	30.750

7. *Net annual income from farming operations.*

Details	Gross income	Expenditure	Net income
	£P. Mils	£P. Mils	£P. Mils
Plantation crops	83.300	25.650	57.650
Annual crops	51.650	20.250	31.400
Stock and poultry	42.100	30.750	11.350
Total	177.050	76.650	100.400

Total net income = £P.100.400 mils.

Schedule 'B'.

NON IRRIGATED FAMILY FARM IN THE JENIN SUB-DISTRICT.

SURFACE AREA = 135 DUNUMS.

1. *Division of surface area of 135 dunums.* dunums
   (a) Site for house, buildings, fuel plantation, etc.   5
   (b) Plantation crops on rocky land unsuitable for annual crops   10
   (c) Annual crops in 3 course rotation :

Winter cereals	40 dunums	
Legumes, hay, vegetables	40 dunums	
Summer crops	40 dunums	120

   Total surface area   135 dunums

2. *Stock and poultry.*
   2 selected *baladi* cows and 1 calf.
   2 tethered Damascus goats and 1 kid.
   20 *baladi* hens.
   1 mule.
   10 beehives.

284

CHAPTER VIII.

3. *Yields and gross annual income at pre-war prices from crops.*

PLANTATION CROPS.

Crop	Area in dunums	Total yield in kgs.	Value in mils per kg.	Gross value £P. Mils
Olives	5	1,480 fruit = 360 oil	40	14.400
Mixed fruits	5	—	—	12.000
Total	10	—	—	26.400

ANNUAL CROPS.

Crop	Area in dunums	Total yield in kgs.	Value in mils per kg.	Gross value £P. Mils
Winter cereals.				
Wheat	30	3,000	8	24.000
Barley	10	1,200	4	4.800
Legumes, hay and vegeables.				
Berseem (*jahli*) hay	5	1,500	4	6.000
Lentils	5	300	9	2.700
Beans	5	375	9	3.375
Kersenneh	5	300	5	1.500
Vetch and oats hay	15	5,250	3½	18.375
Potatoes	5	5,000	5	25.000
Summer crop.				
Millet (*dura*)	20	3,000	4	12.000
Sesame	10	400	20	8.000
Water melons	5	7,500	1½	11.250
Cucumbers	5	4,000	4	16.000
	120	—	—	133.000
Tibben from cereals, lentils and *kersenneh*	—	4,500	1	4.500

Total gross value = LP. 137.500 mils

4. *Costs of production.*

PLANTATION CROPS.

The following are the estimated costs of production of the plantation crops exclusive of labour. The expenditure is mainly for the cost of fertilizers, insecticides and depreciation of tools and implements. The cost of ploughing does not include wages :—

CHAPTER VIII.

Crop	Area in dunums	Annual expenditure in mils/dun.	Total annual expenditure £P. Mils
Olives	5	200	1.000
Mixed fruits	5	500	2.500
Ploughing	—	—	3.500
Total	10	—	7.000

ANNUAL CROPS.

The estimated cost of production of the annual crops is 550 mils per dunum. The total annual cost of production on 120 dunums = £P.66.000.

The various items included in the cost of production are detailed in paragraph 4 of Schedule 'A', and in addition there is the cost of tractor ploughing and cost of hiring mechanical implements.

5. *Stock and poultry.*

The expenditure and income from stock and poultry is the same as is given in paragraphs 5 and 6 of Schedule 'A', viz :—

    Gross income   LP.   42.100
    Expenditure   LP.   30.750
    Net income   LP.   11.350

6. *Net annual income from farming operations.*

Details	Gross income £P. Mils	Expenditure £P. Mils	Net income £P. Mils
Plantation crops	28.000	7.000	21.000
Annual crops	137.500	66.000	71.500
Stock and poultry	42.100	30.750	11.350
	207.600	103.750	103.850

Total net income = LP. 103.850 mils

Schedule 'C'.

FAMILY FARM IN INLAND PLAINS.
(*Surface area* = 87 *dunums.*   12 *dunums irrigated*).

1. *Division of surface area of* 87 *dunums.*   Dunums

   (a) Site for house, buildings, fuel
       plantation, etc.   5

   (b) Plantation crops on rocky land unsuit-
       able for annual crops   10

CHAPTER VIII.

(c) Annual crops in 3 course rotation:
　　Winter cereals　　20 dunums
　　Legumes　　　　　20 dunums
　　Summer crops　　 20 dunums　　　　　60

(d) Irrigated annual crops　　　　　　　　12

　　Total surface area　　　　　　　　87 dunums

2. *Stock and poultry.*
2 tethered Damascus goats and 1 kid
2 selected *baladi* cows and 1 calf.
20 *baladi* hens
1 mule
10 beehives

3. *Yields and gross annual income at pre-war prices from crops.*

PLANTATION CROPS.

Crop	Area in dunums	Total yield in kgs.	Value in mils per kg.	Gross value £P. Mils
Olives	5	1,430 fruit = 360 oil	40	14.400
Mixed fruits	5	—	—	12.000
Total	10	—	—	26.400

Annual crops — Non-irrigated.

Crop	Area in dunums	Total yield in kgs.	Value in mils per kg.	Gross value £P. Mils
Winter Cereals.				
Wheat	15	1,500	8	12.000
Barley	7	840	4	3.360
Legumes.				
Lentils	5	300	9	2.700
Beans	9	675	9	6.075
Vetch and oats hay	4	1,400	3½	4.900
Summer crops.				
Millet (*dura*)	15	2,250	4	9.000
Sesame	3	120	20	2.400
Water melons	2	3,000	1½	4.500
	60	—	—	44.935
Tibben straw from cereals and lentils.	—	1,500	1	1.500
		Total gross value	=	46.435

CHAPTER VIII.

IRRIGATED CROPS.

Surface area = 12 dunums
Annual cropping area = 21 dunums.

Crop	Area in dunums	Total yield in kgs.	Value in mils per kg.	Gross value £P. Mils
Green fodder.				
Berseem (*mesquawi*)	4	20,000	1	20.000
Maize	1	5,000	1	5.000
Wintersome	2	12,000	1	12.000
Vegetables.				
Carrots	2	3,000	7	21.000
Egg plant	2	4,000	4	16.000
Tomatoes	4	6,000	5	30.000
Cauliflower	2	3,000	4	12.000
Potatoes	4	6,000	5	30.000
Total	21	—	—	146.000

4. *Costs of production.*

PLANTATION CROPS.

The costs of production of the plantation crops are as shown in paragraph 4 of Schedule B, viz. total annual expenditure = £P.7.000.

ANNUAL CROPS.

Non-irrigated.

The estimated annual cost of production is 550 mils per dunum. The total annual cost of production on 60 dunums = £P.33.000. See paragraph 4 of Schedule B.

Irrigated.

The estimated cost of production per dunum of irrigated land is £P.4.000 per crop dunum (not surface dunum) including the cost of water but exclusive of labour. The total annual cost on 21 dunums of crops = £P.84.000.

5. *Stock and poultry.*

The expenditure and income from stock and poultry is the same as is given in paragraphs 5 and 6 of Schedule A, viz :

Gross income	LP. 42.100
Expenditure	LP. 30.750
Net income	LP. 11.350

CHAPTER VIII.

6. *Net annual income from farming operations.*

Details	Gross income £P. Mils	Expenditure £P. Mils	Net income £P. Mils
Plantation crops	26.400	7.000	19.400
Annual non-irrigated crops	46.435	33.000	13.435
Irrigated crops	146.000	84.000	62.000
Stock and poultry	42.100	30.750	11.350
	260.935	154.750	106.185

Total net income = LP. 106.185 mils

(b) Legislation designed to protect cultivators against eviction.

128. The earliest legislation in Palestine concerned with the protection of tenants from eviction was the Land Transfer Ordinance of September, 1920. This Ordinance and that which amended it in the following year (The Transfer of Land Ordinance, 1921)* were designed to secure the protection of agricultural tenants from eviction when land was sold by the landlord. The object of the legislation was political rather than economic, namely to maintain tenants of long standing on land, large tracts of which were being sold by absentee Arab landowners to Jews during the first substantial immigration of Jews into Palestine after the British occupation. Under this legislation the consent of Government to all dispositions of immoveable property was required; and the Governor of a District (later the Director of Lands) was required to withhold consent to any transfer of agricultural land unless he was satisfied that the tenant would retain sufficient land for the maintenance of himself and his family. This legislation failed to achieve its purpose because tenants for the most part did not avail themselves of its provisions, but preferred to divest themselves of their rights thereunder by declaring, usually before a Notary Public, that they were not tenants entitled to its protection and accepting monetary compensation for so doing. Tenants were often induced to do this by unscrupulous pressure brought to bear upon them by their Arab landlords, to whom they stood in a quasi-feudal relation, and by their state of indebtedness. The principal Jewish land purchasing bodies at that time adopted a policy of not purchasing land unless all agricultural tenants had been removed therefrom by the vendor before the sale. Thus the provision of the law requiring retention of sufficient land for maintenance of the tenant and his family was evaded.

* Bentwich, Vol. I, p. 62.

Chapter VIII.

129. However, this ineffective legislation remained on the statute book until 1929, when the relevant section was replaced by the Protection of Cultivators Ordinance*. This Ordinance provided for the payment to certain classes of tenants of compensation, not only for any improvements but also for disturbance, on their receiving a valid notice to quit a holding. It further provided for the constitution of Boards to decide disputes as to whether or not compensation for disturbance or improvement was payable and as to the amount of any such compensation. The previous requirement that a cultivator must retain a subsistence area elsewhere found no place in the new Ordinance. But in 1931** this requirement was restored mainly by reason of the recrudescence at that time of large scale land sales by Arabs to Jews and the emergence into prominence of the problem of the landless Arab. (In 1933 a committee of enquiry found that some 664 Arab families who had been displaced by land sales had been unable to obtain other holdings on which they could establish themselves, or to find other equally satisfactory occupation). The amending Ordinance of 1931 also protected from eviction persons who had exercised continuously for a period of five years a practice of grazing or watering animals or the cutting of wood or reeds or other beneficial occupation of a similar character, unless the landlord had made equivalent provision towards the livelihood of such persons. Subsequent amendments tightened up the Ordinance on various points in favour of the tenant and stopped certain loopholes through which it had been found that evasion was possible.

130. This legislative action in favour of tenants culminated in the repeal of the 1929 Ordinance and its amendments, and its replacement by a new comprehensive piece of legislation, the Cultivators (Protection) Ordinance of 1933***, which is substantially the law as it exists to-day. The salient provisions of this existing law are as follows :—

(a) It defines a "statutory tenant" as any person, family or tribe occupying and cultivating a holding otherwise than as owner thereof. The term includes the relatives of any person occupying and cultivating a holding who may have, with the knowledge of the landlord, cultivated such holding : it includes the heirs of a tenant; and also any person who is hired by the landlord to do agricultural work and receives as remuneration a portion of the produce of the holding which he cultivates.

* Laws of 1929, Vol. I, p. 299.
** Laws of 1931, Vol. I, p. 3.
*** Drayton, Vol. I, p. 506.

CHAPTER VIII.

(b) It provides that a "statutory tenant" who has occupied and cultivated a holding for a period of not less than one year shall not, provided that he has paid his rent and that he had not grossly neglected his holding, be ejected therefrom unless he has been provided with a subsistence area approved by the High Commissioner. Such subsistence area is to be, as far as possible in the vicinity of the land from which he has been displaced.

(c) The Ordinance also provides for the protection of the rights of persons who have exercised on land the practice of grazing or watering animals, or cutting wood or reeds, unless provision of equivalent value is secured towards their livelihood; provided that such persons have exercised the practice concerned, by themselves or their agents, habitually, at the appropriate seasons, for not less than five consecutive years within a period of not more than seven years prior to the date when any application is made to a court for their eviction.

(d) The constitution of Boards to decide certain questions which might arise between landlords and tenants and for the determination of subsistence areas is provided for.

(e) The High Commissioner is empowered to appoint one or more Commissions consisting of not less than two persons to decide disputes on the following matters :—

(1) as to whether any person is a statutory tenant of a holding; or

(2) as to the length of time that any statutory tenant has occupied and cultivated a holding; or

(3) as to whether any person is the landlord of a holding; or

(4) as to whether any person has exercised continuously any practice of grazing or watering animals or cutting wood or reeds or other beneficial occupation of a similar character by right, custom, usage or sufferance.

These Commissions have consisted for some time past of an Assistant District Commissioner and a District Officer in each subdistrict. Appeal lies therefrom only on a point of law to the Land Court by leave of that Court. The practice and procedure followed in any enquiry before these Commissions is set out in Regulations*.

131. Landlords still found means of evading the intention of the Ordinance, principally by giving leases for periods of less than one year, generally for nine or ten months, sufficing for the cultivation

---

* The Protection of Cultivators Regulations, 1934, Volume of subsidiary legislation 1934, p.99.

CHAPTER VIII.

and harvesting of both a winter and a summer crop. A Bill was therefore published in 1936 amending the definition of "statutory tenant" so as to extend protection to any person who cultivated a holding "for one year or a period necessary to raise two successive crops". The Bill was not proceeded with on account of the recommendation of the Royal Commission * that a Committee should be set up to consider the whole question of land legislation in Palestine, including the Cultivators (Protection) Ordinance.

132. During the war the application of the provisions of the Cultivators (Protection) Ordinance has been circumscribed in two respects by means of Defence Regulations :—

(a) In February, 1942, State Domain was excluded from the scope of the Ordinance**. The reason for this was that it had become impossible to prevent trespassers on State Domain from acquiring rights under the Ordinance, thereby preventing Government from utilising these State Domains in the best interests of the community. It was considered that it was undesirable to tie the hands of Government, who, when determining the use to which State Domain should be put, would naturally safeguard the position of occupiers of long standing.

(b) Consequent upon the introduction of this Defence Regulation exempting State Domain, other landlords pressed for similar protection, and in the result, so as to enable all available land to be put under cultivation during time of war, a second Defence Regulation*** was introduced in December, 1942, withdrawing the protection of the Ordinance from persons who occupied or cultivated a holding for the first time subsequent to the date of the Regulation.

133. With the tightening up of legislation in favour of the occupier there has been increasing criticism, particularly from Jews, that "it affords too great an opportunity for bogus claims and puts a premium on trespassing, with the result that endless delays and great expense are incurred in resisting and buying off these claims before a clear title and undisputed possession of land can be obtained"†. In 1941 the State Domain Committee expressed the view that the Ordinance had become what they described as "a serious obstacle to the reasoned development of the country" in that it placed in the hands of tenants

---

* Paragraphs 29 and 69 of Chapter IX of their Report.
** Defence Regulations, 1939. Regulation 48A(2). Kantrovitch, Vol. I, p. 73.
*** Defence Regulations, 1939. Regulation 48A(1). Kantrovitch, Vol. I, p. 73.
† Royal Commission Report, page 243.

CHAPTER VIII.

and trespassers a weapon with which they were able to victimise the landlords. The view was also expressed that the Land Transfers Regulations alone gave sufficient protection to Arab tenants and that with their enactment in 1939 there was no longer need of the Cultivators (Protection) Ordinance. In view of these criticisms, the High Commissioner appointed a Committee in February, 1942, to consider whether the Ordinance should be amended. This Committee was under the chairmanship of Mr. R. E. H. Crosbie, C.M.G., O.B.E., the members being the Directors of Land Registration and Land Settlement and the Legal Draftsman.

134. The Committee reported in January, 1943. They expressed the view that, although before 1933 it was the landlord who had abused the legislation and the tenant who accordingly needed increased protection, since that date "it had been the landlord's rights which have increasingly stood in need of protection, so that to-day the Ordinance is widely regarded rather as an instrument to facilitate the exploitation of landlords by tenants than as an instrument for the protection of tenants from the exploitation of landlords".

135. They showed that the outstanding abuse lay in the exploitation of the Ordinance by trespassers and squatters whom it was never intended to benefit but who, by the definition of "statutory tenant", are legally entitled to its protection. Such persons enter upon land without the knowledge or consent of the owner, often without paying rent, and sometimes remain on the land not as *bona fide* cultivators but rather with a view to exploiting the pecuniary value of their gratuitously acquired rights. The provisions of the Ordinance make their eviction by the landlord a process which is not only lengthy but which is not assured of success, owing to the difficulty of finding alternative subsistence areas as required by the Ordinance. The landlord is normally obliged to have recourse to buying the occupier off the land; he has, however, no effective guarantee that the occupier will not return to the land and acquire fresh rights and a fresh nuisance value as a "statutory tenant".

136. The Committee found that the protection afforded by the Ordinance was also being abused by tenants who, having entered into a lease agreement with a landlord, refused to honour their obligations under the lease once they had acquired the rights of a "statutory tenant", and availed themselves of the provisions of the Ordinance to remain in occupation without paying rent. The Committee reported that abuses of this nature were tending to

Chapter VIII.

retard agricultural development in that landlords prefer to let their land lie vacant and fallow until they are able to develop it themselves rather than to lease it to tenants whom they will not be able to remove. This criticism has been met temporarily by the Defence Regulations to which reference is made in paragraph 132.

137. The Committee also found that the protection afforded by the Ordinance to rights of grazing and watering animals and of cutting wood and reeds operated to the detriment of sound agricultural and forest development.

138. They were also of opinion that the procedure under which disputes are dealt with by various Boards, Commissions and courts is cumbersome and constitutes the major cause for delay in the eviction of a statutory tenant. They reported that proceedings can be dragged on from one tribunal to another for years, at great expense, without any finality, the decisions of one tribunal being often reversed or annulled by an alternative or higher one.

139. The Committee made various recommendations for amelioration of the state of affairs disclosed by them, and submitted a draft of a new Ordinance to give effect to their recommendations. The principal recommendation was that protection should be confined to persons who have already acquired full rights as statutory tenants under the existing legislation and whose continued enjoyment of these rights is morally defensible, i.e., *bona fide* cultivators mainly depending on agriculture as a livelihood who have either (*a*) been statutory tenants for a period of one year with the consent of their landlord, or (*b*) been statutory tenants for a period of five years whether or not they ever obtained the consent of the landlord; but that the protection should not extend to trespassers and squatters who have been on the land for less than five years without ever having obtained the consent of their landlord; and should not extend to the wives and relatives of tenants.

140. The report has been under the consideration of Government, but consideration of the measures necessary to give permanent effect to the Committee's recommendations was deferred until after the war; the problem is a complex one and of political consequence, and the principal drags imposed by the Ordinance upon agricultural development have been temporarily removed by the Defence Regulations of 1942.

Chapter VIII.

(c) **The re-settlement of displaced Arab cultivators.**

141. Sir John Hope Simpson, in chapter II of his Report of 1930, recommended that the development of the land could best be ensured by the appointment of a Development Commission invested with the necessary powers. As a result of this recommendation, Mr. Lewis French, C.I.E., C.B.E. was deputed by His Majesty's Government in 1931 to investigate and report on the problems pertaining to development and land settlement in Palestine.

142. Mr. French was appointed Director of Development with the following duties :—
 (i) To prepare a register of "landless Arabs".
 (ii) To draw up a scheme for re-settling such Arabs.
 (iii) To ascertain what State and other lands could be made available for close settlement by Jews with reference to the obligation imposed upon the Mandatory by Article 6 of the Mandate.
 (iv) To report on the improvement and intensive development of land in the hills in order to secure to the *fellaheen* a better standard of living without, save in exceptional cases, having recourse to transfer.
 (v) To report on the feasibility and advisability of providing credits for Arab cultivators and Jewish settlers, and, if so, the best methods of achieving this purpose.
 (vi) To put forward proposals for draining, irrigating and otherwise reclaiming land not at present cultivated or cultivated only to a limited extent.

Mr. French presented a report in December, 1931, and a supplementary report in April, 1932.

143. The Arab Executive and the Jewish Agency were both invited to nominate one member each to assist Mr. French in an advisory capacity, but no progress was made with these appointments. Before Mr. French reached the country, the Arab Executive had made it plain that they would have nothing to do with the development scheme. They declined to enter into any discussions on the subject unless Government assented to their condition that such a scheme should not be based on the principles embodied in the letter addressed by the Prime Minister to Dr. Weizmann*. The Jews, on their part, took no effective steps to appoint a representative.

---

* Mr. J. Ramsay Macdonald's letter of the 13th February, 1931.

CHAPTER VIII.

144. The first duty of the Director of Development was to ascertain the number of "landless Arabs" in Palestine and to make a register of them. "Landless Arabs" had been defined as "such Arabs as could be shown to have been displaced from the lands which they occupied in consequence of the lands falling into Jewish hands and who had not obtained other holdings on which they could establish themselves or other equally satisfactory occupation". The Director, in preparing the register, was given the assistance of a legal assessor whose duty it was to scrutinise claims and advise him as to the sufficiency of evidence in each case before the claim was admitted.

145. As the first step to obtaining particulars of displacement, the District authorities were asked to ascertain in what villages displacement of Arab cultivators had occurred and to see that, if claims were made, some *prima facie* evidence was forthcoming which satisfied the conditions prescribed in the preceding paragraph.

146. The following categories of Arabs, though in fact landless, were not considered :—

(1) Persons who had been displaced in consequence of purchases by non-Jews.

(2) Persons who at the time of the sale to Jews were not tenant cultivators, e.g. owners who habitually let their lands, ploughmen and persons who, from debt or bad seasons or other causes, had ceased to be cultivators and had become labourers, etc.

(3) Persons who were able to obtain other lands after the sale, but subsequently gave up cultivating owing to bad seasons or for some other reason.

(4) Persons who had obtained employment of a fairly permanent nature.

Consequently, up to the 1st January, 1936, although 3,271 applications for re-settlement had been received from landless Arabs, only 664 had been admitted to the register, while 2,607 had been disallowed.

147. The policy of His Majesty's Government as formulated in 1930, after the presentation of Sir John Hope Simpson's report, contemplated the initiation of a comprehensive development scheme to be financed from a guaranteed loan of £P.2,500,000: it was visualised that, during the first years of that scheme, provision should be made from His Majesty's Exchequer of such annual amounts as might be required to meet the interest and

Chapter VIII.

sinking fund charges upon the loan. But in January, 1932, the Secretary of State intimated that conditions had changed in the interim, and that it could not be assumed that it would be found practicable to make £P.2.500,000 available for development purposes.

148. The Director of Development left Palestine in June, 1932, and the Department of Development was re-organized and placed in the charge of a development officer. This officer was instructed to draw up schemes for the resettlement of the displaced Arab cultivators admitted to the Register which schemes were to be financed from a sum of £P.250,000 made available for the purpose as an advance against the proposed £2,500,000 loan.

149. As suitable State Domain lands were not available, land on which to settle the displaced cultivators on the Register had to be purchased from private owners. An area of 17,868 dunums was accordingly purchased in the Beisan and Jenin sub-districts at a cost of £P.72,240. It was calculated that this area would provide subsistence areas for some 400 families.

150. The Department of Development was abolished in 1939 and the management of the settlements which had already been started devolved upon the District Commissioners, whilst to the Department of Land Settlement fell the task of attempting to regularise the occupation of Arabs who had been allowed to occupy the land without the terms on which they would hold it having been settled. The keeping of the Register of landless Arabs was discontinued and sporadic cases of landlessness are now dealt with as and when they occur.

THE ARABS OF WADI EL HAWARITH IN THE TULKARM SUB-DISTRICT:

151. The first landless Arabs to be dealt with were the Wadi Hawarith Arabs, whose landlord had disposed of his land to the Jewish National Fund. Judgment for their eviction had already been passed as early as the end of 1929, and it became imperative to find other land to which they could move. Government thereupon undertook the reclamation and deep ploughing of some 10,000 dunums of the land which it had purchased in the Beisan sub-district, with a view to settling these Arabs upon it, and by the 31st of August, 1933, the major portion of the area was ready for occupation. On being evicted from the Wadi Hawarith, the Arabs, however, refused to settle on the lands prepared for them on the grounds that they were used neither to the climate nor to irrigated cultivation; their settlement in the Beisan sub-district had accordingly to be abandoned.

Chapter VIII.

152. In view of this refusal, the possibility of making other arrangements for the settlement of the tribe on land lying in the vicinity of the Wadi Hawarith was investigated. The northern section of the Wadi Hawarith Arabs was accordingly settled on a State Domain in the Tulkarm sub-district known as Basset Sheikh Mohammad (GP/5/62—Wadi el Hawarith). This area consisted mainly of swampy land bordered by sand dunes and is 1,568 dunums in extent. After it had been drained and deep ploughed the land was allotted equally among the ninety families. The southern section, numbering 109 families, are camped on an area of 250 dunums (GP/5/54—Ma'baroth) taken by Government from the Jewish National Fund in exchange for a parcel of State Domain. These Arabs are cultivating land in the neighbouring Wadi Qabbani and elsewhere which they rent from the owners. Both the northern and southern sections of the Wadi Hawarith Arabs have declined to enter into any lease of the Government land which they occupy, but they pay a nominal rent.

The Arab Zubeid of the Safad sub-district.

153. These Arabs, numbering some 68 families, having been evicted from their camping grounds, Government authorised the provision for them of a new camping site in the Safad sub-district near an area of land which the owner was willing to allow them to cultivate. This site, which was the property of the Palestine Jewish Colonisation Association, was received by Government in exchange for a neighbouring parcel of State Domain of which the Association had already a long term lease. The Arab Zubeid were given a loan of £P.100 per family; they have settled permanently on the new site and built houses there, although in the past they had been tent-dwelling nomads. In 1944 the ownership of the land was transferred by Government to the new occupiers.

Other re-settlement Schemes.

154. In addition to the Arabs of Wadi el Hawarith and the Arab Zubeid, some 100 families, evicted from different parts of the country, expressed their willingness to take up land under Government schemes, and for these families three settlements were started in 1934, one at Tel esh Shauk in the Beisan sub-district and the others at Muqeibla and Beit Qad in the Jenin sub-district.

CHAPTER VIII.

155. The Tel esh Shauk scheme (GP/10/26) covers an area of 2,181 dunums of irrigated land divided into 51 plots varying in area between 15 and 52 dunums each of which is leased to a family. The settlers have been provided with accommodation for themselves and for their animals and a system of irrigation has been laid out. On their arrival they were provided with advances of money to enable them to make a fair start. The settlers are undoubtedly enjoying better conditions since they have been re-settled than they ever experienced in the past.

156. Some 4,225 dunums were purchased for the Muqeibla scheme (GP/7/2) and 2,094 dunums for the Beit Qad scheme (GP/7/1). A number of settlers were placed by the Development Officer on both areas but, later, the settlers of Beit Qad were transferred with their consent to Muqeibla in order to leave the Beit Qad land free for direct agricultural production by Government. There are now 50 families settled at Muqeibla occupying plots nearly all of which measure 80 dunums. The settlers have entered into 49 year leases with Government and are satisfactorily cultivating their allotments. As in the case of the Tel esh Shauk scheme the settlers at Muqeibla were also granted loans.

157. The Arab Sabarji are a semi-nomadic tribe consisting of about 120 persons who had been subsisting mainly on their flocks and herds and who had been trespassing on privately owned land. Although they were not landless in the sense of having been displaced from land which they formerly occupied owing to its being transferred to Jews, Government has settled them on a State Domain at Kafr Misr in Beisan sub-district. (The area of land allotted to them is 1,802 dunums for cultivation (GP/10/16/9 and 10) and 30 dunums for a camp site (GP/10/16 (25)). Leases have been concluded between Government and thirty heads of families representing the tribe.

(d) An illustration of the complexity of the land problem— the case of the Ma'lul Arabs.

158. The following case, that of the Arabs of Ma'lul village in the Nazareth sub-district, is described below as an example of the difficulties by which the Administration may be faced when attempting to give effect to the dual obligations of Article 6 of the Mandate and to ensure the retention for Arab peasants of a sufficient area of land for their subsistence. The areas quoted throughout this sub-section are in terms of old Turkish dunums; an old Turkish dunum is 919.3 square metres.

CHAPTER VIII.

159. Ma'lul is situated on the Haifa-Nazareth road in the foothills which bound the plain of Esdraelon on the northern side. It has an area of about 16,000 dunums of which nearly half is cultivated land. It has at present a population of about 900 persons, all Arabs; there are about seventy principal cultivators, the rest of the men of the village being hired ploughmen and labourers who do not own or lease land.

160. The lands of the village were originally the property of the Sursok family of Beirut. The villagers of Ma'lul were their tenants. In 1921 the Sursoks sold the lands to a Jewish company, the Palestine Land Development Company, with the exception of an area of 2,000 dunums which was excluded from the sale and remained in Arab hands. This area of 2,000 dunums, only part of which was cultivable and which contained the village built-on area, was insufficient to support the Arabs of Ma'lul and, as a result of intervention by Government, the Palestine Land Development Company agreed to lease to these Arabs an additional area of 3,000 dunums of plain land and 150 dunums of grazing land. The lease was to run for six years from 1921 to 1927, the rent payable being one-fifth of the crop. The Company was to instal a water supply for the villagers' animals, and, if the Company failed to do this, they were to be liable to pay £P.200 a year damages and the rent was to be remitted. The Arabs were to be entitled at any time before the expiry of the lease to purchase the land at £P.3 a dunum.

161. During the period of the lease the water was supplied and the rent was regularly paid. On the expiry of the lease an advocate who had been engaged by the Arabs claimed that he had notified the Company of his clients' readiness to purchase the land, but that he had received no reply; the Company maintained that the Arabs had failed to exercise their option. But, at the instance of Government, the Company agreed to extend the lease until 1931, provided that the right of option to purchase was not thereby restored. However, no formal extension of the original agreement was ever executed. The Arabs have remained on the land from then until now, paying no rent and receiving no water.

162. In 1927 the Ma'lul lands were transferred from the Palestine Land Development Company to the Jewish National Fund. By the terms of its constitution the latter organisation is not entitled to sell any of the land in its possession.

CHAPTER VIII.

163. From time to time various issues relating to the rights and wrongs of the parties have been before the courts. In 1931 the Jewish National Fund brought a case in the courts against five of the principal cultivators and obtained a judgment to the effect that rent at the rate of 150 mils per dunum should be paid. The Arabs on their part sought to establish that their option to purchase was still valid or, in the alternative, that they possessed rights under the Cultivators (Protection) Ordinance : they denied that rent was due from them since water had not been supplied, and they counter-claimed for damages for this failure to supply. The Fund's claim for rent since 1927 and interest thereon amounted to some £P.10,000 at the end of 1945.

164. The Ma'lul Arabs also claimed grazing rights over an area of 5,000 dunums of rocky land which lies to the west of the village and on part of which the King George Jubilee Forest had been established by the Jewish National Fund. The Arab el Mazareeb, a tribe of herdsmen, also claimed grazing rights and the right to pitch tents in the same area. The case came in due course on appeal before the Supreme Court, who on 15th February, 1940 found in favour of the Arabs in respect of grazing only. The Jewish National Fund was granted leave to appeal to the Privy Council; on 24th June, 1943, the latter confirmed the judgment of the Supreme Court.

165. In 1937 the late Mr. Andrews, Development Officer, with the consent of Government, attempted to negotiate a settlement between the parties. The arrangement at which he aimed was that the Fund should make over to Government the ownership of an area of land in Ma'lul village, part suitable for cultivation and part suitable for grazing, sufficient for the needs of the villagers. Government would then lease this land to the villagers. In exchange for the land, Government would make over to the Fund the ownership of an area of State Domain of equivalent value in the south of Beisan. Provisional agreement on this basis was reached between the parties, but before any action was taken on it the report of the Royal Commission was published (June 1937). Under the Commission's tentative proposals of partition, the land in Beisan fell within the Arab area; Government therefore directed that the negotiations initiated by Mr. Andrews should be suspended. In October, 1938, following the receipt of the report of the Partition Commission, the proposals for partition of the country were dropped by His Majesty's Government; they therefore no longer constituted a barrier to negotiation; but the restrictions

CHAPTER VIII.

imposed upon land transfers by the policy of the White Paper of 1939 introduced a further complication. The lands in Beisan which it had been proposed to exchange for the Ma'lul lands lay within zone A (the prohibited zone) of the Regulations which were introduced in February, 1940 in implementation of the White Paper policy. The boundary between zone A and zone B fell across the Ma'lul lands, the hilly areas of the village being assigned to zone A and the plain to zone B.

166. In 1940 the acting District Commissioner of the Galilee District reported that the parties had again been negotiating with one another and that virtual agreement had been reached on the basis of the arrangement proposed by Mr. Andrews, but with some variation in detail, the Arabs having increased their demands on the strength of the judgment to which reference is made in paragraph 164. The question of the proposed exchange was then referred to the State Domain Committee for consideration of three alternatives :—

(a) The exchange with the Jewish National Fund of 3,400 dunums of Ma'lul land (half in the hills and half in the plain) for an area of State Domain equivalent in value situated within zone A in the Beisan sub-district.

(b) The exchange with the Fund of 3,400 dunums of Ma'lul land for an area of State Domain equivalent in value situated somewhere within zone B.

(c) No exchange, the Arabs and the Fund to be told that they must settle the matter themselves.

In their report, submitted in July 1940, the State Domain Committee pointed out that, while it was true that the Land Transfers Regulations did not apply to State Domain, it had been accepted as a general principle that State Domain should not be alienated to Jews unless the transfer was of such a nature that it would be permitted were the State Domain in question Arab land; and that to permit exchanges of Jewish land in the free or restricted zones for Arab land in the prohibited zone would be contrary to the intention of the Regulations. The Committee were furthermore of the opinion that it was not incumbent on Government to find other State Domain, either in the free or the restricted zone, which the Jewish National Fund might be prepared to accept in exchange for the Ma'lul land. They considered that in land transactions such as those from which the situation in question

302

CHAPTER VIII.

had arisen both parties should be treated as private citizens and expected to abide by the bargains made. The State Domain Committee therefore recommended that, in view of the Land Transfers Regulation, the exchange suggested should not be countenanced and, moreover, that Government should not negotiate for an exchange of the Ma'lul land for State Domain elsewhere, and that the parties to the dispute should be left either to reach a compromise between themselves or, in the alternative, to obtain and abide by the judgment of the Courts. In September, 1940 these recommendations were considered by the High Commissioner in Executive Council and in accordance with the decision then taken it was made clear to both parties that in no circumstances would State Domain land be made available for the purpose of settling the matter, and it was suggested to them that they should submit the dispute to independent arbitration. The suggestion of arbitration was rejected and, although various alternative proposals for negotiating a settlement were subsequently put forward and examined, there was no substantial change in the position or in the attitude of Government until 1944.

167. In that year, however, the villagers of Ma'lul having finally failed, after protracted proceedings, to establish in the courts rights of cultivation claimed by them under the Cultivators (Protection) Ordinance, were faced with the prospect of eviction from the land on application by the owners, the Jewish National Fund, to whom the land had in the meantime been finally adjudicated in the course of land settlement. Since Government had played an active part from 1920 onwards in retaining the Ma'lul Arabs in occupation of this land it was represented that there was an obligation on the part of Government to take steps to ensure the future support of these agriculturalists. Apart from the lands now definitely awarded to the Jewish National Fund there remained for the subsistence of the Arabs an area of 2,000 dunums of which only about 900 dunums were arable land, the balance being either rocky grazing land or built upon. This area of arable land was considered to be far short of the minimum needs of a rural community of 900 persons.

168. The situation was therefore reviewed in September, 1944, by the State Domain Committee, who revised their previous recommendation in regard to an exchange of State Domain and proposed, in view of the changed circumstances, that the Jewish National Fund should be offered, in exchange for the 3,000 dunums of plain land (zone B) in Arab occupation at Ma'lul, areas of State Domain in Beisan which in total were almost equivalent in extent, which

Chapter VIII.

had been encroached upon by Jews and which could probably only be recovered by the use of force. The State Domain in Beisan is in zone A, but the Committee considered that, in view of the special considerations in this case, there was justification for a departure from the principles laid down by Government that the spirit of the Land Transfers Regulations should be applied to State Domain. In making their recommendation the Committee attached particular importance to the consideration that Government would acquire an equivalent area of land also in the restricted zones owned by persons other than Palestinian Arabs and would use this area for the benefit of Palestinian Arabs.

169. In October, 1944, this recommendation was accepted by Government after consideration in Executive Council and the Director of Land Settlement was authorised to negotiate the exchange proposed. But the Jewish National Fund declined to negotiate an exchange which included land upon which Jewish settlers had trespassed and were in occupation.

170. In December, 1944, the Jewish National Fund put forward counter proposals. These fell into three parts :—

(a) The lands to be given up by the Jewish National Fund at Ma'lul. The Fund proposed to make available for the Ma'lul Arabs 1,700 dunums in the plain (zone B) and also 1,700 dunums in the hills (zone A). The District Commissioner considered that these areas, together with those of which they were in lawful occupation, would be sufficient for the subsistence of the Arabs of Ma'lul and that it was unreasonable to expect the Jewish National Fund to give up the whole of the 3,000 dunums in the plain which had been leased by them in 1921 and of which the Arabs had ever since been in occupation.

(b) Land in Beisan to be acquired by the Fund in exchange for 1,700 dunums of plain land at Ma'lul. The Jewish National Fund asks that an area of 3,775 dunums in the undermentioned villages of Beisan sub-district should be transferred to them :—

Masil el Jisl — 1,690 dunums estimated by the Fund to be equivalent in value to 563 dunums at Ma'lul.

Ghazawiya — 760 dunums estimated as equivalent to 380 dunums at Ma'lul.

CHAPTER VIII.

Safa — 1,000 dunums estimated as equivalent to 400 dunums at Ma'lul.

Tel esh Shok — 325 dunums estimated as equivalent to 325 dunums at Ma'lul.

These lands were not in occupation by Jews but some of them were leased by Government to Arabs. Government considered that the valuations placed by the Fund on the Beisan lands on comparison with those placed on the Ma'lul lands were too low.

(c) Land on the northern frontier of Palestine at Buleida and Meis in Safad Sub-District to be acquired by the Fund in exchange for 1,700 dunums of hill land at Ma'lul. The Jewish National Fund asked for 5,000 dunums. Land settlement operations in this area are not complete and the lands at Buleida and Meis have not been registered as State Domain : for this reason alone the exchange proposed could not be entertained by Government.

171. During 1945 the Jewish National Fund pressed for settlement of the problem, and it was thought that, unless negotiations were pursued, there would be danger that the Fund would start cultivation of the plain land at Ma'lul which hitherto had been in Arab ownership. In the District Commissioner's view this might result in a serious local security situation. As the counter proposal of the Fund did not offer a basis for a solution likely to be acceptable to Government the problem was again considered by the Executive Council on the 10th October, 1945. The High Commissioner (Lord Gort) then decided that a solution should be sought by way of a further offer of an exchange of lands. Despite the Land Transfers Regulations and the decision that the provisions of these Regulations should be applied to State Domain, Lord Gort considered that it was right to offer to the Jewish National Fund lands within zones A or B, provided that an equivalent area of land at Ma'lul owned by persons other than Palestinian Arabs would be obtained thereby for the use of Palestinian Arabs. But his view was that the offer of an area of State Domain in the restricted zones appreciably in excess of that to be acquired in exchange would not be justified and that any difference in values should be made up by the offer of additional State Domain situated in the "free" zone. Accordingly, the following proposition was put before the Jewish National Fund on 22nd October :—

(a) The Fund to transfer to Government their title to 1,700 dunums of plain land (zone A) and 2,000 dunums of hilly land (zone B) situated in the village of Ma'lul.

CHAPTER VIII.

(b) The Government to make available from these lands, for the use of the inhabitants of Ma'lul, 1,700 dunums of plain land and 1,700 dunums of hilly land, for the Mazareeb tribe (see paragraph 164), 300 dunums of hilly land on such terms and conditions as Government shall deem fit, but provided that one of these conditions shall be that the inhabitants of Ma'lul and the members of the Mazareeb tribe shall resign formally and absolutely all claims and established rights to grazing within any part of the village of Ma'lul the ownership of which remains registered in the name of the Jewish National Fund.

(c) The Government to transfer to the Jewish National Fund the title to 3,700 dunums of State Domain situated in Beisan Sub-District or elsewhere within zones A or B of the Land Transfers Regulations.

(d) The Government to place a value upon the 3,700 dunums of Ma'lul lands to be surrendered by the Jewish National Fund and upon the equivalent area within zones A and B to be offered in exchange therefor.

(e) Should the Government and the Jewish National Fund disagree over the valuation of the lands, the difference of opinion to be referred to a British Judge for assessment in accordance with the procedure of the Land (Acquisition for Public Purposes) Ordinance, 1943.

(f) Should the determined value of the 3,700 dunums offered by Government be less than the determined value of the 3,700 dunums at Ma'lul surrendered by the Jewish National Fund, an area of State Domain within the "free" zone of the Land Transfers Regulations to be transferred by Government to the Jewish National Fund. The extent of this area of State Domain within the "free" zone would be determined by the difference in value between the areas exchanged within the restricted zones.

172. The reply of the Jewish National Fund to these proposals was to the effect that they declined to negotiate on the basis of the Land Transfers Regulations and would not accept the proposal that any dispute over comparative values should be submitted to any third party. They proceeded to make three alternative offers. The first two were for the exchange of 6,372 dunums and 4,153

CHAPTER VIII.

dunums respectively of land in the Beisan sub-district within zone A for 3,700 dunums at Ma'lul. Apart from the question of the relative land values upon which the Fund had computed these areas and to which Government would not have agreed, the basis of exchange whereby a larger area to be acquired by the Fund in zone A than was to be surrendered at Ma'lul (where only half the area is zone A and half zone B) was not acceptable to Government as it was contrary to the spirit of the policy underlying the Land Transfers Regulations. The third alternative was for 2,646 dunums at Ashrafiya and 354 dunums at Tel esh Shok (a total of 3,000 dunums in Beisan sub-district within zone A and all good irrigible land) for the 3,700 dunums at Ma'lul (of which 1,700 dunums was unirrigated arable land in the plain and 2,000 dunums hill country). The Jewish National Fund assessed the value of the 3,700 dunums at Ma'lul at the same figure as that of the 3,000 dunums in Beisan. but the Director of Land Settlement (who is the official valuer of Government) placed the former area at £P.59,400 in comparison with £P.73,938 for the latter. The land at Ashrafiya was originally purchased by Government for the settlement of landless Arabs. It was leased on short term to Arabs and was in their occupation until taken over by the military authorities in 1942 for the production of fodder required by the Forces. The Arabs expect to be allowed to go back on to the land when it is no longer required by the Army and, in July, 1945, following rumours that the land was about to be transferred to Jews, a number of enquiries were made by Arabs as to Government's intentions and there was also some agitation in the Arab press on this subject; a reply was given on behalf of Government to the enquiries that no change in the holding of this land was contemplated at that time. The land is still required by the military authorities for the production of fodder and it is not known when it can be released from such use. Moreover, the transfer of the Ashrafiya lands to the Jewish National Fund would not have effected the consolidation of Jewish lands in the Beisan area which was a subsidiary objective of Government's proposals for exchange. In all these circumstances Government was unable to accept an offer of exchange which involved the Ashrafiya lands.

173. On 24th November, 1945, the Jewish National Fund obtained a Court order of possession of the lands at Ma'lul and on 5th December, on their application, the Execution Officers went on to the land to take possession on the Fund's behalf. The

Chapter VIII.

mukhtar of Ma'lul and a number of the elders of the village thereupon refused to yield possession of it and an application was subsequently made by the Fund to the Chief Execution Officer for delivery of the land by force. It was evident to Government that here was the makings of a serious incident in which blood might be shed, and the problem was therefore again discussed in Executive Council on 13th December and, after considering and rejecting a proposal that the Ma'lul lands should be acquired by Government by proceedings under the Land (Acquisition for Public Purposes) Ordinance, it was decided by the High Commissioner that a further attempt should be made to negotiate an exchange, valuable State Domain in Haifa Bay (free zone) together with small parcels in Beisan being offered. Negotiations on this basis are proceeding.

Section 12: Memorandum on land registration at the termination of the mandate

12.01

76452/1M48

MEMORANDUM

on the history, law and practice of land registration in Palestine and the organisation of the Department of Land Registration, with a note on the custody of the records of title to land at the termination of the British Mandate.

By

Mr. J.F. Spry, formerly Assistant Director of Land Registration, Palestine.

October, 1948.

Contents.   Paragraph.

The history of land registration in Palestine;
    the Ottoman system   1 - 6
    defects in the system   7 - 10
    the British Occupation   11
    enforcement and reform of registration   12
    settlement of title   13 - 14
    control over dispositions   15 - 17

The law and practice;
    the law relating to registration   18 - 20
    intended revision and codification of the law   21 - 23
    the form of the registers   24 - 29
    procedure in the land registries   30 - 36

The organisation of the Department;
    territorial areas of jurisdiction   37 - 40
    staff   41 - 44

Accounting; the deposit accounts   45 - 48
The Ghor Mudawwara Agreements   49 - 50
Statistics   51
Conclusion   52

Appendices.

    I.   Note on the restoration of the Jerusalem Land Registry records.

    II.   Note on the custody of the records on the termination of the Mandate.

    III. Note on the photographing of the land registers, with indices.

The history of land registration in Palestine.

The Ottoman system.

Land registration was introduced into the Ottoman Empire in 1858, although it does not appear to have been applied to the area now known as Palestine until the year 1869 to 1873.

2. It would not be appropriate here to consider the very complex Ottoman land laws, but it may be noted by way of introduction that the law recognised private ownership of land (mulk) as well as a form of tenure from the state (miri). Ownership (mulk) was, with some exceptions, confined to land within the walled towns, although the Sultan had the power in his discretion to divest himself of his residual ownership (ragaba) of any state land. The owner of land could dedicate it for religious and charitable purposes (as waqf), when it was deemed to become vested in God. Miri tenure, which was intended for agricultural land, was heritable and alienable but subect to determination on failure to cultivate. The right to miri tenure could be acquired by cultivation for ten years, and the state encouraged the extension of cultivation both for the sake of food production and for the revenue derived from tithes.

3. Registration was based in the first instance on the investigations of commissions of enquiry (Yuglama or Shamwiya) which proceeded from village to village. Entries were made in bound books, and showed the area, boundaries and proprietorship of all land in private ownership or private tenure. Waste land and land applied to public purposes, such as roads, were not registered. All entries required formal confirmation.

4. Once land was registered, every disposition required official approval and registration. The form of such registration was that of registration of deeds rather than of title, entries being made in chronological order in books known as the Daimi registers. (The system may be compared with that of the former Middlesex Registry in England). The method of reference was by serial number and date.

5. Registration carried no guarantee, but it constituted prima facie evidence of title which it was not easy to rebut.

6. Land registries were maintained in all administrative centres, but their work was subject to confirmation from Stamboul, where duplicates were maintained of all the land registers. These duplicates are now preserved in Ankara.

Defects in the system.

7. In theory, the system had much to commend it, but in practice it failed, largely for two reasons. In the first place, the original investigation was not based on a survey of the land and was carried out in a very perfunctory manner. Areas were given only approximately, and the description of boundaries usually consisted of the names of adjoining owners by reference to the four cardinal points. Secondly, it was soon realised by the people that the land registers provided the Government with information of value as a basis for taxation and conscription. In consequence, registration was not always sought, and when it was, fictitious figures were given for the area (under

/the

2.

the Ottoman Land Code the boundaries shown in the land registers, if definite, prevailed over the area), while persons liable to military service often procured registration in the names of nominees.

8. In consequence, the land registers, at the time of the British Occupation, were both inaccurate and incomplete.

9. It should also be noted that the Turks, in their withdrawal, removed many of the land registers, not all of which were subsequently recovered.

10. As a commentary on the failure of the Ottoman system, it may be remarked that the German colonies of Sarona and Wilhelma, and many of the Jewish colonies, kept their own, unofficial, land registers.

The British Occupation.

11. On the British Occupation, the land registries were temporarily closed, to be reopened in September 1920 with the enactment of the Transfer of Land Ordinance 1920 (later known as the Land Transfer Ordinance). The system remained substantially unchanged, although the form of the registers was altered and the procedure modified in minor respects. No duplicates were kept, although weekly returns of dispositions were made by the land registries to headquarters in Jerusalem.

Enforcement and reform of registration.

12. In order that the land registers might correspond with the position on the ground, ordinances were enacted to enable beneficial owners, whose lands were registered in the names of nominees or whose title appeared only in the unofficial registers, to procure registration in their names. For the future, attempts were made to remedy the two principal defects in the Ottoman system. In the first place, the Transfer of Land Ordinance, 1920 imposed severe penalties on all parties to a disposition which was not completed in compliance with the provisions of the Ordinance, and declared any such disposition void. (The penalties were, in fact, never exacted, while the avoiding provision was mitigated by the application of the principles of equity). In the second place, plans were required, at first administratively, and when this was challenged before the Courts, by an amendment of the Ordinance.

Settlement of title.

13. The Transfer of Land Ordinance 1920 had, in its recitals, anticipated land settlement, town planning and the establishment of credit banks. All three came to pass, although their evolution was still incomplete at the end of the Mandate. Of the three, land settlement is the only one that needs consideration here. This provided for a general investigation of title to all land, whether or not then registered, on the basis of a cadastral survey. Both public land and village common land were subject to the investigation, the settlement officer being charged with the duty of protecting the interests of the state. The main objects of the undertaking

/were

were to determine obscure and complicated titles, to define boundaries and to encourage partition. Settlement officers were given wide judicial powers, subject to a right of appeal to the Courts. Their decisions were embodied in Schedules of Rights, in accordance with which new registers were opened.

14. By the end of the Mandate, settlement of title had been completed in respect of some four and three quarter million out of Palestine's twenty-six million dunums, the latter figure including desert and uncultivable land. The area covered included almost the whole of the coastal plain and the greater part of the Galilee District. It should also be noted that prior to the enactment of the Land (Settlement of Title) Ordinance, the title to the Ghor Mudawwara lands in the Jordan valley had been settled by a body known as the Demarcation Commission, whose work was completed, not preceded, by a cadastral survey.

Control over dispositions.

15. There has never been complete freedom of disposition in Palestine. As noted above, dispositions in Ottoman times required the consent of the appropriate official. Under the provisions of the Transfer of Land Ordinance 1920, all dispositions were again made subject to the approval of the Administration. The Ordinance clearly explained the objects of the restriction, the principal being the desire to prevent speculation and to protect the cultivators of the land. The Governor of the District (later renamed the District Commissioner) had to satisfy himself that a proposed transferee was a resident of Palestine, that he was not acquiring land in excess of his needs, that he intended to cultivate the land and that the transferor, or his tenant, would retain sufficient land for the maintenance of himself and his family.

16. The Ordinance was prepared at a time when Palestine was a very backward country, and envisaged a paternal government examining in detail every one of a limited number of transactions. Such examination did, in fact, take place and undoubtedly did much to prevent the dispossession of tenant cultivators. With the development of the country, however, the measure of control which had been fitting in 1920 became inappropriate. The consent of the Director of Land Registration was substituted for that of the District Commissioner, the economic prerequisites to that consent were abolished, and applications came to be considered in the light of their legal validity, rather than their social or economic desirability. The protection of cultivators was not forgotten, but became the subject of separate legislation.

The Land Transfers Regulations 1940.

17. Freedom of disposition was again restricted, though for a different reason, by the enactment of the Land Transfers Regulations 1940, following the White Paper of 1939. The country was divided into three zones: only in the central coastal strip, the town planning area of Jerusalem and in municipal areas was freedom of disposition allowed; in Zone B, which included Eastern Galilee, the Vale of Esdraelon, two small areas of the coastal plain and the southern half of the Negev, dispositions by Palestinian Arabs in favour of persons not

/Pal-

Palestinian Arabs were subject to the consent of the High Commissioner; in Zone A, which comprised the greater part of the country, dispositions by Palestinian Arabs to persons not being Palestinian Arabs were with very limited exceptions forbidden, while dispositions between persons who were not Palestinian Arabs were subject to the consent of the High Commissioner. A Palestinian Arab was defined as an Arab ordinarily resident in Palestine, the High Commissioner being given the final discretion to determine in case of doubt whether any particular person was an Arab or was so resident. The policy underlying the giving or withholding of consent was outlined in an explanatory statement published with the Regulations. The duty of enforcing the Regulations necessarily fell on the Department of Land Registration.

The laws relating to registration.

18. The registration of all deeds effecting dispositions of land, whether or not the title had been settled, was required by the Land Transfer Ordinance, but there was no ordinance defining the manner of registration, or the powers and duties of the Director, nor, apart from the Land (Settlement of Title) Ordinance which prescribed the form of the new registers, were there any statutory forms. The procedure was, in fact, largely customary, although still based on the so-called Tapou Law (The Law as to the Granting of Title Deeds for State Land of 8 Jamazi'ul Akhir 1275 AH), the Regulations as to Title Deeds of 7 Sha'ban 1276, the Law as to Title Deeds for Pure Mulk to be issued by the Deftev Khane of 28 Rejeb 1291 and the Law as to Title Deeds for Moussagafat and Mousteghilat Waqfs of 9 Rebi'ul Evvel 1293, which, although largely obsolete, had never been repealed. These, and other relevant Ottoman laws and regulations, are available rendered in English in editions prepared by Fisher, Ongley and Tute: no translation has ever officially been adopted, although translations of individual articles have from time to time received judicial recognition.

19. These laws must be read with the Provisional Laws introduced by the Young Turks, which were accepted as binding by the Courts of the Mandatory, and with a considerable number of ordinances and rules enacted by the Mandatory. Of the former, the Provisional Law regulating the Right to Dispose of Immovable Property of 5 Jumad il Awwal 1331, which defined and extended the powers of a holder of miri land, is especially noteworthy. Of the latter, apart from the Land Transfer Ordinance (as amended) and the Land (Settlement of Title) Ordinance (as amended) and the rules made under them, mention should perhaps be made of the Bankruptcy Ordinance, the Charitable Trusts Ordinance, the Companies Ordinance, the Co-operative Societies Ordinance, the Credit Banks Ordinance, the Land (Acquisition for Public Purposes) Ordinance 1943, the Land Law (Amendment) Ordinances, the Land Registers Ordinance 1944 (mentioned further in Appendix I below), the Mining Ordinance, the Mortgage Law (Amendment) Ordinance, the Oil Mining Ordinance, the Partnership Ordinance, the Survey Ordinance and the Town Planning Ordinance, but this list is by no means inclusive; indeed there were comparatively few ordinances of general application

/which

which did not require to be considered in connection with land registration. The very controversial Town and Country Planning Bill 1947 dealt at length with matters of registration, and it was mainly because of differences of opinion on this subject that it was not enacted.

Case law.

20. There is a great wealth of case law in Palestine regarding land, especially on the application of English principles of equity. Also, as was to be expected, the Land (Settlement of Title) Ordinance gave rise to much litigation. Issues regarding registration came less often before the Courts, but several High Court decisions have been reported from cases in which the Director was a respondent, usually concerning the discretion vested in him by section 4 of the Land Transfer Ordinance. These decisions may be found either in the official Palestine Law Reports or in the privately published Annotated Law Reports.

Intended revision and codification of the law.

21. The revision and codification of the law relating to land registration were considered at intervals over a long period and tentative drafts prepared, but on every occasion circumstances led to the postponement of the project. When it became clear that the end of the Mandate was approaching, an entirely new Bill was drafted, intended as a record for any future administration of the practice which had been evolved during the Mandate, and of such reforms as experience had shown to be desirable. This draft was being considered by the Law Officers when the Mandate ended.

22. The law and practice applied in Palestine differed from the Torrens system in three respects: first, that registration did not cure defects in title and hence did not absolve a purchaser from the duty of investigating title, secondly, that the registered title was not supported by a Government indemnity, and finally, that there was no system of caveats. It was in these as well as many minor respects that it was proposed to introduce changes.

23. As an appendix to the Bill, there was attached a complete redraft of the fees rules, intended to achieve greater precision, consistency and comprehension. It was unfortunate that financial necessity led to the use of land registration fees as a source of revenue, as the very high level of these fees inclined the public to think of land registration as a liability to be evaded rather than as a protection to be sought.

The form of the registers.

24. The form of registers used by the Turks has already briefly been noted, and the fact that two forms were used during the British Administration. Of these, the first, used in respect of land the title to which had not been settled, was known as the Register of Deeds. It consisted of bound books, each folio of which was ruled in columns providing for the Petition and Deed numbers, the date of registration, the category and description of the land, the description of the boundaries, the area, the names of the parties, the declared consideration, the assessed value and finally a column for remarks.

"Category", in this connection, has a technical meaning, the commonest categories being mulk, true waqf, miri, untrue waqf and matrouka. The remarks column was used both for cross-references and for the entry of attachments and other orders of courts. Deeds and other instruments were entered in chronological order, but a separate folio was used for each parcel. The method of reference was by village, volume and folio.

25. It will be seen that the form of these registers represents an advance on that of the Daimi registers, where no attempt was made to group entries by reference to parcels. Unfortunately, owing to the multiplicity of interests which frequently arose in respect even of the smallest parcels (largely, but not exclusively, because of the Moslem law of succession), entries in respect of one parcel might occupy many folios, possibly scattered over a number of volumes, and in such cases investigation of title might be a laborious task. Another defect was that subsisting entries tended to be obscured by cancelled ones, particularly entries of ownership by cancelled encumbrances. A minor defect was the waste of labour and space in repeating items, such as the description of the land and its boundaries, which do not normally change.

26. These defects were as far as possible removed on the introduction of the new registers, known as the Registers of Title, under the Land (Settlement of Title) Ordinance. These were loose-leaf, enabling all the pages relating to one parcel to be grouped, and were divided, as in the English and the Torrens systems, into three parts: the description of the land, the ownership and the encumbrances. The method of reference was by block and parcel, a block being a unit convenient for plotting, usually containing about five hundred dunums and containing from one to a thousand parcels.

27. Settlement of title was, with very few exceptions, limited to agricultural and undeveloped land, and the sites of villages were excluded. In consequence, even where settlement operations were complete, the old registers sometimes still contained a few valid entries relating to houses and gardens in villages. Since the Schedules of Rights issued by settlement officers did not contain references to previous registration, it was not possible to make cross-references between the old and the new registers. The question may therefore arise, although in practice it seldom happens, whether an entry in an old register is subsisting or has been replaced. Also it is not possible to destroy the old registers, since it is impossible to be sure that any one does not contain valid entries.

28. It should, perhaps, also be noted that no separate leasehold registers were kept, leases exceeding three years being entered against the mulk or miri title as encumbrances, as, for lack of any other place, were subsequent dispositions and transmissions of the leasehold interest. It is only comparatively recently that leasehold interests have become of importance in Palestine, since the

/Arabs

7.

Arabs rarely make registrable leases of agricultural land. On the other hand, land registered in the name of Keren Kayemeth Leisrael Limited (the land holding company of the Jewish Agency) is always leased and never transferred. An even more important change came through the building of blocks of flats. The registration of a large number of leases against a single parcel would in itself cause excessive complication, but the situation is made still worse because the people of Palestine, Jews and Arabs alike, prefer ownership to a leasehold interest. Since the separate ownership of a flat is not allowed by law, the custom has grown up of acquiring a share in common in the ownership of the parcel, together with a lease of the particular flat. The machinery of registration must be adapted to meet this situation, and there seems no good reason why a leasehold register should not be introduced. It is suggested that in the case of new registers it would be convenient to interleave sheets of a different colour into the existing registers, each immediately to follow the sheet bearing the mulk or miri title, and with, of course, the appropriate cross-references.

29. Another change in contemplation at the end of the Mandate was the introduction of registers similar in form to the Registers of Title for use in connection with urban properties. Such registers could be based on the Urban Property Tax Assessment block plans. The change could be made gradually, and while it would be difficult in respect of the old cities, little difficulty was anticipated in respect of the newer residential and industrial quarters. Such a change should lead to greater efficiency, and should prove of convenience to the public.

Procedure in the land registries.

30. The procedure on dispositions and other transmissions may very briefly be summarised. It was set in motion by an application in writing. This was given a number, known as the Petition Number, and entered in a journal known as the Petition Book. A file was opened. Evidence of title (either a Certificate of Registration or an official Extract) and of payment of taxes was produced by the applicant, verified in the Land Registry, and any necessary requisitions made. The fees payable were assessed, and when they had been paid a deed was executed before the Registrar of Lands and attested by him. This was given a Deed Number and entered in a second journal known as the Deeds Book. In transmissions where no deed was executed, the appropriate instrument, as, for example, a Certificate of Succession, was treated as a deed. Finally, the disposition or transmission was entered in the Register of Deeds or the Register of Title, as the case might be. Where the title to the land had passed, a Certificate of Registration was issued to the transferee; in other cases, certified copies of the deed could be obtained by the parties.

Duties of the Registrar.

31. The Registrar of Lands, before attesting a deed, had to satisfy himself, first, as to the title of the transferor and his personal capacity to effect the disposition; secondly, that the

/Proposed

8.

proposed disposition was lawful and that the deed by which it was sought to be effected was in proper form; thirdly, in the case of an application for the sub-division of a parcel, or entailing such sub-division, that the sub-division would not conflict with an approved town planning scheme or offend against an order by a settlement officer prescribing a minimum area for parcels in the neighbourhood; fourthly, that the transferor was not liable for any taxes due to the Government, or, where the land was in a municipal area, for rates (the extension of this to the areas of local councils was under consideration); fifthly, that the proposed disposition would not offend against the Land Transfers Regulations 1940; and finally, as to the identity of the persons appearing before him. He had also to value the land, as fees were assessed on the value, not on the declared consideration.

Certificates of registration.

32. It may be noted that a Certificate of Registration was, as its name implies, a certificate that a particular registration had been effected: it was not a certificate of title and its production was not indispensable to future dispositions. This is a matter in which changes were in contemplation.

Binders of valuable documents.

33. In the case of settled land, the deed, and any other document of enduring importance, was extracted from the file when registration was complete, and placed in a binder; in the case of unsettled land, the documents were all retained in the file. Files from which the valuable documents had been extracted were no longer of any importance, and all those more than a year old were destroyed at the end of 1947, after checking by responsible officers.

Orders of Court.

34. Orders of Court were entered in a special book, known as the Register of Writs and Orders, before being entered in the Register of Deeds or Register of Title. They did not appear in the Petition Book or in the Deeds Book.

Objections.

35. It has been noted above (in paragraph 22), that there was no system of caveats in Palestine. A record was, however, made of objections in what was known as the Objection Book, and an attempt was made to settle any issues, or direct them to the courts, before a disposition was completed. Although an objector had no legal rights, and although the practice was open to abuse, it did prove helpful to the public in preventing fraud, but having no legal authority, tended to be an embarrassment to the Department.

Searches and Extracts.

36. The right to search the land registers and to obtain official extracts was customarily confined to "interested persons", an expression interpreted somewhat liberally to include all persons having a registered interest in the land in question and such other persons as could satisfy the Director that they had reasonable need of the information, such as persons instituting legal proceedings.

/37.

9.

The organisation of the Department.

37. Turning to the administration of the Department, it has already been noted in paragraph 6 above that the Turks established land registries in the administrative centres; in all, there were thirteen, situated at Acre, Beersheba, Gaza, Haifa, Hebron, Jaffa, Jenin, Jerusalem, Nablus, Nazareth, Safad, Tiberias and Tulkarm. All these offices were re-opened in 1920, and the correspondence between the district boundaries for administration and for land registration was generally maintained, any change in the former being followed by the appropriate transfer of land records.

Territorial areas of jurisdiction.

38. An additional land registry was opened in Beisan after the conclusion of the Ghor Mudawwara Agreement, but it was later closed on account of political disturbances, and the records moved to the land registry at Nazareth. The records of Beisan were, however, always kept distinct from those of Nazareth, in the hope that circumstances might permit the re-opening of the Beisan office; indeed, it had been agreed in principle shortly before the end of the Mandate that the office should be re-opened, and this was only postponed because of the lack of suitable accommodation.

39. The policy of identifying administrative and land registration districts had to be abandoned, however, in respect of Jaffa and Tulkarm as a result of the 1936 disturbances. Both these offices served a considerable Jewish public, but both were situate in towns which became unsafe for Jews. Since every transaction had to be completed in a land registry, it was decided to open new offices at Tel-Aviv and Nathanya. In the case of Jaffa and Tel-Aviv particularly, it was not possible to make the division on any broad geographical line, and the principle adopted was to transfer to Tel-Aviv the records of these areas which appeared in the land registers as substantially in Jewish ownership. On the same principle, further records were from time to time transferred to Tel-Aviv, and the situation was finally reviewed, as thoroughly as circumstances permitted, and the appropriate transfers made, immediately before the end of the Mandate.

40. With the outbreak of disorders in November, 1947, however, with the end of the British Administration in sight and in view of the possibility of an interregnum, it was the safety of the records rather than the convenience of the public that assumed overriding importance. The registers were photographed, so that they might be restored in case of destruction (see Appendix III) but it was also decided that certain administrative changes should be made. These were to embody the principle that records of title should so far as possible be left in the custody of the community having the paramount interest in the land concerned irrespective of any suggested lines of political demarcation. These proposals, and the final disposition of the records, are described in Appendix II.

Staff.

41. As may be seen from the preceding paragraphs, the work of land registration was decentralized, and local Registrars of Lands had considerable powers and discretions. They were, however, required to

/refer

10.

refer to headquarters in a number of matters, generally speaking, those of great magnitude, those of political significance, and those of legal or technical difficulty. Since Registrars could not be expected always to appreciate the existence of political or legal difficulties, they were required to submit to headquarters all cases within those classes where such problems were to be anticipated, and they could, of course, refer any others.

42. A headquarters staff was maintained in Jerusalem for administrative work, including the inspection of the land registries, accounting and the preparation of statistical records, for the technical work of examining and ruling on files submitted by Registrars, and for certain subsidiary matters, including the preparation of grants of public land, the administration of the Ghor Mudawwara Agreement and the realization of the assets of the former Ottoman Agricultural Bank. Latterly, the copying into the new registers of schedules of rights was also performed at headquarters.

43. The organisation of the staff was complicated by the need, first, to maintain both Jewish and Arab officers in every office likely to be frequented by Arabs and Jews, and, secondly, to maintain in the staff as a whole, and in any particular grade, a balance of Christians, Moslems and Jews. Any failure in either respect was liable to become a political issue, but too faithful adherence to what was in itself not an undesirable principle entailed loss of efficiency and sometimes injustice in the promotion of individuals.

44. Details of the staff employed may be found in the approved Estimates: in brief, the nominal staff comprised ten First Division officers, one hundred and twenty-four Second Division officers, a varying number of temporary clerks and some thirty-six messengers, caretakers, cleaners and watchmen. The clerical staff was divided between the different offices as follows:-

Acre	3 (2.5%)	Nathanya	5 (4.5%)
Gaza (including Beersheba)	9 (8%)	Nazareth (including Beisan)	4 (3.5%)
Haifa	16 (14%)	Safad	2 (2%)
Hebron	1 (1%)	Tel Aviv	17 (15%)
Jaffa	19 (17%)	Tiberias	5 (4.5%)
Jerusalem	24 (21%)	Tulkarm	4 (3.5%)
Nablus (including Jenin)	4 (3.5%)		

Accounting.

Deposits.

Waqf fees.

45. The method of accounting employed was that laid down by Financial Regulations and does not call for special comment. Three classes of receipt credited to Deposit accounts should, however, be noted. First, where land was

/dedicated

11.

dedicated to a Moslem waqf or where any disposition was registered of land subject to a Moslem waqf, one half of the fee was credited to a deposit account in the name of the Awqaf Administration. This procedure related both to true and to untrue (takhsisat) waqfs, but was particularly important in connection with the latter, since land subject to a true waqf was normally inalienable. The original authority for the practice was contained in Article 4 of the Ottoman Land Code, amended by the "Schedule of Fees to be applied in the Land Registries", published in 1920 and validated by Article 46 of the Palestine Order in Council 1922.

Mortgage moneys.

46. A deposit account of a different nature was kept to assist mortgagors who wished to redeem their mortgages but who could not otherwise obtain a valid discharge owing to the death, absence or disability of the mortgagee. The practice which, although mentioned in the Land Transfer Fees Rules, lacked specific legal authority, was derived from Article 8 of the Provisional Law for the Mortgage of Immovable Property of 1 Rabi'uth Thani 1331. Such mortgage moneys were only accepted where the Director was satisfied that hardship would otherwise be caused; in such cases, the entry in the land registers relating to the mortgage was cancelled on the deposit of the mortgage money and all outstanding interest. This account was similarly made available in connection with the statutory charge for compensation imposed under the Land (Settlement of Title) Ordinance where a settlement officer excised land from one parcel in order to enlarge an adjoining parcel less than the minimum in size or with boundaries which prevented its proper exploitation. The ledgers relating to this deposit account were photographed before the end of the Mandate; the reference to the negatives being spool A/561.

deposit a/c

The Ottoman Agricultural Bank.

47. The third account was for receipts in connection with the realization of the assets of the Ottoman Agricultural Bank. These included payments on account of capital and interest, as well as the rents for properties previously mortgaged to the Bank and bought in by the Bank when sold in satisfaction of the mortgages. Although retained on deposit, these sums were in fact the property of the Palestine Government, by virtue of the provisions of the Treaty of Lausanne, embodied in the law of Palestine by the Treaty of Peace (Turkey) Ordinance.

48. The Bank was originally incorporated by and was, in fact, a branch of the Ottoman Government, and it was as such that its assets in Palestine passed to the Mandatory. The realization of the assets was first entrusted to the Custodian of Enemy Property, later to the Accountant-General and finally, in 1935, to the Director of Land Registration. The position was reviewed at that date, when it was found that many of the debts would have been difficult to prove. All such debts were written off. The remaining debtors were treated with generosity: in many cases, where the

/debtor

12.

debtor was considered too poor to pay, the debt was written off; in the remainder, the debtors were excused all or most of the interest due. In spite of these concessions, great difficulty was experienced in obtaining payment, and the sum of LP.2,898.119 mils was still outstanding at the end of the Mandate. Two cases were then pending before the Courts and one before the Notary Public.

The Ghor Mudawwara Agreements.

49. With the Ghor Mudawwara Agreements it is not necessary to deal in detail. The history of the Ghor lands has been set out on several occasions. Briefly, these lands, situate in the Jordan valley, settled, abandoned and resettled in Ottoman times, were held by persons whom the Sultan regarded as his tenants but who maintained with great obstinacy that they had older and greater rights equivalent to miri tenure. A compromise was reached with the cultivators by the Mandatory, under which the former were to pay by instalments amounts corresponding to the unimproved value of the land and were to receive immediate miri titles. As mentioned in paragraph 14 above, the parcels concerned were marked out and the ownership determined by a Demarcation Commission, whose work was followed and completed by survey. The cultivators, however, feeling secure in their possession, showed no inclination to pay. The Government were reluctant to take drastic measures, and prolonged negotiation led to three revised agreements, under each of which the cultivators obtained concessions. Even so, few payments were made except on behalf of cultivators who wished to sell their land, when the payments were, in fact, made by the purchasers.

50. The procuring of the signature of the several agreements by the cultivators was entrusted to the District Administration, as was the collection of the instalments; the Department of Land Registration was responsible for the preparation of the agreements and for the maintenance of accounts. Various books of account were kept in respect of the earlier agreements, merely showing gross receipts, but new ledgers were opened in respect of the third revised agreement, showing the appropriation of all receipts between capital and income and to any particular parcel, or in the case of a deceased signatory to the credit of any particular heir, as the case might be. All receipts, whether capital or income, were credited to revenue. The accounts are complicated by the fact that many of the signatories are dead and as a result of concessions allowing the sale of part only of the property comprised in an agreement.

Statistics.

51. Lastly, a small section of the headquarters staff was devoted to the compilation and analysis of statistics from the weekly returns of transactions submitted by Registrars. These included the number and nature of the transactions completed, the consideration or value passing and the amount of the fees collected. Separate figures were kept in respect of urban and rural lands and for each land registry. Returns were sent monthly to the Department of Statistics for inclusion in the bulletins issued by the Department, while annual figures were included in the reports

/prepared

prepared for the League of Nations. The last annual report issued was for the calendar year 1946, to which were appended graphs showing the growth in the work of the Department during the first twenty-five years of its existence. Statistics for 1947 became available too late for analysis before the end of the Mandate.

52. It is not easy to assess the measure of success achieved by the Department. Although in law the registration of all dispositions was compulsory, it cannot be denied that a great deal of conveyancing took place off the register, especially in rural districts where settlement of title had not taken place. Many reasons might be given, but undoubtedly the two most important were the conservation of the fellah and the high level of fees. The Mejelle, providing that powers of attorney were irrevocable where the rights of third parties were involved, suggested an alternative system of conveyancing, and many purchasers were content to rely upon such powers although they knew that they had no legal title and although purported revocations were the cause of constant litigation. On the whole, however, the system of registration worked reasonably well, and in a country of exceptional problems, instances of loss through fraud or mistake in registered transactions were remarkably few. That the system enjoyed a fair degree of public confidence was shown not only by the steady growth in the number of registered transactions, but even more by the fact that a registered title, although it carried no indemnity, was usually accepted without investigation by advocates as well as by the general public.

53. This memorandum has been written in England since the termination of the Mandate, partly from notes brought from Palestine and partly from memory. The information it contains is believed to be correct, but could only be checked by reference to records which it was not thought proper to remove from Palestine and which it was not possible to copy in the comparatively short period when it was known that the Mandate was coming to an end. In this connection, it should be on record that no registers, documents of title, files or departmental records were removed from Palestine nor were any destroyed before the withdrawal of the British Administration. It is hoped that all such records may survive for the use of future governments and the benefit of the people of Palestine.

APPENDIX I

Note on the restoration of the Jerusalem Land Registry records.

In July 1944 a bomb, believed to have been intended against the police billets situated over the Jerusalem Land Registry, destroyed that office and caused great damage to its records. Some registers were destroyed, while others were damaged by fire and water. Fortunately, very few files were lost.

2. A similar disaster, though on a smaller scale, had previously taken place during rioting in Tel Aviv. On that occasion, the registers were restored by administrative action: on the destruction of the Jerusalem office, however, it was decided that enabling legislation was desirable, and the Land Registers Ordinance 1944 was enacted. Under the powers conferred by the Ordinance, the registers which had been damaged by fire or water were copied, missing particulars of minor importance, where known, being inserted in ink of a different colour. Where any material particular was destroyed or rendered illegible, a quasi-judicial enquiry was held after public advertisement in the Gazette. Every new entry, whether copied or restored on enquiry, was certified by a senior officer authorised under the Ordinance.

3. Detailed procedure was laid down departmentally for the copying of the registers and the checking of the copies so made. The actual copying had largely to be done by temporary clerks engaged for the purpose, but every entry was to be checked by two clerks, of whom at least one was to be a permanent member of the staff. Copies were to be exact, even of patent errors, such errors being later corrected after the process of restoration was complete. The last entry on every folio was to be initialled by the clerk who copied the folio, and by both the clerks who checked it. Later, almost a complete recheck was made by experienced officers. The work was not wholly satisfactory, but although many minor clerical errors were found, only two errors or omissions of a serious nature came to light from some thirty thousand folios copied.

4. The procedure for quasi-judicial enquiries proved satisfactory, although shortage of senior staff and pressure of other work made it possible to deal only with cases for which application was made. About fifteen hundred enquiries were heard, and although the Ordinance provided a right of appeal to the courts from the decision of an authorised officer, no such appeal was ever made. In a very small number of cases (probably about a half of one per centum), the authorised officer refused to make a new entry, on the ground that insufficient evidence had been produced. A considerable number of entries remained to be reconstructed when the Mandate ended.

5. In view of the incompleteness of the Jerusalem registers, the Deeds Books for Jerusalem, themselves copies, were photographed (see Appendix III).

APPENDIX II

Note on the custody of the records on the termination of the Mandate.

As soon as it became known that the Mandate was drawing to an end, a policy had to be formulated for the disposal of the records in the custody of the Department, in the event of there being no successor authority recognised by the Government capable of accepting responsibility for them. Those records were doubly important, both to any future government and to the hundreds of thousands of individuals whose title to land depended on them.

2. The first decision taken was that no such records should be removed from Palestine; the second was that they were likely to be safer decentralized than in a central store, since there was no place in which one could be sure of their security, while the desire of both Jews and Arabs to possess them might well lead to their destruction in a struggle for their possession. The solution seemed to lie in asking the appropriate Municipal Corporations, which it was hoped would continue to operate, to assume responsibility for the safety of local records until such time as there should again be a recognised government in the country.

3. The first practical step was to decide what records it was most important to preserve and to ascertain their numbers and locality. The records were treated as falling into two classes: the registers, of the first importance, and the documents on which they were based, of the second. It has already been noted (paragraph 33) that in the case of unsettled land, the documents remained in the files, while in the case of settled land, they were extracted and placed in special binders. The deeds books and the registers of writs and orders were also included in the second class. The following table shows the position as on 17th November 1947. Additional registers and files were, of course, opened after that date, but precise figures of these are not available.

Registry	Turkish Registers	Registers of Deeds	Registers of Title	Registers of Writs and Orders	Deed Books	Binders of Documents	Files (unsettled land)
Acre	66	126	32	2	42	13	9,600
Beersheba (1)	2	59	-	1	5	-	1,600
Beisan	(2)	122	16	3	21	11	4,400
Gaza	57	83	308	3	49	175	4,700
Haifa	30	311	282	5	170	252	49,900
Hebron	42	53	-	2	7	-	2,900
Jaffa	128	279	139	6	140	657	55,700
Jenin	75	68	2	2	9	3	2,400
Jerusalem	59	335	15	3	28	6	58,100
Nablus	96	106	2	2	20	2	5,800
Nathanya	3	31	72	2	23	210	-
Nazareth	60	159	87	4	26	37	7,700
Safad	79	135	59	2	21	20	5,800
Tel Aviv	-	81	224	5	47	409	22,000
Tiberias	37	163	94	3	33	33	9,000
Tulkarm	110	81	92	2	49	78	8,000
Totals	844	2,192	1,424	47	690	1,906	247,600

(1) Kept at Gaza.
(2) Included with Nazareth.

From these figures it was obvious that the bulk of the records made their movement undesirable except in case of necessity.

4. The second step was the implementation, as far as possible, of the policy of placing the records relating to any substantial area of land in the custody of the community having the paramount interest in it. The proposals were as follows. First, the abolition of the Safad Land Registry, since it was feared that Safad would be the scene of fighting, and the division of its records between Acre and Tiberias. A line was chosen running north and south along village boundaries, comparable with, but not the same as, the boundary between Zones A and B under the Land Transfers Regulations 1940. The villages to the west, listed in Table A to this Appendix, were to be attached to Acre, and those to the east, listed in Table B, to Tiberias.

/Secondly

Secondly, it was proposed to separate the two villages of 'Ailabun and Mughar and al Mansura from Tiberias and to attach them to Acre. Thirdly, it was proposed to remove the Beisan records from Nazareth, an exclusively Arab town, to Tiberias, then a mixed town. Fourthly, it was proposed to remove the records relating to the Jewish settlements in the Plain of Esdraelon (listed in Table C) from Nazareth to Haifa. Lastly, it was proposed to remove from Jaffa the records relating to rural areas, and to open a new land registry at Ramle. The immediate reason for this change was the insecurity of the twon of Jaffa, but apart from the question of security, the change had much logically to recommend it, since Ramle is the natural centre of the area, while Jaffa is separated from the rural lands by a belt of Jewish-owned land

5. It will be appreciated that these changes were planned at a time when it was supposed that Haifa and Tiberias would remain mixed towns. When Tiberias was abandoned by the Arabs, a further modification was made to the plan, and the registers of Beisan were divided.

6. In the meanwhile, however, the photographing of the registers, described in Appendix III below, had led to a drastic and unexpected modification of the general plan. All the registers, except those of Nathanya and Tel Aviv, had been brought to Jerusalem for photographing, partly by the British Army and partly by the Palestine Police. The registers of Beersheba, Gaza, Nablus and Tulkarm were duly returned, but by the time the remainder had been photographed, the rapid deterioration in the safety of the roads and increasing calls on armoured or escorted transport precluded their return. The result was that a large proportion of the land registers was collected in Jerusalem, at a time when fighting for the city seemed imminent. In these circumstances, the only course seemed to be the application in a more general way of the principle already adopted, and the Supreme Moslem Council and the Jewish Agency respectively were asked to accept the custody of the records which could not be returned to their stations. Happily, both agreed.

7. Before the registers were handed over, the adjustments outlined in paragraph 4 above were effected in respect of them (they could not be effected in respect of files and other documents), and the registers of Beisan were divided, those listed in Table D being handed to the Jewish Agency, and the remainder to the Supreme Moslem Council. Apart from those of Beisan, the registers handed to the Supreme Moslem Council were those of Acre (including half Safad), Hebron, Jaffa, Jenin and Nazareth (excluding the Plain of Esdraelon). Those handed to the Jewish Agency were those of Tiberias (including half Safad), certain registers transferred from Jaffa to Tel Aviv (see paragraph 39 of the Memorandum) and those of Haifa (including the Plain of Esdraelon). The registers of Haifa were handed over not for custody but for transmission to Haifa, where the Municipal Corporation had agreed to assume responsibility for them, and it is understood that they were duly delivered.

/8.

8. It may be noted that the registers handed to the Supreme Moslem Council were placed for safety in the women's section of the mosque Al Aqsa in the Haram ash Sharif? the Jewish Agency had not, at the end of the Mandate, decided on a permanent store for the registers in their custody.

9. There remained the problem of the registers of Jerusalem. The records of Arab and Jewish interests were there so closely intermingled that any division was quite impracticable in the time available, while to hand all the registers either to Jews or Arabs would have been interpreted as an act of political significance and would have caused very great resentment in one or other community. This problem was solved when the General Secretary of the Young Men's Christian Association agreed to allow the registers to be stored in the main building of the Association, which was then under the flag of the International Red Cross of Geneva. The registers were in fact stored in the gallery of the Association's library.

10. The steps described in the four preceding paragraphs were taken after consultation with and generally with the concurrence of representatives of both Arabs and Jews.

11. Departmental records and statistics, and the ledgers of the Ottoman Agricultural Bank and the Ghor Mudawwara Agreement were left in the headquarters office in the Russian Compound in Jerusalem.

12. All furniture and equipment was left in the various land registry offices. The photostat camera belonging to the Department could not be moved from the former Palace Hotel, and was therefore left in the custody of the Supreme Moslem Council.

13. The following table summarises the whereabouts of the registers and valuable documents, while in parentheses are shown the responsible authorities.

Land Registry	Registers	Files
?	Haram ash Sharif (Supreme Moslem Council)	Taggart Building, Acre (Municipal Corporation).
BEERSHEBA	Taggart Building, Gaza (Municipal Corporation).	
BEISAN	see Table D and paragraph 7 above	Government Offices, Nazareth (Municipal Corporation).
GAZA	Taggart Building, Gaza (Municipal Corporation).	
HAIFA	Jerusalem (Jewish Agency)	Municipal Offices, Haifa [1] (Municipal Corporation).
HEBRON	Haram ash Sharif (Supreme Moslem Council)	Taggart Building, Hebron (Municipal Corporation).
JAFFA	Haram ash Sharif (Supreme Moslem Council)	Ramle Airport [2] (Municipal Corporation).
JENIN	Haram ash Sharif (Supreme Moslem Council)	Land Registry, Jenin (Municipal Corporation).
JERUSALEM	Y.M.C.A., Jerusalem	Law Courts, Jerusalem.
NABLUS	Taggart Building, Nablus [3] (Municipal Corporation).	
NATHANYA	Land Registry, Nathanya (Township)	
NAZARETH	Haram ash Sharif [4] (Supreme Moslem Council)	Government Offices, Nazareth (Municipal Corporation).
SAFAD	see Tables A and B	Government Offices, Safad (Municipal Corporation).
TEL-AVIV	Land Registry, Tel-Aviv (Municipal Corporation).	
TIBERIAS	Jerusalem [5] (Jewish Agency)	Taggart Building, Tiberias (Municipal Corporation).
TULKARM	Taggart Building, Tulkarm (Municipal Corporation).	

/Notes:

Notes: (1) Transfer approved and presumably completed.

(2) Transfer from Jaffa Land Registry arranged; it is not known if it was completed.

(3) Except certain Turkish registers omitted to be returned, handed to the Supreme Moslem Council and stored in the Haram ash Sharif.

(4) Except the registers shown in Table C, handed to the Jewish Agency in Jerusalem.

(5) Except the registers of 'Ailabun and Mughar and al Mansura, attached to Acre, handed to the Supreme Moslem Council and stored in the Haram ash Sharif.

TABLE A.

Villages the registers of which, formerly in Safad Land Registry, were attached to Acre.

'Akbara	Hurfeish	Ras al Ahmar
'Alma	Jish	Rihaniya
'Ammuqa	Kafr Bir'im	Sabalan
Dallata	Khirbat al Higab	Saliha
Deishum	Malikiya	Samui
Dhahiriya at Tahta	Marus	Sa'sa'
Fara	Qabba'a	Shuna
Farradiya	Qaddita	Sufsaf
Ghabbatiya	Qudeiriya	Teitaba

TABLE B.

Villages the registers of which, formerly in Safad Land Registry, were attached to Tiberias.

Abil al Qamh	Jahula
'Abisiya and Kefar Szold	Ja'una
Aiyelet hash Shahar and Yarda	Jubb Yusuf
'Arab ash Shamalina	Kefar Gil'adi
Beisamun	Khalisa
Biriya	Khan ed Duweir
Buweiziya	Khisas
Dafna	Khiyam al Walid
Dan	Kirad al Baggara
Darbashiya	Kirad al Ghannama
Dardara	Kirad al Kheit
Dawwara and Amir and Kefar Nehemuya	Lazzaza and Beit Hillal
	Lubya
Dhahiriya al Fanga	Mahanayim
'Ein Zagha	Mallaha and 'Arab Zubeid
'Ein Zeitim	Manara
'Ein ez Zeitun	Mansura
Fir'im	Mansurat al Kheit
Ghuraba	Mazari ad Daraja
Harawi	Meirun
Hatsor	Metulla
Hula	Mishmar hay Yarden
Hunin	Muftakhira

/Mughr al Kheit

TABLE B (continued)

Mughr al Kheit
Nabi Yusha
Na'ima
Qadas
Qeitiya
Rosh Pinna
Safad
Salihiya
Sanbariya
Shanga at Tahta

Sho'ar Yashuv
Tuba
Tuleil and al Huseiniya
'Ulmaniya
Weiziya
Yesud ham Ma'ala
Zanghariya
Zawiya
Zug al Famgani
Zug at Tahtani

TABLE C.

Settlements in the Plain of Esdraelon the registers of which, formerly in Nazareth Land Registry, were attached to Haifa.

'Affula
Balfuriya
Gevat
Ginneigar
Kefar Barukh
Kefar Gid'on
Kefar Yeladim
Mahane Yisrael

Merhavya Group
Mizra'
Nahalal and Shimron
Ramat David and Hash Sharon and 'Ayanot
Sarid
Tel 'Adashim

TABLE D.

Villages the registers of which, formerly in Beisan Land Registry, were handed to the Jewish Agency.

Beit Alfa
Beit hash Shitta
'Ein Harod
Geva'

Heftsi Bah
Kefar Yehezgel
Sakhina and Nir David
Tel Yosef

APPENDIX III

Note on the photographing of the land registers.

The photographing of the land registers was first considered as a security measure after the destruction of the Jerusalem Land Registry in 1944, but no action was then taken. The question was reopened as soon as it became known that the Mandate was to be determined, in view of the possibility of an interrognum and consequent disorder. Approval was given to the proposal in October 1947, and in December three Watson Recording Cameras were bought in England and flown to Palestine. These were later supplemented by two cine cameras specially adapted. It was thought impracticable to move the cameras from office to office. They were therefore set up in Jerusalem, and the British Army and the Palestine Police were asked for their assistance in transporting the registers. The operation and maintenance of the cameras was given out to contract, although the work remained throughout under the control of the Department, generously helped by the Public Information Office. Photographing began in January 1948.

2. In the meanwhile, serious disorders had begun. Uncertainty as to the future and the imperative need for speed made it impossible to build up an orderly procedure from experiment. The initial rules to be adopted were simple, the main provisions being as follows. No photographing was ever to take place unless at least one member of the permanent staff of the Department was present, and unless a British officer was present, there was to be at least one Arab and one Jew. A certificate signed by the Acting Director was to be photographed by way of identification at the beginning and end of every film and of every register. Spools were to be numbered and a complete record made by Departmental staff of every register photographed. Test strips were to be made several times daily with each camera, developed and handed to the Department. The exposed films were to be delivered to the Department for development and storage in England.

3. The proposals for supervision unhappily proved impossible of fulfilment. Although the cameras were placed in a central position thought to be accessible alike to Arabs and Jews, Arab officers from the beginning expressed reluctance to work there and attended only irregularly. Jewish officers worked throughout, except at times of exceptional danger. It should, in fairness to the staff, be pointed out that the building came under fire on numerous occasions and that many of the staff who lived at a distance had to pass through dangerous neighbourhoods. In consequence, photographing sometimes took place with only Jewish officers of the Department present, sometimes with only temporary officers and occasionally with no departmental representative present. It may be added that while the contractor who undertook the photographing was a Jew, the majority of his employees were Arabs. It was rarely, therefore, that both communities were not represented.

4. A record was made of the work done, although it was obviously incomplete and may not be wholly accurate. From it, the indices contained in Tables E, F, G and were compiled. (Indices not copied - originals in Colonial Office).

/5

5. It was clearly impossible to photograph all records of value, since their volume was too great. It was decided, therefore, to photograph only the Ottoman registers, the Registers of Deeds, the Registers of Title and the Registers of Writs and Orders. In the case of Jerusalem, the Deeds Books were also photographed to supplement the incomplete registers (see Appendix II). The Deposit Ledgers relating to mortgage moneys were also photographed (see paragraph 46 above).

6. In the circumstances, the programme adopted was to photograph first the registers of those offices whose areas of jurisdiction included land in mixed ownership and those offices which by reason of their situation were thought to be in the greatest danger. In the event, all the land registers were photographed except those of Hebron, Jenin, Nathanya and Tel-Aviv. A plan to send the two ciné cameras to Tel-Aviv was frustrated when the road from Jerusalem was closed by Arab irregular forces.

7. Of the records filmed, the Ottoman registers, the Registers of Deeds and the Registers of Writs and Orders were bound books, while the Registers of Title were loose-leaf. The bound books, with few exceptions, were too large to permit of the photographing of the double page, and photographing the reverse after the obverse of each sheet would have entailed great delay, as the books would have had to be moved from right to left or from left to right after each exposure. It was found quicker to photograph first all the obverse pages in a book, and then to work backwards through the reverse pages. In some books, the folio numbers appeared only on the obverse pages: instructions were given that in such cases the numbers were to be entered also on the reverse, but this was certainly not done in all cases. Since the pages were photographed in order, it is thought that no great difficulty should be experienced in reconstructing the books should the necessity arise. It must, however, be borne in mind that pages were sometimes photographed twice, where there was any doubt as to the success of the first exposure. Where bound books were not completely filled, one or two blank pages were photographed after the last entry, in proof that they were blank. Every page of the reconstructed Jerusalem registers were photographed, however, since folios on which entries had not been restored might appear in any part of a book and the existence of blank sheets was no proof that entries might not appear on later folios. In the case of the loose-leaf books, each folio was photographed in turn, first the obverse and then the reverse. Block and parcel numbers did not appear on the reverse, and for lack of time no attempt was made to insert them.

8. Although few registrations were completed after the registers had been photographed, the photographic record must be read with the weekly returns of dispositions and the weekly returns of court orders for 1948.

9. In all, over seventeen hundred spools of film were used, each of a hundred feet, and between a million and a quarter and a million and a half exposures were made. It was originally estimated that the work would cost between six and nine thousand

/Palestine

Palestine pounds; the actual cost is not known but it was probably a little over eight thousand Palestine pounds.

10. Of the three Watson cameras, one was sold, with the unused film, to the Jewish Agency. The other two, as being likely to be of use to a future government, were retained and stored in the Rockefeller Museum. A reader, purchased with the cameras, was given on loan to the Museum.